MW00986868

# Christ and Sophia

# Christ and Sophia

## Anthroposophic Meditations on the Old Testament, New Testament & Apocalypse

Valentin Tomberg

SteinerBooks
2006

SteinerBooks
Anthropososophic Press, Inc.
610 Main Street, Suite 1
Great Barrington, MA, 01230

*Christ and Sophia* is a translation from the German of
*Anthroposophisch Betrachtungen über des Alte Testament;*
*Anthroposophische Betrachtungen über das Neue Testament;*
*Geisteswissenschaftliche Betrachtungen über die Apokalypse des Johannes.*
Revised for this edition from translations by R. H. Bruce.


Library of Congress Cataloging-in-Publication Data

Tomberg, Valentin.
[Anthroposophisch Betrachtungen über des Alte Testament;
Anthroposophische Betrachtungen über das Neue Testament;
Geisteswissenschaftliche Betrachtungen über die Apokalypse des Johannes.
English]
Christ and Sophia : anthroposophic meditations on the old testament, new testament, and apocalypse / Valentin Tomberg.
p. cm.
Includes bibliographical references and index.
ISBN-13: 978-0-88010-565-1
ISBN-10: 0-88010-565-8
1. Jesus Christ—Anthroposophical interpretations. I. Title.
BP596.J4T6613 2006
299'.935—dc22
2006003762

First Edition

10 9 8 7 6 5 4 3 2 1

# Table of Contents

The publisher acknowledges with gratitude
generous gifts by the Sophia Foundation of North America
and several anonymous donors, without which publication
of this volume would not have been possible.

# Introduction

Christopher Bamford

THOUGH RELATIVELY UNKNOWN to the general public, Valentin Tomberg, the author of these anthroposophical studies (or, more accurately, *meditations*), is an important, complex, and somewhat controversial figure in twentieth-century spirituality generally, and in Anthroposophy in particular.[1] In the world but not of it, he led a mostly hidden, ordinary life, remaining largely unknown to the public during his lifetime, while intensely involved with his times and a circle of intimates.

It is difficult to judge the importance of spiritual figures. Esoteric researchers, saints, initiates, and channels of grace cannot be rightfully weighed on the scales of the world. Their consequence, if we can use such a word, is not quantitative or to be measured in material terms. It is qualitative, interior, and above all, invisible. Thus, the effects are difficult to assess. On the earthly plane, Tomberg was certainly a person of intense spiritual discipline, practice, and dedication and extraordinarily accomplished in prayer and meditation. He possessed a brilliant mind, which he coupled with profound qualities of heart, two attributes he never allowed to become separated, always uniting feeling with thinking in service to the divine. A student of the occult traditions of the West and an intellectual, he was learned in many traditions and languages and was able to put his mind to whatever he chose—or, rather, to whatever his conscience called him. At the same time, he was in every respect a person of intense moral probity and conscience. Last but not least, he was a single-minded seeker whose love, reverence, and devotion for Christ and Sophia, the wisdom ground of the world, was the fruit of selfless dedication from his earliest years.

Born in Russia at the turn of the twentieth century, Tomberg was by temperament and destiny in equal measure an occultist, a religious, a mystic, and a deep, clear thinker. He was also a person of exceptional will and compassion; in studying him, one has the sense of a moral force. Intimate with disappointment, loss, suffering, and rejection, he was forced into exile after the Bolshevik revolution and spent the first half of his life in the service of and devoted to Anthroposophy, for which he was a tireless, idealistic, and dedicated worker, lecturer, and writer. The fruits of those years are contained in a number of penetrating, still relevant, but hard-to-find, and consequently little-read publications. Besides the astonishing meditations contained in this volume, there is a collection of "early articles," some single-lecture pamphlets, a series of studies on Rudolf Steiner's "Foundation Stone Meditation," and a lecture cycle titled *Inner Development*. Other items continue to circulate in typescript.[2]

All of this work has a unique power, a fiery, adamantine, brilliant quality, stemming from the being of the author who, working within and for Anthroposophy, is always doing new work. Inspired by Rudolf Steiner, thoroughly immersed in Steiner's work, and following Steiner's meditative spiritual scientific method of research—while always acting in the service of Christ, whom he called "The Master"—there is never a sense of mere commentary or exposition in his writings. We always feel the author speaking from his own experience and making it new. It is not surprising, then, that during the uncertain decade and a half (1925–1940) following Rudolf Steiner's death—a time when the stakes were high as to how and who should protect, continue, and enhance Steiner's great legacy in the face of the looming tragedy of Central Europe—Tomberg's independence and individuality would become not only controversial, but also open to being interpreted (or misinterpreted) as arrogance or worse. It is difficult with hindsight to say exactly what spiritual claims Tomberg made for himself (especially given the claims made for him by others after his death) and in what sense he made them during these years.[3] Undoubtedly, he undertook his own spiritual research, and he spoke and wrote from his own spiritual experience. However, though this set him apart, it did not make him unique; other anthroposophists who did the same, each in their own way (for example, Walter Johannes Stein, George Adams, and the Koliskos), suffered the same fate: ostracism from the Anthroposophical Society. On this question, as on all such questions, readers will have to make up their own minds based on his work.

On another level, the facts are clear; a combination of internal and external politics (the split in the Anthroposophical Society, paralleled by the rise of the Nazis in Germany), culminating in the outbreak of World War II, led to Tomberg's departure from Anthroposophy as the context of his spiritual work and to "joining" the Roman Catholic Church, where he continued his work. After a stay in Germany as a displaced and stateless person (1944–1949), during which he studied law and wrote four works on jurisprudence (one being the publication of his doctoral thesis), he moved to England, where he lived until his death in 1973 while vacationing on the island of Majorca. Largely hidden and forgotten, during that period he worked for the foreign service of the BBC, while leading an intense inner life of prayer, meditation, and esoteric study. The visible fruit of that work is his acknowledged masterpiece, *Meditations on the Tarot,* which was written in French during the 1960s and published anonymously, first in a dubious 1972 German translation and then in French in 1980, to considerable and widespread acclaim. With the English edition of 1985, its classic status was confirmed, and hence it was not surprising to see it appear on the HarperCollins list of the "100 Best Spiritual Books of the Twentieth Century." In 1985, a posthumous collection of four short "Catholic" works appeared in German under the title *Lazarus, Come Forth!* (first published in English as *The Covenant of the Heart: Meditations of a Christian Hermeticist on the Mysteries of Tradition*).[4]

As for controversy, Tomberg is controversial among, above all, anthroposophists (primarily in retrospect) because of his "defection" to Catholicism, which is seen as a "betrayal" of Rudolf Steiner.[5] He was, however, already controversial before that (as mentioned) because of his moral and spiritual independence—for *who* he was. He was "different." Perhaps this impression arose partly because, as formed by Russia, he was a "Platonist" in a movement that was then, and largely remains, predominantly "Aristotelian."

According to Rudolf Steiner, these two "schools of souls" represent different approaches to Christ and to the spiritual world.[6] The Platonists of the Middle Ages, as exemplified by the School of Chartres, were souls whose previous incarnation had taken place during the first centuries after the Mystery of Golgotha. They started from Christ as a gnostic cosmic reality, permeating nature, at it were, from above. Aristotelians, on the other hand, were souls whose last incarnation was during "pagan" times. They started from below, from nature as given by the senses, in order to uncover the working of the Cosmic Christ. Platonists were drawn not so much toward nature as to the moral sphere. Their path was from the universal to the particular—a downward path of purification through the heart into the depths of the soul—a path of "wisdom." Aristotelians, however, worked through nature's moral lawfulness to science. Their path was one of purification through precise observation—a path of "knowledge." From the Aristotelian point of view, therefore, esotericism is rather the mystery of outer things, and true esotericism (one's true task) lies in the outer world. For Platonists, by contrast, it lies within. Rightly understood, however, the two are complementary aspects of a single reality. Inner and outer are but two sides of one coin, as are nature and grace, self-power and other power, and so on.

Aristotelians and Platonists should work together, but during the period when Tomberg was active in Anthroposophy, the mood was Aristotelian. As a Platonist, he was controversial almost by definition. Likewise, as a Platonist (and a Russian) he had an ineradicable affinity for Russian Orthodoxy, which again made him "different." It presented the problem of a "religious" temperament (again essentially Platonist), which, rather than turning toward nature and to visible history as the Aristotelians did, turned to Christ and the Christ Event as the heart of Anthroposophy, and hence to the heart and inner meaning of history, nature, and cosmos. On this basis, in the meditations collected here, Tomberg sought to ground Anthroposophy in biblical revelation. Startling in its ambition though this might have been, it certainly was not orthogonal to Steiner's own intentions, because for Steiner, too, the Mystery of Golgotha was indisputably "the turning point of time."

All this, however, is perhaps only by the way. Despite whatever was "controversial" about him, Tomberg was probably forced out of Anthroposophy (or he left) as part of the general crisis in the Society at that time. Whatever it was—and whoever he was—he took it with him into Catholicism, through what must have been a kind of void. He had always served a higher reality: the reality of Christ, Sophia, and the divine spiritual worlds. To serve this reality on Earth required a form. Anthroposophy, when he discovered it (or it discovered him), seemed to provide a form perfectly suited both to the times and to his personal temperament and mission. He entered it with his entire being. There is no question that he held anything back. But it was not to be. Anthroposophy in its earthly form rejected him and cast him out. As devastating as this must have been, he had no choice but to continue his spiritual search and his work.

In the end, after unsuccessful attempts to find a home in Orthodoxy and in the Christian Community, Tomberg found a hidden place in the great stream of Christ's activity in the West, the Petrine Church. Here, too, he could not but be "controversial." After all, he did not become a theologian or a servant of the Church in any conventional sense. Tomberg always remained, at heart and by vocation, an esotericist who sought to put the wisdom of the esoteric—the Johannine and the Hermetic traditions, odd bedfellows from an orthodox point of view—at the service of the exoteric Church. That Church, if it paid any attention at all, cannot have been completely at ease to find various, "shady" occult figures of French Hermetism (Eliphas Lévi, Saint-Yves Alveydre, Papus, Maître Philippe) proposed as Christian "masters." At the same time, paradoxically, but not perhaps surprisingly in light of his idealism, after Vatican II Tomberg became, if not disenchanted, then at least critical of the Church, which he felt had lost its "vertical dimension." He wrote: "The Council for which Pope John XXIII prayed did in fact fail; it failed to fulfill the highest and most responsible task of the Church's leadership, to guard the portal where the way begins that leads to degeneration, to exhaustion, and to death."[7] Just as he had done as an anthroposophist, as a Catholic Tomberg preserved his independence. His allegiance was always to the truth as he experienced it.

Because of the controversy—not to mention the mystery—surrounding the person of Valentin Tomberg, this introduction must deal mostly with the facts of Tomberg's early and "anthroposophical" life. That one can now in some measure tell his story is owed largely to the labors of Elizabeth (Liesel) Heckmann, the author of a recently published two-volume biography of Tomberg.[8] Deep thanks are owed to her and her publisher for gathering so many details of a fascinating and inspiring life, of which, sadly, only a few may be recounted here. Readers of *Meditations on the Tarot* must therefore rest satisfied with some insight into the early life of their author. For his later life, they must consult the second volume of Heckmann's biography, unfortunately available only in German.

Tomberg was born in St. Petersburg, Russia, on St. Valentine's Day, February 26, 1900 (according to the old Russian calendar), to German-Estonian parents. Baptized Valentin Joseph, he adopted his father's name, Arnoldevitch, in accordance with Russian tradition. His father Karl Arnold (b. 1865) was an official in the Tsar's Interior Ministry. Karl Arnold was from Paide, a small rural town fifty miles from the Estonian capital, Tallinn. Valentin's mother Julianna Johanna (b. 1868) came from Tartu, the second largest city in Estonia and 150 miles south of Tallinn. Valentin was the second son; his brother Richard had preceded him.

The family was Lutheran and, according to their father's wishes, the children were brought up in the Evangelical tradition, though without narrowness or dogmatism. Blessed with a warm, intuitive spirituality, their mother ensured an atmosphere of openness and spiritual freedom in the household. From Valentin's earliest years, it was she who nurtured her young son's burgeoning, broad interest in the spirit. She sensed a desire and openness in him that his Lutheran heritage alone could not meet. She therefore began to take him to both Catholic and Russian Orthodox religious services. Each liturgy, she felt, offered its own depth as well as its gifts and teaching. Thus, as he recalled with gratitude in his later years, it was she who formed his spiritual search:

> One day, sixty-eight years ago, when the author was a four-year-old child [1904], the child was playing before a wide-open window through which a cloudless blue sky could be seen. Suddenly, he stood up and, gazing at the blue heaven and without any prompting, asked his mother: "Where then is God? Is he in the sky? Is he floating there? Or is he sitting there? Where?" His mother stood up and answered: "God is present everywhere. Just as the air is invisible yet penetrates everything, and thanks to it we live and breathe in the air, so our souls live and breathe in God and live out of and thanks to him."
>
> This answer was so enlightening and convincing that, like a breath, it blew away all conceptual difficulties, leaving behind the certainty that the invisible God, who is the life of the soul, is everywhere present. This seminal idea later grew into the heights, the depths, and the breadths. It was, so to speak, the primal cell from which over the decades there grew a many-branched tree of insight and a life of faith.[9]

From the first through the twelfth grades, Tomberg attended the humanistic Evangelical Lutheran Petris School, where he was taught in German and Russian and learned English and French. Founded in 1709, Petris was one of four prestigious Protestant German schools in St. Petersburg. He graduated in 1918. During his last year at St. Petersburg University he pursued courses in law, history, and philosophy. Clearly, he had an exceptional mind. He was also already a seeker; as he wrote to Rudolf Steiner in 1924, "My esoteric strivings began in 1915."

His first and, for a long time, over-lighting interest—the initial compass of his mind and heart, his search—was Russian Orthodox spirituality, which, as he makes clear in his *Early Articles,* includes more than what we usually think of in the West as "religion." Tomberg, it must never be forgotten, was always deeply and thoroughly Russian in his soul; Russian was his mother tongue, and Russian "Orthodox" culture—at once religious, philosophical, existential, social, and artistic—was his "mother culture." Not only was he the contemporary of the great triad of philosopher-theologian-mystics Pavel Florensky, Nikolai Berdyaev, and Sergei Bulgakov; he was also their brother and peer—like them a lover of Christ, freedom, and the Divine Sophia.[10]

Orthodoxy, from the Russian perspective, is more than a religion. It is both an attitude, or mood of soul, and a culture. It is best exemplified perhaps by the story of how

Christianity first came to Russia. In 988, Grand Duke Vladimir decided to convert to monotheism. Uncertain of which path to take (everyone was wooing him), he sent representatives to examine the various faiths in practice. When they returned, the representatives reported that they found Islam too austere and abstemious; Roman Catholicism was too formal and without glory. After attending services in Hagia Sophia in Constantinople, however, they thought they were in Paradise. So moved were their *feelings* by the *beauty* of what they experienced that they exclaimed, "We did not know whether we were in Heaven or on Earth. For on Earth there is no such splendor or beauty, and we are at a loss to describe it. We know only that God dwells there among human beings."

The Russians were thus converted not by a sermon or a philosophy, but by the beauty of the liturgy—by an imaginal soul experience of the living Christ in their hearts. Individual and free striving—a deep heart-felt love for Christ—became the central motive of Russian spiritual life. Ecclesial organization did not rigidify as it did in the West, but remained a soul-spiritual, "Sophianic" reality expressed by the untranslatable word *sobornost*, which means unity as well as catholicity, community, and the gathering together of all into one, the body of Christ. Two ideals flowed from this: first, the simultaneous unity and interdependence of all humanity, so that every human being owes a debt of gratitude to every other human being; and second, the redemptive and universal power of compassionate suffering, in which every instance of suffering is for the sake of the whole. *Every sufferer suffers for all. Whatever the crime, everyone is guilty.*[11]

Such deep-seated compassion is the epitome of the Russian spirit. It is best expressed, perhaps, in Dostoyevsky's famous speech in praise of Pushkin as the founder of the Russian spirit. Lauding Pushkin's "universal responsiveness" (his ability to reincarnate his spirit in the spirit of any and all human beings), Dostoyevsky saw in him the quintessentially Russian, panhuman, universal characteristic that would enable Russia to save Europe and "pronounce the final word of great general harmony, of the final brotherly agreement in accordance with the law of Christ's Gospel."[12]

Despite this emphasis on feeling, Russia is not limited to the heart alone. In the seventeenth century, Peter the Great opened the door to modern Western thinking, thereby planting the seeds of the tensions between the "Europeanizers" and the "Slavophiles" and beginning the ongoing struggle to resist materialism by reconciling the head and the heart.[13] Throughout the nineteenth century, these tensions built until, in the generation before Valentin Tomberg, they reached a prophetic and paradigmatic climax in figures such as Tolstoy, Dostoyevsky, and Solovyov, who, seeking to overcome materialism, were for the young Tomberg "figures of the greatest possible significance for the development of Eastern Christianity."[14]

Such was the framework within which Tomberg was led at a very early age into occult, or esoteric, study and practice, whose long tradition in Russia dates back to the seventeenth century. When the Rosicrucian Fraternity disappeared from Western Europe during the Thirty Years War (1618–1648), rumor had it that it removed eastward to the Baltic States and beyond. Freemasonry arrived in 1731. Over the following decades, many different streams—drawing on Rosicrucian sources, Jacob Böhme, Martinez de Pasqually, and the "Unknown Philosopher" Louis Claude de Saint-Martin—vied for the control of Russian esotericism. In 1822, however, as part of the lead-up to the Decembrist Uprising of 1825, all Masonic and occult organizations were banned. They went underground to emerge after 1900 with renewed vigor, as exemplified by the Tsar's relationship with the French occultists Papus (Gerard Encausse) and Maître Philippe.[15]

Where and how Tomberg began his own search is unclear. We do not know what impelled him. Many are called, but few are chosen. Tomberg's call must have become conscious very early, even before the exchange with his mother quoted earlier. One suspects that he must have felt from the beginning the intimate presence of the spiritual worlds and been given the desire "to know God" for himself, not just in a "mystical" sense, but in all the complexity of the demands of the divine will: God's incarnation in creation through cosmos and nature, history, and human life. He must have understood that presence as suffering and known in his heart that "one should not go too quickly from the many to the one," but suffer with and for each gradation.

It is most likely that he started with Theosophy, which by then had become firmly established as a cultural, if divisive, presence in Russia. By 1916, as the philosopher Nikolai Berdyaev noted, any account of spiritual striving in Russia was bound to take account of it.[16] Madame Blavatsky, who founded the Theosophical Society in 1875, was both Russian born and controversial.[17] Throughout the 1880s, her sister Vera Zhelikhovskaia worked tirelessly to defend, explain, and publicize the Theosophical movement and its founder. By 1890, both had become culturally important enough for Blavatsky's *Key to Theosophy* to warrant a largely negative review by Vladimir Solovyov. His critical stance, however, did not prevent Russian Theosophists from later interpreting his "Sophia, the Wisdom of God" as a variant of their "Theo-Sophia." The fact that Solovyov's brother Vsevelod continued his attempts to discredit the movement did not help. Nevertheless, by 1900 the climate had changed, and Theosophy continued to grow during the next twenty years.

Beginning in 1902, Rudolf Steiner's work, Anthroposophy, became an important part of Theosophy. Not only was Steiner a leading Theosophist and "theosophical" author until his break with the Theosophical Society in 1913, but more important, from a practical point of view, Marie von Sivers, his closest associate and later his wife, was herself Russian. One of her closest friends in St. Petersburg was Maria Strauch-Spettini. In 1902, Strauch-Spettini held an afternoon tea that included Olga von Sivers, Marie's sister, as one of the guests; eight years later, that group became the Russian Theosophical Society. Through Marie von Sivers, Steiner's connection with Russia was always inwardly strong. Outwardly, it was enhanced by the fact that many Russians were affiliated with the German Society, and many of the leading cultural figures of the time took an intense and educated interest in it. In 1904, 1905, 1906, 1912, and 1913, Rudolf Steiner gave lectures designed especially for the Russians. The 1906 lectures in Paris were especially important, because the flower of the Russian spiritual intelligentsia were present. "Many of the Theosophists who attended took notes, which they later read in circles at home, accounting in part for Steiner's high profile among Russian occultists." Not only among occultists, however; while the bourgeoisie tended to remain "faithful" to Blavatsky and Besant, it was primarily artists and intellectuals who were drawn to Steiner.

Three months after the official founding of the Anthroposophical Society in Germany on February 2, 1913, the Russian Anthroposophical Society was founded. Solovyov's poem "The Three Encounters," in which he describes his three meetings with Sophia, was read at the opening meeting (May 8, 1913):

> Let it be known: today, the Divine Feminine
> Is descending to Earth in an incorruptible body.
> In the unfading light of the new Goddess,
> Heaven has become one with the depths.[18]

Tomberg had begun visiting the Theosophical Society in 1915. However, as he wrote to Rudolf Steiner in 1920, he soon turned to Anthroposophy:

> Three years ago, I joined the Russian Theosophical Society, making "spiritual culture" my goal. But I could work neither with theosophical one-sidedness nor, especially, Theosophy's unrestrained suppression of every free movement of thinking. On the other hand, your writings (*How to Know Higher Worlds, An Outline of Esoteric Science, Theosophy,* and *A Way of Self Knowledge*) showed me that, besides Theosophy, there existed another movement in which precisely what I missed in Theosophy was to be found: regard both for the requirements of reason and also for the uniqueness of the Individuality. For this reason, I turned to Anthroposophy.

About this time (1917–1918), Tomberg had a profound spiritual experience, as he wrote in 1933 to Marie Steiner in a letter whose idealism, passion, and dedication are palpable:

> Fifteen years ago (in St. Petersburg, in Russia) it happened—on the street, amid many passers-by—that I experienced an awakening of deep soul forces. I felt the awakening. I became conscious of a powerful will force within me that I united in the depths of my heart with a holy vow *to dedicate my whole life to the cultivation of spiritual knowledge and its manifestation to the world*. I have never forgotten this vow—others may say and think of it what they will. I can only say, before my conscience and my angel, that I have remained true to it in all decisions and questions of life. It shines in me like a radiant sun that irradiates and illumines all.

While Anthroposophy and Rudolf Steiner remained the heart and context of Tomberg's youthful spiritual endeavors, initially he did not limit his path to them. There was the Russian spiritual and philosophical tradition on the one hand and, on the other, the tradition of modern occultism. As he later recounted, in St. Petersburg at this time a school of serious students of the occult had gathered around a professor of mathematics at Pages College, G. O. Mebes (or Meubes). Tomberg met members of this group and became friends with them. "The friendship being true, based as it was on unreserved mutual confidence, they (those who belonged to the so-called Rosicrucian elite of this group) transmitted all they knew and recounted everything concerning the work of their group." This work was based on the Tarot. On its basis, they studied kabala, astrology, alchemy, and magic—all the so-called Hermetic arts. As Tomberg himself says, this work was also a "general impulse received in his youth."[19]

Following the Russian Revolution (October 1917), life in Russia became untenable for the Tombergs, who fled to Estonia. It must have been after March 3, 1918, for on that date the Treaty of Brest-Litovsk, Germany, returned Estonia to Russia. To leave when they did was therefore a tragic decision. The family found its way inland to Rakvere, where they were forced to hide from the Russians; they had entered the lion's mouth. At a certain moment in Rakvere, Tomberg's mother set out to find her son. The Red Army immediately spotted and identified her as an enemy by her dress. They tied her to a tree and shot her, along with the little dog she had brought with her. It was Valentin who found the body. It was a shattering and decisive experience. Thereafter, he was on his own.

He went on to Narva, the first town across the Estonian border. "In 1918, I went to Narva, where I lived until the Russians attacked. There I joined a voluntary regiment of Estonian intellectuals. About a month later, I fell ill and was imprisoned by the Russians. My captivity was of short duration. The Army of the North liberated me. After this I went to Tallinn, where I worked as a medical assistant in the military hospital in Juhkental." In February 1920, in accord with the Versailles Treaty, Estonia regained its independence.

Tomberg worked at the hospital from April 20, 1920, until May 1, 1922. He quickly learned Estonian and, while continuing to work, began to study law, comparative religion, and languages at Tartu University. (By the end of his life he would be able to speak Russian, Estonian, German, Dutch, English, and French fluently; he was also able to read and understand Spanish, Polish, and Ukrainian and to read Latin, Greek, Hebrew, Sanskrit and Old Bulgarian Church Slavic.) After he left the hospital, he took what work he could find, becoming a farm laborer and a pharmacist's assistant. Finally, in 1923, he obtained a job in the Estonian post office, which he kept until he left for Holland in 1938. These were difficult years. Indeed, hardship and poverty would accompany him his whole life. Yet, whatever he earned went toward books and study.

He was not alone for very long, however. He had, almost immediately upon arrival in Tallinn, met a friend of his mother from St. Petersburg: Helene Glasenap, recently divorced and nineteen years older than he. She took him in. They were married in December 1922 in the Vicarage of the Lutheran community. It was a union of convenience, companionship, mutual respect, and support. It was probably never consummated.

Anthroposophy now became the guiding center of Tomberg's life. On July 4, 1924, he wrote to Rudolf Steiner:

> Most Honored Doctor!
>
> With this letter, I turn to you to request admission into the School of Spiritual Science in Dornach.
>
> First, I must tell you that I am not a member of the Anthroposophical Society, although I know several members, some of whom are my friends.
>
> My esoteric strivings date from 1915. Since 1920, I have worked actively for the advancement of the anthroposophic work. I understand this work to be essentially the dedicated activity whose goal is to deepen human consciousness by means of independent, selfless, creative, cognitive work, free of all dogma and authority and combined with the practice of self-criticism. I have striven to work in this way for a long time in two, small, closed circles.
>
> What prompts me to write is not to seek "connection" with a human group or relief (though it is certainly nice to pass responsibility on to others), but the conviction that I have a life task that—as far as I know now—consists in being useful in my own way to the work that Dornach serves. Thus I have decided on a difficult task, one that claims all my powers. I do not wish to enter a "spiritual boarding school," where spiritual food is served ready-made. Whatever spiritual truths or spiritual validity I may discover, I hope to bring to realization, along with the duties that follow, and bear them as seeds into the future. I perceive what is coming as something difficult. Therefore I will gratefully accept your decision, whatever it may be, regarding my fate.
>
> I am twenty-four years old. I have no profession, for, as yet, there is none for me. I dedicate my available time and powers to spiritual science and its demands.
>
> I have done many different kinds of work—clerk, teacher, farm worker, pharmacist, artist. I am poor, and therefore cannot come to Dornach.
>
> Awaiting your decision I remain, and will remain in the future, your grateful and humble coworker in the work of the realization of humanity's vocation and destiny.

Rudolf Steiner died the next year; Tomberg never met him. It is unknown whether Steiner replied personally, but Tomberg received word that he should first join the Anthroposophical Society, which he did on January 1, 1925. Rudolf Steiner signed his "pink card." The Estonian Society had been formed only the previous year under the leadership of Otto Sepp, who quickly became a trusted friend and mentor. It was a small group. Tomberg soon found himself vice president, lecturing frequently, and leading study groups. He and Sepp grew very close. He also began to write and, in 1926, with Otto Sepp and Harald Rennit, founded the first Estonian anthroposophic journal, *Antroposoofia*. For Tomberg, however, Anthroposophy was never an intellectual affair, but an individual, social, and cosmic path of transformation and inner development. From the beginning, his life of spiritual practice was arduous, assiduous, and profound.

In 1927, Tomberg reapplied to Marie Steiner for admittance to the School of Spiritual Science and was accepted. The membership card, however, could not be sent through mail. Marie Steiner herself, therefore, would personally hand it to him at the Danzig Conference of the Polish Anthroposophical Society, which she would attend with other prominent board members such as Elizabeth Vreede (with whom Tomberg would later form a deep friendship) and Günther Wachsmuth. Despite what would later occur, at that time and for the next few years, Tomberg was extremely close to Maria Steiner and enjoyed her complete trust, which made their subsequent alienation only the more painful.

At the Danzig Conference, Tomberg (along with Otto Sepp) was to speak on the topic of "the problem of the East European border states and its solution in a free spiritual life." From that point on, it became part of Tomberg's spiritual task to elucidate the mission of Russia and Eastern Christianity and the nature of "Russian" Anthroposophy. He wrote many articles on the subject and worked tirelessly to bring together in a "Russian movement" the various groups of Russians dispersed across Europe—in Paris, Berlin, Prague, Warsaw, Riga, and his own Tallinn. During this process, he met many people and made many friends, none more important than Nikolai Belozvetov and his wife Maria. Seven years older than Tomberg, Belozvetov would become one of Tomberg's closest friends.

Invited by Marie Steiner, Tomberg visited Dornach for the first time in the summer of 1929. Upon leaving, he wrote to her:

> Before leaving Dornach, let me tell you what moves my soul deeply. I leave with the feeling of certainty that I was able to grasp Dr. Steiner's intentions more deeply than before and that the clear, conscious objectivity that you represent so nobly and uncompromisingly is the right one for all the branches of anthroposophic work—in art as well as in cognition. These few meager sentences contain a whole world of experiences I lived through in Dornach. Thank you for making it possible. Let me now inscribe (with full consciousness of the responsibility of such words) the ripe decision of my gratitude-filled soul:
>
> *I will dedicate myself wholly, as a person and a human being, to the service of Anthroposophy as the union of the two worlds in sun-clear human consciousness. I will dedicate all my power, ability, time, and means to the work, for which Dr. Unger died and for which you, dear honored Frau Doctor, live.* (emphasis added)

He was as good as his word; in the next two years, thirty-three penetrating articles (still well worth reading) appeared in the main German anthroposophic journals. Those articles cover a wide range of topics and give evidence of an extraordinary soul seeking a home in Anthroposophy. Their author is not so much an expositor as he is a seeker, an explorer. He does not write finished, conclusive statements but, as it were, open-ended reports on ongoing spiritual research. There are themes and tensions. Anthroposophy—as teaching, method, and culture—provides the frame; love of Christ, the motive; and the very real, historical situation of a Europe divided into three (Western, Central, and Eastern) provides the problematic.

Whether it is Anthroposophy or love of Christ that one aspires to, Tomberg is very aware that it makes a difference where one stands. He writes: "It is true that, when consistent in its inner principles with Rudolf Steiner's spiritual science, meditation is always the same; yet the relationship of the person in question can vary, according to which cultural sphere one belongs to—the Eastern, Western, or Central European. For the difference of the soul attitude reaches right into the intimate realm of meditative life."[20]

The first article, "The Gospel of John as a Way to Understanding the Spiritual Hierarchies," sounds the primary themes that will echo through all of Tomberg's work: the reality and unity of divine, cosmic, and human history; the interrelationship of "emptiness" and "fullness"; the spiritual hierarchies; the centrality of Christ; the Johannine mission; and the transforming *moral* power of the Logos.

Today, we experience the universe as "an immense void, in which certain spaces are filled." But, in earlier times, interplanetary space was experienced as "full" with spiritual substance. The cosmos was a "plenitude surrounding the void of the Earth." Matter, rather than the "stuff" of reality, was a "hole," or "imprint," in the fullness. As such, it was a sign and could be read. What was above was like that below. Then things changed. What was full, the cosmos, became empty; "The human soul was deserted by fullness, both outwardly and inwardly. She became surrounded by fields of emptiness, where the material and abstract confronted her as pale reality." In other words, the human soul became the lonely source of light in an otherwise dark, meaningless world and lacked the power to fill it.

Such was the desert in which John the Baptist, "the voice of one crying in the wilderness," proclaimed the coming of Christ, through whom the emptiness could be filled—for "in him the fullness of the Godhead dwelt bodily." Tomberg takes John's Gospel as his guide. He shows how John teaches that the fullness is now open to human beings once more. According to the principle, "the deeper the effect, the higher the cause," the fullness; for Tomberg, this is the working together of the spiritual hierarchies and the Trinity, now made available to us through the incarnation of the Logos, in Christ, the Word "made flesh."

After the Baptism (the birth of the "I"), the third hierarchy, working through the signs or miracles, purifies the soul, or astral body, opening our cognitive faculty of *Imagination*. Then, in the "Farewell Discourses," through the work of the second hierarchy, the Word becomes living, moral speech: *inspiration*. Next, at Golgotha, living, moral speech, the power of *imagination* and *inspiration*, becomes *intuition* through the work of the first hierarchy. The physical body is transformed. Finally, through the resurrection, the power of the Godhead becomes manifest. Thus, for Tomberg, Christ is at the center of cosmic, human, and divine history and Anthroposophy, as way and substance, or content, is the path to revealing his activity.

Tomberg's remaining articles dealt either with specifically anthroposophic topics or with Anthroposophy in relation to various aspects of Eastern Christianity, Eastern

Europe, and Russia. Always aware of the difference between East, West, and Center (Central Europe), he wrote of, among other topics, meditation, occultism, Theosophy, and the metamorphosis of logic and thinking; of Christianity; of the evils of totalitarianism and materialism; and of the Russian soul and its unique understanding of suffering. The implicit theme is always how to make spiritual experience concrete and truly grounded in its place and time.

The immense range and depth of his articles—and their sheer quantity, with at least two published every month during 1930 and 1931—made Tomberg known suddenly in anthroposophic circles. He became a visible "exponent" of Anthroposophy and, therefore, privy to the political infighting endemic to spiritual institutions and increasingly rampant at the time.

1932 marked a turning point. Otto Sepp, Tomberg's first mentor, died, and Tomberg and Maria Belozvetovna decided to unite their destinies.[21] Both, of course, were married. The Belozvetovs, however, had been estranged since at least 1928. On the other hand, for Elena Tomberg her husband's decision was so unexpected and unwanted that she wrote about it to Marie Steiner, veiling her grief and shock in terms of the general confusion surrounding Sepp's death. Marie Steiner heard her cry of despair. At this point, Tomberg, too, wrote to her about the situation:

> Naturally, I will never abandon Elena Eduardovna Tomberg, and will never leave her without the assistance and attention she needs and has earned. I will take her with me to Berlin.... I know that you cannot receive this news with any but mixed feelings. Too many divorces and such have happened in our society. I understand that very well. But what should I do? I can say only one thing (and it is the truth): My conscience is absolutely clear. I know that I am acting correctly, that I cannot act otherwise than I am doing. Naturally, then, why conceal it? It would pain me deeply if you would condemn us. You are the only person in the world whose condemnation would be a great blow to me. If you were to condemn me, which I would quite understand and am ready to accept, nothing will change in our relationship to you and the work you are doing. We will remain your faithful coworkers.

True to his word, Tomberg did not abandon Elena Eduardovna. Until he left Estonia in autumn 1938, she lived with the new couple, received about a third of Tomberg's meager income, and, when Alexis Tomberg was born, assumed the role of grandmother. In the eyes of the world, it must have appeared an odd arrangement that did little for Tomberg's reputation. Rumors circulated. Marie Steiner felt betrayed: "I liked Herr Tomberg very much, and I trusted him." Up to that point, she, who was the most powerful person in the society, had supported him. They had been very close. Indeed, in a sense, Tomberg had been her protégé. Increasingly, she would begin to turn against him—as she would against many others. For now, however, as Tomberg continued to report on his anthroposophic work in Estonia, their relationship seemed unchanged. From Tomberg's side, it was a new beginning. He had found in Maria a life companion who not only shared his deepest spiritual interests and strivings, but also was practical and gifted in innumerable ways. At the same time (September 25, 1932), he was elected the General Secretary of the Anthroposophical Society of Estonia. He intensified his lecturing activity, giving (for instance) a three-month course on Rudolf Steiner's *How to Know Higher Worlds*.

Meanwhile Elena Eduardovna justifiably felt left out. Jealous, she made her unhappiness known. Somewhat naively, or idealistically, Tomberg had not reckoned with her dissent. He regarded the marriage, which, as far as is known, was unconsummated—she was nineteen years older than he—primarily as a social arrangement. That arrangement would continue. Nevertheless, she naturally felt deceived. She had dedicated her life to keeping house for her husband and supporting him behind the scenes. Introverted, intelligent, and warmhearted, she was much loved in the anthroposophic community. Maria, by contrast, was very different: aristocratic, artistic, an intellectual, and fluent in many languages. Above all, she and Tomberg loved each other very much. In love, they were always together. Members and friends in Tallinn, therefore, naturally felt that they had lost "their" Valentin. Then, when Nikolai Belozvetov and his new wife Anna von Stockmar came on an extended visit to work with the Tombergs in Tallinn, rumors began to fly and complicate matters even more.

These were difficult years for Europe and for Anthroposophy. Since Rudolf Steiner's death in 1925, two tendencies had struggled for dominance on the board of the General (or Universal) Anthroposophical Society, founded a year and a half earlier by Steiner himself. One tendency was expansive; it sought to develop Anthroposophy in a comprehensive, inclusive direction. The other was contractive and sought above all to protect Rudolf Steiner's legacy.

Almost immediately upon Steiner's passing, the overwhelming sense of responsibility for what he had initiated—intensified by issues of power and personality—began to make it impossible for members of the board (the *Vorstand*) to work together and resolve their differences. The situation is far too complex to explain in any detail here; suffice it to say that the board, personally selected by Rudolf Steiner, consisted of five members: Marie Steiner, Albert Steffen, Günther Wachsmuth, Ita Wegman, and Elizabeth Vreede. By 1928, things had already deteriorated to the point that Wegman and Vreede were effectively marginalized and no longer attended meetings. Over the following years, until the expulsion of Wegman and Vreede (and others) in 1935, things simply got worse.

Tomberg's first relationship was with Marie Steiner; when it soured and died, his main support would come from Elizabeth Vreede. Consequently, as far as Dornach, the anthroposophic center, was concerned, he was on the "wrong" side.

As this debacle unfolded and reached its climax, the greater European debacle also loomed on the historical horizon. It, too, would soon climax. Hitler acceded to power on January 30, 1933. Eleven days before, Tomberg had written to Marie Steiner to see if there was any way he could spend a year in Dornach, working where Rudolf Steiner himself had worked. He had also written to her a few months previously, saying he hoped to come at Christmas and, mysteriously, that he had something very important to tell her. "You are the only person in the world to whom, quite often, I can say everything." What he had to say is unknown, but it probably concerned insights into both Anthroposophy and the European situation. To Anthroposophy, National Socialism meant more pressure and that it was time for the already beleaguered *Vorstand* to circle the wagons. Personal attacks on Rudolf Steiner and on the anthroposophic movements generally began almost immediately and, on February 16, Günther Wachsmuth wrote to Tomberg that, for many reasons, his wish to come to Dornach could not be accommodated. A few days later, Marie Steiner, still appearing warm and friendly, confirmed that a visit at that time would not be possible. Later, Albert Steffen, too, wrote. It became clear that Tomberg's work was not needed in Dornach. His place was to work on and from the periphery. With the birth of his son Alexis in August and with the ever-strengthening Sophia-Christ–centered collaboration with his wife Maria, his spiritual work would take on new, multifaceted depth.

In November 1933, the first chapter of the "Anthroposophic Meditations on the Old Testament" appeared and was circulated. The following chapters would appear over the next year and a half, and the series would continue. As soon as the first appeared, however, a heated debate arose over the legitimacy of such a work. It cannot be said that Tomberg did not anticipate the furor; his original "Author's Note," addressed to the members of the Anthroposophical Society, makes this clear:

> These "Anthroposophic Meditations on the Old Testament" are intended to represent the beginning of a series of ongoing publications to which the author knows he is committed. The purpose of such a regularly occurring series of publications is to meet the need, existing in wide circles of the Anthroposophical Society, for pure *anthroposophic* research. The content of the "meditations" did not come into being through intellectual speculation and the establishment of hypotheses, nor by merely collecting facts drawn from Rudolf Steiner's lecture cycles, but through *anthroposophic* research.
>
> The writer is not in the position to indicate all Rudolf Steiner's cycles, books, and individual lectures on which he worked to achieve the results made public in the "meditations." Suffice it to say, once and for all, that the writer owes Rudolf Steiner *everything* that was allowed to become insights for him. *Everything* that he has to say *is rooted* in the life work of Rudolf Steiner, to the extent that he was even led, through Rudolf Steiner, to *new* sources of insight from which he was allowed to draw. As the air that we inhale is difficult to separate from the air in the outer world, so it is difficult for the writer to draw a line between what he gained for himself and what Rudolf Steiner communicated. Anyone who knows anthroposophic literature will be able to distinguish between what is new and what has been given already. Others will have to be satisfied with the question of *the truth of the contents* of the "meditations," irrespective of the matter of their origin. It is certainly also anthroposophically *correct,* when taking up facts and ideas, to ask first concerning their *truth,* rather than about the authority of the person conveying them.

> It must also be said, right at the beginning, that the writer will in no way be drawn into any polemics. Letters with a polemical content will remain unanswered. He simply does not have the time to answer them. He has no reason to fear any criticism, however, for everything essential that has been able to be made public has already undergone the criticism that precisely the anthroposophic way of knowledge brings with it.
>
> Finally, the writer must ask German readers' indulgence with regard to the language of the "meditations." He is a foreigner, and his knowledge of the German language is incomplete. But he has made the effort to express himself as carefully as possible in order to attain at the very least clarity of expression.

With this foreword and the accompanying first chapter, Tomberg's fate in the Anthroposophical Society was effectively sealed; the die was cast. It was only a matter of time before he could no longer work in any official capacity in the society. Though it was characteristic of him never to engage in contentious behavior, it was also characteristic never to allow himself to be moved from his purpose by it. No matter what was happening around him, he simply continued to do what he felt he had to do.

That he anticipated difficulties is quite clear from the foreword. These were (and still are) "fighting words." He states that he is "bound" to his task, with all that such a prophetic "call" implies and is, thereby, also publicly putting his "will" to the test. At the same time, he criticizes the society (and implicitly the *Vorstand*) by asserting that it lacks *anthroposophic* research, a need that he will meet. He then makes it clear that the content of his work is neither scholarly nor speculative, but original spiritual research. At the same time, he makes it clear that he has made Steiner's work his own. He has, as it were, confirmed it for himself. This in itself is a disturbing claim when one considers both the level of inner work it implies and the fact that Steiner is usually held to be so far "above" anyone else that the best one can do is to follow the traces of his coattails. Tomberg says it is difficult for him to tell where Steiner ends and he begins. In other words, he is not writing "secondary" anthroposophic literature or explanatory commentary on Rudolf Steiner; he is writing an "original" *anthroposophic* work and asks to be judged accordingly. That is why he is not interested in footnoting and acknowledging every debt, although he acknowledges gratefully that he owes *everything* to Rudolf Steiner's "lifework" (itself an interesting choice of words); this suggests that, in addition to Steiner's work, he means also the "person" and the earthly event that constituted Steiner's life. As an "anthroposophic" work, then, the "meditations" arise according to the method and from the whole worldview and contents established by Steiner; but it is the author's work and whatever it contains that should be judged above all on its own truthfulness. Finally, as if to forestall but, in effect, to arouse criticism, Tomberg states that he will not answer any criticism of a polemical nature.

For about sixteen years (in the scale of things, a relatively long time), he had worked intensively with Rudolf Steiner's indications. Assiduously, even ferociously, and with great inner discipline and dedication, he had practiced *seemingly successfully* Rudolf Steiner's transformative exercises for the attainment of the higher states of consciousness known as *imagination, inspiration,* and *intuition.* Deeply and widely read, passionately concerned with the world in all its aspects, he had sought to make the vast diversity that Steiner had brought into the world as spiritual science his own. The *Early Articles* show how deep, broad, and existential was his understanding of the path of spiritual scientific research and how seriously he took it as a path of initiation.

Reading the *Early Articles* and the "meditations," we become aware of the extent to which Tomberg was able to speak out of, and for, the whole of Anthroposophy. Anthroposophy was not just a "study" or a "hobby" or a "club" for him; it was his life—his total and wholehearted commitment. It was truly an initiation, and he saw that the future of Anthroposophy would depend on others taking it up with the same dedication. Therefore, he stressed in his first chapter: "The highest initiates are here; they have students through whom they can speak; there is even a deeper wisdom and higher discipline than what lies before us in the scripture we possess. *Everyone who works hard enough and is found worthy can gain access to this wisdom and discipline.*" And quoting Rudolf Steiner: "We can be certain that, if our striving for knowledge is sincere and worthy, initiation will find us whatever the circumstances."

Clearly, besides being gifted with a penetrating intelligence and a deep sense of the morality and wisdom of the heart, Tomberg was enormously gifted *spiritually.* But had he overreached himself? He was still very young—only in his thirty-third year. Was he ready to step forward as a teacher? Was he, in fact, doing so? Such were the questions raised by the opening chapter and introduction. If he was making such claims, even implicitly, was he simply being brash, idealistic, overzealous, and even arrogant (with the arrogance of youth)? Or was he justified? Readers of the "meditations" will have to make up their own minds. Certainly, no matter what else was at stake, it was a startling and courageous act to herald the world-historical, cosmic, and divine mission of the Jewish people as National Socialism brazenly strutted and consolidated its power and shamelessly instituted its lethal "final solution" of Anti-Semitism.

The "series" of publications to which the author was committed, however, is not limited to the Old Testament. It was to continue and include both the New Testament and the Apocalypse: a major anthroposophic undertaking. In other words, Tomberg is proposing a program that, extending through lectures on the "etheric Christ" and the unpublished "Our Father Course," will take ten years to fulfill—clearly, a significant project. Thus, as one begins to read the first chapter, it is not surprising when one realizes (and it must have been as clear then, as it is now, though the historical context is very different) that a new spiritual note is being sounded, one that seeks to deepen Christianity in a new way and to midwife a transfiguration of the world through our moral understanding of it.

Scripture, Tomberg begins, provides us with the evidence—or "facts"—of the divine spiritual worlds' ongoing and mutually transformative interaction or conversation with humanity and the Earth. As such, it constitutes a continuation of the ancient mysteries, through whose suprasensory revelations human culture and civilization have always evolved and "whose methods alter with every epoch but persist in an unbroken line to the present day."

The method for Tomberg is the one outlined by Rudolf Steiner and called anthroposophic spiritual science. This science is not a body of knowledge or information, but living *human* experience, *a way of knowing*, that leads to moral action in the world. Just as human experience, the unified human field, consists of body, soul, and spirit, so spiritual science—or "occultism"—likewise consists of a unity made up of three realms, traditionally called the eugenic, the hygienic, and the mechanical. The eugenic path is that which harmonizes the relations between humanity as a whole and the spiritual world; the hygienic path does the same for the individual human organism; while the mechanical regulates "nature" so that it harmonizes with true human destiny. The three paths are unfolded for us in the three great spiritual documents of our time: the Hebrew Scriptures, the New Testament, and the Apocalypse. The Hebrew Scriptures teach the esotericism of the "holy birth"; the Gospels teach the esotericism of healing humanity of its sickness; and the Apocalypse unveils the esoteric consequences of this healing of humanity for nature and the cosmos. In other words, Tomberg assumes a vast and dual task: on the one hand, to reveal the deepest, esoteric meaning of the Old and New Testaments and, in this sense, to contribute to a renewal of Christianity; on the other, to place Christianity—the love of Christ and Sophia—at the heart of Anthroposophy. Thus, the aim of the "meditations" is nothing other than to place Anthroposophy at the service of the Christ: to serve Christ and Sophia out of Anthroposophy.

It is impossible in the compass of an introduction to recount the depth and riches that flowed through Tomberg during this period. Readers will have to study for themselves these "meditations" as they continued to flow unabated during some of the most painful years of human history—years that placed their author continuously under the greatest personal and historical pressure. The "meditations" are not the fruit of an ivory tower existence but arise from a spiritual necessity during extraordinary times. Indeed, it is difficult to imagine the inner strength of spiritual purpose required for such a task. Nevertheless, the context, however moving, is incidental. Readers will have to decide for themselves as to the value of Tomberg's work, through the work they themselves do in coming to terms with it. Certainly, there are great riches here that demand repeated and meditative reading. The themes are vast and huge and concern nothing less than our human past, present, and future. At the same time, this vastness is always brought down to concrete, individual moral and spiritual experience.

In the anthroposophic world of that time, attitudes toward the "meditations" differed, and opinion was divided. There was opposition, suspicion, slander, and resistance; but also a growing circle of new friends. Chief among these was Elizabeth Vreede, the embattled *Vorstand* member of whom Rudolf Steiner repeatedly said she understood him better than anyone else.[22] She would become a close spiritual companion for Valentin Tomberg. Receiving the first chapter, she engaged Tomberg honestly and frankly, writing that, though she found his language overly rigid and conceptual for her taste—and had other criticisms—she could nevertheless recognize that what he was saying arose from authentic spiritual experiences. Tomberg responded with gratitude, saying how much he appreciated her friendly objectivity, out of which free and open discussion might flow. As for his language, he had had to choose between two "evils": whether to be classified an "intellectual" or a "fantasist." He consciously chose the former, believing it the only one that had a chance of being heard in the Anthroposophical Society.

The society was suffering extreme divisions. As Tomberg continued serenely to issue chapters of his "meditations," increasing internal and external pressures were in the process of splitting the society apart. Ita Wegman and Elizabeth Vreede had already been effectively excluded from the governing *Vorstand;* that exclusion would become official with their "expulsion" in 1935. Preceding this, a year earlier, a movement had begun to create Free Anthroposophical Groups. With the expulsive *Memorandum* of spring 1935, such groups would gain strength under the coordination of Elizabeth Vreede. Many national societies and prominent anthroposophists would participate. Tomberg, naturally, was among them. Attacked personally, his work defamed, he resigned as the general secretary of the Estonian Society and as "class reader" and ended his group work. His focus now became twofold: his own spiritual research and his growing and close collaboration with Elizabeth Vreede. As he concluded his Old Testament "meditations" and began on the New Testament, on November 1, 1935, the Anthroposophical Society was banned in Germany. It was a seismic symptom whose ominous aftershocks reached from East to West.

But life went on. For a moment, up to the outbreak of World War II, the Free Anthroposophical Groups, acting independently of Dornach, seemed to promise a new possibility and new life, both for inner spiritual work and for collaboration and community. The Free Anthroposophical Groups arose first in Germany and continued to build on Rudolf Steiner's own establishment of a "second" free society for young people in the 1920s. In July 1934, groups in Holland, England, and Germany gathered to form a "union," with the blessing and support of Elizabeth Vreede (at that time still on the *Vorstand*). Free groups in other nations would join them. In this new milieu, Tomberg continued to make new friends—Elizabeth Vreede above all, who recognized in him someone who was both a new significant figure in Anthroposophy and personally sympathetic. She organized lectures for him, in a way becoming his "sponsor," and distributed his "meditations" from her home in Arlesheim, where he was received as a guest and a collaborator. Through her, Tomberg came to know many of the leading independent anthroposophists of the time. And, as awareness of the "meditations" began to spread more widely, he met other "karmically" significant figures such as Stefan Lubienski (affiliated with the Dutch Free Anthroposophical Group) and, above all, Ernst von Hippel, a jurist, with whom he was clearly linked by destiny and who became, with Belozvetov, one of his two closest friends: a soul brother.

Von Hippel, an early opponent of Nazism, was a student of Rudolf Steiner and a member of the Christian Community, though not of the Anthroposophical Society. After the war he, too, would become a Catholic. He had discovered the "meditations" and wrote to Tomberg to express his appreciation, inviting him to visit him in Königsburg and enclosing a copy of his own book of 1935 on the subject of humanity and community. Deeply religious, von Hippel was a stalwart advocate of a universal spiritual perspective on law and morality. A lover of Christ and the truth, he opposed materialism in all its forms. Tomberg and von Hippel met the following year (1936) in Tallinn. In his letter of thanks, Tomberg, now working on his New Testament "meditations," spoke of "a warm and bright feeling of friendship and an unshakeable conviction of being united and remaining united on all the ways of destiny."

Despite traumatic historical conditions, these were fruitful years. Tomberg's friendships with Ernst von Hippel and Elizabeth Vreede continued to deepen. Under Vreede's patronage, in 1937 and 1938, Tomberg lectured in Free Anthroposophical Groups in Holland, England, Germany, and Switzerland. He gave courses on "Inner Development" and on "The Spiritual Hierarchies" and began intensive spiritual research (unpublished) into the chakras. He also prepared for publication the first part of a study of Rudolf Steiner's "Foundation Stone Meditation." In his foreword (Christmas 1936), Tomberg writes that, for eleven years, he has "not only regarded it as the foundation stone of all anthroposophic study, but has also endeavored to make it the foundation of all his written or spoken work. In whatever task he has had to perform, he has taken the Foundation Stone as his guide." That this was not just a passing obligation is made clear by the publication of a second part in 1937, and a third, concluding part in 1939—this despite his resignation from the General Anthroposophical Society in 1938. His growing friendship with English Free Anthroposophists such as George Adams meant that his work began to appear in England in English translation, with Elizabeth Vreede writing the introduction of the Old Testament Studies and Adams introducing the work on "The Foundation Stone." Meanwhile, of course, his New Testament "meditations" continued to appear.

In late fall of 1938, Tomberg left Estonia for Holland, where in 1939 he took over the direction of the Estonian Consulate in Amsterdam. There he continued his work, but now, significantly, in a "Western" context. He completed his New Testament chapters and began his "meditations" on the Apocalypse. Meanwhile, he continued his anthroposophic lecturing and teaching activity, including the fascinating and important lecture cycle (at the turn of the years 1938–1939) on "The Four Sacrifices of Christ and the Appearance of Christ in the Etheric" (see the appendix in this volume). Tomberg was, in fact, one of the first anthroposophists to take up Christ's reappearance in the etheric, this most precious fruit of Rudolf Steiner's spiritual research. Although Tomberg had alluded to Christ's etheric return previously in two (1931) articles reprinted in *Early*

*Articles* ("The Deepening of Conscience, which results in Etheric Vision" and "Suffering as a Preparation for Etheric Vision"), in this lecture course, he went into it in great detail. Interestingly, two pages of the typescript from lecture 6 entered circulation with the heading "From a lecture by Rudolf Steiner, Stockholm, 1911." As such, until the mistake was realized, people quoted from them as if they were by Steiner himself.[23]

On September 1, German troops crossed into Poland, and German planes began bombing Polish cities. On September 3, England and France declared war. As Holland remained neutral, Tomberg lectured tirelessly on Hitler, National Socialism, and evil, trying to awaken his listeners to a heightened consciousness that could combat the evils arising from the unconscious. At the same time, he strove to deepen the spiritual understanding of the realities he felt most important.

On May 10, 1940, Germany invaded Holland (the evening before, Tomberg gave his last public lecture, "The Human Being as Trinity"). By May 14, the resistance had ended. Ten days later, on May 24, Zeylmans von Emmichoven dissolved the Dutch Anthroposophical Society and burned the records. The same was done for the Free Groups. It was in those days, too, that Valentin Tomberg and Zeylmans von Emmichoven had a fateful conversation. The result was that Valentin Tomberg, asked by Zeylmans not to work with the Dutch groups, terminated his formal association with Anthroposophy. No one knows exactly what the point of dissension was. One rumor suggests that Tomberg's circle had been discussing various people's previous incarnations, including his own and those of Zeylmans von Emmichoven. This is possible, but there is no written evidence for this. Indeed, there is no evidence that Tomberg ever went beyond Steiner in speaking of historical incarnations. Another idea places blame on the themes of Tomberg's lectures to the Free Groups—perhaps his increasing focus on Christ and Sophia, but more likely his occult analyses of Hitler and National Socialism. For Tomberg, Hitler was satanic, one of the seven stages of the manifestation of the Antichrist. For his part, Zeylmans mistrusted "independent esotericism that went beyond Steiner." He felt it was important for Holland, at that moment, to stay close to Steiner's own work. For Tomberg, Steiner's work was, above all, increasingly a bridge to experiencing Christ, Michael, Sophia, and all the angels. Whatever the cause, the die, again, was cast.

He continued with his work, nonetheless. With a small group, he deepened his biblical, Christological, and Sophiological research, as well as his prayer and meditation practices. In Christmas 1940, he gave the "Our Mother" prayer:

> Our Mother,
> You who are in the darkness of the underworld,
> May the holiness of your name shine a light anew on our remembering,
> May the breath of the awakening of your kingdom warm all homeless wanderers,
> May the resurrection of your will enliven eternal faith unto the depths of matter.
> Receive today the living remembrance of you from human hearts,
> Who pray you to forgive the sin of forgetting you,

And are ready to fight against the temptation in the world
That has led you to existence in darkness,
That through the deed of the Son, the immeasurable pain of the Father be stilled
In the liberation of all beings from the misfortune of your withdrawal.
For yours are the homeland, the generosity, and the mercy
For all and everything in the Circle of All. Amen.

Sometime in May or June 1940, he began what would be a three-year course with about ten people on The Lord's Prayer, studied in connection with the Old and New Testaments and brought into focus with the union of Christ and Sophia and the Persons of the Trinity. This was a different kind of work. Intimate, prayerful, meditative, it was intended to create a Christic stream to counter Hitler's satanic counter stream. Throughout the war years, this little group would deepen its Christian esoteric path, beginning in the mornings with *meditation* (especially Steiner's so-called supplementary exercises) and ending in the evenings with *prayer*. At the center of this work lay the idea of "communion": *our daily bread*.

Thus it became clear to Tomberg—especially in the face of the evil shamelessly visible in the increasingly vicious persecution of the Jews—that to realize a complete path required a liturgical *community* that, orienting Earth toward Heaven, could embody Heaven on Earth. For him this became a heart's need that would lead him mysteriously to the Catholic Church.

He had always loved, and for many years intensively studied, the Russian Orthodox liturgy. Thus he turned first to Orthodoxy, to Father Dionysii, the priest of the Russian Orthodox Church in Amsterdam who had often spoken against National Socialism in his congregation. There was much they could agree on; there was a meeting of hearts on many things. But when Father Dionysii learned that Tomberg's philosophy included reincarnation, he drew the line; he would not give him the sacraments.

Tomberg turned next to the Christian Community, with which his two "best" friends, Ernst von Hippel and Nikolai Belozvetov, were connected and which, since 1936, had been under strict surveillance by the Nazis, who knew that, with the dissolution of the Anthroposophical Society in Germany, many members would seek refuge and a place to gather there. Tomberg had long wanted to meet Emil Bock, who had taken over the leadership of the Church after the death of Friedrich Rittelmeyer in 1938. In February 1942, Bock returned to Stuttgart after eight months' imprisonment ("protective custody"). Because Belozvetov lived in Stuttgart, he could set up a meeting and accompany Tomberg. Von Hippel was also present at one meeting. Again, we do not know exactly what passed; nothing was written down. Certainly, the question of religious renewal was discussed, especially what would be done after the defeat of Germany, when the ban on the Christian Community would be lifted. Liturgical questions, too, must have been addressed. Tomberg evidently made a plea for the inclusion of the Mary-Sophia being. Bock apparently would have nothing of it: "We have Michael. That suffices. We do not need Mary-Sophia." For

Tomberg, Mary-Sophia was the foundation of any authentic religious, spiritual striving and alone ensured that any gnosis—even Michaelic gnosis—was complete and not one-sided. Emil Bock, however, would not be swayed. Although interested in, and even devoted to, the Mary being, "Sophia," in Tomberg's sense, meant little to Bock. The upshot was clear. The Christian Community did not "need" Valentin Tomberg.

In fall 1942, Tomberg inwardly "entered" the Catholic Church. He made a formal but, as far as one can ascertain, still only inward commitment at the Church of Mary Magdalene in Amsterdam. It was unexpected. His closest friends, Belozvetov and von Hippel, were surprised, but they understood. They knew their friend. But they also understood that such a move would shock many anthroposophists. Anthroposophists, for the most part, felt that organized religions (churches in general and the Catholic Church in particular) were regressive forces, belonging to a previous age and state of consciousness. Rudolf Steiner himself had often, though by no means always, spoken to that effect.

Here it must be noted that Tomberg at this point was not "leaving" Anthroposophy; he was only "joining" the Church. When and how and to what extent he actually "left" Anthroposophy remains an open question. Certainly, he abandoned the more "Aristotelian," spiritual scientific mode of research and expression and turned to a life of intuition and prayer and a more "Platonic," mystical, imagistic, and poetic form of communication. Equally unknown is how and to what extent his relationship with Rudolf Steiner changed. For the moment, these things must remain mysteries. According to Charles Lawrie, sometime in the 1950s in London, the Russian anthroposophist Eugenia Gurwitsch asked Tomberg, "Why did you become a Catholic?" He replied very simply, "Rudolf Steiner wanted me to."[24] Who knows whether this is true, and if it is, what it means? At the very least, it seems to imply that Tomberg retained a connection with the individuality of Rudolf Steiner. Though certainly critical of anthroposophists in his *Meditations on the Tarot,* Tomberg speaks highly of Steiner in his last work, *Lazarus, Come Forth!* There, writing of the angelic hierarchies, he states: "The teaching on the heavenly hierarchies was renewed in the first quarter of this century through the lifework of the great Austrian seer and thinker Rudolf Steiner. The depth and profundity of Steiner's contribution to a new understanding of the spiritual hierarchies is such that this theme cannot be taken up today without taking into account his remarkable accomplishment." He goes on to call Rudolf Steiner's achievement incomparable—"a cathedral (on the level of thought) to the celestial hierarchies"—and unique in human spiritual history.[25]

High praise, indeed, but it should not, of course, be taken to imply that little had changed; everything was changed. Tomberg experienced an inner evolution, one so great that, as he put it, it divided his life in two, making his earlier "anthroposophic" life seem like a previous incarnation. He had gone from being a spiritual scientist to becoming a "mystic." His path changed from meditation to prayer. Yet he remained an "occultist," or esotericist. In this sense, he did not change; his life, from the earliest manifestations available to us, is clearly continuous. As late as 1952, he wrote a manuscript (unpublished) titled "Mars and Buddha," which by its title appears still clearly within an anthroposophic framework.

The move toward Catholicism was not expected—yet neither was it unexpected. In his "Our Father Course," Tomberg had already revealed that his spiritual scientific research was leading him to view Catholicism in a different light. Previously, in the *Early Articles*, he had been critical. He had written of how Eastern Christianity was an inner communion with the living Christ that left Christians free to think as they would. In the East, there was no "infallible" teaching; the individual was left free. The love of Christ was all. But in the West, according to Tomberg's view at that time, Christianity had taken on a more dogmatic, authoritarian form. Now, however, as he ended his "Our Father Course," he began to see things differently. He spoke of the tasks of the two streams, Petrine and Johannine, exoteric and esoteric, one caring for the sheep and the other waiting, both stemming from a single founder—Christ—and each with its own tasks.

On a more personal level, when the Waldorf schools were forbidden in Holland in 1941, the Tombergs sent their son Alexis to a parochial school, which led to his entering the Catholic Church—the Dominican church of St. Thomas Aquinas—in May 1943.

Reading this, one might think that life in Holland was passable. But life in occupied Holland was almost impossible for the Tombergs. They struggled simply to exist. In November 1943, Ernst von Hippel, who was academically well placed, suggested Tomberg come to Germany to pursue a doctorate in law at Cologne University. The Hippels were fortunate to have a big house. Tomberg chose a dissertation topic, "Degeneration and Regeneration in Jurisprudence," which he hoped would lead to further work on the moral foundations of law. In February 1944, he moved to Germany, and, as the bombs dropped, registered as a law student at the University of Cologne. He got a job as an assistant at the Institute of International Law, and by November, as bombs continued to drop, he had completed his dissertation. In March of the following year the Allies took Cologne, which, on June 21, 1945, was given over to the British to supervise. In July, Tomberg began to work as an interpreter in the Cologne-Ossendorf Camp for Displaced Persons. It was there, through the kind offices of an unknown (perhaps Polish) Catholic priest, that Valentin Tomberg formally entered the Catholic Church. Here again there are mysteries. Both Valentin and Maria Tomberg had been married before. It is unknown whether these previous marriages were annulled (by "external forum") or whether—as seems more likely given the circumstances—the priest determined, after confession and conversation that, according to the dictates of the "internal forum" of consciousness, they had remarried with a clear conscience.

At the end of that year (1945), the Tombergs moved to Mülheim, about thirty miles north of Cologne. It was a new life in a new world, though many things remained the same. Tomberg continued to teach, study, write, and conduct esoteric research. His dissertation was published in the fall of 1946. Early in 1947, his second work of jurisprudence, *The Foundations of International Law as Human Rights* appeared. Meanwhile, reflecting his inner life, he wrote (still unpublished) texts on "Inner Work," "Work on the Way to the Jordan" (both 1946) and, significantly, on "Sophia-Maria" (1947).

For the purposes of this book, the rest of his life must remain unexamined. Briefly stated: In 1948, the Tombergs moved to England, where Valentin Tomberg would work in the monitoring service of the BBC. Life would then assume an unaccustomed regularity and stability. Family life, professional life, inner work and esoteric research all flowered, despite failing health and various crises. Prayer and some smaller projects seem to have occupied him then until, in 1958, he began work on a manuscript on the Tarot. By 1965, he had completed *Meditations on the Tarot,* his great work—or rather, his *second* great work if we rightfully count these "meditations" as his first great work. Finally, between 1967 and 1970, he wrote the texts contained in *Lazarus, Come Forth!* On the morning of February 24, 1973, while on holiday, he died of a stroke on the Island of Majorca.

In her introduction to the first English translation (1939) of *Anthroposophical Meditations on the Old Testament,* Elizabeth Vreede wrote:

> Valentin Tomberg's *Studies of the Old Testament,* intended primarily for members of the Anthroposophical Society and other readers well enough acquainted with modern spiritual science as given in the fundamental writings of Rudolf Steiner, represent the beginning of an extended work. They are the first of a number of serial publications which the Estonian author has been issuing for several years past—written and duplicated originally in the German language. The twelve studies on the Old Testament, begun in autumn 1933, were followed by another series of twelve on the New Testament. In their original form, these works are already known and valued by students in many countries. It is therefore greatly to be welcomed that the Anthroposophical Society in Great Britain has undertaken to make them more widely accessible by issuing this English version. The anthroposophical movement has produced many valuable works upon scientific, social and educational subjects, and we may hope that these "Anthroposophical Studies," entering as they do into sublime realms of ethical and religious life, will also be met with due appreciation.
>
> It should go without saying, and the author himself has made it clear, that such communications as are here contained do not absolve the reader from the responsibility of exercising his free judgment—submitting them to the test of independent thought and meditation and experience—even as Rudolf Steiner required us to do with his own teaching upon spiritual science.
>
> Those of us who often heard Rudolf Steiner's lectures and made a practice of thus examining and testing what he said, by and by became so convinced of the essential truth of his communications that we were able to receive his further statements always with open mind and heart, without embarrassment. Even when things he said seemed very strange at first, we knew from past experience that the initial strangeness would presently be transformed into real understanding and recognition. Therefore in spite of all the limitations of his listeners and pupils, there always was about Rudolf Steiner that atmosphere of trust and confidence in which spiritual truths can ripen and find due expression.

> For these "Anthroposophical Studies," such an atmosphere must, of course, first be created, and this can happen only gradually, by dint of open-minded study and examination, and at the same time by our refraining from over-hasty judgment or premature conclusions. Readers will do well to apply to them the methodic principle we also learned from Rudolf Steiner: that the truths of occultism must sustain *each other,* for in this sense alone can occult statements be "proved." The very fact that these studies—as the author pointed out in his preface to the original (1933) edition—are founded on the Anthroposophy of Rudolf Steiner, will make it easier for the reader, from the basic truths already known to him, to understand and weigh whatever in these pages reaches out beyond Dr. Steiner's teaching.
>
> If then these studies of the Old Testament—to be followed, we may hope, by those of the New Testament also—are taken in this way with open mind and independent judgment, the reader will surely find in this "searching of hearts" a still greater enrichment, to add to the many deeply spiritual and sublime reflections that are here contained.

Finally, a few words concerning the title and subtitle. Originally, the works in this volume appeared simply as *"Anthroposophische Betrachtungen...,"* which was translated as "Anthroposophical Studies." *Betrachtungen,* however, are not "studies" in any academic sense; there is a perfectly good German word, *Studien,* that means studies. Literally, a *"Betrachtung"* means a "view, inspection, or examination"; figuratively it implies "reflection or consideration." However, qualified as *"besinnliche"* or *"nachdenkliche"*—or, for instance, *"Anthroposophische"*—it means "contemplation or meditation."

Thus, these are "Anthroposophic *Meditations"* or *contemplations.* They are the fruit of spiritual work; they grow out of spiritual research and are in some sense "Spiritual Scientific Research Papers." They represent spiritual scientific meditative research. Tomberg calls them "Anthroposophic," not because they are anthroposophic in *content*—though they are that—but because the fruit of "spiritual scientific" meditative activity is practiced according to the anthroposophical or spiritual scientific *method.*

We have chosen the overall title *Christ and Sophia* to encompass Tomberg's whole Anthroposophic-Christological endeavor. For Tomberg, these two spiritual beings underlie and determine his entire creative work, as indeed they do the whole of creation itself. In a way, Tomberg's universe is quite simple. It reflects the mutual interdependency and simultaneous coexistence in eternity and time of four elements that seek to become one through human beings: the Godhead, the Trinity, the nine angelic hierarchies, and the divine holy being, Sophia, she who unites all through knowledge and participation in all. Sophia, the ground of knowing and of the union of all with all, is thus also the servant of all.

Christ and Sophia run throughout these "meditations." No "abstract concept or merely pious mystical state," Sophia is an actual transcendent being, acting in the cosmos as an archangel and communicating "Unity"—the unity of the Trinity, of the cosmos, of humanity with all. It is she, close relative of the Holy Spirit and grace, who gives meaning to cognition, for she is true wisdom, cosmic intelligence, the "plan of the temple." Everywhere in Tomberg's work, she who is the servant of all is above all the servant of the master, Christ.

For Tomberg, Sophia is indissolubly united with Christ. Drawing on his Russian heritage, he recognized this very early. Writing in 1930 ("The Metamorphosis of Thinking") about the moral unity of humanity and human history through Christ—"Christ is the meaning of the Earth"—he adds:

> A remarkable figure lives in Eastern Christian thought. She is Mary, the Mother God, who is also Sophia, the Holy Wisdom. This figure is also the "Church," the principle of the community of all humanity, and thereby of the same essence with Christ. She is the principle of community (*ecclesia*), She is that which *unifies* Beings.

According to Pavel Florensky, Sophia's motto is *Omnia conjugo:* I unite all. Christ, too, unites all. They are inseparable.

In another article (1931), Tomberg extends his vision of Sophia. Writing of Eastern Christianity he calls her the "soul" of the human community (the "Church") as Christ is its "spirit:"

> The outer "Church" is only the body, in and above which live both a soul and a spirit.... This body is fragile and imperfect.... But in this body its soul lives and its spirit works. Sophia is the soul of the Church.... And Christ is the spirit of the Church. As the soul of the Church, Sophia also belongs to Christ. She is the breath who goes out from the being of Christ and is directly received by souls. She is the effective radiance of Christ, the aura of his Being.

For Tomberg, Christ and Sophia are members of a single being—whose third member is humanity, the visible community, suffering and dying. It is the story of this being—the story of our evolving cosmos—that he meditates upon in this book through the revelations given to us in scripture.

Something must still be added in conclusion. For Tomberg, as an anthroposophist, Sophia—as cosmic intelligence and ultimately, therefore, the source of our cognitions—is closely connected with the Archangel Michael. The Archangel Michael for Rudolf Steiner and for anthroposophists is at once the regent (or ruler) of our age, the Guardian of the Threshold who mediates cosmic intelligence to humanity, and the founder of a cosmic spiritual school, whose earthly reflection Anthroposophy seeks to be. In the first lecture ("The new Michael Community") in *Inner Development,* Tomberg shows the intimate interrelationship among Michael, Sophia, and Christ. He speaks of Platonists and Aristotelians coming together to form a new "spiritual knighthood" under the name *Michael-Sophia in nomine Christi:*

> The men and women of Sophia, of revelation, will walk the path together with the men and women of knowledge: the Platonists will stand guard with the Aristotelians at the threshold of the spiritual world. They will have to guard the secrets of the spiritual world. In this community, guardianship will involve neither keeping silent nor revealing everything. Instead, it will mean that a living rampart or

wall will be erected—consisting of steadfast human forms, who will stand as a vertical connecting link between the spiritual and physical worlds. On the one side they will open the gates to the authorized; on the other they will close them to the unauthorized. This community of knights—this future community of knights of the threshold—will be fully realized only in the sixth [next] epoch. This community was begun through Rudolf Steiner, through the founding of the anthroposophic movement, through the revelation of the mission of Michael and through the misfortune that we later experienced. We are summoned by the voice of Rudolf Steiner; we are tested by the misfortune now (1938) coming to us.

What we must awaken in the depths of our souls is *earnestness* concerning the spiritual and outer worlds, and *fidelity to the spirit,* each according to his or her position in life. We can conduct ourselves in every way, in speech and action, according to the demands of everyday life. But let us keep one province free from compromise; *let us remain true to the spirit,* independent of all teachings and teachers, of all organizations in the world. *Let us remain faithful to the inner voice of truth and conscience.* Then we will be in the school that is preparing for the future Michael Community: the community that will bear the motto: *Michael-Sophia in nomine Christi.*[26]

# Introduction Notes

1. See Sergei O. Prokofieff, *The Case of Valentin Tomberg: Anthroposophy or Jesuitism?* (London: Temple Lodge, 1997); and *Valentin Tomberg and Anthroposophy: A Problematic Relationship* (London: Temple Lodge, 2005). Also, T. H. Meyer and Elizabeth Vreede, *The Bodhisattva Question: Krishnamurti, Rudolf Steiner, Annie Besant, Valentin Tomberg, and the Mystery of the Twentieth-Century Master* (London: Temple Lodge, 1993). For an outside perspective on the later Tomberg, see Antoine Faivre, "Analysis of the Mediations of Valentin Tomberg on the Twenty-Two Major Arcana of the Tarot of Marseilles," in *Theosophy, Imagination, Tradition: Studies in Western Esotericism* (Albany, NY: SUNY Press, 2000).
2. See bibliography.
3. For the kinds of claims made on Tomberg's behalf, see Robert Powell *Hermetic Astrology: Toward a New Wisdom of the Stars* (Hermetica: Kinsau, Germany, 1987, 1989); *The Most Holy Trinosophia* (Great Barrington, MA: Anthroposophic Press, 2000); and Dafydd Griffiths and Keith Harris, *The Western Shore: Christian Hermeticism*, vol. I (U.K.: Western Shores, 2005).
4. See bibliography.
5. See Prokofieff's works on Tomberg (note 1).
6. See Rudolf Steiner, *Karmic Relationships*, vols. 3, 4, 6 (London: Rudolf Steiner Press).
7. See Valentin Tomberg, *Lazarus, Come Forth!*, part I, chapter 3 "Causality and Miracles in the Spiritual History of Humankind."
8. Liesel Heckmann (with Michael Frensch), *Valentin Tomberg: Leben, Werk, Wirkung*, Band 1.1 1900–1944, Band 1.2, 1944–1973 (Schaffhausen, Switzerland: Novalis Verlag, 2001 and 2005); see also *Valentin Tomberg: Leben, Werk, Wirkung*, vol. 2, Quellen und Beitrage zum Werk (Schaffhausen: Novalis Verlag, 2000). All biographical details are drawn from these two works.
9. See *Lazarus, Come Forth!*, introduction to part four, "The Breath of Life" (extract translated from German by C. Bamford).
10. The Russian Sophiological tradition, which has been called the twentieth century's most important theological contribution, begins with the work of the Slovophiles (Aleksei Khomiakov and Ivan Kireevksy), comes to flower in Vladimir Solovyov, and then fruits in, above all, Sergei Bulgakov and Pavel Florensky (see bibliography). Bulgakov and Florensky, as well as Berdyaev, were very familiar with Rudolf Steiner's work, indicating perhaps an inner connection between Anthroposophy and Sophiology. Readers may also recall that, for Rudolf Steiner, the next cultural epoch is to emerge from Russia. See Valentin Tomberg, *Early Articles*, for his view of this tradition,
11. See T. J. Binyon, *Pushkin: A Biography* (New York: Knopf, 2003).
12. See Boris Jakim and Robert Bird, *On Spiritual Unity: A Slavophile Reader* (Hudson, NY: Lindisfarne Books, 1998).
13. See, Valentin Tomberg, *Early Articles.*

14. See Harrie Salmon, "Valentin Tomberg und die neue hermetische Philosophie" in *Valentin Tomberg: Leben, Werk, Wirkung,* vol. 2, Quellen und Beitrage zum Werk (Schaffhausen: Novalis Verlag, 2000); also Maria Carlson, *"No Religion Higher Than Truth": A History of the Theosophical Movement in Russia.* (Princeton: Princeton University Press, 1993); and Lauren G. Leighton, *The Esoteric Tradition in Russian Romantic Literature: Decembrism and Freemasonry* (University Park: The Pennsylvania State University Press, 1994).
15. See Berdyaev "Theosophy and Anthroposophy in Russia (1916)." On the web at http://www.berdyaev.com/berdiaev/berd_lib/1916_252b.html.
16. For this and what follows, see Maria Carlson, *"No Religion Higher Than Truth": A History of the Theosophical Movement in Russia* (Princeton: Princeton University Press, 1993).
17. See Paul M. Allen, *Vladimir Soloviev: Russian Mystic* (Blauvelt, NY: Garber, 1978).
18. See Harrie Salmon, "Valentin Tomberg und die neue hermetische Philosophie" in *Valentin Tomberg: Leben, Werk, Wirkung,* vol. 2, Quellen und Beitrage zum Werk (Schaffhausen: Novalis Verlag, 2000); also Valentin Tomberg, *Meditations on the Tarot,* letter 21, "The Fool."
19. See Valentin Tomberg, *Early Articles.*
20. A union that inspired numerous rumors.
21. This is what I have been told. I cannot of course vouch for its accuracy.
22. As reported by Robert Powell in an article, "Valentin Tomberg als Sündenbock der Anthroposophischen Gesellschaft," which is to appear in *Valentin Tomberg: Leben, Werk, Wirkung,* vol. 3, Quellen und Beitrage zum Werk (Schaffhausen: Novalis Verlag, 2007). Powell tells how two pages of Tomberg's *Four Sacrifices of Christ and the Reappearance of Christ in the Etheric* were extracted and copied and began to circulate with the heading "from a lecture of Rudolf Steiner in Stockholm in 1910." At one point, Wilhelm Rath, a well-known anthroposophist, received the extracted pages from his stepmother, and they began to circulate in Dornach. The papers were even read by Rudolf Grosse at a Goetheanum conference for teachers of religion. This was in 1980, before the erroneous attribution was discovered. For Powell, the misattribution serves as circumstantial evidence that Tomberg and Rudolf Steiner drew from the same source. Once again, readers will have to make up their own minds. It is certainly interesting and true that Tomberg was among the first to meditate and write about the importance of the reappearance of Christ in the etheric, as Thomas Stoeckli notes in the collection *Das aetherische Christenwirken* (Dornach: Verlag am Goetheanum, 1991).
23. Charles Lawrie, "Valentin Tomberg—einige Tatsachen, einige Fragen" in *Valentin Tomberg: Leben, Werk, Wirkung* ["Valentin Tomberg: Some Facts and Questions"], vol. 2, Quellen und Beitrage zum Werk (Schaffhausen: Novalis Verlag, 2000). This article appeared in English originally in the short-lived British anthroposophic journal *Shoreline* (no. 2, 1989, "The Vision of Europe.")
24. See Valentin Tomberg, *Lazarus, Come Forth!*
25. See Valentin Tomberg, *Inner Development.*

# PART ONE

# ANTHROPOSOPHIC MEDITATIONS ON THE OLD TESTAMENT

# Chapter 1

# The Old Testament

## The Nature of the Old Testament

The fact that first strikes the unbiased reader of the Bible—the best known and most misunderstood book in the world—is that it speaks throughout of interaction with the spiritual world. It is a document that bequeaths to posterity the witness of an interaction with the spiritual world maintained for thousands of years. The deity, Yahweh Elohim, speaks to humankind; reveals himself, face to face, with the human being; angels appear and speak; prophets see the future and hear messages from suprasensory beings. The most superficial students of the Bible know this, so that even they must admit that the Bible tells of a constant interaction between humankind and spiritual beings.

But interactivity with spiritual beings is precisely what is presented by the content and practice of the ancient mysteries. Neither did the mysteries of antiquity rest on "faith," but were based on conscious interactivity with suprasensory spiritual beings, spiritually seen, heard, and received into themselves. By this means, revelations flowed into humankind, upon which great civilizations were founded. These revelations were preserved and taught, and the whole of them constituted the sacred wisdom of the mysteries—the spiritual science whose methods alter with every epoch but persist in an unbroken line to the present day. The science based on conscious interaction with the spiritual world—that is, on suprasensory experiences—is known in the West as *occultism*. In what follows, we shall use this expression, hoping that the reader will, for the moment, understand its only meaning to be a science based on conscious suprasensory experiences.

Studied from this point of view, the Bible is a book that describes *facts* belonging to the realm of occultism. Not that it contains the teaching of occultism; rather, it contains the facts upon which the teachings of occultism are based. The interaction with the spiritual world described in the Bible is not a doctrine or occultism; it is a fact upon which its doctrines are based. Thus, for instance, the Bible contains no instruction concerning karma and reincarnation, yet it manifestly gives evidence or the facts of karma and of the reappearance on Earth of the same individualities. That this is actually so, will be shown in these meditations.

To make anything of the facts contained in the Bible, we must employ the means offered us by occultism. Neither a literary and historic nor an abstractly philosophic means of study can serve any obvious purpose for us in this task; only real occultism offers results. Access to real occultism has been thrown open to wider circles in the present epoch by Rudolf Steiner's life work. He presented a large part of it to the public in the form of anthroposophical spiritual science. Anthroposophy as it lies before us in Steiner's writings and printed lecture cycles is not in itself actual occultism. It becomes so only in the soul of those who not only acknowledge its truths, but also discern them. True occultism is present only in the presence of living occultists. Otherwise it becomes a mere matter of anthroposophically directed religious, philosophic, or aesthetic convictions. True occultism does not involve fostering convictions but discernment of the facts, interdependencies, and entities of the suprasensory world that engenders them, as well as the fulfillment of those duties and missions that result from them.

If we conceive of occultism in this sense, we find ourselves concerned with a trinity. The trinity in the human being, or the occultist, corresponds to a trinity of occultism. Just as human beings consist of spirit, soul, and body, likewise occultism is divided into eugenic, hygienic, and mechanical occultism. And just as the threefold human being represents a unity, likewise the three great realms of occultism also represent a unity. Anthroposophy, as presented in the writings mentioned, makes it possible to access these three regions of true occultism.

The three realms of occultism are distinct in regard to their missions and their methods. The task of mechanical occultism is to regulate the outer forces of nature in a way that corresponds to the true destiny of humankind. Hygienic occultism does the same with respect to the forces of the human organism. Eugenic occultism, however, has the mission of establishing a correct relationship between spiritual forces and humankind—that is, it must regulate human karma by means of birth and death. Mechanical occultism, therefore, is related more to the forces outside humanity, the forces that work in nature. Hygienic occultism is concerned especially with humankind. And the special theme of eugenic occultism is the human relationship to the tasks set by the superhuman spiritual world—in other words, one's destiny.

It must be understood that the three realms of occultism are always represented by living personalities, each being the leader of an appointed realm. These (the highest authorities of human spiritual science) work, for the most part, silently for the health and welfare of humanity. The characters Benedictus, Theodosius, and Romanus in Rudolf Steiner's mystery plays are portrayed as the three most advanced initiates. They are supposed to represent the three realms of occultism. It is easy, too, to perceive how each of the three realms of occultism corresponds to each character; as one watches the mystery dramas, it is easy to quickly solve this matter unequivocally.

The Bible itself is equally clear in showing us the concerted activities of the three occultisms through the three personalities who preside over them. In Genesis, chapters 18 and 19, we read of Abraham's encounter with the "three angels" in the Grove of Mamre and the destruction of Sodom. Now if we picture this episode as it can be with the help of spiritual science, we will be able to understand it as an episode of the cooperation among the highest initiates of the three occultisms.

In ordinary daytime consciousness, without leaving his body as one does during sleep, Abraham has a spiritual experience of the presence of Yahweh Elohim. The suprasensory vision now disappears and, instead, three men stand before him. He recognizes them as messengers whose advent was heralded by the suprasensory experience. They are messengers of the deity whom he had just seen. In this way, the suprasensory merges into a sensory experience. Whereas God had spoken a moment ago, now three men are present. Abraham transfers to God's messengers the reverence he had felt toward God. Reverently, he offers them hospitality. This is accepted, and the three men partake of his food. Then one of the three informs him that, within a year, Sara will bear him a son. Sara hears this, but because of their advanced age it seems incredible to her. He who knows the secrets of eugenic occultism, however, repeats the promise and eventually it comes to pass. If the laws of eugenic occultism are kept, births are possible until an age that "merely scientific" modern science would call impossible. In a not very distant future, however, science will be forced by facts to allow its findings to be revised.

Thus the mission of the first of the three is fulfilled. They depart, and the two others go to Sodom. They recognize that their task is to decide the fate of that town. Specifically, it must be decided how badly its civilization is diseased and whether, indeed, it is still viable. Thus the question was whether there might still be hope of curing Sodom or, as an infected center, it should be destroyed.

As the episode progressed (it is unnecessary to repeat the details), he who represented hygienic occultism found ample opportunity to assess the condition of Sodom. He found Sodom to be morally beyond cure. The representative of mechanical occultism then acted on this diagnosis, and, once Lot and his family had left the city, Sodom was destroyed by the power of the fire element. The "three angels"[1] are, in fact, the three highest initiates of the three branches of occultism, whose concerted action was needed to decide Sodom's fate. Moreover, we cannot grasp the significance of the worship of the Jesus child by the three "wise men from the East" (of whom we read in Matthew's Gospel) unless we understand that it refers to the united wisdom of the occultism of those days that, in the persons of the representatives of its three realms, greeted the advent of its highest individuality.

Anthroposophists should contemplate these facts with deep earnestness. They should not only acknowledge that there are still three initiates living on Earth, but they should also be able to feel it within themselves. An attitude of mind should be maintained in the Anthroposophical Society that could be expressed in this way: The highest initiates are here; they have students through whom they can speak; there is an even deeper wisdom and a higher discipline than what lies before us in the scriptures we possess. Everyone who works hard enough and is found worthy can gain access to this wisdom and discipline. And we should give due weight to Rudolf Steiner's words in *How to Know Higher Worlds:*

> Many people believe that they must seek out masters of higher knowledge wherever such masters may be found in order to receive teachings from them. There is a twofold truth to this. On the one hand, if our aspiration to higher knowledge is sincere, we will certainly spare no effort and avoid no obstacle in our quest for an initiate able to lead us into the higher mysteries of the world. On the other hand, we can be certain that, if our striving for knowledge is sincere and worthy, initiation will find us whatever the circumstances. (p. 15)

If every earnest and worthy seeker can find an initiate, there must always be initiates. If Rudolf Steiner had been the only initiate with no others to come, the sentences just quoted would be false. But they *are* true, notwithstanding that the inner organization of many anthroposophists today is such that they seem to doubt their truth. In other words, they hardly face the possibility that new initiates may arise. In fact, however, it is not just a possibility, but a necessity. To see this is an aspect of every anthroposophist's responsibility; it is more important than one's personal wishes.

After this necessary digression let us return to the matter of the Bible's nature. If we accept the Old Testament as a record of occult facts, we are naturally faced by a question: Which of the three realms of occultism is especially characteristic of the Bible? In other words: Is the Bible a book of mechanical, or hygienic, or eugenic occultism? To answer this question, we must for a moment look at the Bible as a whole. The Old Testament tells us about the fulfillment of a task that was worked out over fifteen centuries or so and based on a covenant agreed upon between a human community and the spiritual world. It is the story of a contract between a group of people and a divine spiritual being. The spiritual thread of that contract unifies everything that the Bible had to say about the incidents, trials, revelations, and destinies. Two statements express the substance of the contract made with Abraham and renewed during the times of Moses, David, and the Babylonian captivity: "I AM is the Lord," and "The Lord shall become Man; He shall be born of the seed of Israel." The first contains the obligation of the Israelite community toward the spiritual world; the second contains the promise of the spiritual world made to the Israelite community.

The obligation incurred by acknowledging the "I AM" defines the fundamental character of the Israelite spiritual impulse in history. That spiritual impulse was distinguished from the other influences by the fact that it owed its whole essence exclusively to the I-forces of humankind. Whereas the spiritual was revealed to other races through nature and the stars by means of the astral body, the universal spirit was revealed solely through the I to those who were the leaders in the spiritual movement of the Israelites. In Israel, the greatest sin against the obligation of adherence to the I was seen in the functions of nature, or star worship (the high places, "groves," and so on). In other races, however, these were the most important parts of religious life, because the object of these functions was interaction with the spiritual world through the forces of the astral body, with the I-forces eliminated. The kind of interaction with the spirit that the Israelites were supposed to foster was possible only by eliminating the forces of the astral body, or subconscious forces, so that, unhindered, the I might become the channel of interaction with the spiritual world.

It was through this interaction that the Israelite civilization was created and maintained. Those who were able to practice this interaction consciously were the prophets, of whom there were many more than are mentioned in the Bible, for there was an unbroken line of prophets from Abraham to Malachi. The prophetic mission was handed down in this way through a school of prophecy, and this made it possible for each prophet to prepare a successor. The training of those prophets was, in many ways, similar to that of modern spiritual science. It also excluded everything subconscious, everything physical, and addressed itself exclusively to the forces of clear human consciousness. In serene tranquility, without commotion, the schools of the prophets performed their exercises, studying to master a deep silence in the presence of the spiritual world. Once the silence reached a certain stage, the spiritual world began to speak. What the prophet received in this way was imparted to others. Thus the community of Israel was guided to its goal.

That goal was to realize the promise of the Messiah's holy birth. Everything in the life of the children of Israel was to be ordered so that, after many generations, the race might produce a body suited to the work of Christ on Earth. And we cannot properly understand the countless details of the instructions contained, say, in the books of Moses concerning food, hygiene, sexual relations, and so on, unless we first understand them not as forms of asceticism (there was no asceticism in Israel, just as today there is no physical asceticism for students and initiates of true Christian occultism), but as a rule of life directed in such a way that it would prepare for the future birth of the body intended to receive the Christ. The remarkable significance attached in the Bible to correct marriage and correct birth can be understood only by very seriously accepting the fact that the history of Israel was a story of the preparation of Jesus' body. We see in it a conscious application of the laws of heredity, subjecting the destinies of individuals to that particular purpose.

Because it describes the preparation for a holy birth, the Bible is the only great work of eugenic occultism extant in the world. Today, there is no writing that contains more of the mysteries of eugenic occultism than the Bible. The profound interrelationships that exist between birth and karma, with their obligations enduring through many incarnations, are most clearly recognized through the Bible. This is especially true of the Old Testament. It is the most valuable document of eugenic occultism handed down to us from the past. Another significance for true occultism is found in the New Testament (in the four Gospels), for although the New Testament indeed narrates facts that indicate the end of one era in the history of eugenic occultism and the beginning of another, the center of gravity is no longer found in the region of eugenic occultism but in another realm. The facts it contains lead to knowledge of the deepest mysteries of hygienic occultism. Quite apart from the many healings of infirmed body, soul, and spirit that the Gospels describe, the main event, at the very center of the Gospel picture—the Mystery of Golgotha—can and must be accepted, above all, as the supreme act of healing of the worst human sickness. The four Gospels contain the most valuable knowledge obtainable concerning the occultism of healing. There is no document from the past that preserves for humankind more mysteries of occult healing than the Gospels.

Now the Bible as a whole consists of three parts, for the Revelation of John is as clearly distinct from the Gospels as they are in turn distinct from the books of the Old Testament. The Old Testament depicts the preparation in secular history for the Christ event, and the Gospels depict the event itself; likewise, the Apocalypse depicts the consequences of that event. The Apocalypse, however, contains no history of the generations, as does the Old Testament, nor does it contain a delineation of the life and death of any particular being, as do the Gospels. The Apocalypse portrays future human and cosmic events and shows the cosmic results of the Christ's incarnation. Those results are not only of a spiritual and moral kind; they also partake of the character of natural phenomena. The Apocalypse describes the influence that spiritual and moral impulses will in time exert upon natural forces. The Revelation of John accurately describes alterations in the strata of Earth's interior and in the etheric strata surrounding the Earth as effects having moral causes. The cosmic drama of the Apocalypse deals not only with a struggle that concerns humankind, but also with the struggle that concerns nature. It points to facts beyond the regions of eugenic and hygienic occultism; for the effect of the humanly spiritual on external natural forces is the theme of mechanical occultism. The Apocalypse is the only authoritative document that preserves for us the knowledge contained in mechanical occultism.

The purpose of these meditations is not to discuss hygienic occultism, and even less mechanical occultism. The author will thus limit himself more strictly to a consideration of the Old Testament as the authoritative exponent of eugenic occultism, using the other two parts of the Bible only insofar as it is impossible to keep them or the three divisions of occultism entirely distinct from one another. The Bible forms an indivisible whole precisely because it contains the principal truths of the three realms of occultism, which in themselves present an indivisible whole. We cannot understand the Old Testament without the Gospels, and likewise we cannot understand the Gospels without the Apocalypse. The Old Testament tells the history of the preparation for the events recorded in the Gospels, and the Apocalypse shows the purpose of those events.

Equally indivisible are the three realms of occultism as we see them in life. It is impossible for anyone to be healed without considering that person's karmic and hereditary history; nor can one be healed without the means of healing, and these can be procured only through the agency of mechanical occultism. This is just one example; many others could be cited to show that the three realms of occultism present a whole, and that only by cooperation can their purpose be duly fulfilled.

In these meditations it will be necessary to deal with just one realm of occultism with the help of the Old Testament, but the author begs his readers to keep in mind that, however painful it may be, it is inevitable today that it does a certain violence to these things just by describing them. In what follows, we shall deal with the Old Testament as the authoritative document of eugenic occultism. Before we begin to study the details of this document, however, we must answer a general question about the "chosen people" with whom the covenant we spoke of was made: Who are the "chosen people," and what is the nature of that "choosing"?

## The Chosen People

The history of Israel is the history of a "chosen" people, whose mission it was to prepare an event of human significance. After that event took place, however—that is, after the Mystery of Golgotha—there seems to be no further reason for the existence of a chosen people. We might think that, since the Mystery of Golgotha, the whole of humanity had become such a people. This idea, however, contradicts the apocalyptic picture of the future, which shows a final choosing of the twelve tribes of Israel, after humanity has gone through all the tests of earthly destiny. "Twelve times twelve thousand" in the Apocalypse represents the last phase of Earth's evolution in its transition to the Jupiter stage.

So the Apocalypse confronts us with the puzzling fact that the "chosen people" will exist even into the most distant future. To understand this, we must first answer this: If a "chosen people" is to exist in the distant future, how far back can its history be traced into the past? Where do we find the origin of that "chosen people?" Is the moment of their exodus from Egypt actually the beginning of the history of the "chosen people?"

In the sense of the Apocalypse, we can best understand the choosing and the significance of the chosen people, or the undying Israel, by studying the history of humankind with the purpose of discovering the origin of the chosen people. We must go back to the time when a unique civilization flourished in Atlantis, the continent west of Europe, which was later submerged. That civilization was especially distinguished from that of today by the fact that it was based on very different human faculties. Modern civilization is founded on the human faculty of thinking and the experiences that reach us through the mind, whereas the Atlantean civilization was based on faculties that would be viewed today as "magical." The faculties of the Atlanteans relied on a far more intimate relationship between humankind and the natural environment than exists in modern times. For Atlanteans, an external natural event was a direct inner experience; similarly, the inner experiences of Atlanteans exerted an influence on the outer events of nature. The will had the power of not only moving a person's limbs, but it could also affect the forces of nature. Likewise, the spoken word had a power that, today, when speakers lecture or declaim—we can no longer conceive of. It could heal or kill, build or destroy, through the natural force that accompanied it.

The use of such magical powers was the basis of Atlantean civilization; their misuse caused the destruction of the Atlantean continent. The capacity to influence the life processes of nature became an integral part of a self-interested development of power and was largely misused. The misuse of magical powers went so far that it threatened to split the whole population of Atlantis into two groups: a smaller group ruling by the power of magic, and the greater population forced into obedience. If this had occurred, every chance of human evolution toward freedom would have vanished. If the Atlantean catastrophe had not taken place, black magic would have blocked the progress of human evolution; it destroyed a civilization that was evolving increasingly in that direction.

But that catastrophe did not affect all the inhabitants of the Atlantean continent. There were those who escaped, and this was no accident. A community had gathered round an exalted leader who, at the right moment, led them to another area. These were the individuals who neither practiced black magic nor became its passive victims. These people became the community that, under the leadership of Manu, abandoned Atlantis and moved to Central Asia. Thus a part of the Atlantean population was "chosen" to bring about the migration from Atlantis. So here we have the epoch during which a "chosen people" first appears; it is the first choosing and the first exodus.

Those who left Atlantis with this migration had the task of reaching a specific region where a new civilization, capable of evolution, could be established. Under the leadership of Manu, the "chosen people" journeyed to its "promised land." After long wanderings, they finally reached it. There, in Central Asia, the first colony of Aryan civilization was planted, the root of all later post-Atlantean civilizations.

This most ancient Aryan community had, like the Israelites later on, also established a covenant with the spiritual world. The obligations undertaken in this covenant formed the substance of the Code of Manu. This code especially stressed that life should be ordered in such a way that heaven and Earth, the spiritual world and the sensory world, should be kept in balance. It is only through this equilibrium that the evolution of free personality is possible, and in Atlantis this had become virtually impossible. On the other hand, to maintain the purity of the Aryan impulse, they had to avoid mingling with the other races left behind at a lower stage. The first covenant of the first chosen people after the first exodus was based on these two precepts: fidelity to Earth and heaven and severance of the chosen people from the races infected by the decadence of Atlantis.

The ancient Indian civilization, whose evolution did not accord with Aryan precepts, developed later on from the Manu community. This Indian evolution developed a strong preference for spiritual things, with a corresponding contempt for earthly phenomena. Thus the Code of Manu was broken. The harmonious relationship between heaven and Earth ceased to exist. Consequently, the Indian civilization could no longer be used to accomplish the task of post-Atlantean humanity. A new civilization capable of conducting its evolution in a right way had to be established. Thus a second exodus occurred and a second chosen people arose who remained faithful to the original Aryan impulse, establishing a new civilization on the plateau of Persia. This civilization received its spiritual foundation from the great Zoroaster. It involved a command to fight Ahriman on the side of the divine Sun being, Ahura Mazda. But the struggle against Ahriman involved not only an inner readjustment and a specific conduct of life, but it also included the defense of the Aryan civilization against the Turanians.[2] The Turanian races had preserved the dark side of the Atlantean culture and thus existed as the polar opposite of the impulses emanating from the great Zoroaster. The conflict with the Turanians, therefore, was a matter of life and death for the civilized community of Persia. Only by heroically opposing the smallest compromise with the Turanian spirit could the existence of the Persian civilization be preserved, because a spiritual current can be effective only so long as it is not drawn into compromise. This is true today and was no less true in the time of the conflict between Zoroaster's doctrine of pure spirit and the dark-nature magic of the Turanians. As time went on, however, the heroic spirit of the ancient Persians weakened and a conciliatory mood of compromise set in. They sought respite from the never-ending tension of volition needed to remain faithful to the spirit of the great Zoroaster. This inner weakness resulted in outer defeat; Turania was victorious in the struggle against Persia. This blocked any further evolution of the ancient Persian civilization in regard to its true mission. So it happened once more; those who remained true to the spirit of the great Zoroaster left Persia and founded new civilizations in Mesopotamia and Egypt. Another chosen people, unwilling to accept alien impulses, abandoned the region of Persian culture to establish a new civilization elsewhere. This new civilization split into two streams, Chaldean and Egyptian, established by the great Zoroaster through two of his disciples.

The Egypto-Chaldean culture had the task of preserving the sanctity of the two great gateways to the spiritual world—the gate of birth and the gate of death—until a holy birth and a holy death would open these gates forever for all humanity. The races under the Egypto-Chaldean civilization were to prepare for the birth of the being who would bring supreme health to humankind through his sacrificial death. The mysteries of birth and death were to be held unsullied by these races, so that the Christ event might take place on prepared ground. Chaldea was appointed guardian of the mysteries of birth, Egypt the mysteries of death. Both guardians, however, broke faith. The Turanian element penetrated Chaldea and poisoned the spiritual life of that land. The worship of Baal and Ashtaroth,[3] widespread among the races of Mesopotamia and Syria, led to a concept of birth that contrasted in the greatest degree with the view that should have been fostered.

The details of that dark cult cannot be discussed with decency; suffice it to say that in every detail, it was designed to banish everything spiritual or holy from the relationship of father, mother, and child. Sex life was intended to be torn away from its divine source, leaving it prey to demonic forces, and birth was to be mechanized. This was supposed to be attained by killing all the firstborn—a purposeful measure designed to destroy the conscious, loving expectation of the soul descending among humanity, to be replaced by unconscious, mechanical human reproduction. If this had succeeded, the appearance of eminently spiritual individuals on Earth would have absolutely come to an end, because eminently spiritual souls can be born only when they are expected consciously. The cooperation of the free human consciousness of the parents is a fundamental condition of their appearance. So now we see clearly what was the intention of these cults: to hinder the birth of Jesus.

As birth was materialized in Chaldea, so death was materialized in Egypt. The sublime thought of overcoming death through resurrection—as cherished in the holy mystery schools of Egypt—was replaced by the desire to preserve the outer bodily form. By introducing mummy worship, Egypt committed the same kind of sin against the mystery of death as Chaldea had against the mystery of birth by becoming enslaved to Baal worship.

Thus in Chaldea, birth was desecrated; in Egypt, death. Thus the foundation upon which Christ Jesus should appear could not be laid down, neither by the Chaldean nor by the Egyptian spiritual stream. Once more, there was a need for a chosen people and an exodus. This occurred when a small band of Chaldeans led by Abraham separated from the Chaldean nation and formed a new tribe. That tribe traveled to Egypt, where it grew into a nation. The reason it had to be in Egypt in order to become a nation can be understood when we recall that the sin of Egypt was the degradation of death, not birth. In Egypt, the new race was protected from the destructive Chaldean influence. It would be able to preserve its particularly pure relationship to birth. But it could not coalesce with the Egyptian civilization, which would cause it to lose the true concept of resurrection. Hence it had to migrate as a race out of Egypt, just as it had migrated as a tribe from Chaldea. This occurred under the leadership of Moses, who guided the fourth chosen people, the people of Israel, to its promised land. This race, however, was also unfaithful to its calling and was carried away into Babylon, whence a chosen section was eventually led back. This was the final choosing before the advent of Jesus Christ, whereby birth and death regained their divine significance in human consciousness.

Is this, then, the end of the story of the "chosen people"? To answer this question, we may, for the time being, disregard the Middle Ages and the present epoch, since they do not yield any relevant facts. We will turn our attention, instead, toward the future and the epoch of the sixth civilization. That post-Atlantean epoch will be distinguished from the present one mainly by the fact that humankind will be divided into two separate communities: a smaller community consisting of those who have received the Christ impulse into their consciousness, and a larger one consisting of those who have rejected it. The spiritually minded community will establish a civilization based on social justice, morally distinct from the civilization belonging to the rest of humankind—just as, say, today's civilization of Europe appears distinct from the native cultures of Africa. Even physically, the two types will be distinct, so that, in body, soul, and spirit, two separate human races will arise.

These matters should not be considered abstractly, but in the most specific way possible. Indeed, anthroposophists should have long ago seen the real significance of the anthroposophic movement for the future. It is not concerned merely with beliefs and ideas, but with the beginning of an actual race construction—the establishment of race stocks that, in succeeding generations, will be spiritualized to the full capacity of human beings of the sixth epoch. The future requires not just ideas, but also bodies; such ideas are to be realized, not just in heaven, but also on Earth, and ideas can prove their power only by taking hold of the terrestrial. When the grown children of anthroposophic parents turn their backs on anthroposophic teachings (which is not infrequent) and devote themselves to other pursuits, we should not necessarily talk of "karma" and "free will." Rather, we should ask ourselves: Was the Anthroposophy of the parents sufficiently convincing for the children? Did more life flow into their souls through it than from other sources in the outer world? If the question is asked in this way, we realize that only so much of the anthroposophic teaching that has been apprehended by the *hearts* of one generation can be passed on to the next. Anthroposophy of the *head* has no place in the current of anthroposophic life that must flow through the generations; for this, only Anthroposophy of the heart is viable. Thus, only what has become a matter of the heart can flow on, "body forming," from the present into the future and as far as the sixth epoch. Anthroposophy of the head is a concern of the individual; Anthroposophy of the heart is the concern of all humankind. It is Anthroposophy of the heart that, in time, will become the power that supplies people of the sixth epoch with the organism required for life on Earth.

We live in an epoch when a new covenant with the spiritual world has been established—a covenant that has as its object the preparation of the sixth civilization. It calls for fidelity toward the spiritual world, and requires a continuous effort to maintain uninterrupted conscious interaction with it. The sources of ever-new and truly spiritual perceptions must never be quenched. Only through a continuous influx of spiritual knowledge can the anthroposophic community remain alive. Despite its rich store of literature, it would perish if the direct flow from the spiritual world were interrupted for a significant length of time. Nothing can take the place of this influx; it is indispensable to the viability of a spiritual scientific movement, which cannot fulfill its missions as described unless it captures hearts. And this is impossible unless conscious interaction with the spiritual world is maintained unceasingly in the movement. Tradition alone cannot keep it alive; should the revelation from the spiritual world be silenced, the hearts will also be silenced; this would lead to the spiritual death of the movement.

Now the mystery of the chosen people continues into the distant future. It is the history of the karmic stream of souls specifically associated with the Christ impulse. It is the same individuals who, through numerous incarnations, accomplish the work of Christ. The prophets of Israel will all reappear so that interaction with the spiritual may be preserved, uninterrupted, today as it was in their time. Thus, the karmic stream, the chosen people, the undying Israel, will continue to flow from epoch to epoch to give to humanity, in moments of crisis, fresh roots for a new civilization when the old one falls.

We have built up the idea of the chosen people, and we have seen its true nature. This is essential to understanding the Bible and what the Bible is in truth. The Bible contains the history of the chosen people, which is the history of the Christ impulse. The chosen people constitute the karmic community that, during the Atlantean Epoch, stood in a special relationship to the Sun oracle—the community of the Sun individualities. It is they who, throughout all of earthly evolution, are called to be forerunners, upholders, and heralds of the Sun being we know as Christ.

Having reached a true concept of the Old Testament as the book of eugenic occultism, and having a view of the chosen people as the karmic stream of the Christ impulse, we come to the third fundamental question, whose answer is essential if we are to understand the Bible: Who is the God that the Bible calls *Yahweh* [or *Jehovah*]? And what is his relationship to the karmic Christ impulse and to Christ himself? The next study will deal with the nature of Yahweh, and his karmic and historic significance.

# Chapter 2

# The Yahweh Being in Cosmic and Human History

## Yahweh as the Cross Bearer

To understand the being of Yahweh, the subject must be studied in relation to the whole of cosmic history. If we wish to understand spiritual beings, we must not isolate them from their own and other hierarchies. In the physical world, an object may be studied in isolation, but in the spiritual world an individual can be known only in relation to the universal. Thus, this study, which is dedicated to the Yahweh being, must first demonstrate the need for collaboration among the spiritual hierarchies. It will try to show this so that the reasoning does not seem philosophically abstract but allows its truth to speak directly to the heart. For there are areas in which argument is just as out of place as work clothes would be at a celebration of festive joy or solemn mourning. Consequently, part of this study will reveal certain important interrelationships in a narrative.

In the beginning of all that exists, the Father being *thought* the ideas of all beings and things. After he had thought the ideas of the whole world, he rested. The Father now no longer creates new thoughts, for all the ideas, even to the end of the world, were thought, or created, by him in the very beginning. The resting spoken of in Genesis of the Creator on the "seventh day" simply means that all thoughts of the creation had been thought out. But the thoughts of the Father would have remained as mere thoughts unto eternity if the Son had not breathed life into them. The Son breathes life, inspiring it into the thoughts of the Father. In this way they become living beings. There are however, still many thoughts remaining in the sphere of the Father into which the Son has not breathed life. The vivifying of the Father's thoughts by the Son continues, and thus new things appear in the being of the cosmos.

But the Father's thoughts that have become entities can enter the stream of cosmic events only through the power of the spirit that materializes them. They receive a body when the will of the spirit penetrates and guides them into the world of action. Thus, cosmic events occur through the activity of the eternal Trinity. But this is a very complicated process involving innumerable beings. The beings of the spiritual hierarchies work under the guidance of the divine Trinity, but they work so that their activity is divided according to the persons of the Trinity who guide them. There are hierarchies of the Father, the Son, and the Holy Spirit whose tasks are distinct one from one another. In general, the first hierarchy (seraphim, cherubim, and thrones) is especially subordinate to the Father; the second hierarchy (dominions, dynameis, and exusiai) is subordinate especially to the Son; and the third hierarchy (archai, archangels, and angels) is especially subordinate to the Holy Spirit. The three hierarchies work in harmony with the impulses that issue from the Trinity. This is the general picture, but if we study the details, we discover that in reality the three divine persons are active in all three hierarchies. Each of the three hierarchies is divided within itself into a trinity; and each of these subdivisions is again subject to one of the three persons of the Trinity. Thus, the vivifying love impulse of the Son works especially through seraphim, exusiai; the archangels, the enlightening wisdom of the spirit, works through cherubim, dynameis, and angels; while the will of the Father is revealed through thrones, dominions, and principalities. If we now review the general arrangement of the three spiritual hierarchies, we find the following classification according to the three primal cosmic persons:

The *seraphim* belong to the hierarchy of the Father, within which they represent the Son.
The *cherubim* represent the spirit, within the hierarchy of the Father.
The *thrones* are pure representatives of the Father principle.
The *dominions* are Father spirits within the hierarchy of the Son.
The *dynameis* are representatives of the Holy Spirit, within the hierarchy of the Son.
The *exusiai* (*elohim*) are pure representatives of the Son, within the hierarchy of the Son.
The *archai* are Father spirits within the hierarchy of the Holy Spirit.
The *archangels* are Son spirits, within the hierarchy of the Holy Spirit.
The *angels* are pure representatives of the Holy Spirit.

A plan of this arrangement shows that the hierarchy of the exusiai (to which the elohim belong) is the Christ hierarchy in the cosmic system. Mainly, the Christ being is active through it, for the exusiai are the Christ spirits within the Christ hierarchy.

Now the exusiai are divided into seven hosts, corresponding to the seven planetary spheres, which are their fields of action. Each of these hosts is drawn into unity by one being who takes the lead within the corresponding planetary sphere. Hence, in occultism we speak of the "seven elohim" who together represent the "fullness" (*pleroma*) of cosmic life and embrace the seven planet spheres. When we speak of the seven elohim in the following meditations, therefore, it must be remembered that we refer to these seven guiding beings of the hierarchy of the exusiai; but it must not be supposed that the hierarchy consists of only seven beings.

If we wish to understand the cosmic Christ correctly, we must look to the seven elohim, as the revealers of Christ in the cosmos. Similarly, if we wish to understand the seven elohim, we must look to the earthly life of Jesus Christ as described, for instance, in the Gospel of John. For if the "fullness" of the seven elohim dwelled in Christ, his earthly activity must have been revealed by these seven. The experiences derived from meditation on what is revealed to us by the life of Christ on Earth constitute the seven stages on the path of Christian initiation. This path is still walked today; but it belongs to higher stages than those for which Rudolf Steiner gives exercises in the first part of his book *How to Know Higher Worlds.* There is only one path of Christian esoteric teaching, but the stages of this path are distinct one from another. The Christ stage of the path of Christian initiation consists of seven exercises, which in their turn consist of meditation on the seven phases of the passion of Jesus Christ. These phases are:

the washing of the feet
the scourging
the crown of thorns
the bearing of the cross
the crucifixion (mystic death)
the resurrection
the ascension

The cosmic Word, or Logos, speaks through these seven events, each of which provides a subject for meditation at each stage on the path of initiation. It speaks through seven tones whose harmony reveals the "fullness" that dwells in Jesus Christ. To understand these seven events means understanding Christ as the "fullness" (*pleroma*) or combined activity of the seven unified elohim. Thus the first elohim being is the one who guides the spiritual etheric impulse of "foot washing" in the cosmos, which is not merely human but also a cosmic process. The foot washing exists wherever the higher serves the lower instead of ruling it by force. Thus, foot washing has its place in the destiny of everyone, for the angel always serves the human being. Guardian angels do not *rule* over those they protect, but serve them, stooping from spiritual heights to the depths of earthly destiny.

Authentic occultists cannot be understood unless their mode of action is accepted as foot washing. The desire to rule is the very first thing they lay aside; even the instinctive stirring of their subconscious is aware of the hollowness of any wish to make an impression or to acquire external importance. They wish to serve and nothing else. Hence the most exalted initiates work silently: in silence, they bear the burden for humankind; in silence they render the highest service. Just as the foot washing is a cosmic process guided by the first elohim, likewise the other six stages of the path of Christ are cosmic processes, behind which stand the six remaining elohim. Thus we may speak of the elohim of the foot washing, the elohim of the scourging, the elohim of the crowning with thorns, the elohim of the carrying of the cross, the elohim of the crucifixion, the elohim of the resurrection, and the elohim of the ascension.

When we study these stages in the path of Christ, one fact strikes us: Christ himself washed the feet, was scourged, crowned with thorns, and crucified. He rose again and ascended into heaven. The cross, however, was carried for him by another. He walked six stages of his path alone, but another took his place at one stage—the cross bearing. This fact leads us directly to the mystery of Yahweh and the six Sun elohim. For it is one of the fundamental truths of spiritual science that the "fullness" of the six elohim dwelled in Christ as the spirit of the Sun; one elohim worked alone, apart from the hexarchy of the Sun elohim. This elohim standing alone is the being whom the Bible calls Yahweh [or *Jehovah*] Elohim. He is the fourth elohim, the cross bearer in the cosmos. This is the being who has taken the cosmic cross bearing upon himself.

To understand the nature of Yahweh Elohim in its significance for the cosmos and for humankind, we must study the process of cosmic cross bearing, which gives us a principal key to understanding the Old Testament.

## The Moon Mystery

The idea generally associated with the fact of death is that of the decaying corpse; and the process of decay is generally accepted as an image of the way death functions in nature. But this is not a true picture of death; decay is merely the transition of an individual's living, organic substance into the living organic whole of the Earth. Death is not present there; rather, a life process occurs. Through decay, the substance of a corpse is delivered from death and received into the cycle of living nature. Hence the correct picture of death would not be that of the processes of decay, but mortal remains in which there is no decay. In decay, the Earth's life is active; death is revealed only in rigidity. When a part of cosmic history is torn away from the flow of time and becomes a rigid portion of space, then we have a truly dead body, or corpse. Life is space with time flowing through it; death is rigidified time in space. When time becomes space and surrenders control over form, it dies and becomes a corpse. This was realized in ancient times. Hence the cross—as an image of the cooperation between space and time become rigid—was the symbol of death.

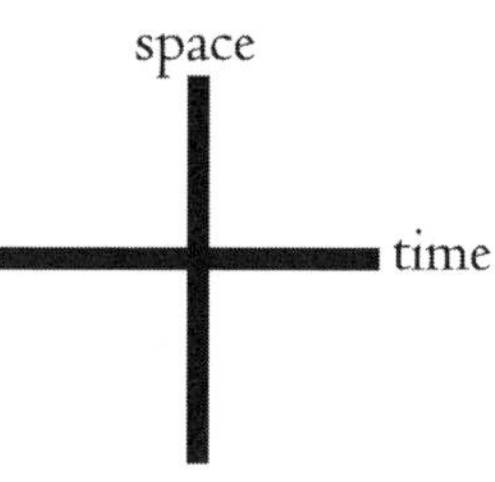


If we view the cross as indicating time grown rigid in space, then we have formed a true idea of bearing the cross. Cross carrying is connected with a dead portion of the past—a bit of the past grown rigid—that must just be carried because, in itself, it is incapable of movement. Thus, for instance, the incarnation of a human being in a mineral body is an example of cross bearing. Since we have received mineral substances into our physical body, we continually bear our "cross," the body. Thus all embodied human beings are cross bearers, for throughout life they carry with them a dead, mineral body, which is alien to the true nature of the physical body.

But being incarnated in a mineral body is not the only instance of cross bearing; it can also occur in other realms of existence. Cross bearing in human spiritual life, for example, is represented by a doctrine that was once alive but then became rigid dogma. The cross of religious and scientific dogmatism weighs heavy on human souls born under the influence of Western culture. Like foot washing, however, cross bearing is not merely a human process, but also cosmic. Where, then, do we see this cross bearing in the cosmos? Are there phenomena in cosmic life that bring about cross bearing? In other words, where in the cosmos can we find that dead body, or corpse, that must be "carried" by living, cosmic beings?

For thousands of years, poets have sung the praises of the "chaste Queen of Night." The Moon, dispenser of night's silver light, has always been an object of poetic admiration, but what, in fact, is the Moon as a cosmic body? It is a dead body, a corpse circling around the Earth, which carries it along in its cosmic orbit. The Moon is a rigid clod of Earth's past, carried about with her. If the substance that has agglomerated to become the Moon had not detached itself from the evolution of the Earth during the Lemurian epoch, all life on Earth would have died. Terrestrial life would never have been able to control so much rigidified substance had the Moon's substance remained with the Earth's substance. Thus, the surplus of death was removed from the Earth through the beneficial intervention of the spiritual world. Radiating cosmic formative impulses, one of the seven elohim left the Sun fortress to which he rightly belonged in order to sever the Moon—that rigidified Earth corpse—from the Earth, so that in the future he might work from it at a distance from Earth. The Earth and earthly humankind owe the possibility of further evolution to this sublime sacrifice of Yahweh Elohim. If Yahweh Elohim had not renounced the Sun existence and assumed the burden of the Moon, the Earth's cross, the essential nature of Earth would have been crushed under the weight of that cross.

Today, the most highly esteemed personalities are disparaged and slandered, and their words are falsely interpreted as the opposite of what they mean. Consequently, now more than ever, it is an extremely solemn obligation of all anthroposophists to rediscover words that reverently represent to humankind the true character of the sublime, cosmic cross bearer Yahweh Elohim, who has been misunderstood, misrepresented, misinterpreted, and maligned. Human beings need gratitude not only toward one another, but also toward spiritual beings. It is true that spiritual beings do not actually need our gratitude, but we need to show it for the sake of our human dignity. It is inconsistent with human dignity to be ungrateful and to silently ignore lies and slander against those highly exalted spiritual beings to whom, as human beings, we owe such an immense debt. The Moon exusiai, who belong to the host of Yahweh, do in fact have the right to bear, gleaming on their brow, the exalted sign of the Sun; but for the benefit of humankind they bear the silver Moon sign instead. Indeed, it was no preference for death that caused them as the primal bearers of life to choose the Moon—that rigid corpse in the cosmos—in which to live and breathe; this was done to save and protect the feeble flame of humanity on Earth.

Poets have made the Moon an inexhaustible source of human sentimentality, but where are the poets to write appropriate words for the true beauty—the moral depths—of that cosmic sacrifice, the Moon? Where are the hearts that, instead of dissolving and becoming depressed by melancholy, are conscious of the flame that glows in the Moon, the flame of the sacrificial love of Yahweh Elohim? The sacrifice of Yahweh Elohim is more sublime than one can grasp directly through human understanding. To fully understand it, the heart must cooperate with the mind, for not only is Yahweh Elohim the bearer of the cross of the dead body in the cosmos, but, more than that, he banishes evil from the cosmos by keeping the "Eighth Sphere" at a distance from the Earth. Here we enter an area that belongs to the mysteries of true occultism, but even the part of this we are able to discuss will be enough to help us more deeply understand the nature of Yahweh Elohim.

## The Eighth Sphere

The stream of cosmic evolution flows through seven phases, or "manvantaras." These phases are described in Rudolf Steiner's *Outline of Esoteric Science.*[1] He calls them the Saturn, Sun, Moon, Earth, Jupiter, Venus, and Vulcan phases. These phases of evolution may be called "spheres," though they are not contemporaneous, but manifest one after another. Thus, once evolution has run its normal course, it will have passed through seven spheres, or stages, of existence. It is always possible, however, for cosmic history to stray from the path of normal evolution because of the activities of the three hierarchies of "evil," which resist the hierarchies of "good." And insofar as such resistance succeeds, another sphere is formed in the cosmos that does not belong to the seven normal spheres of evolution. It represents an independent sphere outside the normal stream of evolution. In occult science, therefore, it is called the "Eighth Sphere."[2]

In certain circles of occult scientists there are two half-true ideas about the Eighth Sphere—ideas that may lead to dangerous consequences, precisely because each contains some truth. One identifies the Eighth Sphere with the Moon. The result of this half-truth is a tendency that, widespread in such circles, finds expression in the slander of Yahweh. This, again, leads to a denial of the Old Testament, without which the true depth of the New Testament cannot be understood. The idea that the Moon is the Eighth Sphere causes a feeling of antipathy toward the Old Testament, which deals a deathblow to comprehension of the Gospels. We must realize that every *thought* in the process of time evokes *feelings* that determine the path of the *will*, leading it in either the right direction or the wrong direction. Here, however, we are facing a preconceived large-scale plan to sway the wills of many away from the path of Christianity.

The other half-true idea about the Eighth Sphere places it within the Earth. According to this theory, the innermost strata of the interior of the Earth form the Eighth Sphere. This view leads to a misrepresentation of the Moon, a denial of Yahweh's mission, which results in a tendency to dismiss the Old Testament, and this again makes a deeper understanding of the Gospels impossible. Identifying the Moon with the Eighth Sphere leads to false statements about Yahweh; identifying the interior of the Earth with the Eighth Sphere leads to the denial of Yahweh; and both ideas have the common result of delaying the world's discernment of Christianity's importance.

As we said, these two views are half-truths. They contain just enough truth to entice the instinct for truth from the depths of human souls, and enough falsity to guide that instinct in the wrong direction. The truth about the Eighth Sphere is this; it is located *between* the Earth and the Moon; it is both dependent on the Moon and associated with the Earth's interior. It is true that the Earth's interior is the part that has fallen under the power of the Eighth Sphere; but the Moon is the cosmic fortress from which the Eighth Sphere is kept under control. Certain strata of the Earth's interior represent the domain of the Eighth Sphere within the terrestrial planet, while the Moon, in fact, draws the Eighth Sphere toward itself, and thus keeps it at a distance from the Earth. To understand this process, to a certain extent we must understand the properties of the *substance* of the Eighth Sphere.

The physical matter with which we are familiar is in fact the solidification of spiritual substance; the astral becomes etheric, the etheric becomes rigid, and physical substance manifests. This is spirit that has become fixed. Physical matter does not arise from an assemblage of elements, but from the disintegration of elements. As the living etheric substance stiffens and crumbles, constituents of physical matter are formed. Today, chemistry is interested only in the phenomena of disintegration; the organic genesis of matter is beyond its sphere.

Besides organic and inorganic substance, there is still the possibility of a third kind of substance. In addition to life (organic substance) and death (inorganic substance), there is also the possibility of the "phantom." The substance of the phantom is neither alive nor dead; it may be compared to electromagnetic substance. A phantom does not live, nor is it dead; rather is it formed of electricity endowed with sensation and consciousness. The chief characteristic of this substance is absorbency, which, in contrast to ether, is inherent in it. Just as everything etheric tends to radiate, the substance of the Eighth Sphere tends to absorb. This tendency to absorb is an external expression of the ahrimanic principle. For Ahriman is a being in the cosmos who strives to absorb into himself all that exists. Hence the substance of the Eighth Sphere, Ahriman's cosmic citadel, exhibits the same main characteristic.[3] This characteristic of the Eighth Sphere allows us to understand the means by which it can be confined to a definite place in the cosmos. This made it necessary to create and effectively position a body with enough inner power of resistance to withstand the absorbing influence of the Eighth Sphere—that is, strong enough not to be engulfed by it. This is a body that the Eighth Sphere tries to absorb, but it is suffused with a force that is able to stand firm against it. This cosmic body is the Moon, and the power from the Moon that offers resistance to the Eighth Sphere is the spiritual power of Yahweh Elohim.

From within the Moon, Yahweh Elohim holds the Eighth Sphere in check. As a result, the Eighth Sphere is kept away from the Earth until a particular epoch of time. There is no direct connection between humanity and the Eighth Sphere; such a connection can be only indirect, by way of the sixth stratum of the Earth's interior. For humankind, therefore, Hell is always below, because no human being has ever been in the Eighth Sphere. For this, we owe gratitude to Yahweh's sacrifice, which protects humankind from the Eighth Sphere.

## Yahweh in the Course of Earthly Events

The foregoing sequence of ideas makes it clear that Yahweh Elohim is the antagonist of Ahriman in the extraterrestrial cosmos. The consequences of this extraterrestrial conflict benefit the Earth and the earthly human race; but the conflict itself takes place beyond the terrestrial planet. The Bible nevertheless speaks often of Yahweh's direct intervention in earthly events; he reveals himself through earthly elemental forces, speaks to the prophets, and guides the destinies of nations. These facts lead to a question: What is the role of Yahweh Elohim in terrestrial events—not indirectly through the Moon, but directly through interventions such as those recorded in the Bible story? To answer this we must consider the epoch of terrestrial evolution that began the karma of the human race. It is the epoch of the "fall" of humankind and the beginning of the luciferic intervention in human affairs. The effect of this intervention appeared when the human astral body gained independence from the spiritual hierarchies. The astral body was detached from its close association with the region of the hierarchies, and this initiated the karma of the human race (though not yet individual karma), since the separation of the astral body from the hierarchies led to error, disease, and death.

The luciferic intervention became apparent in the spiritual world as the result of an event traditionally known as the "fall of the angels," which occurred in the region of the hierarchies. This event can be understood spiritually if we picture it as a conflict between wisdom-filled love and emotional commiseration. During the Moon period, the hierarchies of angels were so closely associated with the astral bodies of humankind that they controlled the functions of the I, or Ego, in the human organism; but during the first half of the Earth's evolution, they renounced their power over the human astral body in order to give place to the human I. From that time on, although the angels still inspire the human I, they do so without encroaching upon its freedom; they are counselors and guardians, but never rulers.

Now, of course, it is easy to find facts that "contradict" this truth, and we may say the same of all of the thoughts and facts we have discussed. For example, it may be argued that there are cases when an angel not only speaks, but also acts. Yes, there are indeed cases when an angel acts so vigorously that it influences even the physical body. There is nothing to be said against these facts; they are perfectly true. But insofar as comprehension of them is concerned, it must be argued (even if they are regarded only as influences) that angels merely strengthen the goodness that is in the human being; they do not compel one to goodness. It is for human beings themselves to recognize goodness as good; the *magic* of goodness belongs to the angel (or to any other hierarchical being, under whose protection humankind may be).[4] In this way, the hierarchy of angels renounced the alliance with humankind that existed during the old Moon period. This renunciation must be considered an act of wisdom-filled love, or loving foresight. The angels withdrew from humanity to give the human I, or Ego, room to evolve.

One section of the hierarchy of angels acted differently. They were deterred by the trials and dangers that freedom would bring upon human beings. They felt sorry for humankind and, moved by compassionate feelings, assumed the task of guides to save human beings from the sufferings that lay before them. They rebelled against the decree of the highest gods, and took a path of opposition to that of the spirits who served true human well-being. Whereas the angels who were aiding the true progress of humanity renounced power and withdrew from human affairs, the luciferic angels plunged even more deeply into the human organism to free human beings by force. Since then, every human being has, in addition to a guardian angel, a luciferic angel so closely allied with the astral body that the angel has come to be called the "luciferic double."

Because of the "fall of the angels" (the process through which luciferic angels became luciferic doubles), the human astral body became, as we have said, detached from guidance of the gods. This was manifested as egoism, a quality that, toward the end of the Lemurian epoch, mastered the human individual with the intensity of a natural force. Humankind would have succumbed entirely to this egoism if the hierarchies of good had not struck back. This involved the creation—from below, out of the human etheric and physical nature—of a countercurrent that opposed the egoism flowing down from the human astral nature and "I" being. In the depths of the human subconscious, a force was planted that restored the balance needed for the evolution of a free I-being. If the elemental force of love had not been planted in human beings, we would have completely succumbed to the elemental force of egoism. Through the luciferic impulse, humankind receives a strong tendency toward self-esteem; through the Yahweh impulse, we receive an equally strong tendency to esteem others. For it was Yahweh Elohim who planted the capacity for love in earthly human nature, whereby we are able to focus not only on ourselves, but also on others. To counterbalance the luciferic tendency toward self, the "Thou" tendency sprang up in humankind, receiving its impetus from Yahweh Elohim.

We may consider how crudely egoistic human beings would have become if husband and wife, parents and children, brothers and sisters and relatives had not been able to love one another—in short, if individuals, surrounded by an abstract "humanity," had only a living self-interest. Owing to the earthly activity of Yahweh Elohim in the earliest days, long before the Christ event, humankind became capable of sacrifice; it was Yahweh Elohim who infused the faculty of love into the human bloodstream. On Earth, he overcomes the disintegration of humanity; in the cosmos, he overcomes the "Eighth Sphere." From the Moon, he resists Ahriman; on the Earth, he resists Lucifer.

We can never understand the spirit of the Old Testament if we misrepresent the historical significance of Yahweh as the opponent of Lucifer on Earth. This is exactly what distinguishes the Bible from the sacred writings of other civilizations (for instance, the sacred writings of India); in style, form, and content, it is free of luciferic influence. Compare, for example, the story of King David in the book of Kings with the life story of Krishna or the Buddha as preserved in Indian tradition. The former is a record of actual spiritual reality, without embellishment of the terrestrial human being and without abasement of the divine spiritual; the latter is a record in which a terrestrial human is present only insofar as this is absolutely essential to the expression of the supersensory divinity. In the former, the point is to picture spiritual and actual facts; in the latter, the presentation of supernatural events is especially emphasized and, moreover, intensely aestheticized and conventionalized.

The Bible, however, is also distinguished from Eastern scriptures by its content. The ascetic, world-renouncing character, which is a feature of both Eastern and Early Christian ecclesiastical literature, is entirely absent in the Bible. No prophet or Old Testament hero is an ascetic in the Eastern or Christian ecclesiastical sense. The mortification of desires is not regarded as having the slightest value in the Bible; rather, it esteems the subordination of desire to high and distant ideals. There is, indeed, in the Bible a kind of asceticism, but it is an asceticism of the soul, a purely moral kind. It involves subordinating one's personal inclinations to the call of duty. Fear, anger, and self-indulgence must be overcome in order to accomplish acts that will hasten the fulfillment of Israel's mission. This is why the Israelites were a peaceful race. They hated war and had a horror of bloodshed. And yet this race waged wars of annihilation against those who followed corrupt cults. This—overcoming of one's own interests for the sake of objective requirements—is asceticism in the biblical sense. Only this kind of asceticism is free of the luciferic impulse, from which asceticism in the usual sense is never free. Asceticism, as it was understood in the Europe of the Middle Ages was, in truth, a preparation for the "ahrimanizing" of European humanity. For if the axiom "Every spiritually minded person must be an ascetic" had been carried to its logical conclusion, the result would have been that incarnating souls would find acceptance only with spiritually inferior parents; in other words, they would have been brought up under conditions of heredity and education that would have stifled their spirituality. Ahrimanic birth is the inevitable result of luciferic asceticism.

True Christian asceticism, therefore, can be found only in the history of the Grail line, which began with Joseph of Arimathea and ended with Lohengrin, not in the cells of the monks and hermits of the Eastern and Western Catholic churches. Similarly, the asceticism of the Bible is higher than what is contemplated in the Upanishads and Puranas. The asceticism of the Bible reveals the spirit of the cosmic cross bearer, Yahweh Elohim; and it is therefore, at heart, nothing less than a cross bearing in life. Cross bearing is the subordination of personality to the karmic decree to spiritual duty, and this indeed can be done with joy; it is the basic moral impulse of the Old Testament. Unless we understand this basic moral impulse of the Bible by realizing the cosmic and terrestrial mission of Yahweh, the Bible remains not only a mystery, but also a stumbling block for the modern human being, in whose subconscious mind still echoes the notions of the Catholic ecclesiastical worldview.

It may easily be argued that the age of the Old Testament is past; since the Mystery of Golgotha, humankind is freed from the ties of blood. The Yahweh impulse working in the blood has given place to the purely spiritual Christ impulse.

Before raising this objection, however, we should consider that the Yahweh impulse does not oppose the Christ impulse, but represents a part of it. Just as white light can manifest the seven primary colors, likewise, the Christ impulse can be revealed in a sevenfold way through the seven elohim. The Yahweh impulse is simply one of the seven ways in which the Christ impulse reveals itself. And the process that was brought about by the advent on Earth of the "Fullness" (the six other ways of revelation) in Jesus Christ was that the six others were added to the Yahweh impulse. Freedom from blood ties does not mean that the blood loses its importance, but that it is now able to be not only the bearer of the Yahweh impulse, but also the bearer of the united entity of the seven elohim, the complete Christ impulse. The freedom from blood ties that was exoterically built up during the Middle Ages was a luciferic concept; the esoteric view of the Grail teaching was inherently Christian. In Grail lore there was no question of separating the soul life from the blood, but rather of ennobling the blood by bringing into it not only the life of the soul, but also the life of the spirit. Thus blood ties become the express image of spiritual karmic bonds. Being freed from blood ties after the Mystery of Golgotha means that human beings can no longer be bound karmically through ties of blood; rather, human beings are bound in karmic bonds that have the same nature as blood ties. During pre-Christian times, a marriage in which there was no blood tie was a crime; similarly, in times to come it will become increasingly clear that a karmic marriage outside the tie of blood is not only a moral crime, but also a crime against nature. In the sixth post-Atlantean cultural epoch, a spiritual karmic marriage within the blood ties will represent the principle of evolution throughout generations, just as, say, during the early Egyptian period, marriage between blood relations was the principle of evolution throughout generations.

We have thus studied the nature of Yahweh Elohim as the cosmic cross bearer who opposes the Eighth Sphere in the cosmos and, on the Earth, the disintegration of humanity. By doing so, we have answered the questions concerning the relationship between Yahweh and the Christ, the hierarchies of good and evil, and the Earth. We have still one question to answer in connection with the Yahweh being—namely: What is the relationship between Yahweh and human consciousness? How can we discern Yahweh in human consciousness?

## Knowledge of Yahweh

In the foregoing analysis, we tried to show how the Yahweh being bears the cosmic cross on which Christ was later crucified. Before Christ became the spirit of the Earth, that spirit was Yahweh Elohim. It was his influence that was active in the terrestrial element at the time when the Moon was still a part of the Earth, before the epoch when the Moon had to be temporarily cast out of it for the benefit of the Earth. In ancient days, seven planetary spheres were spoken of—Saturn, Jupiter, Mars, Sun, Venus, Mercury, and the Moon. Earth was not yet mentioned among them, but we must not imagine that the Earth was viewed as the Eighth Sphere. It was not mentioned, because the Moon took its place as a separate sphere among the others. The Moon sphere, which reaches from Earth to the orbit of the Moon, is actually the Earth's ether body. Thus, when the suprasensory part of the Earth was intended, it was not the word *Earth* that was used, but *Moon.* The Moon was considered (quite correctly) to be Earth's conscience. Earth's conscience bore witness to the nature of Yahweh, who had established the Moon fortress to protect the Earth from the Eighth Sphere.

To discern Yahweh's nature, it was not necessary to abandon the human physical etheric bodies, the medium of daytime consciousness, and rise to the higher astral body and I. His nature could be discerned by a watchful I in that part of the human physical and etheric organization situated *between* the physical and the etheric bodies. The blood is the substance that forms the boundary between the physical and the etheric; it needs little to become etheric, yet the firmest parts of the physical body are built up by the blood.

Yahweh Elohim functioned in the etheric portion of the blood, where human consciousness could meet him. But blood is the physical organ of the human I, just as the nervous system is the organ of the astral body and the glandular system of the ether body. Blood consciousness is also I consciousness; the human blood impulse is the capacity for love, implanted by Yahweh, and about which we spoke in the previous section. We can understand the whole history of our human relationship to Yahweh, as described in the Bible, by thinking of it as two parallel lines drawn right through the entire Old Testament—a line showing the influence of the Yahweh impulse on the blood as it works in the subconscious; and a line showing discernment of Yahweh in the I, working consciously. The first line reveals Yahweh as the "wisdom of the blood"; the second reveals him as the "wisdom of the I." The figures of Tamar and Ruth, for example, belong to the first line, that of the intuition of Yahweh through the blood. The prophets belong to the second line, that of the inspiration of Yahweh through the I.

In the first line, Yahweh functioned as leader of the children of Israel; in the second line, Yahweh spoke to the prophets—*life* and *knowledge,* the two gates through which human beings encountered the Yahweh being. We must picture this double relationship with Yahweh as clearly as possible. Yahweh meant *life* to the members of the Israelite community. The words of Job's wife, "Curse (or deny) God and die," contain literal truth; denial of God meant death, because such a denial caused the etheric life force of the blood to disappear. As a being of the second hierarchy, Yahweh had power over the life force; this is exactly what was expressed in the words of Job's wife. Thus the Israelite race was bound to Yahweh through its life force and bound equally through its consciousness. The whole spiritual life of Israel, even its outer civilization, was rooted in the revelation of Yahweh. Not just the law, but also all of the details concerning the allotting of land, the special duties of various towns, the building of the temple in Jerusalem, and so on were all based on conscious interaction with the Yahweh being, the source of all knowledge, art, and legislation in Israel.

There was also another side to this deeply rooted union with Yahweh—the attitude toward death, especially for the Old Testament characters. They vehemently resisted death; existence after death lay beyond the scope of their interest, to say nothing of their hopes and longings. It would be a mistake, however, to think of this attitude toward death as materialistic. Materialism affirms the material and denies the spiritual. This was not the case for those of the Old Testament. They affirmed the spirit as perceptible by any whole human being—that is, by anyone consisting of body, soul, and spirit. To them, a disembodied human being was incomplete; they believed that the more complete one was, the more complete would be the revelation of the spirit. They had experienced interaction with the spirit on Earth, and to them death was a distressing interruption of that relationship. They did not value earthly life for the sake of material things, but for the spirit revealed in earthly things. Yahweh Elohim, the sublime spirit they knew, revealed himself only in earthly life; death meant being severed from Yahweh Elohim, to whom they knew they were bound by all the threads of their being. Was this feeling an illusion? To answer this, we must now study the cosmic character of Yahweh Elohim from a different perspective.

When Yahweh left the Sun, descending from the Sun sphere to the Moon sphere, he ceased to be a god of day (as the other six Sun elohim are) and became a god of night. In a cosmic sense, Yahweh renounced the sphere of light and plunged into the sphere of darkness, thus bringing light into the darkness, so that he became the "light god of the night." This is how this act of Yahweh appears from a cosmic perspective. From the terrestrial point of view, however, the opposite is true; by renouncing the activities of the spiritual Sun—which shines brightest at midnight and at Christmastime, the darkest times on earth—he became, terrestrially, a god of day—that is, he became one of those beings who can be perceived by human daytime consciousness. Human beings could encounter him while still in the physical and etheric body, or the waking state. But earthly day is cosmic night; thus Yahweh became a night god who revealed himself to Abraham at midday.

Yahweh Elohim will not be found in the world of spiritual light, the Sun sphere to which the souls of the dead rise after the Kama Loka period.[5] For he left this sphere, and passed to the Moon sphere, which is, indeed, Kama Loka, experienced subjectively by human souls after death. There, a soul is concerned with one's own destiny and not free to contemplate the nature of Yahweh Elohim.[6] Thus we see that it was no illusion on the part of Biblical characters to sense death as a severance from Yahweh. It is perfectly true that human beings were separated from Yahweh by death. This was the tragedy of death for Israel's leaders; it was not a material mode of thinking, which is frequently the superficial supposition. The tragedy of this severance from Yahweh can hardly be expressed with more feeling than it is in Psalms 6: " Return, O Lord, deliver my soul: oh save me for thy mercies' sake. For in death there is no remembrance of thee: in the grave who shall give thee thanks?" The prophet Isaiah sounds the same tragic note: "For the grave cannot praise thee, death cannot celebrate thee: they that go down into the pit cannot hope for thy truth. The living, the living, he shall praise thee, as I do this day: the father to the children shall make known thy truth" (Isaiah 38:18–19).

Union with Yahweh ceases after death; only the living can discern Yahweh. Knowledge of him is knowledge for the living, because it is between birth and death that he is to be encountered, not between death and birth. Yahweh Elohim is the god of cosmic night. He shines in the darkness, and the life between birth and death is a night of the soul. But in this night a light shines on the soul, which gives it life. This light in the darkness is the Christ light of Yahweh Elohim, the reflected moonlight of the world's spiritual Sun.

And so we have established the most essential concepts to guide us in understanding the Bible. These thoughts—the Bible as a book of eugenic occultism, the chosen people as a karmic stream, the Yahweh being as the cosmic cross bearer—all serve to awaken tones in the reader's soul, quickening for many a deep understanding of truths that might otherwise pass unnoticed. In the next study, we will try to understand the essential impulse of the Old Testament as it appears at the beginning of Israel's history. That impulse is revealed in the careers of Abraham, Isaac, and Jacob, and the study of these three will form an important chapter in the archives of eugenic occultism.

# Chapter 3

# Abraham, Isaac, and Jacob

## Comprehension of the Trinity

Like the substances of the human body, thinking, feeling, and willing, the three primary forces of the human soul life, are rooted in the cosmos. Just as bodily life is inconceivable without light, air, and food from the surrounding world, the soul's life is inconceivable without an influx of forces from the surrounding suprasensory spiritual world—from the fountainhead known as Father, Son, and Holy Spirit. If light, air, and food are withheld from the human body, it will die; if cosmic thinking, feeling, and willing are withheld from the human soul, it withers like a snapped twig. Just as the nervous system needs light, the rhythmic system needs air, and the digestive system needs food, likewise, thinking, feeling, and willing need the light of the Holy Spirit, the love of the Son, and the power of the Father. The meditation presented at the 1923 inauguration of the Anthroposophical Society by Rudolf Steiner as a spiritual "foundation stone" is, in fact, a means of enabling, kindling, and illuminating the primary forces of the human soul. Its content, choice of words, and rhythm enable it to link, as perfectly as possible, the soul with the cosmic spirits that illuminate, animate, and strengthen it. The triangle of Father, Son, and Holy Spirit in the rectangle of east, west, north, and south is a spiritual figure that can lead to important developments in spiritual knowledge. It can also lead to developments that prove the following.

Human beings are directed toward cosmic spirituality in three ways, and so long as they remain in union with the spiritual Trinity, human soul life maintains its harmony. But when human beings are partial or biased toward the spiritual world, they are exposed to certain dangers. For example, if we adopt a partiality toward the Holy Spirit, we risk falling under the power of the evil spirit Lucifer. This can be understood easily by clearly understanding the essential significance of the conscious presence of the Father, Son, and Holy Spirit. Joy is the fundamental characteristic of the realized presence of the Holy Spirit—a realization of the joy of freedom. In traditional Christendom, this experience has been called "joy in the Holy Spirit." This term is literally accurate, since experience of the Spirit is always accompanied by joy. It is a blissful experience of freedom.

The Son is experienced as a pattern for the whole of humankind. This experience is not joy but one of conscience, which always includes an exhortation to action. It is activity that flows into the soul from the experience of the Son.

The Father is experienced neither in joy nor in activity but in the deepest contrition of the soul. Human beings come to know the Father by realizing that, in themselves, they are nothing when they are cast down so that there is a desire to be annihilated on the threshold of the realm in which the breath of the Father is perceived. Thus, the experience of the Father is reconciliation with *death*. We are reconciled to the fact of death, because we know that the Father is present. Tears of bitter penitence bring an experience of the Father; tears are always an indication that the soul has reached the boundary of the realm where the Father's breath is felt.

But when we are partial in our efforts, instead of striving for the Holy Spirit, for example, we may strive for the *joy* of the Holy Spirit. Such effort would be luciferic. It is a luciferic temptation to seek the joy of the Holy Spirit instead of the Holy Spirit himself. This is what happened to the spirituality of the ancient Indian civilization. It had an impulse to rise to knowledge of the Father, but it never did so because ancient India adopted a partiality in spiritual life. Consequently, that civilization became luciferic, which led to the rise of the ancient Persian civilization. Thus began the karma of the post-Atlantean civilizations.

Partiality in experiencing the Son results in an attitude that might be described as follows: Earth is the realm of action. Error, suffering, and evil hold sway on Earth, but not in heaven; it is on Earth that they must be actively fought against. The hierarchies are active in the spiritual world, and human actions are less important in that world. On the Earth, however, human actions are decisive. In the spiritual world everything is ordered; consequently, one's undivided attention must be given to the physical world. The truth is, however, that one's lack of interest in the spiritual world and exclusive focus on the sensory world are the results of partiality toward the Son principle; the result may be surrender to Ahriman's allure.

One-sided emphasis on the Father principle in our present epoch does not lead to being ensnared by opposing spiritual powers. In the present epoch, only the false Holy Spirit and the false Son—Lucifer and Ahriman—function as antichrists. In the karmic future, however, those who in the present epoch tend to be fatalistic will fall victim to the third hostile power. Fatalism is the fruit of partiality toward the Father principle; it is the expression of a complete inner passivity toward the world. Such passivity, however, will one day become a tremendous danger once the false Father begins to function in the world. A time will come when Asura will appear as the karma of Ahriman, just as Ahriman appeared as the karma of Lucifer. The three dangers of spiritual one-sidedness can be avoided only by conceiving of the universal deity as "Three in One." The Trinity of eternal goodness is a unity, and the human soul must think of it as a unity. If this unity is disintegrated, it falls under the power of the evil trinity.

In the stream of time, however, human beings are always partial to some extent. True, such one-sidedness evens out in the course of time, but in any given epoch, humankind constantly places special emphasis on one of the three persons of the divine Trinity. And, with this, certain inclinations of the soul appear that, if allowed free reign, lead to the kinds of errors discussed here.

To understand Abraham, Isaac, and Jacob, we must bear in mind both the positive and the negative means of experiencing the Godhead. From these three individuals flows the stream of Israel's inheritance *and* its karma, which leads to the birth of the Messiah; they represent the threefold divine intervention in this stream. The secret of the lives and destinies of these three persons involved their participation with the forces of Father, Son, and Holy Spirit in the work of eugenic occultism, as was summarized in the genealogy of the two Jesus children in the Gospels of Matthew and Luke. Deep spiritual impulses first appeared in those three patriarchs and worked through generations of forefathers toward the Jesus children. There are *three* patriarchs in whom they first appear, because there are three spiritual impulses whose cooperation prepared the advent of Christ on Earth. These three impulses are rooted in heaven and are the expression of the Divine Trinity. Consequently, we must first study the light and shadow of the human soul's experience of the Trinity, so that we may understand the figures of Abraham, Isaac, and Jacob—not just as biographical or even historical personalities, but also in the cosmic sense.

## The Father Thought of Abraham and the Son Sacrifice of Isaac

We are now in a position to answer these questions: Why would *one* patriarch be insufficient to supply the primary impulse for the history of Israel? Why does the Bible speak of "the God of Abraham, of Isaac, and of Jacob"?[1]

*Three* personalities stand at the beginning of Israel's history because, if there had been only one, the whole course of its evolution would have fallen inevitably into one of the three dangers of the spiritual life: spiritual egoism, materialism, or fatalism. The Three in One is a unity, and if we cut off any one of its sides, we inevitably stray into one of the three paths of error. To avoid this, there were three personalities through whom the three primal impulses of Israelite history flowed into its hereditary and karmic streams.

To preserve Israel's evolution from fatalism, materialism, and spiritual egoism, three impulses had to be active from the beginning. If, for instance, the primal impulse had been transmitted only through Abraham, it would have taken a turn toward fatalism. If the obedience of Abraham to the will of the Father had been the singular foundation of Israel's spiritual life, it would have resulted in a fatalistic race. The willfulness of Jacob—even to the degree of conflict against God—was needed to balance that danger. Further, the spiritual life of Israel would have become astrally abstract if it had been rooted only in Abraham and Jacob. It would have exhibited a duality of *law* and *power*. *Love* would not have been present to hold them in unity.

Without the impulse that Isaac transmitted, the spiritual life of Israel would have lacked heart. Just as Abraham embodied the thought of Israel, and Jacob its will, Isaac embodied the very life of Israel. Israel received its purpose from Abraham, and in Isaac that purpose became life; the power to accomplish it was given through Jacob. The mission of Israel could never have taken hold of the ether body if only the Abrahamic impulse had been active. It would have functioned only in the astral body, but through the impulse of Isaac it was able to descend into the etheric body. It could never have penetrated the physical body, however, without adding the impulse of Jacob. Only the combined activity of three impulses could render the whole human character of Israel's mission effective. It was in Abraham, Isaac, and Jacob that the threefold stream of inheritance through the generations of Israel began—the inheritance of Israel's thought in the subconscious of the astral body; Israel's sacrifice in the subconscious of the etheric body; and Israel's victory in the subconscious of the physical body. The thought of the Father, the sacrifice of the Son, and the victory of the Spirit were thus all reflected in history.

The entire mystery of the Old Testament period is nothing but the consummation of the Father's thought in preparing the sacrifice of the Son for the future victory of the Holy Spirit. So we may say that the Old Testament is primarily the book of Abraham's thought, and the New Testament is the book of the consummation of Isaac's sacrifice, while the Apocalypse represents the book of the future victory of Jacob. The Old Testament is the book of the Father's thought; the New Testament is that of the Son's sacrifice; and the Apocalypse is the book of the Spirit's future victory. Hence, we cannot understand the entire Bible unless the Old Testament is understood. The Old Testament reveals the thought that inspires the whole. This fact also sheds light on the dangers connected with repudiating the Old Testament, a tendency that is growing continually stronger today. Moreover, the Old Testament reveals the true reasons for such repudiation, which resolve into the intention (concealed behind various masks) of eradicating the *thought* of the Bible from human consciousness—that is, recognition of the Christ impulse. Let the reader take this as a warning: every spiritual tendency that dismembers the Bible and declares any of its three parts to be less valuable than the others is working on the side of hidden evil in the world; for the harm to humankind that will ensue outweighs anything noble and true that such a tendency might bring with it.

Thus, the biography of Abraham should be studied as a revelation of the *thought* of Israel. This does not mean that Abraham's thoughts represent the thought of Israel; rather, it means that the career of Abraham *embodied* the thought of Israel. It is important to grasp the significant truth that prophecy does not mean proclaiming the future only through words, but also through conduct. There are not only prophetic sayings, but also prophetic life histories that are themselves objective prophecies. Such biographies are not important just to knowledge; they are important also to the seeds of destiny planted within the suprasensory organism of Earth so that they will develop in the course of human history. The career of Abraham should be regarded as "lines of force" in the astral organism of the Earth, representing the general directions of the future history of the Children of Israel. They form the astral ground plan for Israel's destiny. Abraham's career, viewed as a picture, makes the whole history of the Israelites intelligible. Consider, for example, the spatial scene of their history—Palestine, Egypt, and Mesopotamia. Within these three lands, the drama of Israel's destiny was enacted—from its beginning up to the Mystery of Golgotha. Now this was the very location of Abraham's wanderings. The wanderings of the little tribe under the leadership of Abraham as prince were confined to Mesopotamia, Canaan, and Egypt. The limits of Abraham's wanderings marked the limits of the spatial scene of the history of Israel. This is no accident but a measure with definite bearing on the future, and this may be discerned from the following passages in the Bible (Yahweh is speaking to Abraham): "Go forth of the ark, thou, and thy wife, and thy sons, and thy sons' wives with thee. Bring forth with thee every living thing that is with thee, of all flesh, both of fowl, and of cattle, and of every creeping thing that creepeth upon the earth; that they may breed abundantly in the earth, and be fruitful, and multiply upon the earth" (Genesis 8:16–17). In other words, Abraham was commanded to wander over the land in order to mark out a region that should belong to his descendants. Thus his wanderings assumed the significance of an appropriation for the future. Abraham must *see* the land that is to belong to Israel. He must absorb it into his consciousness. His astral body must collaborate with the auric configuration of the land. Once this is done, he has assumed possession of it. For the true, not merely the outer, possession of a country takes place gradually. First, a definite astral purport impregnates the astral being of the land; as the second step, that astral impregnation descends into the etheric forces of the land so that, finally, it manifests on the physical plane. When the third stage is reached, we have defined a region where a specific karmic community can accomplish its mission unhindered. In other words, its members will have come into possession of a "promised land."

In this way, guiding spirits prepare special places and regions for specific purposes. First, an astral covering embraces a certain place, which then becomes etheric so that it will be populated eventually by physical human beings. Spiritual centers thus sprang up in human history. But we must not confuse the center with its inhabitants. We must never forget that it is the *place* that is consecrated, not those who assemble there. The duty of the people is to work in harmony with the intent of the consecrated place. Whether they fulfill that duty depends on human free will. One strict law, however, functions objectively in the consecrated place; such a place takes revenge on those who are unfaithful to its spirit. Even in a relatively short time, the dogmatism that manifests in a place designated for spiritual life leads to astral indolence; when the spirit of compromise is thus admitted, it leads to reverses that make it impossible for those particular people to carry on the work in that place. The hallowed place overthrows and drives out all who are unworthy of it. Thus stood the ruins of the Temple of Jerusalem, awaiting the advent of more worthy successors than those who had been carried away to Babylonian captivity. Those who had been disobedient to the divine guidance of Moses in the wilderness had to die before the Children of Israel could enter the Promised Land under the guidance of Joshua. On the other hand, besides the worship of Yahweh in Palestine, there were only the lowest cults of indolent spirituality.

So far we have barely touched the whole concept of karma. We cannot begin to deal with reality unless we can conceive of karma as a tissue of numerous cooperating laws in many realms of existence. And the law of the consecrated place belongs to the laws of karma. From the days of Abraham onward, Palestine was under this law. The particular purpose of Abraham's wanderings in Palestine was to sanctify that country because, thousands of years ago, it was chosen as the soil upon which Jesus Christ would walk.

But it was not just through those wanderings that the seed of the future was implanted in Palestine. Abraham also dug wells (Genesis 26:18), built altars (7:7 and 8:18), planted groves and "called there on the name of the Lord, the everlasting God" (21:33). In other words, during his wandering, Abraham established centers for the doctrine and worship of Yahweh. His wanderings, therefore, promoted the spread of a new mystery cult—that of Yahweh—wherever he went. Thus the tribe, of which Abraham was prince, grew. People of various tribes and races gathered around him, but they had one thing in common: an understanding of the new revelation. The teaching of Abraham laid the foundation on which the new race was built. The Yahweh mystery was a magnet that attracted those who were called to form the nucleus of a new people.

Thus, by means of the *Word*, Abraham linked the people in the land of Palestine with the mission of the future. Nevertheless, teaching was not Abraham's only effort to prepare for the future. He also acted in ways that affected the three kingdoms of nature in that land. The altars that he built were intended for the sacrifice of animals, whereas the trees he planted and the wells he dug were actions that affected both the vegetable and the mineral (water) kingdoms. During his wanderings, Abraham worked for the future through four media: speaking, sacrificing, planting, and digging wells; these corresponded to the four kingdoms of the Promised Land: human, animal, plant, and mineral.

These activities of Abraham must not be considered external or ceremonial; he accomplished mystic actions. Their meaning becomes clear when we consider that the spiritual world works in the physical world through karma. Forces of the spiritual world cannot work on the physical plane unless the human will allows them entrance. Human actions, performed in full consciousness, are gateways for the work of the gods on Earth. Thus digging a well at the very place where spiritual *inspiration* had been experienced was a mystic action that allowed the presence of that inspirational force there in the future. We must not think that the conversation between Jesus Christ and the Samaritan Woman occurred by accident at the well Jacob had dug. The woman who was drawing water from the well was able to perceive Christ with her soul, because the conversation took place at this well that, in the distant past, had been dug for reasons connected with the mysteries. Nor will we underestimate the significance of planted trees if we picture Rudolf Steiner's explanation (in *Christ and the Spiritual World*[2]) of how St. Paul could work only in regions where the olive tree grows.

Now, if we study the life history of Abraham we find four very important events: the meeting with Melchizedek, the encounter in the Grove of Mamre, the birth of Isaac, and the sacrifice of Isaac. These are the weightiest events in the life of Abraham, and they have a significance that is more than just personal; they are objectively decisive for the future.

In his lecture course on Matthew's Gospel, Rudolf Steiner told us what is needed concerning the meeting with Melchizedek and the mysterious being who appears in the Bible with this name.[3] But there is one point of view from which we must still consider this encounter: from the perspective of the genesis of Israel's prophetic tradition, which began with Abraham and ended with Malachi. That tradition started when Melchizedek blessed Abraham, transmitting to him the faculty that was later handed down through the whole history of Israel, either by blessing or by anointing. Thus, Isaac blessed Jacob; Moses blessed Joshua; Samuel anointed David and blessed Nathan; and so on. The meeting of Abraham and Melchizedek is thus the prototype of the Israelites' spiritual tradition of prophecy. The Order of Melchizedek was an obligation that every prophet had to fulfill in his successor. The time of the meeting with Melchizedek began the historic practice of this "order"—that is, the history of Israel in the true sense of the word. The history of Israel is the path leading from the prophetic "evening meal" of Melchizedek to the true Last Supper of Jesus Christ. At the beginning of Israel's history, the exalted Sun initiate gave bread and wine; at the end of that history, the Sun being himself gave bread and wine. From the communion of wisdom to the communion of love, this is the history of Israel.

Wherein consisted the gift of prophecy that was transmitted in the way indicated? Through interaction with the spiritual world, perception is distinguished from revelation; likewise, in the physical world one's real experiences are distinguished from a description of them. In the physical world, we can either travel for ourselves, or listen to accounts of the travels of others; likewise, in the spiritual world we may investigate for ourselves, or we may receive revelations from spiritual beings. In the first instance, we depend on our own efforts; in the second, we depend on the favor of spiritual beings. In the case of perception, one investigates; in revelation, the spiritual world speaks.

The faculty of being receptive to revelations was a large part of the gift of prophecy. Prophets, in the real sense of the word, did not research the spiritual world, but spoke for that world. This was why the universal law of reincarnation, for instance, was unknown in the schools of the prophets. It had not been revealed to them; they knew only that *prophets* were born again, but not that reincarnation is a fact that applies to everyone. Nevertheless, not all of the Old Testament individuals whom we call prophets were actually prophets in this sense. Daniel, for example, was not a prophet in the usual sense of the word. He was an initiate and researched the spiritual world on his own. He *read* in the spiritual world and thus resolved his questions. This is why the beings of the spiritual world called him the "man of will." Neither was King David a prophet; he also claimed suprasensory experience through his own efforts. This is also true of Joseph, the son of Jacob, who was born with the karmic faculty of dream interpretation, or the ability to read the records of the spiritual world.

Those who were "blessed" became prophets by that means. This blessing must not be thought of as a mere expression of good will, but as an influence that set in motion a certain organ, or "lotus flower," of the ether body. The spiritual world was thus able to speak through that organ. A certain organ in Abraham's ether body (which also has a physical expression) was set in motion by the blessing of Melchizedek. Thus Abraham became the first prophet of Israel and founded the prophet tradition.

Based on these facts, however, we must not jump to the conclusion that prophets were less important than spiritual investigators; this is not, in fact, the case. The revelations given to humankind through the prophets were, in many cases, more important to humanity than were the results of individual initiates' investigations. Furthermore, initiates sometimes gave up their own researches in order to impart higher revelations to humankind. They renounced their own learning, so that the spiritual world might speak through them. It is because of such a renunciation that humankind was given revelations through Isaiah. With Isaiah we are dealing with one of the highest initiates of the ancient mysteries who appeared as a prophet in Israel. Rudolf Steiner informed us of the important fact that several initiates of the mysteries appeared as prophets in Israel, and Isaiah belonged to that number.

On the other hand, we must not conclude that individual learning and revelation are mutually exclusive in an individual lifespan. In fact, it has happened that, in a single life, periods of revelation have alternated with periods of knowledge gained through research. A discussion of such complicated relationships to the spiritual world would lead us too far from our immediate purpose, but it can be said, in general, that prophets, in the sense indicated, were primarily dispensers of revelation.

Thus the line of revelation in Israel's history began with the meeting between Abraham and Melchizedek. It was an independent line of interaction with the spiritual world, clearly distinguished from that of the old mysteries. In the mysteries of Egypt, for example, the goal was to free an individual from the physical body during the three-day temple sleep; in Israel, however, the goal was for spiritual beings to descend into the physical body. During the temple sleep of the mysteries, the astral body stamped its suprasensory impression into the ether body while it was free of the physical body; in the Israelites' spiritual cult, on the other hand, impressions were transmitted through the ether body to the I, within the physical body. This led to the Israelite tradition in which Melchizedek (who bore in himself the ether body of Shem) gave bread and wine to Abraham and blessed him. In other words, he exerted a strong influence on Abraham's ether body. This is why Moses assumed the ether body of the great Zoroaster; it was done so that new and powerful revelations would flow into the spiritual life of Israel. The perception made possible through the astral body was called "air" or "spirit," and initiation into the mysteries was seen as being born again of the spirit or air. But the perception made possible in Israel through the ether body was called "perception by water," and the new consciousness awakened in this way was meant to be born of water.

Now, however, the line of the old mystery initiation—which took place in the dark night of the temple—reached its consummation in clear daylight with the resurrection of Lazarus brought about by Christ, who thus appeared as the highest initiate of the cult of air perception. Similarly, it was Christ who brought to its consummation the line of water perception by initiating Nicodemus while freed from his physical body in the dead of night. Then the words ring forth concerning the need for *both* impulses; we must be born again of water *and* of air. And just as Christ brought mystery initiation out of the darkness of the night into daylight, he also led the Israelite initiation out of daylight into night consciousness. Abraham and Nicodemus are the names that mark the limits of Israelite initiation. But Nicodemus is also an initiate of the new night initiation that grew out of the old day initiation, just as the Lazarus-John event was also an initiation of the new day initiation that grew out of the old night initiation.

The method called the "order of Melchizedek" thus found its culmination in the suprasensory episode of Christ's conversation with Nicodemus. In that conversation it reached its goal—it led to Christ. But the abstract term *method* really means "destiny"—Israel's destiny begun by Abraham. Now if the line of Israel's revelation led to Christ, its essence was the *promise of the Son's birth.* And the promise of a son's birth was what Abraham experienced, in his old age, as the second great event of his life at the meeting in the grove of Mamre. The significance of that meeting was shown in our first study, which considered the ongoing collaboration of three initiates. Here it is necessary to mention only the fact that Abraham and Sara received the promise of a son.

It is difficult to discuss these things in sharply defined concepts. Yet it is certainly the author's intention to speak in that way, because this is the mission of our age. But there are circumstances in which it is difficult to avoid the appearance of speaking vaguely. This is not the result of vague thinking, however, but an imperfection of the instrument that expresses it. In this case, the point is to clearly and truthfully say that the son promised to Abraham also included the promised birth of the eternal Son. The son of Abraham indicated (to him personally and objectively to humanity) not only an event in his personal life, but also a revelation by means of an actual event. The birth of Isaac was itself a revelation, awaking in Abraham's soul an understanding of the mystery of the relationship between the eternal Father and the eternal Son. How was this possible?

The descent of the soul to earthly birth takes place in stages. Ordinary, secular consciousness is, in fact, related only to the last stage of that descent. It is not implanted into the physical plane until just before the actual birth. But this is only the lowest link in the chain that is the birth process. Before the soul reaches the region of actuality, it descends through the regions of *imagination, inspiration,* and *intuition.*[4] In the past, this descent was not always hidden from the parents' consciousness, and it will not always remain so in the future. In the past, the birth process could be experienced consciously even before it reached the physical world. The descending being was *recognized* in the suprasensory world. Thus it became possible to give the new earthly being a true name. The name expressed the knowledge revealed in the suprasensory world through that descending being. In the future, this faculty will reappear—especially in the East. Eugenic occultism will be so widespread that there will be a continual increase of human beings who are aware not only of the lowest levels, but also of the suprasensory stages in the process of birth. Not only will it be known that someone is being born but also the purpose of that birth. The mission, or "inner word," of the descending soul will be perceived. And, again, names will be sought that correspond with each word. It will be recognition of karma.

But karma has two sides. It is, on the one hand, an expiation of past guilt; this is the earthly karma that began with the "fall" of humanity. But there is also a heavenly form of karma, or eternal karma, that represents the primal thought of every human soul. Every soul is a thought of the Father, shining through all incarnations as an ever-radiant star. The meaning of existence—earthly karma—is contained in the very fact that temporal, terrestrial karma is united with eternal, celestial karma.

If the birth of a soul on Earth is awaited consciously, it can show itself in its eternal thought through *intuition* and *inspiration* before it is revealed as character, temperament, and physical form. Thus through the I, or ego, of Isaac, Abraham discerned the Father's thought of the Son. Abraham was able to recognize in the birth of Isaac the mystery of the eternal Son's earthly birth and sacrifice. Isaac's star revealed to him the mystery of the Son's sacrifice, and this revelation became the essence of Israel's whole history.

The analogy between death and initiation is often cited. Indeed, it is easy to see that the spheres through which human beings travel after death are the same as those of initiation. But it is seldom understood that birth can be a process of initiation. Nevertheless it is true; just as the stages of the ascent of the human path to knowledge correspond to the stages of the ascent after death, the stages of descent in the revelation of the spiritual world correspond to the stages of the descent to birth. Now the main point in the tradition of the prophets was revelation, and that was experienced not in death, but in *birth.* Death had no great significance for the spiritual life of Israel; through the gate of birth alone shone the light of the spiritual world. Therefore, we will not find in the Bible the wisdom that shines through the gate of death; but of all human documents, only the Bible allows the revelation of the spiritual world to shine through the gate of birth with such pure light. Thus the mystery of the Son was revealed to Abraham through the birth of Isaac. To him it meant an initiation process that turned the whole stream of history for Israel.

Even more important for prophecy was Abraham's experience of preparing his son for sacrifice upon an altar. It presents a comprehensive picture of Israel's prophetic thinking. Superficially, it seems to be a historical image of this thought. Generations to come were able to see that image of the father sacrificing his son, and thus they prepared their souls to grasp the Mystery of Golgotha. To understand this event—not only in its prophetic significance, but also as a human action—we must once again consider the divine Trinity, especially in relation to human freedom. Strictly speaking, occultism views the Trinity not as a "concept" or principle but as the collaboration of three cosmic spheres. The sphere of the Father functions above, where the genesis of primal thought takes place. The sphere of the Son functions in the middle, where life is breathed into the thought descending from the Father sphere; this is the sphere of primal life. Below the Son sphere is the sphere of the Holy Spirit, into which the Father thoughts—endowed with life in the sphere of the Son—have descended; there they receive form and become primal images, or archetypes. Thus we may speak of the spheres of primal thought, primal life, and primal images, or archetypes.

The process of conscious human perception, however, is the opposite of the divine process of creation. Thus it is the power of thinking that enables human beings to perceive the sphere of the Spirit, while feeling can rise to the sphere of the Son, and, through *intuition,* only volition is able to penetrate to the sphere of the Father. To the inner eye, the sphere of the Holy Spirit appears as a circle, shining iridescent in all the colors of the rainbow; the rainbow is, in fact, the image of the Spirit sphere and renders it perceptible to the senses. The sphere of the Son should be pictured instead as a cloud-forming process in blue and white. This sphere contains no finished forms, however, but is a cloud realm that rings with sound.

Through their powers of perception, the ancient Indians reached the Son sphere, the sphere of formlessness, or the sphere of form death. But they could not rise to the sphere of the Father, or sphere of resurrection. This was possible in Christendom only after Christ went to the Father through death, so that "where I am, there ye may be also" (John 14:3).

Human consciousness bears a different relationship to each of these three spheres. For instance, in the third post-Atlantean epoch, freedom was possible only in the sphere of the Holy Spirit. Only in thought could human beings be free. The spheres of the Son and the Father were, however, unavailable to human freedom. It was not until New Testament times—after the Mystery of Golgotha and Christ became the Lord of karma—that the sphere of the Son was also opened to human freedom. In the future, the sphere of the Father will also be open; but in Old Testament times human freedom was possible only in the sphere of the Holy Spirit.

Abraham, however, rose to *intuition* of the Father sphere. This momentous event occurred when he went with Isaac to the mountain to sacrifice his son there. Abraham was in a state of consciousness in which his whole being was dominated by *intuition* of will. Consciously, he acted from within the Father sphere. When he lifted his hand to sacrifice Isaac, it was not he who raised the hand, but the Father, the eternal First Cause of the universe. No freedom or choice existed in the sphere of the Father. And just as Abraham—representing eternal Fatherhood—lifted his hand for the sacrifice, Isaac at that moment represented the eternal Son, for he did not refuse to be sacrificed; he was filled with the *inspiration* of the Son. His consciousness was in the Son sphere, where, likewise, there was then no freedom.

So we can say that Abraham's sacrifice of Isaac was not merely a symbol; it was actually the thought of the Father within the will of Abraham. And the sacrifice of the eternal Son, who offers his life to eternity, was present in the feeling of Isaac. Thus at that moment, the Father and the Son were indeed present on the physical plane as a true prophesy of sacrificial death and resurrection. The processes of willing and feeling do not forecast only sacrificial death, but also resurrection. Because the sacrifice was not accepted, Abraham experienced within himself the resurrection of his son. In his will, Abraham had already sacrificed Isaac; he experienced the miracle of resurrection when Isaac was instead restored to him alive. The sacrifice of Isaac is the main prophetic event in the life of Abraham. In it, the "Father thought" of Abraham and the "Son sacrifice" of Isaac became visible to the senses. Thus was the prophetic mission of Abraham fulfilled.

Now if we study the life of Isaac, we find that he was striving for one particular thing—to restore the work of his father where it had fallen into ruin. Thus Isaac also wandered, reopening the wells that Abraham had dug but had since filled with earth. Isaac restored them and replenished them with water. This picture gives us a deeper understanding of his character. Just as the divine Son breathes life into the thoughts of the divine Father, Isaac brought new life to the wells of Abraham.

> And Isaac digged again the wells of water, which they had digged in the days of Abraham his father; for the Philistines had stopped them after the death of Abraham: and he called their names after the names by which his father had called them. And Isaac's servants digged in the valley, and found there a well of springing water. (Genesis 26:18–19)

This "well of springing water" is a picture of Isaac's life work; it speaks clearly and profoundly. Isaac's mission in life was to *live* what Abraham had learned. His calling was to absorb into the life body all that Abraham had borne in his astral body. The life body bears *memory,* and Isaac created living tradition, the "springing water" that would quench the thirst of generations. Isaac also revived the old names of his father's wells he restored, thus *remembering* the past. But this was not his only mission. He found the well of springing water in the present, for this true tradition reveals not only a restoration of the past, but also penetration into the present to discover "wells of springing water." The spiritual life of Israel involved more than recording the sacrifice made by Abraham and transmitting it from generation to generation; it also included the appearance of many prophets who found the "springing waters" of inspiration, each in his own time. Truth is seen as a river whose spring must forever yield new water; otherwise the waters stagnate and die. This is what had happened to the Israelites' stream of spiritual life, represented by the Scribes and Pharisees. They were exactly the ones who substituted dead tradition for living, flowing water. By freezing the rivers of truth in Time, and by limiting moral imagination to the confines of outer manifestations of righteousness, they fulfilled their karmic calling of erecting, in the spiritual life of Israel, the cross on which Christ was crucified. The wooden cross of Golgotha was merely the outer expression of the spiritual fact that Israel had long ago prepared—in the form of rigidified knowledge and morality—a cross for the Messiah.

In comparing the lives of Abraham and of Isaac, we find a characteristic common to both—they were both highly obedient to the spiritual world. They were not apostles of freedom but established obedience in the world. We can understand this by keeping in mind the fact that, in the sense of the foregoing exposition, they were representatives of the Father and the Son. As such, they could not be free during the third post-Atlantean epoch. For Jacob, it was different. In contrast to Abraham and Isaac, Jacob brought the impulse of freedom into Israel's history. He represented the Holy Spirit, whose sphere was the only one in which freedom was possible. The concrete relationship between Abraham and the spiritual world was the opposite of Jacob's relationship. In Abraham, it was the will—an impulse from the Father sphere—from which the stream of revelation flowed into the current of his thinking. From willing into thinking—this was the path revelation took for Abraham. With Jacob, on the other hand, thinking came down into willing. But because freedom in thinking was possible (we will discuss the reasons in detail later), awakened by thinking, Jacob's will was free.

Abraham's path led from the Spirit to the Father. He fulfilled his calling when he surrendered fully to the Father. This was the highest point of his life work. Jacob's path, however, led from the Father to the Spirit. He reached the highest moment of his career when he attained the highest degree of freedom. After the night of wrestling with a Messenger of God, he triumphantly turned the stream of his life in a new direction. Freedom of spirit was the new direction that Jacob gave to the history of Israel.

We can understand this because Jacob had absorbed much of the luciferic impulse. He had not fallen victim to it, but absorbed and transformed it. Jacob's spiritual conflict with the Messenger of God was mainly an opposition, or rebellion. But how did this conflict end? "I will not let thee go, except thou bless me" (Genesis 32:26). These are the last words of the struggle. And the Messenger of God blessed Jacob; he expressed his recognition that the luciferic impulse in Jacob had been transformed. The conflict between the divine hierarchies and the luciferic impulse does not involve overcoming the latter by force; it leads to inner transformation. The beings of the divine hierarchies accomplish sacrifices that compel Lucifer's wondering love. Through the example of sacrifice, the luciferic impulse is overcome; through the love that compels him to sacrifice, he is transformed inwardly.

The words "I will not let thee go, except thou bless me" show that the luciferic impulse has been transformed. The essence of luciferic transformation is the love of the Spirit that will not surrender until the Spirit accepts it. After that fateful night of spiritual conflict at Ford Jabbok, Jacob followed the Spirit in freedom, compelled neither by inner nor by outer necessity. From that time forward, he followed the Holy Spirit out of love. This is why he was called Israel, and his name became the name and characterization of the race into which Jesus would be born. Free love of the Spirit was the goal of this people's history and the eventual fruit of the tree of law. It was this free love of the Spirit that rendered souls susceptible to the actual presence of Christ on Earth. It was the freedom of Jacob-Israel that caused fishermen on the Sea of Galilee to leave their nets and their boats to follow him, whom they recognized neither from the Scriptures nor from the prophets' predictions, but from within their loving hearts (Matthew 4:18). Nor did they ask whence he came or the name of his father and mother; these fishers of Galilee were children of Israel and chose his path out of love.

In Israel-Jacob lived the union of the "Father thought" of Abraham and the "Son sacrifice" of Isaac as freedom in the Spirit. In it, the purpose and life of Israel received the power given only through freedom. It is not effort that invokes true power in the spiritual world, but the will working in freedom.

We must not think, however, that this characteristic in Jacob contradicts what was said at the beginning of the second chapter of this study. We should instead think of

Jacob as the son of Isaac—that his freedom was the daughter of obedience to the divine love that descended upon Isaac from on high. Only because he was the son of Isaac, Jacob could enkindle that personal love of the Spirit we have been discussing. If Isaac and Abraham had not preceded Jacob, his freedom would have been mere rebellion. Had Jacob been the son of Abraham and not the son of Isaac, he would have been a fanatic about the law. Only as the third could he become what he was. Abraham's thought and Isaac's love became the quality of free personality in Jacob. As the first, Jacob would have been an incarnation of uncontrolled self-will; as the second, he would have been fanatical about the law; as the third, he came to bear spiritual power—freedom in the Holy Spirit.

Thus Israel-Jacob stands at the beginning of the history of Israel as one who, not without reason, gave his name to the people whose history is recorded in the Old Testament. Consequently, the next study will deal with the record of Israel-Jacob.

# Chapter 4

# The Spiritual Triumph of Jacob

## The Origin of Falsehood in Humanity and in the cosmos

The main characteristic that strikes us when studying the life of Jacob is that, with his very first breath, he is engaged immediately in a struggle. Even at birth, he had to fight for the rank of firstborn; he had to fight for his inner birthright against his brother's outer right. And again he had to fight for Rachel, whom he loved; he had to endure twenty years of hard labor with Laban before he could return to his homeland, at whose gates he experienced the greatest fight of all—his fight with the Messenger of God. We can rightly say that Jacob was able to attain to his true destiny only through conflict; he received nothing gratis, but had to achieve everything by overcoming hindrances. Jacob's true destiny was girded, as it were, by false circumstances and facts; to reach the truth, he always had to cut through a layer of lie. This was true of his position in his own home, where—by right of the "blessing" and his father's spiritual bequest—he was really the firstborn; but external conditions contradicted spiritual reality. Likewise, he encountered falsehood when he was wooing Rachel; through deception, Leah was brought into his tent (Genesis 29). Thus he had to wait long for his true wife to bear sons, with whom he felt himself in real sympathy. Joseph and Benjamin were his last sons and the only ones he loved. But even here, a dividing wall of lies stood between him and his beloved children. Joseph was sold into Egypt, but for many years his father lived in the belief that a wild beast had torn him to pieces. Eventually he had to surrender Benjamin as well, because he believed the lie that Benjamin was the price required by a powerful, unknown Egyptian for the deliverance of the whole tribe.

These facts clearly show Jacob's whole path of destiny and how it always led him to decisions related to his attitude toward lies. Every opening on the path to his true destination was blocked by falsehood; as he traveled toward his goal, a layer of lies overshadowed every event in his life. Some of the most staggering stories of the Bible involved Jacob's life. His story reveals powerful twists and turns—not just in terms of human tragedy, but also for cosmic karma. These statements of fact lead us naturally to ask: *Why* was Jacob's destiny like this? And what was the karma that formed the basis of his destiny?

The last study indicated the luciferic nature of Jacob's soul life. He possessed a great deal of *personality,* and in the days before the Mystery of Golgotha, a strong consciousness of personality was possible only in souls deeply imbued with a luciferic impulse, which leads the astral body to a certain independence in relation to the surrounding spiritual world. This occurs because strong feelings of sympathy and antipathy flow from such an astral body, enveloping it with a kind of mist like a cloudy wreath. A surrounding cloud is formed about the astral body, separating it from and making it independent of the surrounding spiritual world. These sympathies and antipathies do not arise from association with the guardian angel, but from association with the luciferic angel. The inspiration of the luciferic angel does not enter through the door of the human I but flows directly into the astral body—that is, he works down to a greater depth than the normal angel. And so the current of his inspiration flows directly from the astral body into the ether body without deflection at the boundary between the two. Here, however, it is changed to its opposite, for here the law of reflection holds true in the interrelationships among the various members of the human being. If, for example, an upward-pointing triangle lives in the consciousness of the astral body, so long as it is not properly brought down by the I itself, it will be reflected in the ether body as a triangle pointing downward.

So it happens that the luciferic angel leads to lying. He makes the astral body independent of the spiritual world around it in order to keep it entirely under his own influence. Then, through his inspiration, which penetrates as far as the ether body, he causes lies. Consequently, a garment of false images surrounds the ether body. An encompassing sphere is formed that mirrors what the luciferic angel has poured into the astral body. The luciferic angel does not inspire deception; his inspiration is perfectly valid within the astral world. But the way he does it leads to falseness in the etheric body, materializing as the garment encircling the etheric body. The garment is not transparent but casts a shadow into the etheric body, causing darkness in certain parts of it. This darkness is the very space upon which Ahriman is able to seize. The ahrimanic double takes up his abode in the parts of the etheric body darkened by the presence of the luciferic angel. Thus Ahriman makes his appearance as the karma of Lucifer.

The ahrimanic double is a being endowed, very often, with subtle intelligence, fastening upon the darkened portion of the etheric body, and from there working outward into human consciousness. But we must not imagine that the darkness issuing from the ahrimanic double is merely an absence of light. Rather, it is an opposing light—even an intelligence—against the intelligence of the hierarchies, to which purely human intelligence also belongs as the fourth hierarchy. When the luciferic angel conceals the light of the hierarchies, the "active"darkness of the ahrimanic double streams forth. This darkness quenches the consciousness of the spiritual in objective reality and pours lies into the surrounding physical, objective world. So it happens that the subjective falsehood caused by the luciferic angel is changed by the ahrimanic double into objective lies.

This is the process by which lying originated in human history. The cosmic process is similar. First we must conceive of the world of the hierarchies as light flowing from the Godhead. Now what happens within that light world is that—insofar as human guidance from the gods is concerned—Lucifer opposes them. He wishes to guide humankind in a different way from that of the gods (see second study). This is the reason why Lucifer becomes a hindrance to the light of the gods. He casts a shadow from the spiritual world onto the world below. That shadow gives Ahriman a cosmic point of attack to intervene in evolutionary progress. If it were not for Lucifer's shadow, Ahriman would have been unable to interfere in evolution; he would have always been eclipsed and dazzled by the light of the hierarchies. Neither could he have worked, since there would have been no field for his activities, nor could he have watched, because the light of the hierarchies is impenetrable to the gaze of Ahriman. But wherever Lucifer clears a space of light, Ahriman can gain a foothold on which to flourish.

How should we imagine the shadow that Lucifer causes in the cosmos? The Sun shines not only at midday, but also at midnight. Its daylight is physical, but its light at night is spiritual. It was Lucifer who brought the spiritual light of the Sun to a lower level, causing a part of it to become physical. This physical light of the Sun is the shadow cast by the Sun in the spiritual world. The visible light of the Sun is the luciferic shadow in the cosmos. The fact that Lucifer extended his influence to a lower level, however, had important consequences for the etheric organism of the Earth. Because of the law of reflection already mentioned, an etheric sphere grew to become a garment surrounding the Earth. There, lies that reflect the truth of the spiritual world surround the etheric body of the Earth. The luciferic sphere encircles the Earth, and it is this that casts the shadow of the Sun's spiritual light into earthly life.[1]

The shadow cast by Lucifer enables Ahriman, as we have said, to intervene not just in cosmic but also in terrestrial happenings. Just as an individual human being may have an ahrimanic double, as a living being the Earth has one as well. The Earth's ahrimanic double is the Eighth Sphere, which Yahweh keeps away from the Earth. Within Lucifer's shadow arose the Eighth Sphere of the cosmos, the ahrimanic double of the Earth. In the second study, we spoke of the substance and chief characteristics of the Eighth Sphere in relation to the mission of Yahweh Elohim. But how are we to imagine the luciferic sphere?

## The Luciferic Sphere

To understand a "sphere" of the cosmos means to be able to answer this question: What moral and spiritual purposes are at the root of that sphere? A superficial description of any spiritual reality is useless unless it is based on a specific truth. Concrete facts are important only insofar as they contribute to an understanding of truths; initiation does not mean multiplication of incomprehensible facts, but insight into the mystery they reveal. Perceptual penetration is not merely a review of a factual panorama, but the goal of initiation. The path of initiation leads to union with cosmic intelligence—that is, to understanding of the *purposes* of the spiritual hierarchies. True, those purposes become intelligible only with the help of symptomatic facts in nature, regardless of whether they are perceptible to the senses; but then, facts have a clear symptomatic significance as a medium for the expression of definite moral and spiritual truths.

Consider, for instance, the description of suprasensory worlds offered by C. W. Leadbeater in such works as *The Astral Plane* and *The Mental Plane* and compare those with the picture given by Rudolf Steiner. Leadbeater describes suprasensory worlds in such a way that the memory of the reader is enriched by a number of facts without intellectual effort. In Rudolf Steiner's picture, on the other hand, the reader can perceive the moral and spiritual meaning of the suprasensory worlds—that is, one knows that the *intellect* is enriched. The principle of Rosicrucian initiation (Rosicrucian in doctrine, not in the traditional sense) is based on *understanding* the great mysteries of existence. This certainly does not cover the whole ground, for the great initiates are not those who have only knowledge but also love and sacrifice. Nevertheless, the foundation is laid in the Michaelic principle of broadening the intellect. Thus, when we investigate the moral, spiritual purpose underlying the luciferic sphere, it is not an intellectual speculation but a loyal adherence to the aforesaid principle of our spiritual movement.

Two important volitional tendencies may be observed in human civilization. One is expressed in the search for ways and means to eliminate *death* from human destiny. The American Mulford, for instance, has written a booklet entitled "The Crime of Dying."[2] In it, he expresses his conviction that, if the will of humanity were to change directions, death might be banished altogether from the world. The indecency of being separated from the body would thus no longer exist; human beings could live an *eternal* bodily life. Immortality in the body is the aim of one volitional tendency. The other looks for eternal blessedness in an existence freed from the body. In the East (and also in ecclesiastical Christendom) there are many who look yearningly toward heaven, fervently fulfilling the injunctions of their religious creed in the hope of entering eternal bliss. Deliverance from this earthly vale of tears—the prospect of never again being born—constitutes the deep desire of those individuals.

If the first volitional tendency were to be completely developed, humanity—at the end of its earthly evolution—would enter the Eighth Sphere. The Eighth Sphere is precisely the part of the cosmos that is beyond the sway of human karma, including death and birth. There, the soul no longer needs to leave the body, since it no longer draws its powers from the realm of the hierarchies; rather, it draws them from Ahriman, whose tool it would have become. If, on the other hand, the other will tendency were to reach complete maturity, humankind would enter the luciferic sphere as early as the sixth epoch of civilization. The luciferic sphere is the "paradise" of all who despise life and of all who have lost their way in life. It is the sphere of "satisfaction" that makes a descent to rebirth unnecessary on Earth.

The luciferic sphere is the false Devachan in the cosmos, while the Eighth Sphere can be regarded as a countersphere to Kama Loka. The endeavor to avoid death is actually a flight from the judgment of the kama loka state, the desire to avoid encountering the cosmic conscience. The Eighth Sphere is precisely the place to which the cosmic conscience has no access. The luciferic sphere, by contrast, is devachanic (at least for a certain period of cosmic evolution), out of which nothing can be obtained for the further evolution of the Earth and the preparation of future incarnations, but in which the bliss of emancipation can be enjoyed. In fact, it is the moral reverse of the true Devachan. For whereas a being of the true Devachan turns toward humankind, the gaze of the being of the luciferic sphere is turned away from humankind. Within the true Devachan, a tremendous work is performed for the good of human evolution; its bliss is the bliss of active service. In the luciferic sphere it is, instead, the bliss of resting in contentment; its bliss is that of a dream.

*Flight* from the cosmic conscience is the conscious effort of the Eighth Sphere: to lose sight of the cosmic conscience in *dreaming* is the way to the luciferic sphere. Seen from the perspective of cosmic reality, the luciferic sphere is that of objective cosmic fantasy—the kingdom of lies (for mere fantasy is a lie) in the universe. Specter and falsehood; these constitute the character of the Eighth Sphere and the luciferic sphere. Now every lie in process of time becomes a specter. Ahriman pursues his activities in the shadow of Lucifer. Therefore, it is the final destiny of the luciferic sphere (unless the hierarchies capture it) to become the prey of Ahriman. Thus it will be in the macrocosm; thus it is in the microcosm, in humanity. One of the most astounding processes we can observe in life is the "ahrimanizing" of those who, over a long period of time, have been in thrall to their luciferic tendencies. The luciferic soul life becomes mysteriously transformed to an inner technique that serves ends having nothing in common with the original intentions of that individual.

The luciferic sphere shares a boundary with the sphere of the Holy Spirit, representing, as it does, its reflection. To reach the sphere of the Holy Spirit, consciousness must first pass through the luciferic sphere that covers it. To arrive at truth, it must first conquer the surrounding lies. The conquest requires that the astral power of the conscience recognizes the fact that the luciferic sphere is a mere reflection and thus advances to the truth reflected by it. The interpretation of the luciferic sphere by the power of the conscience signifies the opening of a window onto the sphere of the Holy Spirit. Thus, for instance, human beings are faced with the choice of rising to greater heights or sinking down to Earth. If we choose to rise to "the regions of the eternal spirit," we enter the luciferic sphere. In reality, however, we do not rise to these heights, but move in a circle around the Earth. Rising, in that case, is merely an illusion. But if we choose a self-sacrificing descent, casting a solicitous glance on the Earth of our fellow human beings, by that very gesture we ascend to the sphere of the Holy Spirit, where spiritual rising bears a resemblance to descent.

Now the luciferic sphere is not merely a ring moving round the Earth; it is also the sum of the forces that influence earthly events. Wherever falsehood occurs in human destiny, those forces exert their influence. The possibility of taking a wrong path of destiny enters the karma that indicates true human progress. This is the karma of the luciferic intervention, and the stronger the influence of that intervention in a former life, the more densely the garment of falsehood encircles all that is true in the destiny of the individual concerned. And the very reason why humankind is educated to freedom is that we may make the choice between the sphere of Lucifer (influencing our destiny) and the sphere of the Holy Spirit. In his life, Jacob was faced, to a marked degree, with this choice. This is why he was picked to represent the impulse of freedom in Israelite history.

Note: Just as the Eighth Sphere acts indirectly by means of certain spheres in the interior of the Earth, so the luciferic sphere does not directly affect human destiny, but also acts indirectly through the medium of certain subterranean spheres.

## Jacob's Threefold Spiritual Victory

In the sense implied by these meditations, the realm of falsehood is not just within humankind but also a karmic current, a tributary to the cosmic as well as to the human life stream. And it was necessary that Jacob should be born within this current. Even within their mother's womb, the twins, Jacob and Esau, wrestled for the birthright, but falsehood won the victory; Esau was born first. It is clear, however, that his birthright bore no relation to inner truth, both because Esau sold his right as firstborn for a mess of pottage, and because it was really Jacob who later carried on the tradition of Israel. The whole course of Israel's history is a proof that Jacob was the true firstborn.

Jacob knew this; his mother also knew it. Israel, however, went blind and could not see the true state of affairs. (Isaac's gradual blindness indicated a definite law of Israelite revelation—that the revelation ceased, as a rule, after a certain age.) Thus Jacob had to wrestle for his true position in his parental home. He succeeded in this struggle, but to escape his brother's vengeance he had to leave his home and journey to Mesopotamia. This was the first conquest in Jacob's life: the victorious issue of the conflict between inner conviction and the maya of outer circumstance. The thought that gleamed within him proved more powerful than the actualities surrounding him. Now, however, this victory had definite spiritual results. Because Jacob was not misled in the first stratum of his destiny of falsehood, he was granted his first insight into the sphere of truth—the sphere of the Holy Spirit. As he penetrated through a part of the luciferic sphere, the view into the corresponding part of the sphere of the Holy Spirit was revealed to him.

Now the sphere of the Holy Spirit is the sphere of the activities of the third hierarchy.[3] Angels, archangels, and principalities radiate their influence from this sphere as representatives of Spirit, Son, and Father within the sphere of the Holy Spirit. Because Jacob maintained the thought of his destiny against the external facts that opposed him, therefore the sphere of the angels was revealed to him as the lowest part of the Spirit's sphere. This happened at Bethel, when he fell asleep on his flight to Mesopotamia, and experienced the revelation of the angelic hierarchy described in the Bible as Jacob's Dream.

> And he dreamed, and behold a ladder set up on the earth, and the top of it reached to heaven: and behold the angels of God ascending and descending on it. And, behold, the Lord stood above it, and said, I am the Lord God of Abraham thy father, and the God of Isaac: the land whereon thou liest, to thee will I give it, and to thy seed;... and in thee and in thy seed shall all the families of the earth be blessed. (Genesis 28:12–14)

As Jacob had conquered the falsehood connected with his birth, the mission to which his birth called him was revealed to him through the realm of the angels—that is, his conscious perception of the angels came to him from the perspective of eugenic occultism. The first stage of eugenic occultism is attained when one enters conscious interaction with the beings of the angelic hierarchy. Eugenic occultism does not involve knowledge of universal laws, but entering conscious interaction with the beings who know the mysteries of birth. The true horoscope will not be reached by a path of calculation but through a path of interaction with suprasensory beings. What angels have imparted to humankind, that is the "horoscope" in the true sense. Apart from a karmically necessary interruption in the thirteenth and fourteenth centuries, this connection was maintained continuously, and consequently there is an unbroken "tradition" of eugenic occultism in the West, a tradition that made progress in proportion to its knowledge. It would, however, be incorrect to conclude that this tradition was cherished only within a dark and gloomy occultism. We must do justice to the *good* wrought by its influence in the present history of humankind, especially since Rudolf Steiner has imparted to us so much of the spiritual stream of Rosicrucianism, which with every century has a further step in the progress of knowledge to record.[4]

The knowledge granted to Jacob in night consciousness represented the stage of eugenic occultism corresponding to knowledge of the angelic hierarchy. By its means, the fundamental characteristic of the angels was revealed to him; it is this: the line of movement of the angels is vertical. Angels are constantly moving either up or down. Their mission is to unite the spiritual world with the human I-being dwelling here on Earth. An angel soars upward to obtain a broad insight into the spiritual world, then sinks down to guide earthly events through the medium of the human I in the spirit of that insight. Verticality is the law that governs the activity of the angelic hierarchy.

We understand angelic activity when we imagine a line that binds the human heart to the star shining above one's head. This line corresponds to the movement of the angel whose charge it is to maintain a link between the higher and the lower. With a sympathetic understanding of this line, we can understand the tragic position of the angelic hierarchy. With the growth of materialism, the two ends of this line are increasingly contrasted; it is increasingly difficult for angelic beings to unify the two poles of their realm. The lower pole constantly threatens to develop in a way that has nothing in common with the higher. The disruption of two irreconcilable realms of being constitutes the deep suffering of the angels and their bitter pain. If help had not come, that pain and suffering of the angels would have led inevitably either to a denial of the higher world (blotting out the angels) or to a repudiation of the lower world (forsaking humankind). Help arrived, however, through the sacrifice of an archangelic being who, filled through and through by Christ nature, descended into the angelic hierarchy. When the being of Jesus (the Nathan Jesus) descended into the angelic hierarchy without forfeiting his archangelic nature—which he was enabled to do through the Christ impulse with which he was filled—a new possibility arose in the realm of angels. This possibility was brought about by the raising of the cross within the angelic sphere. To the vertical line of conflicting higher and lower was added the horizontal line of "I and Thou." The great fact of the cross in the crucifixion was the possibility of redeeming the angelic hierarchy—the fact established by the Nathan Jesus for the angelic hierarchy. Through the redeeming, sacrificial act of the Nathan Jesus, the Christ impulse was revealed to the angels.

This sacrifice—raising the cross in the realm of the angels—may be understood if we study the fundamental principle of the archangels, the archangelic hierarchy. In contrast to the angels, whose primary movement is vertical, archangels move horizontally. Archangels are not beings who unite the physical world with the spiritual, moving upward and downward between the two; they move through space in such a way that human beings are united in spatial groups (or races). And the archangels, reaching hands to one another, form a chain around the Earth, through which the full inspiration of Christ's revelation to humankind may circulate. The consonance of all folk spirits is the only complete revelation of the Christ impulse. Thus the Christ inspiration flows from East to West around the whole Earth, bringing about consciousness of universal brotherhood. The divisions, or barriers such as languages and political frontiers erected between nations, do not originate with the true folk spirits but with luciferic archangels.

Now let us suppose that this horizontal line of brotherliness—the fundamental characteristic of the archangelic hierarchy—is introduced by an archangel into the angelic hierarchy, whose fundamental characteristic is the vertical line. Then, within the angelic hierarchy, two simultaneous movements spring up: one, the union of two surfaces, and the other, the union of being on *one* surface by love. Thus arises the cross—that is, the revelation of the Christ impulse within the angelic hierarchy as the result of the sacrifice of the Nathan Jesus.

Now we return to Jacob's "dream" and see that his dream reveals not only the basic principle of the angelic hierarchy moving in tragic tension upward and downward between the two worlds, but also the fact of the redemption of angels through the Christ impulse. For it is *from* the angels' ladder that the Lord speaks to Jacob. In other words, the angels descend to the lower end of the ladder and ascend again to the upper end; but the being whose visage was Yahweh Elohim is neither above nor below but in between, where the two lines, the horizontal and the vertical, cross. And what does this being reveal? He reveals the fact of the future redemption of the whole human race through the events that were to take place in the race of Jacob—events that would free humankind from the discord of irreconcilable opposition of body and spirit, as humanity freed the angels. The cross was given to human beings just as it was given to the angels; that is the great revelation that Jacob received. Moreover, he became aware that an exalted spirit being must descend so that the cross could be given to humankind on Earth. But a long preparation was needed over generations to prepare a suitable body.

After this tremendous revelation, Jacob's life path led through the *second* stratum of falsehood, which he had to overcome in the household of Laban. Jacob's task was to find and fulfill his true destiny, not just as a single individual but also as a member of human society. To become settled in proper domestic conditions as a member of a proper nationality, to establish a home at a specific place on the Earth—this was Jacob's mission. Now, however, he had to overcome enormous obstacles that blocked his way at every step. Not only was Leah set between him and Rachel through deception, but Laban also wanted to bind him to the place, using various means to prevent his return to Canaan. Jacob and his family were supposed to become members of a different race in a different land from that of his destiny. He was to be kept at a distance from the Promised Land, in this way striking into a different path from the one it was his vocation to follow. When Jacob forcibly tore himself away from those false ties and connected with his family, he overcame the *second* layer of lies in his destiny. His feeling recognized the true link as opposed to the false, proving stronger than the fetters forged by Laban or the fear of his brother's wrath awaiting him in his homeland. This victory had its first results immediately. As at that time a part of the sphere of the Holy Spirit was revealed to sight, so at the same time was a part of the spirit sphere revealed: on the way home he met the "hosts of God."

> And Jacob went on his way, and the angels of God met him. And when Jacob saw them, he said, This is God's host: and he called the name of that place Mahanaim. (Genesis 32:1–2)

How should this encounter be understood? We have tried to describe the principal characteristics of angels and archangels. According to these characteristics, angels are beings who unite two worlds, while archangels work in space. They are spirits of space in the sense that they endow space with moral quality. True spiritual geography is knowledge of the activities of the archangels and the spatial boundaries of these activities. The spiritual map of Earth is quite different from the political or national map, which shows only the realm of the Lucifer's archangelic activity. The correct division of space remains hidden behind that false map. The true interrelationships among the archangels is also hidden behind outer maya. The archangels do not split humanity into races but bind it into unity. Their influence does not induce contentment with what one nationality affords but arouses a deep interest in other nationalities. Their mission is to bring concord among variously constituted groups of human beings. Such concord is the inspiration of the Christ impulse, which can no more be nationalistic than, say, the wind. Just as the breeze is for everyone, Christ is present for all. This is why we picture the normal archangels correctly by thinking of them as unified hosts moving horizontally over the surface of the Earth like a wind of inspiration. The rushing current of the archangelic host is a powerful experience of inspiration, blowing once every year as a breath of enthusiasm for all that is good through the whole of humanity. On Christmas night, the rushing current of the archangelic host flows around the whole Earth. It was this rushing current of the hosts of God that Jacob experienced on the way to his homeland. The great social inspiration of human brotherhood was given to him then, once he had overcome the false social inspiration represented by Laban. "In thy seed shall all the nations of the earth be blessed"—these words of promise became a spiritual reality to him, for he saw the bond that unites the spirits of all nations and that this would become a reality with the coming of the Promised One.

Even greater than the first and second victory was the *third* victory that Jacob won, for it was achieved in a struggle against the flow of destiny—occasioned not by human beings but by gods. This was the victory gained during the night before he met his brother Esau at the Jabbok Ford (Genesis 32). A complete understanding of Jacob's lonely wrestle that night by Jabbok Ford presupposes knowing the facts of true occultism (a discussion of which is beyond the scope of these meditations). Nonetheless, we will endeavor to bring out the meaning of this wrestling from the perspective of karma. We can grasp its meaning by considering death as it is affected by the participation of the spiritual hierarchies.

Death, whether seen from the spiritual or the earthly side, is the cessation of physical breathing in a human being. But the physical breathing of human beings is a reflection of spiritual breathing, which is a harmonious collaboration of knowledge and love. Breathing, in the spiritual world, is the harmonious result of existence within and outside the self in regard to the beings of the hierarchies. The first state is knowledge, the second is love. In human beings, it is the human spirit expressed in breathing. But the human spirit consists of three parts. Spirit self (*manas*), life spirit (*budhi*) and spirit body (*atma*) are the three parts of the eternal spiritual quintessence of human beings.[5] The collaboration of this trinity is the spiritual cause of breathing. Manas is the essence of human knowledge; budhi, the essence of love; and atma maintains a balance between manas and budhi. Therefore, the primal cause of breathing lies in atma.

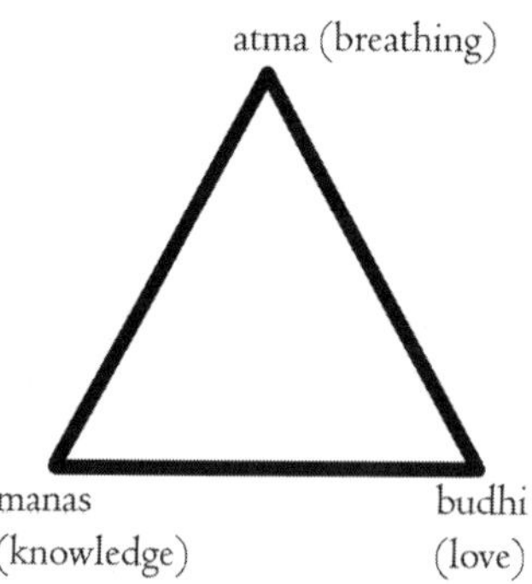


The three main spiritual hierarchies participate in human breathing. The spiritual components of human beings rest (as a rule) in the womb of the hierarchies. Manas is represented by the third hierarchy; budhi is born by the second; and atma lives in the womb of the first hierarchy. The time spirits (archai), however, represent the first hierarchy (that of the Father) within the third hierarchy. They determine the period of breathing in time—that is, the moment of one's death. Just as the archai harmonize the work of angels and archangels in a person, it is they who provide for the duration of one's breathing. The moment of death is the moment of meeting with the beings of the archai. The vision of one's life tableau, which begins then—a simultaneous picture of one's whole life course—is that meeting. It is the power of the time spirits that places the period of earthly life before the soul as a whole; and we owe to that same power the sublime consciousness of personality awakened by this experience. The time spirits are also the "spirits of personality." Jacob met one of those spirits of personality that night prior to the encounter with his brother. It was death with whom he wrestled during that fateful night.

How should we understand the karmic sense of this meeting? The current of destiny that brought falsehood into Jacob's life was threefold: it was physical lies that he had overcome in his parental home; he overcame astral lies in Laban's house; now he was facing spiritual lies on the path of life—the karmic consequence of his action toward his brother. By means of outer deception, Jacob wrestled for the inner truth of his birthright. His fidelity to truth reaped the karmic reward of the revelations that came to him from the angelic realm, but the requital of his deception awaited him in the form of death. For this is how karma works—simultaneously rewarding and punishing for the same deed. The balance of karmic justice is an exact balance; nothing remains unpunished, nothing unrewarded.

Jacob recognized this and separated himself from his family so that they might remain unscathed. He waited *alone* on this side of the river, because he knew that he was destined to death. But he did not succumb to the temptation of fatalism; he defended himself against death. He did not allow himself to be led astray by the spiritual falsehood of fatalism, but set *love* against the *knowledge* of inevitable death. The power that preserved his breathing is expressed in the words indicating the successful issue of his wrestling: "I will not let thee go, except thou bless me" (Genesis 32:26). If he had yielded to the knowledge of death, his breathing would have ceased, and he would have died. The balance of the first principles of breathing—knowledge and love—would have been overthrown in favor of knowledge. But as he resisted knowledge with the whole force of love, at the "breaking of the day" the angel of death, the archai being, surrendered. Love proved itself stronger than death.

> And Jacob called the name of the place Peniel: for I have seen God face to face, and my life is preserved. And as he passed over Penuel the sun rose upon him, and he halted upon his thigh. (Genesis 32:30–31)

Through love and humility, Jacob caused the angel of death to surrender to Christ, the Sun of the World. Whereas Jacob recognized the justice of the requital by death, the angel of death recognized the justice of inner change through love and humility.

Jacob's victory consisted in this: avenging justice retreated before the sun of expiatory justice. But the measure of love was stronger in Jacob than was the recognition of death; thus he was obliged to restore the balance; after the wrestling he " halted upon his thigh."

Through the compensating power of his love, Jacob was granted the capacity, not only to breathe—that is, to go on living—but also to expiate his trespass against his brother. Karma "pardons" nothing; it merely substitutes an inner, free atonement for a superficial one. It was thus for Jacob. As he met his brother humbly, and subjected himself to him as the elder, he won over the human heart of Esau in the same way as he had won the divine heart of the hierarchies—the sun, which "rose upon him."

> And he [Jacob] passed over before them, and bowed himself to the ground seven times, until he came near to his brother. And Esau ran to meet him, and embraced him, and fell on his neck, and kissed him: and they wept. (Genesis 33:3–4)

On the human plane occurred only the reflection of what had originally occurred on the divine. The angel of death who is the messenger of the Father, blessed Jacob instead of depriving him of breath; Jacob's brother, who came to meet him with four hundred armed men to kill him, ran to him and kissed him. And Jacob had overcome death in the spirit, death turned from him even in human events on Earth.

Jacob's threefold victory signified for him knowledge of the mysteries of birth, life, and death—that is, knowledge of angels, archangels, and archai. The last stage, the meeting with the hierarchy of the archai, had imparted to him the cognition revealed in his twelve "blessings" of the twelve tribes of Israel. This is the cognition of the mysteries of *time*. For Jacob's twelve "blessings" contained prophetic decisions of the destiny of each of the twelve tribes in time to come. "Gather yourselves together, that I may tell you that which shall befall you in the last days" (Genesis 49:1). With these words Jacob addressed the twelve. Why should there be *twelve* personalities who followed the three patriarchs, Abraham, Isaac, and Jacob?

## The Nature of the Twelve

Meditations three and four were devoted to Abraham, Isaac, and Jacob as representatives of the three primal impulses in the history of the Israelites. These three impulses are those of the Father, the Son, and the Holy Spirit. Through the three personalities we have studied, these three impulses were implanted in the children of Israel. But their work had to be carried out in the time that followed their planting. Carrying out the work in time, however, is a process that cannot be grasped by studying only the physical world. It can be comprehended only if it is considered as a collaboration of the spiritual, astral, elemental, and physical worlds. The archetype of this process is based on the impulses of soul forces—thinking, feeling, and willing—to obtain the elemental power with which to carry out its technique on the terrestrial plane. The ideas of the spiritual world (the higher Devachan) must become impulses of the soul (the lower Devachan), so that physical happenings may be shaped by elemental forces (the astral world).

Now if we picture the ideal trinity, revealed in Abraham, Isaac and Jacob, as realized in time, it has to work in four worlds. To become completely real, the *thought* of the Father, the sacrifice of the Son, and the victory of the Holy Spirit must be active in all four worlds.

This collaboration of the four worlds gives the number *twelve* as the law of the complete realization of the Trinity in time. This is why there had to be twelve tribes through which the destiny of Israel should be realized. That is why the number *twelve* is the key that opens the way that leads to realization of the Old Testament mission. It is also the key, however, to understanding the realization of the New Testament impulse. For the twelve apostles of Christ are the "fathers" of the *karmic* twelve tribes of Israel, who in time to come will embody the Christ impulse (see the Apocalypse of John.). Since the Mystery of Golgotha, the apostles of Christ have exercised by turns an inspiring influence on humankind, in succession from Judas to John. Thus there is a John era, a James era, and so on. Today, we live in an era of Judas. This is shown especially by the fact that we live in a time when there are enormously strong inclinations toward treachery. In almost everyone of the present age, the potential for treachery is present in one form or another. This can be seen very clearly if we consider the fact that human confidence is becoming increasingly rare. Everything new, whether in people or in ideas, is first received with suspicion. Today, confidence must be won; it is no longer the first natural impulse of the human heart. Suspicion today does not require anything special to be evoked; it arises immediately, of its own accord. This lack of confidence is an unmistakable sign that the Judas tendency is secretly present. Those who approach others with groundless suspicion are always the ones who have a hidden basis for distrusting themselves.

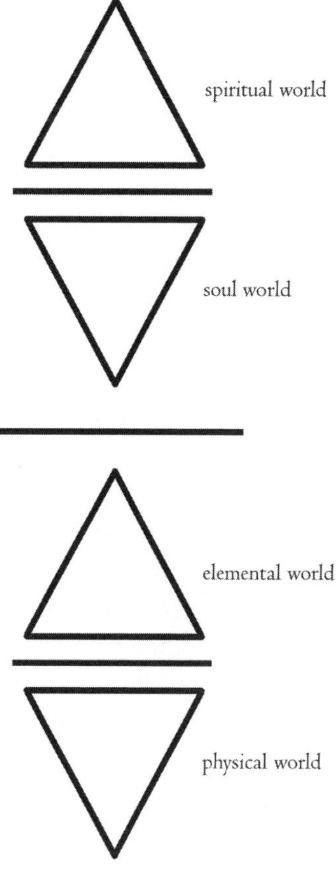


The Christ impulse influences the future through the twelve. This means that human consciousness must openly accept it in thinking, feeling, and willing within the four worlds. The mission of humanity is to think, feel, and will Christ in the four worlds. Those who carry it into effect become the thirteenth.

This fourth study accomplishes an aspect of the purpose of these meditations—characterizing the Trinity of original good in the world by means of its expression in the three occultisms and in the individuals of Abraham, Isaac, and Jacob. But the trinity of good stands in opposition to the trinity of evil; and the subject of the next study will be the trinity of evil, as it may be found in the Bible.

# Chapter 5

# Evil in Cosmic Karma as Presented in the Bible

## The Unique Character of Daniel's Spiritual Knowledge

In the foregoing meditations we considered evil as expressed by luciferic beings and ahrimanic power, from one definite side. The point was to consider evil insofar as necessary to understand the nature of Yahweh Elohim and the basic spiritual impulses of Abraham, Isaac, and Jacob. Now we will move on to the knowledge of evil contained in the Bible and translate it into the concepts humanity owes to Rudolf Steiner. Naturally this task can be achieved only within certain limits, conditioned both by the content and by the range of the subject.

As a whole, the Bible is a book of facts. It pictures events and actions and, as a rule, leaves it to the reader to understanding them. There are, however, parts of the Bible that impart definite information concerning future generations. Some of this has significance only for the time when it was written; some is concerned with a future that has already passed; but some refers to the whole future of terrestrial evolution. Therefore, this information cannot, even today, be viewed as merely historic, because from the depths of these writings solutions may be drawn for the problems of cosmic karma. The parts of the Old Testament that bear an apocalyptic character are to be found mainly in the books of the prophets. There are apocalyptic passages in almost all the prophets' writings, but, in the author's opinion, the books of the prophets Isaiah, Ezekiel, and Daniel have the greatest apocalyptic significance. If, however, we are seeking especially explanations of the karma of cosmic evil, the Book of Daniel is the best able to give profound answers to our questions. In what follows, therefore, we shall study a part of the Book of Daniel.

Before we begin we must consider the sort of knowledge of cosmic karma that the Book of Daniel presents. The common views of "revelation" or "spiritual insight" are insufficient for truly understanding the perception of cosmic karma as we have it in Daniel. For a concrete understanding of the process we must be aware that there are several kinds of perception of cosmic karma. One involves a welling of inner memories of things experienced in previous lives. Such memories may arise in the form of a succession of thoughts that, with the greatest possible clarity and with organic coherence, offer positive certainty of the truth of the objective experience. Only in this form, for instance, could the very important knowledge of the wisdom of the mysteries have risen again and been imparted to others during the thirteenth century, when there was no possibility of spiritual clairvoyance. At that time, the whole of the wisdom possessed by humankind was rescued by twelve individuals who revived all the wisdom of the seven Atlantean periods and the five post-Atlantean civilizations by means of an inner rush of memory, and imparted it to a thirteenth, from whom proceeded the collective wisdom of Rosicrucianism later on.[1]

A different kind of perception of cosmic karma is the reading (that is, the seeing and deciphering) of the akashic record. This perception presupposes a stage of initiation that can be reached by very few individuals. Only the highest initiates of humankind (for instance, those of whom we spoke in the first study in connection with the three occultisms) can attain it. There is, however, a third kind of perception of the mysteries of cosmic karma. To those who possess a lower degree of initiation than needed to read the akashic record, knowledge concerning the cosmic karma may be imparted by *imagination* and *inspiration* in cooperation with beings of the spiritual hierarchies. In such a case, beings of the hierarchies *show* the individual concerned, through *imagination,* and interpreting through *inspiration,* certain mysteries of karma that they wish to impart to that particular person, or through that person to humankind.

Now if we study the Book of Daniel with a view to the kind of perception that has produced it, we see that Daniel's perception was the third kind. The pictures of the "kingdoms" of evil, for instance, were described to him by the Archangel Gabriel (Daniel 8, 15, and 16), and the last revelations of his book he owed to an elohim being, whom he had been able to meet through the help of Michael, "prince" of the people of Israel (Daniel 10, 13, and 14). Thus pictures were shown and interpretations given to Daniel through beings of the angelic and archangelic hierarchies; but it was the archai who presented the substance of the revelations. It was the mysteries of *time* about which Daniel was inquiring; he was trying to understand the "days" of the cosmic karma. But he put his questions to the spiritual world, not from himself as an individual but in the name of the Israelite race. This happened as the result of a definite stage in the evolution of conscious responsibility, which at that time corresponded to conscience. For instance, those who felt responsible only for themselves and their own actions were in alliance with the angel. But those whose sense of responsibility was extended to include the destiny of a race were interacting with the archangel; this was true for Daniel. Thus in chapter nine of his book, his penitential prayer for the people of Israel is quoted. In this prayer, Daniel addresses the highest being he knows—not in his own name but in the name of the people. "*We* have sinned ... we do not present our supplications before thee for our righteousnesses, but for thy great mercies" (Daniel 9:5–18). These words are taken from the prayer that shows the temper of Daniel's mind. Now, as Daniel asked in the name of the people, the answers he received were revelations about the future of this people. But this was a very special people: it was a "chosen" people, comprising a karmic community of people who, from the earliest ages, had been associated especially with the Christ impulse. Thus, not only was the future of

Israel revealed to him, but also the destiny of the karmic community of the eternal Israel, the whole effect of the Christ impulse in human karma. These revelations were imparted to Daniel by an elohim being of the host of Yahweh (Daniel 10:5, 6). But as his inquiries arose from race consciousness, it was archangels who interpreted the communications for him, insofar as the creation of corresponding conditions in space made it possible. The subject of the communications, however, was represented by the future actions of the archai beings, who themselves never speak; for the Father does not speak. The archai can be seen only in time; to human beings they are silent.

The questions that Daniel asked were certainly not theoretic; he was in bitter earnest about them. Thus the revelations depicted in chapter 10, for instance, were preceded by a severe struggle. "In those days I, Daniel, was mourning three full weeks. I ate no pleasant bread, neither came flesh nor wine in my mouth, neither did I anoint myself at all, till three whole weeks were fulfilled" (Daniel 10:2–3). Daniel tells us the condition of his soul when the spiritual world had stirred him to the communications recorded in chapter 10. That questions concerning impersonal cosmic affairs should arise from the pain and anxiety of personal problems, this was the necessary condition preceding the revelations granted to Daniel. Such questioning is also essential today, for the spiritual world will be compelled to silence if it is not questioned. And humanity owes Rudolf Steiner an enormous debt for raising among humankind—by the imparting of spiritual facts—such as would not otherwise have been awakened. Steiner's Anthroposophy is a path that not only answers the questions that already exist, but also places new and greater questions before the soul. Because of this, the spiritual world will not lapse into silence; the truth that flows from it will not dry up. Such a question is the one concerning the cosmic karma of evil. It was alive in the soul of Daniel and led him to significant conclusions. To make these conclusions our own is the task we shall attempt in what follows.

## The Trinity of Cosmic Evil

The truth of Rudolf Steiner's statement that Ahriman is the karma of Lucifer has been considered in the foregoing meditations, from both the cosmic and the human side. We tried to show clearly how Lucifer had caused the intervention of Ahriman, both in cosmic evolution and in human destiny. Now, however, the question arises: What is the destiny of the beings of the luciferic hierarchy?

If we think of cosmic evolution as a collaboration among the spiritual hierarchies, we realize that a continual ascending and descending of beings is occurring within this evolutionary process. The ascent and the descent, however, are of two kinds. The descent may signify a sacrifice, but it may also be the result of degeneration. On the other hand, the ascent may be the result of ripening for higher activity, or it may be a phenomenon of regeneration, or rebirth. Thus the luciferic hierarchy is in a process of degeneration as well as one of regeneration. The Mystery of Golgotha has exercised most profound influences on that hierarchy. Because of the Mystery of Golgotha, a spiritual event of enormously far-reaching importance took place: the inner conversion of Lucifer. Lucifer conceived a love of Christ and acknowledged the wrong he had done him. The Mystery of Golgotha convinced Lucifer that he was in the wrong. This is indicated in the Gospels when one of the crucified thieves acknowledged his guilt and the innocence of the third crucified one. It was Lucifer's conscience, revealed in this malefactor.

Since that time, the influence of Lucifer is felt by humankind as the result of its past activity. The luciferic angels long for deliverance through humanity. They are bound to the consequences of their past activity; they *cannot* exercise any influence other than what they formerly exerted. But humankind can free its luciferic angel. This happens when we absorb the Christ impulse into ourselves. Then the luciferic angel is set free and becomes the servant of the proper angel. We place ourselves humbly at the service of the angel, just as before we were proud in opposing him.

This is true both of Lucifer, who is a being of the second hierarchy, and of the luciferic angels. Lucifer recognized Christ immediately; but the luciferic angels must come to recognize him through the human beings with whom they are individually united. It is different, however, for the luciferic beings of other hierarchies—for example, the archangels and the archai. Among them are beings who have *not* changed; they have retained their former organization. Moreover there are beings among them who have made an alliance with Ahriman. We can understand this alliance correctly by viewing it not as a mere treaty but as a partial ahrimanizing of the inner organization of the beings concerned. They become beings of an ahrimanic and luciferic character.

We can understand why this has happened when we consider that the karma of the luciferic hierarchy will, as such, eventually disappear. It cannot maintain its existence throughout eternity by denying the gods on the one hand and, on the other, by refusing to take part in the radical opposition to the spiritual world led by Ahriman. There are only two lines that the luciferic beings can take: either they have to be converted and join the hosts of Christ, or they must persist in opposition to the gods, even to the ultimate consequence of an alliance with Ahriman. One way is that of regeneration, the other of degeneration. First, however, a process of transition takes place, in which the two natures—luciferic and ahrimanic—amalgamate before a luciferic being degenerates into an ahrimanic being—that is, before he is devoured by Ahriman, who allows no great number of beings to exist in his neighborhood, but consumes them. Those luciferic beings who have formed an alliance with Ahriman are at this stage of degeneration. They are, in fact, no longer luciferic beings but form a separate hierarchy.

Thus, today there are *three* hierarchies of evil at work: the luciferic, the luciferic and ahrimanic, and the ahrimanic hierarchies (and this last must be seen as merely the sum of the parts of the Ahriman being). If we wish, therefore, to understand thoroughly what is happening in the present era, we must consider that today there are not only luciferic and ahrimanic impulses at work, but also impulses that outwardly appear luciferic, but behind which an ahrimanic influence is hidden, impulses in which luciferic enthusiasm serves ahrimanic purposes.

But the karma of evil is not exhausted with the degeneration of the luciferic being to the stage of the ahrimanic being. Just as the luciferic, carried through to its last consequence, inevitably becomes the prey of Ahriman, so the ahrimanic, carried to its ultimate consequence, becomes the prey of a *third* being in the cosmos. Rudolf Steiner designated this third being Asura, which represents the third stage of cosmic evil (not counting the transition stage from luciferic to ahrimanic). Just as Ahriman is the karma of Lucifer, Asura is the karma of Ahriman. Very little can be said about the qualities of Asura; the possible descriptions of his nature are limited. Nevertheless we must speak clearly of Asura, even though we are limited, because it is a duty of the present age; a clear picture must be given, or none at all; vagueness must be avoided at all costs.

To form a concept of the nature of Asura, we must study the four parts of the human being in their relation to cosmic evil. The human I encounters evil in the three bodily parts of the human being. If the I-being had not stooped to the astral, etheric, and physical body, it would not have come into contact with cosmic evil. This happens first in the astral body, where the I encounters luciferic activity. The meeting with ahrimanic influences occurs in the etheric body. The luciferic double has an astral nature, but the ahrimanic double is etheric. The whole drama of human vulnerability to evil in the past and in the present depends on the I-being having come to terms with these two doubles. The third encounter with evil is, however, impending in the future. This will take place in the physical body, when the I begins to seek an understanding with the power of Asura.

This understanding has not yet been attained; the conflict between good and evil in human nature has, at the present time, reached no further down than the etheric body. The three encounters with primal cosmic good experienced by human beings between birth and death do not affect the physical body. By night, human beings experience in the I, the meeting with the Holy Spirit, whose light is transmitted by his angel; at Christmastime, human beings meet with the Son in the astral body. His warmth is transfused into human beings by the archangels; and once in human life, or at the hour of death, we meet, in our etheric body, the Father, represented by the beings of the hierarchy of archai. Encounters with cosmic good as well as with cosmic evil take place outside (above) the inner being of the physical body. In other words, the conflict between good and evil has not yet descended into the physical body. Only the results of that conflict are mirrored in the physical body, insofar as it depends on what takes place in the higher members of the human being. If, for example, the gallbladder or the liver is out of order as the result of this conflict, the cause cannot be found within the physical body; it is merely the reflection of what is happening in the astral-etheric region.

Now the physical body is the area that is under the influence of the Father, just as the etheric body is under that of the Son, and the Holy Spirit is revealed in the astral body. The astral body is therefore the scene of the conflict of the Holy Spirit against Lucifer, while in the etheric body the war of the Son against Ahriman is fought. That the physical body is not yet a scene of conflict indicates the significant cosmic fact that, at the present time, there is no being in the universe strong enough to enter the lists against the Father himself. Ahriman does not venture; he shows respect to the Father. He opposes only the

Son, hoping that the course of cosmic karma will justify him in relation to the Son in the eyes of the Father. Ahriman's hope is that he will succeed in creating a current of cosmic karma that will convince even the Father. It is not a conflict with the Father to which he aspires but the creation of cosmic conditions in which he may be able to say to the Father, "Behold, you gave existence to beings so that they might be free; but they have chosen not your Son, but *me.*"

Lucifer was even less inclined than Ahriman to enter the lists against the Father. Neither has Lucifer operated *directly* against the Son; it was the Holy Spirit with whom he was in conflict. His intention was to guide humankind so that individuals might find the *love* without attaining the *truth* of the Holy Spirit. The Christ deed convinced him, just because it was a revelation of love in perfect consonance with the truth of the Spirit. Lucifer recognized that this is not a revelation of true love that would try to spare humankind the knowledge of the truth. Therefore he changed his character and became a *Paraclete,* giving inner help to human beings who have received the Christ impulse.

It is impossible for a being to oppose the Father in the cosmos unless the current of cosmic evil has been so developed that a karmic region is established, giving that being a foothold. Such a region does not yet exist, but it is being formed. It is made up of the *physical* results of ahrimanic activity. Not physical in the sense of diseases, which indicate the karmic balance, but in the sense of ahrimanic *health,* producing a physical body no longer dependent for its existence on the inflow of forces from the region of the first hierarchy, but able to draw them from another source. When the physical body has been brought into this condition—as the result of its ahrimanizing—the moment of time will have been reached at which the Asura being can make his attack.

This condition of the physical body cannot take place until, in the far future, a change occurs in the current relationship between the etheric and astral bodies (expressed in the facts of sleep and death), a change that will result in sleeplessness and deathlessness of the etheric body. When the I *never* quits the two lower regions—in sleep or in death—the possibility of an influx of spiritual forces from the realm of the first hierarchy will cease completely, leading to a condition that will give Asura a point of attack.

The influence of this third force of evil will be distinguished from that of Lucifer or Ahriman, especially in its relationship to the bodily parts of the human being as well as to the changed human I-being itself. When the luciferic influence, working through the astral body, leads the human I astray and tears it from its union with the spiritual hierarchies—when Ahriman through his influence on the etheric body, enslaves the human I—then Asura will completely disintegrate the I thus torn from the spiritual world by Lucifer and enslaved by Ahriman, absorbing it into his own being. Just as Lucifer brings the I out of the waking condition into the dreaming condition, and Ahriman brings it out of the dreaming into the sleeping condition, likewise Asura brings death to the human I. For humanity, the spiritual death of the I-being is the danger of the third stage of evil.

In a lecture in Berlin, March 22, 1909, Rudolf Steiner spoke of the karmic paths of the three stages of evil and of the dangers they represent for humanity.[2] But the Bible also speaks of these paths and these dangers, notably in the description Daniel left for future generations: his vision of the four beasts. The preceding considerations (as well as the lecture by Rudolf Steiner) will help us understand the seventh chapter of the Book of Daniel to a certain degree.

## The Karma of Cosmic Evil as Presented by the Prophet Daniel

The purpose of the prophet Daniel was to preserve for the future certain important truths he had experienced. In accordance with a decree of the spiritual world, he embodied all his revelations in "signs," so that they might be deciphered at a time when people not only believed things, but also *perceived* them. The substance of his records is the revelation of a series of important future events in the cosmic karma of good and evil. The utilization of the whole treasure of knowledge bequeathed to us by Daniel must be preserved for the future; here we are concerned only with the part that involves the karma of evil in the sense of the previous section.

The spiritual revelation recorded in the seventh chapter of the Book of Daniel affords us what we need for our task. In that chapter, the karma of evil is boldly outlined. The delineation begins with the picture of "the four winds of the heaven [that] strove upon the great sea" (Daniel 7:2). This figure shows us the cosmic *scene* of the conflict between good and evil. Space—with its four cardinal points of north, south, east, west—is neither one of the three abstract categories of Kantian philosophy, nor is it merely the distance that must be covered to reach some particular point; it is an ocean of forces at rest, set in motion by four *active* forces. These four active forces are the spiritual influences within the elemental world—the "winds" that cover the elemental world. The currents caused by the four "winds" in the elemental world give rise to the four elements, which are impregnated by the four realms of elemental beings (salamanders, sylphs, undines and gnomes).

These four groups of elemental beings are simply the lowest expression of the "four winds." Their origin is rooted in the eternal Trinity, from which issue the cosmic impulses called "north," "south," "east," and "west." The Father being works through the cosmic impulses of north and south; the Son and the Holy Spirit are active in the impulses of east and west. When these impulses work *together*, cosmic good results; when the "four winds" work *against* one another, the result is cosmic evil. This is why the description of Daniel's night vision begins with this image: "The four winds of the heaven strove." These winds striving against one another are the four currents of cosmic evil. They are not controlled from Heaven, but from the depths of the "sea"; their origin must be sought in the "four ... beasts" that appear out of the depths of the sea: "And four great beasts came up from the sea, diverse one from another" (Daniel 7:3).

The first beast is represented as a lion with eagle's wings. It is the current of evil active above, in the air. In this figure, the lion's courage is winged, having become arrogant and proud. Lucifer is a being who is essentially a stranger to fear; not until he is faced with the matured karmic consequences of his rebellion against divine guidance will he learn to know fear. Then he will be obliged to experience in himself the ahrimanic element of fear. Thus he will have to experience the karma of his act inwardly as a kind of "Kama Loka." This Kama Loka—in which he must experience the horror of the potential results of his action, and fear lest they should be irreparable—transforms Lucifer into a humble being; his arrogance disappears completely. This is imaginatively depicted by Daniel, when he says: "I beheld till the wings thereof were plucked" (Daniel 7:4).

This naturally leads to a question: In the second study, the "fall of the angels"—the luciferic rebellion—was represented as a result of emotional compassion; here, arrogance or presumption is alleged as its cause. How can these two explanations be reconciled? *Compassion* is not really the right word to express precisely the reason behind the defection of Lucifer from the gods. The appropriate term is not contained in the English, French, or German languages. The Russian word *shalostj*, by contrast, gives an exact idea of the essential cause of Lucifer's rebellion. It means pity for a being who is felt to be too weak to free itself from a painful situation. This feeling is distinct from compassion (which in Russian is *sostradanie*), because compassion may also be felt for someone who is respected, whereas the feeling intended here is a contemptuous pity. It contains within itself a hidden scorn for the being for whom this kind of compassion is felt.

This feeling—as well as the ideology it evokes in most important human affairs—becomes intelligible when we read the chapter about the Grand Inquisitor in Feodor Dostoevsky's book *The Brothers Karamazov*. There, more clearly than anywhere else, the difference between the love of Jesus Christ and the love of the Grand Inquisitor is shown. Whereas Christ, by his action, shows the greatest possible respect for humankind—not working by miracle and power, but by *sacrifice* (the temptation in the wilderness)—the Grand Inquisitor, on the other hand, is convinced that humanity is incapable of coming to Christ in freedom; Christ's error must be remedied through those who are prepared to bear the cross of guardianship and assume sole responsibility for humankind. The Grand Inquisitor does not love humankind as Christ does; he feels a burning but contemptuous compassion for human beings. Freedom, he is convinced, should be reserved for the few chosen ones; but the mass of humanity should be *led*. And if Christ were to appear again, it would be the Grand Inquisitor's duty—even though he had recognized him—to imprison him as a dangerous heretic, whose coming would bring confusion to the masses of humankind under his tutelage; the specter of freedom would arise again and destroy his work of compassion.

This chapter of Dostoevsky's work helps us understand, deep in our heart, the reasons for the luciferic opposition to the divine purposes. This understanding of the heart shows us that luciferic compassion in its true form is nothing but arrogance and overweening pride; it is based on a low esteem of humanity, of which Lucifer was to assume the guardianship. Hence, it is no contradiction to say that Lucifer rebelled against the gods out of pride, while at the same time he pitied humanity. What the soul experiences as luciferic compassion is overweening spiritual pride. The fact that Lucifer becomes a humble being who sees the need of terrestrial reality for the human evolution as planned by the gods is expressed by Daniel in this imagery: "And it [the first beast] was lifted up from the earth, and made stand upon the feet as a man, and a man's heart was given to it"—that is, a heart that, through error and fear, has found access to love (Daniel 7:4). The "feet" are two currents of will, now directed *downward*. Lucifer's karma involves changing the "eagle wings" to "feet," causing his will to flow in service down to Earth.

Different, according to Daniel's images, is the destiny of the second beast, which is not "winged" but "like to a bear, and it raised up itself on one side" (Daniel 7:5). Much is contained in this picture—among other things, the knowledge that Ahriman does not exhaust all his forces over earthly events. Only a part of the nature of Ahriman is active on Earth; the remaining (and greater) part functions in the Eighth Sphere, between the Earth and the Moon. It is therefore correct to describe Ahriman as "raised up *on one side*" only, because the other side cannot be found on Earth. And this is why humanity today (and even more so in the past) cannot see Ahriman as a complete personality. It is quite possible to meet with the personality of Lucifer, but for Ahriman one can never encounter more than part of the personality. The whole personality of Ahriman cannot be seen, but its parts may be experienced in various forms. The form in which it is generally seen is a caricature of the human figure. Even the ahrimanic double is an individual caricature of the one to whom the double belongs. Daniel, however, had an imaginative perception of the part of the ahrimanic nature that is perceptible; he saw him as the double of humanity as a whole. This is why he speaks of a figure that is "like to a bear"—a caricature of the human form.

Ahriman's activity toward humanity constitutes a continuous effort to destroy it. The luciferic influence on humankind evokes illusions and passions; that is, Lucifer *enriches* humanity from a quantitative point of view. Ahriman, on the contrary, endeavors to reduce humanity to the annihilation of his own individuality; he *subtracts* forces from the human personality, and appropriates them to himself. This is not noticeable in the life of an individual person, because the forces absorbed by Ahriman remain unchanged in that individual until the moment of death. After that moment, one might become aware of the extent to which the affected soul has been impoverished. During earthly life, the forces stolen from a person by Ahriman become faculties of the ahrimanic double; *he* uses them in human beings, so that, to the external observation, there is no lacuna in the one concerned. If, however, the double were withdrawn, the loss would be externally visible. For instance, a brilliantly gifted journalist or lawyer would suddenly become a mediocre, insignificant hack. Such a one would suddenly feel helpless in the face of a task that had previously been fulfilled brilliantly, having always been able to twist, bend, and shape facts according to one's goal. Now, one would stand confused before the facts, because the capacity to twist and bend them would be gone.

The destruction of human forces by Ahriman occurs not chaotically in human history, but according to plan. This organized realization of ahrimanic purposes takes place with the help of the occultism that entered into human destiny during the Atlantean period (especially in the ancient Turanian epoch). It will not surrender its position until it is overcome by humanity itself. Black occultism is the tool by means of which Ahriman accomplishes his work of destroying humanity. Such occultism is likewise threefold; it is the cooperation of black eugenic occultism, black hygienic occultism, and black mechanical occultism. As it is irrational to refuse to believe that there are, and have always been, three occultisms of good, likewise is it irrational to believe in the existence of only one or two forms of evil occultism—say, mechanical and hygienic occultism. There are, in fact, three forms of evil occultism, and these represent the means through which Ahriman exercises his power in human history. This study does not wish to describe the three occultisms but to read the signs of Daniel. We can read the signs of the second beast when we understand, in the command given to "Arise, devour much flesh," an expression of the essential tendency of ahrimanic destruction. In this image, the other beast "had three ribs in the mouth of it between the teeth of it." These are the instruments of Ahriman, or the three black occultisms, which are used to sieze the object to be devoured (Daniel 7:5). Seizing must come before the devouring, and the three ahrimanic occultisms are the cosmic instruments with which Ahriman seizes his victims.

After Lucifer and Ahriman have intervened in the current of cosmic karma, there arises, as a result of the compromise between the two tendencies, a third evil tendency of a luciferic and ahrimanic nature. Of the beings of this tendency, it may be said that they possess a combination of the luciferic power of flight with the ahrimanic calculating power of the brain. This power of flight is dependent on brain power; the wings are subordinate to the heads. Now, however, the head knowledge of these beings is not concerned with the threefold unity of the spirit, but with the four-sidedness of the material, elemental world. Therefore Daniel says of them in speaking of the Third Beast: "Lo another, like a leopard, which had upon the back of it four wings of a fowl; the beast had also four heads" (Daniel 7:6). The four heads represent the faculty of analytic thought carried to its logical consequence in the formation of these organs. Each of the four elements implies a distinct branch of knowledge (four separate heads), or four independent realms held together solely by practical intent: the *will*. To each of these heads a wing is assigned—the uplifting power of inspiration.

Then Daniel describes the fourth beast, which appears as the last in cosmic karma: "dreadful and terrible, and strong exceedingly; and it had great iron teeth: it devoured and brake in pieces, and stamped the residue with the feet of it" (Daniel 7:7). In this picture we can recognize those qualities of the Asura being mentioned—namely, the power to disintegrate, or "break in pieces," as Daniel says, the human I-being. But it is the I-being that binds together the threads of past, present, and future. This continuity of consciousness in time, as the karmic interdependence of yesterday, today, and tomorrow—the previous life, the present life, and the next life—human beings owe to the nucleus of their being, the I, which continues on through sleep and waking, death and birth. Time, as the unity of past, present, and future, is under the law (karma) on Earth, so long as the archai, or time spirits, can keep the human I-being from forsaking the kingdom of karma (or "law," as Daniel calls it). If they had ever done that (in the sense of the ahrimanic immortality of which we have spoken), the continuity of time would have risked being annihilated in terrestrial development. Ahriman, whose character is most clearly expressed in the machine, mechanizes time; he excludes the morally creative from it, but does not disintegrate it. In the machine, time certainly becomes amoral, but it remains in existence. It is the same for the I-being of those who have surrendered themselves entirely to Ahriman. The I-being of such individuals sleeps a dreamless sleep; it is in the same condition of consciousness that existed during the period of the ancient Sun, the condition of plant consciousness. It is incapable of developing any kind of morally creative activity; it works by necessity, like a machine, but it still exists as a *potential* possession.[3] The danger that Asura represents for humanity lies in the effective severing of the threads that bind past, present, and future into one. Imagine the situation if every moment were to bring something different, something having no connection with what is past, or what is to come—if, for example, there were no rhythm of the years nor any mechanical rhythm to it all. Everything would be arhythmic, like the pulse of a sick man at the point of death.

"And he shall speak great words against the most High, and shall wear out the saints of the most High, and think to change times and laws," says Daniel of the ruler of the last "kingdom" of evil (Daniel 7:25). In other words, time as a unity and a rhythm will be destroyed, and the karmic principle will be discarded. The last representative of evil will oppose the Father himself. While Lucifer endeavored to create a relationship between human beings and the spiritual world, different from that which the Holy Spirit brings into effect by means of the angels, and while Ahriman resisted Christ, by marshaling humanity in mechanized space—as distinct from the grouping of humanity by the archangels of Christ—Asura will endeavor to break the chain of the archai, the representatives of the Father.

But Daniel also speaks of the karmically predestined issue of that attempt. In majestic imagery, he pictures the court of justice that will be held by the Ancient of Days:

> Whose garment was white as snow, and the hair of his head like the pure wool: his throne was like the fiery flame, and his wheels as burning fire. A fiery stream issued and came forth from before him: thousand thousands ministered unto him, and ten thousand times ten thousand stood before him: the judgment was set, and the books were opened.... I beheld even till the beast was slain, and his body destroyed, and given to the burning flame.... I saw in the night visions, and, behold, one like the Son of man came with the clouds of heaven, and came to the Ancient of days, and they brought him near before him. And there was given him dominion, and glory, and a kingdom, that all people, nations, and languages, should serve him: his dominion is an everlasting dominion, which shall not pass away, and his kingdom that which shall not be destroyed. I, Daniel, was grieved in my spirit in the midst of my body, and the visions of my head troubled me. (Daniel 7:9–15)

These sentences have an immense substance. Among other things, they contain not only a description of the asuric revolt, but also the reasons why his defeat was inevitable.

When the cosmic hour strikes in which "the books are opened for judgment," the sacrifice of him who is "like the Son of Man" will already have been consummated. When Christ became human, he created a karmic current that decides the issue of the Last Judgment. As a result of the conquest of Ahriman, the results of Ahriman's influence in the cosmos (the coming of Asura) will also be conquered. In the flame of the Father's wrath, the personality of Asura will be brought to nothing. So the one who wished to bring annihilation to others will meet that fate himself.

Thus the Mystery of Golgotha has three results in cosmic karma: the inner conversion of Lucifer, the conquest of Ahriman, and the annihilation of Asura. This is not brought about by force, but through justice. The Mystery of Golgotha is an event within karma and turns the scale for the deliverance of humankind before the judgment seat of karmic justice. The very reason Christ became Man was that he might enter the realm of human karma and alter it. Daniel shows the consequences of this change in the picture of the court of justice that the Father will convene.

Knowledge of the trinity of evil is contained in the Book of Daniel; not *only* knowledge of the trinity of evil, however, but also the knowledge of the eternal trinity of good. In the chapter quoted, there is pictured also the imaginative vision of the Father being, the inspiring knowledge of the Son, and the intuitive union with the Spirit, which Daniel experienced. The Father being could be seen by Daniel in *imagination* only, because human beings can approach the Father only as closely as *imagination* allows. *Intuition* of the Father, for instance, could not be borne; *intuition* signifies an inner acceptance in one's own being. Daniel could approach one step closer to the being who "came with the clouds of heaven" (that is through the sphere of the Son); he recognized him in *inspiration.* The meaning of his vision of future dominion was explained to him by "one of them that stood by." But the Holy Spirit was experienced by Daniel within himself; he was allied with him by direct *intuition.* Daniel can speak of the "spirit in the midst of my body."

If we study the whole Book of Daniel, we can understand in what way Daniel recognized the Father being. He saw him as the Ancient of Days, the being who reveals himself through all the Spirits of Time (the archai). And Daniel saw the series of "days" in endless perspective; the pictures of the cosmic days were unrolled before his spiritual sight. Epoch followed epoch in unbroken succession, but through the pictures of past and future cosmic days was revealed to him the countenance of the Ancient of Days, the primal cosmic entity, who in each "day" reveals but a small fragment of his being. The flaming wheels of cosmic happenings revolve unceasingly, but on the throne of fire they carry, the primal cosmic entity remains at rest. Then, when the cosmic hour strikes, his word will flash forth into the world, and the world will stand still for judgment. The books of cosmic memory will be opened, and the Father will administer justice to all the beings of his creation standing before him in freedom.

Art originated in such experiences, and it will arise again from such experiences. In future times, people will not allow themselves to create out of mere fantasy; the earnestness of cosmic events will silence fantasy in the face of the signs becoming visible in the heavens of eternal being. The spirit of such an art breathes through many passages in the Bible; that this spirit will arise again is a hope we may cherish.

In this study we have tried to picture cosmic karma as it was perceived by Daniel. The author hopes at least to have made the reader feel that the Bible contains not merely a section of human history, but also deep truths concerning cosmic events. Many mysteries of cosmic karma can be found in the Bible. Now that—with the help of the Bible—we have studied a chapter of cosmic karma, it is natural to move on to a study of human karma as seen in the Bible. Can a deeper knowledge of human karma and reincarnation be found in the Bible? This question will form the subject of the following study.

# Chapter 6

# Spiritual Guidance in Old Testament History

## The Birth of Conscience in Human Nature

In our previous meditations, the Old Testament was described and considered as the book of eugenic occultism. It has become obvious that the mystery of the messianic birth is at the center of the Old Testament as a whole. On the other hand, however, we must see that the realm of eugenic occultism is not exhausted by the mysteries of physical birth, but that it includes *every* birth, even that of new consciousness. For even the birth of a new consciousness takes place according to definite laws, and needs the preparation of physical and soul conditions to make it possible. Every descent from the spiritual world, every incarnation—be it of a soul, or of a new consciousness, or even the manifestation of a new idea on the physical plane—belongs to the realm of eugenic occultism. For the laws of birth are always the same; only, to individual cases their application is different. These "laws" cannot, of course, be abstractly formulated; or, rather, they may be formulated in thousands of different ways, in which there would then be hundreds of contradictions. They are contained in spiritual forms and figures, and it would need delineation from many points of view to produce a picture by means of which the inner figure, the "law," should appear in the consciousness. This is why Rudolf Steiner pointed out on several occasions that the study of spiritual science is in itself a means toward clairvoyance. When the facts offered by spiritual science are received into the consciousness, the inner figure that combines them into unity reveals itself through these truths, as though through a language. To learn about the evolutionary stages of Saturn, Sun, Moon, and Earth does not merely mean we can outline a scheme of activity for the hierarchies, but, by picturing this activity, we lift it to an inward vision of *law*—not a vision of lines forming a figure, but cosmic purpose. This happens when the head's imaginative thinking descends to the area of breathing. It does not lose clarity and precision, but acquires the quality of consciously following the cosmic lines, or currents, of thought that flow through a person and become clear, well-defined figures. This is the function of the perceptive force whose central currents are in the area of the larynx. This is what makes it possible for people to perceive anthroposophic truths *directly*. This descent of the head's consciousness into the area of the larynx was what Dr. Carl Unger meant when he referred to "breathing in pure thinking as the first, albeit a shadowy, clairvoyance."[1] Such breathing in pure thought is, in fact, the basis of our hope that spiritual science will be accepted in the world. If the existence of formative etheric forces can be proved through scientific experiment—if it can be proved by philological and historic research that, for example, there really was an Atlantean civilization, and still it cannot be proved by experiment or by philology and history that, say, thrones, cherubim, and seraphim shape the just consequences of human life on Earth for the next life—nevertheless, we do not need merely to "believe" but can *know*, if we have the perceptive courage to steep ourselves in these suprasensory facts with all the force of calm thinking. The important thing is to have the courage to accept spiritual facts without requiring "sources" and "proofs." Pure spiritual science can have no source but itself. It is the strength of Rudolf Steiner's life work that its source is in itself; it contains in itself all that is needed to arrive at an honest and independent conviction.

We gain an honest and independent conviction when we are prodded by the teachings of spiritual science to accept its inner truth without hesitation. It is this unhesitating acceptance of the inner truth that we need to stimulate a more profound understanding of certain laws through these never-ending meditations on Old Testament truths. One of these laws has to do with birth, and it shapes all of the Old Testament. But, as we have said, this includes not just the physical, but every kind of birth. In this way, we can understand the Old Testament more exactly by adding to the previous explanations—that, although the Old Testament does indeed present the preparation of a birth, it is the birth not just of a body, but also of a new consciousness. This alternate side of the Old Testament shows the preparation of the birth of conscience in the human soul.

> Behold, the days come, saith the Lord, that I will make a new covenant with the house of Israel, and with the house of Judah: Not according to the covenant that I made with their fathers in the day that I took them by the hand to bring them out of the land of Egypt; which my covenant they brake, although I was an husband unto them, saith the Lord: But this shall be the covenant that I will make with the house of Israel; After those days, saith the Lord, I will put my law in their inward parts, and write it in their hearts. (Jeremiah 31:31–33)

These words of the prophet Jeremiah strike the very center of the other aspect of the Old Testament's purpose: to prepare the birth of conscience as "the law that is written in their hearts"—*the birth of a human organ, within which the perfect conscience can be born*. This would be a more complete expression of the Old Testament's mission.

Now if the Old Testament evolution had to prepare the way for the Christ's coming, in connection with the foregoing thoughts we must ask: What did the coming of Christ require? The answer that would suggest itself immediately is that a *body* would be needed—one organized in such a way that the Christ could live and work within it. But this answer does not go far enough, since we must consider not just the physical, but also the astral and etheric bodies. Nevertheless, we should not consider these only in terms of substance and structure (indeed, this applies as well to the physical body), but also as a means of giving soul and life forces on certain spiritual truths in the physical realm of existence. The whole organism that the Christ needed for life on Earth had to be an expression of the forces with which he could unite. It had to serve as a gate through which to enter the domain of human events. The human organism had to be structured in such a way that it could provide an inner relationship with the *elemental* being of the Christ.

So, what is the gate through which the Christ could enter the domain of human events? Upon what ground could he stand as a starting point for his association with the Earth? The gate through which the Christ could descend to Earth was *conscience*—one so powerful that its effect was *physically* formative. Fire, air, water, and earth alone could never accomplish what was achieved by the force that the nature elements cannot offer: the force of conscience. From a superficial perspective, one could say that Christ entered the body of a human being, but if we look more deeply, we must say that the Christ entered the human conscience. Conscience is the gate that admitted the Christ being into union with the being of Earth. Humankind owes the possibility of Christ's descent to Earth to the fact of there is a conscience on Earth, completely awake in the three bodies—yes, and keeping those three bodies awake.

To understand this fact, we must keep in mind that conscience is not just a "feeling"; rather, when it is fully awakened, a condition of human nature in which the spirit knows the truth, in which the soul, *as soul*, knows the truth, in which the body, *as body*, knows the truth. The conscience is the joined knowing of spirit, soul, and body. In conscience the whole nature of the human being speaks the truth, radiating simultaneously from spirit, soul, and body. Should the "I" forsake the bodies, they continue to work on their own in the light of truth. This was the condition of the three sheaths of Jesus of Nazareth. Forsaken by the "I" of Zoroaster, he walked the path to the Jordan to receive the Christ into himself through the baptism by John. It was the conscience of humanity that walked the path to the Jordan, undeterred by the misfortunes of those individuals it encountered, because this was the conscience of humanity going to the Jordan, and in the name of all humankind and the consciousness of all human guilt, crying to Heaven for help for all—until the words sounded from on high: "This is my beloved Son; this day have I begotten him."

After the Christ had entered the conscience-awakened sheaths of Jesus at the baptism in Jordan, however, his first experience of the reality of earthly existence was specifically the element of conscience. The fullness of the spiritual world withdrew, replaced by the loneliness of the life of conscience. Thus abandoned by the spiritual world and after forty days of loneliness in the wilderness, Jesus had to undergo the three primal temptations of conscience on Earth. The three temptations in the wilderness required neither perception of the spiritual worlds nor power over earthly nature, but the decisive voice of conscience. It was not until he had—alone and forsaken—withstood the temptations through his own inner strength that "angels came and ministered unto him"—that is, the spiritual world once again opened and encompassed him. It was during the period of forty days in the wilderness that Christ permeated conscience with his own being. This period contains the mystery of Kali Yuga, the dark epoch in human history. But it also contains the mystery of the individual Kali Yuga of the separate human souls that must continue to hunger and thirst for the spiritual world until the conscience has withstood the temptations in the wilderness, at which point it will have gained strength to open the gates of that world without the risk of losing the independence and freedom it has acquired.

Three steps must be taken toward awaking one's conscience before one step can be taken in spiritual experience. Before every revelation of the spiritual world, life must enter the question set by conscience; only after conscience has passed through thinking, feeling, and volition will the spiritual world impart the experience that reveals the answer it will give to this question. So, it is meant literally, not figuratively, when Rudolf Steiner says, "For every single step that you take in seeking knowledge of hidden truths, you must take three steps in perfecting your character toward the good."[2] But perfecting one's character for good requires, above all, that it become the expression of the conscience. The birth of conscience must precede the ascent into the spiritual world. Now, because the karma of the "Fall" has led to a complete darkening of the spiritual world for humankind, it is due solely to the coming of Christ to Earth that we are able to ascend into that world at all. Thus, matters of conscience concerning the Fall and the reparation to be made for it had to precede any possibility of such ascent; that is, they had to precede the coming of Christ.

There must have been, before the descent of Christ, a conscience on Earth that eventually concentrated all its force on this question: Humanity has become darkened. Human eyes are no longer able to see; human ears can no longer hear. The consequences of the Fall roll on inexorably. The flames of memory and desire still live in human hearts, but memory will grow dim, and desire will fade. Then hearts will have become like stone. The most sublime revelation of the highest wisdom will be in vain, for there will be no one to receive it. The downfall of humankind is inevitable unless a new force descends to give sight to the blind, speech to the dumb, hearing to the deaf, and the ability to walk to the lame. Humanity cannot do this; fire, air, water, and earth cannot do it. The Sun being in heaven alone is able. Will he do it?

This question was anguish for the one who was baptized in Jordan. It constituted the whole force of his being, for the awakened conscience of humanity was the force that breathed in Jesus, moved his limbs, gave sight to his eyes and hearing to his ears. In him was the perfect revelation of conscience. He was the representative of humanity, both in the sense that the whole suffering of humanity dwelt in him, and in the sense that he took upon himself the whole healing of humanity. This must be understood as fully as possible. For we can imagine only his outer appearance, even when we view it as the visible expression of the human conscience. It had not the classical beauty of an Apollo, nor the calm of a Jupiter, careless of the world. No, it expressed the pain of a conscience awake to all the consequences of the Fall of humankind. And after the baptism in Jordan, when this countenance of selfless anguish received the lines of sublime repose traced by the presence of the eternal, world-embracing love within him, it became

what may be discerned by studying the *Representative of Humanity,* carved in wood in the "Goetheanum group." It is not classic beauty that Rudolf Steiner placed there for future generations of humankind; it is a picture of perfected human conscience, which knows it is one with the will of cosmic godhead. Thus this presentation of the conscience of humanity stands as an exhortation to tread the path which leads through pain to peace. On every side, however, people seek a painless path to peace.

The Old Testament is a history of the preparation for the birth of the sort of human organism that could be called a "conscience organism." Only in such an organism could the Christ live. The preparation for the birth of the perfect conscience followed various and complicated paths over long periods of time. In what follows we will discuss those paths.

## Buddha, Elijah, Jesus

In the lecture cycle *The Christ Impulse and the Development of Ego Consciousness,* Rudolf Steiner said that, in the course of evolution, the divine spiritual leaders of humanity would be confronted by the fact that something unknown to them was present in humankind: conscience.[3] And if they were to understand it, they would have to descend to Earth and incarnate, because the human conscience could not be perceived by them from the spiritual world. Now we might conclude from this that beings of the spiritual world have no conscience—that conscience can be developed only on Earth by earthly humanity. This view is justified insofar as we are speaking positively of the human conscience; it is not correct, however, to deny the attribute of conscience in hierarchical beings. In fact, all the beings of the world possess conscience—that is, the force of moral imagination in the sense that Rudolf Steiner uses this term in his *Intuitive Thinking as a Spiritual Path* (or *Philosophy of Freedom*).

Every being bears the mystery of its individuality within itself, and it is conscience—the inner creative source—that gives individuality to all beings, even to the beings of the hierarchies. Individuality exists only insofar as it can add something to the cosmic life around it that could not manifest without assistance. The hierarchies of cosmic good are not automata, even though for them there is no question of a choice between good and evil. They serve the good by seeking in their conscience ever new and more perfect deeds of sacrifice. There is no limit to the moral imagination of goodness; the beings who serve the good are distinguished by the acts of sacrifice they choose. They freely renounce the rights they possess in the cosmos in order to achieve by sacrifice, on a higher level, something greater than they could have attained had they remained within their rights. Something like this is also true of a certain group of human souls who, in the disembodied state in Devachan, make decisions concerning the next earthly life that awaits them.[4] For example, a human soul may have a karmic right to a harmonious life of sunshine, surrounded by friends and in a milieu congenial to its character; this is the *right* of that soul. But it may happen that, after examining the life before it in the light of conscience, this soul may freely renounce the destiny offered by karma. The conscience of such a soul may say, "I have before me the possibility of a harmonious life on Earth. I will not need to expend my forces in conflict and pain. Meanwhile, however, humanity will go through trials in which I will not actively share. My help in the fight for truth is more necessary to humankind than my happiness." Such a soul may choose a mission involving a very different course of life from that to which it had a right. The consequence of this may be that that soul is placed by destiny in the middle of a conflict on Earth and may never meet success during a whole lifetime. Here it is not a question of a choice between good and evil, but between good and better. And the faculty that can decide between good and better is the conscience of spiritual beings who have not incarnated.

So it is not conscience in general that puzzles the spiritual beings, but the *human* conscience standing between good and evil. This position between good and evil is possible only in the human organism, which not only stands face to face with evil, but has absorbed it into itself. Spiritual beings cannot absorb evil; they can *face* evil and they can recognize it in its effects, but they cannot experience it in themselves. If a spiritual being were to absorb evil, it would become an evil being; spiritual beings are an undivided whole. Only human beings can combine two natures within themselves. This is because of the "Fall," which led to a new fact in the cosmos—the existence of beings who can experience evil as well as good within themselves. Indeed, human beings are sinful because they have absorbed evil into their nature. But because of this, a possibility arises for humanity that does not exist for other beings—the possibility of the intuition of evil, along with the intuition of good. This involves a tremendous cosmic risk, because it may happen that humankind grows to *love* evil. So that this does not occur—so that the balance between good and evil in the human organism is not weighted in favor of evil—from the earliest times, help has been given to human beings from the spiritual world. This help has been mainly in the form of ever new forces flowing from on high to strengthen the good in human beings. To accomplish this, beings from the higher hierarchies renounce their higher rights and come down to unite directly with humankind. Among these are the three beings to whom we owe an infinite debt—beings indicated in occult world history by the names of Buddha, Elijah, and Jesus.

Since the Lemurian Epoch, the Jesus being, who was partly embodied in the Nathan Jesus, has exercised a harmonizing influence on the human organism. He was an archangelic being who descended to the angelic hierarchy in order to be associated directly with humankind. Rudolf Steiner describes the effect of the threefold permeation of the

Jesus being by Christ (during the Lemurian epoch, the first third of the Atlantean epoch, and the final third of the Atlantean epoch) as harmonizing, accordingly, the *senses*, the *life processes*, and the *soul forces*. The twelve senses were harmonized in such a way by the Jesus being that they maintained an inner balance, a capacity that animals, for example, do not possess. The seven life processes were similarly brought into an equilibrium, whereby the human soul life could experience itself without being absorbed entirely into the separate life processes. One result was the faculty of the vocal expression of the soul by means of speech. Eventually the three soul forces of the astral body—thinking, feeling, and volition—were harmonized so that an "I" experience could manifest. The "I" was no longer submerged completely within the three soul forces, but could have an independent identity. From this arose the faculty of human speech, whereby human beings, through the use of vowels and consonants, could give expression to *objective* phenomena.

During the fifth post-Atlantean epoch, the fourth permeation of the Jesus being by the Christ occurred. The point was to harmonize the "I" just as the physical, etheric, and astral bodies were harmonized before. But the "I" expresses itself through the three aspects of the human being as the forces of the sentient soul, the rational soul, and the consciousness soul, and in such a way that the "I" force, reaching down to the physical body, is experienced as consciousness soul, while the "I" activity reaching into the etheric body is experienced as rational soul, and the "I" being present in the astral body is experienced as the sentient soul. It is the force of love that harmonizes these aspects of the soul, because it is love that holds a person together as a complete being, within whom purposes, feelings, and actions are in accord. Only through love can human ideas and actions be unified; knowledge alone cannot do it. The harmonizing of the "I" forces is accomplished by the love impulse that Jesus Christ brought down into the earth's evolution.

The Coming of Christ would have been impossible, however, if it had not been preceded by a long preparation of awaking conscience. The three parts of the soul had to be awakened fully before love could be born. And in the pre-Christian age, spiritual beings worked toward awaking conscience in the human sentient soul, the rational soul, and the consciousness soul, to make possible the incarnation of Christ. The strongest influence was exerted by three such spiritual beings who effected, out of the angelic hierarchy, the preliminary transformation of the human heart. One of these beings was the one who had worked for long ages through individual human beings, until he incarnated in the sixth century and brought about the event in world history called the "Buddha awakening."

In Gautama Buddha, we are dealing with a being of the third hierarchy. He permeated a human organism *completely*—that is, permeated even the physical body. To form an adequate image of the process by which Prince Siddhartha, son of King Shuddodana Gautama, became a Buddha, we must view the process as an awakening through the power of conscience. Before his enlightenment under the bodhi tree, the prince was a man to whom the spiritual world was closed. The sight of sickness, old age, and death aroused him to inquire, with superhuman strength, into the suffering of humanity and its cause.

It was not through *knowledge* that the hierarchical being living in the Buddha was revealed, but mostly through the *strength* of the questions awaking in him. What distinguished the Buddha from other human initiates of those days was not, to begin with, his outstanding knowledge, since he knew less than the others. For teachings, he went to both Brahmans and penitents; it was the superhuman force of his questions. The superhuman revealed the power of conscience in him. It was the power of conscience that guided him to awaken Buddha consciousness, which revealed a higher wisdom to him. Thus we might say that in the Buddha we see a human consciousness whose human questions were bestowed with a superhuman power of conscience. But if we also recall that a hierarchical being had taken possession of the Buddha's physical organism, we can understand the Buddha event as the origin of the symbolic conscience of the consciousness soul, because the consciousness soul is the aspect of the "I" being that is expressed in the physical body. This also explains the main quality of Buddha conscience—its individuality. The consciousness soul is not social in itself; while living its life in the physical body, it experiences itself as a separate individual, not united to humankind through a community of breath.

And this is why Prince Siddhartha asks this question when he sees a corpse: "Will I die, too?" His questions are about the fate of a single individual, and this is exactly the nature of the consciousness soul. Later, of course, he turns to humanity and preaches the Four Noble Truths of suffering, the cause of suffering, deliverance from suffering, and the paths leading to deliverance from suffering. But even so, both his demeanor and the essence of his teaching are such that he is really addressing separate individuals. The truth of his buddhahood is there for all humankind; the significance of his teaching could never be common to all of humanity. Insofar as it was inevitable that at one time or another humanity would develop a consciousness soul, to that extent the symbolic consciousness soul of the Buddha concerns all human beings; but insofar as the Buddha teaches a path leading to pre-Christian goals, to that extent his teaching concerns only a certain number of individuals of the pre-Christian evolution.

The being who incarnated as the Buddha placed before humankind the awakened individual conscience of the consciousness soul. The activity of another being, whose task was to waken the sentient soul, was quite another matter. To accomplish this, he did not need to descend into a physical body, but worked in the "I" forces of the astral body. Indeed, it would be more accurate to say that, just as the Buddha worked in the physical body (which is interpenetrated by the etheric body), the being named in the Bible as Elijah worked in the astral body, which acts through the ether body. The activity of the Elijah being, as described in the Bible, expresses itself especially by overshadowing a person without merging with the individual, while at the same time bestowing elemental power. The Elijah being does not incarnate, but works through the "I" organization of the astral body, encircling and hovering over it. Like a cloud, it encompasses the person through whom it works, but it does not wholly enter the individual.

When we study the Bible and the persons through whom the Elijah being worked, the impression we get is one of hovering power. But the natural forces through which Elijah's power was exerted—as expressed in the various miracles described in the Old

Testament—is not our essential understanding of the Elijah being. More important than his power over elemental forces is the *moral* activity of the Elijah being. This mainly involves awakening—not the individual but the national conscience of the people of Israel. Thus when, for example, the prophet Naboth Elijah withstood the prophets of Baal (I Kings, 21–22), he was not acting as a mere man, but also as the voice and power of the being who represented the *national* conscience. As he kindled drenched wood on the altar through lightning, by this sign he proclaimed that, although the hearts of Israel were almost inconceivably estranged from the guidance of Yahweh because of service to Baal, they might yet be caught up as by a natural force and enveloped in fire, just as the wet wood had been. If the spiritual and moral force of Yahweh has power to ignite incombustible material in the natural world outside of human beings, will it not have power to kindle the estranged heart of human nature?

In this connection, it will not be out of place to make some essential observations concerning the relationship between the Elijah being and Yahweh. The spiritual guidance of the children of Israel was really far more complicated than is implied by the image—correct certainly, but incomplete—of the "nation led by Yahweh." Picturing this guidance more exactly, we see, in addition to the human leaders, four spiritual beings in particular (a fifth was working in a very hidden way) who control the guidance of the Israelites. Those beings are so closely interwoven that the higher can be seen working *through* those who are subordinate to them, as if they were within them. Thus the "I AM" who spoke to Moses through Yahweh Elohim was the Christ being himself. From the very beginning of the Old Testament, Christ was working through Yahweh, who was as it were the countenance of Christ. Just as the Moon passes sunlight to the Earth during the night, Yahweh passes on the light of the I AM, the Christ.

Now, although the Hebrew people were a "chosen people," they were nevertheless a definite race with their own "folk spirit." It was essential that this folk spirit be one who would be able to embody the universal impulses of humanity in one race. Michael was such an archangel; in a sense, he functioned as the countenance of Yahweh. The Archangel Michael was the folk spirit of the Hebrew race, because he was particularly able to represent and accomplish, as folk spirit, the universal human purposes to be achieved by this race. Now, races have not only folk spirits, but also folk souls. We must not think of the folk soul as a kind of cloudlike aura around a race, merely representing the sum of the individual souls of those who belong to it. The folk soul is a concrete spiritual being who belongs, as a rule, to the angelic hierarchy. To understand this, keep in mind that the evolution leading from a normal individual guardian angel to folk spirit (or archangel) does not occur by fits and starts, but runs its course through certain stages. Before an angel rises to the dignity of archangel, he goes through the folk soul stage, which must be considered the transitional stage from the angelic to the archangelic hierarchy. The folk soul works in a different way than does the folk spirit; it also works differently from the individual guardian angel. What distinguishes it from the individual guardian angel is its comprehensive activity within a race; but what distinguishes it from the folk spirit is the fact that it works more according to angelic than to archangelic methods. We must notice also that not all archangels are folk spirits; some among them are at the transition stage of evolution to the hierarchy of the archai. For instance, there are seven archangels who become time spirits for relatively short periods of time—three or four hundred years. The archai themselves are spirits of epochs, lasting about twenty-two centuries. During this period of an archai being's regency there are seven shorter periods governed by the seven archangels who are rising to the dignity of archai. Something like this also applies to other hierarchies.

This digression was intended to stimulate in the reader not only a schematic picture of the hierarchies, but also an appreciation of their individual multiplicity. It is especially important to recognize this individual multiplicity in relation to the angelic hierarchy, which stands, of course, next in order to humankind. To begin with, we must distinguish at least three groups of angelic beings: angels with specific missions; those who work for cosmic groups of humanity; and those who function as guardian angels. These last, as we have said, are at the stage of preparing for the archangelic hierarchy. To get a clear understanding of the activity of the folk souls, we must compare it with the activity of individual guardian angels and the folk spirits. The guardian angel's special work is to inspire the human "I" while it lingers in the spiritual world during sleep. Archangels, on the other hand, inspire the human astral body once each year at Christmastime. But the folk soul inspires the "I" present in the astral body—that is, it functions in the sentient soul in particular. While the angel meets the human being in sleep, while the "I" and astral body are freed from the etheric and physical bodies, the folk soul meets the human being at the boundary between the astral and etheric bodies, where the astral is associated with the etheric but has not yet descended into the physical; this is where dreams arise. Hence, the folk soul expresses itself mainly through the oracle dreams of a race and in the myths and fables that spring from them. It is not only individuals who dream; races also dream. Through folk dreams, the folk soul attempts to interpret the inspirations of the folk spirit for human consciousness. The folk soul is the interpreter of the folk spirit's purposes, mainly through the symbolic element of creating myths and fables. It communicates the dreams of the race, which dwell in the consciousness soul. For the rational soul, myths and fables are rather insignificant; for the consciousness soul, they have no importance; but for the sentient soul, they have a vigorous life and represent the conscience of a race. Just as the individual conscience in feeling and volition is an inner memory of what a human being has received in sleep while meeting with the angel, likewise the myths and fables of a race are the memory of what its consciousness has retained from meeting with the folk soul, which interprets the folk spirit. In this connection, it is important to mention that around no other character of the Old Testament have more myths grown up among the Jewish people than around the figure of Elijah. Moreover, even in the Bible, the figure of Elijah bears a mythological character. He is the only man in Old Testament history who went alive up to Heaven and on horses of fire.

And there we have the fact enunciated that Elijah was the folk soul of the Hebrew people. The mission of the Elijah being consisted mainly in awakening the popular conscience of that race. But he fulfilled this mission with greater power than that of a normal folk soul being, because the Elijah being was not an angel risen to the rank of a folk soul being but an abnormal angel endowed with archangelic powers, but who had descended to the grade of folk soul. This is why Elijah possessed a power surpassing that of normal folk souls. He was an angel through whom the I AM force of the elohim worked. Hence, he had the power of the second hierarchy; he had power over the elemental forces of fire, air, water, and earth. Within his human personality, Elijah also had more strength than a normal folk soul. Whereas a normal folk soul works by creating myths and fables, Elijah not only produced images in the consciousness of the sentient soul, but he also endowed these images with objective elemental power, so that they became events, or "miracles." In this way, emotions of the human soul were to be evoked, through which consciousness of Israel's vocation would be awakened. Elijah's effect on humankind was like thunder and lightning; into stirred human hearts flashed a lightning-like perception of the forgotten covenant with Yahweh. They were converted; they experienced a change of heart. This characteristic of Elijah's activity lived long in human memory. The peasants of pre-Revolutionary Russia still thought of the Elijah being as the spirit that revealed itself in thunder. "Elijah is angry," they would say when a storm was raging.

This saying is more profound than it appears at first sight, because the force of Elijah that evoked the emotions of human souls was the force of the righteous wrath of the spirit world. In Elijah was manifested the herald of the coming world "storm," the day of judgment for the Earth and its dwellers. Creative lines of force mounted up from the Elijah being into the Father sphere. The highest source of the Elijah forces can be found in the sphere of the Father, because the Yahweh Elohim who upheld Elijah was not only the countenance of the Christ, but also the directing hand of the Father. That Yahweh had taken Israel under his protection meant not only that the eye of the Son rested on this people, but also that the hand of the Father, guarding and punishing, was outstretched over its destiny. Humankind as a whole, however, cannot comprehend the love of the Father. The highest perception of love to which human beings can rise in the life between birth and death is to perceive the love of the Son. Yet humankind experiences the love of the Father in the righteous wrath that represents the highest power in the cosmos. That highest power was active in Elijah when, through the emotions of the human sentient soul, he brought about national penitence and national humiliation. When, through spiritual insight, the Buddha set the ideal individual conscience before humankind when Elijah, through emotions, stirred from without and awakened to life the conscience of the community, a third being was working to prepare for the birth of the perfect conscience in a way that would unite the two polarities.

To understand the activity of the Nathan Jesus (as distinct from Zoroaster) during the period before his fourth sacrificial permeation by the Christ being, we must first notice that even while he was preparing himself for the mission of harmonizing the human "I" forces—even during this preliminary activity—he was already exercising a harmonizing and balancing influence. This was possible especially because the rational or intellectual soul already in itself represented a balance between the sentient soul directed outward and the consciousness soul directed inward. This is precisely why Rudolf Steiner chose the name "rational soul" (or intellectual soul) for this member of the human soul. It unites within itself a dual nature: reason, inclining more toward the sentient soul, and intellect, inclining more to the consciousness soul. These two poles of the rational soul may also be seen as the polarity of artistic imagination versus logical apprehension. While the special influence of the Jesus being on the rational soul was the awaking of its conscience, the work was carried on from two directions: on the one side by rational impulses evoked by outer impressions, and later metamorphosed into faculties of thought; and on the other side, by spiritual insight awakened by thoughts that, later on, would lead to actions arising from the consciousness. The first side of Jesus' activity is seen especially in the spiritual tendency handed down in the figures of Apollo and Orpheus, the "son of Apollo." The expression of this activity was the powerful musical influence that prepared human minds for the evolution of thought in Europe, of which Rudolf Steiner spoke on several occasions.[5] The art impulse that preceded the luxuriant thought life of Hellenism can be traced to its source in the inspiration of the Jesus being.

The other line taken by the activity of the Jesus being can be seen in the figure of Krishna as it has been preserved for us in the Bhagavad Gita, for example. The Bhagavad Gita, the book about Krishna, does not deal with art but contains doctrine that instills an epitome of thoughts for guidance. These thoughts, however, are not an end in themselves, but have the purpose of effecting a definite change in the consciousness of those who accept them. When Krishna expounds to Arjuna his teaching on the three *gunas* (the three conditions of the soul), he points to a fourth condition wherein the soul rises to become a free "I" self above those three *gunas* that human beings have in common with nature. By urging the human individual toward freedom from the group soul mentality, he prepares the way for individual conscience. The conquest of the group soul mentality was of primary importance for Arjuna as he stood wavering at the head of one army and opposite another in which the enemies confronting him were really his nearest and dearest. It was only after he had received the whole teaching of Krishna, which had been inspired by the Jesus being, that he decided to fight. The individual insight proved stronger than the group soul mentality—this is the event in the spiritual history of humankind that was enacted on the battlefield of Kurukshetra. Spiritual understanding of *dharma* (the law of karma) prepared the way for individual conscience as inner knowledge, brought into being by Krishna.

Thus the Jesus being was, on the one hand, active in the reason, preparing the experience of the communal conscience, and, on the other, active in the intellect, preparing the experience of the individual conscience standing and thus effectively acting between the great polarities, Elijah and the Buddha.

Thus three beings worked together to prepare the birth of the conscience by means of which the Christ was able to descend to Earth. For the conscience which was to receive the Christ into itself must be fully awake, that is to say, it must be awake in the sentient soul, in the rational soul, and in the consciousness soul. But what does it mean when we say that the conscience must be fully awake in these three members of the soul? It means that the consciousness of manas, budhi, and atma are all present. Before we can realize the true depth of the stirring spectacle of the three sheaths of the Nathan Jesus as he walked the path to baptism in the Jordan, we must first recognize the atma power, the budhi life, and the manas light acting on the physical, etheric, and astral bodies of the one who walked the path to the Jordan baptism. This wakefulness of the outer threefold conscience resulted from the collaboration of the three beings who had been preparing for this wonderful eventuality throughout long ages. The Buddha rays were active in it; the Elijah power prepared the way before it; and the Jesus life filled it. All of the sacred melodies of Orpheus, all the enlightenment of the Buddha, the whole-hearted readiness of Jesus for willing, generous sacrifice—and, yes, even the ripest fruits of the great Zoroaster's experience—all lived in the figure of the awakened conscience of humanity as it walked the path to the Jordan.

The lines followed in preparing the birth of this conscience were, in reality, complicated even more than it would seem from the processes we have tried to outline in these meditations. But regardless of how complicated they were, they all had one thing in common: like every birth, the birth of conscience, which had to manifest before the incarnation of the Christ, was a painful process. This has been the law of all birth since the Fall of humankind—the law of physical birth as well as the birth of a new consciousness; any new thing that is to come into the world will have its place prepared by pain. Ever since the Fall, every position in the world has been occupied; there is no room for anything new; place for any new thing must be paid for by sacrifice. Consequently, the path leading to spiritual perception, to spiritual revelation, is a path through pain to the high happiness of a sunlit conscience. Joy is the promise given to humanity by divine guidance; but joy can come to birth only when a way is opened for it by pain. Conscience is the highest human good; humankind sees it from only one side by thinking of it as a source of inner unrest—the "sting of conscience." This is true, but human beings will learn through time that it can be an inexhaustible source of joy as well. It is the inner Sun, which has power to irradiate all the dark places of life. This was the Sun by whose light Paul fell, blinded to the Earth as he journeyed toward Damascus. He spoke of this Sun when he wrote, "Not I, but Christ liveth in me" (Galatians 2:20).

# Chapter 7

# The Karma of the Israelites

## The Two Main Karmic Currents in Human History

In the previous study, we tried to suggest the inner structure of the activities of spiritual forces—the spiritual forces that helped form a human organism capable of receiving the Christ. The reflections of the last study should show, moreover, that such action was not confined to the Israelite community, but included all the progressive spiritual movements among human beings, which brought us to the baptism at the Jordan. This guidance by suprasensory beings from the spiritual world is, however, only one side of the history of Israel seen as a whole. The other side comprises the action of human forces, either uniting with the higher guidance or setting themselves in opposition to it from below. The conjunction of these two currents leads to the reality of all events described in the Bible—the *karma* of the children of Israel.

Now we might be tempted to think of karma in this way: Above is spiritual guidance; below are human forces that either resist or do not resist the purposes of this spiritual guidance. They resist when the purposes are too high for them, and fall in with them when they can rise to that level. In other words, we might assume that only divine and human forces are concerned. In reality, however, there is yet a third set of forces, neither divine nor human in nature: the forces of cosmic evil, which also strive to influence human nature, not, like the hierarchies of good, from the various spheres of the spiritual world, but from the different strata of the Earth's interior. If we are to understand human attitudes toward spiritual guidance, we must consider this third factor—that is, the counter-guidance of humankind from within the Earth.

In his lecture "Good and Evil: Individual Karmic Questions," Rudolf Steiner gives us the help we need to understand enough about the interior of the Earth for the purposes of this study.[1] There, he indicates the main characteristics of the nine spheres of the Earth's interior. Because all readers of these meditations are no doubt familiar with the substance of that lecture, we do not need to repeat it and can simply state the question that arises: What is the significance of the nine spheres of the Earth's interior for individual human karma and for that of humanity as a whole?

If we contemplate the function of the nine spiritual hierarchies in their relationship to humankind, we see it as a realization of the divine archetype of the human being's ninefold nature. The goal of the hierarchies is the ideal human being—that is, one whose physical, etheric, and astral bodies, and whose sentient, rational, and consciousness souls have become the perfect expression of the spirit body, the life spirit, and the spirit self. In the spiritual world, there are thus nine archetypes of the nine parts of human nature; and the realization of these archetypes in humankind is the prime purpose of the whole spiritual cosmos of good. The primal purpose of cosmic evil, on the other hand, is to establish in the nine parts of human nature a tendency to oppose this. Hence the archetypes of good are confronted by nine counterparts, which may become models for shaping the human being. We must not think of the nine archetypes of evil as merely empirical polarities of the divine archetypes, but rather as corresponding forces and substances contained in the nine spheres of the interior of the Earth. The nine spheres of the interior of the Earth are the cosmic storehouse of the forces and substances from which the powers of evil will form the ninefold nature of the *evil* human being who is their victim.

Thus the mineral stratum of Earth is the sphere that supplies substance and forces for the evil counterpart of the physical body. Because we have absorbed mineral substances into our physical body, we are already involved in the first sphere of evil. And because of the Fall of humankind, human beings have bound the physical body to a mineral body. The true physical body is the volitional organism (not the personal will but its organism) of humanity, and it is this organism to which Rudolf Steiner applies the term *phantom.*[2] The fact that it is bound to a mineral body is, on the one hand, the cause of weakness in human beings, who must always carry their prison around with them. On the other hand, however, it is a pledge to the future triumphal glory of spiritual force over material inertia.

The second stratum of the interior of the Earth (fluid earth) contains the counterforces of the etheric body, while the third stratum (gaseous earth) contains the counterforces of the astral body. The next three strata (form earth, fruit earth, and fire earth) contain the counterforces of the sentient soul, the rational soul, and the consciousness soul. The sixth stratum of the interior of Earth contains the opposite of the consciousness soul, and is, in fact, the ahrimanic stratum of the Earth's interior. In the present epoch, this stratum projects very dangerous impulses to the surface of the Earth, while the next three will not reveal their activity in human history until a future time. The ninth stratum of the interior of the Earth (the core) contains spiritual evil—that is, forces standing as high on the ladder of evil as the forces of the spirit body (atma) stand on the ladder of good. This classification can be presented and left only in a tabular form; the task before us does not allow us to go into greater detail, but it is quite possible to pursue the subject further by means of Rudolf Steiner's lecture, "Good and Evil: Individual Karmic Questions."

Now we can ask how the ideal human archetype can be pictured. Occultism offers this answer: Work steadfastly to place Jesus Christ before you in his reality, to understand him, and to experience him, whereby you will realize that the archetype of the human being was, by the will of God, present on Earth in the person of the one who arose from the dead. He is the prototype not just of the human being, but also of the gods, who have to make the human being in his image, and human beings must strive to be like him. The nine aspects of his risen nature present the ideal embodiment of the nine parts of human nature. Therefore Jesus Christ is the interpretation of human evolution. The hierarchies of evil, however, set up an opposition to this interpretation. It consists in the incarnation of the ninefold organism of the Antichrist—which is neither a fable nor merely a principle or a universal impulse, but a real being with the mission of presenting an absolute prototype for the evolution of humankind toward evil. In him, a human creature will appear in the cosmos, formed entirely from the nine strata of the Earth's interior. Just as Jesus Christ represents the concrete revelation of the nine hierarchical spheres, the Antichrist will represent a concrete revelation of the nine strata of the interior of the Earth.

This is why there have been, since the Atlantean epoch, two main occult tendencies that have become karmic currents. True, there is still a third, which might be called a "compromise tendency," but this will disappear entirely in the future. When the time comes for the division of humanity—first into two civilizations (during the sixth culture epoch) and then into two main races—there can be no compromise tendency; everyone will have to make a decision as to which of the two types of human evolution one will choose.

The two tendencies indicated initially found expression in the white and black forms of magic during the Atlantean epoch. Those who left Atlantis under the guidance of Manu and established post-Atlantean settlements in Central Asia belonged to the movement that tried to realize the human archetype according to the will of God. This movement was continued in the Persian civilization founded by the great Zoroaster. The other movement, however, took the form of the Turanian civilization. The conflict between Persians and Turanians was a karmic continuation of the primal Atlantean antagonism. The same conflict reappeared later in the antagonism between Yahweh worship and Baal worship. The fact that this conflict, despite numerous temporary setbacks, ended with the victory of Yahweh worship is because of the advent of Jesus Christ on Earth. Even after that, however, the spiritual conflict certainly has not ceased. In the later Persian Empire, a stronghold was set up in defense of the Antichrist, when a center of occult and cultural activity was formed in Gondishapur by the leaders of this movement, whereas the activity of the other movement radiated mainly from Ireland. The central region, however (the Mediterranean countries), was then under the political and spiritual dominion of Rome. After the influence of Gondishapur had been "blunted" (Rudolf Steiner's term) by the seventh-century tide of Islam, it made its way slowly through the centuries by the roundabout path of Arabism into the Christian world, until the nineteenth century, when it celebrated triumphal progress over the Earth in the outer form of Western materialism.[3]

These are the main lines of activity of Christian and anti-Christian inspiration in human history. What we called the karmic current of "immortal Israel" in the first study is really the movement described here; it strives to realize the human archetype intended by the hierarchies of good. This movement could equally be called the karmic current of "immortal Iran." In terms of the purpose of these meditations, however, the first term is preferable.

Once we have come to recognize the existence of the two main currents of human evolution, we are confronted by this problem: How can there be a karmic tendency toward evil? After death, everyone passes through the purification of kama loca and prepares the next incarnation from the realm of good, or Devachan. So, if an individual cannot take the evil of one incarnation into the next, the thread of evil must certainly be broken with each death. In the next life, is it not the case that one bears only the *consequences* of the evil from the former incarnation, not the evil itself?

To solve this problem, we must consider not only what happens in the spiritual world when we pass into the state between two incarnations, but also what happens during this time in the interior of the Earth. While individuals are in the kama loca state and receiving moral impulses to correct the wrongful acts they have committed, the "double" in the interior of the Earth is simultaneously receiving the reflection of these impulses, or antagonistic inspirations. Thus, when we are born once again on the Earth, we arrive with, on the one hand, the inner experience of the spiritual world of good, but also, in opposition to this, the experience that our double has undergone in the realm of evil. Consequently, during the life between birth and death, one must *overcome* evil; we can never "free" ourselves of it merely by escaping from it. The evil that is not overcome in earthly life endures, and human beings will repeatedly find themselves in close association with it until they have conquered it during the time between birth and death. This clearly shows that there is an unbroken current of evil. The threads of evil in humankind are drawn from one incarnation into the next through the strata of the Earth's interior, just as the threads of good in humankind are drawn through the incarnations by way of the heavenly spheres of kama loca and Devachan. So we can understand how it may happen that, for example, a man takes revenge on another in his next incarnation.[4] Most certainly, this man did not form his idea of revenge in the kama loca state, much less in the devachanic period, but it may happen nevertheless (though it need not happen) that the man avenges himself in the next life. The thread of revengeful thought will not have passed through the heavenly realm, but through the underworld of the interior of the Earth. In this way the continuity of evil arises in human karma, and so a karmic current of evil is also present in humankind.

We might anxiously ask: If this is the case, then isn't almost everyone certain to be involved in the karmic current of evil? It is immensely important to understand that what human beings call "righteousness," even "holiness," is not "righteousness before God." We need only remember the words of Jesus Christ: "None is good, save one, that is, God" (Luke 18:19). In determining to which of the two karmic tendencies certain people belong, it is not the external faults and virtues that must be considered, but their inner attitude toward the spiritual world. It is not faults that decide the matter, but denial and denunciation of the spirit. The Gospel word is quite literally true that says all sins may be forgiven except sin against the Holy Ghost; and the decision depends upon this. It is fundamentally wrong to regard a Lenin, for example, as a criminal in the *human* sense. He was, by contrast, a man who was freed from many human weaknesses simply because he abandoned himself completely to the influence of that horrible movement, so inimical to the human race. Indeed he was less subject to such weaknesses than many who stood on a Christian and humane footing. Human defects and sins are compensated by personal human karma—people may either annul them of their own free will through acts of sacrifice, or they may need to cancel them through suffering—the spiritual world pities people for this, but does not condemn them. Sin against the Holy Spirit, on the other hand, is a crime against the whole cosmos; through it, one becomes an enemy to the whole spiritual world.

By learning to distinguish "righteousness before men" from "righteousness before God," we also come to understand why the saints of the Bible (including the Gospels) are so far from "saintly." King David, for instance, is mentioned in many passages of the Old Testament *and* in the Gospels as a model of righteousness. But if we read the story of his life we must admit that the traditional idea of a "saint" does not apply to his character. The key to this problem is supplied by the fact that "saintliness" in terms of the Bible means something fundamentally different from what we imagine as a result of the influence of ecclesiastical Christianity. The Bible does not mean "righteousness before men"—righteousness in the soul's relationship to the material world—but "righteousness before God"—righteousness in the soul's relationship to the spiritual world. The soul is situated between two worlds, oscillating continually between the higher and the lower. There are thus two kinds of merit and two kinds of sin. In this lower world, humankind as a whole cannot be "saintly," or faultless, so long as the consequences of the "Fall" endure. People can make an honest effort to be *healthy*, but not saintly. On the higher level, however, human beings can be united in truth and reverence with the spiritual world. Thus, "righteousness before God" is the right relationship between a human being and the spiritual world; it is the fulfillment of the spiritual mission of humankind on Earth.

This is the sense in which we can understand the two spiritual karmic currents. The standard established for them is not human virtue but spirituality, or genuine human morality, ringing true not only on Earth, but also in heaven. Therefore, the philadelphic community of the sixth cultural epoch will consist not of "saints" but of spiritually minded people, just as "evil" humanity will consist not of criminals but of those who deny the Spirit. The philadelphic community will establish and realize a standard of innocence that many will attain.

The choice of the karmic current depends on this true morality, springing up and growing in secret. It does, of course, produce also an outer morality—a wakefulness of conscience in all the details of life—but this external morality is, nevertheless, merely a karmic consequence of the inner morality, just as the disappearance of many symptoms of disease is a consequence of the inner cure of the organism. It is the healing of human thinking, feeling, and volition through the force of inner morality. In the eyes of the spiritual world, "sinners" are sick and must be not judged, but healed. From the perspective of truth, all human weaknesses are symptoms of disease; they will not be overcome by the contrary symptoms of health, or human virtues, but by inwardly healing the life of the soul. It is the health forces of the spiritual world that effect the cure, not precepts, principles, and judgments.

Once we really comprehend these truths, we can answer, at a higher level, the question concerning the character of those who form part of the "white" karmic current. Then the decisive factor will no longer be looked for and found in human nature, since it still contains within itself the consequences of the "Fall," but rather in the conduct and demeanor of the free human "I." And this gives a completely different picture of the facts, because now we can see the fundamental truth that all human beings may belong to the "white" movement.

This is also the reason why the expression "immortal Israel" should not be understood in the sense of Calvin's doctrine of predestination—that a certain number of individuals are "elect" for all eternity. In reality, fresh individuals attach themselves to the "white movement," just as there are also karmic traitors who forsake it and join the opposite side. The two main karmic movements offer continual opportunity for entering and leaving. Nor is this contradicted by the fact that there are a number of individuals (and this is especially true of the leaders) who from the earliest ages have belonged with complete decision to one or the other side.

These two movements are the visible expressions of the two sources of inspiration in human history: the spiritual world and the interior of the Earth. The inspirations from below are, as it were, inverted copies of the true inspirations from the spiritual world. So it may happen that when gods are speaking in the heights of the spiritual world, demons in the depths below are turning what they say into its opposite. When we can consider, from this point of view, the grand picture of tragic world history that shows Moses on the mount receiving the revelation from Yahweh Elohim, and at the same time the Israelites at the foot of the mount worshipping the golden calf, we put our finger on the point in time when the lower inspiration entered the spiritual life of Israel as a national experience. From that moment on, the inspiration of the false Messiah found a way into the Israelites' spiritual life. After that, the whole history of the children of Israel involved conflict not just with surrounding hostile forces, but also with this other inspiration within the community itself. The other inspiration was the opposite of the expectation of Christ; it was the expectation of the highest incarnation of the principle of force on Earth. Even after the fulfillment of the Christ's coming, the influence of this other inspiration continues; even now the expectation of a Messiah is still alive. The moment they dedicated themselves to the golden calf, an entry for Baal worship was opened in the hearts of the people of Israel. That was the moment when the tragic karma of the Israelite race began.

## Yahweh and Baal in the Destiny of Israel

The more deeply we investigate the picture of Moses on the heights receiving inspirations from the spiritual world, with the people below dedicating themselves to the golden calf, the more clearly can we recognize in our hearts the basic impulse of Israel's destiny. True, the golden calf is not yet Baal worship, but it opened the door to Baal worship. When the Israelites chose the symbol of the Bull as an expression of what was to be held in the highest honor, a change of direction took place in the current of their communal will; the will current, which had been directed toward the future, was now reversed toward the past. The inner meaning of the Exodus from Egypt was precisely a renunciation of the Bull cult, or the past, represented by the zodiacal forces of Taurus. In the desert, where no influences of past civilizations could reach them, the Israelites would immerse themselves in the movement of the future, the cult of the Ram, represented by the zodiacal forces of Aries. By directing their will toward the past, the Israelites severed themselves from the spiritual source of inspiration (to become incarnate in the future) from which the revelations of Moses were drawn. As a consequence of this severance, however, a door was opened for another inspiration of the future. The inevitable result of ceasing to strive after future progress, with all its risks and conflict, is to set up another future, differing from the one originally intended. Nothing can be *without* a future; if the future intended by the spiritual world is renounced, human beings find themselves on paths leading to a different future, one designed from the interior of the Earth. This situation can be more clearly represented in this way: Imagine a horizontal arrow from left to right as the spiritual guidance incarnating in the future, and below it another arrow representing the corresponding human will current striving toward the future.

The resulting figure shows the conditions of a lasting and correct inspiration (see first figure). If, on the other hand, the will current turns toward the past, a hiatus occurs—an empty space in the relationship between the higher guidance and the will. This empty space can then be filled from *below* by a force that replaces the absent human will (second figure).

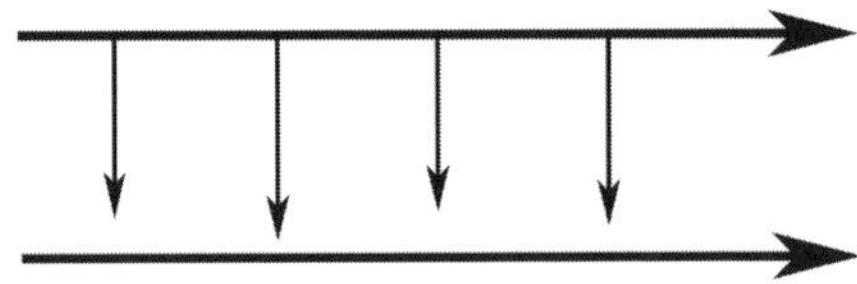

Something like this happened with the backsliding race in the wilderness; it developed a spiritual inclination toward the Baal impulse, an inner urge toward the Baal future. From that time on, the will was always present in the chosen race to give themselves up to Baal worship; potential readiness to accept the Baal movement was thenceforth a constant danger to the spiritual mission of Israel.

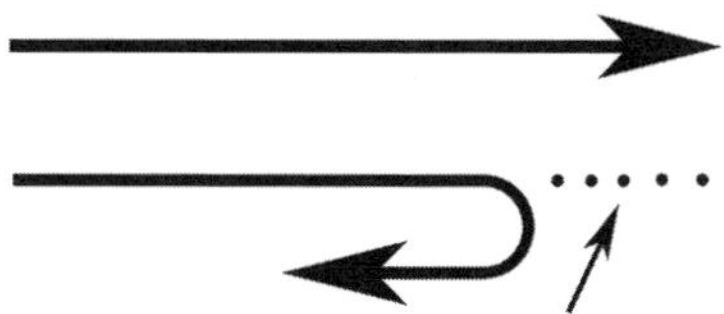

To appreciate the seriousness of this danger, it is essential to understand the nature of the Baal cult as the opposite of the Yahweh cult; and for this, we must grasp the truth that each epoch of human evolution has a certain mission, not just in the realm of general civilization, but also in the realm of occultism. This mission may be viewed as the correct "method" for the average student of mystery wisdom in that particular epoch. For example, the method that was used until 1879 was to develop the logical initiative forces of the *head,* with the response given out of the *heart* forces. The mission of the last epoch was to create a circulatory system of question and answer between head and heart. Today, the mission is again different. It consists of an insight depending upon thought, attained by the development of conscience forces whose power is to be exercised in the creative word.

During the time of the ancient Israelites, the mission was to produce a direct current of influence from the consciousness center of the head to the will center of the metabolic system. What was outwardly known as "the law" was also a method of inner evolution. In reality, "law" meant simply that the will had to subject itself to certain revealed thoughts. It did not include the heart culture of free morality, which did not become possible until a later epoch of evolution. In the time of the Israelites, the instinctive will life was governed directly by specifically revealed thought contents, imbued by the power of Yahweh with a force that was, in fact, able to control the life of will. We can clearly understand the nature of this method if, as a starting point for deeper study, we consider Rudolf Steiner's discussion of the work of the prophets and sibyls.[5] Those lectures as a whole offer one of the most important keys to the understanding of the Old Testament, if the impetus to further study is received from within.

Every method of every epoch runs the risk of being changed into its opposite. In the Old Testament epoch, that risk was represented by the Baal method. This involved raising the instinctive will life directly into the head, allowing it to dominate the human life of imagination and thinking. When the unpurified will struck upward from below, the powers of the Earth's interior were able to pervert the whole imaginative life. As a result, another "law" arose, infusing the most perverse ideas into the minds of human beings. The precepts of this "law" seemed right to those concerned, precisely because their natures were filled with the very will power that had created those precepts. This was the origin, for example, of the command that the firstborn children were to be sacrificed.

If the Baal method had ousted the Yahweh (or "I") method—if the state of mind expressed by the words "devouring fire of the will fills me and drives me to action" had conquered the frame of mind represented by "reverently I bow before the wisdom of God and yield myself to his will"—then the incarnation of Christ on Earth would have been impossible, and *perhaps* some other being might have incarnated. This would have been disastrous for humankind.

Now, if we study, for example, the Books of Kings in the Old Testament in this light, we realize the enormity of the risks that attended the continuation of the Yahweh mission. Often the Yahweh current was merely a thin thread in imminent danger of breaking; it seemed many times that it would certainly be overcome by the Baal current. In this conflict there were, in fact, moments when the whole future of Israel's mission hung by a slender thread. Such an instance was the betrayal of Yahweh when, under the guidance of Moses, Israel lived in Shittim (Numbers 25:1). The betrayal was brought about by the Midianite and Moabite women who, through the counsel of the Magus Balaam, son of Beor of Pethor (Numbers 31:16), were abducted from the leaders of Moab and Midian as a means to an end. The end in view was actually attained, "And Israel joined himself unto Baalpeor: and the anger of the Lord was kindled against Israel" (Numbers 25:3).

Karmically, the "pleasure" and the "anger" of the Lord indicated prosperity and destruction, life and death. In this case, death would destroy the greater number of the Israelite community. Indeed, if death had struck down all those who were corrupted by the Baal influence, the history of Israel might even have had to begin afresh as a small tribe of a few thousand, where Abraham, Isaac, and Jacob had begun. And they would have died because they were no longer fit for further service to the mission of Israel—indeed, they had actually become a danger to it. This was because the direction of the current in the ether body was altered for all those who were victims of the magic exercised consciously by the hostile priest kings. The Yahweh current, which flowed downward from above, was replaced by the Baal current directed upward from below. Those who were affected became *organic* antagonists of the Yahweh mission.

Now, in a flash, a change took place in this disastrous destiny. Phinehas, the grandson of Aaron, acted in a way that changed the course of the karmic current (Numbers 25:11). To understand the mystery behind this change of destiny, we must go even more deeply than before into the work of the Elijah being.

## The Karmic Mission of the Elijah Being in Old Testament History

In the previous study, we tried to describe the Elijah being as the folk soul of the ancient Israelites, though an abnormal folk soul, descended from a height and using forces greater than those of a normal folk soul. These greater possibilities lay, on the one hand, in the forces that the Elijah being possessed and, on the other, in the intimate relationship he had established with human individualities. Functioning not only as a folk soul, but also as the protective spirit of a single human being, he was able to work so that the actions of one man held karmic significance for the whole race. Through his special connection with the individual, the acts of that individual could gain the significance of racial actions for the karmic history of Israel. Thus, the Elijah being became a bond between the spiritual guidance of the Israelite race and its human will current. He was concerned with both the one and the other side of its complete karmic history.

We can picture him as the inward lightning of spiritual guidance, flashing into the human will with the significance of a racial event.

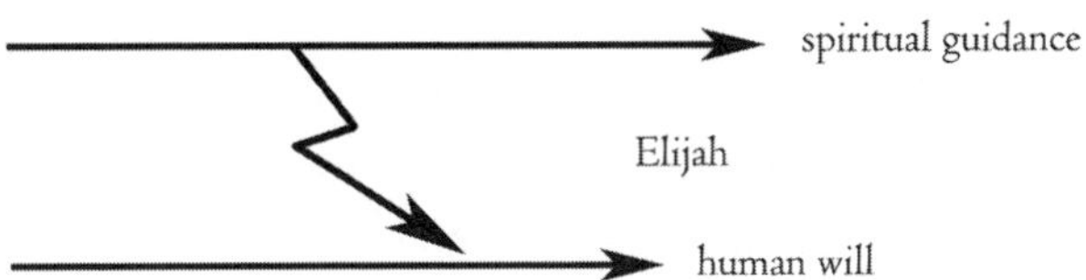


In this way, the Elijah being caused a strengthening and turning of the racial will in the direction of right. This happened the moment Phinehas, the son of Eleazar, took a javelin in his hand. His hand performed an act that had not just individual but also universal significance.

> So the plague was stayed from the children of Israel. And those that died in the plague were twenty and four thousand. And the Lord spake unto Moses, saying, "Phinehas, the son of Eleazar, the son of Aaron the priest, hath turned my wrath away from the children of Israel, while he was zealous for my sake among them, that I consumed not the children of Israel in my jealousy." (Numbers 25:8–11)

With these words, the Bible expresses the situation described. This was not the result of any outer action by Phinehas; indeed, twenty-four thousand were killed. Outwardly, it did not in itself bring about an exemption; its power consided in fact that the act was performed by the folk soul in the human will.[6] It changed the direction of the race's karma, because in it the will of the folk soul acted in cooperation with the individual human will. We must bear in mind that, at the moment of Phinehas's intervention, a shock convulsed the whole of Israel and healed it from the inner effects of the Baal influence. The ether bodies of the people were altered by the shock to the degree that they again became "Yahweh ether bodies." In other words, the direction of the circular current within them was altered. The "forgiveness" that came to the race was in fact healing. It is mainly true, even today, that every act of forgiveness signifies a healing of the soul or body. We have only to think in the sense of Christ's words, "Thy sins be forgiven thee ... arise and walk" (Matthew 9:2, 5).

Again, in the second period of Israel's history, the Elijah being intervenes to save. In the time of the kings (from David to the Babylonian captivity), the time of the government of Ahab and Jezebel was spiritually the most dangerous. During that period, Baal worship was the official national and state religion. The condition of the Israelites' spiritual life at the time is most clearly indicated in the words of Elijah Naboth:

> And Elijah came unto all the people, and said, "How long halt ye between two opinions? If the Lord be God, follow him: but if Baal, then follow him." And the people answered him not a word. Then said Elijah unto the people, "I, even I only, remain a prophet of the Lord; but Baal's prophets are four hundred and fifty men." (I Kings 18:21–22)

This then was the proportion between the two currents at that time: one prophet of Yahweh against four hundred and fifty prophets of Baal, confronted by an undecided race seeking compromise and easily led. In the previous study, we spoke of the meaning of Elijah Naboth's act on Mount Carmel. Here the point is to understand that act from another point of view—one that is quite natural when we compare the deed of Phinehas with that of Elijah Naboth. In the first case, it was the impulse of a human soul to which was given the power of an event in nature, by which the corrupt ether bodies were restored to health. In the second case, however, it was a natural occurrence (lightning from heaven) to which a humanly moral effect was given. It brought about the decision in favor of Yahweh in the souls of those present. The first act was a purification of the ether body; similarly, the second was extended to the astral body. Thus the astral body was cleansed from the Baal impulse, and the mission of Israel was saved once more.

We may realize that the action of Elijah Naboth was concerned mainly with the astral body, not only from the description in the Bible, but also from the stage of development the Israelite race had reached. If during the first stage of growth (from the Exodus to the reign of David) the ether body could be corrupted because it was not yet fully formed; thus during the era from David to the Babylonian captivity the astral body could be corrupted, because during that time it was in process of formation. Evil, in fact, always works *in advance*; its constant endeavor is to secure deformity. Thus, for example, during a period when the ether body is already "born" (or self-dependent), it makes a special effort to attack the astral organism, so that the appropriate birth of the astral body may be prevented, and a deformity is produced instead. This was precisely the task of the Baal worship carried on by Jezebel and Ahab. During the time when Israel was passing through the stage in which the astral body is prepared (corresponding in a human life to the period between the seventh and fourteenth years), an astral quality was to be injected into the race, and this would have given the astral body a form different from that intended by the spiritual guidance. We can understand the whole activity of both Elijah Naboth and Elijah Elisha if we think of it as a healing of the astral body.[7] This activity is described in detail by Rudolf Steiner in the fifth lecture of his *Turning Points in Spiritual History*. Hence, in general, it is not necessary to go more deeply into the subject. Only one detail needs mention—the violent death of Naboth at the hands of Jezebel and Ahab. That event is important insofar as it is an example of the karmic continuity of evil (as mentioned at the beginning of this study). In this event, we see how the past can avenge itself on the future. Overshadowed by Elijah, Phinehas kills the leader of the tribe of Simeon, who has prostituted passion to the service of Baal worship; and now Naboth, overshadowed by Elijah, is killed by Jezebel and Ahab, who have given themselves up to Baal worship. The activity of Elijah could not, in any case, have been interrupted by this, because he could continue his work through a different personality, Elisha. But the act of vengeance was accomplished nevertheless. This shows us how impulses from the past persist and work out in the distant future.

The Elijah being appears a third time on the stage of Israel's history in the critical years just preceding the advent of Christ on Earth. In arresting words, the prophet Malachi speaks of the necessity for Elijah's appearance and of the solemnity of the time:

> Behold, I will send you Elijah the prophet before the coming of the great and dreadful day of the Lord: And he shall turn the heart of the fathers to the children, and the heart of the children to their fathers, lest I come and smite the Earth with a curse. (Malachi 4:5–6)

The folk soul of Israel functioned as a folk soul for the last time in the figure of John the Baptist. Thus it is appropriate to study as Old Testament history all that took place up to the moment of the baptism of Jesus in the Jordan. That event is the exact boundary between the Old and New Testaments. Until the moment of the Jordan baptism, even the thirty years of Jesus' life was part of the preparation for Christ's coming and, therefore, part of the Old Testament. This digression is needed to justify the study of John the Baptist in a work devoted to the Old Testament. The mission of John the Baptist is linked so closely to the Old Testament that it cannot be separated from it. It is easy to see this when we realize that it was the Elijah being who was active in John, rounding out the work of preparation—that is, the work of the whole of Old Testament history. And we can understand the nature of this rounding out by studying the procedure at the Jordan baptism.

The baptism was merely the last stage of a certain change of heart that the disciples of John were bound to pass through. Before they attained the baptism with water, they had to experience a certain relaxation of hold in the ether body; the loosened ether body needed to free itself partially from the physical body at the moment of baptism. The preliminary loosening of the ether body—assisted even further during the first century of our era through a natural facility—was brought about by the power of the awakening conscience. The word of John possessed, in particular, the power of waking the conscience of the face. The preaching of the Baptist should not be considered merely as a criticism of the time, and even less a moral sermon; it possessed the quality of lightning force we saw in the Elijah being. True, this force no longer expressed itself in outer miracles, because it had been raised to the highest miracle—the awakening of conscience. It was neither in actions nor in prophecies that the mysterious power of John the Baptist was revealed; it was in his *voice*. In response to the question of who he was—whether a prophet (a foreteller of the future) or Elijah (the miracle worker of the past)—John answered that he was neither a purveyor of revelations nor a doer of miracles; rather, he was the *voice* of one who speaks out of the loneliness of conscience. Indeed, the whole power of John was in his voice. John spoke outwardly as conscience speaks inwardly. No one could forget his voice; it penetrated to the most hidden depths of the soul. John did not say: It is written, the kingdom of heaven is at hand. He did not even say: God has revealed to me that the kingdom of heaven is at hand. No, John simply said: The kingdom of heaven is at hand. And everyone who heard him could discern in his *voice* the presence of the kingdom.

To understand this, it is essential to know that all human faculties pass through three stages in maturing—the stages Rudolf Steiner calls *imagination, inspiration,* and *intuition.* These three stages may appear in very different ways, according to which faculty (out of the seven human faculties) is functioning in a given situation. In fact, there are twenty-one modes of expression of the seven suprasensory faculties. One of these faculties is the *Word.* Likewise, the faculty of the Word evolves through three stages. The first stage of the Word involves being able to impart to others what we have learned of the spiritual world. The second stage of the Word is attained when the spiritual world also speaks through the human being. The third and highest stage of evolution of the Word is a language whereby a new revelation is granted to the physical as well as to the spiritual world. In that stage, human and spirit world speak and listen simultaneously; the spirit world reveals its mysteries to humanity, and humanity reveals its secrets to the spirit world. The human being is not a tradition monger or a prophet, but a voice that speaks from and for both worlds at once, a voice that has its source in the loneliness of a conscience become one with the spiritual world.

John spoke from his own being in the deepest sense; as he did so, the Elijah being spoke through him. The lightning of Elijah's revelation functioned in the voice of John. His words lived in human minds and worked changes of thinking—an awakening of conscience. The forces of conscience—experienced to begin with as an enlightened courage conquering shame and fear—loosened the ether body through the shock of this conquest. When the ether body had been sufficiently loosened by this means, one was prepared to experience baptism. This experience involved viewing the life tableau, the true picture of one's whole life. At the baptism, as those being baptized experienced their own being as a spectator outside their life current, the baptism signified to them the awakening of the true "I." Thus John Elijah prepared the "I" human, so that Christ might find those who had awakened from the delirium of life. If John had not made this preparation, there would have been no ears opened to hearing the Christ. Because of John's work, a group of individuals were able to gather around Christ Jesus, able at least to meet him in such a way that he could manifest himself to humanity through the Word.

The mission of the Elijah being thus stands before us in bold outline in the karma of the children of Israel. Through the personalities of Phinehas, Naboth Elijah, Elijah Elisha, and John the Baptist, he is active at the critical moments of the race's destiny, healing and awakening it, step by step, with his elevating influence—first exercising healing on the ether body, then cleansing on the astral body, until, eventually, activity reaches the point of awakening the "I." These steps correspond to the three stages of growth in the Israelitish race organism.

In the following sections, the three epochs of the Old Testament evolution will be studied in relation to typical characters.

# Chapter 8

# Moses

The history of the Hebrew race begins with the Exodus from Egypt. This event may be considered the hour of its birth, because that hour began the independent life of the new race, which had emerged from the sheath of Egyptian influence. But this was a painful and complicated process, and it did not end with crossing the Red Sea. It was not until the fortieth year of wandering in the wilderness that the emancipation from Egyptian influence—which began with the exodus from Egypt—was completed. It was the mission of Moses, the Egyptian initiate who had risen to the perceptive knowledge of Yahweh, to introduce and carry through this emancipation and to give the new race a new culture for all time. Just as Abraham, Isaac, and Jacob had supplied the basic impulses that formed the subconscious tendencies of the Israelites' thinking, feeling, and willing, so all the thinking and striving of the race in day consciousness was based on the wisdom of Moses. The activity in the *blood* of the race was derived from the three patriarchs; the worldview and outlook on life that lived in its *consciousness* was derived from Moses. The contribution of Moses to Old Testament history is related to the contributions of the patriarchs just as the "I" is related to the astral, etheric, and physical bodies. What was active in the three members as volition, feeling, and thinking impulses was raised by Moses into the daylight of wisdom. True, this wisdom was *revealed* in accordance with the evolutionary conditions of the times (a logical thought life was not yet possible), but it nevertheless had the sort of nature that appealed to the intellectual sense, which is a daylight sense.

In connection with this, it may be necessary to say that the epochs of human history that can be called "pre-logical" (before there was logical thought in concepts) were neither thoughtless nor illogical. On the contrary, minds were stirred by great thoughts to a higher degree than they are today; and the consistency with which they were worked out reveals a force of logic that the modem age of empirical experimentation has lost. Thoughts were there—great thoughts, majestically shining like guiding stars above all human effort and endeavor, deciding all its details with a logical and admirable consistency. But those thoughts were not produced by human beings; they were *revealed* and placed before human thought sense with cosmic logic, from cosmic heights. But the thought *sense* is not synonymous with the faculty of judgment and logical thinking. The latter, in fact, is the activity of the human "I," whereas the thought sense belongs to the senses of the human organism.

If, today, we were to use only the old type of thinking, we would be treating our thought faculty (which includes the perceptions of the thought sense as well as the power of judgment) in the same way we would our hands if we were to use them only to touch objects instead of working with them. The faculty of touch might be developed to great delicacy in that way, but in time the hands' efficiency would atrophy. If, today, thoughts are merely *accepted* without being honestly worked out to their final consequence by the individual power of judgment, then a false thought life is the results. Such individuals are then filled with thoughts that they hold in memory as perceptions of the thought sense, but they are actually without thought. They might feel very satisfied with themselves for such a comfortable state of mind; but if they find themselves in situations that involve the need for initiative of judgment, they are more helpless than others who "know" less but take the trouble to think independently. In general, such people become the victims of mass suggestion.

The "Old Testament" attitude toward perceptive knowledge is, in the present age, a serious danger; it is a poison that can paralyze the best forces of today. In practice, however, even the most orthodox persons of our time feel the need to judge for themselves, but their judgment is pushed down out of the realm of knowledge related to humanity and the cosmos and into the area of personal affairs, where it expresses itself as the unhealthy affirmation and negation of personalities; one is condemned, another deified. This is how the one-sided acceptance of thought as the substance of revelation works today. In Old Testament times, however, it acted in an essentially different way. At that time, the thoughts shone through the thought sense and deep into human minds. The light force of thought worked directly—with suggestive force, as it were—on those people. And they bowed reverently before the thought as a symbol of the Word of God. The Bible tells us that the God of Israel wrote the Ten Commandments himself, with his own hand, on Moses' tablets of stone. This is *literally* true, and in a deeper sense than is usually attached to the interpretation of the passage. Whereas thoughts today enter the blood through the nerve system, in those days they were engraved in the nerve system alone, as mere perceptions of the thought sense. Now, the nerve system is the part of the human organism that is most highly mineralized. It supplied the "tablets of stone" on which God could write his commandments with his own hand. Those commandments *shone as thoughts* in the truth of their content (not as the inner voice of conscience, for no such thing existed then). We must not imagine those "tablets of stone" as opaque stone, but crystal. The astral bodies, whose physical expression is the nerve system, were, in the case of the Israelite community, purified beforehand by the "heavenly manna," the force coming down from manas. Therefore the nerve system, through which the manas force shone, must not be pictured as "tablets of stone" in the sense of opaque stone, but as crystalline tablets through which the words of God's commandments could shine. The commandments did not need to be confirmed; their divine origin was recognizable through their light force. Although inner moral feeling was not present at that time, there was instead a strong feeling for the authority of divine thought.

This thought was not, of course, received in the form of abstract ideas, but through *images.* Today, from the perspective of knowledge, no value is ascribed to pictures; they are valued only as illustrations. The picture is seen merely as raw material for shaping a concept that will become part of an abstraction. From many pictures, or concrete images, one concept is distilled. We receive the idea "human being," for instance, when we divest all images of individuals and their various idiosyncrasies. The process today is: From several pictures we get *one* concept. But if the concept sense (or thought sense) swings in time with the image sense, the opposite takes place, and out of one picture several concepts are obtained. For example, the old Biblical image of the Garden of Eden produces a host of concepts when the picture is transposed into the language of concepts. To begin with, "garden" is a condition of nature that is distinguished from "forest," because it was not produced by nature alone, but resulted from the intelligence that shaped it. It is thus a matter of relationship between the human and natural forces interwoven in human nature; the inner human being has exercised a formative influence upon nature, while nature, on the other hand, has appeared in the human being as *inwardness.* A city is an aspect of existence where human intelligence forms and governs everything; a forest is the free domain of nature, without the cooperation of human intelligence; a garden, however, signifies the harmonious collaboration of nature and human beings.

But this collaboration is not possible without a shared circulation system. Paradise was possible because the four streams of the etheric formative forces (life ether, sound ether, light ether, and warmth ether) had a rhythm common to nature and human beings. The four rivers of the Garden of Eden were "garden" streams in the sense that they possessed both human and natural significance. Thus we receive a second concept of the Garden of Eden—that of an etheric system of circulation common to human beings and nature.

Such a confluent alliance of the human with the natural signifies, from the moral point of view, human *innocence.* This was the pre-karmic condition of humankind; only with the first sin does human karma begin, as the path of experience of the knowledge of good and evil. But *cosmic* karma was already in existence. The Tree of the Knowledge of Good and Evil grew in the midst of the garden of innocence. True, this cosmic karma was the affair of the gods, who rule in nature (the "tree"), not a human affair. And it was in the realm of nature, apart from the human being, that the karmic tree of luciferic guilt grew. A person may eat the fruit of all the trees except this one—that is, humankind was in confluent alliance with the whole realm of nature, except the part of it that was entangled in the luciferic karma of the gods. Humanity dwelt in an "extra-karmic" region of existence. Human beings overstepped the boundaries of this region because of the temptation arising from the subconscious. It was not the Tree of Knowledge that tempted, but the *animal,* or serpent. Thus it was a force that belonged neither to pure nature nor to conscious human beings, which caused the infringement of the karmic boundary. "Animal" is the force of the subconscious in the astral body, which insinuates itself into consciousness as temptation. By eating the fruit of the Tree of Knowledge—by entering the same confluent alliance with this tree as with all the other trees of the Garden of Eden—humanity became subject to karma. Human karma began, and the state of innocence ceased. Human beings were driven out of this garden and into a condition of existence in which the double curse, human karma, held sway—the realm of sweat and tears. Since then, work and pain have been the universal karma of male and female on Earth.

But when human beings—who had been allied with divine nature—allied themselves with luciferic nature, it was not humankind alone that fell, but all of nature with which it was in alliance. Humankind dragged the three kingdoms of nature with it into the realm of karma. Nature still trusted humanity at that time and followed where it led. The bonds with which human beings were connected to nature in Paradise pulled nature down with them in the Fall. During the very long lapses of time that followed the Fall, a different relationship was formed, step by step, in human evolution between humankind and nature. Human beings severed themselves from nature and became isolated. But this isolation of humankind in relation to nature was not merely the result of a one-sided withdrawal from nature; there was also a distrustful withdrawal from human beings on the part of nature. At one time, nature trusted human beings and followed them, but nature had to suffer disappointment in humanity. Thus it has come about that the beings of the elemental world have for a long time had no confidence in humankind. The real tragedy of all this is that the redemption of nature can take place only through human cooperation.

Nature awaits redemption when humanity is once more united in love with nature, and, thus united, rises along with nature to that place from which, because of its love for humanity, nature once fell. Nature is now waiting for human beings to requite her former love for humankind; but thousands upon thousands of years have passed, and the nature beings still see no indication that human beings are willing to bring them redemption. Instead, humanity wants to enslave nature, increasingly demanding more of the fruits of nature than she freely offers. Humanity is not satisfied with the gifts that nature offers, but wants to extort from her all she has and to subjugate her entirely to its egoistic purposes. Do not think that the "white" mechanical occultism of the future will include the evolution of new forces that compel nature to greater efforts of production; the true mechanical occultism will allow elemental beings to regain their confidence in humankind, serving out of free love. White magic does not command but offers a reciprocal service of love between humanity and nature. If the soul of the nature beings again becomes subject to humanity, if nature again hears the sounds of "His" voice mingled with the human voice—the voice of the one who once spoke on Earth with the voice of human sounds that nature will never forget—then mechanical occultism will replace modern technology. The "mechanics" of mechanical occultism will consist in reuniting the bonds of confidence and love between nature and humanity.

The relationship between nature and humankind, however, will never again be the one of the "garden," as it was in the beginning. In the future, nature will have completely surrendered to humanity, who will determine the face of nature. If the "garden" stands at the beginning of the story of the relationship between humanity and nature, the "city" stands at the end of it. "heavenly Jerusalem" is the city of the future, just as "Eden" was the garden of the past. This is the secret of the structure of the whole Bible—the path from the Garden of Eden to the heavenly city of Jerusalem. The Bible's structure is identical to that of human evolution. Thus the Bible is correctly called "divine scripture," because divine purposes can be found there. On the one hand, the genesis of humanity presents a whole; similarly, the Bible that describes it also presents a whole. It is the mission of the anthroposophic movement to restore the Bible as a whole to the people of today.

The wisdom of Moses, as we have seen, was addressed to the concept sense (or thought sense), with which the image sense kept pace. It is not that Moses' disciples actually believed that humanity once lived in a garden and was driven out of it; in those images, they understood the idea of the cosmic connection between the human primeval condition and the beginning of human karma. On the other hand, the picture was not as important to them as the thought it communicated. The Israelite mind, in contrast, for example, to the Egyptian mind, already had a strong tendency toward intellectual matters and had drifted considerably from the intense life of imagination. This is the nature of the wisdom of Moses as a phenomenon of spiritual history.

Now, if we inquire into its nature, we can look at the answer given by Rudolf Steiner in his lectures on the Gospel of Matthew.[1] The wisdom of Moses revealed the mysteries of *time,* whereas the wisdom of Hermes was a revelation of the mysteries of *space.* In another lecture course, Steiner shed light in a magnificent way on the cosmic secrets of the Mosaic record of creation.[2] It is assumed here that the reader is familiar with the reasoning of this course of lectures, and in what follows we will approach matters in a way that presumes at least a basic knowledge of the principles of Steiner's tenets on the wisdom of Moses.

If Moses' teachings (as found in the Bible and as Rudolf Steiner has translated them into the language of spiritual science) are placed as a whole before the inner eye, one thing above all others strikes us in these teachings—the thought toward which all details are directed: that humankind is the crown of creation. Moses shows the stages of ascent in the work of creation, until humanity, the highest stage, is attained. But the story of this highest effort of creation begins, according to Moses, with the Fall and the divine "curse" pronounced over this highest created being. If these two thoughts are considered together—that human beings constitute the highest effort of creation, and that human beings were constructed in such a way that they deserved the curse—we may be tempted to think that the human being is an abortive effort by creation and that all that follows is the history of correcting this failure.

Some may accept this thought lightly as a mere theoretical possibility, but, unfortunately, it has played a large role in human history. No matter how it is formulated, this thought is present behind every manifestation of pessimism and misanthropy. Even "frames of mind" express (often subconsciously) ideas. And the idea that humankind is an unsuccessful experiment in the diverse expressions of its formulation has had a devastating effect through the millennia. But, in fact, the thought that Moses presents to us in the Bible is that the destiny of humanity involves creating the possibility of a close encounter between good and evil, thus initiating an arrangement, called karma, between good and evil. Moses wanted to interpret the cosmic sense of the fourth hierarchy to human perception, and the solution of this problem is the very core of Moses' wisdom. The mystery of karma is the central revelation that reached humanity through Moses. This is precisely the reason why Moses' wisdom is the wisdom of time; it deals with the origin of the karmic current and the currents which flow from it into the future.

To understand the wisdom of Moses is to understand the nature of karma. Thus we will turn to another question. But first, another question may greatly lighten our task of understanding karma. What would the world be like if karma did not exist? What would be the situation for all the hierarchies whose actions determine what we call "the world"? For an answer, we must first be clear that each hierarchy, however exalted, has something higher to which it looks up, as it were. On the other hand, each has something lower that constitutes its field of activity. Now let us imagine karma—arrangement between good and evil—as nonexistent; although the hierarchies would be able to look up, they would have no task below them. They could still look toward higher and higher ranks of godhead, but they would have no battle to fight for the realization of what they saw, for there would be no hindrances to overcome. What is the significance of *contemplating* the divine without striving for it? It signifies *cosmic sleep.* All the hierarchies would sink into cosmic sleep if there were no karma.

This is true not only of the hierarchies of good, but also of the hierarchies of evil. If there were no karma, there would be no ground on which the hierarchies of good could encounter the hierarchies of evil; the hierarchies of good would adopt the standpoint of good, and the hierarchies of evil, the standpoint of evil. Thus they would confront one another in stasis, since there would be no debatable ground on which the truthfulness of good could be exposed to the untruthfulness of evil through objective events. If there were no area where the arbitration of the primal cosmic being could be convincingly revealed to *both sides,* neither the hierarchies of good nor the hierarchies of evil would have anything to do; all of them would then be sunk in cosmic sleep. This cosmic sleep is precisely the cosmic condition that preceded the condition of ancient Saturn—or, more exactly, the cosmic condition from which that Saturn condition emerged. Cosmic evolution, from the time of ancient Saturn until the Earth period, is essentially the process of creating the cosmic karma organization, or the preparation of an area where the understanding with evil might be arranged. The hierarchies who, as creators, are engaged in this work originated in an earlier world; Ahriman also came from an earlier world. We may picture Ahriman as an iceberg from a long-past world, appearing from afar in the southern waters of this world. Ahriman was lured into this world by the fact that Lucifer (who became "Lucifer" in this world) had created the conditions that allowed Ahriman free entry. The shadow that Lucifer cast in the divine light was Ahriman's entryway into the present cosmos. Ahriman's approach was gradual; on ancient Saturn his presence was perceptible at a great distance because of the physical *cold* that issued from him as a herald of his coming. Even on the ancient Sun it was through images of darkness that the approaching being was perceptible. On the ancient Moon, the approach of Ahriman was even clearer; it manifested as the hardening of the part of the ancient Moon that was turned away from the Sun. The sound of Ahriman's hardening *Word*—the *Voice* of Ahriman, so to speak—was perceptible to the sense of inspiration on the ancient Moon. It was not until the evolution of *Earth* that Ahriman himself entered this world. Thus it is only on the Earth that the nature of the ahrimanic can be recognized. But that was when the creation of karma was accomplished; evil entered this world to acquire an area of existence, which had in the meantime been constructed so that it was "neutral." In other words, it could be just as easily acquired by good as by evil. What area was this?

In the language of the mysteries (that is, in the language in which the gods speak to men) the condition of existence that corresponds morally to zero—that is, neither good nor bad—is called a "dust" condition. Thus, for example, there is dust knowledge, dust art, and dust religion. The best way to understand what *dust* means in the spiritual life is to study from this point of view the *Faust* monologue in the first scene of part I. Goethe enumerates most of the dust phenomena in the spiritual life, and does it in such a way that we can understand the meaning of *dust.*

In the Bible, Moses expresses the significant truth that the man was created out of *the dust on the ground,* and that he became a living soul when God "breathed into his nostrils the breath of life." With these words, Moses tells us that the archetypal human organism is constructed so that it presents a dual nature. On the one hand, it is rooted in the divine; on the other, it exhibits a spiritually empty space that belongs to neither good nor evil. Thus, it was human beings themselves who, like magnets, attracted evil into the world. They offered it a ground of which to take advantage. If Lucifer opened the gate into this world for Ahriman, it was humanity who provided the footing for Ahriman to take a stand. Dust originated in the shadow of Lucifer. Earthly humanity was formed from dust and thus provided the battlefield for good and evil, or karma, in the world. The reason for creating humankind, therefore, was to begin the process of karma—to make possible an understanding between good and evil. In the sight of the primal cosmic being, who stands above good and evil as these are understood by the consciousness of all cosmic beings, human beings will be shown which of the two is true. Karma is the perpetual arbitration of the deity in the strife between good and evil. Karma is the purpose of this world; but it is only through humanity that it could come into the world.

Humankind caused the current of guilt and atonement in the world, but it is not an abortive creation of God; human beings fulfilled the purpose—at enormous cosmic risk—of making possible within themselves the encounter between good and evil, so that evil might be overcome. An immense spiritual heroism underlies the basic human impulse to incarnate on Earth; *reverence* for the human being arises in the hearts of those who recognize these cosmic truths—and this is true and genuine reverence, because nothing leads it off course. *True* reverence for humanity does not honor only the saints, but flows from recognition of the primal purpose of human nature, which has humbled itself to the level of sin. We should not think that the spiritual hierarchies look down on humankind as, say, "an angel in the preparatory stage." No, the spiritual hierarchies esteem humanity more highly than human beings have yet learned to esteem any being. Beings of the spiritual world know human sins, but their joy in everything positive that humanity accomplishes is greater than what they suffer at the sight of everything uncomely that we create in the world. The good that human beings make real in the cosmos has greater value to the spiritual world than does the good of that world, which exists as a matter of course. The parable of Jesus Christ in which he tells us of joy over the lost sheep accurately expresses the cosmic truth that good is more valuable to a sinner, or those who have absorbed evil into their system, than it is to a saint, or one who has not thus absorbed evil. The finest expression of this was given by Rudolf Steiner: "Humanity is the religion of the gods."

So, it was *intentional* that human beings become "sinful," and the Fall is really the birth of humanity. "Original sin" is the destiny of every human being born on the Earth; otherwise there would have been no point at all to human incarnation on Earth. Out of the spiritual world, which is the home of human individualities, souls descend to Earth with a conscious determination to plunge into the current of evil so that, with each incarnation, they can wrest a fragment from evil and take it with them after death as a trophy, as it were, into the spiritual world. Individual karma determines the forces of good, and how much of them, one appropriates or forfeits in that struggle. It is the universal karma of humanity, however, that with each birth we must plunge into the current of evil. This current of "original sin" has flowed through the generations since the Fall; it is not an individual matter but concerns the generations. It is the dark will power that flows through the generations from the past to the future. This dark will power is in itself evil; human beings are destructive and evil to the degree that only the will, without thought, is active in them. Those evil beings are joined by the thought-radiating human being who descends to birth in order to convert the evil will nature into thought. This is why the *head* is the part of the limb system that remains unchanged from the previous incarnation (a fact Rudolf Steiner has spoken of from various perspectives[3]). Nonetheless, if the thought life proves too weak and, instead of directing the will, becomes its tool, then a *negative* thought life results, which brings evil ideas into the world.

Thinking must direct volition, which is dark. This is why Moses gave the commandments of the law to the children of Israel. The Law of Moses causes thinking, which is divine in origin, to confront the will, which is naturally evil. By causing the starlight of thinking to oppose the dark current of original sin, Moses gave rise to the moral feelings of fear, shame, and repentance. People are not just thinking and willing beings, but also beings who can feel. If we had no feeling organization, we would be centaurs. The centaur is really a being made up of only thinking and willing. What distinguishes human beings as human is the power of feeling.

The image of Moses receiving the revelation of *divine thought* on the heights of Mt. Sinai in contrast to the people worshipping the animal at the foot of the mountain expresses the tension between thinking and volition in the human organism. Feelings of fear and shame could make those people obedient, because at the time of Moses the link between human thinking and willing had not developed enough for anything higher than obedience. The people of the Old Covenant were beings of obedience. By displaying this sharp contrast through the Law, however, Moses awakened the first yearning of the human heart for a condition that later the prophets called the condition in which the Law is written in the heart. Moses presented, in the sharp contrast between *divine claim* and *fallen* human nature, the problem of pre-Christian human existence by showing the need for a reconciling force that would spring to life in human minds sometime in the future.

The wisdom of Moses shows the beginning of humanity as an innocent "garden," then exposes the nature of fallen humanity, and finally points prophetically to a future reconciliation. The "time wisdom" of Moses is knowledge of the human path through the whole of earthly evolution. That path involves, first, the human organism becoming a victim of sin—becoming a karmic organism—so that it could develop as an *obedience* organism, then as a *conscience* organism, and finally rising to the freedom of a *love* organism. The path of humanity leads from the pre-karmic "garden human" to the fallen "karmic human," who becomes a "conscience human" by consciously taking part in the conflict between good and evil, finally evolving into the "love human," the *victorious* human. While the garden of innocence stands at the beginning of the path as a picture of relationship between humanity and the environment, the end of the path is the City of Love, the heavenly Jerusalem archetype of the Jupiter existence, which will follow the Earth existence.

We may truly call the books of Moses the "Song of Songs" of humanity, because they reveal the magnificent cosmic purpose accomplished by the human hierarchy, and they show the direction of the future divine victory that humankind can win. The spirit inspiring humankind lives and breathes in the Pentateuch; it issued from that great leader of humanity, who, approximately seven millennia in the past, guided a small community of Aryans in their conflict against the cosmic sovereignty of Ahriman. The courage of the great Zoroaster is the etheric bloodstream that gives life to the words of the Pentateuch; the resurrected wisdom of the great Zoroaster is the essential wisdom of his disciple Moses.

## The Path of Moses in the Wilderness

This study must be limited, so we can emphasize only what offers the best foundation for understanding the most essential points. Consequently, we cannot go into the many details of Moses' life as described in the Bible. To understand the development of Moses' life work at the time, we must single out three significant events as the children of Israel wandered in the wilderness: feeding the people with heavenly manna; quenching their thirst with water from the rock; and deliverance from the fiery snakes through seeing the brazen serpent. These three events represent the stages of a path that the chosen people had to walk, under the guidance of Moses. If we recall that we are dealing with the beginning of a new stream of spiritual culture, it is enlightening that they were able to follow his path only in the wilderness. Such a stream could not be born in the context of an old culture; it had to have free space, a cultural vacuum, in which to develop. Egypt, Babylon, and Phoenicia had old, obsolescent cultures; their traditions would have overwhelmed the tender seed of a new culture. This is why it was necessary to wander so long in the wilderness, away from the great civilizations, until the Israelites' revelation culture had reached a certain degree of maturity. That maturity would be impossible until the generation that left Egypt had died out. Once those who had lived in Egypt had all died, the new current would be clear of Egypt's influence.

The purpose of the wilderness was to prepare a generation who would consciously renew the Covenant of Abraham, Isaac, and Jacob. The three primal impulses of the patriarchs thus had to be experienced again in the wilderness by the people as a whole, but in such a way that they would be lifted out of the subconscious in which they had been functioning and into consciousness. The renewal of the Covenant in the wilderness meant, essentially, that Moses would lead the whole race to the knowledge that Abraham, Isaac, and Jacob had possessed in their time. The whole race in the wilderness had to experience the three stages of the first Covenant. Therefore, we must study the three events already mentioned as stages on the path of renewing the Covenant.

Those who wander through a physical wilderness must overcome three dangers. Barrenness, drought, and heat represent the dangers of hunger, thirst, and prostration. Certain dangers also threaten the spiritual side of wandering in the wilderness. They appear as loneliness that gradually affects the astral, etheric, and physical bodies. Human beings depend on a myriad of influences in the environment; when that environment shrinks to the singularity of a wilderness, hunger arises externally as a stimulus. The lack of external impressions constitutes the first trial—loneliness. In time, however, the lack of impressions affects the general condition of the inner life. As the inner life becomes increasingly self-dependent, it hardens within itself. Its agility may disappear, and the lonely individual begins to long for a fuller life. One thirsts for more dynamic movements in experiences, and the temptation may arise to create this movement out of one's wishes. In an ardent play of fantasy, one may then create a subjective world to replace the unsatisfying environment. The ardent wish life is thus made to glow, and a condition of psychic inflammation is established. This is the greatest danger of loneliness; hypertrophy of the volitional life at the expense of the life of feelings and thinking. The passions are all fanned to fever heat, and a burning fire fog clouds the senses. The wholesome coolness of thought, and clear-hearted feeling will be driven out by the consuming fire.

The absence of external influences was needed for the revelation of new knowledge. Meanwhile, however, this need was accompanied by the spiritual dangers of the "wilderness": hunger, thirst, and heat, which the chosen people had to suffer. Nevertheless, their suffering was also necessary. The way of every revelation must be prepared for by suffering. Since the Fall, the human organism is made up in such a way that it must be transformed by effort and pain whenever a new spiritual revelation is to occur. Happiness makes people strong for earthly work; but pain shows them glimpses of heaven. We gain such glimpses when we read about the wandering of the children of Israel through the wilderness, guided by Moses. Happiness went before them as the Pillar of Fire; suffering afflicted them in the camp and in their tents, forging a bond with the renewed Covenant. Thus it was possible for a revelation of the manas, or spirit self, to occur in the wilderness. That revelation was not individual but common to all. The first stirring began with evening twilight, and with the first sunlight, it vanished. A new kind of sleep began for the Israelite community; to the degree that they hungered from a lack of impressions during the day, impressions were granted to them at night. The wilderness was silent during their daily wandering, but it whispered great promises at night. The dusty horizon of the daytime spoke only of a monotonous road to an uncertain destination; the starry heights of night spoke the secrets of a great future, filling their souls with the power and courage to continue on the endless paths of the wilderness. The poverty of experience in the horizontal plane conditioned the wealth of life in the vertical. The desert plains caused hunger, but the manna that descended from heaven fed the hungry. The souls who experienced the manas revelation with Moses in the wilderness form the community of "manas humanity" in future times. The impressions of that time continue to live in those souls; but they will not attain the maturity of their innermost possession until the sixth epoch. They form the karmic rootstock of the philadelphic manas community. This became their destiny when, thousands of years ago, they received the night revelations in the wilderness under the guidance of Moses. Souls who have tasted the heavenly manna form a community that, in the future, will again become a historic fact.

The manas revelation in the wilderness was a revelation of the future. The people, however, could not live exclusively by and for the future; they thirsted for a day life in the present. If the astral body can, as it were, project itself into the future (which is the manas process in the astral body), likewise, the etheric body depends on an influx of life force in the present. If this does not happen, it becomes hard. In the Israelite community, this influx was interrupted externally. The ether bodies of its members had to depend on themselves. Because of this, "thirst" set in as the longing for a current flowing in from etheric life forces. Moreover, this influx took place, but not in the old way, from outer nature; it flowed from within outward. Moses struck the rock, and invoked a stream of living water. The origin of this water was not in nature, but in the innermost human spirit, functioning in the ether body. The "thirst" was quenched by the force of the life spirit, or budhi, flowing into the ether body—not through *knowledge* of budhi (no such thing was possible yet), but through the presence of the power of the budhi being in the ether body. What is the power of the budhi being? It is the breath of Christ. The living water that flowed from the rock was the first contact with the living Christ being, pointing prophetically forward to his presence in the Earth organism. It was a prototype of the "living water" mentioned in the Gospels.

Abraham's revelations received new life through the activity of the manas, but now they became an experience of the whole race. The Son force of Isaac likewise became a racial experience in the symbol of water flowing from the rock. A third such experience in the wilderness repeated the incident of Jacob's wrestling. Just as the issue of Jacob's spiritual conflict was determined when he saw a truth higher than that of the messenger of death, it was the sight of a higher truth in the brazen serpent that delivered the Israelites from the deadly bite of the fiery snakes. We will discuss the mystery of this last incident only to the degree that it furthers our research.

The third danger of loneliness discussed here is the soul becoming inflamed. The inner life becomes luciferic, which again may influence the corresponding condition of physical health. It will form a basis for a destructive fever if the equilibrium of the human organism gives way one-sidedly to the fire of the will. This fire will rise in a spiral, snake-like movement into the head. Moreover, the physical sickness is the least of the evil consequences of this process; at least, it checks and resists the physical effects. It is worse when "uplifting the fiery serpent" is used as a method. Current literature on Indian yoga disseminates such methods throughout the world. Nevertheless, if this is actually done, it can lead only to death or a kind of spiritual sickness that does not yet have a name in psychiatry. This was certainly the danger that threatened the children of Israel. The deadly bite of the "fiery serpents" was a kind of madness that spread among the people—like a physical epidemic—that ended in the death of those affected. The manifestation of this disease was luciferic in the extreme.

The danger of loneliness is that it admits the possibility of an extreme form of luciferic qualities. In the desert wandering of the children of Israel, this danger was indicated by the plague of fiery serpents; consequently, only the healing of this luciferic sickness could save them. This healing involved an inner transformation of the luciferic nature, as in Jacob's spiritual wrestling. Everything said in the fourth study about transforming the luciferic is also true of healing through the brazen serpent; nevertheless, we can say more for an understanding of this symbolism.

Through the Mystery of Golgotha, Lucifer became the Paraclete—a spiritual being who serves Christ from love. This is the inner transformation of Lucifer; but luciferic *karma* continues in its original direction. Gradually, the inner makeup of Lucifer will also cause a change in the luciferic influence; but this transformation will not reach the plane of objective phenomena until the distant future. The Venus condition of earthly evolution is the point of time that occultism indicates as the final stage of Lucifer's karmic transformation. Then Lucifer will also work in the area of outer phenomena as Christ's ally. He will then function with a healing force in nature, showing himself in the spiritual power of copper, which is allied with the power of Christ. The serpent that appeared as the seducer of humankind in Paradise will become a means of healing as the brazen serpent.

Nevertheless, the inner process of converting the luciferic hierarchy is a gradual one. Lucifer's first transformation was through the Mystery of Golgotha, but there had been individualities belonging to the luciferic hierarchy who experienced such transformation earlier. Indeed, from the very beginning—with the first defection of the luciferic hierarchy—there were beings who had remained loyal to the Holy Spirit. From the beginning, those beings constituted (under the guidance of one who rose to the highest act of sacrifice) the conscience of the luciferic hierarchy. They belonged to this hierarchy, but remained faithful to divine guidance, thus acting as a warning of imminent danger for the apostate beings of the host of Lucifer. They are the living goal of the luciferic spirits; they accomplished the conversion of the luciferic at the beginning. Thus, the symbol of the brazen serpent is not just a symbol of the evolutionary future of Lucifer, but also a monitory symbol of luciferic conscience in the past. Moreover, the sight of this image healed; it transformed the luciferic in human beings, because it awakened the forces of remorse in the conscience of the luciferic hierarchy.

Therefore, Moses led the people of Israel toward a renewal of the Covenant, in that they experienced the perceptive knowledge of Abraham, the life of Isaac, and the conversion of Jacob through the incidents of the manas food, the water flowing from the rock, and the healing through the sight of the brazen serpent. The path of Moses in the wilderness had significance not only for the people, but also for Moses himself, because he also experienced certain trials on his path as an individual. Of course, he pursued his path for the benefit of the people, because the attainment of higher stages required it. This is true today as well. The saying "If the rose adorn herself, she adorns the garden also" is true only in a limited way. The higher stages cannot be attained unless there is an effort in the will to perform certain service for humankind. The higher the ascending step, the wider must be the sphere of humanity to be served.

This was the challenge given to Moses. By serving the Israelites he was able to interact through sight and hearing with the being mysteriously named "I AM." Through *imagination* and *inspiration,* he perceived the countenance of the being Yahweh Elohim. To recognize the mysterious being behind Yahweh, however, he had to rise to *intuition;* this was impossible unless he could identify himself on a higher level—not just with the Israelites, but also with humanity as a whole. He could not do this; when the spiritual guide presented Moses with his intention to abandon *this* people and raise another from Moses' posterity, Moses opposed this, saying that if it were done he would perish with the people. He argued, "What will the Egyptians say when they learn that this people has perished in the wilderness?" For him, it was *this* people who should fulfill the mission; he could not lift himself to see that only the work itself matters, not the group of people who do it. Tragically, Moses was forbidden entry to the Promised Land because he did not believe the Lord (Numbers 20:12) and was unable to rise to *intuition* knowledge of the I AM in the spiritual world. For Moses, the way through the wilderness meant ascending from the first to the second stage of suprasensory consciousness; entry to the Promised Land meant attaining the third level, *intuition* knowledge of the Christ being. Because he did not believe and could not rise to perception of the invisible and inaudible, he was allowed to see the Promised Land from a distance but could not enter it.

Thus, Moses died in the wilderness, having reached the boundary of Christ knowledge without passing over it. This was the tragedy during the age of the old Covenant—in general, direct knowledge of Christ was still unattained. Knowledge of Christ was at that time Moon knowledge; only a reflection of the Christ light was perceptible. However, such perception penetrated ever more deeply during the course of Old Testament history. The purpose of the following meditations will be to demonstrate this.

# Chapter 9

# David and Solomon

## Judges and Kings

The previous study showed the significance of Moses as a person in the spiritual history of humankind. It must be acknowledged (attentive readers will have noticed this) that, in that study, which was dedicated to a particular individual, there was in fact little said about that individual himself. He was considered merely the bearer of a certain code of wisdom; his individual life did not demand attention. There is, however, a definite reason for this—one that can be easily understood if we compare, with the help of the Bible, the lives of three important people during the time of the judges—Moses, Joshua, and Samuel—to the lives of the kings Saul, David, and Solomon. Indeed, the fact strikes us that, because of the impersonal nature of their missions, it is almost entirely unimportant to understand the judges as persons. When studying the judges, we really do not need details of their personal lives, but this is not the case when studying the kings. There the personal aspect stands out so strongly that it is impossible to understand their mission without considering it. The writers of the Bible knew this; they merely sketch the lives of Moses, Joshua, and Samuel as a background to the history of the whole race. But they describe the lives of these kings so that the history of the race becomes a background to their life stories.

With the institution of the kingdom, the personal aspect gains importance. This happens so radically that, along with the usual epic presentations of the Bible, lyrical pieces begin to be interwoven into them. The Psalms and Solomon's Song of Songs are parts of the Bible where the personal experience of individuals finds unlimited expression. This leads us directly to a question of the difference between the period of the judges and that of the kings in the history of Israel. The period of the judges lasted from Moses up to Samuel, showing an authority that, today, would simply be considered theocratic. True, this term does not tell us much, but it points us in the direction we must look for an understanding of this kind of authority. The judges' authority relied on the relationship between the race of people and Yahweh Elohim, whose representatives were the judges. When the consciousness of the race was turned away from

Yahweh, the authority of the judges was weakened; when Israel returned to Yahweh, the judges became strong again. The judges did not really possess temporal jurisdiction; they were simply speakers and delegates for Yahweh, whose destiny they shared in the consciousness of the race. Thus in the life of Moses, for example, there were times when his authority almost reached the zero point, to be righted only through an extraordinary intervention of spiritual guidance. The power of the judge was, therefore, not persistent; which was one reason why the establishment of a kingdom was sought after in the time of Samuel. "Kingdom" represented a steady, unalterable power, independent of the vagaries of racial piety. The other, deeper reason for establishing a kingdom was that the Israelites had reached a stage in their history where mere confidence in divine forces was no longer enough; a need arose for human forces to share in their destiny. Human forces had to have a greater scope than they had been given thus far. Those human forces, of course, had to be the best, and so the choice of the king had to be left to the deity. When the choice was made, however, the king would represent not only the deity, but also the best will and capacity of humankind. There was a need to look up not only to the deity, but also to a *person,* which was natural to the stage of evolution the Israelites had reached at the time of Samuel. By that time, the law and jurisdiction of the judges would no longer satisfy the people; they wanted to see a man through whom the human forces would be authorized to act in collaboration with the divine.

This requirement of the people was conceded. Through Samuel, an individual was chosen to be king, and the people accepted the choice. Saul, the first king of Israel, was an eminent representative. "From his shoulders and upward he was higher than any of the people" (I Samuel 9:2) indicated not only his physical development, but also his outstanding personality. Indeed, the personality of Saul carried all the possibilities of the Israelites' spiritual nature. Saul represented Israel in the sense that he was able to lift himself to the race's highest heights, as well as sink to its deepest depths. The angel and the demon of Israel were joined in his nature. For example, although he dearly loved David, he also hated him and sought to take his life. Likewise, he loved his son Jonathan above everything, yet he threw a javelin at him when Jonathan contradicted him. He had genuine devotion for the God of his fathers, yet it was not beneath him to ask a witch to conjure up the deceased Samuel. Yahweh and Baal lived in him simultaneously, and in this sense he represented a people that, for centuries, had acted as an arena for the conflict between two forces in consciousness and the blood. For this very reason, the fact that Saul was chosen king, therefore, met the need of the people, in the highest sense, to see the forces peculiar to determining their own destiny. When Saul became king, all the human forces in the Israelites' souls rose, with and through him, to sovereignty. It was not because the Israelites were dissatisfied with Saul that he met a tragic end and another was chosen to replace him as king; rather, it was because the God of Israel was dissatisfied with him. The result of the first trial of human freedom was negative; the demon proved stronger than the angel.

Now, however, it was necessary to maintain the kingdom—in other words, the rights of personality, which had matured in the meantime. During the time of the judges, the

Moon relationship to cosmic spirit light was in keeping with the times, but after that, the development of the Israelite spiritual life had advanced a step. By this time, the simple reflection of spiritual light was no longer felt to be completely satisfying; spiritual light must be received from the human being's own forces, and in such a way that the Spirit should flow into the spiritual life of the race—not as spirit alone, but as spirit and soul. The need for spirit impregnated with soul was an outer expression of the step from the Moon to Mercury, which the Israelites had made in the meantime. In the history of Israel that followed, two more steps were taken: the transition from Mercury to Venus at the time of the Babylonian captivity, and the contact with direct sunlight during the time that Jesus Christ lived on Earth.[1] These steps indicate, in fact, the gradual intensification of the Christ light experience, first received from above as commandments and promises, then moving gradually closer to humankind—that is, penetrating ever more deeply into human consciousness until it finally radiated *from* the man Jesus of Nazareth. On this path of intensifying Christ light, the Mercury stage was the first step in the path toward union with the individual. Behind the demand of the people that judges no longer lead them, but kings instead, there is the fact of the inner evolution of Moon to Mercury—that is, a growing desire to look up to a human being who could speak in the name of God so that the human speaks of God, and not only God speaking through the human individual. Human experience and wisdom would unite with divine revelation; the human word would be granted the right not only to impart the divine Word, but to speak in harmony with it.

This was the deeper reason for instituting Israel as a kingdom. It is the reason why, from the time of the kings' beginning, the Holy Scriptures allotted space for the human word. The Psalms and the Books of Ecclesiastes were received into the Holy Scriptures because, at the time, the human word and human wisdom were esteemed sufficiently holy to stand alongside God's Word. The narrow-mindedness of later schools of Scribes and Pharisees did not yet exist when the dawning of the coming divine human was first proclaimed by sounding the word of human individuality. At that time, people welcomed the evolution of individuality and incorporated the documents that bore witness to it into the Holy Scriptures.

## David

The Bible draws the outer life of David in such detail that it is unnecessary to repeat that description. By adding the Psalms to it, we get a complete picture of David's life, in relation both to the outer world and to the spiritual world. His life represents an extraordinary multiplicity of trials, hardships, triumphs, and blunders in the world of ordinary activity, but it shows an equal multiplicity of trials and triumphs, suffering, and joy in his inner relationship to the spiritual world. Both the biblical biography and the Psalms make it easy to see that David lived two lives at the same time, and that each brought him great trouble and great happiness. One was the life he lived in the outer world of action and events; the other was superimposed on the first by his inner connection with the spiritual world. This second life was really the decisive one; the position David holds in the spiritual history of humankind as a model of "righteousness" arises mainly from his unique relationship to the spiritual world. That relationship attested to his faithfulness to the spiritual world, despite his many trials. Because of it, the cognitions and revelations that came to him were pure. There were times, in fact, when David was unable to see into the spiritual world, but when he could see it, he saw it truthfully; illusions were not allowed to enter his interactions with the spiritual world. It was possible to keep illusions at bay, because he kept *everything* (desires and personal matters) far from his interactions with the spiritual world. Because he preserved the purity of the part of his soul turned toward heaven, preventing it from coming into contact with the other part, his interactions with the spiritual world were also pure. This consisted especially in meeting with an elohim being from the host of Yahweh Elohim. When David prays in the Psalms for the Lord to "cause His face to shine upon" him, we must not think that this is a poetic or mystical figure of speech.

This is no poetic adornment of an imaginary interaction with a mere being of belief; it is *real,* with a *real* being, and face to face. Just consider the following words as a reflection of reality, and we cannot fail to see that they refer to an interaction with an exalted spiritual being, maintained by a strenuous exercise of every force:

> O God, thou art my God; early will I seek thee: my soul thirsteth for thee, my flesh longeth for thee in a dry and thirsty land, where no water is; To see thy power and thy glory, so as I have seen thee in the sanctuary. (Psalms 63:1–2)

This Psalm speaks of the yearning expectation of a renewed meeting with the elohim while wandering through a "dry and thirsty" region, both literally and spiritually. Such meetings were numerous in David's life; indeed, they were times when he sought counsel of the guiding being for every action. This may be clearly seen, for instance, from the following passages of the First Book of Samuel:

> Therefore David enquired of the Lord, saying, Shall I go and smite these Philistines? And the Lord said unto David, Go, and smite the Philistines, and save Keilah. And David's men said unto him, Behold, we be afraid here in Judah: how much more then if we come to Keilah against the armies of the Philistines? Then David enquired of the Lord yet again. And the Lord answered him and said, Arise, go down to Keilah; for I will deliver the Philistines into thine hand. (I Samuel 23:2–4)
>
> Then said David, O Lord God of Israel, thy servant hath certainly heard that Saul seeketh to come to Keilah, to destroy the city for my sake. Will the men of Keilah deliver me up into his hand? Will Saul come down, as thy servant hath heard? O Lord God of Israel, I beseech thee, tell thy servant. And the Lord said, He will come down. Then said David, Will the men of Keilah deliver me and my men into the hand of Saul? And the Lord said, They will deliver thee up. Then David and his men, which were about six hundred, arose and departed out of Keilah. (I Samuel 23:10–13)

The point to notice in these passages is that the spiritual world answers only David's questions and offers no spontaneous advice. David was no prophet in the sense of being continually inspired by the spiritual world; he had to ask for counsel from the spiritual world. His connection with the spiritual world was free, which is why he did things that he had not consulted the spiritual world about (for example, his marriage with Uriah's wife and the numbering of the Children of Israel). He atoned for his transgressions, but it was obedience to the counsels of the spiritual world that resulted not only in the realization of his objective mission, but also in the prosperity of his personal destiny. Indeed, during sleep, every human soul has similar interactions with the guardian angel, but it happens at night and remains hidden from the day consciousness, whereas for David it occurred in waking consciousness, including waking consciousness at night.[2] David had the same relationship to his guardian being, whether in day consciousness or, as is normal, in sleep.

This relationship, however, demanded constant effort and spiritual exercise. The Psalms that he bequeathed to posterity are the visible traces of those efforts and exercises. To understand the origin, character, and meaning of the Psalms, we must become clear about something more.

The evolution of the manas (the spirit self) will be perfected by humankind only toward the end of the Jupiter period, which will follow the evolution of the Earth. The manas will then form a unity with the human "I," so that human beings will not merely receive manas revelations nor even seek after and attain manas knowledge; they will perform manas acts. The manas being in human beings will become the human creative force with which they will work. Before this stage is reached, however, humanity will have to go through a process involving several steps. As far back as the Lemurian epoch, humanity experienced the activity of manas, and this led to the genesis of the sentient soul. At the end of the Atlantean epoch, it was manas guidance that was followed by the hosts of those who were led by manas. The ancient Aryans acknowledged the authority of the manas being, and that authority led them away from the destruction of doomed Atlantis. Under the guidance of Moses, the Israelites experienced the reality of the manas being as they wondered in the wilderness. They experienced it as an inner nighttime revelation that extended into the daytime life of feeling and volition as *power,* or "strengthening food from heaven." On the other hand, a manas revelation came to the apostles during waking day consciousness through their experience at Pentecost. Nevertheless, part of humankind will not participate in conscious manas *knowledge* until the sixth cultural epoch. Then, there will be a great number of individuals who will no longer merely receive revelations, but will carry on conscious interaction with the spiritual world through the manas being. During the waking daytime, they will be conscious citizens of two worlds; it will be within their will power to open their eyes to the spiritual world and to close them again and turn their attention to the earthly world. This will become a human faculty; human beings, and no other, will be able to open and close the gates of the spiritual world to their sight. In the Revelation of John, this human faculty of the sixth cultural epoch is called the Philadelphia:

> And to the angel of the church in Philadelphia write; These things saith he that is holy, he that is true, he that hath the key of David, he that openeth, and no man shutteth; and shutteth, and no man openeth. (Revelation 3:7)

The "key of David" is exactly the faculty that David possessed—the ability to freely interact with the spiritual world. No one can close or open the way to those who possess the key of David, or those with manas *cognition*, not just manas revelation. Manas knowing is, in essence, different from that attained by means of the rational soul, or even by the consciousness soul. If cognition can be reached by means of these soul forces (whose characteristic is gradual ascent), then manas cognition is a gradual descent. Thus, in ascending cognition, for instance, nature (mineral, plant, animal) would be recognized first, then human beings, and finally the suprahuman spiritual world. But in manas cognition, the process would be reversed. Spirit would be recognized first, then human nature, and finally mineral nature. In the path of manas cognition, the highest soul forces are first apprehended, and a gradual descent follows. Thus the beings of the suprasensory world are recognized first, and only later the phenomena of the world in which they express themselves. Cognition gained through ordinary soul forces is attained by ascending from cognition of the phenomenal to the beings behind it.

Thus the kingdoms of nature must be studied first to find definite archetypal forms expressed in them. Once the archetypal forms are found, it becomes possible to ascend from there to cognizing the spirits of form, or elohim. In manas cognition, however, the beings of the elohim will be recognized first, and only later (sometimes after a long time) their revelations in nature processes. King David's cognition was of this kind. He consciously interacted with the elohim being, but his knowledge of nature was meager. This type of knowledge could reach his soul forces only in the areas of human history and human morality; he lacked the forces needed by the rational and consciousness souls for a comprehensive knowledge of nature. Centuries later, Pythagoras, once he himself had heard the music of the spheres, was able to realize natural phenomena by the awakened forces of the rational soul, bringing the mysteries of the archetypal form (*peras*) closer to cognition by means of human soul forces and actively working through numbers and figures. Nevertheless, for David this was impossible and unnecessary; during his time, no one inquired into the concrete expression of the divine in individual phenomena. To find answers in a worldview tuned to the Spirit, such questions had to begin in the rational soul or consciousness soul, to find the solution in a science attuned to Spirit, or spiritual science. It was direct perception of the voice of the spiritual world forming cosmic phenomena that led Pythagoras to work out a system of numbers and figures that could interpret the external world. Likewise, that same voice some five hundred years earlier caused David to write a psalm, in which the majesty of the creative voice of God is expressed in stirring words:

> The king shall joy in thy strength, O Lord; and in thy salvation how greatly shall he rejoice! Thou hast given him his heart's desire, and hast not withholden the request of his lips. Selah. For thou preventest him with the blessings of goodness: thou settest a crown of pure gold on his head. He asked life of thee, and

> thou gavest it him, even length of days for ever and ever. His glory is great in thy salvation: honour and majesty hast thou laid upon him. For thou hast made him most blessed for ever: thou hast made him exceeding glad with thy countenance. For the king trusteth in the Lord, and through the mercy of the most High he shall not be moved. Thine hand shall find out all thine enemies: thy right hand shall find out those that hate thee. (Psalms 21:1–8; see also Psalms 19)

To experience the "voice of the Lord" directly and know that it affects everything in the outer world satisfied David, and he felt no need to build that knowledge into a cosmic concept. Consequently, his whole effort was directed toward maintaining a constant living interaction with the elohim being; it was all he needed. "One thing have I desired of the Lord, that will I seek after; that I may dwell in the house of the Lord all the days of my life, to behold the beauty of the Lord, and to enquire in his temple" (Psalms 27:4). The Psalms also tell of how David suffered when that communication had to be interrupted.

The pain of those interruptions did not arise only during times of disfavor, but even more so as follows: Manas knowledge is, as we have shown, a descending cognition. This brings experiences that are sharply distinguished from the experiences of ordinary knowledge. In manas cognition, the supraconscious strata of the human being are filled first with a form of knowledge that does not penetrate ordinary consciousness until the final stage of its journey. This is its course in the season of "flood tide." At the time of the "ebb," however, it is ordinary consciousness that first loses it, whereas the deeper strata remain pervaded completely and ringing with that knowledge. Nevertheless, a condition of suffering arises from this process, about which we can form an idea (if only an approximate one) by acknowledging the following words, not as poetic exaggeration, but as a description of actual fact:

> I am poured out like water; all my bones are out of joint; my heart is like wax, it is melted in the midst of my bowels. My strength is dried up like a potsherd; and my tongue cleaveth to my jaws; and thou hast brought me into the dust of death. (Psalm 22:14–15)

When we experience the contrast between supraconsciousness and ordinary consciousness—whereby the supraconscious is filled with cognition so that ordinary consciousness feels even emptier—the yearning that takes hold of us is greater than that of a soul completely untouched by the spirit. Then we feel our ordinary nature to be an obstacle that must give way to the spirit. Indeed, it is not the body that we feel in this way, but more particularly the soul, since this is what causes the body's yearning; because of its inner structure, it hinders the incoming flow of strengthening and enlightening spiritual force. Both the spirit and the body place responsibility for this yearning on the soul. Thus the soul becomes aware of its guilt—not just against the body, but also against the spirit. When the soul can be *touched* by the spirit—so distinctly that, although the spirit does not penetrate into the full awareness of the soul, yet the soul nevertheless yearns for it with all its might—and when the body shows that it inwardly hungers and thirsts for the spirit, then the soul is able to realize its offence against God and nature. The soul then "confesses its sins," and because of this suffering, a new force springs up within, a powerful force that will have the most profound significance in the destiny of human beings and humanity as a whole—the force of penitence. If it is *guilt* that keeps the spirit at a distance from the soul (as it does in day consciousness), it is the force of penitence that reopens the doors closed to the spirit world. No one on Earth is without blame; if spirit knowledge were imparted only to perfect saints, there would never be spirit knowledge on Earth. The gates of the spirit world would always be closed to humankind. Yet there is a key that can open those gates—true inner repentance for human guilt in the sight of Nature and of God, both in one's own name and in the name of humanity. The faculty of penitence, properly understood, is the very force that in the future (beginning in the twentieth century and continuing into the sixth cultural epoch) will open, for an ever increasing number of people, the gates that close out the spirit world. For this faculty is none other than "the key of David ... that openeth, and no man shutteth," about which John speaks in the Apocalypse in relation to the philadelphic cultural community (Revelation 3:7). This faculty is called the "key of David" because, in the Christian current of human history, David was its first bearer and representative.

If we look at Psalm 51, for example, and study it sentence by sentence in the light of what we've just discussed, we get a vivid impression of what especially concerns David.

> I acknowledge my transgressions: and my sin is ever before me. Against thee, thee only, have I sinned, and done this evil in thy sight: that thou mightest be justified when thou speakest, and be clear when thou judgest. Behold, I was shapen in iniquity; and in sin did my mother conceive me. Behold, thou desirest truth in the inward parts: and in the hidden part thou shalt make me to know wisdom....
>
> Create in me a clean heart, O God, and renew a right spirit within me. Cast me not away from thy presence, and take not thy holy spirit from me.... Deliver me from blood guiltiness.... For thou desirest not sacrifice, else would I give it; thou delightest not in burnt offering. The sacrifices of God are a broken spirit; a broken and a contrite heart, O God, thou wilt not despise. (Psalms 51:3–17)

Insofar as David is concerned, the essential point is the "sacrifice of the broken and contrite heart that will not be despised." The faculty of penitence he possessed was his "key"—the key that opened the gates of the spiritual world. In David there was a deep feeling for the "law" far in advance of his times. Just as Mercury (what astronomy calls Venus), as the morning star, heralds the appearance of the Sun, through the knowledge that was his through penitence, David was the herald of the Christ Sun. Now, David's Mercury wisdom was manas knowledge. That manas knowledge was not, however, confined only to him. His son Solomon (whose very name means *manas wisdom*) also possessed it. But there was an important difference between the wisdom of the father and the wisdom of the son. David experienced the manas light in a way that revealed his own imperfection and guilt to him, whereas Solomon saw the imperfection in the surrounding world. While the one, because he saw the imperfection *in himself*, never despaired of the world or lost courage in life, the other saw the imperfection in the world, and as a result, at the end of his life he viewed the world's restless movement with the indifference of a wise man who, having claimed the manas light for his own, shut himself away from all illumination that the world had to offer. By studying the character of Solomon we can understand the danger of manas knowledge; but this does not mean that we should not consider it with deep human sympathy. Indeed, no other type of study is admissible with regard to human beings and their destiny; antipathy or cold indifference blinds the observer's soul to human nature and destiny.

## Solomon

When the light of manas irradiates the astral body, astral revelation occurs. If this results from the initiative and effort of the human "I," we are dealing with manas knowledge. But if the "I" gathers the rays of manas light into a singular focus within itself and then radiates it as its own light, the manas wisdom becomes the peculiar wisdom of the individual concerned. This was the situation for Solomon. He is the only one in the Bible with *human* wisdom; others were either spirit-filled prophets or "men of God"—that is, those who had had face-to-face interaction with the spirit world. They could not be called "wise," because the only thing peculiar to them was the faculty of conscious intercourse with the spirit world; what they drew from that interface was not their own wisdom, but that of God. Consequently, David was called "the lamp of Israel," but not "the wise man of Israel." He had not made the light of manas wisdom his own; he allowed the light common to the whole spiritual world to shine through him, and thus he reduced his own judgment to silence. The title "wise man" was applied correctly only to Solomon, who became wise by appropriating the manas light to himself. True, the preponderance of self supervened in Solomon's cognition only gradually—it was selfless at first. It was only with time—especially in the second half of his life—that it became egocentric. The Solomon who in his dreams at Gibeon had prayed to God during the night to give him a heart obedient to the spirit (I Kings 3:5–14) stands in sharp contrast to the Solomon who says, "Therefore I hated life; because the work that is wrought under the sun is grievous unto me: for all is vanity and vexation of spirit" (Ecclesiastes 2:17). A stretch of life's path lies between the dream seer Solomon in Gibeon and the Solomon of Ecclesiastes. That path led the originally submissive soul to the loveless worldly knowledge of an indifferent observer. This is Solomon's tragedy—that instead of becoming, as a judge of human nature, the preacher of wisdom to be attained by penitence, he became, as a judge of life and the world, the preacher of vanity and nothingness.

The failure of Solomon, however, should not be seen (as is common) in a one-sided way that merely claims he was not "pure" and "high" enough to fulfill his mission. It is easy to dismiss someone in a sentence like this, and no doubt it will be done frequently. The important thing is that we should study a great soul from this perspective: What was this great soul's purpose? And what was the real reason this purpose miscarried? Rudolf Steiner's way of talking about such individuals will always be a model. Take, for example, the way he spoke of Ernest Haeckel (1834–1919) or of Friedrich Nietzsche (1844–1900), and you will understand what must be considered in studying the life and work of another human being. Reverent love sharpens the eyes for studying humankind. And if we take the trouble to penetrate the soul of Solomon in this way, we find an amazing story of a great soul on Earth.

Solomon's soul was Promethean in character, one that lived a distant future in advance—not in such a way that it merely experienced a future that would one day come down from the spiritual to the earthly world, but in such a way that the future was in fact brought into the earthly world, where it was prematurely developed. This soul brought down "fire from heaven," and thus had to suffer as Prometheus did; we recognize the vulture gnawing at the liver of Prometheus when we read of Solomon in the book of Ecclesiastes. His indescribable weariness of the world and his impotent yearning to change things—which strike the book's keynote—are simply divine punishments for bringing heavenly fire down to Earth. A word, a primeval word, sounded at the decisive hour of human destiny, making itself heard again as the essential impulse of Solomon's soul: "Ye shall be as gods, knowing good and evil" (Genesis 3:5). Solomon followed this word, no longer asking what heaven said of Earth but climbing every height and exploring every depth of the earthly and the human, to test for himself "every work that is done under the Sun" (Ecclesiastes 8:9). To walk in all the ways of wisdom and of folly, to prove all pleasures for himself, to taste for himself all that is sweet and all that is bitter in life—this was the desire of the Titan Solomon. He built the temple according to the instructions that his father had left behind, and Solomon surpassed them in beauty and splendor. Along with the temple, however, he built a palace for himself that was no less magnificent than the house of God. And he had a throne erected in it—a throne of gold and ivory such as no ruler on Earth possessed. He collected immense wealth and surrounded himself with every kind of beauty, the works of both human and God. It was not his excesses and his dissolute character that led Palestine, Phoenicia, Syria, and Egypt to give Solomon their fairest daughters, but his insatiable thirst for knowledge.

Nevertheless, before the gray dawn, Solomon left his kingly palace and roamed as a simple soldier of the royal guard through the narrow lanes of the city, through the fields, and through the surrounding vineyards. There he came to know the other side of life—the lives of the humble, the widows, and the orphans. There he discovered Sulamith, who was able to awaken in his soul something that the Queen of Sheba and the Pharaoh's daughter could not arouse.[3] The Song of Solomon tells of this. But his urge for knowledge was not confined to his environment.

> For he was wiser than all men ... and his fame was in all nations round about. And he spake three thousand proverbs, and his songs were a thousand and five. And he spake of trees, from the cedar tree that is in Lebanon, even unto the hyssop that springeth out of the wall; he spake also of beasts, and of fowl, and of creeping things, and of fishes. And there came of all people to hear the wisdom of Solomon, from all kings of the earth, which had heard of his wisdom. (I Kings 4:31–34)

This soul roamed far and wide seeking to know what was profitable under the sun. But its questioning was based not on the possibility of accruing profit to heaven from earthly events, but on the value of earthly experiences within the realm of Earth itself.

This soul reflected that God in heaven is divine; therefore, all that we need to trouble about is to find divine happiness on Earth.

> Twice have I seen God face to face; my father also has seen Him. Yet the soul of my father *froze* within him after he had accomplished his work, and should have been happy. What is in heaven, belongs to heaven; but what man may find on Earth, that will I seek. Surely man comes to Earth for the sake of Earth, not for the sake of heaven. What is there profitable on Earth, for the sake of which man is born and lives? Why is it worthwhile to be born on the Earth?*

Solomon certainly did not deny the Spirit, nor was he an egotist who demanded personal happiness. His soul beheld the tragic picture of his aged father, having accomplished his work as the anointed of God and surrounded by a group of people devoted to him in life and death, ruling over the very hearts of a nation grown great. Yet, at the end of his days, he suffered the frost of life in loneliness. His friends looked anxiously for any remedy that Earth might afford, but everything failed; nothing could be found to warm the freezing soul. This picture confronted Solomon as the great question of life: What is the earthly lot of humankind? Can one find anything at all that brings happiness?

Thus, the question that arose throughout Solomon's inner life originated in the earthly life of David. In fact, however, David's condition was not caused by despairing of life's value, but by the loss of that which he valued most of all: his friend Jonathan, the son of Saul. Throughout his life, he had missed him, and nothing could atone for that loss. The words of his lament, "I am distressed for thee, my brother Jonathan; very pleasant hast thou been unto me; thy love to me was wonderful, passing the love of women" (2 Samuel I:26), sang through the whole of David's life, and took the living warmth from his soul at the end of his days. Nevertheless, this was the yearning for a love which had once been found; it was not despair of finding anything at all of value upon Earth. Grieving for something which has been possessed, and is now irreplaceable, is fundamentally different from the mood which prompted the words: "Vanity of vanities, all is vanity." Solomon's grand experiment in life led to his conviction that all of life's profit is mere vanity. But it is no less vanity to turn from earthly life to the heavens, for "he that observeth the wind shall not sow, and he that regardeth the clouds shall not reap" (Ecclesiastes II:4).

What, then, remains to human beings if, during earthly life, neither Earth nor heaven offers any goal for human striving? Solomon's answer is that we should not set a goal. "Rejoice, O young man, in thy youth, and let thy heart cheer thee in the days of thy youth; and walk in the ways of thine heart and in the sight of thine eyes; but know thou, that for all these things God will bring thee into judgment" (Ecclesiastes II:9). In other words, let nature be nature within you; live out your life naturally, but always within the limits prescribed by the law of God—for fear of judgment, "or ever the silver cord be loosed, or the golden bowl be broken, or the pitcher be broken at the fountain, or the wheel broken at the cistern. Then shall the dust return to the earth as it was, and the spirit shall return

* The source of this quote was not found in the King James Bible. The author often used the Russian authorized translation of the Bible in quoting the Old Testament, and some passages were altered by the original editor to correspond more closely to the author's translation. — Ed.

unto God who gave it" (Ecclesiastes 12:6–7). Thus, after having striven for many years to leave behind him for posterity a book vindicating life, Solomon actually left a book for suicides—in Ecclesiastes, anyone contemplating suicide can find an argument in favor of doing it. If everything is vanity, and if one focuses only on the dearth of the enjoyment derived from small ordinary pleasures, who can go on living? Is fear of judgment likely to be enough reason for enduring life until the end?

Solomon's path is that of luciferic manas knowledge. The test that manas knowledge brings is the necessary inner decisive understanding with Lucifer. Two ways remain open to humankind: the path of penitence and humility and the path of sitting in judgment on life and the world (with the exception of oneself). Our human consciousness of guilt before nature and the spiritual world is the soil in which the true manas knowledge can flourish; to sit in judgment on life and the world is to surrender to luciferic temptation. The choice between these two paths will be the great test of the sixth culture epoch, when humankind will experience the greatest exposure to the temptation of disappointment in human endeavor, human ability, and human perception. Humankind *must* experience this; only those in whom all the lights of life are extinguished will find the new and true power to live—to live by *love*. But first, human beings must wander through the wilderness; the descent of the "heavenly manna" is possible only in the wilderness. Then (and to many it will come even earlier) people will set aside the things they value today—scientific progress, prosperity, society—as childish toys. Either they will stand humbly as complete beggars before the spiritual world, or they will turn away out of contempt for the world and life. If we choose the first, the gates of the spiritual will world open, and a force will flow into life that gives new worth to all its values. Then—as once he did in Paradise, before the fall—human beings will give new "names" to all the things of Earth. The "reevaluation of all values" is the result of manas knowledge, but it can lead to either a positive or a negative result. In the nineteenth century, the tragedy of such an alteration of manas knowledge (in a negative sense) took place before the eyes of the entire world. The reevaluation of all values by Friedrich Nietzsche was a repetition of the Solomonic reevaluation. When Nietzsche took up his purpose of leading the present cultural epoch toward awareness of guilt and to deep penitence, he set up the ideal of the "superman" (*übermensch*), who was not Zoroaster but Solomon, freed from the fetters of a "fear of judgment." If we think of Solomon as free from the consciousness of judgment and come to maturity in the age of Darwin and Haeckel, we recognize him in *Thus Spake Zarathustra* (1883–1885). Isn't the "joyous science," free from the "spirit of heaviness," simply a remodeling and extension of Solomon's final exhortation: "Rejoice, O young man, in thy youth, and let thy heart cheer thee in the days of thy youth"? Isn't Nietzsche's idea of "eternal recurrence" simply a new form of the Solomonic teaching turned into optimism: "The thing that hath been, it *is that* which shall be; and that which is done, is that which shall be done, and *there is* no new thing under the sun" (Ecclesiastes 1:9). Indeed, the resuscitation of Ecclesiastes in the person of Nietzsche's Zarathustra is carried so far that even the words of Solomon may be encountered again in Nietzsche: "And I find more bitter than death the woman, whose heart is snares and nets, and her hands as bands ... one man among a thousand have I found, but a woman among all these have I not found" (Ecclesiastes 7:26–28).

Thus Nietzsche can be deeply understood through Solomon. Moreover, through Solomon and Nietzsche, we can also understand luciferic manas knowledge, which ultimately succumbs to Ahriman. If Prometheus brought fire from heaven, if Solomon burned up all human values in this fire, it was in Nietzsche that it was finally transformed into the fire that glows in the Earth's interior—a fire of hatred. When Nietzsche wrote *Anti-Christ* (1888), the fire of this writing was no longer inspired by the pity of Prometheus for humanity, nor was it driven by the fire of Solomon's disillusionment, but by the fire of hatred toward the Christ spirit. Solomon's disillusionment was thus changed into the hatred that guided Nietzsche's hand when he wrote *Anti-Christ.* This is a staggering example of the path of luciferic degeneration, from pity for humanity to subjection to the power of Ahriman, as, essentially, it was described in our fifth study. Expressed there is universal truth that can be understood and realized here through a living example.

The period of the first book of Kings was the period of Mercury revelation—in other words, the time when the manas being made itself felt. The period of Babylonian captivity leads us a step further and closer to the direct Sun revelation through Christ Jesus. The next study will, therefore, have as its subject the spiritual side of the Venus epoch, the period of the Babylonian captivity.

## Chapter 10

# The Babylonian Captivity & the Wisdom of Zoroaster

Both the third study, "Abraham, Isaac and Jacob," and the eighth, on Moses, discussed the significance of the Promised Land. In the former, we saw that Palestine had been made a "holy place," and in the other that, for Moses, entering that land was the third stage, which he was nevertheless denied. We should now see in the Babylonian captivity a new aspect of the Promised Land and its significance. It was a matter of neither preparing the area for sacred purpose nor entering it, but mainly a consideration of *evacuating* the area. That evacuation was necessary in the destiny of the Israelites, as death and sickness are necessities in the destiny of individuals. To regard it merely as a punishment, however, would be both one-sided and shortsighted; nor would such a concept help us understand the continued destiny of the people. On the other hand, much may be learned from the idea that may be derived from suggestions in Rudolf Steiner's lecture cycle on Matthew's Gospel.[1] Steiner tells us there that the mission of the Babylonian captivity was to introduce the Venus sphere into Israel's destiny; while in Babylon, the people came into direct contact with Zoroaster working through Zarates. This suggestion, apart from anything else, shows the *direction* in which the meaning of the evacuation of the Promised Land must be sought. But before plunging into the question of the significance of its evacuation at the time of the Babylonian captivity, we must shed a certain light on the significance of the Israelites' *occupation* of Palestine.

First, it is important to understand the essential relationship between the people of Israel and the region of Palestine. The association of the Israelite community and its mission with the territory of Palestine cannot be explained by common considerations (though correct in themselves) of the history of civilization—for example, the remarkably advantageous position of Palestine, situated between the three main spheres of civilization: the Mediterranean (through Phoenicia), Egypt, and Mesopotamia. We can, for example, probably explain the phenomenon of laughter correctly in terms of the muscles' movements at the corners of the mouth, yet this explanation is entirely inadequate to anyone who has laughed, because one also experiences the merriment that causes those muscles to move. Similarly, in the bond between Palestine and the children of Israel, we cannot explain it by means of facts on the same level as the phenomenon to be explained; we would merely give a description of the process, but not explain it. The explanation must be looked for on a different level. Therefore, here we must leave unconsidered much that might be correctly and appropriately said from the perspective of outer historical research, while devoting our undivided attention to the spiritual and karmic side of the question.

By doing this, we find that the problem resolves itself into a trinity of mutual relationships: first, the Christ being descending to his birth; second, the Israelites; and third, the area of Palestine. The mere juxtaposition of these relationships clearly shows that neither the destiny of race nor the destiny of region should be sought in themselves but in Christ. If the whole cosmic activity of the Old Testament history of the children of Israel was intended to prepare for the birth of Christ, then the area where the work was to be accomplished must also be seen from the perpsective of this task. Here an important question arises: Why did the Christ being need Palestine? This question becomes even more important when we recall that for centuries the Israelites had managed to live and thrive outside the Holy Land (in Egypt, in Mesopotamia), but that the three years of Christ's sojourn on Earth were spent only in Palestine. The race, therefore, was not assigned to this area as much as Jesus Christ was himself.

This fact points directly toward the mystery of the bond between the mission of Christ and Palestine. The perception of the relationship of Jesus Christ to that territory is one of the most amazing understandings related in a factual history of Jesus Christ. He needed this area, not for life but for death. In order to live on Earth he needed the generations of the race—the ancestors in the lines of Nathan and Solomon—to die on Earth, however, he needed the land on which the Mystery of Golgotha was accomplished. Palestine was the burial place of Christ—prepared over many centuries—just as generations of the people of Yahweh signified the preparation of his birthplace.

If we are to understand this, we must be aware of the fact that, at birth, human beings receive the etheric body from the heavenly realm, the physical body from heredity, and the mineral body from their physical environment. The first represents one's life, the second one's share in human karma (or "original sin"), and the third, death. The outer mineral world can mean only death to human beings—death is the singular reality of the mineral world.[2] Thus the heavenly world gives human beings the capacity to live an earthly life; their ancestors handed down the cross to bear; but the outer mineral world renders death necessary. Even the Christ being had to receive this from the outer world. Palestine was the only area on Earth that allowed the type of death inherent in his mission. For many centuries, Palestine was being prepared as a "holy place" for that purpose. For a long time, this region was being prepared, on the one hand, to increase the flow of "milk and honey"—the revelation current from the spiritual world—until the coming of the "bread of heaven"—the Christ; on the other hand, it was being prepared as a place for the death of Christ.

Now, what was the nature of that preparation? The mineral stratum of the Earth's surface is the first of the nine subterranean spheres and represents the bulwark of the Earth's interior against heaven. It is not, in itself, evil; it is, however, a sphere of moral nothingness, so to speak, which presents an obstacle to heaven through the sheer inertia of its solidity. Nevertheless, the wall of mineral matter is not impenetrable; just as it is possible for the evil of the subterranean spheres to appear above the mineral stratum, it is also possible for the good of heaven to function below it. To facilitate this, much is done from above. And in this sense, all of humanity works by shedding their corpses at death, thus counteracting this stratum's tendency to solidify. The strongest influence in this direction, however, is produced through the effort of individual human beings. This occurs when individuals employ the "I" method of occult practice; a stream of light flows downward from the "I" center between the eyebrows, which is able to pierce the mineral stratum and penetrate farther into the subterranean spheres. By sending down a light stream of this kind, Rudolf Steiner was able to describe the subterranean spheres (which appear in the lecture course titled *Founding a Science of the Spirit*[3]).

A similar method also existed in ancient times. This was the Yahweh method, practiced in the spiritual life of Israel since the days of Abraham.[4] The idea at the time was to set up a stream of consciousness in the limb and metabolic system and beyond it. The mystery schools then had a different goal. Humankind was striving upward so that the soul, freed from the body, might receive impressions in the spiritual world. In the mysteries, human beings had the special task of keeping the gate of heaven open. The Yahweh school, on the other hand, guarded the "gate of Hell," of which Christ spoke to Peter. Thus earthly humankind was doing the same as Yahweh does in the cosmos, in which, from the Moon, he guards the entrance into the Eighth Sphere by guiding the sunlight into the darkness of night. Thus the Yahweh initiates guarded the "gate" of the subterranean spheres, which was held open through their efforts.

We must imagine this "holding open" concretely. It is a kind of "inverted volcano," heaven toward Earth. Just as a volcano is a place in which the subterranean has forced a way upward, Palestine is a place where the higher world broke through downward as an effect of the Yahweh current. This work points to the fact that, during the Old Testament epoch of preparation, activity was needed not only in the direction of eugenic occultism, but also in the direction of mechanical occultism. In other words, the Spirit and the Father worked together to make possible not only the death but also the birth of the Son. Thus, when an earthquake took place during the Mystery of Golgotha, we must look for its source not on Earth but in heaven. In fact, it was a "heaven quake," which, although it shook and clove the Earth, was quite distinct in its origin from any previous earthquake. That event at that moment was a visible expression of the long-prepared suprasensory actuality—a cleavage in the interior of the Earth, which now manifested as an outer event. Through that cleavage, the Earth received the sacrament of holy communion, and through this it was eternally united with Christ.

This is the sense in which Palestine was the "Holy Land" (this is no longer true since it fulfilled its task): it was to be the burial place of Christ. It was the mortal body of Christ, or the mineral body, that he received from the Holy Land. Now, this fact had significance also for the Israelites. To the Israelites, this land had just the opposite significance; to them it was the land "flowing with milk and honey." The forces that overthrew the resistance of the subterranean powers were experienced by humankind as a flow of blessing—"milk" flowing as an *astral* blessing, "honey" as an *etheric* blessing, and expectation of the third, the "bread of life," whose blessing would extend deep into the *physical* body.

The experience of the mysterious flow of the currents described as "milk" and "honey" hovered over the land like a breath of magic, felt as a breath of cosmic childhood and innocence, especially at the sunset hour by souls on whom silence had fallen. The memory of it lived on in the natural love between husband and wife, and the joy of it lived on in the child; this was characteristic of the Israelites. This magic breath lay silently over the land in expectation of the one who was to come. It was no illusion, nor was it a revelation from Yahweh Elohim, who spoke to Moses in clouds great with lightning. No, it was the presence of the astral and etheric forces, carried later by Christ in his astral and etheric bodies—forces that belonged to the soul of the Nathan Jesus. It was the sister soul of Adam, stooping from heaven to unite itself ever more and more closely, through its forces of pure childlikeness, with the land that would give it the mortal body of mineral matter. Before the Nathan Jesus was physically born, he had long hovered over the land of his birth, uniting with it (and that in innocence) by sending down a current of tender love that wove a delicate tissue binding him to the land. These currents were felt by humanity and named "milk" and "honey."

And Isis Sophia, the Mother in heaven, immortal sister of the one who made the sacrifice—the archangel who bore the childlike soul on his bosom—blessed all birth and all the fruitfulness of the land. She breathed veneration of the mother into the etheric soul of the land, speaking deeply into the hearts of Israel's women—the mothers of the one who was to come—and filling them with the silent knowledge: holy is all the joy of the mother, and holy is all her pain. And while the prophets spoke in words wherein the flames of Yahweh Elohim might be detected, the women of Israel maintained a hallowed silence concerning the unwritten, unuttered revelation of Isis Sophia. Thus, in the Holy Land, the milk of Isis Sophia and the honey of Osiris flowed through the innocent being of the Nathan Jesus.

Before the mystery could be perfectly prepared, however, the spiritual life of Israel had to absorb the words and offerings of heaven, as well as what had existed as earthly experience from the beginning of human evolution. In Jesus Christ, the revelation from heaven and the ripest fruits of wisdom acquired on Earth were intended to meet. The most perfect representative of earthly wisdom for the whole post-Atlantean cultural epoch can be seen in the personality of the great Zoroaster. He is the "first Aryan," because he gave reality to the mission of Aryanism—that is, the post-Atlantean civilization. Not only did Zoroaster absorb all of the wisdom of the ancient Indian cultural epoch, he also made it an attribute of himself. This is why, after the ancient Indian civilization had taken a direction not in accordance with the mission of post-Atlantean humanity, Zoroaster was able to establish a new civilization in opposition to Indian apostasy and Turanian hostility.[5] The Zoroaster impulse was established between the apostasy of one and the hostility of the other. It is thus easier to consider the nature of Zarathustrian wisdom by studying it in its relation to the ancient civilizations of India and Turania.

These two contrasting currents provide material for a moral and conceptual outline of Zoroaster's wisdom, which is significantly furthered through an understanding of its essential characteristics. The essential contrast between India and Iran on the one hand, and Iran and Turania on the other, may be gathered from the study of the primeval event of earthly human destiny, referred to as the fall of humankind.[6] This was the birth of earthly human karma, described as the "curse" of the Father. It contains three necessities for earthly humanity: pain with all birth, toil in all work, and death for everything that was born. Since then, the advent on Earth of anything new, whether in being or in thinking, is fraught with pain; all creation, material, or spiritual, requires effort to overcome hindrances; and everything born or created on earth passes away sooner or later. What the great Buddha said concerning the lot of humankind is really nothing but a repetition of what was said in the first Book of Moses; Buddha simply recalled the Father's "curse" to human consciousness.

This primal karma of terrestrial humanity is behind all karmic currents and, ultimately, behind all individual human destinies. The formation of individual karma depends on its relationship to primal karma. Since Lemurian times, however, there have been two basic karmic currents in humankind, and since Atlantean times three (after the sixth cultural epoch, there will again be only two), determined by their concept of the "curse." Even in the first epochs of primal karma, two different concepts had already arisen: one feeling the "curse" as an actual curse, the other sensing it as the highest expression of the Father's love, and thus as a blessing. The story of Cain and Abel illustrates the contrast of these two concepts, indicating the beginning of two karmic currents. The incense of honest gratitude for the earthly situation rose to heaven, while the incense of dissatisfaction with the earthly life hung over the Earth. These are the attitudes that initially led to the two great karmic streams for humanity.

The third great karmic current—that of active hostility toward primal karma—began during the Atlantean epoch. The sin of Atlantis was essentially nothing more than rebellion against the necessities imposed by primal karma: pain, toil, and death. The dark eugenic occultism of the Atlanteans endeavored to rid life of pain, while their mechanical and hygienic occultism resisted death through illicit means.

Thus, two karmic currents began as legacies from the distant past; one was expressed as a longing for emancipation from the vale of tears of earthly life; the other as subnatural forces opposing natural suffering of pain, toil, and death. It was the first of these streams that turned the ancient Indian culture away from its original direction; the second ran its course in the Turanian civilization. On the one hand, therefore, a culture arose that longed to leave the Earth behind, setting as its highest goal freedom from pain, toil, and death; and on the other hand, a culture came into being that grasped at any possibility of circumventing those necessities.

In this connection, we must see that the meaning of the Christian current on Earth may likewise be found in overcoming primal karma. The mission of humankind on Earth is to resist karma. But the only battle cry expected from humanity is, "Forgive us our trespasses as we forgive them that trespass against us." Cosmic karma is a balance that weighs accurately; it is only when "forgiveness" lies on the one scale of human initiative that the spiritual world can place "redemption" on the other side of the balance. The spiritual world has waited nineteen centuries for this moment—the solemn moment, long desired, in which humankind will make forgiveness possible. If the karma of the past is a burden to insolvent humanity, it is an even heavier burden to the spiritual world. To the world of love, not being allowed to forgive causes greater suffering than the expiation of guilt causes to human beings. This is why the Christ became human and offered the awful sacrifice; it was done to emancipate both worlds by bringing freedom from guilt to the world of earthly humanity, and by bringing to the spiritual world freedom from the bondage of the will to give. For endless ages, the beings of the spiritual world have held inestimable gifts ready for humankind; they await the hour when they may whelm humanity with happiness, but that hour will not strike until the voice of humanity rings out with truth with, "Father, forgive us our debt, as we forgive our debtors." Therefore, we may never comment on the misfortune of another by saying, "It is that person's karma." The gods may say this, because they do so with divine pain; it is our business, however, to mobilize all the initiative and force we possess to mitigate—indeed, to prevent—any negative karma that has been earned by another. What would be the purpose of the healing arts, for example, if they were not humanity's fight against karmic consequences that have been earned? Indeed, the whole future of occult healing is based on the sentence from Luke's Gospel:

> That ye may know that the Son of Man hath power on earth to forgive sins (he said unto the sick of the palsy) I say unto thee, Arise, and take up thy couch, and go into thine house. (Luke 5:24)

The right kind of fight against human karma is accomplished by carrying forgiveness and remission into human, worldly affairs; if people are able to abandon the principle of "an eye for an eye, a tooth for a tooth," this principle will no longer be used against them.

The resistance to karma established by the Turanian culture was, nevertheless, quite a different kind. In it, human beings tried to flee from individual karmic responsibility into "we-consciousness," and "we-humanity" was in turn trying to escape universal human karma by fleeing to subterranean spheres. The suppression of individuality in the womb of the "we-consciousness" was the one side of the Turanian endeavor; the other involved turning that we-totality toward the principles and forces of the subterranean spheres, especially the subterranean sphere called "fire earth," representing the area of Ahriman's limitless power in the earthly organism. It would never have occurred to humanity to seek refuge in the interior of the Earth if not for the betrayal of the Vulcan mysteries (of which Rudolf Steiner writes in *An Outline of Esoteric Science*), which took place during the Atlantean epoch. The spiritual basis of the Turanian civilization was precisely the "betrayed" Vulcan mysteries (given over to evil and wrongly interpreted by evil), though in a weakened form compared with that of the Atlantean epoch. The essential truth of the Vulcan mysteries was that the highest goal of earthly evolution involved the complete conversion of the Earth's interior through humanity. This, moreover, is why Steiner chose the term "Vulcan" for the seventh and highest state of

Earth's evolution. This name remains a mystery as long we are trying to find a planet that corresponds to the future Vulcan condition, in the way that "Jupiter" and "Venus" indicate two future conditions. This enigma disappears, however, when we look for the heavenly body not in the heavens but within the Earth, which is where Greek mythology places it. The fact of the matter is that there is no planet Vulcan; instead, the "planet" is concealed within the the Earth. When the time arrives for the Earth to turn completely inside out, the objective phenomenon of the Vulcan planet will appear.[7] It will appear surrounded by a spiritualized ring of former earthly humanity. Humankind, in conjunction with the cosmic Father forces, will then be faced with the tremendous task of converting the lowest evil into the highest good.

The fundamental thought of the *betrayed* Vulcan mysteries was exactly the misinterpretation of the spiritual condition of things as just discussed, so that it would become its opposite. They did not consider the Earth's interior to be the *object* of the highest conquest of future humanity, but rather the *source* of forces for humanity's highest conquest. This "highest conquest" to be attained, hypothetically, with the help of the Vulcan forces, involved overcoming the "curse" of the Father—overcoming pain, toil, and death. A desired goal, for example, was to end all pain through the forces of the "air earth" (the third subterranean sphere), which kill feeling. And by applying, in conjunction with the "technical" forces of the "fire earth," the energy and luxuriant growth of the "fruit earth," they hoped to achieve freedom from all work. Further, it was hoped that even deeper strata of the Earth's interior would give the earthly immortality that Rudolf Steiner calls the "ahrimanic ideal of immortality," which would, in fact, not be immortality at all but "deathlessness," or an escape from the primal karmic necessity of death into a region into which that necessity does not extend.

These intentions functioned in the foundations of the Turanian civilization and determined many of its details—for example, the sort of communism that extended even into family life and was peculiar to the Turanian civilization.[8] The "we-consciousness" of Turanianism was expressed in this—for instance, its inner bias toward the interior of the Earth was shown in its hostility toward agriculture. If human hands furrow the Earth with ploughs and scatter seeds that are brought to growth and fruition through the warmth, light, and rain of the heavens, they are acting in conjunction with Heaven, in deepest contrast to the alliance with the Earth's interior. This is why the great Zoroaster taught *agriculture* as a human religious duty to the small Iranian community that had gathered round him. To the ancient Indians, agriculture meant servitude exacted by nature; to the Turanian, it was hostile; to the Ancient Persian, whose life was necessarily spent in hard toil among sterile mountains, it was nevertheless the earthly expression of fidelity to Ahura Mazda.

The fact that Zoroaster attributed religious significance to agriculture points to the essence of Zoroaster's wisdom and that of the ancient Persian culture impulse that resulted from it. It points, specifically, toward the *third* relationship between humankind and primal karma, which distinguishes the karmic community of ancient Persia from the ancient Indian culture, placing it in opposition to Turanianism. The positive relationship to the "curse" of the Father, the root of Zoroaster's wisdom, was made possible by the perception of the true significance of the fall of humanity. This perception shows that toil, pain, and death are the great auxiliaries that keep humanity from falling into the bottomless abyss of evil. Through toil, human beings are preserved from irresolute passivity; through pain, they are protected from the danger of excessive subjectivity, because through pain they are reminded of the surrounding world; and through death, they are rescued from a complete severance from the spiritual world. Toil, suffering, and death preserve the human will from passivity, feeling from aloofness, and thinking from obscurity. Thus the "primal curse" simply represents a threefold protection of humankind from harm. One experienced it as a prison; another as the enemy's stronghold; but the third recognized it as a protective wall against evil. Thus the three karmic currents arose, which determined, about seven thousand years ago, the three basic cultures of the post-Atlantean epoch.

The positive relationship between humanity and primal karma resulted not merely in appropriate gratitude toward the guiding cosmic powers, but also something else—the inner conversion of work, suffering, and death into joy, quietude, and peace. This came about through the influx of the Holy Spirit into human destiny as determined by the Father. Because of the Holy Spirit's entrance into work, suffering, and death, "work in the Spirit," "suffering for the Spirit's sake" and "death into the Spirit" all became possible; in other words, the mysteries came into their true character. The mysteries arose originally from the relationship between the Holy Spirit and the requirements of the Father. Thus through the spiritualizing of work, *meditation* arose, the "spiritual exercise" of the mysteries; through the spiritualizing of suffering, the *trials;* and through the spiritualizing of death, the *initiation* of the mysteries. The principle of occult method is the inner spiritualizing of work into spiritual exercise, of suffering into mystery trials, and of death into the initiation process.

The method alters with every epoch, but the principle is, up to a certain point, the same today as it ever was. The three primary stages of the mysteries, *preparation* (purification), *enlightenment,* and *initiation,* have their origin in the uplifting of the three "curses" of the Father into the light of the Holy Spirit. The Aryan method of initiation, the basic principles of the most advanced post-Atlantean mysteries, was devised by the great Zoroaster. During the Egypto-Chaldean epoch, this method was continued by his students Hermes and Moses, who adapted them to the needs of other peoples. During the fourth cultural epoch, it was renewed by Zoroaster himself in Babylon, and the leading personalities in Israel, as well as Pythagoras, participated in that renewal. Zoroaster's work, however, was not limited to recognizing the primal karma of humankind as the expression of the Father's healing will and to developing a method of initiation to unite the primal ordinances of the Father with the Holy Spirit; he was also the first spiritual leader of humankind to offer a prophetic indication of the approaching birth of the Son.

The Old Testament account of the post-Atlantean evolution, however, signified the preparation of the birth of the Son. When we say that, in Old Testament times, the Father acted through karma and the Spirit in perceptive knowledge to bring about the birth of the Son, we are describing the most significant event of that time. This was accomplished from the spiritual world; it was also prepared consciously by humankind. And the one who was able to perceive the mysteries of this preparation most deeply was Zoroaster, who thus became leader of the mystery current embodying the thought of the post-Atlantean epoch. In the seventh and sixth centuries before Christ, the content of this mystery current involved the recognition of cosmic karma—the "days" and "nights" of the cosmic year and the Sun being who was about to descend to Earth. Zoroaster's "time wisdom" was recognition of the karma through which the Father was acting, and his "space wisdom" was recognition of the relationship between Sun and Earth within the stream of time.

This is why the one who rose to recognition of the Father's cosmic karma was (in the language of this mystery current) given the name "Father," while the one who attained perception of the secrets of space was named "Sun Hero." In Genesis, therefore, Moses—who was able to describe the creation and development of primal karma through the fall of humanity—was called "Father." Hermes, who was able to make known the Osiris mystery, was called Sun Hero. But one who could recognize, in the preparation of the Son's birth through humankind, the mission of a karmic community as the work of a *people* was called by the name of the people whose spiritual mission he had perceived—for example, "Persian" or "Israelite." This was the stage Nathaniel had reached; he recognized Christ as the expected one.[9] Of these three stages, only the first, the "Father stage," represented the spiritualizing of death. The other two were attained by spiritualizing suffering. This was done in such a way that the stage of Sun Hero was reached through suffering responsibility for all of humankind, and the stage of "Persian" by suffering responsibility for a karmic community of human beings. Four preparatory steps (raven, occult, warrior, and lion) led to these three higher stages, representing the stages of spiritualizing work. Thus, those who could rise to the thought faculty directed toward the darkness of the unknown were called "raven." Those who attained *perception* in such darkness—that is, found a hidden light there—were called "occult," or hidden ones. If that attained perception ripened to the power of representing it in opposition to cosmic evil and error, they were called "warrior." And finally, those who attained the highest degree of spiritual activity—imperturbable courage that does not shrink from work—were called "lion."

During the Babylonian captivity, the Yahweh current of the Israelites met the school of Zoroaster. That meeting was one of the most significant events in human spiritual history. Not only was it a physical meeting of the representatives of two currents, but, more important, the current of Israel's *revelation* encountered the current of the *perceptive knowledge* of the Zoroaster mysteries. This was the preparation for the union of Nathan Jesus with Solomon Jesus—the innocent sister soul of Adam meeting the individuality of the great Zoroaster. And before this encounter could take place, the children of Israel, for a time, had to leave Palestine, the land of milk and honey. They had to be outside the revelation currents of milk and honey, so that they could appreciate the highest effort of human perception. The astral revelation of the sister soul of Adam was to be silent during this epoch; only the spiritual revelation of Yahweh, through "I" being, could and would continue its activity. Human perceptual experience was to end, whereas the divine Yahweh revelation was to be communicated to the outer world.

Therein lay the "encounter" in Babylon. For example, Daniel had to experience a "trial by lions" in the lions' den, on the one hand, and, on the other, was able to communicate revelations about which the Chaldean magi were ignorant; these two facts point to the spiritual nature of the encounter in Babylon. Daniel's endurance of the lion trial of courage led him to be seen as worthy of the fifth rank in the mystery, as well as being elevated to be the king's counselor and joint governor. Because he imparted revelations in the name of the Jews' God, he came to proclaim the Jehova mystery to non-Jews. Thus, because those two currents met in Babylon, a spiritual exchange occurred; after that, the mysteries of other peoples had initiates who looked for the birth of the Savior of humankind among the Israelites. Conversely, in Israel there were initiates who recognized the significance of the coming Messiah to all humankind. This is why the three "wise men" from the East could travel, as representative of the mysteries, to Bethlehem to greet the Solomon Jesus child. This is also why schools of perceptive knowledge could be established in Palestine—for example, the school of the Essenes.

At first, the Essene school had held a high position, but later on it lost its purity, and another mystery, Egyptian in nature, assumed the mission of preparing for the recognition of the coming Messiah's significance for all humanity. These schools consciously worked to unite the innocence of the "non-fallen" sister soul of Adam with the wisdom of the mysteries. The three wise men came to Bethlehem because the Yahweh revelation had entered the Zoroaster mysteries; the shepherds were able to hear the heavenly message because hearts in the "land flowing with milk and honey" had long been conscious of a bond with the innocent sister soul of Adam; and the two Jesus children were able to be born—and find conscious acceptance—only because of the existence of those who could establish an alliance between revelation and perceptive knowledge, between innocence and mature consciousness. This alliance, however, would have been impossible had it not been prepared much earlier, as described, by the Babylonian captivity.

For the children of Israel, the Babylonian captivity represented the passage through a certain stage of life. If the exodus from Egypt represented the Moon stage and if the period of the first kings represented the Mercury stage, the Babylonian captivity represented the Venus stage.[10] This means not only that the history of Israel immediately preceded the Christ event—which could occur only at the Sun stage—but also that in the consciousness of the average Israelite an encounter with wisdom had taken place that reached almost to the Christ being. The meeting with the Zoroaster wisdom during the Babylonian captivity was precisely the consciousness event of "Venus." At the same time, this event signified change in the spiritual moral essence of Israel's tradition. At the beginning, it was especially directed toward protecting and preserving its unique character from the threat of the neighboring races' traditions; now it acquired the character of a universal human institution. This fact is all the more understandable because of the meeting with the Zoroaster school already described, but it may become even clearer if it is grasped not only through the horizontal flow of human history (even the history of the mysteries), but also through truths from the world of spiritual hierarchies—that is, the vertical flow. We grasp it vertically by considering that the Moon, Mercury, and Venus stages (periods of time) also represent stages in the spiritual "space" that unites the Sun and the Earth. These are *spheres,* each representing the world of a spiritual hierarchy. Thus the Moon sphere is the realm of the angelic hierarchy, whereas the Mercury sphere is the realm of archangels.

Now, from this perspective, consider the first two periods of the history of the children of Israel. We see that, during the time of the judges, the "law" lay upon human beings as a moral code, while at the beginning of the period of the kings it began to be heard within their souls. We may also say that, during this second period, the revelation light of the law received astral warmth. This change reveals the entry of the archangelic sphere into human consciousness. Now, however, the Israelite consciousness at this stage recognized that it carried a definite racial mission. Nevertheless that recognition changed during the Babylonian captivity; it rose to apprehension of the fact that the mission was for all humanity. This happened specifically as a consequence of the ascent into the Venus sphere, the sphere of the archai hierarchy. Let us study the revelations of Daniel from this perspective.

We spoke in detail of Daniel in study 5; the descriptions there shed light on the nature of the Babylonian captivity as a stage in the history of Israel. Nevertheless, we should not neglect another spiritual figure of that period. The great revelations of Ezekiel show us the spiritual origins of that period from a viewpoint that is different from that of the Book of Daniel. Daniel recognizes the birth of the Son, brought about by the Father. Ezekiel, on the other hand, perceives the Son through the sphere of the Holy Spirit. Daniel shows the karma of humanity at that time, whereas Ezekiel describes the power of the Holy Spirit shining in on human karma. Thus Ezekiel reveals a certain truth, which is one of the greatest treasures hidden in the Bible. For this reason, the next study will be devoted to prophet Ezekiel's revelation.

# CHAPTER II

# THE HOLY SPIRIT & THE SOPHIA

## THE SAGA OF THE PROPHET EZEKIEL

WHEN WE STUDY the history of human cognition, we find that a problems runs through this history, as an unbroken thread, concerning the common source of the outer world and human consciousness. The cosmic Godhead in relation to the world and humanity was, and ever will be, the most important question for earthly humanity. Since the moment of the birth of thought this question has been answered in various ways. But, regardless of how manifold the answers to the question may be (apart from Atheism, which is a manifestation of spiritual disease rather than knowledge), they may ultimately be combined into three categories. The Godhead may be considered pantheistically, theistically, or deistically; it is the cosmic entity in itself, or it guides the universe it has created from outside, or it is the creative being at rest above the universe who, having created the world, has lost interest in its fate. In the first instance, we have the Godhead of all consciousness, enlightening the world and all life that flows through the currents of the world; in the second, we have the highest being with whom humankind is confronted; in the third, we have the transcendental originator of the cosmic system present in the cosmos, the same way a watchmaker is present in the constructed watch. These views depend on certain basic feelings that are peculiar to human souls in their views of life. One soul feels inundated and irradiated by the divine; another has the experience, as an independent being, of confronting the divine in free exchange; and yet another feels neither the flow of the divine in the cosmos nor its revelations in free interaction, but merely a memory of the divine as the rational principle that governs the universe. Those who hold these fundamental conceptions often stand in irreconcilable opposition, believing that the truth of their own view unmasks that of the other as mistaken. Thus, the pantheist views the theistic concept of God as anthropomorphic; the theist regards the pantheistic concept as naturalistic and vague; and both reject the concept of a deist (say, Voltaire) as an insubstantial abstraction. The deist, on the other hand, considers both the other concepts unscientific and philosophically unsound.

Real Christianity, however, means more than preaching peace; in truth, it brings peace into the conflict of ideas. The Christian idea of God—the "three in one," which is really the view of God taught through the holy wisdom of the primal mysteries—is a concept in which deist, theist, and pantheist can all clasp hands in friendship. The light of the Christian Trinity reveals that a deist acknowledges only the Father, a theist only the Son, and, with the same exclusiveness, a pantheist stands for only the Holy Spirit. All three representatives of these fundamental ideas of the Godhead are correct insofar as they say something positive, but they are wrong to the degree that they refuse to acknowledge other viewpoints. In fact, the Godhead dwells outside the course of world events, is present as the highest example for all beings in the world, and also flows and vibrates through all that exists. The threefold Godhead is the highest point to which human thinking can soar and find rest; it is the highest view that the human heart can grasp and that human beings can acknowledge with their whole being. But people must not assume that they can gain a true idea of the Trinity by only one path. They will never find the Trinity by devoting themselves entirely to the study of outer nature; that path leads only to recognition of the Father. And those who devote themselves solely to observing their own inner life will gain an idea of the Holy Spirit's universal power. But those who study the outer as well as the inner worlds, beginning with the question of what is lacking in the outer world and what is missing in the inner world—not asking what is *present*, but what is missing from the universe and from humankind—will attain a cosmic concept of the Son.

A gaze directed reverently toward the source of consciousness and life must lead to recognition of the Holy Spirit; an observant, perceptive gaze directed to the outer world leads to conviction of the Father's existence, the Creator, to whom his work, displayed to perceptive insight, points; but a gaze that views with warm sympathy the misery and imperfection of life leads to certainty of the Son. Whenever piety is lacking in the soul, the Holy Spirit becomes merely an abstract concept; when truth is weak in courage, the Father cannot be acknowledged; and when there is no love in life, the Son cannot be confessed. To acknowledge the Three in One means being able to soar aloft, to see life in a religious, objective, and therapeutic way. Christianity confronts humankind with this claim when the idea of the Trinity is placed before us.

If the paths leading to acknowledgment of the three persons of the Trinity are different, so also are the inner processes that bring about the acknowledgment of each person of the Trinity. Thus the Father cannot be fully understood, but only acknowledged. The *activity* of the Father can bring strength to human beings, but the earthly, physical human eye cannot see the Father himself. The Father's activity is revealed in human beings, in that the soul is pervaded alternately by light and by darkness from above. When a soul is first illumined and then plunged into darkness and silence, the strength that remains in the soul after these states is the strength of the Father's activity. The Father reveals himself neither in light nor in silent darkness, but through light *and* darkness. The direct experience (as distinct from acknowledgment in thought) of the Father being that is possible to human beings on Earth is confined to the experience of his activity in the alternation of highest happiness and deepest loneliness. One cannot know the inner repose of the soul that reflects the repose of the Father in heaven unless one also knows both the bliss of ineffable clarity when the soul is illumined by the spirit and the indescribable loneliness of the soul waiting motionless like a ship with sagging sails in a dead calm, with no urge to action or perception. This repose is the human experience of the Father; it is this that makes people strong for the trials of life and death. It is the vertical adjustment of the human will, which forms one into a pillar, as it were, that unites heaven and Earth. Thus, in the time of world war, Rudolf Steiner stood as a pillar of will power, imperturbable as the storms raged about him. It was the *reality in life* in the words of the Lord's Prayer: "Thy will be done, in Earth as it is in heaven." This was expressed in the attitude of Rudolf Steiner's soul.

Nor can the Holy Spirit become an object of perceptive knowledge; for it is the activity of the Holy Spirit that is behind such knowledge and makes it possible. The Holy Spirit is the light that illuminates consciousness in perceiving, making visible the objects of perception. Therefore, we never read of *knowing* the Holy Spirit, but only of being "filled with the Holy Spirit." Human beings cannot experience a *meeting* with the Holy Spirit; one can only be filled inwardly with his light. Then, in this light, one recognizes the objects, processes, and beings of the universe. But then it is not the Holy Spirit we recognize, but the cosmic objects, processes, and beings *through* the Holy Spirit. The Holy Spirit is always flowing through and irradiating all beings; everyone is interpenetrated continually by the Holy Spirit, but people fail to notice this simply because the current of the Spirit's activity is not intercepted by one's consciousness. When this happens in such a way that the "I" becomes the focus for the Holy Spirit's light, people are "filled with the Holy Spirit." In our present era, the manifestation of this condition is not the same as it was in ages past, when the phrase was coined. In the present age, it no longer means "speaking in tongues," but rather a condition of the greatest possible clarity and certainty in the knowledge of the great spiritual and moral questions of existence. Human beings simply acquire a much stronger light of consciousness than they possessed before. One becomes more awake, and this heightened wakefulness (which makes ordinary consciousness seem like idle dreaming) is the modern means of being "filled with the Holy Spirit." The fact that this fullness reveals itself simultaneously as calm bliss does not in any way change the fact that the condition is a heightening of waking consciousness.

It is different for knowledge of the Son; a meeting occurs between a human being and the Son, in which the Son stands before one as an example. Such a meeting results from the attitude toward the universe and the life we have called therapeutic. We encounter the Son when we ask what is lacking in the universe. This is not an abstract problem but a combination of many concrete, living questions, all expressing the condition of a soul that makes an effort not to find life perfect but to *make* it perfect. Similarly, for instance, we can study stones, the mineral kingdom, beginning with the question: What is in a stone? This will lead to understanding the principles of the mineral kingdom as constituted in the present cosmic epoch. We can also study the mineral kingdom starting with the question: What is lacking in it? What is missing that should be present? We should perceive that the stone is cold, that it is without the warmth it possessed long ago during the period of ancient Saturn. Warmth left the earth later on with the Sun, and the mineral matter that was left cold became stones. So we recognize the mineral kingdom as a manifestation of the cosmic process of disease. And we realize that what it needs to return to its true condition is that warmth of will spoken of in the Gospel when Jesus Christ speaks the significant words that faith can move mountains. Mountains are motionless simply because they have been deprived of the original will fire of ancient Saturn, and it is humanity's mission to restore to the mineral kingdom this fire that becomes faith as it passes through the human "I."

If we investigate the plant world with the same insight, we see that the light is missing in it—light that once belonged to it during the cosmic epoch of the ancient Sun and then, later, left the Earth with the Sun. Since then, the plant longs for light, and the Sun bestows it from above, but its true condition is attained only when it is bearing sunlight within itself. The true yearning of the plant world is not exhausted in the mere aspiration that the Sun should shine upon it, but extends to a desire that plants should have sunshine internally. The plant world is a visible expression of the manifold desire of the terrestrial organism to be reunited with the Sun. But this desire of the Earth is without hope unless human beings allow the love light of the Sun to radiate through and out of them.

Next, if we direct a therapeutic glance toward the speechless animal world, we realize that it lives in the dim hope of one day surrendering entirely to the word, so that it may be able to no longer live by vague instinct but under the guidance of the clear thought impulses. The obedience of domestic animals to human beings is an instinctive expression of this hope; the animal world desires to become an effective force of active thought, the Word.

And even human beings themselves reveal to such a glance what is lacking in them as well. The fact that people think points to the fundamental condition behind their existence—that the meaning of this existence has not been granted directly to humankind. We would not need to busy ourselves with thinking if the revelations of thinking were given to us directly. If the meaning of life already lived in human consciousness, we would indeed direct our activities in accordance with it, but we would not look for it through thinking. What human beings need in order to be *human* in the truest sense of the word is to have the living presence of life's meaning within. The fall of both humankind and the kingdoms of nature provides knowledge of what has thus been lost. The fall into sin is visible in the three kingdoms of nature and in humanity, because each of these four realms of existence must be completed before its true condition is reached. However, we combine them and ask: What is lacking in Nature and Man? The complete answer to this question is true humanity.

True humanity is lacking in terrestrial existence; it can complete, or redeem, all the beings on Earth. Long ago, all terrestrial beings arose from the great human being, Adam Cadmon, and all earthly beings still long for what they lost at that time. If the animal kingdom is stunted humanity, and if the plant and mineral kingdoms are in a similar condition, then the redemption of those kingdoms is not possible until they are restored to their lost human condition. But earthly human beings have also fallen. They, too, represent a stunted manifestation of the true human being, Adam Cadmon. Thus, earthly humankind is the stage in terrestrial existence whereon the longing of all creatures attains consciousness of itself. The fact that human beings stand erect upon feet is a phenomenon in the course of natural events, signifying that the cosmic tragedy of congealing stones, the darkened yearning of the plants, the dumb hope of the animals have all become a conscious effort toward redemption. But for human beings to fully recognize their responsibility toward nature, they must take one very conscious step—that of fully recognizing their own imperfection as stunted, fallen human beings. Not until this recognition has taken place will humankind become fully alive to its responsibility. Rudolf Steiner describes the process of this recognition in *How to Know Higher Worlds,* in which he pictures the meeting with the one called the "Lesser Guardian of the Threshold."[1]

The test of this encounter is that human beings should know themselves just as they have become because of the Fall. Knowledge of one's nature as it has become leads us to knowledge of what we will become. Those who can endure the recognition of the stunted human will thus be led to realize true humanity. If that cognition is experienced in full consciousness, it becomes that meeting with the Son described in *How to Know Higher Worlds* as the meeting with the "Greater Guardian of the Threshold." If this encounter is not accompanied by the control of *all* the forces of perception, cognition, and memory in the soul, then the meeting with the Son is less definitely conscious; nonetheless, it gives one's soul an imperturbable certainty in the recognition of Christ as the meaning of the Earth.

This encounter with the Son is for human beings an objective event in cognition. In it, we encounter our archetype with perceptive recognition. At the same time, we also recognize that this is the archetype for all earthly being, because within it is hidden the warmth, the light, and the word, for which the three kingdoms of nature yearn. It is in the character of the "new Adam," the resurrected Adam Cadmon, that the Son meets the human being. But this figure is not just an archetype to humankind; it is also an archetype to all the beings of the spiritual hierarchies, because there is something lacking even in the beings of the spiritual hierarchies. What is lacking in them must be brought into their sphere of existence by humanity. It is the mission of the fourth hierarchy, humankind, to satisfy the essential need of the first, second, and third hierarchies. That need is the *freedom* that will have achieved its cosmic destiny once it has overcome karma in the universe. This is the desire of the beings of the higher hierarchies, but to bring it to pass they require the help of human beings. Only a blind, earthly human being can annul the karmic consequences of the blindness of any other terrestrial human being. The higher hierarchic beings cannot do this, but they desire it so that the law of justice can be established through love, to the very ends of the natural world. This, however, can be accomplished only by incarnate human beings, yet they will not do it, because, since the Fall, the will has been the evil element in human nature. Consequently, the will of the Son, revealing himself as the highest elohim, is the highest example of love given to humanity; and thus, on the other hand, the power of the highest elohim—previously becoming and now having become human—is the highest example for the beings of the spiritual hierarchies. The divine human is the evolutionary ideal of all beings in the universe, spiritual as well as earthly. In a certain sense, all spiritual beings strive to become human in the sense of having the power to overcome karma; but the task of humankind is to become divine, to absorb the divine love into the human will.

Ezekiel recognized this central truth of the universe when he saw, as the center of his cosmic vision of the hierarchy of the Holy Spirit, the Son enthroned in "the likeness of a man." No doubt, he saw this archetypal picture prophetically, as a cosmic purpose for the future, because at the time the Christ had not yet become human; but he saw it as the center of the sublime tableau of the activity of the Holy Spirit, directed toward the fulfillment of this purpose.

If we study more closely the central figure of Ezekiel's vision by the River Chebar (Ezekiel I:3), we find that this figure presents a certain answer to the question of existence asked by nature and humanity. The aspect missing in nature and humankind is contained in this figure. The various elements of the figure are those we have already mentioned as absent from nature and humankind. Ezekiel not only speaks of one in "the likeness of a Man," but also speaks of the *voice* that sounds above the four cherubim where the throne is set and on which the one sits who has a human likeness. He speaks, too, of *fire* that shines in glowing metal in the limbs of the one who is like a human being, and finally of the *light* proceeding from him, like "the bow that is in the cloud in the day of rain."

The true, divine, human countenance, the voice sounding above the beings that represent the four group souls, the metallic fire and the light—these four elements that complete the central figure of Ezekiel's vision are precisely those of the essential gifts missing from the mineral, vegetable, animal, and human kingdoms of the Earth, for which all terrestrial beings are longing. The "metallic fire" of the limb system, or will, that he saw is that warmth of will that the mineral kingdom lost at the fall of humankind; the light he saw gleaming in rainbow colors is the light for which the plant world has been yearning since Earth's severance from the Sun; the voice that sounds above the group souls is the Word, the hope of all animal existence; and the divine human countenance is the image of the goal of all true earthly human effort.

Ezekiel thus established a true image of the meaning of earthly existence for the future "reader"—that is, for the inspired cognition of future generations. He did this as a "Son of Man," by which title he is always addressed in the spiritual world, and this has a very definite significance.[2] Rudolf Steiner gave the explanation of this title, in relation to the Gospels: "Son of Man" represents a future condition of consciousness that will be born from the present consciousness as its posterity, or "Son." In this sense, therefore, "Man" represents the four members of the human being—the physical body, ether body, astral body, and "I" being. "Son of Man," on the other hand, would indicate one who experiences and represents also the manas principle, the spirit self, as a fifth member. This was exactly the case with Ezekiel. It was not just because of the subject of his revelations that he lived in the future, but also because he was able to perceive and know it by means of this additional member belonging to the human being of the future. And the whole fundamental character of his revelation depends upon this fact.

To begin with, his revelations refer to the highest, he who is enthroned above the cherubim, and then they descend as far as to human concerns. This descending scale of cognition is very much characteristic of the cognition of the "Son of Man," or manas cognition. In study 9, "David and Solomon," we spoke of this characteristic; here we need only to show why the reader, together with the author, will have to follow a descending path in continuing the study of Ezekiel's revelations. In order to be clear about an important point, however, there is one more thing to mention before we move on. The descending scale of cognition indicated here has nothing in common with speculation and is, in fact, its very opposite. Speculation (philosophic speculation, for instance) begins with experience of our lower world and draws conclusions by threads of analogy about the higher world. But in "descending cognition," binding threads are drawn from the higher world to the lower. It is distinct from speculation in that it endeavors to perceive the events and facts of the lower world by means of the higher, whereas speculation typically explains the higher world by means of the lower. To see this clearly is even more important, because today there is a great deal of confusion about this. Today the prophets and the Apocalypse are often explained by merely projecting the content of our lower world into them. Consequently, sectarian, pseudo-scientific interpretations arise that have nothing at all to do with the revelations themselves, because their meaning cannot be found in this world. The pictures and parables of the revelations must speak for themselves; if they are silent, every interpretation arbitrarily projected into them from the substance of ordinary experience is really no more than an arbitrary interpretation.

If we are to understand the complete tableau of Ezekiel's vision, it is not enough to understand only the central figure; in conjunction with the central figure we must also study all the various details of the vision. These details refer to specific beings of the spiritual hierarchies and to the particular ways they function. We must, therefore, first get a clearer idea of the beings referred to and of their activities.

In our tenth meditation, events of the Old Testament period of human spiritual history were described in general as an expression of this thought: At that time, the Father was active in the destiny in which the Holy Spirit was preparing the birth of the Son. The second part of this sentence ("in which the Holy Spirit was preparing the birth of the Son") contains the whole meaning of Ezekiel's vision at the River Chebar, up to the point where commissions destined for those around him were laid upon him. The vision shows the Son at the center of the Holy Spirit's activity. All the incidental figures surrounding the central one are related to this activity. As we have shown, the Holy Spirit in his own nature cannot be an object of cognition; his activity can be recognized only through beings appointed to that end. The nature of the Holy Spirit at that time was filling Ezekiel himself, who was the *subject* of the cognition; it could not therefore be at the same time its *object*. This is the condition expressed in the Bible by the words "the hand of the Lord was upon him." The Hand of God, therefore, was upon Ezekiel from the first moment of his visions (Ezekiel I:3.), and it was these that were made possible by this "Hand."

The activity of the Holy Spirit we are considering extends to all the hierarchies, yet there are hierarchies that are united with him in a particular sense. Just as the archangels, elohim, and seraphim, for example, represent the Son in a special way, the angels, dynamoi (spirits of motion), and cherubim represent the Holy Spirit. They in particular fulfill the cosmic mission of the Holy Spirit, whereas other hierarchies have devoted themselves to the fulfillment of the missions set up in the cosmos by the Son and the Father. The mission of the Holy Spirit to incarnate human beings involves filling them with the light of consciousness, which, in its least clouded form, manifests in human *thought.* This light is a gift to human beings; we can freely use it or misuse it. Human beings can either freely subject their will to it or, conversely, master it through the will, which works through misusing the light of consciousness. But however people use it, they owe every influx of the light of consciousness to that source, which we know as the Holy Spirit.

Now, before this light reaches humankind, it is worked upon by the spiritual hierarchies, and brought down to humanity in such a way that human beings are able to endure it. *Three* hierarchies in particular are concerned with bringing the light of consciousness to human beings: the cherubim, the dynamoi, and the angels. The cherubim breathe out light, radiating eternal light toward the material world. The dynamoi control the strength of their action in the human world. The angels guide the various beams of this light to human individuals. If the angels' activity were to fall away from this joint process, individual differences in the inner current of the light of human consciousness would disappear; everyone would simultaneously receive the same effect of the light, without distinction of color, quantity, or epoch. Most human beings would be blinded by the white light of surging consciousness. If the activity of the dynamoi were to fail, humanity would grow rigid in the light of eternity and stand breathless in the light of eternal stillness; every movement would die away, making progress along the path of human evolution impossible.

Humanity depends on the spiritual hierarchies, just as the hierarchies depend on one another. The angels rescue humankind not only from a complete darkening of consciousness of life in the material realm, but also from the blinding of consciousness by the direct, unmediated light of spirit. The spirits of motion add the power of movement, or progress, to the cherubim's eternal light. The cherubim radiate light into the dark material world—the light that flows from the eternal Trinity. The angels represent the light of the Holy Spirit at the ultimate end of its activity in relation to the confines of darkness; they are literally the "Sons of Twilight."[3] They represent the many nearby eyes of the spiritual world directed toward earthly matters. An eye of the spiritual world, one's guardian angel, rests on each human being. No one is forgotten; the eye of God (to use the language of religion) really does rest on every human individual. And it is not just an observing eye; it is an enlightening, irradiating eye. The angels not only have the task of recording what they see of the minds and actions of human beings for the higher ones of the spiritual world, they must also bring word to humankind concerning the purposes and activities of the beings in the spiritual worlds. They are "messengers," both for the world of the hierarchies and for the world of earthly humanity. They continually work to move the souls of earthly humanity in harmony with the great cosmic purposes; they try to bring the stirrings of human souls into consonance with the great cosmic impulses. Nevertheless, the great cosmic impulses originate especially in the hierarchy of the dynamoi, or spirits of motion. It is these spirits who give the real force to the supreme light of wisdom.

The impelling force of the dynamoi must be mentioned, because they renounced their share in the evolution of this force; their "dynamic force" must be seen as an activity that merely awakens longing, not as "movement." It is Ahriman who moves beings "dynamically"; Lucifer moves them through allurement. The dynamoi, however, move beings on the paths found for them through the yearning for the light of the true, the beautiful and the good. The history of great cosmic yearning—from birth to fulfillment—is also the history of a certain cosmic evolutionary cycle. Thus, for example, the Earth, as the fourth evolutionary cycle, is essentially (from the polarian epoch to the period of its transition to the pralaya condition) the history of a particular cosmic longing that entered the stream of cosmic events with the fall of humankind; it received the hope of fulfillment in the Mystery of Golgotha. We have already tried to describe this longing; now the point is to recognize its connection with the activity of the spirits of motion. Its cycles of movement are revelations of the spirits of motion. These cycles, were also called "wheels" (*rotae*), so that the spirits of motion may be spoken of as "wheels" whose rims are full of eyes; the angels are the "eyes" on the rims of the dynamoi's wheels.

Encouraging movement, the activity of the dynamoi, is conditioned by the cherubim, who radiate the light of *harmony* in accordance with which the dynamoi activate longing. The spirits of harmony (as Rudolf Steiner names the cherubim in *An Outline of Esoteric Science*) provide the *substance* of the yearning of all beings. They reveal the archetype of harmonized humanity, the complete human being, to humankind. But human beings are not harmonized unless the four members of their being are in harmony; the "I" must be allied with, not in conflict with, the astral, etheric, and physical human being. The language of primal occult symbolism would say that harmonious human beings have the "human," the "eagle," the "lion," and the "bull" in equilibrium within. The human being has four forces: human forces in front, eagle forces behind, bull forces on the left, and lion forces on the right. Those who are harmonized are ready to attain an even higher state, since harmonizing is the preliminary requirement for the entry to a higher force. Before the person of harmony can become a person of love, the four essential human forces must provide a stage for the fifth. Once the Holy Spirit has brought about the harmonizing of the human being, the time has come for the Son's birth. Once an earthly human organism has realized the archetype of the cherubim, the Son, or Christ, it will be born on Earth. But before this could happen, the history of Israel (as Ezekiel perceived) had to be continued in a certain direction. Ezekiel's mission developed out of the perception of *how* it had to be continued.

If we take the text and examine it sentence by sentence, Ezekiel's vision at the River Chebar will become understandable. Nevertheless, for lack of space we cannot do that here. Instead, the author hopes that by now the task will not be too difficult for the reader, who will be able to understand the coherence of every sentence in Ezekiel's description if the fundamental truth of the revelation has been understood—that Ezekiel sees the activity of the Holy Spirit through the cherubim, the dynamoi, and the angels, and that the goal of that activity is the birth of the Son in a harmonious human organism. This birth of the Son, however, means to fulfill the desire of all earthly beings—not just humankind, but all the kingdoms of nature.

The vision of Ezekiel, therefore, represents one of the most valuable documents possessed by humanity, because it contains such specific information concerning the function of the Holy Spirit. In connection with these considerations (especially those dealing with the various methods and types of cognition related to the three persons of the Trinity) a question arises: If various methods and qualities of soul are needed to recognize the Father, to perceive the Son, and to acknowledge the Spirit, how does one perceive the Trinity as a unity? Is it possible to receive undivided wisdom—not just a combination of three different forms of perceptive knowledge gained by different means, but perception leading to a view that synthesizes the whole? This leads us to consider an important spiritual fact in Old Testament history by examining the nature and function of the Sophia.

## The Nature and Function of the Sophia in Old Testament History

Rudolf Steiner once spoke of the various kinds of perception of Jesus Christ in Western, Central, and Eastern Europe. The West, he said, recognized especially the human Jesus of Nazareth; Central Europe, by contrast, regarded the Christ impulse to be a universal myth-forming spiritual current; and Eastern Europe comprehended the fact that Jesus Christ is both God and human. In relation to this, Steiner mentioned three men as representatives of these three spiritual tendencies: Joseph Ernest Renan, David Friedrich Strauss, and Vladimir Solovyov.[4] These reflections by Rudolf Steiner provided this author with a strong impulse to closely study the work of Vladimir Solovyov. A result was the conviction that this author had never encountered a work written before the time of Rudolf Steiner that contained such a profound concept of the nature and mission of Jesus Christ, a view presented against the background of cosmic history. That study included, for example, Solovyov's *Lectures on Divine Humanity*,[5] the deepest and most comprehensive statement on this subject before Steiner's works. For this very reason, however, a question now arose: How did Solovyov come to this amazing cognition of the more profound mysteries of the Son and even the divine Trinity as a whole? In studying all the works of Solovyov, we find no actual path or method leading to this perceptive knowledge. We can indeed follow his thoughts and thereby be convinced of their truth, but the works of Solovyov offer no explanation as to how we can reach similar new knowledge. One has this knowledge, or one does not; this is the only answer we can gather from Solovyov's writings.

Nevertheless, the impression remains that Solovyov gained his knowledge on quite a different path from the one he follows to make it understandable to others. For him, the language of thought is *only* a language; he states the facts of cognition in crystal-clear logic, but he did not receive them along the path of logic. *How* they have come to him, however, we do not learn from Solovyov's works, but from his biography. In his poem "Three Conversations," he uses his humor and wit to protect what is greatest and holiest in his life from the ill-natured wit of others.[6] He speaks of the three suprasensory experiences he had in 1862, 1875, and 1876. The first experience came to him as a boy during divine service in church. The being appeared to him then whom, fourteen years later, he came to know in another form as the Mother of God. He had the second experience while doing research in the British Museum in London on certain questions related to the sources of human spiritual history. On that occasion, he heard the inner word, which directed him to Egypt, where in the loneliness of the wilderness he had his third, decisive experience. He saw—and immediately understood what he saw—the cosmic Sophia being as a revelation of the Wisdom of God. This experience was the true source of Solovyov's "philosophy"; the remainder of his work was merely a struggle to form his thoughts so that the essence of what he had seen might be *told*.

What did Solovyov see in the Egyptian desert? Who is the Sophia? The Sophia is no abstract concept or merely a pious, mystical state of mind, but an actual archangelic being who performs a particular spiritual task. A part of this special mission is the anticipatory manas revelation, given through certain individuals. Various other beings are also involved in this revelation, but it is Sophia who brings about the revelation by means of which the *unity* of the Trinity (and also the unity of the three occultisms) becomes perceptible. For humankind, Sophia does not represent separate cognitions in distinct areas, but the knowledge of what gives meaning to all cognitions. Indeed, the separate cognitions—insofar as they do not serve practical purposes—have only the meaning of an alphabet by which the sublime cosmic mysteries of the Trinity may be read.

The total knowledge of those mysteries, by which the temple of the universe is built and whose stones are the separate cognitions, is imparted by the Sophia, called (in the language of the Bible) the "Wisdom of God." The plan of the temple was drawn up before the building was done; the *Wisdom* was there as a whole before wisdom-filled objects and processes came into being. Solomon, the builder of the temple in Jerusalem, expressed this when he put these words into the mouth of Wisdom:

> The Lord possessed me in the beginning of his way, before his works of old. I was set up from everlasting, from the beginning, or ever the earth was. When there were no depths, I was brought forth; when there were no fountains abounding with water.... When he prepared the heavens I was there, when he set a compass

> upon the face of the depth.... When he appointed the foundations of the earth, then I was by him, as one brought up with him. (Proverbs: 8:22–30)

"Wisdom hath builded her house, she hath hewn out her seven pillars" (Proverbs 9:1). For Solomon, this is wisdom that speaks and builds, a "master worker" with God. Thus Solomon understands it not merely as a sum of knowledge but as an actual spiritual being. That being of whom Solomon speaks, and whom Solovyov saw, is the same hierarchical being who, during the first centuries of Christian era, was called Sophia by the Gnostics. For humankind, the "house" of Sophia is the complete knowledge of the plan for building the universe and one with the goals of evolution. We encounter this "house" in Rudolf Steiner's mystery dramas, as "the suprasensory Temple of Wisdom," from which arise the high impulses of the three initiates, the characters of Benedictus, Theodosius. and Romanus. The temple has stood since primeval times; it is the place of initiation of human souls; to "enter" it means simply to acquire the knowledge of the sublime plan of cosmic evolution. To be initiated does not mean to know all things; no one can do that, not even the beings of the spiritual hierarchies. It means, rather, to perceive in a single survey the main outline of the evolutionary movement of everything. This survey is made possible by the suprasensory "buildings" of the Temple of Wisdom, constructed on the lines of *intuition*. The "buildings" of the temple (if we imagine them as visible shapes) form an inverted bowl, out of which the seven streams of revelation flow. These streams are the pillars of the temple, and the bowl is its dome. The seven pillars of the House of Wisdom, about which Solomon spoke, are also seven paths, or methods, of absorbing the streaming contents of the bowl, or the temple's dome.

What we understand as "logic" is, in fact, one of these streams, directed downward from above. When this stream reaches the conscious "I" point, real Aristotelian logic begins. But when the stream of logic is brought even lower by human beings—down to the level of digestive activity—a certain type of logic does arise, but it is logic in which the stomach and the interests of the stomach determine logic and conclusions. The basis for the logic of Marxism, for example, arose on this path. And if the stream of logic is brought even lower—into instinctual life—the peculiar type of logic as expressed by Freudian psychology arises.

Logic can, however, descend even further. When this happens, human beings are beginning to use a type of logic that is directed from the subterranean spheres. This may even be an irrefutable logic and may have an enormously convincing effect. This is the logic used by those whom Rudolf Steiner speaks of in his three lectures of November 18, 19, and 25, 1917.[7] These are the stages of the process which, in his lecture cycle "The Karmic Relationships of the Anthroposophical Movement," Rudolf Steiner calls "the rape of the cosmic intelligence by Ahriman." If the cosmic intelligence (the consonance of all the Hierarchies, as Rudolf Steiner defines it) reaches the feet, through which the forces of the subterranean spheres work upward within an individual, then the cosmic intelligence, or "logic," is stolen by Ahriman. Thus, one no longer thinks independently, but Ahriman is thinking through that person.

The part of the cosmic intelligence that has descended to the "I" being and even lower is the "fallen Sophia," the Sophia Achamoth of the Gnostics.[8] The *pure* Sophia remains in the heights of the spirit worlds. During the present era, her work of revelation is under the protection of the Archangel Michael, who is the "administrator of the cosmic intelligence" in the sense that he guides the whole revelation of the Sophia so that it may be absorbed by the best forces of the human consciousness soul. He creates the bridge between the manas light and the consciousness soul by pouring strength of will into the moral essence of thought revelations. He strengthens the will power of thinking, thus protecting it from intrusion, because it is difficult to introduce an alien content of will into a thought strengthened by Michael. During Old Testament times, the Sophia was equally active. This may be seen not just from the Proverbs of Solomon we have quoted, but also from the deeper fact of the birth of Jesus of Nazareth, which represents the goal of Old Testament history.

The birth of the Nathan Jesus was possible only because there was already an awareness of the meaning of his birth. What we may call the "immaculate conception" was a birth brought about not by unconscious forces but by the forces of consciousness. Nevertheless, it was not the head's consciousness forces, but the *heart's* conscious forces that were active in the mother of the Nathan Jesus. It was a revelation of the Sophia, present as a heart revelation in the mother of Jesus. That revelation had been in preparation for a long time, because along with the "I" revelation of the prophets there had always existed another current of revelation; this was the current of heart revelation of the mothers and grandmothers of the expected Messiah. The Messiah was not promised only prophetically, but was also discerningly loved and lovingly discerned in the silent depths of the heart. Nor was this a dim discernment; it was a wordless, silent cognition. This does not mean, however, that it was vague or uncertain. Although a great clarity and certainty may exist in the heart's discernment, there may nevertheless be no organ to express it in words. Such wordless, unspoken discernment lived for many centuries alongside the cognition spoken by the prophets. Indeed, side by side with the written book of the Old Testament we must consider another, unwritten book—one containing the wordless revelation of the heart of Sophia. A radiant comprehension of this invisible book lived in the heart of Mary, whereas an intellectual comprehension of the written book was present in the consciousness of Joseph, who is, for this reason, traditionally represented in art as an old man. The fundamental quality of Joseph's consciousness is correctly imagined in this way, as a very mature consciousness that embraced the experiences of long ages.

In the figure of Jesus of Nazareth, pressing on to his baptism in the Jordan, we have the consummation and completion of the Old Testament. This figure is the result of the activity of all the forces, currents, and beings described or indicated in these meditations. The activity of Yahweh Elohim, the archangelic being of Jesus, the immaculate sister soul of Adam, the Elijah being, the great Zoroaster and his disciples, the Buddha, and finally the Sophia all resulted in the human Jesus of Nazareth, who was able to absorb into himself the being of the Christ at the baptism in Jordan. This is why the next and last study of the Old Testament (which will summarize the whole work) will be devoted to the figure of Jesus of Nazareth before the moment of the Jordan baptism. That moment of the Jordan baptism is the boundary between the Old Testament history of humankind and the New Testament. Everything that preceded it belongs to the Old Testament section of the history, and everything that followed belongs to the New Testament era of human history. It is the moment of the living consummation of a great past absorbing the living seed of a great future into itself. The purpose of our next study will be to bring this moment one step nearer to understanding.

# Chapter 12

# Jesus of Nazareth

## The Descent of the Christ and the Jesus Being

The Old Testament is a document that describes the preparation for the descent of the Christ being. But, to be understood, this descent must be studied from two perspectives. On the one hand, we have the horizontal current of Old Testament history and preparation for this event; on the other, the path, which we must keep clearly in sight, by which the Christ being descends, step by step, in a vertical direction toward Earth. Even Christ's descent involved a series of acts and sacrifices. His approach to the Earth was certainly not one that could simply be determined in space; every step in the direction of Earth implied entering a phase of consciousness that sacrificed individuality to "make room" for the Christ. Even the final step, entry into a human being, could take place only because the "I" of Zoroaster had renounced its place in that human being. Just as humankind had to offer the Christ a body in which he could live and work and had to make a sacrifice in order to afford him room, similarly the spiritual hierarchies also had to act. The path of Christ as he approached his earthly life involved the sacrificial offering of the body's members and a renunciation and withdrawal on the part of certain beings of the spiritual hierarchies. Thus the Sun elohim Yahweh renounced his Sun activity and left the Sun to work from the Moon sphere.

Thus, the elohim hierarchy was able to receive the Christ into the Sun sphere as the seventh elohim. By giving up his share in the spiritual Sun aura, Yahweh made it possible for the Christ not only to work through the hierarchy of the elohim, but also to be present in that hierarchy as the seventh elohim. He surrendered his "Sun body" to the Christ. But from the Moon he kept contact with the body that would become the bearer of the Christ. In this way he was able to receive the Christ light from the Sun and, with it, illuminate earthly events more deeply. This was the relationship between Yahweh and Christ when Moses asked the true "name" of the God under whose influence he had come. The name given to him was "I AM THAT I AM" (Exodus 3:14), and this was the esoteric name of the Christ. He whose influence was felt in the background was in fact Christ.

This was the path of the Christ through the second hierarchy. His path through the third was also made possible through sacrifice and renunciation. The spirit of the age renounced his function of revelation; he "became silent." The silence of the spirit of the age was expressed by the fact that no more prophets arose, no more oracles sang, and the shrines of the mysteries no longer spoke. No great ideas flashed forth in philosophy, and no great works appeared in the arts. There was silence in all of human spiritual life; only what was old continued—everywhere the sources of revelation ran dry, except when, through *special* human faculties, a perception of the spiritual managed to be reached.

We might say the spiritual side of the time was at a standstill; it lost its future, and only the spiritual present remained. The fact that the spirit of the age had renounced its claim to act in the future allowed the presence of Christ into the flow of time. Because the spirit of the age surrendered his future will, Christ was able to enter the current of time as the future of humanity. Yahweh sacrificed his "Sun body" to Christ and likewise the spirit of the age surrendered his "future body" (the sum of his future intent) to Christ. This is why, had it not been for the Christ impulse, the fourth cultural epoch would have had no future after the Christ event. The whole force of the future was saved only by the Christ impulse; all mystery beings, all philosophy, and all art were doomed to destruction unless imbued by the Christ impulse. This is the great lesson that the tragic figure of the emperor Julian the Apostate left to posterity. The reason behind Julian's tragic history cannot, however, be found in his abhorrence of the main forms of Christianity at the time, nor can it be found in his preference for Hellenic forms, but in the profound spiritual fact that there was no possibility at that time of continuing the relationship between the past and the future. What the Greco-Roman forces had created could not be taken any further by the forces of that genius, though its time was not nearly at an end. No, we must look for the future forces of that genius in another being—the spirit whom the Galileans proclaimed. Thus the emperor Julian failed to continue the future according to the sense of the spirit of the Greco-Roman age, because the spirit of the age had himself renounced such continuity in favor of guaranteeing the entrance and dominion to a new impulse, thus maintaining a vertical relationship to the horizontal line of continuous evolution.

The fact that the spirit of the Greco-Roman age surrendered the continuation of its original impulse explains not only the tragedy of the Emperor Julian and many others of that time, but also the significant fact in the spiritual history of humankind that—in contrast to other antecedent civilizations—the Greco-Roman civilization was not repeated; it happened only once. Thus it stands alone, also, because the spirit of that age (or, as we might say today, the "spirit of antiquity") surrendered its future volition. The Greco-Roman "antiquity" can never be repeated for the simple reason that the spirit of antiquity did not will a future for it.

Thus the gate into the third hierarchy was opened to the Christ. The continued descent of the Christ being was made possible by the sacrifices of an archangelic being, who had in past earthly history already effaced himself three times before the Christ in such a way that humanity was enabled to share in the greatest blessings. Because this archangel had devotedly sacrificed himself three times in the past, and had then descended into the angelic hierarchy, the greatest dangers resulting from the fall of humanity could be averted for humankind. The activity of the Christ through the angelic being Jesus in the Lemurian Epoch harmonized the human senses; at that time Jesus Christ exercised a harmonizing influence on the *physical* body through the "I" forces. It was during the first half of the Atlantean epoch that the Christ was able to penetrate the Jesus being more deeply and descend for the second time. At that time, Jesus Christ harmonized the life processes of the ether body through the forces of the astral body. In the second half of the Atlantean epoch, when the union of the Christ with Jesus effectively took place for the third time, the human astral body was harmonized through the forces of the ether body, so that the faculty of objective speech could manifest. The fourth union of the Jesus being with Christ occurred in Palestine nineteen hundred years ago. His mission then was to harmonize the "I" through the physical body; thus the being of Jesus Christ then had to incarnate in the physical body.

This last paragraph (insofar as it refers to the various *kinds* of influence exercised by Jesus Christ each time) can be better understood if we recognize that the waking human being in fact represents a duality: the "I" present in the physical body forms one part (generally called the "conscious" part) while the other is formed by the astral body functioning in the ether body (a combination generally thought of as the human "subconscious"). This leads to the following diagram, which also serves the purpose of explaining, to a certain extent, the different kinds of influence exercised by Jesus Christ in his fourfold intervention in the destiny of humanity.

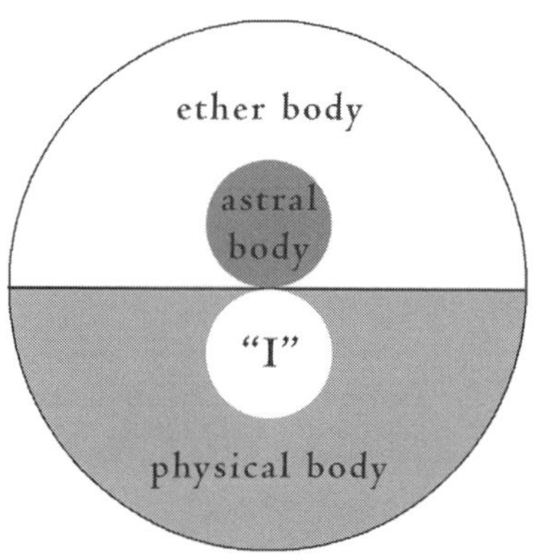


This diagram shows clearly that harmonizing the "I," or converting the "I" from a dividing being into a combining being, could not happen outside the physical body. This is why the incarnation of Christ was needed for this mission, and had been so long awaited and prepared—which is precisely what is conveyed to us by the Old Testament.

These introductory explanations lead us directly to the nature of Jesus as the being of the third hierarchy—the one who from the earliest times made it possible for the Christ to function in the fourth hierarchy, humankind. And now, to begin with, a question arises. It is understandable that the archangelic nature of Jesus could provide the Christ a possibility of entry to the third hierarchy, as far as the angelic stage; but, from what we have discussed so far, it does not appear that it also signified for him an even greater possibility of intervening in the destiny of the fourth hierarchy. Why could Christ do more for the destiny of humanity when he was in union with Jesus than without that unity? What is the special relationship between the Jesus being and humankind? For an answer, we must consider the immaculate sister soul of Adam, the link that bound Jesus in a very special way to humankind.

## The Jesus Being and the Immaculate Sister Soul of Adam

In his *Outline of Esoteric Science,* Rudolf Steiner speaks of the various inner structures of the human soul as well as its various paths in the cosmos at the time of the event described in the Bible as the fall of humanity. At that time, human souls who were not strong enough to incarnate in the altered conditions of Earth had to leave the Earth and "wander" on other planets. Consequently, seven communities of souls arose in the history of human destiny; among them, the Sun souls alone had the power to remain on Earth. At the same time, those Sun souls were constituted inwardly so that they had, in stable equilibrium, both the incomplete structure of the human groups that went to the outer planets as well as that of the groups that left for the inner planets. Because of this, they might be thought of (once the destiny of all humanity on Earth was established) as representative of humanity as a whole. Then, when the most important juncture of this critical epoch was reached—when only Adam and Eve, the strongest pair of the Sun souls, could remain on Earth—those two souls represented the destiny of humanity as a whole. The changes that affected the astral, ether, and physical bodies of that pair through the "fall" concerned all humankind, forming the beginning human karma, or the "original sin" of biblical literature.

But that "fall" is only one side of this transaction. There was another side that involved the fact that, whereas certain members of the pair representing humanity "fell"—that is, absorbed evil into themselves—other members were "raised" at the same time. In other words, they were united with certain beings of the spiritual hierarchies. Those "members" were the seeds of the Spirit body (atma), implanted in the physical body during the period of Old Saturn; during the Old Sun, formed into the part of the ether body that carried the life spirit (budhi); and reorganized during the phase of the Old Moon as the part of the astral body to bear manas. At the "fall," the atma organization of the physical body, the budhi organization of the ether body, and the manas organization of the astral body were all placed under "protection," while the rest of the organization of the three bodies succumbed to the fall. Thus, the whole process of the fall of humanity was twofold; the fall of three members of the human being was accompanied by the rise of three others. In a manner of speaking, we could also say that, if a homogeneous object is set on fire, smoke, steam, and ashes are formed, there is also a soaring flame producing light and warmth. Along with the "smoke" of the fallen astral body, the "steam" of the fallen ether body, and the "ashes" of the physical body returning to mineral, something else rose into higher regions: the *immaculate* warmth of will of Old Saturn, the light nature of the Old Sun, and the kindled Pentecost flame of manas. In those higher regions, they were placed under protection and "stored away" for the future; in other words, they were absorbed there by higher spiritual beings. The *immaculate* astral nature of Eve received the spiritual being who was worshipped in Egypt as the goddess Isis, and in the Christian Church today as the Mother of God, the Queen of heaven. In the previous study, we spoke of her as the Sophia.

The immaculate etheric nature of Adam was absorbed by the archangelic being Jesus, who has also been known and worshipped under various names and figures since the earliest ages. The *immaculate* physical nature of the human being was raised even higher and absorbed by a higher being above Jesus and Sophia. This physical body, preserved from the fall into sin, is called the "phantom" by Rudolf Steiner in his lecture course *From Jesus to Christ.*[1] It was returned to humankind by the highest elohim himself at his incarnation in Palestine. This is the resurrection body of the "last Adam," a term used by the Apostle Paul.[2]

Thus the "fall" did not just dim the astral, ether, and physical human organizations; it also lifted the human manas, budhi, and atma principles from the sensory world into the suprasensory world, thus withdrawing them from earthly humanity. This withdrawal, however, is merely a temporary means of preservation with a view toward the future. For instance, if the pure budhi nature of one person is preserved for the future, it means that the pure budhi nature has been preserved for all of humankind, waiting the time when earthly conditions have been prepared for the budhi revelation. As long as the spiritual is present and remains pure, it can be transmitted. Just as we can communicate our thoughts without becoming poor in thought, even though the thoughts have become the property of another, likewise the life spirit (budhi) is not exhausted by transmitting spiritual life or living spirit to others.

The pure sister soul of Adam, who was preserved from earthly incarnation until the birth of the Nathan Jesus in Palestine, is therefore not only an individual being, but also the individual being of the human budhi principle. Through the repeated entry of the Christ into human destiny during the Lemurian, Atlantean, and post-Atlantean epochs, this being formed both the link that bound the Jesus being to humanity and the instrument through which he worked, since it united him with the sister soul of Adam, while he also surrendered himself unconditionally to the Christ.

Now we can answer our question concerning the special relationship between the Jesus being and humanity: It was the close connection between the Jesus being and the sister soul of Adam—representing the pure life spirit of humankind—that allowed him to heal the various consequences of the fall of humanity. It was possible to bring the fallen human organism into harmony again and again, because the forces of the human life spirit, which had not fallen, could be used for healing by Jesus Christ, since they represented the connecting channel through which the Christ could function in human destiny.

## The Jesus Being and the Nathan Jesus

The descent of the Christ through the third hierarchy can be seen as a constellation of the sacrifices of the spirit of the Greco-Roman age and of the Jesus being (in collaboration with the Sophia). This leads us to ask: What aspect of his descending path led him into the human being? To answer this question, we must acknowledge the two sides of human nature and the fact that either may serve as a portal. There is a physical side—the physical, ether, and astral bodies—and a spiritual side—the atma, budhi, and manas principles. Humanity as such stands between them in the focus of the "I," to which both gates lead. Impressions reach the "I" through the outer gates of the physical organism; moral intuitions, on the other hand, reach the "I" through the inner gate of the spiritual aspect. In his *Intuitive Thinking as a Spiritual Path* ("The Philosophy of Spiritual Activity"), Rudolf Steiner describes how these two currents for perception and action are united by the activity of the human "I."[3]

If we conceive of human nature—as described in the essential message in *Intuitive Thinking as a Spiritual Path,* we can see that the entry of Christ into human nature took place through the "inner gate"—not as an external event but as an exalted moral intuition. In other words, the path Christ followed in order to take possession of Jesus of Nazareth at the baptism in Jordan led through atma, budhi, and manas, not through the physical, ether, and astral bodies. We may say, in the language of the Bible, that the baptism in Jordan was a baptism "with the Holy Ghost and with fire," in consummation of John's baptism "with water."[4] What happened, therefore, was substantially the same as the process of cognition that Rudolf Steiner describes in *Intuitive Thinking as a Spiritual Path* as the union of perception from without and intuition from within. The profound Christian content of *Intuitive Thinking as a Spiritual Path* may be understood by studying the baptism in Jordan; on the other hand, we can scarcely arrive at an understanding of the Jordan baptism, free of dogma, unless every angle of our thinking and feeling has been irradiated and prepared by the essence of that work.

The descent of Christ into the human being, therefore, followed the path of atma, budhi, and manas—that is, his path led first to inner union with the "phantom," or the "Saturn" soul, then with the immaculate Sun nature of the human being, and finally with pure human Moon nature, before he could take possession of the human "I" organization. It was not until the "I" being had been secured that the three bodies were penetrated by the Christ. The three temptations in the wilderness did not take place until after the baptism in Jordan. This fact removes certain seeming contradictions when comparing series of Rudolf Steiner's lectures—that it was during the Jordan baptism that the Christ penetrated the bony system of the body; that he first entered the three bodies during the temptation in the wilderness; and even that he was not fully incarnated in the physical body until the agony in Gethsemane. This only seems to be a contradiction until we realize that what is called simply "the physical body" really has two sides: the force system of the spirit body (atma) and the force system of the material physical body. Rudolf Steiner is speaking of the first side of the physical body in connection with the baptism in Jordan, and of the second side in relation to the event in Gethsemane. The exalted intuition whereby the Christ was able to enter the human being was preceded by a comprehensive perception of human destiny. Before the baptism in Jordan, Jesus of Nazareth had renounced all previous paths of the past and had accepted the inevitable dissolution of the mystery organization. This powerful perception thus became the question that was answered by the Christ's descent.

How was Jesus of Nazareth able so to experience the destiny of humankind and how did this experience bring with it the descent of the Healer? He carried within himself both a comprehensive knowledge of the Zoroaster "I" and, united in his physical nature, the conscience of humankind and the third hierarchy. The fact that this conscience lived in his physical nature indicates its highest development. The conscience is not perfectly developed if it has to act according to deliberation and reflection, but only if one's physical nature moves in obedience to the conscience just as the plant moves in obedience to the Sun. A plant does not deliberate and discuss, but simply allows its leaves to grow toward the sunlight. Thus the whole soul and physical organization of Jesus of Nazareth leaned toward the conscience of the world, the "Christ Sun." Within itself, his astral body continued the inner impulses effected in it by the hierarchical being Jesus in his former unions with the Christ. This astral body was made up of the condensed inspirations of the Archangel Jesus, who, while functioning as an angel, had in the past been interpenetrated by the Christ three times. The active aftereffects of this earlier interpenetration made the astral body of Jesus of Nazareth a body of "longing after Christ." On the other hand, the whole organization of this body (likewise the result of its participation in the earlier healing influence of Christ on humankind) participated fully in all human destiny. We could even say: In its upward flow, the astral body of Jesus was human longing; in its downward flow, human suffering.

No physical body could have borne such an astral body had the "I" living within it not possessed an unusual power of cohesion, and had its superhuman sensibility to shock not been balanced by a force able to return it to equilibrium. Because the Zoroaster "I" could give a wisdom-filled direction to the immense forces of the longings of the Nathan Jesus, the physical organization was empowered to bear those longings; because the being of Buddha radiated into the astral body of the Nathan Jesus, the tranquil calm of Buddha flowed into the intensely agitated life of the soul. This current of calm preserved the physical organism from destruction by a fiery excess of pain; the centralizing Zoroaster force preserved it from congealing in an excess of longing. Thus the astral nature of the Nathan Jesus united within itself the greatest possible capacity for *ecstasy*—for expanding in purest self-surrender—with the greatest capacity for *enstasy*, or concentrated repose in the self.[5] The first faculty made it possible to sustain the ordeal of the baptism in Jordan, that is to say, the absorption of the cosmic being of the Christ; the other gave proof of its power soon after, during the temptation in the wilderness.

The ether body of Jesus of Nazareth bore the innocent life spirit of the sister soul of Adam, and hence the forces of human youth bestowed the freshness of the first day of creation on every impulse in the soul of Jesus. When he spoke, he did so as only the most childlike child would be able to speak if it also possessed the most mature wisdom of the ages. The wisdom of the great Zoroaster shone in him with all the freshness of youth, without weariness, without the wounds of innumerable disappointments, and without the heaviness of soul that must be experienced and endured on the paths leading to such wisdom. Experience leads to wisdom, but it wearies even souls. Therefore, from very early ages, the soul of Zoroaster had carried within itself the experience of terrestrial history, but it surrendered that earthly experience to a soul that was without it. Thence the wonderful combination of the most mature wisdom arose along with the most childlike mind. Here was a man who could speak in such a way that not only did he speak the truth, but in speaking, restored the life that animated it on the first day of creation. Cosmic dawn lived in the great Western concepts of human destiny when he spoke during the time before the baptism in Jordon.

This wondrous being lived in a physical body that, from the earliest times, had been prepared to be able to absorb it. The preparation had had many different aspects, including the guidance of heredity forces to preserve *positive* parts of humanity's past. Heredity was employed in such a way that it served the purposes of spiritual guidance. Heredity served those purposes as, in one genealogical line, a number of individualities repeatedly incarnated, inheriting the positive qualities over many generations while eliminating what was negative through effort and work. Thus a line of positive heredity arose leading, as Luke puts it, to Adam and to God.[6] The divine, who worked formatively in the body at the time of Adam, could also work in the body of the Nathan Jesus, and this is what is expressed in Luke's Gospel. Now the spirit being who preserved and fiurther developed the good in the inheritance was the being Yahweh Elohim. Ever since the moment when Melchizedek restored the hereditary current of primal good through Abraham, Yahweh Elohim was the power (*exousia*) who preserved and propagated this primal good from generation to generation. It reached its highest development in the physical body of the Nathan Jesus. This appeared especially in a property of the physical body of Jesus, which must be described as the highest degree of mutability in respect of the soul and spirit—a mutability so complete, in fact, that no definite, continued outer semblance could be ascribed to Jesus. His external appearance so perfectly mirrored his soul that, when speaking of it, one could not say just "Jesus" in a general sense, but had to say "Jesus of Pain," "Jesus of Compassion," "Jesus of Devotion," "Jesus of Wisdom," and so on. But this quality was not confined to expressions of the face and body; it penetrated deeply into the inner organization of the body so that in fact there was nothing mechanical about it. Now, of course, this would be considered a great disadvantage; today the "strong man" is valued and admired above everything. But the physical strength of Jesus was the very opposite of a modern man's strength. When he had to carry the cross, he was too weak to do it; his "strength" or "weakness" did not depend on his muscles but on the state of his soul. He was physically strong when the soul and spirit was aflame in him, and physically weak when people's hate and blindness oppressed him. Nevertheless, he had the healthiest of human bodies; in fact, his was the first truly healthy body—if by "health" and "strength" we understand something other than their usual meaning today. Today, bodily health implies as close as possible to the animal state. To understand the true meaning of human health, however, we must see bodily perfection as an expression and instrument of the soul and spirit, not as competition with the animal condition. It is not the mission of humankind to possess a better muscular system than does a lion or bull; rather, the human purpose is to bring about the true *humanizing* of the human body and life.

Thus the Nathan Jesus possessed an organism we could call an organism of love, as distinct from an organism of force that reverts to the centaur. The nature of the Nathan Jesus, however, is not exhausted by a study of his astral, ether, and physical bodies. Something more belongs to the organism of every incarnate human being, something that envelops that being just as the bodies do. Every incarnate human being brings another kind of "body" that may be called a "karmic sheath." This sheath is made up of the forces of good and evil, which are not rooted in the three human bodies but are drawn by past karma into one's environment as a circle of influence, so to speak. There may be certain exalted spirit beings whose influences surround a person, and there may be other beings whom individuals draw into their environment through an inner affinity. The forces and beings that form one's karmic sheath may be quite diverse, but we get the essential idea of the "karmic sheath" by understanding that it is the *activity*, conditioned by the past karma, available to nonhuman beings in one's environment. But the Nathan Jesus was an exception. He had no individual human karma from the past; thus his "karmic sheath" was very different from that of other people. Because he was without past *individual* karma, he was not surrounded by an individual karmic sheath, but by the karmic sheath of humanity as a whole. This meant, however, that a vast range of human impulses were active in his environment, born by spirit beings who represented them quite accurately.

Three particular impulses were active around him, "making smooth the way" for the Christ within him.[7] These impulses revealed themselves in the simple forms of "insight," "the spirit of sacrifice," and "penitence." Later, St. Paul—after being transformed by the presence of Christ—understood the scope of these impulses and described them as "faith," "love," and "hope."[8] Behind what was so simply described, however, were certain spiritual beings who represented the most comprehensive impulses of humanity. Thus, within the astral mother sheath that enveloped the Jesus child, the being of the Sophia, bringer of all perceptive knowledge, was already active. Later, she would surround him with her influences (in processes that are impossible to describe here) until the baptism in Jordan, and even later, up until the hour of his death upon the cross. The "faith" that Jesus Christ found surrounding him was the work of the Sophia. And the imperturbable certainty conferred on the souls of the disciples by the recognition of the Pentecostal flame was likewise bestowed through the cooperation of the Sophia being.

Another spiritual being was behind the "spirit of sacrifice" that Jesus Christ needed unconditionally in his environment for the completion of his task. This was the spiritual being whose astral structure Jesus carried within him, though its "I" being had already been active through John the Baptist. The forces of Jesus the hierarchical being worked partly in the inner life of Jesus of Nazareth and partly in his environment. Outwardly, the "I" forces were active; inwardly, the astral forces were active. The bond of love that bound those around him to Jesus was real—a reality broken into fragments to form a mutual relationship between Jesus and those around him. What bound the disciples of John the Baptist to Jesus of Nazareth was the hierarchical Jesus being, who was present as "I" in John the Baptist, and as astral nature in Jesus. Hence the disciples of John moved quite naturally to Jesus Christ; they sensed the soul of John the Baptist's thought in him. After the death of the Baptist, the "I" of the hierarchical Jesus being continued to influence those who surrounded Jesus Christ.

It was not only the Jesus being, however, whose activity made itself felt through John the Baptist. In our seventh study of the Old Testament, we tried to show just how the Elijah being was operating in the power of the Baptist's word. This was the spiritual being behind the forces of penitence that surrounded Jesus. After the death of John the Baptist, he became the group soul of the circle of disciples around Jesus Christ. The tremendous transformation that the disciples had to experience could occur only through a conviction—common to all of them—that a "change of heart" was needed. And behind that conviction (the soul of their group) stood the Elijah being, who had to keep the disciples alert so that they were ready to see that yesterday's accomplishment was no longer complete and, consequently, that they had to overcome it. The question of whether this task could be accomplished is one that must be addressed in our meditations on the New Testament; here it is enough to indicate the mission of the Elijah being in order to show that his activity was comprised in the karmic sheath of Jesus of Nazareth as well as in the activity of the Sophia and the Jesus being. Thus the most comprehensive impulses of humanity functioned in the karmic sheath of Jesus of Nazareth—a karmic sheath common to all of humanity.

It was enlightened by the Sophia, warmed by the Jesus being, and awakened by the Elijah being. They worked together in different ways, while always making smooth the ways for the Christ. And, in fact, the Sophia worked in the same way that the Holy Spirit works in the cosmos, and the method of the Jesus being corresponded closely to the nature of the Christ himself—that is, to the cosmic nature of the Son—while the Elijah being worked in the sense of representing the Father principle. Thus we can say that the karmic sheath of Jesus of Nazareth was made up of the activity of the eternal Trinity, and through three specific beings, it formed an environment receptive of the words and activities of Jesus Christ.

## Jesus as the Receptacle of Christ

If we now wish to review all that has been said in order to see the complete image of Jesus of Nazareth as the consequence of all the forces and beings we have mentioned, we must see this figure as the vessel for the descending Christ; the task of receiving the Christ was what unified the many forces in Jesus. Those forces arose from diverse sources, but they were all unified in the purpose of forming the vessel of Christ. This was the spontaneous resolution of the Zoroaster "I," which entered the being of the twelve-year-old Nathan Jesus for this purpose—and for this reason abandoned it again at the baptism in Jordan, leaving to the Christ the "I." This was the desire of the astral body, too, in which lived the primal surrender of the archangelic being Jesus, in Christ, and in which the rays of the Buddha (as the teacher of wisdom, compassion, and love) pointed to the living essence of compassion and love in the heart's serenity. This was also the deep inner life necessity of the immaculate sister soul of Adam present in the ether body; the immaculate Sun being loved the guiding being of the Sun with all the forces of her nature. This was also the language of the blood—spiritualized through many generations—in which the great impulses of the whole Yahweh tradition were active.

No member of the Jesus being was subject to compulsion; every part of his nature strove freely for union with Christ. It was he, the guiding being of all the world's love, who had no use for anything given through compulsion, not even physical love, unless it was prepared to surrender itself through its own volition. And this was the most wonderful thing in the nature of Jesus of Nazareth—that *every* member of his being freely accepted the Christ. Before such a being could even exist, the whole evolutionary preparation of the Old Testament was needed. This was, and is, the mission of the true eugenic occultism: the free human being. The Jesus being expressed as living reality what Goethe expressed allegorically in his fairy tale "The Green Snake and the Beautiful Lily," what Schiller described in the thought language of his *Letters on Aesthetic Education,* and what Leo Tolstoy presented to humanity as the tragic problem of destiny.

What is the real essence of Goethe's enlightened dreams, Schiller's ideals, and Tolstoy's tragedy of life? It was Jesus of Nazareth—as a being in whom the body affirmed truth and loving kindness, in whom loving kindness was truth, and truth kindhearted, and in whom the bighearted truth was expressed even more powerfully and warmly through flesh and blood. If we study his character in the light of perceptive knowledge, it is impossible not to love Jesus of Nazareth. He is the realization of every yearning of the better human nature—all that is wholesome in his body, soul, and spirit. Indeed, the rule of spirit over soul and body will never satisfy human beings in a lasting way, because all "asceticism" of the spirit toward the body is intensely cynical, and all "asceticism" of the spirit toward the soul is complete cruelty. Those who try to follow "only truth" straight as an arrow are, to begin with, strict toward themselves, then strict regarding others, then cruel toward themselves, and finally cruel to others. They will then perhaps have great ideas and intentions, but in working out these ideas and intentions, they ruthlessly cast aside much that deserves life and prosperity. Neither can the soul's "asceticism" toward the body ever satisfy; it becomes either fanatical mysticism or fanatical morality. Even the soul's "asceticism" toward the spirit (which does also exist) today leads not to a "holy simplicity" but to cunning and hypocrisy. Those who deny themselves any development of a free thought life begin to think with the subconscious, becoming crafty while their "pure soul" becomes merely a means to an end. What all true, healthy human beings desire, however, is a free and loving alliance of body, soul, and spirit. Such an alliance was perfected in Jesus of Nazareth; thus the Jesus organization was, and is, the object of the conscious or unconscious desire of the best representatives of humankind. Nevertheless, this was also why Christ, the Heart of the World, was able to enter Jesus of Nazareth; the descent of the Christ was heaven's answer to love in the spirit, soul, and body of the Nathan Jesus.

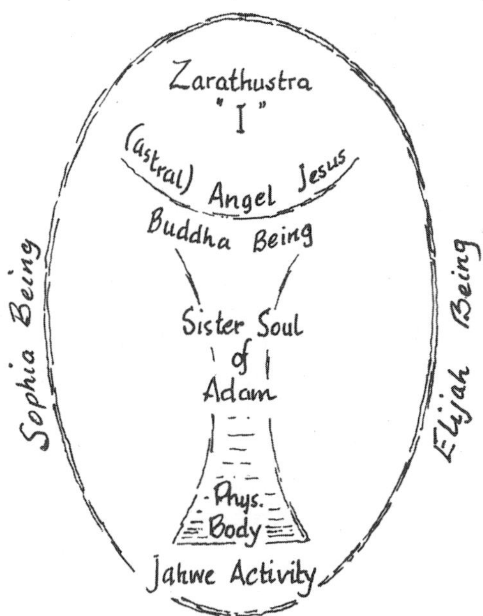


Now, as we conclude our work on the Old Testament, if we study the nature of Jesus of Nazareth as the vessel of Christ, we find that the "bowl" of this receptacle was formed from the astral body of the archangelic being Jesus, while the interior of the bowl was formed by the Zoroaster "I," and the outside by the Buddha. This bowl was supported on a pedestal of the ether body, in which lived the immaculate sister soul of Adam. The lower part of the pedestal was made up of the physical body, previously prepared through Yahweh's activity. The vessel was wrapped in a threefold sheath, made up of the combined activities of the Archangel Jesus, the Elijah being, and the Sophia. The unsheathed vessel, formed by seven spiritual beings, was, at the baptism in Jordan, filled with the substance destined for it. The fact that this wondrous vessel would receive the Christ within it at the baptism in Jordan meant, too, that it received immortality within itself.

When Joseph of Arimathea brought a marvelous chalice from the hill of Golgotha to the distant west, it was this chalice that forever retained the property of filling itself with the Christ's spirit. The mystery of the Holy Grail is the mystery of the members of the being of Jesus, which received the Christ into themselves. The "imprints" (as Rudolf Steiner calls them) of these members form, when united, the whole Grail mystery; they form the sacred vessel that can receive the "Holy Grail"—the "I" imprint of Jesus Christ.

These matters form the subject of our meditations on the New Testament, which directly follow this final study of the Old Testament. At the moment of the baptism in Jordan, a voice sounded, heard spiritually above Jesus of Nazareth, saying, "This is my beloved Son, today have I begotten him." Thus the Old Testament history of humanity closes, and the New Testament history begins.

# Addendum

Many questions have been addressed to the author, by readers of these meditations, questions arising not from a polemical spirit but from a genuine desire for knowledge. Essentially, these questions may be reduced to two: What authority is there in the works of Rudolf Steiner, since much that is stated in these meditations contradicts the prevailing concepts and tendencies of today? And, what authority is there in other, ordinary, experience? It is impossible for the author to substantiate everything quoted in these meditations from Rudolf Steiner's works or verbal statements; to do so would necessitate the writing of a thick volume, at least twice as long as these meditations. The author will, therefore, confine himself to showing, by means of a few basic thoughts and facts from the first study, that the basis for what has been said *can* be found both in Rudolf Steiner's works and in life itself if sought with attention and an open mind.

The principal statements in the first study may be summarized as follows:

1. The white occultism of the world presents a threefold unity that, from the earliest times, has been accepted in the progress of knowledge, and in the farthest future will continue to be accepted.

2. This occultism is always represented by a "council" of three guiding beings, each of which stands for a distinct branch of its threefold entity.

3. The unbroken transmission of the complete white occultism is not construed from the conservation of earlier knowledge, whether in memory or in writing, but from continued conscious communication, through *imagination, inspiration,* and *intuition,* with the spiritual world.

4. The mission of the anthroposophic movement is not limited to a general survey of the spiritual world and the spiritual history of humankind; it looks for ways and means to do justice, through genuine occultism, to always new and expanding purpose in life. This, however, requires advanced knowledge in terms of eugenic, hygienic, and mechanical occultism.

5. In this task, the three parts of the Bible (the Old Testament, the New Testament, and the Apocalypse) may prove a great help, because in them we can discover, or rediscover, the most profound truths of the three branches of true occultism.

Now that we have set down these five points, we can approach the question of whether they are based on the authority of Rudolf Steiner and on ordinary experience.

Did Rudolf Steiner stand alone, or were there others who had such knowledge? In a lecture titled "The Nature of the Christ Impulse and the Michaelic Spirit Serving It," Rudolf Steiner spoke of the murder of the Archduke Ferdinand as a symbol of broadest range.[1] "I did not know of it beforehand, either by the direct method or through other occultists," he says, and therewith indicates two paths by which he might know beforehand about significant matters—in other words, his own research and communications from other occultists, who evidently existed and whom Rudolf Steiner took seriously.

But Rudolf Steiner did not, of course, speak directly of two other great initiates in his lectures, since that was part of the more intimate side of his life. Nonetheless, he did so in private conversation. Dr. Friedrich Rittelmeyer tells of such a conversation in his valuable book *Rudolf Steiner Enters My Life.*[2] There he points out,

> It was remarkable to hear, in so direct detail, that there really are such spiritual leaders of humanity, who, well protected in their secrecy, maintain a foreseeing and guiding rule behind the history of mankind. Specially do I remember the look with which Rudolf Steiner said of one of these two master minds, "He was a very great man." His eye saw him, as it were, in the distance; and in his glance lay the reverence which one great sage pays to another. To my question whether either of these two was still alive, and whether he ever saw him, he answered, "I do not need to."

In a later conversation, Steiner mentions the significant fact that, in the present age, only one of the three can work in public, while the other two must remain in obscurity.

Who are these three guiding individualities? In his lecture "The Bodhisattvas and the Christ," Steiner says that the plan for the future evolution of the Earth was preserved in the school of Rosicrucianism.[3] Their teachers were Scythianos, the Buddha, and Zoroaster. Now, since the beginning of the seventeenth century, the Buddha personality has abandoned Earth in order to work on Mars.[4] Thus only the Zoroaster being and the Scythianos being remained on Earth. But Steiner, nevertheless, speaks of a *third* being. In lecture 8 of his course on the Apocalypse, Steiner says,

> Mani is that exalted individuality who is repeatedly incarnated on the Earth, who is the guiding spirit of those whose task it is to transform evil. When we speak of the great leaders of mankind, we must also think of this individuality who has set himself this task. Although at the present day this principle of Mani has had to step very much into the background, because there is little understanding for spiritual work, this wonderful and lofty Manichean principle will win more and more pupils the nearer we approach the understanding of spiritual life.[5]

Thus the three guiding beings who are "repeatedly incarnated" are Zoroaster, Mani, and Scythianos (and by "incarnated" we do not refer only to embodiment in flesh, but also to activity that can reach into the physical through another human being). This applies to Rosicrucianism as a spiritual stream. For instance, in the last lecture of *The Mission of Folk-Souls,* Steiner points out the identity of the "sources of Rosicrucianism" and his spiritual science.[6] It can therefore be regarded as well authenticated when we say that Steiner speaks of three beings—and states their "names"—who guide the stream of Christian occultism. Therein the "Mani principle" today stands more than ever in the background, and even farther into the background is the "scythianos principle."

But what are these principles in reality? Not individuals, but principles represented by individuals? Well, in the lecture quoted above, the Mani principle is sufficiently characterized as the principle of the transformation of evil into good—that is, the principle of healing. And what is the Zoroaster principle? Zoroaster was the being associated as a guide with the birth event of Jesus of Nazareth and who made the incarnation of Christ possible; he is the representative of eugenic occultism. Only in the distant future will the scythianos principle come into the foreground as the principle of "mechanical occultism."[7]

Now, regarding the three occultisms, the following argument might arise: In *The Challenge of the Times,* Rudolf Steiner speaks of the mechanical, eugenic, and hygienic faculties that are to be established in the future, but not of three branches of white occultism in the present.[8] How can the existence of these branches of occultism be proved? It can be proved, both from lectures of Rudolf Steiner (some that have yet to be published) as well as from other facts. The author must refrain from quoting from archive lectures, because they are not at his disposal; but he would like to point to one fact in life, which in itself says all that is required.

At the beginning of 1893, a series of lectures was given in London by C. G. Harrison, president of the "Berean Society," in which appears not only the same terminology as that employed by Rudolf Steiner, but also exactly the same system of formulae. These lectures have also appeared in a book in German (two editions, Leipzig). Harrison says the following, word for word:

> It is the knowledge that pertains to the region beyond about which there are differences of opinion as to how much it is prudent to reveal. Much of this knowledge it would be a plain duty to communicate to the world, if we were sure it would not be misused. Certain facts connected with human generation it would be useful for everyone to know. Many of the evils which spring from ignorance of the causes of disease might be easily averted, and the diseases themselves removed without recourse to drugs. Much time and labor might be saved if the ratio of consonant etheric vibrations were known, and our skillful mechanicians thus in a position to avail themselves of "nature's finer forces."[9]

Now, what is Harrison actually saying here? He says that there are three items of knowledge of practical importance that ought to be revealed when the conditions for it are favorable. These three branches of knowledge refer to reproduction, health, and mechanics. Indeed, the knowledge of such matters exists; it is the substance of tradition. Harrison says much more on the subject, but whole chapters of the book cannot be quoted here; the point is to show, by examples from Harrison, that there is at the present time (that is, in 1938) knowledge of the three regions of occultism. Steiner has, in fact, communicated much of this knowledge—enough, at any rate, to provide a sure fulcrum for the work moving in this direction. (The author could show this by many examples, but he must refrain from doing so and leave this to the readers themselves.)

So much for the three realms of occultism and for the beings who guide them; now for the question concerning the progress of spiritual knowledge. In this connection, it should be enough to quote only one statement of Rudolf Steiner: "Progress in spiritual knowledge—this is one of the impulses that underlie the whole of our spiritual science movement" (*Background to the Gospel of St. Mark*). We can place this statement alongside the following: "We will not merely study books written centuries ago, but develop in a living way the spirit which has been given us."[10] These two statements give us the unequivocal expression of Steiner's attitude toward the tendency to dogmatize and deny as applied to advancement of knowledge. When he spoke of books, he also meant his own books and himself as an author. He himself never considered that spiritual knowledge was definitely fixed by the results of his researches, otherwise how could he have said: "Many occult teachings have been gathered together here; in fifty years, possibly, one point or another may have been investigated still more closely, may have to be differently expressed"?[11] There are many passages in which Rudolf Steiner speaks of progress in knowledge as the life nerve of the movement. The statement that, if Anthroposophy is not accepted by humankind now, it will have to wait a hundred years (which is interpreted as meaning that humankind is provided for, for a hundred years) really means simply that only after a hundred years will the opportunity again be offered to absorb spiritual knowledge from its beginning into the cultural life of the general public; the statement does not refer at all to those who have accepted it at this opportunity.

Concerning the possibilities of new spiritual knowledge, Steiner has indeed said a great deal; he spoke of the new clairvoyance (the "etheric clairvoyance," able to perceive karmic collections) that will be established in a number of human beings from the thirtieth year of the twentieth century; he spoke of the rapid increase of knowledge through the reappearance in the second half of the century of the great teachers of Chartres; he wrote of the constant influx of the "knowledge of the Grail" during the whole of the fifth post-Atlantean epoch, and into the sixth.[12] And Steiner spoke of many other things that need not be mentioned here, because attention may be very easily diverted from the correct treatment of the question, to the study of detail—but the facts are well known to hundreds of Anthroposophists.

These indications, however, are enough to show that the statements or fundamental matters in our first study do not contradict in the slightest the teaching of Rudolf Steiner. And to the attentive eye, the reading of non-anthroposophical literature will yield sufficient facts to give them authority. Here, single points only have been picked out to indicate the lines that will give complete clarity, while the purpose behind this appendix is precisely to stimulate the reader to the task of testing them by reference to Rudolf Steiner's works, as well as by the universal spiritual life of humankind.

Adit ing erostrud tin velit am incidunt am, quatue core magnim dit prat delestrud duisisc illuptatum ipit alit lore vel ut iril ullaore tat ipit la faciliquatue delessecte min henis autpat. Magna faccum augait lut ut accum quam quatin velenis nim velis nulput ullamet ipsuscil iril dolorti ncidunt num in veniscipis aut do odo odit, si ex et elit vel do odignis nis dolore cortie ming er ilissed magnis nim amconul lutpati ncilisim venim ipsuscilit del eugait, volore consenim ipisseniam vercing enim zzrit augiat exercilisci bla feum et, veniam iustrud ex exercilit wis ea commodo lessed dolesequis delisit luptat lutpatis diat eu feum enis am ad essissenibh eugiamc ommolummod tio elit veliquisi.

Patum augait adiam zzriuscin er sim enit lum vel duipissi tetum zzrit, consed tat.

PART TWO

# ANTHROPOSOPHIC MEDITATIONS ON THE NEW TESTAMENT

# Chapter 1

# The Temptation in the Wilderness

We need not consider in detail the baptism in the Jordan, which was discussed in our previous series of meditations as a completion of the Old Testament. We will, however, go into the incident that immediately followed it. That great spiritual event was the temptation in the wilderness. After the Christ being entered Jesus of Nazareth at the Jordan baptism—through which he became Jesus Christ—he was, as the evangelist says, led by the spirit into the wilderness where he fasted forty days.

Let us try to see the greatness, the power of what is expressed by the evangelist in this short sentence: "Then was Jesus led up of the spirit into the wilderness" (Matthew 4:1). First, we must study matters related to the intimate experience of the human heart on its path toward the spiritual world. After the Christ being had joined the stream of humanity through the baptism in the Jordan, his later destiny can be comprehended only through the most profound understanding of humanity. Comprehension of the characters in the Old Testament required us to begin with suprahuman facts—the activities of the hierarchies, even as far as the eternal Trinity—before we could understand actual human characters and events. By contrast, comprehension of the New Testament necessitates a different approach; we must start with the human characters and carry threads drawn from the human upward to the suprahuman, or divine. In studying the Old Testament, the human could be understood only through the divine; in studying the New Testament, the opposite is needed, and the suprahuman, or divine, can be understood only through the human.

It is often overlooked that, in the Old Testament, characters and events are studied in a way that places the human element in the foreground, whereas in the New Testament, it is primarily the divine that is sought. This leads to a common misconception of the Bible, expressed as a feeling of aversion toward the "profane" and "all-too-human" nature of the Old Testament, while the New Testament is seen as a source of dogma and a document of miracles performed by God made flesh, serving as proof of his divine power. On the other hand, however, it is no less false to see only the human element in the New Testament; the "man of sorrows from Nazareth" is not the true image of Jesus Christ. To penetrate to his true nature, we must not stick with the human element, but press through it to the divine within. Similarly, we cannot understand the patriarchs Abraham, Isaac, and Jacob by thinking of them as merely human individuals living out their personal destiny; we must also consider the three basic impulses of the world of spiritual hierarchies—impulses needed to explain why they are included in the Holy Scriptures. On the other hand, we will never understand the temptation of Jesus Christ in the wilderness if we see only the God in Jesus Christ. This explains why the Gospel of John, which above all shows the God in Jesus Christ, tells us nothing about the great event of the temptation in the wilderness, and why Mark's Gospel mentions it only briefly.

If the record were only of God, or Logos, there would be nothing to say of the temptation scene in the wilderness; it was not God who was tempted there, but the divine submerged in the human. The point of attack for the temptation was the human in him, not the divine. Thus the writer of the Logos Gospel is right to keep silent about the temptation in the wilderness. But the authors of Luke's Gospel (the Gospel of the sickness and healing of all humanity) and Matthew's Gospel (the Gospel of original sin and redemption) are just as correct when they describe the temptation scene. Without this scene, it is impossible to comprehend the unity of the divine human drama enacted in Palestine. Not only are the Transfiguration and the resurrection connected with the Mystery of Golgotha, but also Gethsemane and the temptation in the wilderness. We comprehend the divine human story of the New Testament as a unity only by keeping both sides of the "divine human" in view.

Having made these necessary remarks on the distinction between our work on the New Testament and the preceding work on the Old Testament, we can now move on to consider the matters we need to know and understand for an understanding of the temptation in the wilderness.

If we study the human being within the combined organism of human and nature, we may say that the human condition is connected in body, life, and soul with this combined organism (and this applies even more to the human being of nineteen centuries ago). Countless binding threads pass to and fro between the thought of one person and many others of the present and past; countless threads of sympathy bind a human being to a myriad of beings in this world; our wishes and actions bind us to things and beings near and far. Family, friends, nationality, and culture all provide supports on which one can lean; they accord us fullness of life and the necessary relationships. Our consciousness, and even more, our subconscious, receive a constant influx of "nourishment"—impressions, thoughts, encouragement, refreshment, stimuli, life impulses, and forces. We breathe and draw substance, images, and forces from our environment, and what we seek and find refreshes the weary, calms the restless, stirs the languid, and soothes the angry. We drink the colors of light, sounds, and words—we drink from the great colored, sounding, moving stream of life, and the more deeply we drink from this stream, the healthier we are. This is the situation for human beings and their relationship to their world environment, and it is proper that this is so.

Nonetheless, in human life everything can change. We may become severed from the universal life stream so that it no longer nourishes us, and we become isolated. Such isolation is felt when we no longer recognize the spirit world merely through thought or even through its reflections in the etheric, instead being inwardly permeated and stirred by it directly—and not by the etheric world, which in fact represents the fullness of the life flow, but by the spiritual world, whose relationship to the etheric world is no different from the wind's relationship to waves. When we are first stirred and then permeated and filled by the reality of the spirit, a great change takes place in our whole being and human organism. The whole human organization—especially the organization of consciousness—is no longer just receptive and absorbent, but becomes active and radiant. The channels that previously received currents from the cosmos now become paths for one's forces to flow out into the world, or they may dry up completely. Thus one becomes isolated in the physical etheric world; the influx from the cosmos becomes increasingly weakened, whereas the individual becomes increasingly active, radiating more and more into the cosmos. The inner organization is converted in from one that takes to one that gives. But the more we become givers in the horizontal plane of the life flow, the more we become receivers in the vertical plane of revelation current from the spirit world. Now Leonardo's dictum, "Great love is the daughter of great knowledge," is reversed; it now becomes, "Great knowledge is the daughter of great love." This is the only way that, as human beings, we can recognize the degree to which we are irradiating beings and processes through the inner light of love—that is, the degree to which we make them visible through the light we radiate. Then, all other sources of light in the world are extinguished; until we can find the inner power to suffer as love demands, the surrounding world remains dark and empty, an unending cold and silent wilderness.

In the nineteenth century, there was a man at the center of the stage of European culture, standing before the eyes of the whole world and enacting a tragedy of desolation and loneliness. He found it impossible to surrender himself to the impulse that could have transformed the wilderness surrounding his soul into a flowering paradise. This man carried in himself immense potential for revelations from the spiritual world. His whole organism was ripe for spiritual reality. It would have required only a humble acceptance of the spiritual world's love, and a great spiritual initiate and herald of the spiritual world could have arisen. The world would have been given a great seer and teacher of the spirit if humble surrender to the cosmic impulse of love had opened the spiritual eyes and ears of Friedrich Nietzsche. He knew the wilderness and its temptations, but he yielded to them.

Nietzsche's loneliness was not merely a case of being alone in the world, but an isolation of his whole soul and spiritual organism. It is no poetic outcry, it is most bitter truth when, in his very seriously intended poem, he says:

> Above rooks call
> As cityward they wing their whirring flight.
> Soon snow will fall—
> Ah, happy one who homeward turns tonight.
> You stand benumbed, a fool, casting long looks behind,
> You, who have chosen to flee—facing the wintry wind—
> Into the world— that world that is a door
> To countless wildernesses, mute and cold.
> One who, like you, has squandered his life's gold,
> Is doomed, alas, to stray for evermore:

Nietzsche, however, does not merely experience desolation in his life; he realizes it even to the extent of perceiving some of its causes to some degree. Thus he says, in the "Night Song" from *Thus Spoke Zarathustra*:

> But it is my lonesomeness to be begirt with light! ...
> I drink again into myself the flames that break
> forth from me....
> Many suns circle in desert space: to all that is dark
> do they speak with their light—but to me they are silent.

The actual condition that Nietzche indicates poetically is that his astral-etheric organization was "inverted." To understand this inversion clearly, we may think of the way the eye is arranged. The eye receives impressions from outside, and is thus an entryway for the outer world into the inner human being. Now suppose that the eye has lost its ability to perceive impressions of outer light and that, instead, it is organized in such a way that it can perceive only what it has radiated from inside that human being. The eye would then no longer be the entrance for the outer world into the human interior, but an exit for the human interior into the outer world. Now imagine a similar inversion of all the other sensory organs; we can form an idea of what the reversal of the astral etheric organization actually indicates; the outer world grows dark, and every external impression ceases. One is then either plunged into gloom and loneliness, or one radiates light into the surrounding darkness. It is no mere word play to say that, instead of admitting perceptions, one now emits them. But before this great change takes place, one is "led by the spirit into the wilderness" and encounters the temptations of the wilderness.

These temptations in the wilderness result from the trials of loneliness. Their essence is an ardent longing for fullness that arises from inner emptiness. One "hungers" for the fullness of life, and this hunger may expose a person to the illusion of discerning the fullness of life in the development of power. Those who are thus isolated and emptied stand at a crossroad, between the possibility of either recognizing that, as human beings, we are in fact beggars and must surrender humbly to the love revelation of the suprahuman spiritual world or turning to the forces of the instinctual life to fill the void. The essence of the human instinctual life, however, is power—the will to power. Such will is rooted deep in the instinctual nature of human life. Just as the interior of the Earth is filled with the forces of nine subterranean spheres, similarly the human subconscious is filled with the will to power. This is more than just a parallel, since in this guise the forces of the Earth's interior are projected into the human being. Those forces are the source of a kind of fullness (different from that of the spiritual world) that confronts individuals as a temptation in the wilderness. Those same forces confronted Nietzsche, who assented to them and became the herald of the will to power, the fullness of "this life," and the "superman" who denies everything that counters the instinct and eternal earthly existence.

Nietzsche was then taken up onto a high mountain, and all the kingdoms of the world were shown to him in a moment of time. Nietzsche writes:

> I shall now tell the story of Zarathustra. The basic conception of this work, the *idea of eternal recurrence,* this highest formula of affirmation that can possibly be attained, belongs to the August of the year 1881: it was jotted down on a sheet of paper with the inscription "6,000 feet beyond man and time." I was walking through the woods that day along the lake of Silvaplana; I stopped beside a mighty pyramidal boulder towering up not far from Surlei. Then this idea came to me. (*Ecce Homo*)

What thought? The thought that every situation on Earth invariably repeats itself, that everything comes back, dissolving only to reappear after a time in a combination of the same components. Then time as a straight line disappears, all that has happened is rounded into a closed circle. Looking at this circle as a whole, we see "all the kingdoms of the world in a moment of time" (Luke 4:5), as the tempter shows them. Is this thought a reality? Looked at from the perspective of the spiritual world, it is an illusion, but it is real if we see it as an inspiration for the forces of opposition in their resistance to cosmic evolution. It is the intention of the opposing forces that Earth should have no future; instead, all earthly events should resolve into cycles that go from the surface of the Earth into the subterranean spheres, only to return again to the Earth's surface. And this purpose is not a mere abstraction, but an object of continued effort on the part of the opposing powers in Earth's history. Nor are those efforts entirely unsuccessful. In fact, the present is very much haunted by the past, but it is always specters that rise from the interior of the Earth when anything from the past is seen to live anew. For example, in its time the Mithras cult was an entirely positive phenomenon that advanced the cause of progress; but if it were reintroduced today, it would have to be conjured up as a specter from the subterranean spheres into which its spirit-drained forms have sunk; these would be different from the powers that were once active.

After Nietzsche, "6,000 feet beyond man and time," had seen "all the kingdoms of the world in a moment of time"—after he had conceived the idea of the eternal return, he "worshipped" the majesty of the power that could thus cause the world to appear; he surrendered to that spring of inspiration from which derived the purpose of the eternal return. Then he experienced the fullness for which he yearned:

> Has anyone at the end of the nineteenth century a clear idea of what poets of strong ages have called *inspiration?* If not, I will describe it. If one had the slightest residue of superstition left in one's system, one could hardly reject altogether the idea that one is merely incarnation, merely mouthpiece, merely a medium of overpowering forces. The concept of revelation, in the sense that suddenly, with indescribable certainty and subtlety, something becomes visible, audible, something that shakes one to the last depths and throws one down, that merely describes the facts. One hears, one does not seek; one accepts, one does not ask who gives; like lightning, a thought flashes up, with necessity, without hesitation regarding its form—I never had any choice. (*Ecce Homo*)

And where do these "superior forces" lead Nietzsche? To an "idea of God," conceived as the opposite of life—all that is harmful, poisonous, calumnious, the whole deadly enmity against life brought into a horrible unity in him. An idea of the "true world ...

beyond," conceived to depreciate the only world there is, so that no goal, no reason, no mission is retained for the reality of our Earth. An idea of the "soul" or "spirit" or even of the "immortal soul" was conceived to heap contempt upon the body and make it unhealthy ("holy") in order to confront everything that should be treated seriously in life: "questions of food, housing, spiritual regimen, care of the sick, cleanliness, weather, with a gruesome frivolity" (*Ecce Homo*). In these words, Nietzsche expresses the position to which he was led.

We can study this situation in its entire tragedy by looking at the youthful Nietzsche, who speaks of humankind's highest good:

> O regions of yon holy past,
> Gethsemane and Golgotha. You sound
> The merriest message through eternity,
> Proclaiming: Man with God is reconciled.
> The heart that battled here, the heart that bled,
> Has conquered Death, and made Man's peace with heaven.

Compare this with the Nietzsche who poses "questions of food, housing, spiritual regimen, care of the sick, cleanliness and weather" as the most important of all. We cannot speak of something so simple as a change of mind, but of a tragic downfall. From the "pinnacle of the temple" (Luke 4:9) on which Nietzsche originally stood, and from which he originally surveyed humankind and its history with sublime idealism, he was plunged into the depths of instinctual life, where God, the spirit, and the soul are considered artful inventions.

An unseen, loving hand put an end to it. On one of the first days of January 1889, Nietzsche collapsed on a street in Turin. He wrote crazy notes to his friends and signed them "Dionysos" or "the Crucified." He was then admitted into the psychiatric clinic at Jena University.

Nietzsche's tragic fate is a suitable preparation of the emotions and imagination to understand the temptation of Jesus Christ in the wilderness. For a genuine understanding of the event, however, it is really not enough; for that, we must study the scene against a much more lofty background, with an earnestness that approaches awe. Here we must ask questions and stare facts in the face—facts that may be much more shattering than Nietzsche's distressing fate. At the temptation in the wilderness, the whole of human destiny lay in the balance. We must not think that the forces of temptation had no prospect of success at the time. They have always a chance of success when consciousness—even that of the highest being—is cut off from the spirit world. Jesus Christ in the wilderness was exactly in such a condition of isolation; the spiritual world was not present with him. Angels did not appear "and minister unto him" until after the temptations; they were absent before and during those temptations. He resisted and rejected the temptations, not because the spiritual world was present with him, but through the human forces of waking consciousness. "It is written" are the words he used to answer the tempter. It was thus a time when the spiritual world was veiled; the only defense at his disposal was the written word—truth brought from the spiritual world into the sphere of mineral existence. And this is the way it had to be; the temptations had to be conquered and repelled through the very freedom that is particular to being human. In the hour of the temptation in the wilderness, Jesus Christ was the representative of human freedom, and human freedom must make decisions not from the spiritual world but within itself. The spiritual world was silent during the temptation; it was not through spiritual inspiration that the temptation was overcome, but by the decision of a pure, divine conviction based on the results of human discretion: the ability to make a thoughtful distinction. Once the decision had been made, by this most lofty conviction united with human discretion, "angels came and ministered unto him"; the spiritual world of the hierarchies was opened to him.

The temptation in the wilderness—up to the moment when communication with the spiritual hierarchies began—gives the meaning and contains the positive human karma of the kali yuga, or "dark age." From the perspective of truth, what is the dark age? It is the temptation of humanity as a whole in the wilderness. This age is "dark" so that human freedom can make the decisions concerning temptations. The spiritual world had to be darkened for human experience so that human beings might decide for themselves without its help. The temptations, which must be overcome, are still the three temptations of the wilderness that Christ, as humanity's representative, rejected and overcame (he simply rejected one of the three temptations). Since then, world history has been essentially the story of human encounters, one by one, with the three temptations in the wilderness. It is the responses to these temptations that, in the sixth cultural epoch, will divide humankind into two distinct karmic communities, which will then become two distinct races. The possibility of conscious communication with the spiritual hierarchies will be guaranteed to the part of humankind that has made the right decisions (and the opportunity of deciding will be repeatedly offered to humanity). Those people will no longer have to choose their direction, but will have already made their choice.

We will understand why there is so little spiritual experience today if we understand world history as a preparation, a determination, a judgment, and a consequence of the temptations in the wilderness. Why are there so few, even in spiritual movements, who have genuine suprasensory experiences? Because people have not yet decided for certain whether to serve or rule; whether to possess the kingdoms of the past or to wander destitute into the future; whether to desire miracles or knowledge. Until people have decided for obedience, poverty, and the chastity of knowledge, they remain dependent on what is "written"—unless they have, in fact, decided in favor of power, wealth, and the authority of miracles. It is true that there is much that "is written" today, much more than there was a hundred years ago, and this is because the time has come when decisions press upon us, and they can no longer be postponed.

If, with full moral attention, we study the whole situation of the spiritual life of modern humanity, we can convince ourselves of the fact that people are exposed to the three temptations of the wilderness under the most diverse forms. Thus, today we can realize that in almost every sphere—both in our everyday life and in our cogitative life—there is a growing tendency to substitute a quantitative, numerical value to everything qualitative and specific. Indeed, this has gone so far that a phenomenon cannot be considered "known" until it can be expressed numerically. For example, it is permissible to consider the phenomenon of light "known," because the rate of its distribution in kilometers per second and the frequency and length of its vibrations have been reduced to a formula. This rule is carried so far that, instead of going more deeply into the phenomenon of light in terms of its illuminating power, researchers turn away from the phenomenon itself and work toward results in a row of figures. When they find themselves in a position of substituting (in their minds) numbers for the phenomenon, they consider the act of cognition complete. But what has really been accomplished by attributing the reality of characteristics (the qualitative) to numbers (the quantitative)? They have turned stones into bread. By ascribing to what is dead (quantity) the property of what is living (quality), they have realized in cognition the act of changing stones into bread.

It is not just in their thought life that people change stones into bread; this happens, too, in the ordinary social life of human beings. Everyone, in fact, is in a position to change a piece of metal or paper into a basket of bread. Apart from its "magical" purchasing power, money is a thoroughly mineral phenomenon; it is "stone," but it can always be changed into bread. Money has no more value than the figure arbitrarily assigned to it; but in this way, bread, which bears the properties of food and supports life, is subjected to the power of number.

This fact of life, however, is not confined to the realm of ordinary affairs. It goes further and effects great social movements in the general human worldview. People today are thus divided into two hostile camps—one group adopting "capitalism," the other the "anti-capitalism" in the social life of the state. Between these two camps there is war to the knife, but in fact they both serve the same master: capital. Whether capital is administered by one group (or "class") or by another, or even if it is spread among everyone, the movement nevertheless remains within the framework of the impersonal power of capital; at no point is the realm of its influence exchanged for the realm of life and thought. Whether one is "pro" or "anti" capitalism, the viewpoint is always, in both cases, under the spell of capital. The fact that capital is allowed to exercise such influence over the mind is the tragedy of capital in our time. This is the real problem, and its solution is the most important.

In fairly recent times, the situation was different. For instance, as late as the sixteenth century, Europeans were moved most deeply by religious matters. At that time, Europe was split into two camps that fought over religious ideas with the greatest force and methods. We could almost say that the impetus, the fanaticism, the will to sacrifice exhibited then in defending and resisting religious opinions are now used to defend or fight one or another method of using or distributing capital. Although the religious wars of the sixteenth and seventeenth centuries were unquestionably barbarous, the present wars over capital are no less barbarous; indeed, there is no lack of St. Bartholomew Nights today—in Russia, for example.

Thus the temptation in the wilderness to yield to the impulse to turn stones into bread confronts humankind not only in the life of cognition, but also in the form of capital. The power of this temptation is enormous; it could be said that today's history stands under its sign.

In our present age, however, there is also a strong resistance to abstraction and capital. The cry grows louder and louder, that people must return to life. Life is found not only in knowledge, but also in other areas. Consequently, people turn to the "source of life," which is thought to exist in the instinctual life of the subconscious. For instance, the extreme tendency of Freud's psychoanalysis sees almost nothing in the phenomena of the supraconscious, but only ripples on the surface of the subconscious life of desires. This is where the forces of cause and effect are supposed to be, whereas the thought and judgment of human day consciousness are merely weak surface phenomena. In the West, in America, a similar tendency is represented by Professor James Leuba, an opponent of Professor William James, that also makes itself felt in religious psychology.[1] Leuba explains the mystical state of consciousness by connecting it to erotic phenomena and to the various intoxicating effects of narcotics, while never denying the value of mysticism itself in life.

The most remarkable religious philosophy from this perspective, however, is disseminated among the Russian immigrants of the Greek Church. Its representative is Professor B. P. Vysheslavtzeff (who works with several other professors, including Sergeius Bulgakov and Nikolai Berdyaev).[2] He presents a practical and theoretical philosophy of religion that exhibits an organic union between dark science and dark religion. Vysheslavtzeff has united Freudian psychoanalysis and religious dogmatism, both entirely devoid of cognitive knowledge. In this way, he believes he has established a bridge between religion and science, but, in fact, he points both religion and science toward a common source—the instinctual life of the subconscious. And others seek the "springs of life," which they, too, consider the source of all cultural inspiration—in the instincts of "race," or "folk"—believing that in this way they have found the only viable reality. And there are yet other symptoms of this tendency of human aspiration, seeking in the instincts the true source of human drive and productive forces.

Here we are not concerned with giving a detailed survey of these endeavors, but only point to the fact that today there is a strong, polymorphic tendency to plunge from the conscious into the subconscious. This tendency, however, is really nothing but a surrender to the temptation in the wilderness—to cast oneself down from a pinnacle of the temple into the abyss. The pinnacle of the temple for modern humanity is the free life of thinking, and from that height human beings can acquire mental vision and, in the freedom of clear consciousness, decide the direction taken toward true progress. The abyss into which people are tempted to plunge, however, is made up of the instinctive urges that are hidden from consciousness. And people are tempted to expect miracles from this abyss by simply trusting and surrendering to it. Behind their various masks, the temptations that confront people today are their suspicion of free thinking and their confidence in the instincts. Mostly, people are weary of thought; they would like to see miracles of human nature and eruptions of powerful forces from unknown depths of the subconscious rather than wrestle through toilsome thinking in self-sustained isolation. In our present age, there really is a strong tendency to believe in miracles, and the hope of great things from the unknown (and the subconscious depths are indeed dark) is really no more than a kind of faith in miracles.

These two tendencies—to invest what is dead with the nature of what lives, on the one hand, and to plunge from the conscious into the subconscious—have a common root in a third tendency, which is no less characteristic of today than are the other two. The first case involves an inclination to form a spiritless space where the quantitative replaces the qualitative. The second reverses causality by looking for motivational forces in the subconscious instinctual life rather than in the spiritual sphere. The third tendency is toward an unspiritual configuration of time with no future.

Materialism is not merely the result of thinking, or logic, but a phenomenon that embodies this thought: "The wish is father to the thought." Materialism expresses a tendency of soul to see the world as having no moral or spiritual guidance for direction or order. People are materialistic, for example, because it is logical to say that human consciousness arises from combinations of blind, unconscious matter; they are materialists because they refuse to recognize karma as an actual possibility. And they deny karma in the world because, in the subconscious depths of their souls, they fear karma; they fear judgment. Because the future brings retribution for the past, people deny both the moral world order and the future in the sense of that moral world order.

If people today want to form a concept of the world that corresponds to a desire for freedom from responsibility, they will construct a materialistic worldview. But the idea of modern materialism is not yet finished. It is stuck halfway through its evolution, because, if it continues to evolve in the same direction to its ultimate conclusion, it will be impossible to refute a ruling intelligence behind matter—one that may in fact be amoral, but one that is nevertheless engaged in a consistent effort toward its goal. First, the existence of that intelligence will be noticed and recognized; then, some day, Ahriman will also be discovered; humankind will run up against Ahriman. The name given to this intelligence is unimportant—whether it is called a new kind of electricity that is active everywhere in the Earth organism along with the electricity we already know, or the "potential intelligence of the terrestrial planet"—when materialism has been developed further, the "prince of this world" must be recognized as a reality, and the sovereignty of that reality will have to be acknowledged.[3] In other words, the pursuit of a materialistic way of thinking leads to the "worship of the prince of this world," as referred to in the temptation scene of the Gospels.[4]

The path of Nietzche's destiny is a good example of what precedes the "worship of the prince of this world." The vision of "all the kingdoms of the world in a moment of time" is the preparation leading to this worship. It involves the fact that human consciousness can reach a kind of "mystical" inspiration, imagining, for example, the world as the sum of the movements of atoms (or possibly electricity). No time exists, no future. Every movement repeats itself when all of the possible combinations of its components are exhausted. Every moment is an eternal possession, all the kingdoms of the world are always present; they move in the circles of circles, the ring of repetition.

In a sense, we can speak of three stages on the path of materialistic thought trends. As the first stage of this path we may notice atomism; that is, the control of the consciousness by abstractions such as atoms, electrons, and so on, that corresponds to the *imagination* stage of the spiritually directed path. This might be called the stage of hallucination. There is then a stage that corresponds to *inspiration* in the spiritual path of knowledge. In this we find the counterarchetype, a distorted reflection of Zoroaster's "cosmic year," the rhythm of the cosmos comprehended. This stage might be called the stage of insanity following the hallucination stage. The third stage would involve worshipping the prince of this world, corresponding to the *intuition* stage of spiritual knowledge; but it might justifiably be called a stage of possession. At this stage, one becomes the tool of Ahriman, even though at the beginning it was Lucifer who led the way. Lucifer entices but does not dominate; it is Ahriman who forcibly takes possession of human consciousness. So the path indicated by materialism, which the Gospel calls "the sin against the Holy Spirit," leads through hallucination to insanity and from insanity to possession.[5]

The materialistic worldview itself supplies a formula well adapted to combine all that has been presented on the three temptations in three words of modern speech—three words that express exactly the trinity of materialism: force, chance, and matter. These are the fundamentals of materialism. If we go more deeply into the moral substance of these ideas, we find that *force,* in fact, signifies the age without karma, or the future as it appears through the temptation to worship the prince of this world for the sake of the kingdoms of this world. The concept *chance* means simply the plunge of consciousness into the subconscious and the denial of true causality in favor of the dark, opaque sway of the subconscious. And *matter* is the term for the space, devoid of quality and spirit, which, through the temptation to turn stones into bread, appears as the foundation of life. These three concepts indicate the essence of the three temptations of the wilderness in modern materialistic consciousness; they clearly represent the modern doctrine counter to the Christian creed, which expresses belief in God the Father, the Son, and the Holy Spirit. Those who believe in matter thereby deny the Father, and acknowledgment of force and chance is to deny the Holy Spirit and the Son. Blind force is just the opposite of spiritual light; blind chance is the opposite of the Logos, or Son; and spiritless matter stands in contrast to the cosmic First Cause, or Father being.

Now we can understand the end results of the three temptations to which humankind is exposed. They lead to sleep of moral consciousness by means of unspiritual time (force); its prostration through lack of causality into which it has plunged (chance); and its death through the mechanization of life (matter). The mission of white occultism throughout the centuries has been to combat these tendencies. This is why the Rosicrucian stream compressed all of its knowledge and all of its mission into three sentences. These three sentences were commended to the hearts of anthroposophists in a new form by Rudolf Steiner at the Christmas conference of 1923 as a spiritual foundation stone. The three central precepts of the meditation that he gave to all anthroposophists then are:

> Out of the Godhead is created humankind.
> In Christ death becomes life.
> In Spirit's cosmic thoughts, the soul awakens.

These precepts contain all that human consciousness needs to withstand the three temptations and to persevere against the dangers of sleep, prostration, and death.

## The Temptation in the Wilderness

Now we have the background against which to study the temptation of Jesus Christ. First, imagine the situation of the temptation scene. Jesus Christ finds himself isolated both inwardly and externally. He had been "led by the spirit" into this isolation. At the baptism in the Jordan, through the permeation of a mighty spiritual force into the human organism of Jesus, a process of inner metamorphosis was begun that brings isolation with it. This condition of isolation is manifested mainly in the concentration of all attention, or consciousness, within the human organism itself; it has nothing, no free forces, to spare for the outer world, even for the perception of the spiritual world. Today we might say that the consciousness of Jesus Christ was "subjective" at that time, that it was concerned only with the inner processes of human nature. The dead are in a similar condition during the period immediately following the vision of the life tableau and before the kama loka state. As a rule, they experience this for about forty days as an inner upheaval of their organism that leads to the kama loka condition.

Now, however, the consciousness of Jesus Christ is as clear as imaginable. It is not disturbed by the function of the sheaths into which he has descended. Thus what he encounters there is not experienced as a series of vague urges and inclinations, but as the objectivity of visionary perception. What usually functions in the human subconscious was formed into visions. Thus a figure rose before his mind's eye, showing him from the heights all the kingdoms of the world in a moment of time. The flow of thought (it is not words here, but thoughts) illumined by this vision perhaps might be described as follows:

> You are a spirit being who has become a man. Thus you carry all the forces of the spirit world within yourself, and now, through the members of your human nature, you carry all of the forces and faculties of the lower world. You bear within yourself all the kingdoms of the world. Within you all of the world's forces are concentrated. Unfold them; see how they develop when you unfold them outward from within. In these worlds, you will see nothing foreign and nothing that is not your own. They will be yours, and you will be able to shape them according to your wildest dreams. But I will endow those worlds with immortality and give them to you for an everlasting possession. Suffering will end, but no joy will ever die, because all joy desires itself, and I am the spirit who endows all joys with immortality by leading it back to itself, in a closed circle of repetition. Nevertheless, you will see all the splendor and all the majesty of your

> being unfolded around you; everything will be from you and for you, and—if you will what I will, and if you recognize my will as yours—you shall rejoice in yourself for all eternity.

Jesus Christ recognized Lucifer, and overcame that temptation by acknowledging the will of the cosmic deity, and thus allowed no opening to the spirit of arrogance. In his opposition to cosmic law, or what "is written," Lucifer was recognized. Then another figure appeared that had been standing unseen behind Lucifer as he spoke of the worship of himself. The thoughts of those two beings united into a single stream of doubt, as a challenge to conquer doubt through one hardy, or foolhardy, act:

> If you are the Son of God, then assume a position of complete unity with the will of God, rather than having to make decisions with an isolated consciousness, as you are now doing. Throw off this isolated consciousness and plunge into the fullness of cosmic forces. The will of God is everywhere, and you will surely find it under your feet, just as you find it above. After all, if you are the Son of God, you can certainly plunge boldly into the abyss of consciousness; even the lowest forces of your being—even your feet—will not strike anything alien or be hurt by anything. The will of the Father works everywhere and, when you descend into the depths, his emissaries will be as active in the forces of your feet as they should be in the forces of your head.

These were more or less the thoughts through which the second temptation approached Jesus Christ. Christ, however, also recognized the second figure who had acted as Lucifer's subconscious, so to speak, in the first temptation, and he was now standing next to Lucifer. He recognized in him that being who, in common with Lucifer, tries to turn everything in the world upside down, changing the higher into the lower and the lower into the higher. His answer, therefore, was that the lower cannot give certainty about the divine; the divine alone could do that: "thou shalt not tempt the Lord thy God" (Matthew 4:7). Now that Lucifer had been seen through, and now that the nature of his alliance with Ahriman was recognized, Ahriman appeared alone and had to speak directly in his own language:

> Look at the dead earthly phenomena, the stones; they can come to life as bread if you only command them to do so. They will become as bread because, from the earth's interior, I can supply a lifelike force to all dead matter. You must simply will what is dead to live.

And Christ saw that Ahriman was speaking for the life of the world's "anti-word." He recognized that this is different from the life that comes from heavenly heights through divine Word; it is the life of the anti-word of the world, which from the subterranean spheres wills to kill the living and give life to the dead. Christ therefore rejected that temptation by pointing to the Word of God as the other source of life. But something remained opaque and hidden behind Ahriman during this temptation. Just as, behind the figure of Lucifer, Ahriman was invisibly present in the first temptation, hidden behind the figure of Ahriman was a mysterious being, the subconscious, as it were, of Ahriman, which remained masked. Thus the final cause, the essence of Ahriman's intentions, was immersed in darkness. Christ had indeed rejected the temptation, but something remained unknown and hidden in the temptation. This is why Christ could say, "It is written, Man shall not live by bread alone, but by every word that proceedeth out of the mouth of God" (Matthew 4:4). In this way, Ahriman retains a field of activity and battles for the future. The whole mission of human evolution, right into the Vulcan condition, involves the struggle for this sphere, which has remained contested territory.

The three temptations in the wilderness had powerful consequences for the mission of Jesus Christ himself, as well as for the whole of humanity. We will discuss those consequences in the next meditation.

## Chapter 2

# The Effects of the Temptation in the Wilderness

### The Temptation in the Wilderness and the Temptation in Paradise

The temptation of Jesus Christ in the wilderness had the broadest implications for the whole destiny of earthly humanity, because it was accomplished in the name of humanity for its salvation. In the hour of temptation, Jesus Christ depended on the ordinary day consciousness proper to humankind. The tempters of humanity as a whole confronted him with the temptations intended for all of humankind. Understanding these facts and their explanations in the previous meditation gives a sense of the scope of that temptation incident; but this feeling may be intensified to holy earnestness by taking another step in understanding its meaning.

We will do this by comparing the entire organism of the Old Testament with that of the New Testament. We will thus find that those two organisms show strikingly common characteristics. The Old Testament begins with a description of the six days' labor and its crown, the creation of humankind, or the Old Adam. The New Testament begins with the description of the birth and growth of the new humanity, the New Adam. And just as the Old Testament immediately afterward tells of the temptation in the Garden of Eden, likewise immediately after the event of the Jordan baptism, when the New Adam came into being, the New Testament describes the temptation scene in the wilderness. Little is needed to show us that, if we attribute karmic significance for humanity to the New Adam (significance at least equal to that of the Old Adam), in terms of destiny we must give at least as much importance to the temptation of the New Adam as we do to the temptation in the Garden of Eden. Thus we are led by this simple reflection to the great fact of world history—that, compared to the temptation in the Garden of Eden, the temptation in the wilderness is just the opposite for human destiny. As the original temptation in the Garden of Eden had the fall of humanity as its consequence, along with the myraid of vital changes in consciousness and the human organism that accompanied it, so the temptation in the wilderness had equally vital consequences in relation to changes in the consciousness and the human organism of man—though not in the direction of the "fall," but toward ascent.

Let us now look more closely at the two temptation incidents. In the Old Testament description, the temptation came first to Eve—that is, to the psychic, astral human element. Translated into today's thought language, the temptation approached through this demand and promise:

> Behold the life of your soul; it is displayed around you in images woven from cosmic forces. In yourself, you are nothing, a veritable nothing. Only when you partake of the "fruits of the tree" (the branching world currents that surround you) do you experience your inner life; but it is not your own life, but the life of the world. If you take the fruits of the Tree of Joy, you will be filled with joy; but it is not your joy, but the joy of the world that then flows into you. In this way, you experience nothing of yourself; you are merely a stage for the world's forces. Likewise, when you taste the fruit of the Tree of Hope, it is not you who hopes, but world's hopes shine forth in you; you are yourself just as devoid of hope as of joy. And so you will remain—only a mirror of the soul life of the gods—unless you eat the fruit of the Tree of Distinction between Good and Evil, wherein flows not just the sap of the gods' soul life, but also the sap of the serpent's soul life that has power to say "No" to the purposes of the gods. Eat the fruit of this tree, and you will possess your own life and be able to make decisions just as the gods do. You will be as gods!

And Eve ate of the Tree of the Knowledge of Good and Evil. Then the first temptation of Jesus Christ in the wilderness appears as a sequel to this. Here, too, an appeal is made to self-love, though it is no longer the inner freedom of "I" consciousness that is offered, but "all the kingdoms of the world" as a possession for a soul languishing in desert loneliness. This temptation, however, is met by the human capacity of distinguishing goodness from evil, developed precisely as a result of the temptation in the Garden of Eden. Thereby evil was recognized as evil. (And this sublime capacity Jesus Christ derived from the Zoroaster being, who had been preparing Jesus of Nazareth for eighteen years). Now Jesus Christ repelled the will to power and consciously replaced it with a will that held the same relationship of submission to the deity that it held, unconsciously, before the fall. The submissiveness of paradise, which ended with the temptation in the Garden of Eden, was now restored by Jesus Christ.

The temptation in the Garden of Eden, however, was not confined to Eve eating from the Fruit of Knowledge. "she gave also unto her husband with her, and he did eat" (Genesis 3:6). This is the second part of the primal human drama—that the "I" being is made to absorb the egoism that the astral body has absorbed. The "I" had, as it were, remained on the "pinnacle of the temple" in a reflective contemplation of the sphere of fixed stars, but now casts itself from that height into the surging astral abyss, beset by egoistic instincts. Original (or inherited) sin did not arise until the "I" principle became a victim of astral egoism; as a result, egoism entered the blood and became hereditary. The egoism that had first penetrated the astral nature was now able to enter the blood by way of the "I" organism and, having reached the blood, became an attribute of all succeeding generations.

The temptation to cast himself down "from the pinnacle of the temple" into the abyss of the instinctive also assailed Jesus Christ, but he overcame it by allowing only the clear light of consciousness to be the arena for the covenant between the human and the suprahuman.

The human organization changed because the astral nature absorbed egoism and the "I" principle descended into that astral nature, as indicated in the Bible: "the eyes of them both were opened" (Genesis 3:7). This change involved the development of a faculty for perceiving the outer world. That new faculty was the result of human beings themselves becoming darker, while the world as a whole became correspondingly brighter. Thus far, humankind had been filled entirely with cosmic light and radiated it outward from within. Thus the outer world was irradiated by the light streaming out from humanity and was thus imperceptible, just as during the day sunlight outshines and makes the stars invisible. By absorbing egoism, humankind was no longer translucent to the cosmic light of spirit; the egoism that had entered human beings was now an obstacle to that light. Instead of radiating light, humankind began to cast a "shadow," and that shadow made perception of the outer world possible. Human eyes were opened to the outer world, while the inner world grew dark.

This led to the fundamental condition for a further temptation. True, it was much later that this affected humankind directly; it was not until the Atlantean epoch of evolution that the outer world became the medium of ahrimanic temptation. Until that time, the outer world had been the special object and victim of human wishes and desires; but ever since the Atlantean period, human beings have in turn become victims of the outer world. The dramatic story of materialistic temptation—which assailed Jesus Christ in the shape of the temptation to turn "stones into bread"—began with the Atlantean period. Its possible source, however, can be found as early as the Lemurian period—in fact, it began with the change that human beings experienced when their eyes were opened to the outer world. The initial perception of the mineral kingdom, including mineral vapors, was the essential condition that later gave the mineral realm power over living souls. That power had already been greatly developed when Jesus Christ was tempted in the wilderness. Even after the temptation, it was still active, since the necessity for its existence was acknowledged by the Christ: "Man shall not live by bread alone, but by every word that proceedeth out of the mouth of God." Thus, its existence continues and presents the field for the battle between good and evil beings into the most distant future.

## Transformation of the Spiritual Consequence of the Fall through Christ

With the fall of humanity, human karma began. At first, it was not an individual matter. Individual karma, as it is experienced and recognized today, did not begin until later on, during the Atlantean era, as a defense against Ahriman when humanity first encountered that being. What existed earlier would perhaps be better described as the consequences of the fall of humanity, not karma. The fall, however, was a necessary step for the future hierarchy of freedom. Those consequences were needed for the development of that hierarchy just as water is necessary to the development of a fish. As members of the future hierarchy of freedom, human beings were destined not only to encounter evil, but also to absorb it into themselves. This was essential to the human ability to inwardly recognize both good and evil and thus to make inner decisions. This is because true freedom is not developed by choices that involve external phenomena, but by decisions related to inner knowledge. Humankind had to eat the fruit of the Tree of the Knowledge of Good and Evil; humanity had to absorb it as the basis for freedom. Thus the fall of humanity is actually the point when the predisposition for freedom arose, and the consequences of the fall are the conditions needed for the development of freedom.

These consequences manifested in two directions; within human beings themselves, on the one hand, and in outer destiny, on the other. The external necessities, begun with the fall, are mentioned in the Bible as the "sweat of thy face," "sorrow," and death, or the "return unto the ground" (Genesis 3:16–24).[1] But the changes within human beings because of the fall are also indicated in the Bible. In the third chapter of Genesis, the three essential changes in humankind are described distinctly enough. It says there that, after their "eyes were opened, and they knew that they were naked.... And they heard the voice of the Lord God walking in the garden in the cool of the day: and Adam and his wife hid themselves from the presence of the Lord God" (Genesis 3:7–8). Three things are indicated here: the rise of a new world form, the rise of a new human form, and the rise of a new divine form. The opening of human eyes changed the world; it became objectively external, which had not been the case before. The world had been inner experience, imbued with subjectivity, but now it became objective; it now existed outside, facing human beings, beyond the soul's active weaving. The picture woven of moral forces became a picture of "nature unadorned." At the same time, this unveiling of nature also veiled the sources of nature's origin. As the realm of facts dawned, the world of activity dimmed.

In this new world of outer phenomena, human beings are led to recognize themselves as part of the world. Human beings recognize that they, too, are external phenomena, along with the rest. And the glance that unclothed outer nature—showing it as freed of the moral spiritual element—also unclothed human nature. Human beings became aware that their human nature could not only be experienced by themselves, but could also be observed externally. Nevertheless, the inner experience of the human being and the image produced by the view of it externally were fundamentally different. The inner experience was soul, but the picture of it that appeared externally was only moral and spiritual. Human beings recognized the opaque darkness that they carried within themselves in relation to spirit, and thus arose an elemental urge to hide that darkness from the light of the spirit. And thus began the elemental feeling of shame, which has lived in the human subconscious ever since the fall.

Through the fall, a new picture of the world and humanity arose, and with it a new relationship to divine world guidance, which produced an increasingly faint image of

God that gradually faded completely, as we see in the case of atheism. That change of relationship to the deity that resulted from the fall was really the alienation of humanity from God. Before the fall, the divine being had warmed and illumined human beings through and through; after that point, however, they became increasingly dependent on their own light and warmth. Divine light and warmth withdrew; it was "evening" and "the cool of the day" in the Garden of Eden. Instead of God's light and warmth, human beings were now aware only of his voice and his movement in the Garden of Eden; in other words, whereas the warmth and light ethers were given over to human discretion, the sound and life ethers were still united with the deity.[2] Thus, for human beings the deity became only the thought and meaning of the world, whereas it had formerly flowed as light and warmth through human beings. Because of this alienation of human from divine nature after the fall, human beings no longer experienced the divine as they had in Paradise. The source of benevolent light and kind warmth was now experienced as the power of world judgment. Because human desires and feelings had fallen prey to human discretion, they could now be at odds with cosmic thought and cosmic purpose. Human beings, therefore, learned to experience a new feeling toward the deity, the judge; this became the feeling of fear. It was the chill of fear arising from the warmth that is peculiar to shame. Shame moved human beings to cover their natural nakedness, and fear led them to hide the nakedness of the soul—their wishes and desires—from the face of their judge. Since then, the human ether body—insofar as it has not been transformed—has consisted of the warm currents of shame and the cold currents of fear.[3]

On the one hand the elemental feelings of shame and fear had entered human nature as its constituent parts, and, on the other, thought and purpose—the sound and life ethers—were withdrawn from human discretion and remained in unity with their divine source. Nevertheless, as a direct consequence of the fall, a new spiritual fact of immense scope arose in the world for the destiny of humankind and of all other beings in the universe: "mystery," or secrecy.

It was necessary for secrecy to enter the world only because a higher element had been withdrawn from human choice, and a lower element evaded direct divine guidance. Because the spiritual nature of the sound and life ethers—divine thought and divine purpose—was hidden from the world of human choice, the mystery of goodness manifested; since then, humankind has had to pass through purification, illumination, and initiation—transformations of human nature—to become worthy of fathoming the secret of goodness, which is the mystery of the spiritual world. As light ether and warmth ether—whose nature is essentially feeling and willing—succumbed to arbitrary choice, they hid themselves in shame and fear before the spiritual world. And because shame and fear are opaque to the pure light of the spirit, the other mystery arose in the world, the mystery of the shame and fear that conceal stolen heavenly light and stolen heavenly warmth. The gates between the secret of evil and the secret of good meet in humankind; one conceals itself behind the veils of shame and fear in the human subconscious, and the other is protected by the "sweat" of pure thinking, the sorrow, or pain, of the purification of feeling, and the arbitrariness of death's "return unto the ground."

Since the fall, therefore, humanity has been the key to the gates that lead to the mysteries of the spiritual world for the world of evil as well as to the mysteries of the world of evil for the spiritual world. This is why the Christ had to become a human being: to know the mystery of the subterranean spheres by descending to Hell, the Earth's subconscious. He could then rise proportionately higher in the mysteries of the Father at the ascension that followed his descent into Hell. The fall conditioned human beings in such a way that, through them, the descent into Hell and the ascension to Heaven became possible; it made possible knowledge of good and evil that, for the present stage of human evolution, may be accepted as complete. As a sign that the main consequence of the fall had been annulled by Christ, at the time of the crucifixion "the veil of the temple was rent in twain . . . and the earth did quake" (Matthew 27:51). The mystery of good shall now be revealed—this is the promise given in the image of the curtain rending before the Holy of Holies.

The secret of evil will be irreversibly unmasked; this is the promise expressed by the shock of that earthquake. But unmasking the secret of evil by goodness means the conquest of evil through its conversion into good. It thus means the Mystery of Golgotha—as redemption from the consequences of humanity's fall—will unmask the whole mystery of the world, which comprises all the significant facts of the cosmic mystery. Since then, the history of the spirit world has progressively revealed the secret of the spiritual world; nothing and no one will be able to stop the flow of that revelation. At the same time, evil is gradually being unmasked and thus overcome. Amazing revelations will be made, and, even in the present age, all who are morally awake will see much of that mask removed; moreover, they will be assured important truths from the spring of revelation in the spiritual world.

Before the Mystery of Golgotha could place its seal on the end of this secret, the inner causes of the secret's existence were overcome and transformed through the passion of Jesus Christ. What entered the depths of human nature through the fall acted on Jesus Christ from the outside during the passion. With the fall, human beings became aware that they were naked; likewise Jesus Christ was exposed to every kind of humiliation, and the words of Pilate, *Ecce homo,* ("behold the man," John 19:5) express the accepted judgment of secular world history on human nature as it has been since the fall of humankind. Shame, as it lived in human nature, was experienced by Jesus Christ in the outer world as insult and scorn. Fear, as it took possession of human beings after the fall, fell upon Jesus Christ externally as hatred. Christ's way of passion was to endure the human karma of the fall—that is, the path to overcome the illusion of outer appearance and the elemental forces of shame and fear. Christ took this karma upon himself and suffered it for humanity as its representative.

The words "he took on himself the sin of the world" are meant literally, for the debt of sin was discharged by the passion of Christ. But these words of the Christian tradition are true in an even deeper sense; Christ took not only the consequences of human guilt upon himself, but also the actual guilt itself. The sacrifice of Christ was greater than bearing the consequences of human guilt while he himself was innocent; Christ suffered the karma of the fall, not in the consciousness of his own innocence, but in the consciousness of guilt. His sacrifice went so much the deeper, because he absorbed into his consciousness the guilt of humanity and experienced it as his own guilt. His love was so deep that He had identified himself with humanity. He was the representative of humanity not only as its example, but also as its conscience—filled with the conscience of human guilt before the Father. The consciousness of Christ's innocence was to dwell in those about him—in human beings—but it did not live in him. He did not go to the crucifixion with an awareness of receiving injustice, but of accomplishing divine justice. The words "it is finished," handed down to us in John's Gospel (19:30), were spoken by Jesus Christ as he died on the cross; they do not sound like a final reproach condemning an injustice of human judgment, but more like the solemn proclamation of the justice of divine judgment.

Therefore, it is now the mission of humanity to be the more deeply aware of the injustice of human judgment and the innocence of Jesus Christ. If the conscience of the crucified Jesus Christ was one of the guilt of the fall, then consciousness of the guilt of an unjust judgment in crucifixion of Christ will increasingly become the essential consciousness of all those who wish to be Christians. It is neither sentimentality nor mystic rhapsody, but a fact of every clearly conscious experience in spiritual knowledge that the judgment on Jesus Christ was pronounced by all of humanity, and that the whole of humanity therefore shares the responsibility of it. All the forces of human nature took part in that judgment of Christ; representative characteristics of all humankind sat on the judgment seat at that time, and the result of their collaboration was the crucifixion. This will be discussed in greater detail in a later meditation; for now it is enough merely to state the reason that necessitated the basic moral feeling of post-Christian humanity. It is important (and in the future will become increasingly so) to awaken awareness of the fact that it was *we* who judged Christ. Just as some form of doubt, hatred, and fear exist in every human being, Pilate, the council of the elders, the denying Peter, and yes, even the traitor Judas, live in some form within everyone. And if those forces exist in human beings, should not the conscious guilt of Pilate, the Sanhedrin, Peter, and Judas also exist in human beings? Are we to be thought innocent merely because the forces within us acted at another time and through others? And if we are to speak of those who were directly concerned with the sentence passed on the divine human, would it not be more just to remember when judging them that Judas, for example, judged and condemned himself, and Peter suffered the martyr death of crucifixion, asking in humility that he might be crucified head downward, because he was not worthy to be crucified in the same position as Christ? If we bear this in mind and nevertheless adhere to our intention of studying the question of the crucifixion in relation to particular individuals, then let each look within and ask whether, in truth, one has never betrayed the Christ impulse—and, indeed, whether one has ever judged oneself as sternly as did Judas, or borne karmic suffering with such humility as did Peter?

Through the Mystery of Golgotha, therefore, the great moral balance of the conscience life of all post-Christian humanity is established. On one side of this balance scale is Jesus Christ's guilt consciousness before the Father, as representative of humanity; on the other should be placed the guilt consciousness of human beings for the unjust pronouncement on Jesus Christ. When the hour has come in which the course of Earth's life is ended and all humankind has passed through the Kama Loka that summarizes the whole of earthly existence, then this balance will stand in sight of all the world, and the morality of human consciousness will be weighed. The essence of the Last Judgment will be the trial of human conscience through the symbol of humanity's judgment on Jesus Christ. Human beings will then be divided into two great groups according to whether they experienced their own earthly crucifixion as did the offender crucified on Christ's right or the one crucified on the left. The decision will be made according to whether the voice of one's conscience has been in harmony with the voice of the penitent thief who said, "We indeed [suffer] justly; for we receive the due reward of our deeds, but this man hath done nothing amiss" (Luke 23:41). These words are the highest that one can say out of one's whole being to the Mystery of Golgotha. People may "know much" about the cosmic significance of the Mystery of Golgotha, but out of themselves they can contribute to this mystery only what was expressed in the words of the penitent thief, for these words are the expression of inner transformation of the luciferic impulse that entered humanity through the fall. They represent the result of the Mystery of Golgotha in the human conscience. Only insofar as humankind learns to identify more and more with the impulse of conscience inherent in these words will the Christ force, overcoming the consequences of the fall, enter human consciousness. If the consciousness of the bond with the spiritual world, which was lost at the fall, is called "Paradise" in the Bible, then the direct answer given by the Christ impulse to these words of the human conscience awakened at Golgotha was, and always will be, "Today shalt thou be with me in Paradise" (Luke 23:43).

It is true that the Mystery of Golgotha restores to humanity the Paradise lost by the fall; it is also true that the realization of this possibility depends, for all, upon whether human beings contribute from their free "I" being what is needed for the Mystery of Golgotha. And what is needed is described in the words of the penitent thief; in effect, they are the moral basis by which humankind will be divided—first into two post-Atlantean karmic currents, then into two civilizations, and finally into two races. It will also be the decisive factor when earthly existence has ended and when, according to the Kama Loka (or the last judgment) of all humankind, the division into two planetary spheres of existence occurs.

The karma of humanity's fall was compensated by the Mystery of Golgotha; but before that could happen, identification with fallen human nature had to be experienced. In other words, the *actuality* of the emancipated (though nonetheless alone and isolated from the spirit of the world) human nature had to be experienced; this happened during the night in Gethsemane (Mark 14:36–53). That night, Jesus Christ experienced not only human consciousness, but also the human subconscious, right down to the lowest levels of the physical body. If at the temptation in the wilderness Jesus Christ saw and recognized the forces at work in the human subconscious, he now experienced them within himself as a part of his own being. He experienced inwardly, for example, the active presence of the force that, in the form of the temptation to turn stones into bread, had assailed him in the wilderness. A portion of that temptation was not seen through and was still in force; it persisted in the subconscious corporeal nature of Jesus Christ and caused the inner conflicts during the night in Gethsemane.

The birth of pure human love took place during that night in Gethsemane. Christ brought divine love—the love of the spiritual worlds—to Earth, and now he had to come to know human love on Earth before he could make his divine humanity real. Union of the highest divine love with the highest love of earthly humanity would occur in Jesus Christ. And, to this end, the union of Christ with the being of the Nathan Jesus was necessary. Just as Christ radiated divine love into the human nature of Jesus at the transfiguration on Mount Tabor (Matthew 17:1–9), likewise during the night in the Garden of Gethsemane, the light of human love radiated from the lonely and forsaken human nature into the divine nature of Christ. One mystery of the development of divine humanity is that Christ should not only give, but also receive, not just teach, but also learn. The teaching he had to give was divine love of the Son; what he had to receive, or learn, was human love, born as the sister soul of Adam out of the being of the Nathan Jesus during the night in Gethsemane. At the transfiguration, while the three disciples slept divine love made the decision to suffer death upon the cross of Golgotha; similarly, during the night in the Garden of Gethsemane, the human being out of human love—and during the sleep of the three disciples—made the decision to "drink the cup" of the consequences of the fall for all humankind. And that decision could not be a truly human one unless the battlefield of the temptation in the wilderness to turn stones into bread remained present within the Jesus being. Then because this region was filled with the most sublime love forces, the miracle of changing the dead into the living actually took place: the miracle of the resurrection.

Thus the scene in Gethsemane was the sequel to the temptation in the wilderness. There the battle was fought to the end. The fact that the struggle with the temptation in the wilderness was not yet finished is clearly stated in Luke's Gospel. The Evangelist says that, once the tempter had ended all the temptation he departed from Jesus Christ for a season (Luke 4:13). And this period during which temptation remained in abeyance lasted until the hour of Gethsemane.

## Christ's Transformation of the Outer Consequence of the Fall

If the inner consequences of the fall of humankind, as observed externally, were feelings of shame and fear, then the outer consequences—those that condition human destiny—were toil, sickness, and death. These three, which have been primal necessities of human life since the fall, do not represent punishment, but the protection of humankind from the three greatest dangers on the road to freedom. Elsewhere, we have already discussed (in meditation 10 on the Old Testament) the extent to which these human qualities indicated protection from the dangers of falling into the power of evil. The point here is to show the connection between these three necessities and the effects of Jesus Christ's temptations in the wilderness. This connection becomes evident when we have comprehended the link (pointed out in the previous chapter) between the conquest of death through the Mystery of Golgotha, and night in Gethsemane, and this in turn with the temptation in the wilderness to change stones into bread. If the unfinished nature of this temptation led to a sequel—the sufferings of the night in Gethsemane and the passion as a whole—the other two completed temptations in the wilderness led to the benefits of the revelation and healing, which the Christ was able to give to humanity during his three years. Indeed, overcoming the temptation to acknowledge the kingdoms of this world—seen in a moment of time—made possible the revelation of the teaching of a world of love—not yet existent—that would vanquish and transform this world. The kingdom of God through Christ could be proclaimed only because the alluring sight of the kingdoms of this world "and the glory of them" had been overcome. A way was opened for the proclamation of the kingdom of God when Jesus Christ saw into and, just as fog is scattered by sunbeams, broke the tableau of this world's condition—the condition this world strived toward by means of the forces behind it.

The signs (or miracles) that Jesus Christ performed were made possible through Jesus Christ's temptation to cast himself from "the pinnacle of the temple"—that is, he had to overcome the temptation to work miracles through the opaque forces of the subconscious. The main point is not that the signs and miraculous healings by Jesus Christ were extraordinary and unusual—not the "miracle" itself—but the fact that those signs and healings were accomplished by means of awake "I" consciousness. This could not have happened unless the temptation to rely on the subconscious had already been repelled. Jesus Christ's consciously performed miracles would have been impossible unless those that arise from the subconscious had already been rejected.

Today, if we do not wish to be content with a general impression, but wish to form a realistic idea of the kingdom of God and the miracles of Jesus Christ, we may do so with the help of Rudolf Steiner's writings prior to his anthroposophic publications. Such an idea (like any developed through spiritual activity) can become a window into spiritual reality. For example, after working through Steiner's *Mystics after Modernism* and gaining a clear view of the thought process and the threads with which he wove that picture, we may wonder what he wanted to express through his picture of mysticism.[4] A central idea, stated over and over in different ways in that work, begins to emerge—the sublime idea of the Friendship of God. This idea can be expressed in various ways—indeed, not only expressed, but also experienced by different mystics in various ways. Nevertheless, we have grasped its nature when we realize that the purpose of humankind is to actively intervene at the point where the created—what is finished in the world—ceases, thus furthering what has remained incomplete. In this way, human beings continue the work of God's creation and thus become conscious coworkers, or Friends of God. This is how Tauler, for instance, conceived of the vocation of humankind; it was the significance of

Paracelsus' understanding of alchemy; it is also what Rudolf Steiner wanted to convey to his readers by means of the spiritual individuals in *Mystics after Modernism,* when he presented the souls of his readers with this great, illumining thought: At the point where the given, or completed, ceases, human beings can make real the being of what does not yet exist.

This thought, which shines from Steiner's *Mystics after Modernism,* had already been elaborated by him in the two parts of *Intuitive Thinking as a Spiritual Path,* both for knowledge from cognition and for action out of cognition in all its consequences for today's consciousness.[5] Rudolf Steiner shows that human knowledge comes into existence by adding something not given to observed, given facts—that is, by adding something from a different "kingdom." Thus, an intuition of something hidden is added to what is observed. And this is how ethical human action arises from the fact that the creative results of moral imagination can influence a given situation. In other words, we can say that the finished natural kingdoms are present—as well as the human kingdom as it has manifested—but human beings can manifest yet another kingdom not yet realized: the kingdom of God. That kingdom is just as distinct in character and principle from this formed and finished world as the sermons and signs of Jesus Christ are distinct from nature and the "law of the elders."

Indeed, the mentioned works of Rudolf Steiner lead to Christianity; in them we gain a pure and spiritually youthful relationship with the signs and sermons of Jesus Christ by seeing those sermons as proclamations of the new kingdom—the kingdom of heaven—and the signs as acts belonging to that kingdom. By using the ideas gained from *Mystics after Modernism* and *Intuitive Thinking as a Spiritual Path,* the "miracles" of Christ become revelations of the most sublime *moral imagination,* and his discourses become proclamations from the kingdom of *intuitions,* from which we must draw the necessary strength to carry on the work of life. We can then add to this the idea elaborated in Steiner's *Christianity as Mystical Fact.*[6] This is the idea that Christianity is the realization of the ancient mysteries—that is, the symbols of the mysteries become mystical fact in Christianity. Thus, we experience through this second idea a kind of spiritual communion, free and clear in consciousness, just as through the idea of *Intuitive Thinking as a Spiritual Path* we experience a kind of free, conscious, spiritual baptism. Through *Intuitive Thinking* (and similar works), we connect to Christianity as the impulse to collaborate in freedom with the further development of what has already come into being. Likewise, through *Christianity as Mystical Fact,* we come to Christ as the being behind this impulse, and who through his actions has altered the course of human destiny.

Thus, in Steiner's preparatory works for Anthroposophy, it is thoroughly possible to find Christianity renewed in the present age, and, indeed, to find it as the "word" of the kingdom, as the "signs" of the kingdom, and as the kingdom implanted in earthly events—the Mystery of Golgotha. These three aspects of Christianity are presented in the Gospels; today's way of reading and interpreting the Gospels, however, requires that we find a new path to Christianity, in which the Gospels' significance for humanity can be retrieved. These three sides of the Gospels are the results of the three temptations in the wilderness, as we have said, and they represent the transformation of humankind's inner and outward destiny that followed from its first temptation in Paradise. The Word indicates victory over suffering the "sweat" of labor; the signs and miracles are the healing of suffering sickness; and the Mystery of Golgotha denotes the victory over death.

If we look at the Sermon on the Mount as the central proclamation of the kingdom through the Word and closely study the nine Beatitudes, we find that they contain the spiritual transformation of suffering toil, or work, accomplished by the nine members of the human organism. For example, the blessing on the "poor in spirit" does not mean that one is blessed for being unspiritual, but that bliss arises from the efforts of those who know they are poor in Holy Spirit, and thus continually long for Spirit. Similarly, in the second Beatitude, the reference to those who "mourn" indicates an activity, not a condition. It is the kind of activity intended that offers the strongest resistance to the ether body; overcoming that resistance is the suffering carried by the mourner of the Beatitude. And the Beatitude of the "meek" does not refer to a natural condition, but to the effort to overcome hindrances in the astral body; it is control of the astral body that is called "meekness." And this thought is expressed just as clearly in the following Beatitudes.

A closer study shall be reserved for later, but here the point is to express the basic thought that the Word of Jesus Christ contains the impulse to the spiritual transformation of toil. This transformed toil is called *pistis,* or faith, in the Gospels. Faith here does not mean upholding the verity of one's own (much less others') ideas, but one's grasp of a growing reality of the suprasensory world, making it the focus of one's volition. What is already present can be either known or not known, but what lives as possibility in this world and reality in a higher realm can be (in terms of the Gospels) only believed or not believed. For example, we cannot know whether the Michael impulse will be victorious in the current spiritual conflict; we cannot know this, because the outcome of the conflict depends precisely upon whether the necessary faith in Michael's work exists among human beings—that is, whether both an observant and a cooperative current of volition flows in from the human side. By simply recognizing the fact of that conflict, we are at least aware that it is happening; by making its outcome our personal concern, however, we develop a spiritual force that goes beyond merely witnessing the events to where we also help determine them. Such a purposeful grasp of the future is called "faith" by Jesus Christ.

In his discourses, the point is not knowledge of the kingdom, but faith in the kingdom, because that kingdom has not yet manifested. It is a reality in the heavens, a kingdom of heaven (*basileia ton uranon*), but for the Earth in its present course it is only a possibility, and its realization depends on the voluntary association of human beings with it—human faith. The created world is known through knowledge, and faith reshapes it. Faith can move mountains, just because the same force exists within human beings that once raised the mountains that surround humanity. Nevertheless, it would be incorrect to speak of knowledge and faith as opposed to each other; such opposition does not really exist. Indeed, faith (as this word is used in the Gospels) simply means knowledge that is not merely thought and felt, but also willed. When knowledge awakes to new life (feeling and willing as well as thinking), it becomes faith in the original sense of the word. Faith is thus simply knowledge that has taken hold of the whole human being. When we know—not with thoughts alone, nor with thoughts and feelings alone, but also with our faculties of thinking, feeling, and willing—we then have faith in what is known. What the whole human being has come to know, that is, in the Christian sense, faith.

Thus, what we now call "knowledge" is merely a stage of faith, though the generally accepted meaning of faith today is knowledge that has not yet reached the level of certainty. In our age, such ideas are simply pushed aside; mature knowledge (or faith) has become a stage of uncertainty, a subjective acceptance that something is true. Immature faith, on the other hand (knowledge in the modern sense), is the name given to the highest level of certainty. Thus, the true concept of faith has been lost completely.

Whereas the Word of Jesus Christ wakened faith, his signs and miracles presupposed faith. Their mission was to reveal the effect of faith, not faith itself. This involved transforming, or healing, the sickness of human relationships as well as that of individual souls and bodies. Consequently, at the marriage in Cana in Galilee, for example, the sign of healing was the sanctification of marriage as a human relationship. In the healing of the man born blind, on the other hand, one individual was healed. The raising of Lazarus, however, was the healing of initiation and the mysteries of humankind. The signs and miracles were, in fact, revelations of the kingdom's reality. Just as the kingdom was proclaimed by the Word, its reality was revealed through signs. This genuine revelation of the reality of the kingdom of heaven on Earth is called love, or *agape,* in the Gospels, and preeminently by St. Paul. Love in this sense does not imply a mere feeling, but suggests a condition of the whole human being that makes possible the presence and activity of the kingdom of heaven on Earth.

If human beings could lift their cognition to suprasensory reality and comprehend it with their whole being of thinking, feeling, and willing, then they would have faith. But if that suprasensory reality were to descend into the sensory world and fill humankind, it would manifest as love. Then, if human beings were to see the mystery of the death on the cross and the resurrection of Jesus Christ as the victory of love over death, they would see love's high goal—its great mission in the future of the world. And the force that flowed from contemplating the Mystery of Golgotha and was preserved for the future—when the time comes to conquer death—is the future force of love that will one day conquer death; this is what St. Paul called hope, or *elpis.*

Thus, for St. Paul (who knew the original meaning of these things), the three "theological virtues" of medieval Scholasticism had a sense that soared high above any subjective attitude of soul. The original Christian meaning of *faith* was cognition of the kingdom of heaven with one's whole being; the descent of that kingdom into sensory reality through the human being was the original meaning of *love*; and the future force of conquest over the nonhuman objective force of death was the meaning of *hope* as mentioned by St. Paul. And humankind owes the influx of these three fundamental forces of the spirit and soul to the Word, the signs, and the sacrificial deed of Jesus Christ, which became possible by overcoming the three temptations in the wilderness. Therefore, the three fundamental forces of Christianity are, to put it concisely, the results of the three temptations in the wilderness on human consciousness.

The essence of the spiritual conflict that will be fought out in the present age—and in those that include the sixth and seventh post-Atlantean cultural epochs—is the struggle to develop these three fundamental forces in the positive spiritual life of humanity. And in the present age, the fifth cultural epoch, the conflict concerns faith in particular. In this conflict, it is the mission of Rudolf Steiner's spiritual science to show human beings the way to make cognitive activity take hold of the whole human being—that is, bring faith, in the true sense of the word, to humanity. The reality of love will not be the real issue until the sixth cultural epoch (*Philadelphia*). Social and antisocial forces will then confront each other, just as today spiritual knowledge confronts skepticism.

Today, certainty of knowledge confronts doubt, whereas in the philadelphic cultural epoch, social love, or friendliness, will confront hate. The seventh cultural epoch (called *Laodicea* in the Apocalypse), on the other hand, will have as its main destiny the fight between denial of the future, or hopelessness, and the Christian affirmation of the future's resurrection, or hope. All this is stated directly in John's Apocalypse. This can also be seen directly by every deeply sensitive and thoughtful person who has come to understand that the whole further history of humankind is really nothing but a battle against the Christ impulse and a battle against the establishment of that impulse in the destiny of humanity.

# Chapter 3

# The Beatitudes in the Sermon on the Mount

## The Essence of the Proclamation of the Kingdom by Jesus Christ

In the previous meditation, we considered the three main aspects of Jesus Christ's work in relation to the three temptations in the wilderness: preaching the Word, revelation through signs and miracles, and realization by means of the passion. That meditation showed us that the proclamation of the kingdom made it possible to overcome the first temptation in the wilderness. It must, therefore, be special and entirely distinct from mere instruction, information, or description. It is important now to keep in mind a clear concept of that distinction and to picture and sense the nature of Jesus Christ's preaching through the Word. This is even more important, because without this it is extremely difficult to understand the discourses of Jesus Christ as they have been handed down to us in the Gospels. For instance, the Sermon on the Mount is open to serious misunderstanding if it is considered to be a report, as it were, of a doctrinal "lecture" or "address" abridged into proverbs. By seeing it in this light, we fall into the misunderstandings of its substance as presented to the world by, for example, Leo Tolstoy as his "practical Christianity." If, on the other hand, we view the Sermon on the Mount not as doctrines but as a kind of symbolism, it remains aloft, making it useless in real life. If we take it as a series of injunctions, we pull it down to a level where the burning questions revolve around such matters as military service and eating meat. Considered as mere symbolism, the Sermon on the Mount loses all significance for the striving—the activities and suffering—of humankind and, at best, can be used only for purposes of edification.

In fact, the Sermon on the Mount was neither one nor the other. It was really spiritual activity of the Word, its significance soaring far above admonition by instruction or the stimulus of symbols. The "kingdom" was not presented merely to the disciples' understanding in its essential character, nor was it merely made perceptible to their sensibilities; the very being of those disciples was enriched in ways far more profound than the understanding or sensibility with which it was received at the time—enriched in a way that only gradually, over the course of many lives, would bear fruit in the shape of conscious knowledge and certainty. The words of the Sermon on the Mount were addressed not merely to the personalities present in the body, but especially through them to their intrinsic essence that continues from incarnation to incarnation. The Sermon on the Mount was addressed to the human "I" and was thus the expression of the kind of speech that had power to pierce through the sheaths of the physical, etheric, and astral bodies and reach the "I." It inwardly stimulated the "I" to spiritual movement in ways determined by spiritual lines conveyed to it through the Sermon on the Mount. This moral spiritual movement "form," or gesture, became the experience of the "I." Since that time, it strove through all of its incarnations to give it reality by means of its bodies.

This kind of spiritual form is behind the Lord's Prayer, for example. Rudolf Steiner gave us the essential characteristics of this form in a pamphlet, called "The Lord's Prayer," published in connection with one of his lectures.[1] Another specific suprasensory form is also the basis of the nine Beatitudes. There is no need to wonder that such a form is described in Rudolf Steiner's work as a "simple geometric figure," since the highest spiritual speech can be expressed only in the form of geometrical figures. Colored shapes relate to the ether body, and sound shapes to the astral body. If one wishes to present a truth that can be comprehended at first only through "I" activity, then only the region that lacks the sound and color of geometric figures is available. It is true that in time, with the continued inner activity of such figures, color does flow into their lines—they even begin to emit spiritual sounds. But these are higher colors and higher tones than those that apply to the regions of spiritual forms of expression mentioned here.

The most important effect of the Sermon on the Mount, therefore, was a spiritual, suprasensory stimulation of the inner "I" forces. This stimulation was the result of a movement of the lines of certain moral spiritual forms powerfully displayed by Jesus Christ before the deepest core of the human being. Essentially, the nature of the influence flowing from Jesus Christ was similar to what flowed in ancient times from the exusiai, or spirits of form (elohim), the spiritual parents of the human "I" being. In the very beginning, the spirits of form imprinted into the human "I" the forms of humanity's mission on Earth. But all that was brought about by the exusiai in the devachan state before incarnation now took place in an embodied condition on Earth through Jesus Christ in his Sermon on the Mount. Humankind had already forgotten the "name" given them by their Fathers in heaven; that name was now given to them again on Earth by Jesus Christ, and it was heard once more in the Sermon on the Mount. Through preaching the kingdom, humankind was reminded of this name. The forgotten cosmic mission of humanity lit up in the depths of human souls as their own most special ancient memory—awakened by the power of the forms brought by the Word of Christ concerning the kingdom.

That the spiritual effect of the Word of Jesus Christ was exceptional is emphasized by the evangelists. For instance, Luke says, "And they were astonished at his doctrine, for his word was with power"—literally, "in (or rooted in) the exusiai" (*Kai exeplessonto epi te didache autou hoti en exousia en ho logos autou,* Luke 4:32). It was this Word through exusiai that distinguishes the Sermon on the Mount from the doctrines and discourses of other teachers, such as the Pharisees and Sadducees (and even of the Essenes). The word of those teachers was only a "sheath word," thus penetrating no deeper than the sheaths of the essential human being and abstract to a certain extent. The Word of Jesus Christ, however, was "substantial," communicating with the inner human being. It imparted such a degree of power that the life forces could flow even into the physical body, even into the physical brain. That strengthening influence outward from within—even into the physical body—is called the "bread from heaven" in the Gospels, while the influence that gave movement to the ether body, making it capable of independent movement in the surrounding sea of the elemental world, is called "fish."

Feeding with "bread and fish" was a spiritually real process that took place in the physical and ether bodies as the result of the Word of Jesus Christ. But the word of the Pharisees and Sadducees offered "stone" instead of "bread" and a "snake" instead of "fish," because the rigidified legal righteousness of the Sadducees was like stone to the inner human forces, and the casuistic, straw-splitting agility of the pharisaic logic was like the agility of a snake; it did not strengthen the ether body for independent movement in the etheric, but made it nimble in movement over the Earth's surface with no roots in earthly reality and with no uplift into suprasensory reality. Jesus Christ spoke not as the Scribes and Pharisees. He neither set up a new moral law nor interpreted the old in a new way; rather, through his Word he made the positive karma of humanity fruitful for the future. It was this that occurred during the Sermon on the Mount: he fed humankind with bread and fish; he strengthened the human "I" with the ability to take hold of not only the astral body, but also the etheric and physical bodies from within outward. Essentially, it was not a matter of doctrine and symbolism, but one of outpouring the Christ impulse. That Christ impulse functioned just as the elohim (or exusiai) did during ancient times when they breathed the breath of life into the being of primeval humanity.

## The Nine Beatitudes as the Seed of Positive Human Karma

There is almost no subject imagined or thought of in more ways in the Western world of today than the idea of karma, the law of human destiny. To some, karma represents the totality of ties that bind an individual to earthly matters as the result of past wrongs, leading to a struggle to throw off that karma by disentangling oneself from them. To others, it is the law of compensation, or reward and punishment, leading to attempts to gain merit in order to deserve future good fortune. Still others consider it the benevolent guidance of the world that leads humankind with seeming severity through thick and thin, while preparing behind the scenes an inevitably "happy ending" for all the world. This leads one to strive for confidence in one's destiny and to rely on that.

All of these views of karma are narrow-minded. Though false, they contain some truth about karma, but, whether by design or for convenience, they are narrowed down to the personal element. For a Christian attitude toward karma, the most important thing is to realize that karma is the school of humanity that follows the great experiences of Jesus Christ's passion, step by step, from the humility of "washing the feet," through the crucifixion, and on to the resurrection. However different the karma of single individuals or of groups may appear when viewed superficially, since the Mystery of Golgotha, it is essentially no more than a matter of passing through the seven stages of Christ's passion, preceded by a multitude of differing encounters with the three temptations in the wilderness. The "positive karma" of humanity in the future will thus not involve the appearance of an increasing number of fortunate people on Earth, but an increase of those who are permitted to unite their karma with that of the Christ impulse—to pass through the experiences in their destiny that gradually enable knowledge of the Christian mystery to light up. The human karma of the Christ impulse has, however been laid out beforehand by the stages of the passion and resurrection of Jesus Christ; those who enter the three temptations have decided to follow the will of the Christ impulse in their karma. They do not become "fortunate" but "blessed" (*makarioi*), which means that the positive karma of humanity will not be an escape from suffering and pain, but the experience of a new kind of suffering and pain.

The fact that the Christ impulse can shine into human suffering is the result of the positive karma of humankind since the Mystery of Golgotha. As a result of this inner transformation of suffering, a new type of human being will gradually arise. They are those who, alongside the "fortunate" enjoying their good fortune and the "unfortunate" miserable in their ill fortune, will become a third class called *makarioi*, or the "blessed," in the Sermon on the Mount. These are the ones who, in the joy of their good fortune, will not forget the ill fortune of others, whereas in ill fortune they will have the felicity of the Holy Spirit. The symbolism expressed by the gleaming red roses that spring from the black cross will be constant reality with those who are spoken of in the Sermon on the Mount as *makarioi*.[2] It was the reality of such a one that Goethe wanted to show in the loftiest character of *Wilhelm Meister's Apprenticeship*, and out of his profound knowledge he gave this character the name Makarie, linking her with the Gospel passage mentioned here. Makarie could describe all the movements of the heavenly bodies without seeing them through a telescope, because the movements in the heavens were reflected perfectly in the etheric circulation of her blood. She knew about the starry constellations, because she carried them within her being. She bore them in her own being since her being could allow space for the cosmic world; she was not filled with experiences that had resisted cosmic revelations for so long that the whole personality would have filled with egoistic joys and pains. Because Makarie was so empty, so poor, she was able to know more of the heavens than is normally possible for human beings. Makarie is in fact the realized promise of the first Beatitude in the Sermon on the Mount (Matthew 5), the promise in which Jesus Christ declares the fundamental condition for membership with the *makarioi*—emptiness, inner poverty, and spiritual beggary.

Indeed, the nine Beatitudes of the Sermon on the Mount are really "characterizations" of the ninefold reality of the future *makarioi;* the "characterization" of the conditions that the *makarioi* have to go through in the nine members of their human nature in order to bring to pass the positive karma of humanity.[3] At the same time, it is they who form the foundation of the spiritual school of esoteric Christianity. An occult school is based essentially upon foreseeing the positive karma as potential and, from that insight, devising spiritual exercises that contain the extract of all the effort and experience that exist in the trials and experiences of the contemplated line of future positive karma. From this perspective consider, for example, a classic spiritual exercise by Rudolf Steiner, given in the form of concentration on the Rose Cross in his written work *An Outline of Esoteric Science.* The exercise there is described in three stages, one developing into the next. The first step combines a series of images that evoke feelings into a single image, forcefully built up and retained in consciousness. The next step involves consciously wiping away that living picture, so that the only thing remaining as an object of meditation is the soul's own activity that built and held the picture. Finally, in the third step of the exercise, one blots out even this image-free content from awareness, leaving a perfectly empty consciousness.

This is the spiritual exercise. But what is it? Where does it come from? What is it modeled after? In fact, it is based on the course of the positive karma of humanity during the fifth post-Atlantean cultural epoch. Essentially, it contains the whole drama of the destiny of human souls through a long period leading to the distant future. The exercise arises through foresight of the line of positive human karma during that future time. Indeed, we are justified in stating that the spiritual exercise described in *An Outline of Esoteric Science* contains prophetic content, in a summarized form, equal to that found in many of the prophets' books of the Old Testament. Anyone who carries out this exercise with real awareness will find a way opened to view profound secrets of the world's future history. We should avoid doing this exercise superficially, so that we can say that the positive future of humankind involves finding the way to *imagination,* from *imagination* to *inspiration,* and finally from *inspiration* to *intuition.* It is certainly not this scheme that is important, but the realization of the process in spiritual world history whereby the possibility of gathering a self-sufficient and self-built "treasure" will be guaranteed to human souls, as well as the knowledge that a time will follow when spiritual storms of destiny will extinguish all the lights that have thus far shone so clearly, and that a darkness and emptiness and loneliness will spread within human consciousness, which will be unendurable for some. And after that, souls will be led into a wilderness where even the last refuge, the activity of their own souls, will be taken away. There will be no authority for appeal, no outer teacher, no support—and souls will have to plunge into this nothingness, not knowing if they will ever rise again.

The spiritual exercise stated as humanity's future destiny and shown in a condensed form in fact contains the process of human "beggary," as indicated in the first Beatitude of the Sermon on the Mount. In the first Beatitude we read, "Blessed are the poor in Spirit (those who are beggars for the Spirit), for theirs is the kingdom of heaven" (*makarioi hoi ptochoi to pneumati, hoti auton estin he basileia ton Ouranon*). Likewise, through its three steps, Rudolf Steiner's Rosicrucian exercise says, "Exercise your forces so that you can create your inner kingdom. Surrender that kingdom once you have created it. Then, resign yourself to being a beggar after the Spirit." The Beatitudes and this spiritual exercise have the same message, but the Beatitudes signify the promise of a future karma, whereas the exercise represents an effort to bring about the fulfillment of this promise.

Now that we may hope to have gained a feeling for both the cosmic scope and the spiritually practical significance of the nine Beatitudes in the Sermon on the Mount, it is time to proceed to a consideration of the individual Beatitudes.

## The First Beatitude: The Path of Human Destiny through the Physical Body

During the past two millennia, the conscious relationship of human beings to the physical body has been open to serious misunderstandings. On the one hand, it was customary to view the physical body as the greatest hindrance on the soul's path of surrender to spirit, while on the other, it was the object of rough training in military exercises and feats of strength. Because of these misunderstandings and one-sided concepts of the physical body's significance for humanity, the monastic and knighthood systems came into being. The Grail knighthood, however, was based on a third view of the physical body's significance and was understood by only a few. The essence of this concept saw the physical body as representative of the stage where a complete reconciliation between heaven and Earth could be brought about. When the human "I" is consciously united with the spirit, this is still only the first stage of that reunion; when that union also includes the astral body, the second stage is attained; and when the alliance between the "I" and spirit becomes strong enough to reach not only to the astral body, but also beyond the ether body and deep into the physical body, then the communion is complete. This is why the physical body was seen as the communion body by those who understood the Grail tradition—it was the highest possibility of human communion with the spirit.

Communion, in connection with the Grail tradition, indicates the most significant of experiences at that stage of initiation consciousness, which Rudolf Steiner called the level of *intuition* (the stage of work on the Philosopher's Stone). It is the physical body's existence that makes this stage of initiation knowledge possible. The physical body is not just an instrument for gaining power in the physical world; it is also a place of instruction where high moral and spiritual truths can be learned through experience, which essentially consists of two parts: first, experience of all that the soul passes through because the spiritual world has withdrawn from the world of human experience; and second, the experiences of the soul during the process of comprehending the spiritual world in its immediate presence. The two parts of the first Beatitude contain these two aspects of the path that the soul traverses with the help of the physical body: "Blessed are the poor [the beggars] in spirit: for theirs is the kingdom of heaven" (Matthew 5:3). This first part of the formula comprises the necessary "path to poverty" for humanity as a whole and for each individual. And the second part shows the path to spiritual appropriation of the kingdom of heaven. The phrase "theirs is the kingdom of heaven" does not mean that the kingdom of heaven is allotted to them but refers to their concrete, *intuitive* relationship to the spiritual world. This is clearly expressed by the possessive case in the Greek (*auton estin he basileia ton Ouranon*).

The first Beatitude, therefore, contains the moral spiritual formula of *intuitive* knowledge, while presenting a figure that combines the two moral spiritual lines expressed in this two-part formula. When we think of the path to poverty as leading gradually to the zero point (the "gate of death" as the mysteries express it), and the path to the appropriation of the kingdom of heaven as a process continuing after the zero point, we see the figure of a circle leading from wealth in Spirit, through poverty in Spirit, and to possessing the kingdom of heaven. The figure corresponding to the formula would be as follows:

The path to poverty indicated here, as well as the ascent to the kingdoms of heaven, is shown in the last scene of *Faust.* The whole structure of *Faust* (in its final composition) is, in fact, contained in this figure of the first Beatitude. The path of *Faust,* once he had rejected abstraction, led him through the experience of guilt (in part I) to the knowledge of need in the guise of money and the classical past, which brought him, blinded by care and through death, up to the realms of heavenly love.[4] The tempter intended to lead Faust through false warmth (in the Gretchen tragedy), to false light (the light of the past), and then on through a false impulse from the future (anxiety over the future in a material sense), into a false sphere of existence (Hell). But then it happened that the power of the warmth ether, set in motion by the tempter, led to the knowledge of guilt—that is, knowledge of the moral counterimage in cold, and the alluring light ether figures of the past wakened memory (as the veil of the beautiful Helen). The result was the awareness of present need: the growing consciousness of what had been sacrificed and lost—the meeting with the morally dark counterimage of the luminous past. The whispered suggestions of a false future through the negative sound ether led to an awareness of its moral counterimage, the grey figure of care. The inner warmth and inner light that were kindled by these experiences then led Faust's soul through death—indeed, through death as the gate into the world of real life, not as a gate to the realm of false existence.

Rudolf Steiner spoke of the scenes of Faust's death and ascent into Heaven as an precise description of initiation. It is, therefore, important also to understand initiation in the light of the knowledge of guilt, need, care, and death. And it is no less important to realize that Goethe's description of initiation culminates with "Whoever striving ceaseless toils, him may we well redeem." This only repeats in different words the first Beatitude: "Blessed are the poor in spirit, for theirs is the kingdom of heaven." One who continually toils in the worlds of guilt, need, care, and death is precisely the "beggar, poor in spirit" in the Gospel. The fact that such a one may be redeemed—become *makarios* (blessed)—is shown both by the first sentence of the Sermon on the Mount and by Goethe's life work as a whole.

The experiences that lead to an understanding of human guilt, need, care, and death can be encountered only in the physical body. Only in the physical body can we awaken the force of courage and the humility needed to go through the "needle's eye" of initiation. Only those who are conscious of the range of human guilt and the human need arising from it can develop the necessary humility in the presence of the spiritual world—a necessary condition of acceptance by that world and security against rejection by the spiritual world as a moral alien. Moreover, individuals cannot achieve the courage to enter the kind of gloomy nothingness in which the spiritual world shows itself at the decisive hour, unless they have seen, unparalyzed, not only common day but also cosmic day in the colorless light of care, not flinching from the sight of all that is dying in the cosmos, in humankind, and in themselves. Only in the school of the physical body can we learn the humility and courage needed by free human beings, or initiates, to conclude and realize a free alliance with the spiritual world.

The initiation must be experienced—in a highly concentrated form and time frame—by humanity, step by step, along the path of human spiritual destiny. Humanity must pass through the school of the physical body; it can be spared no stage of this development. The ancient Indian consciousness resisted this need of destiny; it considered the physical body to be an illusion and the soul's union with it a degradation. This was why the ancient Indian culture failed, and a new one, the ancient Persian culture, had to be established.

Here we may ask: Why did the ancient Indian consciousness turn away from the physical body? What was the deeper reason for such an aversion? The reason for this ancient Indian aversion to physical human nature was really the same as what causes aversion to the concrete spiritual world among modern humankind. Today this involves a subconscious fear that deters people from seeking the concrete spiritual world; similarly, in the ancient Indian epoch, it was a kind of subconscious fear that caused them to disparage the physical world. People today flee from the spiritual world, because they are afraid to awaken the conscience, which must, nevertheless, take place on the spiritual threshold (that is, before the meeting with the Guardian of the Threshold). Likewise, the ancient Indian people were afraid of the darkness of the physical body (afraid, that is, of coming into direct conflict with Ahriman). Now, however, the conflict with Ahriman and darkness is also the training ground of the physical body; its stages are guilt, need, care, and death. It was this training that the ancient Indian consciousness feared, and thus they refused to recognize the great truths of primal guilt and the primal karma of humankind.

What was lacking in that Indian wisdom—in all else so wonderfully sublime—was the recognition of those truths of the genesis and destiny of humankind, which shone out later, in the Israelite race, as shown in the first book of Moses. The knowledge of individual karma and individual reincarnation was generally concealed from the Israelites; knowledge of human karma and of the historical future of humankind was generally concealed from the ancient Indians. Thus, the sum of wisdom shines forth only in fragments in various regions and at various times; only the consciousness that can rise above space and time can also meet with it whole, as a unity. St. Paul's statement, "now we know in part," contains a summary of the history of the mysteries, on the one hand, and on the other, a challenge to rise to the mystery that unites all fragments within itself—the Christ mystery.

Knowledge of primal human guilt (original sin in the Bible) was kept from the Indian consciousness and thus did not free that consciousness from the universal human karma, but instead caused it to be experienced with resistance and ill will. Pessimism toward life—which set in relatively early in the Indian civilization—depended not only on the yearning of the Indian consciousness after the spirit, but also on its longing to be free from earthly needs. Thus the ancient Indian culture became an expression of its inner despondency, not because that portion of humanity was especially unfortunate or received a more difficult life from destiny than did the rest of humanity; rather, it was because that culture was discontented with its lot. It was not satisfied, because it could not recognize the secret of that situation and its meaning and importance for the future. Thus, although the ancient Indian civilization had to experience the fact of original sin, it never recognized it.

The nucleus of the ancient Persian culture, by contrast, was composed of people who were permeated by the impulse to do battle against Ahriman. They were not those who despised the body, but were resolved to make the most noble use of it in the realm of action. This disposition was fruitful not only in the realm of action, but also in areas of knowledge. Within the ancient Persian community, a great discovery was made; they discovered Ahriman, who had been concealed from the Indian consciousness. In the ancient Persian consciousness, it was not a matter of placing the pure spirit world in opposition to the impure physical world; rather, it was a matter of distinguishing the pure from the impure, both in this world and in the suprasensory realm. This led the ancient Persians to a deeper understanding of the physical body; they recognized the body as a stage for the conflict between the two powers; from the earliest times, it had borne both purity and impurity. As a result of this insight, the ancient Persians had knowledge of the sin rooted in human nature, but they did not turn away from that part of human nature. They took up the conflict both in the outer world of action and in the inner world of self-mastery.

The step that the ancient Indian consciousness failed to take was thus taken by the ancient Persians. Hence, the point was no longer to overcome the fear of recognizing the existence of original sin, or primal human guilt, but something different.

The test with which the ancient Persian community was confronted was determined by the general situation of that community in its environment. It was a relatively small community that had taken refuge in the mountain ranges and plateau of Iran, away from the numerous surrounding hostile Turanian and semi-Turanian races. When the guidance and instruction of that culture were in the hands of the great Zoroaster himself, its condition was one of extreme oppression and intense poverty. It would be a mistake to imagine the brightest days under the ancient Persian spirit as resembling in any way the kingdom of the Medes and Persians under Xerxes, Cambyses, and Darius—when in Persepolis, Ectabana, and Susa, the Kings spent the seasons of the year in grand palaces and surrounded by thousands of courtiers and splendid bodyguards. A greater contrast is barely imaginable than the one between the little community of ancient Persians—who barely managed to exist in extreme poverty in mountains and glens, and could offer their leader, the great Zoroaster, little more than their blood and the complete confidence of their souls in the ceaseless conflict—and the Persian kingdom founded by Cyrus. The great Zoroaster had no court and no palaces; indeed, there was not even a temple among the poor herdsmen, who longed for agricultural labor but had little possibility of devoting themselves to work they desired. The mystery shrine where Zoroaster held converse with Ahura Mazda and instructed his band of disciples was no temple but a bare mountaintop. The little settlements at the foot of this mountain represented Zoroaster's dwellings.

The Ancient Persian race not only had to contend with material need; it was also under urgent necessity of defending and maintaining its physical and spiritual existence against a far superior foe. Thus for generations it had had to face need in every form. The ancient Persian race had had to drink the cup of need to the dregs, taking its position in the karmic future of humankind by experiencing the struggle not only for material existence and not only for spiritual existence, but for both at once. This experience has a fundamental significance for the whole future of humanity. Experiences of this kind (for instance, that of human guilt and need) will be carried into later incarnations. They will not be carried over merely as ideas, but as moral forces. For example, the experience of human guilt (original sin in the Bible) will become a force that counters the arrogance by which anyone stands aloof from the rest of humanity. Those who have had this experience of human nature must admit, with Goethe, that they bear within themselves the seed of all evil. No matter how imposing their positive potential and achievements may be, they will never look down upon humankind, because they can never forget that, before the highest judgment seat in the world, all human beings are equal.

Only those who have passed through the gates of death and have left the kama loca period behind them can speak of inequality in goodness; in the devachan state, a real distinction in quality may be spoken of; but the devachan state is such that, there, real stages of existence are important, not valuations of them. Thus the experience of human guilt becomes the moral force of humility, in which human beings each know themselves to be either worthy or unworthy members of humanity. Similarly, the experience of need becomes a definite moral force. It becomes the force of endurance, of constancy, of fidelity toward humankind, ideas, and purposes. The experience of care, representing the united forces of doubt and fear, leads to the moral force of courage. Only the experience of death results in the force of love that is more powerful than death.

The experiences leading to the development of these forces formed the tests that were emphasized in the various consecutive cultural epochs. Indeed, the Egypto-Chaldean cultural epoch, which followed ancient Persia, was the age of care, or anxiety, for post-Atlantean humanity. If, for example, from this point of view we study the magnificent Chaldean epic of Gilgamesh, we get an idea of how forcibly care seized upon exactly the most representative people of the age. The whole Gilgamesh epic is essentially one of anxiety; the earlier security and certainty concerning the fate of the human soul was lost to the heroes of that poem, whose whole dramatic action evolved from such uncertainty and care.

Again, if we study the Egyptian priestly culture, we find the same tyranny of care. The "sons of the widow," the Egyptian priestly initiates, wept for the dismembered Osiris; the complete Osiris mystery, which alone could have offered security and certainty, was beyond their reach. The burial places, the mummy worship, the many incantations of the Book of the Dead all speak in various ways of Egypt's anxiety, its care for preservation, saving the soul, and preserving identity, making certain that names would be handed down to posterity.

The black abyss of death and dissolution confronted the consciousness of the Egypto-Chaldeans and filled them with worry over the future of their souls. The "sting of death," however, did not penetrate soul consciousness until the time of the Greco-Roman civilization, when it became not just a matter of uncertainty over the future of the soul, but rather certainty that the soul's existence after death is, in any case, something paler than its existence in flesh and blood. Such an existence without flesh and blood must (so it was felt) be shadowy because it lacks flesh and blood.

The courage of despair inspiring an Empedocles of Agrigentum, who threw himself into the crater of Etna (in the fifth century B.C.), was not an expression of contempt or weariness of life, nor was it a preference for the disembodied existence of the soul; rather, it was a desperate resolve to die in a way different from that of others. Empedocles wished to escape the shadowy life of a bodiless soul; he hoped through that act—the magic, as it were, of the will power exerted in his death—to unite with the elements of Earth in order to be more closely bound up in and with them, and thus be freed from the loneliness of the shadowy existence of the soul. But the magic courage of Empedocles was not enough for emancipation from that "sting of death," the isolation of the soul; nor was the courage of Socrates' cognitive activity enough; a higher force must be revealed to human consciousness. That force was the love revealed by Jesus Christ in the world—love that, passing through death and resurrection, restored to many the radiant certainty through which Paul cried, "O Death, where is thy sting?"

Those who once felt the reality of the Christ impulse had thus regained the certainty that the soul's isolation, the shadow life, can be overcome, and that, where formerly only an existence of poverty and pallor was expected, a rich life could now flourish—one no less warm than the blood and no less clear than the bodily senses. During the Greco-Roman age, however, not everyone could immediately feel the reality of the Christ impulse. First of all, this was possible only for those who possessed a certain foundation. That foundation essentially involved accepting the fact that human guilt must be acknowledged before the Christ impulse can be received. What John the Baptist effected in people through his baptism by water had to be experienced by all human beings in a form suitable to each of them, so that they might be able to receive the Christ impulse. The repentance, or change of heart, to which John the Baptist challenged people, was essentially knowledge of human nature as it had become through the fall of humanity. Such knowledge, which laid in the soul a foundation of guilt consciousness, was the sufficient and inevitable condition for meeting the Christ impulse during the fourth post-Atlantean epoch.

This condition is also the concern of the twentieth century, although it is no longer enough. Today, another stipulation must be added; along with human guilt, human need must also be recognized. It must be taken very seriously when people say that consciousness of guilt before the spiritual world, humanity, and nature is the first requirement for contact with the reality of the Christ impulse, but that the second condition is one's experience and recognition of the need of the spirit, the need of the soul, and the natural need of humankind. Those today who live with an awareness of their own rectitude as their basic soul mood fail to bring what is needed for contact with the Christ impulse in order to prove itself a force of social fraternity in the world. On the other hand, all those who bear this condition within themselves must experience today, according to their destiny, the three forms of need so they can learn yet another part of the truth contained in the sentence "Blessed are the poor in spirit."

It is important today to be fully aware of the fact that humanity must endure a severe malady; this fact is even more tragic because it is not noticed at all by the vast majority of humankind—indeed, most people consent to, and intensify, it. How many people today fully feel the need of the consciousness that is extinguished every night—the consciousness that is obligated to judge and act without memory of the karmic past, without knowing karmic relationships—knowledge without which no one is really able to judge correctly and justly? The spiritual need of humankind—the tragic fact of human blindness, and the even more tragic fact of the preference for that blindness—is a point that must be recognized in our age. The recognition is painful, but it leads to at least one good thing; if we really know who and how many are actually unaware of what they are doing, we become more tolerant, and we learn to rejoice even in the recognition of those several points of attack from which the dominant illusions of the world may be overcome. Almost more serious than recognizing the need of the human spirit is recognizing the need of the human soul. Such insight is needed to perceive that the soul dwindles and disappears today from human consciousness and activity, as did the spirit from human consciousness in the previous millennium. The sun is setting in the human soul; the human heart is becoming increasingly moonlike. The heart is becoming more and more the mirror for the purposes of the head and the lower human urges. Nevertheless, neither the purposes of the head (and today almost everything is governed by purposes, so that even if one is not supposed to have any, one's actions may nevertheless be explained by secret, hidden purposes) nor desires have anything to do with the true soul life. The true soul life is the clear, shining, creative force of the soul, which alone can give to thought and impulses a true direction worthy of humanity. The fact that this force is gradually running dry in all spheres of human life is the experience of the soul's most important need in the present age.

Nonetheless, the need of the present age is not exhausted in the inner life of human beings. Social need and the ever-increasing maladies of the body present a no less startling picture than that of the inner life. Those who are concerned with spiritual science are exactly the ones who ought to keep this side of human need before their eyes with particular intensity, because this is the region from which the most severe attacks of ahrimanic powers are made to darken the spirit and extinguish the soul.

Today the recognition of such need is important; likewise, in the future (especially in the sixth post-Atlantean epoch), the recognition of care will be important. A time will come when, speaking generally, people will have only as much joy in life as is made possible to them by the cultivation of spiritual science. Humankind then will depend entirely on the vertical relationship with the spirit world; the horizontal relationship with the spatial world will offer only anxiety and worry. During the seventh cultural epoch, this "cross of tension" will be the result of not only care but also death. Indurating death forces will work against the forces of love, and the important point will be to recognize death in its manifold activity and, recognizing it, to resist it.

The second half of the post-Atlantean evolution is concerned especially with the recognition of guilt, need, care, and death; but the true conquest of those forces is reserved for the distant future. Indeed, the decisive victory over death, achieved in the resurrection of Jesus Christ, will not be possible to humankind as a whole until the seventh planetary cosmic epoch—the Vulcan Epoch. Only then will humanity be able to fully develop the "resurrection body."

Thus the first sentence of the Beatitudes in the Sermon on the Mount is expanded for our consciousness as the history of guilt, need, care, and death—deepened to give an understanding of initiation, as the realization of the *intuition* stage in the knowledge of the spiritual world by traversing the stages of recognition of guilt, need, care, and death. The first Beatitude represents the formula of *intuition* knowledge on the path of Christian initiation, which itself is simply the concentrated prevenient experience of the positive future karma of humanity.

The next meditation will be devoted to the remaining Beatitudes of the Sermon on the Mount.

# Chapter 4

# The First Three Beatitudes and the Stages of Initiation

## *Intuition* and the First Beatitude

The purpose of our previous meditation was to clarify the first Beatitude and how it represents a formula for *intuition* knowledge and shows karmic paths that lead to that stage of consciousness. To understand the subsequent Beatitudes in a similar way, we need to look at the nature of *intuition* knowledge and comprehend the other two suprasensory stages of knowledge more clearly by considering the second and third Beatitudes. *Intuition* knowledge occurs when, at the moment of knowing, three conditions are present: first, the knowing soul must possess the faculty of not only going out from itself, but also dwelling in another being; second, that other being must be endowed with the same faculty; and, third, this second being must want to enter an *intuitive* relationship with the first.

Although this description may seem short and a bit dry at first, it does in fact indicate a world of experiences and knowledge. *Intuition* knowledge is no poorer than the three other types of experiential knowledge [objective, *imagination*, and *inspiration*], but it is clearly distinguished from the others in that the experience of its approach is impoverishment. The first process to be considered, therefore, is the loss of not only everything that filled the soul, but also everything that could fill the soul spiritually "from without" through substance and experience. The area in and around the soul then becomes silent and void, thus reaching the zero point of experience. Now, nothing would happen if the soul were to remain in this condition, waiting for some event. The soul's discipline on the path to *intuition* is precisely this: the spiritual world creates a silence around the soul, rendering watching and waiting useless. Thus the soul must accomplish an act out of nothingness and go beyond the zero point. The soul must no longer stir up thoughts, pictures, or feelings but set its own being in motion. The soul has to cause a movement of its being that seems impossible to the consciousness it has abandoned, somewhat like causing water to flow from a rock. Yet that is precisely the point; it must find a force never experienced by the soul. A rock is fixed and without water, and this is how the soul experiences its own inner nature. This inner stilled emptiness must find a force that causes *intuitive* knowledge to manifest. This force is needed by the soul to enable it to live outside in another being without losing consciousness.

This process of going past the zero point and sending consciousness outside has been described here from the inner perspective—as it is enacted before the soul's consciousness. Seen externally, however, it may be described somewhat as follows: Before the third stage of rousing the human consciousness in the hidden task of its awakening, the human heart is a spiritual focus where twelve cosmic currents converge, flowing from the constellations of the heavenly zodiac. The central point of the heart is thus formed from without; the focal point at the center of the heart arises as these twelve incoming rays cross one another.

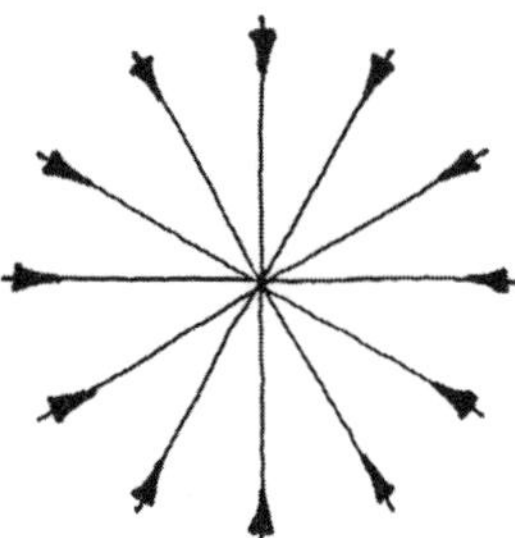

When the third stage in the task of rousing the consciousness begins to manifest in the human being, however, the first thing that happens is a change in the organism of the heart's center, whereby it is separated from the influx of the cosmic rays. When this happens, the zero point of the soul's experience has been reached. The soul experiences itself as a mere motionless point in existence, plunged into loneliness, darkness, and silence. On the other hand, this is also the point when consciousness feels not only alone but also entirely self-reliant and restricted to itself. This complete self-reliance may, in ordinary consciousness, leave the echo of a good sense of freedom; but being restricted within itself may, in ordinary consciousness, produce an echo as a feeling of painful breathlessness in the soul. If these two feelings stay in balance, one is prepared for the test Rudolf Steiner calls the "trial by air" in *How to Know Higher Worlds.* The trial by air may be characterized as the complete absence of motive, rules, and so on—a completely empty consciousness, from which a force for spiritual action must arise. On the other hand, the soul's subjective experience is that it is in, as it were, a space into which no air flows for breathing. One knows that this critical point of the trial by air has been successfully passed when the heart center not only continues to exist after being severed from the cosmic influences, but even begins to radiate on its own from within. The great change that takes place in the spiritual organism of the heart is that the heart itself begins to shine out into the cosmos.

The light force, born of the heart center, then gradually becomes the faculty through which consciousness can live in other beings. It is the revelation of transforming Christ's influence in the human organism; and the test that precedes it is the birth of love, a corresponding change in the whole human being toward love as the central purpose of life and action.

Because *intuitive* knowledge is completley the knowledge of love, it cannot have a passive "object" to be known and into which it might enter without its cooperation. In the case of *intuituve* knowledge, there are no "objects"—only beings who penetrate the knowing human soul just as knowingly as the human soul penetrates them. Therefore, it is a matter of two currents of will meeting each other, flowing together, and remaining within each other. The *intuitive* knowledge of a stone involves a reciprocally interpenetrative contact with the mineral group soul (or with even higher beings who function in the mineral realm). In the process of *intuition*, we not only know, but are known. There is thus enrichment for both parties, through whose cooperation such *intuition* arises. If an incarnated human being "knows" the spiritual world through *intuition*, it means that the spiritual world also "knows" the human being through *intuition*. It is an enrichment of both, not only of knowledge, but especially of volition and capacity. *Intuition* is an act through which both worlds participate simultaneously; hence it always involves a change of nature and the inauguration of new forces.

To "know" the kingdoms of heaven through *intuition* means that they have descended into the human "I" and penetrate it, just as the "I" penetrates them. This is stated in the first Beatitude and is expressed by Rudolf Steiner when he phrases the first Beatitude in this way: "How blessed are the beggars after Christ, for they will discover the kingdoms of heaven through the power of the individual 'I.'"[1]

## *Inspiration* and the Second Beatitude

The act through which the soul goes beyond the zero point and leads to *intuition* comes before the creation of an inner spiritual void. The efforts and trials needed represent the discipline of *inspired* consciousness, made possible for human beings through the ether body. The moral and spiritual experiences that we can have by means of the ether body form a parallel not only through human spiritual history, but also through the inner experiences of initiation with the knowledge gained by training the physical body. To understand the special type of human karma (and the experiences of spiritual discipline) related to the ether body, we must direct our attention for a moment toward the main feature of the ether body: according to its inner structure, it is not a spatial body at all, but a temporal body. And the ether body does not merely carry memory but is actually one's living past. The wisdom revealed in the adjustment of organic processes through the ether body is the past, living in the present, of the ancient Sun period, when the ether body was poured forth by the spirits of wisdom (Kyriotetes). Its inner system of movement is a living memory of the activity of the spirits of motion (dynamis) during the ancient Moon period; and the breathing of the ether body is the preservation of the earthly past when the spirits of form (elohim) permeated human beings with their influence. The past before the fall of humankind, as well as the time after, remains alive in the ether body. The ether body is like a book that contains the whole past and from which it can be read. When the human "I" and astral body are strong enough not only to emerge within the ether body, but also to consciously perceive it within, this perception gradually gives rise to this deepening feeling: Once you were different than you are today. One's consciousness becomes clearer and more certain of the shriveling, dimming, and hardening that has affected the human life realm because of the fall and all that has evolved from it. Out of inner awareness of the ether body a knowledge arises concerning what is lacking in human beings today—what we once possessed and is now lost. This knowledge becomes a tragic aspect of the human soul, because it now knows, not theoretically but by experience, that it has been stunted. Human beings, therefore, becoming aware of their ether body from within, begin to mourn. This mourning of the soul, however, is a necessary postulate for knowing and experiencing, on the path of humanity's positive karma, the side of the comprehensive Christ mystery that meets human beings as consolation and comfort.

The second Beatitude of the Sermon on the Mount expresses it in the following words: "Blessed are they that mourn, for they shall be comforted."[2] We see now that the basic condition needed for knowledge on the path of *inspiration* is to be aware that something is lacking spiritually, and the resulting soul condition is that of one who mourns. This inner mourning of the soul is actually the spiritual incentive to *inspiration.* When, through the ether body, the soul becomes aware of its defects, the first step has been taken toward *inspiration.* This fills up the "empty places" in consciousness, the "comfort" that comes to the mourner. In this sense, every *inspiration* comforts, since it is not only the result of an act of mourning, but also victory over it. The soul's pain is needed not for its own sake, but so that it can become an organ of *inspiration.* The soul becomes the organ of *inspiration* when it accepts pain with calm equanimity and, going through and beyond it, finds the inner silent force to wait and listen in the emptiness of the void caused by loss. This waiting and listening resembles the process of breathing in, since we must always breathe in after we have breathed out and emptied the lungs of air. The term *inspiration* (breathing in) is thus perfectly appropriate, indicating in common fact the essence of the process it refers to. The soul must first experience an emptiness, or lack, before it can discharge into the spiritual world the suctional force (in a moral sense) of waiting and listening. Such an activity is indeed the essential question that arises from pain and is asked in the spiritual world by the soul. By its own nature, it becomes audible in the spiritual world. And this human question, heard in the spiritual world, is followed by an answer from the spiritual world that is audible to the human being. Thus *inspirational* knowledge manifests. It is essentially a dialogue between the human and spiritual realms. It is specially important, therefore, that we learn how to ask—that we learn to ask in such a way that our questions may be heard even in the spiritual world. But the necessary earnestness behind such a question is impossible unless it is born of pain. A painless, satisfied soul can never question with the earnestness needed to converse with the spiritual world. The comfort of *inspiration* knowledge is intended only for those who need it. "They that mourn" shall be comforted (as the second Beatitude expressly states), not those who are contented.

If we look more closely at the whole process by which *inspired* knowledge comes into being, we must distinguish two currents of experience that converge and bring about such knowledge. One current becomes the bearer of memory through the inwardly perceptive faculty of the ether body. It may appear in diverse forms, since there is no less variety in this sphere than, say, in the sphere of ordinary thought cognition confined to the external sensory experience. Thinking, or logic, is the same for everyone, but there is a great difference in the results produced by thinking. One person has a rich thought life and ample insight concerning nature and human existence; another, by contrast, has a few scanty thought formulas that one swears by and refuses to alter. Likewise, there are also such distinctions in knowledge experienced on the path of *inspiration*. Just as we recognize significant or less important thoughts on the path of logical discernment, similarly there are higher, more significant *inspirations* as well as those that have less importance for humanity. Consequently, inner perception, or reading inwardly the book of the ether body, may lead to very different results—solutions to great problems of human destiny, or explanations of individual karmic matters.

If the "I" has become inwardly aware of the ether body through the astral body, a longing, or painful questioning will be wakened in the soul that makes possible the second current of experience. This current involves the "I" having entered into conversation with the spiritual world through the astral body, while imprinting those communications in the memory of the ether body. This is brought from above by the "I" through the astral body and constitutes comfort from the spiritual world; its fusion with what the "I" brought from below from the ether body leads to definite and complete *inspirational* knowledge. Two currents flowing in opposite directions come together in *inspirational* knowledge as it is possible on the Christian path of knowledge. One current brings to the surface observations made within the ether body and the imprint of those observations on the astral body. The other current brings down the observations made by the astral body in the spiritual world and the imprint of those observations on the ether body. In their collaboration today, these two currents show a unity of the two streams of the pre-Christian mysteries that had flowed separately—the way of the southern mysteries based on observing the ether body from within, and the way of the northern mysteries concerned with objectively observing the spirit world through the astral body.[3]

What previously appeared as two schools and two distinct methods in different places on Earth has become a unity through the act of Christ. Thus, cognition on the Christian path of knowledge has become certain and self-reliant since pre-Christian knowledge, because it was only half; it had to be completed and made certain through the collaboration of the priestly initiates. Hence, what that inner spiritual process of knowledge lacked had to be brought in from outside by others. While the neophyte of the Egyptian mysteries was submerged in a world of inner observations, the priestly initiates standing around him spoke formulas and words of spiritual comfort with suggestive force; from outside, they instilled what was lacking in his experience to produce a sure and complete knowing. Thus in Ancient Egypt, a self-dependent spiritual knowledge, or self-initiation, was impossible; initiation had to be brought about with the help of others. This is also true of the northern mysteries of the pre-Christian era. The neophyte was likewise surrounded by a group of priest initiates, taking the place of the force that the neophyte would have provided if he had possessed inner perception of the ether body. Now, in our age, the certainty and self-reliance in the principle of Christian initiation is guaranteed, because today's *inspiration* knowledge includes both realms of experience. Even today, the advice and stimulation of a teacher can be invaluable, but the experiences of learning and knowing are now undergone in free self-dependence.

These two areas of cognition together bring about *inspired* knowledge today; in other words, the sphere of "mourning" and the sphere of "comfort" are experienced in full consciousness only at a certain level of the spiritual scientific path of knowledge. These things are experienced by many on their path of destiny, sometimes consciously but often unconsciously. Thus there are many "mourners" who do not realize they owe the pain they bear in their souls to the perceptions of the ether body, and that the strengthening, comforting insight they are led to by pain is owed to the "I" perceiving through the astral body in the spiritual world. The reality of *inspiration* is expressed in the drama of the soul life and in changes in one's inner character and attitude.

The more sensitive people, therefore, will more easily realize the truth of this process of *inspiration* knowledge. And they will comprehend the process in a higher and holier light if they recognize it in terms of the great archetypal process of all Christian perceptive *inspiration* knowledge—the Pentecost, when the disciples of Jesus Christ recognized the Christ mystery, enabling them to preach it. The Pentecostal revelation was comfort to the disciples after they had sorrowfully mourned for the Master who had departed. Rudolf Steiner spoke more than once of the indescribable grief the disciples experienced between the Ascension and Pentecost. Their grief was even more profound because they remembered the sleep in Gethsemane, the betrayal and denial in their midst, and the desertion of their Master. Because of this knowledge, they deeply felt the inadequacy of their soul forces in contrast to the risen one, revealed to them as the archetype and pattern of true humanity. Thus, the disciples experienced the pure humanity of Adam against the background of seeing their present humanity, so that, after this experience between the Ascension and Pentecost, they could gain knowledge of the silence, the desolation, and the gloom of utter isolation as mourners of humankind, innocent and redeemed. The inner desolation that preceded the Pentecostal revelation was essential for that revelation; the Pentecostal revelation had to fill that desolation, bring comfort to their grief, and give answer to questions born of pain. Recognition of the truth of the old and the new Adam grew in the disciples—recognition of the Mystery of Golgotha as the act that ended the karma of the old Adam and began the new. Yet each could comprehend only one side of the whole revelation; the complete mystery had to be revealed in parts before people could understand it. Therefore, a tongue of fire rested on each of the apostles, imparting one "word" of the Christ mystery that was to be revealed in twelve "words." The event of Pentecost is both a realization and an important basis for understanding the second Beatitude in the Sermon on the Mount: "Blessed are they that mourn, for they shall be comforted." This is the formula of Christian *inspirational* knowledge, and can, when so conceived, be essentially contained in these words of Rudolf Steiner: "Blessed are those who suffer and find their way to the Christ, for they can be filled with the new truth and experience comfort for all their suffering" (*According to Matthew*, p. 154).

## *Imagination* and the Third Beatitude

The inner perception of the ether body described in the previous section is possible only when preceded by a state of stillness and silence in the astral body. When one's "I" is able to bring the activities of the astral body to a conscious point of stillness, it will be able to perceive the ether body's inner movements. The force needed to bring the impulses of the astral body to a standstill is developed on the path of spiritual science—initially through the practice of directing the inner impulses of the astral body from the "I." The concentration exercises practiced on this path have the primary purpose of gaining mastery over the inner movements of the astral body and directing them inwardly from the "I." Acquiring the capacity to determine the astral body's movements from the "I" is a prerequisite for suspending its impulses.

The strongest impulse of the astral body involves everything related to anger. In fact, the force of those impulses in the astral body is so strong that we may consider control or lack of control of such impulses a measure of the control one has over the astral body as a whole. Those who have the inner force to overcome the presence of anger—or the force to evoke anger even when no personal cause exists and one would prefer a comfortable calm—have the necessary force to control the whole astral body. Consequently, anyone who can command the astral body from within from the "I" is a "controller of anger." Another name, expressing the same idea, is "the meek." In this sense, in the third Beatitude Jesus Christ refers to those who are able to control the astral body as the meek (*hoi praeis*). Thus the third Beatitude addresses the discipline that one must go through in the astral body and the future positive karma of the astral body.

Essentially, the karma of the astral body involves the fact that, since the Lemurian epoch of evolution, it has actually been the bearer of the luciferic element in human beings. The most important point in this discipline of human consciousness in the astral body is the need to struggle against Lucifer. The purpose of this struggle is the spiritual conversion of luciferic impulses into "meekness." Anger arises from the pride of opposing the cosmic order, and overcoming it is the purpose of the "I" in its work on the astral body. Thus the meek—those who have brought this work to a certain degree of perfection—are justifiably called the "conquerors of Lucifer." Anger is the concentrated effect of the luciferic element in human beings, and one's conquest of anger may therefore rank as the human conquest over the luciferic element as a whole.

The important point in the conquest of anger is not so much that one should never again be distressed; far more important matters are at stake. For example, one may tolerate the frequent spectacle of human conduct that promotes those of lesser value, while debasing and humiliating those of real merit and vocation. Even more difficult is overcoming indignation on hearing, for example, about crimes against children. It may even happen that one's indignation is directed against heaven itself, crying the ancient reproach, "If your law is the discipline of punishment, what can infants learn by suffering such cruely? If you give freedom to human beings, why do you not protect the little ones from harsh violence? Where is the lightning strike? Why is your thunder silent?" Human anger may be directed against the very guidance of the universe, at which point one has come under the sign of Lucifer. He rose in rebellion against the guidance of the cosmos because of earthly humanity's destiny. To Lucifer, humankind constituted a hierarchy of children abandoned to a harsh earthly fate, and he tried to free humankind from that fate. He wanted to disinherit humanity of the Earth's future—that very humanity for which the Earth's future was designed, the humanity that was intended to inherit it. Thus the conquest of Lucifer has the great karmic significance that his conquerors will not be disinherited in the future of the Earth; they will inherit it. This is the promise of the third Beatitude: "Blessed are the meek [the conquerors of Lucifer] for they shall inherit the Earth [the earthly kingdom]."

Now we may ask: What exactly does it mean to inherit the kingdom of Earth? It is important to begin with the thought that a question of inheritance can arise only after a demise or an end. In this case also, the question involves the planet Earth after its death. The physical planet Earth, as a body, is subject to the fate of all bodies; it is mortal. Consequently, at some point in the future, a time will come when the Earth no longer exists as a living organism. Like any living organism, however, it also has an ether body, which carries the life memory of Earth, just as the human ether body bears the life memory of a human being. When human beings die, their life memory flows from the physical body and reveals itself to the "I," dwelling in the astral body, as a timeless tableau of images of the individual's whole biography. That tableau is thus the inheritance that the soul takes into the spiritual world from its previous earthly life. Seeing this tableau gives the soul the strength of self-reliance in the spiritual world; its moral substance produces the moral content of the Kama Loka period, and the knowledge it leads to in the spirit world represents the substance of consciousness during the devachan period. Thus the soul inherits its previous earthly life by seeing it spread out like a gallery of pictures. This vision (which generally lasts about three days after death) occurs in a soul state that may be called "holy calm." The change in the soul caused by death naturally leads to a condition in which the soul, during this time, is in a state of lofty calm, completely absorbed by that vision of the past life. The astral body is silent and entirely concentrated on the life tableau. While souls are receiving that inheritance of earthly life, they are the "meek." Destiny makes it certain that souls will be in this condition at that point, thus assuring that they will not be disinherited.

At some time in the future, the whole planet Earth will experience a similar event. Its ether body will abandon its physical body, and the tableau of Earth's whole biography will stand in grand images for the consciousness that inherits it. The moral essence of that tableau will then determine Earth's kama loka condition, and the way that this is accepted will determine the height and range of Earth's devachanic period. During Earth's devachan period, her next incarnation, the Jupiter period, will be prepared. That Jupiter period will be the visible karmic effect of the Earth period, the karmic inheritance of the planet Earth.

The tableau of Earth's biography differs in one essential point from the tableau of a past life in the first days after death. After the death of the individual, "meekness" is bestowed in a natural way, but this will not happen in the case of the planet Earth after its death. In the present age, the guardian angel causes the vision of the life tableau and, as a rule, gives the force of "meekness" to the soul. In the future, this will change. The guardian angel will withdraw and—from the "I"—the human being will have to produce the force needed to view the life tableau. The human "I" must be strengthened so that, in the future, it will accomplish from within what was formerly brought about by the angel. Naturally, it is a gradual process for the angel to relenquish a certain sphere of activity and destiny to the human "I." Before the angel withdraws, the "I" will first participate to a certain degree and then collaborate more and more, until the whole activity of the angel is finally taken over by the human being. Nevertheless, a certain karmic hour will strike, after which the type of guidance given thus far will no longer be available. This will also happen at the hour of our planet's death. Human beings will see only as much of the life tableau as the evolved "I" forces can achieve.

Some souls will be able to see only part of the whole Earth life, while others will be able to survey the whole earthly past. These will be the ones who, during their earthly evolution, have been permeated by the Christ impulse to the degree that, before the end of this evolution, they will have reached the *imagination* stage of consciousness. They will not lack the force of "meekness," or control of the astral body as needed for *imagination* and vision of the whole earthly past; they will have developed it during their earthly existence. Before the great survey of their earthly past is placed before their vision as a task, they will have already had frequent occasion to develop the force of *imagination* vision. Essentially, the force of *imagination* vision is the force that gave courage to control and convert anger. Meek human beings are generally the most courageous, since those who carry no resentment against others are not afraid of anyone. Thus it is in ordinary daily life, and even more so in the world of concrete occult work. The ability to bring one's astral body to calm surrender depends absolutely upon whether one has the courage to look truth right in the face.

Presence of mind must be a powerfully developed force before we can go through the trial of courage that represents what is morally essential for training the *imagination.* Rudolf Steiner calls it the "trial by fire" in *How to Know Higher Worlds.* This is, in fact, the trial of courage through which we honestly wish for and are able to endure seeing the unvarnished truth about ourselves—and about others. What human souls experience in this trial might, if the force of courage is lacking, both plunge them into despair about themselves and arouse resentment toward human nature. But this is the very point—not to lose confidence in oneself and in humankind. The trial by fire is a trial of faith; through it, faith in humanity must not only be preserved, but also strengthened, despite and because of the disillusionment in the fire of knowledge. Tolerance, or "meekness," toward human nature must be born from this; otherwise, it would become almost impossible to go on enduring human beings.

This faith in humanity is tested and attains maturity through the trial by fire; it is the Christian truth learned in the school of *imagination.* Christianity is not only confidence in God, but also in humanity. Atheists cannot be Christians, and neither can those who have lost faith in humanity be Christians. The fact that Jesus Christ was both God and human makes it our conscious duty to place confidence in both. In a world where freedom is intended to be realized, it is not only knowledge that is important but, even more so, confidence. Knowledge may strengthen and test confidence, but in this world it is confidence that must speak the decisive word. The fourth hierarchy would become an aborted effort if the powers of evil were to succeed in destroying the world's circle of confidence—human confidence in the spiritual world, confidence in the spiritual world in human beings, and confidence in human beings in one another. The days of human evolution would indeed be numbered.

The hierarchy of freedom cannot fulfill its vocation unless it believes in freedom in a positive sense; it must believe that good will result from the use of freedom. Of course, this belief must endure difficult trials of knowledge based on experience—trials that value both the human and the spiritual worlds. And just as there are those who have lost faith in the spiritual world, there are also beings of the hierarchies who have lost faith in humanity. For example, there are the six planetary archangelic beings (up to the level of spirits of the age) who oppose the Sun being Michael, because they doubted that humankind could be entrusted with the revelation of Michael.[4] Nonetheless, we must look for the source of Christian confidence in other areas; it flows from the Christ being. As long as Christ has confidence in humanity, human beings will maintain confidence in the heart of the world. The confidence of the heart of the world is boundless. Christ is the one being in the world who completely trusts humankind, whereas other beings have various degrees of such confidence. And for us, Christianity means complete confidence in Christ. Christianity depends on confidence, one hundred percent. The primary purpose of all knowledge of the Mystery of Golgotha, the resurrection, Pentecost, and much else is to perfect this complete confidence. Knowledge of Christ's sacrifice—accomplished with confidence in humankind—will become a powerful impulse of conscience that invokes an equally complete confidence to meet it. The measure of Christ's confidence in humanity is expressed in the promise he left us: "I am with you alway, even unto the end of the world" (Matthew 28:20). It tells us that his confidence in humanity will not be withdrawn while the world and time endures. The appropriate human response to this confidence is found in the words of St. Paul: "I live; yet not I, but Christ liveth in me" (Galatians 2:20). These words are the true formula of human confidence in Christ.

The trial by fire is a test of faith through experience, just as the trial by water is a test of hope, through mourning and comfort. And the trial by air tests the capacity to love. The force of confidence is strengthened through the trial by fire; the force of hope in "mourning" leads to the comfort of *inspiration* knowledge; and the force of love is born of the trial by air. This is how the three forces of the Christ impulse are related to *imagination, inspiration,* and *intuition,* the essential experiences of the cognitive stages in spiritual science. The cognitive level of *imagination* is attained when we overcome impatience, anger, and intolerance, and when we develop the necessary courage of faith to endure seeing the truth. The vision of *imagination* is established as the result of a force of concentration greater than that required by ordinary objective consciousness. Such an enhanced faculty of concentration has the moral background of calm courage, possessed by a soul that has become "meek." This is why the fundamental spiritual exercise on the path to *imagination* is the "survey" exercise, in which the past day appears before the inner eye in reversed order.[5] In this way, we lift our consciousness above the level of daily life and no longer identify with it; we view it with the eye of "meekness." By seeing it as alien and outside ourselves, we no longer live in the flow of daily life, but find ourselves outside and above it. We withdraw from the physical and etheric bodies and live in the astral body, from which we look out at the ether body's memory images. This exercise of reviewing the day eventually forms, from within the "I," the force that the angel bestows upon human beings at the important survey immediately following death. On an elemental plane, the exercise is a kind of "inheritance" of the past day, just as the vision of the life tableau after death is an "inheritance" of the life that has just ended, and just as the vision at the end of the Earth's life as a whole will represent the "inheritance of the kingdom of Earth."

The "meek" who are to inherit the Earth, therefore, are those who have undergone the entire trial by fire and who have, during their earthly evolution, reached the stage of *imagination* consciousness. They will be able to see the whole of the Earth's past and to form the conscious threads that bind the Jupiter existence with the Earth existence. They will consciously carry into Jupiter existence the memory of Earth existence and thus make that future the karmic inheritance of the ancient past. The promise of the third Beatitude, therefore, means not only that the "meek" will consciously experience the process of inheriting the Earth's past, but also that they will enter the Jupiter existence with consciousness of its hereditary connection with Earth's past—they will know the karma of Jupiter. And they will want to take up karma and its realization; in other words, they will want to undertake and continue the moral administration and maintenance of the earthly inheritance. Consequently, as the advanced section of humankind, the role of leaders during the Jupiter period will be karmically apportioned to them, since they will have already accomplished (to the degree possible during the Earth period) the true purpose of the Jupiter period, which is to develop *imagination* consciousness.

The third Beatitude contains the promise of positive karma for the human "I" being and its work on the astral body, and at the same time the moral and spiritual formula of *imagination* knowledge that can be attained on the path of Christian esotericism. All that has been said of this Beatitude may be summed up in Rudolf Steiner's words: "Blessed are those who become meek through the power of the 'I,' for they shall inherit the earthly kingdom" (*According to Matthew*, p. 154).

The subject of the next meditation will be evolution of the human spirit and soul in the light of the six remaining Beatitudes.

# Chapter 5

# The Beatitudes and the Human Soul and Spirit

## Inner Transformation on the Path of Christian Spiritual Discipline

Meditations 3 and 4 were devoted to the first three Beatitudes of the Sermon on the Mount as outlines for training human consciousness in the physical, astral, and ether bodies. In this meditation, we will try to show how the next three Beatitudes are concerned with the transformation of soul that human consciousness can experience inwardly on the path to realizing the Christ impulse. The last three Beatitudes, however, refer to the objective changes in the events of destiny that rule outside the soul. In particular, they answer the question: How does the cosmos (suprahuman, human, and subhuman) respond to the Christianization of human souls and bodies? The three central Beatitudes answer the question: How are the members of the human soul (sentient soul, rational soul, and consciousness soul) Christianized? And the first three Beatitudes tell us about the various conditions and trials that the whole human being must pass through before attaining the three stages of evolution in connection with the Christ impulse. Thus we can view the first three Beatitudes as formulas for Christian occultism. The essence of occult initiation knowledge is that it is both inwardly subjective and outwardly objective. And it comprises both aspects, of course, from a cosmic perspective. This is especially clear in this passage: "Blessed are the meek, for they shall inherit the earth"—where an inner soul condition is brought together with a future cosmic fact.

The second group of three Beatitudes might be referred to as "psychosophical," since they deal mainly with the changes in human souls as they pass through the stages of evolution connected with the first three verses. The last three verses may be called karmic, since they address the changes in karma brought about by attaining those three stages of evolution. These verses also refer to the function of the spiritual threefold human being (spirit self, life spirit, and spirit body), which is expressed directly as such in karmic changes.[1] Until these nine verses have been studied as a whole and become the subject of profound perceptive knowledge, one cannot fully comprehend the essential structure of future human beings, who will have absorbed the Christ impulse into their whole being. Human beings will then be able to see most clearly the anti-Christian counter-archetype of the ninefold human being, created expressly as their opposite from within the nine subterranean spheres. When an object is in a combined condition, it is indistinct, but if we can separate one side and see it alone, a clear picture of the other side also emerges.

Now that we have outlined the inner structure of this meditation and the problem it raises, we can continue our meditation on the Beatitudes. We will begin with the central, psychosophical group of verses, since the first three verses formed the subject of the two previous meditations. It is most important to deeply understand the fourth verse, so we will first need to collect certain building stones, which we can find by asking: What does this Beatitude mean by the words *hunger, thirst,* and *filled* in connection with the soul? To answer this question, we must begin with the physical concept and experience of hunger and thirst. This ordinary experience shows us that quenching one's thirst and satisfying one's hunger present a polarity. By quenching thirst, we quench the superabundant fire of metabolic activity in the body, whereas stilling one's hunger brings fuel to that fire. In one case, we put out the fire, and in the other we feed it. However, when the body feels neither hunger nor thirst, a balance of these polarities is achieved, and physical harmony is established in the body.

A similar polarity is present in the experience of the human soul. It consists of impressions flowing into the soul from the outer environment and filling it with sensations and images, on the one hand, and on the other, that current is met from within by the flow of our soul's inner demands (or cherished expectations) on the world. If those impressions supplied to the soul from the world remain unsatisfying, the inner flame of desire will be felt more sharply because of a lack of satisfaction; thus we may speak of the soul's "thirst." On the other hand, a "hunger" of the soul arises when the world brings no new impressions to stimulate the soul, so that it longs less and less for the world and instead concentrates on its own inner life. However, when deeper moral claims, expectations, and yearnings of the soul come into question, the soul experiences equilibrium between its inner claim to the world and the current flowing inward from outside as righteousness. If the soul's organization is preeminently moral, then the relationship between inner impulse and outer reality becomes a question of righteousness. The soul's persistently alternating "hunger" and "thirst" then become "hungering" and "thirsting" after righteousness, since righteousness is a condition of moral harmony in the sentient soul, just as the satisfaction of hunger and thirst is the physical body's state of natural harmony. The sentient soul—soul being living externally in perceptual impressions and inwardly through its expressions of longing for perceptions—is morally just as dependent on righteousness as the body is on food and drink.

The sentient soul, however, is the member of the whole human soul nature that expresses the condition of the complete soul. Cognitions of the consciousness soul and judgments of the rational soul do not alter the soul life until they become living sensations. The sentient soul is the expression of the way the human soul has adjusted to life;

it is the makeup of the sentient soul that shows whether one is harmoniously adjusted to life. Consequently, righteousness is not just the moral element of the sentient soul itself, but also the actual life expression of the whole moral structure of the soul. The measure of righteousness that human beings express in relation to the world—more as demands on the self than on the world—is the criterion not so much of what one wishes to become morally, but certainly of what one has already become. That righteousness expresses the total of one's whole moral condition; it has been known from the earliest times and was taught in the mystery schools. Plato, the initiate of those mysteries, presents the doctrine of the basic moral qualities of the friend of wisdom, or philosopher. He shows how the threefold human being must develop three virtues, and how those virtues completely express their common fruit in external harmony as righteousness (*dikaiosune*). Wisdom (*sophia*), which the human head must develop, becomes courage (*andreia*) in the human heart, and a dominant urge to prudence (*sophrosune*) in the human limbs. But, just as the whole human being finds expression in the environment, wisdom, courage, and prudence are revealed together as righteousness (*dikaiosune*). Thus, the harmonization of thinking, feeling, and volition always produces righteousness. It represents the complete soul life of the human being, maintaining a balance between the soul life as subject to the spirit, the soul life as subject to the body, and the soul life itself.

This is the harmony that the most eminent representatives of spiritual life have ever worked for. In *How to Know Higher Worlds,* Rudolf Steiner tells us what is most essential about how this can be acquired in our time and how important it is on the path of perceptive knowledge. "The soul must become free, poised in perfect balance between the senses and the spirit" (page 128). This is just what human beings hunger and thirst for once they have come into living contact with the Christ impulse. The force that the human "I" is enabled to display through its union with the Christ impulse, and what leads to this harmonizing of the soul, is the force meant in the Beatitude, "Blessed are they that hunger and thirst after righteousness, for they shall be filled" (*makarioi hoi peinontes kai dipsontes ten dikaiosunen, hoti autoi chortasthesontai*). The "satisfying" of that striving for harmony of soul is the very harmony that results when the Christ impulse permeates the sentient soul.

The sentient soul represents the condition of the human soul in terms of its whole attitude toward life; the rational soul represents what can be added to human life as something specific from within. If it is the sentient soul that makes it possible for the soul to participate in life, harmoniously or not, it is the rational soul that assesses the value of this life and one's participation in it. Human experience in the world is owed to the sentient soul; one's response to experience, from within, is the work of the rational soul, which is the speaking soul of the human being. It has something of its own to say to our experiences, or acquired knowledge. Thus it rises above mere experience to assess them. Hence the formation of judgments is the essential activity through which the rational soul expresses itself. This activity of the rational soul is not mechanical, but remains in its proper human, moral sphere; at the base of every decision is a verdict. Whether we are conscious of it or not, our rational soul is constantly active in judging. To use the rational soul means to judge, whether we apply that judgment to ourselves, to others, to nature, or to the universe. It is impossible to judge without either ascribing value to what is judged or withholding it.

If a judgment is based on a healthy sentient soul, harmonized to some degree, one's judgment will be just. If the Christ impulse lives in the sentient soul, the rational soul in a person of good will tends to judge justly, or righteously. And if the rational soul itself has absorbed the Christ impulse, then something enters the act of judgment that allows the "I" to manifest much more, because the rational soul is more related to revealing "I" activity than is the sentient soul. Thus something enters judgment that transcends righteousness. Merely just judgment is formed on the basis of past and present; it is based on what has become of the one under judgment. But kindness, or mercy, soars above righteousness in the sense that it is not only just to the past and present of the one being judged, but also to that individual's future. It does not merely judge on the basis of the past but also relies on positive future possibilities; out of kindness, these are also taken into consideration in judgment. In this sense, kindness, or mercy, is more righteous than simple righteousness, because it also considers the future.

When kindness judges the rational soul, it judges according to the "new law" proclaimed in the Sermon on the Mount. It transcends the Platonic ideal of *dikaiosune,* and grows gradually into a new type of judgment, one in harmony with the spirit of the New Testament. The result of such judgment is that the karmic judgment on the one who is judging becomes kind as well. Those who judge others not only for what they have become, but also for what they are becoming, create a reason why they should be judged in like manner by others. This does not actually occur as a direct effect, but by the circuitous path of karma; nonetheless, it absolutely does take place. The restoration of health—the harmonization of human social relationships—is the result of absorbing the Christ impulse into the rational soul, just as harmonizing the inner soul is the result of its absorption into the sentient soul. The fifth verse of the Beatitudes expresses these fundamental truths concerning the inner conversion of the rational soul, under the influence of the Christ impulse, and its results: "Blessed are the merciful, for they shall obtain mercy" (*makarioi hoi eleemones, hoti autoi eleethesontai*).

Although the Christ-filled rational (intellectual) soul becomes a soul of mercy, it is nevertheless difficult for today's consciousness to comprehend the idea of a merciful intellect. Experience teaches that the very idea of a shrewd intellect carries an unsympathetic lack of consideration, even intrinsic cruelty, in the formation of judgments. Even if we rid ourselves of the thought of hardness and coldness in the intellect, however, it is difficult today to imagine anything positive in a "soft," "warm" intellect. In any case, it is certainly not easy to think of such an intellect as "sharp." The results of "softening" the intellect always seem to be vagueness and subjectivity in forming judgments. Nonetheless, it is possible to judge with perfectly clear concepts that are as clear and warm as sunlight. To show this as a potential social fact to the world is the task that Rudolf Steiner and the spiritual world entrusted to anthroposophic movement and its members' judgment of one another and the world.

And if it is difficult to form an idea of a rational soul that has absorbed the Christ impulse, it is even more difficult to imagine a consciousness soul that shows the influence of the Christ impulse. After all, life today gives us a picture of the inartistic, amoral, and materialistic consciousness soul that dominates materialistic science and other fields. Can the objectivity and pragmatism of today's consciousness soul become creativity, morality, and spirituality? This is the question that arises from the present condition of human consciousness. The transformation that is needed in the consciousness soul through the Christ impulse is the change from the consciousness soul to conscience soul, just as the sentient soul is changed to a righteousness soul, and the rational soul becomes a merciful soul. Indeed, the consciousness soul must become a conscience soul not just in a personal sense of right and wrong, but especially in the sense of taking a conscious and conscientious responsibility toward humanity and nature. The objectivity and pragmatism of the consciousness soul must be maintained, but it will become the bearer of the outwardly projected conscience. In terms of knowledge, modern science has brought an immense accumulation of facts from the kingdom of nature; now, however, it is important to absorb that mass of facts into the realm of conscience. Nature has been placed in the service of humankind by extending knowledge over that world; but by extending conscience over the natural world, human beings will become conscious servants of nature. In fact, human beings will become nature's servant in the sense that they will try to give it the necessary moral and spiritual element, just as nature provides to humankind the needed physical, material world. Conscientious responsibility toward the natural realm results from a deeper knowledge of nature. Natural facts are accurately and exhaustively investigated, and the consequences of the fall of humanity are being investigated in like manner. The investigating consciousness cannot help but stumble upon the fact of the fall of humanity in the sum total of natural phenomena. Just as the law of gravity was once discovered, the law of the fall will also be discovered—that is, the fact that nature as a whole is really decadent humanity. As a result of this discovery, nature will present the claim that human beings should turn their hearts toward the natural world. Then the great catharsis, purification of the heart, will take place. Human hearts will be turned outward, since purification of the heart means that it will no longer be cramped within itself, but opened to the world.

Once the law of the fall of nature becomes a subject of consciousness, it will gain a clear picture of the undivided being that is now broken and decadent in nature. This archetypal human being who contains the whole of nature—the "Adam Cadmon" of tradition and the "image and likeness" of God who is now the desire of all creation—will arise in consciousness from the vision of fallen nature. The pure in heart, those whose hearts have turned toward the realm of fallen nature, will see their God, the ideal archetype. In that image, God will indeed be visible to human beings who have purified their hearts by contemplating the tragic distortion of that image. Thus, in the sixth Beatitude we are told: "Blessed are the pure in heart, for they shall see God." It is not a matter of seeing the cosmic Father God, but one of seeing the divine archetype of humanity, visible in the elemental world as the hope of nature's resurrection in the age of the consciousness soul. The divine archetype of humanity, however, will be visible only to those whose conscience is enlarged to include not only individual and human concerns, but also those of the natural kingdoms. That enlargement will awaken a new natural, "etheric" clairvoyance, which Rudolf Steiner mentioned; the light that will make the elemental world visible, the Shambhala of Eastern mythology, is the light of the conscience of the *katharoi te kardia.*

## Spiritual Destiny and the Last Three Beatitudes

The sixth Beatitude already took us beyond a purely inner soul experience and placed us prophetically within an objectively spiritual event of human destiny. The remaining three Beatitudes lead us even further into this activity.

The sixth Beatitude went beyond the consciousness soul alone to deal with it as directed toward manas (spirit self). While it is the mission of the consciousness soul to make nature an object of conscience, higher powers are needed than those available to the consciousness soul for reconciling nature with the spiritual world. The consciousness soul can certainly realize the fact of the fall of nature, but to bridge the opposition between nature and spirit that resulted from the fall requires something even higher. Such a bridge must be built from both sides—from the spiritual as well as from the earthly side. And if we are to be that bridge, then the part of the human being that is at home in the spiritual world must unite with the part that feels at home in the earthly world. The part that reaches up from below is the consciousness soul; the part that comes down from above is the spirit self, or manas. If the consciousness soul is filled with consciousness of the guilt and need of earthly life, it lifts it like a cup, interceding for the need of Earth. It can then encounter a current descending from above, one that absorbs the darkness of guilt and need into its own clear light, carried upward by the consciousness soul. It may happen then that the ascending darkness and the descending light unite, which leads to a "rainbow" of reconciliation between the two worlds. For example, Goethe, in his soul, carried knowledge of this process of reconciliation and peace between the two worlds. Such knowledge became not only the basis of his theory of color, but also of his fairytale *The Green Snake and the Beautiful Lily.* With this knowledge, he approached the area of light phenomena and assumed the task of showing the great spiritual moral event of reconciliation between the higher and the lower consciousness in external light phenomena, as a reflection of it, so to speak. He was deeply convinced that the natural phenomena outwardly reveal the deepest secrets of the inner life. This is why the world of color was an open secret to him; he contested Newton's theory of light because it threatened to end this sublime parable concerning a way of reconciling the two worlds.

Those who had this kind of vertically directed "rainbow of reconciliation" in their nature were called "knowers of the seven words," or simply "peacemakers." To be a peacemaker, one must have experienced two births: a physical birth from earthly nature, and a heavenly one from God. The higher part of the human being must be borne according to one's individual destiny (not arbitrarily) in human consciousness, just as the lower part is born by natural birth according to one's destiny. The "rainbow of peace" can arise only when both the parts that are to unite are present. Thus, "peacemakers" are not only children of their father and mother, but also "children of God." In this sense, we can now understand the Seventh Beatitude: "Blessed are the peacemakers, for they shall be called the Children of God" (*makarioi hoi eirenopoioi, hoti autoi huioi theou klethesontai*).[2]

If the "birth from above" constitutes a vigorous change of destiny directed downward from above in the suprahuman world, then the eighth Beatitude relates to changes of destiny in the human world and the horizontal realm of human relationships. Indeed this Beatitude deals with the kind of destiny for those who not only unite the higher and the lower as peacemakers, but also maintain, in particular, the balance between right and left. If there are two currents that oppose each other in every area of life, then the harmonization (*dikaiosune*) of human destiny maintains a constant balance between those two polarities. The Christ impulse effects inner harmonization (or righteousness) as an outer condition of the sentient soul. Likewise, those who live by the life spirit (budhi) objectively harmonize the relationships of human destiny. They not only "hunger and thirst" after righteousness, but also help create it in human beings. Thus they act not as representatives of the luciferic human kingdom, nor yet the ahrimanic human kingdom, but with the consciousness of a third kingdom that is not of this world. This is why such individuals must appear inimical to the representatives of the two other kingdoms and even hated by the representative of that kingdom, whose triumphal advance they have frustrated. Thus, for those who bear the life spirit, it is their destiny to arouse a great deal of hostility and hatred around them; in compensation, however, they maintain a constant, intuitive union with the third kingdom, the kingdom of heaven. Life spirit (budhi) signifies the permeation of human nature with the Christ impulse from the "I," right down to the vital body.

Now we can understand the eighth Beatitude as a description of the karma for those who represent the life spirit: "Blessed are they that are persecuted for righteousness' sake, for theirs is the kingdom of heaven" (*Makarioi hoi dediogmenoi heneken dikaiosunes, hoti auton estin he basileia ton ouranon*).

The ninth and final Beatitude also speaks of the persecution that bearers of the Christ impulse must endure. In this case, however, it is not the persecution, humiliation, and slander of the harmony of righteousness, but persecution of the Christ being himself. It is no longer a matter of militant human prejudice and narrow-mindedness, but something else. It is not in the capacity of a human being to consciously hate the being of the Christ; this is possible only for beings of the evil hierarchies. Human beings can indeed become the tools of such beings by taking up the weapons of slander and persecution, but the hatred of Christ that is behind such actions arises from another realm. It is, in fact, a world whose depths no human or any being of the benevolent hierarchies has ever plumbed as deeply as did the Christ himself. It is the realm of subterranean spheres that hates the Christ as an individual, because he is the only being from on high who has ever encountered, face to face, those of the subterranean spheres in their own realm. Thus they recognize the Christ as their greatest enemy.

Human karma is so closely related to the Christ being that human beings, acting, as it were, as carriers of the Christ, likewise arouse the hatred directed against the Christ being. This means that human beings are placed by destiny between the world of evil and the Christ being it opposes. Human karma has been united with the cosmic karma of the Christ impulse. This, however, also reveals the eternal cosmic karmic name, the "star" of humanity—the spirit body (atma). Thus the true, eternal purpose of humanity is revealed as it is written in the "starry heaven" of creation's steadfast purposes, as the primal thought of the Father. And the "great reward in heaven" spoken of in the last Beatitude is that human beings should become conscious of their eternal star and that this fixed star should begin to shine within their constellation. The highest happiness designated for human beings by the Father God shines in the spheres of the heavens that correspond to the fixed stars.

The nine Beatitudes therefore ring out into the starry heavens and command a breathless silence of the soul on the threshold of the Father mysteries. The ninth Beatitude says, "Blessed are ye when men shall revile you, and persecute you, and say all manner of evil against you falsely, for my sake. Rejoice and be exceeding glad, for great is your reward in heaven." This is the karma expressed by forces arising from the subterranean spheres. This Beatitude points to the karmic relationship with the subhuman and the sub-natural worlds, functioning vertically from below upward (between the Earth's interior and the sphere of the fixed stars). The eighth Beatitude, by contrast, is concerned with the karma of the human and natural worlds acting horizontally, from right to left (between the ahrimanic and luciferic forces in humankind), while the seventh Beatitude deals with karma in the suprahuman and suprasensory worlds, acting from above downward.[3]

## The Cosmic Meaning of the Beatitudes

Thus far, we have studied the nine Beatitudes in terms of their significance for human karma; now we must ask: What is their significance for universal karma? They are bound to have such significance if humanity does, in fact, play an important role in cosmic history, and if, in addition, the Christ impulse is more than just a human matter, but a matter of cosmic history as well. We can answer this question by studying the passage directly after the ninth Beatitude in the Sermon on the Mount (as given in Matthew's Gospel). It is a kind of summary of the Sermon on the Mount, culminating in two sentences: "Ye are the salt of the earth.... Ye are the light of the world" (Matthew 5:13, 14). We learn here of the significance that those who have absorbed the Christ impulse will have for the Earth and the universe.

The Beatitudes tell us what happens to those individuals themselves and show the influence that is exercised through them in relation to objective cosmic events. They show us this influence of the Christ impulse on humanity in two directions: the permeation of what is below and the enlightenment of what is above. "Salt" must penetrate the Earth to give it moral "savor." "Light," however, shines upward from the Earth into the cosmos, changing the planet (as seen from the cosmos) from a dark body into a luminous one. The main objective vocation of humankind lies in these two directions—to make the Earth visible to heaven on the one hand, and on the other to thoroughly imbue the Earth with morality. The first aspect of this mission can be understood more easily by remembering that the Earth, seen from the spiritual world, appears as a dark speck in space. It glimmers only in spots where human beings cherish selfless thoughts and feelings, freed from earthly gravity and directed toward the spirit. It is these that create the moral and spiritual illumination by which earthly concerns can be seen from the spiritual world. It is just as difficult for them as it is for earthly human beings to perceive the spiritual world. If selfless spirituality did not exist on Earth, an abyss would make perception of the two worlds impossible in our present age. It is Lucifer who created this abyss, which is bridged repeatedly by nurturing selfless spirituality on Earth. That "cloud layer" of the luciferic sphere covers the Earth and casts a dark shadow from Earth into the cosmos. And a path through this cloud layer can be created only through thoughts and feelings cherished by altruistic motives. Thoughts that are spiritual but harbored in a selfish way reach only the luciferic level, where they are stopped. Considering the great number of individuals who embrace religion, mysticism, and various esoteric streams, we would expect the Earth to shine brightly nearly everywhere; the reason why this is not the case is that the motive behind it all is not selfless.

"Ye are the light of the world" (Matthew 5:14). This sentence from the Sermon on the Mount is, in fact, addressed to the intimate disciples of Christ Jesus. It refers to the light that, issuing from the Earth, must radiate into the cosmos and overcome the luciferic stratum. This verse refers to an altruistic spirituality. To cherish selfless spirituality is, however, impossible unless it is based neither on personal interest nor on the interest of a special group, but is founded on the interests of all humanity. This is expressed in these words of Christ Jesus: "Neither do men light a candle, and put it under a bushel, but on a candlestick; and it giveth light unto all that are in the house" (Matthew 5:15).

When a spiritual life is influenced by the Christ impulse, it cannot serve a private end and is thus always the concern of community. It brings people together and unites them in an organic way. Such a community, however, must not be devoted to the goals and issues that dominate today's ordinary human aspirations and activities. It must instead maintain a level above common practice, like that of a mountain compared to a valley. A spiritual community formed by the Christ impulse should be a "city that is set on a hill" (Matthew 5:14). It is precisely this distinction that makes it visible to the world. Its justification for existence must be the fact that it is present for all, whereas it must also rise above ordinary activities that involve power, conflict, and rivalry. Differing from the common community by shunning the principles of power, conflict, and rivalry, it becomes as visible as a city situated on a hill. An answer to the question of "exoteric and esoteric" in spiritual communities is found in the image of a city upon a hill, which "cannot be hid" *because* it is placed on a hill. It is its *level* that makes a community esoteric. It is its level that justifies the existence of such a community, and it must not be betrayed. Nonetheless, such a community becomes exoterically fruitful by being at this stage. If a selfless spiritual community is cultivated in the world only for spiritual knowledge—as pure spiritual science that does not resort to the usual methods of "demonstration," "scientific proof," and so on—then it completely justifies its existence as a guiding and stimulating phenomenon. Indeed, it will prove even more fruitful in the many areas of life and research by remaining true to itself and beyond the influence of those spheres. If, however, such knowledge is not cultivated for its own sake, just for love of light, but instead to gain an advantage over others in science, society, culture, or some other field, such activity is no longer altruistic, and groups that work in this way no longer create the light that makes Earth visible to the spiritual world.

Kindling light that radiates into the cosmos, however, is just one side of the objective significance of the spiritual stream in humanity. The other side involves inwardly changing the Earth itself. Such a change becomes imbued with morality through its neutral activities—that is, neutral from a moral perspective. The natural processes of Earth are intrinsically neither good nor evil, but stand between the worlds of good and evil (with evil working upward from the subterranean spheres); they are open in equal parts to the influences of both worlds. As long as human beings serve two masters, nature will also serve two masters. It is the mission of humankind to place the determining weight on the scale, thus rescuing nature from its vacillation, which is experienced by nature as a disease.[4] The cause of this disease is nature's neutral attitude toward the conflict of the worlds. This condition is exactly like that of salt that has lost its savor and is "trodden under foot," since it has become merely the object in the struggle between good and evil. And, up to a certain cosmic hour, those who have not yet made the decision will likewise lose the ability to decide as subjects, becoming instead merely the objects of conflict waged by others. In the future, they will form the fourth kingdom of nature, representing objects of the redemption of white magic, which will be practiced by those who have become clear. This undecided portion of humankind is the "salt that has lost its savor" and thus will no longer be an active force but an object of others' activity.

The passage of Matthew's Gospel that mentions "salt" refers to the moral human volition that flows into events on earth. While events in the outer world enter the human organism (by means of food, for example), inner human activities similarly reach out into the events of the outer world by means of human acts. And just as the entry of the outer world into human beings can either build or destroy (depending on whether it is poison or bread), what passes from human beings to the outer world also has a constructive or a destructive effect. But what builds up in the human organism is in fact blood, the organ of the "I." The outer physical world cannot provide blood directly, but only supply the materials with which the blood can build. There is, nevertheless, a substance in the outer world that, to a certain extent, can fulfill some functions of the blood within the human organism. That substance is salt. A salt solution, introduced directly into the blood system, can correct to some degree organic disturbances caused by lack of blood.

If nature cannot provide human blood, neither can human beings provide nature the consciousness of the "I," the spiritual counterpart of blood. Nonetheless, without "I" consciousness, nature cannot gain the ability to distinguish between good and evil, and thus cannot be healed of its disease. Human beings, however, can give nature something that, in effect, approximates "I" consciousness, just as salt within the human organism effectively approximates blood. This substance is etheric life forces imbued spiritually with morality from the human "I." In fact, it is no longer life ether in the sense of natural activity, but the beginning in human beings, through the transformation of the ether forces, of a new, fifth type of ether. This new type of ether that begins in humankind was called "moral ether" by Rudolf Steiner, which expresses its nature most accurately. This moral ether, which comes into being when the Christ impulse permeates human volition and activities, is the "salt of the Earth," allowing the moral element to access nature in a way that has value for nature. The purpose of moral ether is to become an organ for the constructive influence of goodness in nature, just as salt may serve in the human organism as an organ of constructive "I" activity, which normally functions through the blood. By means of actions that express a morally awakened will and with flashes of moral ether, human beings will penetrate natural events. And the beings of nature will direct their way in harmony with those currents of moral ether, which will represent nature's conscience. Nature will then follow humankind freely—not as a slave, but as [in Grail legend] the soul of Kundry might, placing confidence in what is worthy of confidence. Kundry would thus be freed from the curse of serving two masters—Klingsor and the knights of the Grail—and be able to give herself fully to the service of the Grail.

The activity of the moral ether as nature's conscience is the secret of future white mechanical occultism. Machines will no longer rule over natural forces, but natural forces (following the moral ether of humankind) will instead become the motive force of machines. It will be human volition that will bring about the flow of moral ether—volition in which the Christ impulse lives with such power that it will have led to a realization of these words of Jesus Christ: "No man cometh unto the Father, but by Me" (John 14:6). Father forces are activated when human beings have permeated their will with the Christ impulse to the extent that it causes the moral ether current to flow out, just as those forces were active when the prophets of the Old Testament worked and were persecuted.[5]

"Ye are the light of the world" refers to the conquest of Lucifer in the outer, objective world. Likewise, "Ye are the salt of the earth" refers to the struggle against Ahriman in the outer, objective world. Lucifer prevents the light of Earth from shining up into the spiritual world, and Ahriman produces darkness on Earth. This spiritual, moral darkness is carried by Ahriman even into the natural realm. But this is a darkness that is dark only when seen from a spiritual perspective; from an earthly standpoint, it appears to be a certain kind of light, expressed, for example, in electricity. Indeed, Ahriman's main weapon in nature is an earthly electricity more subtle than is known to humanity today. In the conflict with Ahriman over nature, the main weapon of the beings of the spiritual world is celestial electricity. Flashes of celestial lightening often destroy and reduce to chaos the preparations of subterranean spheres that threaten nature and humanity on

Earth's surface. Many plans for evil are brought to nothing by bolts of celestial lightning, whereas nature experiences such events merely as a conflict of alternating success between two powers. Neither the earthly electrical activities of Ahriman nor the flashes of Michael's celestial electricity are convincing in themselves to nature. Driven from one fear to another, nature sighs for redemption while rendering service first to one side and then to the other. Nature will experience only the moral ether revealed through human beings—not as power, but as a call that offers guidance and help. This kind of experience happened once before. A certain amount of the morality working in nature was revealed among the disciples of Jesus Christ after Pentecost. Certain miracles recorded in the Acts of the Apostles and by tradition can be explained only by the fact that, for a period of time, the apostles had a different relationship to nature than would otherwise have been possible during that epoch. When we read the Acts of the Apostles (*praxeis apostolon*), for instance, from the perspective of the relationship between nature and the apostles, we see that this is true. Indeed, we find that the author of the Acts stressed this to make it clear that the apostles had acquired a new kind of magic, always triumphant when in conflict with the old. The writer of the Acts seems to have made it his special task to convince readers that the moral element may affect the events of nature. Moreover, it is not incantations, talismans, amulets, and such that produced this effect, but the name of Jesus Christ and the apostles' spiritual permeation by the Christ impulse—that is, their faith.

The two passages that mention the light of the world and the salt of the earth refer to the universal significance of what the nine Beatitudes describe as human concerns. Indeed, that significance involves the fact that the alienation between heaven and Earth caused by Lucifer can be overcome, and that enslaved nature can be led gradually to freedom by absorbing the Christ impulse. This second task, in particular, cannot be fulfilled until the distant future. "Salt" will appear increasingly active from the sixth cultural epoch, or Philadelphia, onward, but it will not become a dominating factor in natural processes (as, say, gravitation is today) until the Earth's Jupiter incarnation. From the middle of the Jupiter evolution onward, gravitation, as such, will gradually lose its importance in nature. Consequently, gravity will no longer bind natural beings to the scene of the Jupiter events; instead, a moral force will prevent them from floating away. In fact, if natural beings remain faithful to the Jupiter planet, they will affect the moral ether. The moral force of confidence will keep them from floating away, not the compulsion of gravity, which will no longer exist on Jupiter.

In finishing our meditation on the nine Beatitudes, we have taken a step toward recognizing the work of Jesus Christ through his Word. The nine Beatitudes represent the human path to the Son. The next step involves studying the path that leads through the Son to the Father. This step involves the seven petitions of the Lord's Prayer as given by Jesus Christ in the Sermon on the Mount. These petitions show the relationship through which human beings can come to the Father, so long as they have united (in the sense of the nine Beatitudes) with the Son. We can understand the relationship between the Beatitudes and the Lord's Prayer in a deeper sense by using these words of Jesus Christ as a key: "No man cometh unto the Father, but by me" (John 14:6). This gives us the inner connecting thread that leads from the Beatitudes to the Lord's Prayer. In a very deep sense, the Lord's Prayer is a sequel to the revelation given in the Beatitudes; therefore, the next meditation will consider the seven petitions of the Lord's Prayer.

# Chapter 6

# The Lord's Prayer as a Path: Uniting Destiny with the Father

## The Power of the Trinity in Human Destiny

As we ended the previous meditation, we mentioned the relationship between the two most important parts of the Sermon on the Mount: the Beatitudes and the petitions of the Lord's Prayer. We said that the Beatitudes refer especially to the human path to the Son, whereas the petitions of the Lord's Prayer concern the human relationship to the Father made possible through the mediation of the Son. To understand the part of the Sermon on the Mount that culminates in the Lord's Prayer, we must study the relationship between the human being and the Father God. There are real difficulties connected with this, however, because it relates to the sphere of existence in which destiny is woven—an area that ordinary human consciousness is mostly unaware of, just as it is unaware of experiences during deep sleep. But human beings generally experience only the visible effects of destiny, and not the processes that prepare destiny. Those remain hidden beyond the threshold of waking consciousness. It is just as well that this is the case, because in this way no prejudice stifles human initiative and hope. Following death (or the corresponding stages of initiation), however, one gains insight into the processes and dispensation of destiny. To begin with, we experience the transposition of our whole life tableau into the moral sphere. All that lived in the ether body as a series of memory pictures is now illuminated by a light that clearly shows not just the facts of our past life, but especially their moral value. There is no selection or separation of good from bad; the parts of one's biography are merely irradiated by an impersonal light that reveals their moral essence. Such irradiation of the life tableau by the moral light of thought is the work of the third hierarchy. The "reception" given inwardly by the angels, archangels, and archai to the web of destiny of the one who has died involves the fact that the life tableau passes from the light of human memory force into the light of moral evaluation.[1] This network of facts (the "web of destiny") from the past life of one who has died is received by the third hierarchy when it has passed from the realm of memory into the realm of deepened moral intensity.

The subsequent process is a sublime and immensely significant cosmic repetition of the process presented visibly to the senses on the hill of Golgotha, where a sponge filled with vinegar was offered to the crucified one when he said, "I thirst." And he drank the vinegar. Thus the second hierarchy absorbs the human destiny offered from below. The beings of the second hierarchy drink the mingled good and evil from the course of human life. They absorb it directly into themselves, just as a drink is absorbed. The dissolution of the just consequences of one's earthly life into exusiai, dynamis, and kyriotetes means that the substance of earthly life's moral value is absorbed into their starry harmony. All the poison and gall of the earthly life is absorbed by the hierarchies, along with the good it contains. If this were not the case—if heavenly beings did not continually draw "vinegar" from the "sponge"—earthly existence would quickly become completely poisoned, just as the human organism would be if poisons were not absorbed from the "sponge" of the liver and gall bladder.

The third stage of shaping karma in the spiritual world involves the formation of the future life based on the past by the beings of the first hierarchy. The content of the past life vanishes in the midnight darkness of the cosmos, and from it emerge future forms intended to rise as the substance of a future life. This content is poured from on high and received by the second hierarchy, where it becomes sounds—the sound of the trumpets of destiny, as spoken of in John's Revelation. Future karma is written by the beings of the third hierarchy in the "book of the karmic secret" and closed with "seven seals." For each human being, the "keeper of the seals" of this book is one's guardian angel. That being alone has access to the secrets of an individual's destiny, and the functions of guardianship are based on that knowledge. The processes by which the fruits of human life ascend into the spiritual world are characterized in the second lecture of Rudolf Steiner's *Karmic Relationships*. On the other hand, a description of how the matured future destiny descends may be found in John's Revelation. The "vials of the wrath of God," the "sound of the trumpets," and the "seals" mentioned in the Apocalypse are steps in the descent of matured karmic judgment. In the Apocalypse, however, the process described is in reverse to the order indicated here, because knowledge ascends in a direction that is opposite to that of events and revelation.

Thus, the three hierarchies cooperate in the process of forming human karma. Essentially, this involves passing cosmic judgment on the actions of earthly human beings. And three cosmic principles join in this judgment. The Holy Spirit, the Son, and the Father, represented by the three hierarchies, work together in this. The Holy Spirit shows the moral and spiritual balance of the human earthly life; the Holy Spirit gives a complete picture of the earthly life to be judged, or reassessed, in its moral value. Then the Son absorbs it into himself and presents his advocacy to the Father. Human words were heard on Golgotha from the mouth of the crucified Jesus Christ: "Father, forgive them, for they know not what they do" (Luke 23:34). They are heard again and again in the spiritual world whenever an earthly human life is judged. Essentially, it is the cosmic advocacy of the Christ with the Father that bears all the details of the extenuating moral circumstances. Such advocacy means that evil done unconsciously has very different results in destiny from evil done consciously. The fact that they "know not what they do" will always—before the highest cosmic judgment seat—be placed on the scale where extenuating circumstances are weighed. When a human life picture has been illumined by the Holy Spirit, and penetrated by the intercession of the Son, it ascends to the dark area of the cosmic midnight hour. There it is judged by the Father; the decision is in his hands. Once more this experience is foreshadowed to the physical senses on Golgotha. The words of the dying Jesus Christ preserved in Luke's Gospel show, in human speech, the final experience before entering the darkness of death. Before he died, Jesus Christ said, "Father, into thy hands I commend my spirit" (Luke 23:46). In the hour of death, he submitted the human destiny interpenetrated by his being to the decision of the Father, the Lord of Death. And the resurrection was the Father's judgment on the Christ-imbued human being. Similarly, human souls rise again after death from the mysterious darkness of cosmic midnight, enveloped in a newly created "destiny body" woven from forms that have been perfected in resurrection as the just results of the destiny of their preceding life course.[2] Thus the mystery of resurrection takes place in each human destiny between death and birth in the spiritual world, just as it took place nineteen hundred years ago in the physical world.

Something appears in this picture that shows the combined process of forming future karma; the Father God speaks to humankind by means of the fulfilled decrees of destiny. Whereas the Holy Spirit speaks through the moral content of knowing, and the Son speaks through the moral life, the Father speaks only through events—that is, by morally judging events. Thus destiny is the only area in which human beings have a relationship with the Father. Karma is the means by which human beings maintain, develop, and deepen their connection with the Father. This leads to a significant question: If the relationship between humankind and the Father in earthly life is determined by the mature and finished karma of the past, is there any possibility that one can consciously affect that karma through the will? Is it possible to change karma that has matured and been justly shaped according to what produced it? Is it possible to induce the Father God to alter his verdict?

Jesus Christ answered this in the Sermon on the Mount by giving the Lord's Prayer as the prototype and model for conscious human incursion into the realm where the decrees of the Father rule. The seven petitions of the Lord's Prayer are words that affect destiny and can be heard by the Father, thus offering a path through which a deeper, more conscious, and more intense relationship with God the Father may be achieved. The following discussion of the seven petitions of the Lord's Prayer is intended to show how and in what way these petitions can become currents that form destiny and how they contain a human approach to the Father God.

## General Aspects of the Lord's Prayer

If our souls are filled with these questions as we approach the Lord's Prayer, we will be deeply struck by something in the text of these seven petitions; they never mention the individual human "I." There is no talk of *my* Father, *my* trespasses, and so on, a mode of expression that would be a basic condition of mystic absorption and religious fervor in prayer. The petitions always use "we," "*our* Father," "*our* trespasses," and so on. This points to the first, preliminary way we must approach the Lord's Prayer. It shows us that the Lord's Prayer is not at all intended for personal use; consciousness concerned with personal, individual matters cannot use the Lord's Prayer. The Lord's Prayer is not intended for the fulfillment of individual wishes, for the rapturous absorption of lonely mystics, or for personal development. The mere fact that it is addressed to God the Father shows that it is not intended for these purposes. The Father God has to do with the hierarchy of humanity, not its groups and individuals. Separate beings have conscious relationship with the Father only insofar as they represent their hierarchy in its capacity as a community in cosmic destiny. And no one is qualified to represent the fourth hierarchy without having made the concerns of its destiny one's own. When reciting, *in the name of humanity*, the seven petitions related to the seven needs of human destiny, one's consciousness must be occupied with the questions that concern human destiny. Then one's voice becomes the voice of humanity; the unconscious voices of all humankind form a chorus that joins the voice consciously expressing the seven needs of humanity. The hierarchical choirs alone penetrate as high as to the Father God; the sounds of single voices die away on closer thresholds. This is why poets imagine choirs of angelic hosts (though we need not determine here whether those spiritual hierarchies sing "Gloria" and "Hosanna" to the Father God). The fourth hierarchy is no exception; if words are to ascend to God the Father, they must rise morally and spiritually in chorus. What the chorus of humanity has to say to God the Father is contained in the seven petitions of the Lord's Prayer, as spoken by Jesus Christ as the representative of humanity. The Lord's Prayer is the spiritual and moral expression of the chorus of the fourth hierarchy; it contains every cry humankind sends up—even to the threshold of the Father sphere—in all the toil of labor, all the pain of sickness, all the distress and fear of death, and also in every endeavor after goodness, truth, and beauty. This is why the Lord's Prayer offers the best training in selflessness and the surest and most comprehensive source from which the recognition of the true need of humanity can be drawn.

The Lord's Prayer expresses seven needs of human existence, a fact that leads to another essential aspect for an understanding of the Lord's Prayer. If the seven petitions represent human needs, the petitions must also contain something that bears the possibility of satisfying those needs. If human need is conditioned by karma, petitions alone would certainly not be enough to affect karma; they would have to contain something that gives them karmic value. And this karmically effective element can, in fact, be found in the petitions of the Lord's Prayer. Not only is it contained in the petitions, it is also added to the Lord's Prayer as an explanatory note by Jesus Christ himself. Immediately before the Lord's Prayer, Matthew's Gospel quotes these words: "Be not ye therefore like unto them [the heathen]: for your Father knoweth what things ye have need of, before ye ask him" (Matthew 6:8). And immediately after the Lord's Prayer, we read: "For if ye forgive men their trespasses, your heavenly Father will also forgive you: But if ye forgive not men their trespasses, neither will your Father forgive your trespasses" (Matthew 6:14–15). Thus, in the Lord's Prayer it is not merely a matter of petitions, but of justified petitions. And, indeed, it is the principle of moral balance behind the scheme that lends justification to these petitions. The scales are not just a symbol of justice in ancient mythology, but cosmic reality revealed as karma. The constellation of Libra in the zodiac is its cosmic sign, and we cannot understand the Lord's Prayer as a karmic influence unless we study it under this sign.[3]

Now, the very idea of balance is connected to right and left—the horizontal. And this idea is completely appropriate when applied to the karmic relationship between earlier earthly lives and the current one, because it involves an ongoing act of balancing. This idea alone, however, is not enough for understanding the Lord's Prayer, which does not deal with the fulfillment of karma from the past, but with determining future karma now. The seven petitions of the Lord's Prayer represent an active determination of karma, not merely petition for karma to occur; there is no need to be anxious about that. Because the Lord's Prayer deals with the predetermination of karma in the present, the balance that forms the basis of the Lord's Prayer and gives the petitions karmic justification must be imagined not as horizontal, but as vertical. We must picture one end of the scale in heaven and the other on Earth. The higher scale is in the realm of the Father's mercy; the lower in the sphere of human initiative. Between the two and determining the balance is the Son, through whom, alone, human beings can approach the Father. The fact that this karmic balance weighs vertically rather than horizontally is a consequence of the Son becoming the lord of karma. The rule of Christian karma is: "Ask, and it shall be given you; seek, and ye shall find; knock, and it shall be opened unto you" (Matthew 7:7). This differs from the law of the elders, or karma of the old covenant, in that following the sacrifice of Jesus Christ, the weighing was no longer just horizontal, but also vertical. In other words, along with the law whose principle is "an eye for an eye, and a tooth for a tooth," the new law, whose principle is preeminently expressed in the Lord's Prayer, becomes increasingly important. In the following meditations, we will discuss the moral and spiritual meaning of the vertical position of the karmic balance, as well as the nature of the "new law," whose lord is Christ. The task here is to clarify, through the seven petitions of the Lord's Prayer, the nature of the new relationship between humanity and God the Father—that is, the nature of the new covenant as Christian karma, in which the weighing is done vertically.

## The Seven Petitions as a Path to a New Relationship with God the Father[4]

For those who are untouched by spiritual science, it is very difficult in our time to distinguish between thinking of something and meditating on it. This is especially difficult because, while meditation arises as the result of deep thinking, from a certain perspective meditation not only differs from thinking, but it is actually the opposite. Whereas ordinary thinking of an object involves gaining a singular insight into the thing, meditation involves repeated submersion into the insight. Thinking of an object ends when the object is known; it has no reason to concern itself any further with what is already known. Nonetheless, this is the very point where meditation can begin. The purpose of meditation is not to gain new knowledge, but to *live* in acquired knowledge. The discovery of new thought content is not the goal of meditation; the object is to bring thought content down into the life of feeling and volition. The goal of meditation is to make a truth the content of one's whole being. And meditation must be continued for as long as it takes to change a clear thought into a clear force of the will. This is why meditation is considered an exercise, whereas thinking about something is a single, purposeful act.

In the course of an evolving meditation, a transformation occurs, similar to the one that takes place in the evolution of the thinking that develops into meditation. Thinking that has achieved insight may either end at that point, or it may be converted into meditation practice. Thus, meditation that has reached the stage of illuminating the will may either stop at that point or be converted into a different and higher activity. The higher activity that can develop from meditation (as a more advanced stage) begins when the original purpose of the meditation has run dry. If the aim of one's meditation is to completely imbue oneself with something specific, at some point one may be able to say with certainty that the thought now fills one's whole being. That moment, however, may also evoke a purpose for further activity. Whereas the content of meditation permeates one's will, the will is then devoted to the world. Furthermore, devotion of the will to the world brings the challenge of using it, as it has manifested, to serve the world. If the purpose of meditation has been to strengthen the clear and benevolent forces in one's soul, it will now become the will to strengthen those same forces in the world. Repeated exercise of the soul's forces will lead to repeated application of those forces. It is then no longer a matter of doing something to further one's own evolution, but to bring about something essential in the world. Meditation leads to conscious participation in objective world events.

Thus the nature and origin of the idea of God, for example, leads to deep and complex thought. The "name of the Father," imprinted from the earliest ages like a seal stamped in human consciousness, may become a subject of meditation. Such a meditation is lifted to participate in a spiritual event if one's forces of thought, feeling, and volition are allowed to flow into its essence: "Hallowed be thy name." The point is not to discover the name, nor is it merely an exercise for education; the point is simply that the name of the Father may be hallowed. Such an outflow of thought, feeling, and motive, consummated in the name of humanity, is the result of a living union with a higher member of human nature than those said to be part of the soul. Thinking logically about an object is possible because of the rational soul. When such thinking develops into meditation in the sense of intensifying one's consciousness of something already known, then the consciousness soul becomes involved in the meditative effort. And when meditation reaches the stage of participating in macrocosmic events, the spirit self (manas) enters one's spiritual activity. The spirit self is expressed in the devotion of human forces to cosmic interests. The most important cosmic task that human beings can devote themselves to is, first of all, opposition to the alienation of heaven from Earth by trying to unite those two realms. This is the first task of the free human "I": to become a free link between heaven and Earth.

The "I" is the aspect of the human makeup that is exclusively unique to an individual. "I" is one's true name in the cosmos, the name that no one can speak except the one to whom it belongs (a fact that Rudolf Steiner has pointed out in various contexts). No one can say "I" when referring to another; it is a word that has meaning and significance only when said by the one to whom it refers. The fact that this exclusive name of the individual cannot be used by another is an expression of the security and freedom of the "I" as an inner sanctuary. The fact that the name of the other cannot be spoken is the most external expression of the protection from misuse that is given to that name as an individual's exclusive possession; it protects one's freedom from the violation of invasion. Cosmic karma provides that the sanctuary of the human name be hallowed and kept holy so long as individuals do not betray their "name" and so long as individuals do not surrender their freedom, and bow before *another* power.[5] Just as the true human name can be spoken only by the one to whom it refers, the "name" of the Father God likewise cannot in this sense be spoken by *anyone;* beings of the world received their individuality from the Father being, so that the Father being is above the identity of every being; in other words, the Father being stands behind each individual subject, and because of the individualities of these beings, the Father being himself speaks their "name." The various individualities are the "letters" that form the "Word" expressing the name spoken by the Father. The sum total of human individuals forms the name of the Father as he manifests in the world through the hierarchy of humanity.

Thus, the essence of the first petition in the Lord's Prayer implies this: Holy is the freedom of all human individualities, just as the freedom of each individuality is holy, because the freedom of a single being (one's "name") has meaning and significance only when it is in harmony with the great name of human freedom, the name of the Father. "Hallowed be thy name" is thus a petition for realizing the whole hierarchy of freedom; it is a petition for the sublime harmony of the many names in the one name of the Father. That name is not a mere combination of the many names, but a revelation of the Father through the harmony of all beings in the human hierarchy. In the sense of the petition, no single being in this chorus can be absent; otherwise the revelation of the great name would be imperfect. The great name of the Father is to be holy, and with it all single individualities are to be accepted into a holy and secure unity in the name of the Father.

The mission of the "I" is to strive for this unity. In human beings, the "I" reveals the nature of the spirit self (manas), bearing the true individual name of human beings from incarnation to incarnation. The spirit self is actually the member of the human being whose mission is to bring out the individual notes in the cosmic harmony. This note would have made itself heard if a discordant tone, a false name, had not opposed it. While the effort of the spirit self is focused on harmonizing the individual with the world, the luciferic principle of personality in the astral body is focused on an isolated note that ignores cosmic harmony. Because of this luciferic interference, a cacophony arises in the human hierarchy. All divisiveness in humanity occurs as a result of this "false name," which arose from the principle of egoism among human beings. And the petition of the Lord's Prayer ("Hallowed be thy name") is directed against these divisions of humanity and against the false freedom of egoism. This petition is based on the recognition that hallowing the Father name means hallowing every true, individual name. The true name of the individual, however, cannot have real value unless the one whose name it is recognizes the "name," or inner freedom, of every other individual as equally holy. All names are symbols that express the name of the Father.

The principle of balance is at the foundation of the first petition of the Lord's Prayer. We might, therefore, mentally add to the petition "Hallowed be thy name" the words "as we hallow the names of one another." This shows the inner justification of the petition. By maintaining the sanctity of freedom's spiritual source in others, one is justified in speaking the prayer that, through this source of freedom, the Father can reveal himself to all human beings and sanctify them, just as his name is also kept holy. In contrast to the fifth petition of the Lord's Prayer, however, which expresses its justification, this remains unspoken in the first petition. The reason for this can be easily understood if we reflect that, on the one hand, the Lord's Prayer was given during a specific epoch of human evolution, while on the other, it was not supposed to be limited to that period. Can we speak, in a general exoteric sense, about the stage of the evolution toward freedom reached during the fourth post-Atlantean cultural epoch (or indeed the present stage of evolution): "We sanctify the names of human beings"? Was the sanctuary of human freedom so highly valued then, and is it so highly valued today? Do such words fit the actual stage of human evolution at that time, and still fit today's situation? The unspoken aspects of the Lord's Prayer will gradually sound with increasing clarity as humankind reaches the corresponding stages of spiritual evolution. And during the sixth Cultural epoch (Philadelphia in the Apocalypse), the unspoken part of the manas petition of the Lords Prayer will also sound for wider circles of humankind.

If the essential endeavor of the Holy Spirit self involves the holy union of all humanity, the essential mission of the life spirit (budhi) goes even further in that direction. It is not just a question of realizing the unity of the human hierarchy, but one of realizing the mission of the united human hierarchy toward *other* beings. There are beings in the world who depend on human beings. These beings are grouped into the collective concept of "nature." The dependence of the natural realm on humankind arose from the fact that, although nature is subject to "natural laws," moral law is valid only for human beings; nature is exempt. This fact and the consequent tasks and duties of humankind were discussed in the previous meditation (in connection with the "salt of the Earth"). Now it is important to take another step toward a more accurate and profound understanding of these tasks and duties. The first thing we should do in this way is to imagine more accurately the stages of nature's salvation through humankind. The first step is to comprehend the consciousness soul, which has become a "conscience soul" in the connection between nature as decadent humanity and the fall of humanity. From this, the next step follows: realizing the alliance between nature and the moral spiritual element by means of the manas-bearing humanity. This alliance will be made real by introducing into it the "salt of the Earth," or the moral ether.

This, however, does not yet indicate the *redemption* of nature, which is reserved for the future Venus existence of Earth's evolution when the human life spirit, or budhi, principle will be fully developed. Then the moral force issuing from humanity will not only direct nature, but it will also supply moral life force to the very being of nature. Nature will then no longer be guided and confidently follow humankind; rather, nature will have gained possession of its own moral forces. For example, the forms that are heir to the earthly plant kingdom will determine their growth according to moral laws rather than organic laws. There will no longer be types such as phanerogamic and cryptogamic rhizomorphous plants, or leafless and leaf-bearing rootless plants, but forms moved imaginatively by goodness, gratitude, humility, and such, flowering in resounding revelation. The kingdom of nature will be essentially different. It will have grown morally erect and will acquire a self-dependent relationship with the kingdom of heaven—not in the sense of becoming a rigid reflection of the cosmic past, but a present reaction to the spiritual events in the heavens. Nature will awake and no longer depend on dreamy memories of the past, but live in the spiritual present. The kingdom of the Father will be present. "Thy kingdom come," which expresses the fundamental effort of the life spirit, is a petition for the presence of the kingdom of heaven in nature.

To justify this petition, however, it must contain something (even if unexpressed) that can be placed on the other side of the scale. Nature cannot achieve a different relationship to the deity unless humanity has done something. If the petition intends to free nature from the past so that the kingdom of heaven can manifest as a present reality, then something that corresponds to that change in nature's relationship must take place in terms of the human relationship to time. Human beings themselves must renounce the present and live in the future before the kingdom of heaven can manifest in nature—that is, before the *soul* of nature can awake. This is because the *present* is a principle of the soul, the *future* is the principle of the spirit, and the *past* is that of the body. It is a characteristic of budhi consciousness that everything belonging to the present is given to the environment, whereas human beings themselves live only out of and for the future. As budhi consciousness makes itself felt in humankind, the human soul will flow out into nature, whereas that soul itself is devoted to the Spirit. It must renounce the present in favor of nature and submit to the preparation and realization of the future. In this sense, the second petition as a whole may be understood somewhat in this way: May your kingdom be present as we live for the future; may nature be freed from the kingdom of the past and given the presence of your kingdom as we renounce the kingdom of the present and consecrate ourselves to the kingdom of the future. By its very nature, however, surrender to the future means living for the purposes of the future, so that the future is absorbed into the will. Thus, we live the future in advance in the will, while we surrender the heart to our environment. This consciousness is our crucifixion—a sacrificial surrender of the heart forces (of the present) to the environment, while the will reaches into the distant future. This is why a petition for the arrival of the kingdom of heaven always involves a kind of crucifixion of human consciousness. The measure of that crucifixion determines the measure of the justification (the effectiveness) of the petition.

The sacrifice offered by the human consciousness can, however, go beyond renouncing the present; it can also renounce the will to the future. Thus the sacrifice is complete, and nothing is left for the consciousness, and even its existence comes into question. If consciousness attains this highest sacrifice, it experiences death. The miracle of resurrection that may follow is the act of the Father God; it reveals the reality of the spirit body (atma). "Thy will be done on Earth as it is in heaven." This petition is a renunciation of the will; at the same time, however, it transfers the will to beings of the lower kingdom. Just as complete realization of the second petition is reserved for the future Venus existence, complete realization of the third petition is reserved for the future Vulcan existence. The passage "heaven and Earth shall pass away, but my word shall not pass away" expresses a literal truth, and it applies especially to the Lord's Prayer. The words of the third petition are thus true even for the Vulcan period of human evolution. Their validity will be proved during that period by the redemption of the lower, backward human kingdom because of the sacrificial death and resurrection of the more advanced humanity. Then, even the Earth's interior, the kernel of primal evil, will be converted, and the will of the Father will literally be done on Earth as it is in heaven.

Thus, as their spiritual justification, the first three petitions of the Lord's Prayer contain renunciation of our own thinking (our own nomenclature), feeling, and volition. Indeed, renunciation of our own thinking is the necessary requirement for the manas petition; renunciation of our feeling is connected with the budhi petition; and renunciation of our volition is contained in the atma petition of the Lord's Prayer. The atma petition includes not only human beings and nature, but also sub-nature—all evil that works upward in the present age from the subterranean sphere to the Earth's surface. This influence is present in all material existence on the Earth's surface. Nonetheless, the Father influence, which penetrates vertically through the material, is also present in everything. The bread we eat may carry one influence or the other. On the one hand, it may carry the virtue of the sacrament, or holy communion, of the Lord's Supper, while, on the other, it may serve as a medium, for example, to darken the consciousness that unites millions of people, whose banner bears the motto "daily bread," in a community of hatred. Indeed, there are few crimes in the world that have not been committed in the name of "daily bread," while there is nothing in the physical world more holy and more healing—in the deepest sense—than the bread of communion service.

This dual significance of bread was the fundamental reason for the two meanings of the fourth petition of the Lord's Prayer. During the early centuries of the Christian era, there were two interpretations of this: "Give us this day our substantial bread" (*ton arton hemon tov epiousion-panem substantionalem*). It is not, however, a matter of different readings; the important point is that we should understand the fact that two areas of influence converge in the bread. And this is especially important, since it depends on human beings themselves to determine the kingdom through which they enter communion by means of the bread. The meaning of the fourth petition *as a prayer* is precisely that we can receive "today" our bread from the hands of the Father. This petition is thus concerned with the attitude of human consciousness toward the Father influence in the bread as a physical substance; here, it is not a matter of bread as a mere symbol, nor is it merely physical food. Food is needed to sustain life in the physical body on Earth; it is needed so that human beings can live and, moreover, live as human. The physical body is not just a combination of material elements, but also a product of cosmic moral forces of will. As such, it needs material elements, on the one hand, and on the other, moral forces to persist not just as a strictly physical product, but also as an organism concerned with the soul and spiritual nature of being human. The body, as that of a human being, literally "shall not live by bread alone, but by every word that proceedeth out of the mouth of God" (Matthew 4:4). The Word of God sounds in the deepest depths of the subconscious, forming and preserving the body, just as food is assimilated and builds up the physical body in the depths of the metabolic system. In fact, both are equally essential to the life and maintenance of the body. In the present age ("today"), these two bodily necessities must be in balance. In the temptation in the wilderness, the need for such equilibrium was expressed by Jesus Christ: "Man shall not live by bread alone, but by every word that proceedeth out of the mouth of God."

Thus the fourth petition of the Lord's Prayer expresses the need and a petition for this equilibrium. According to its inner sense, this petition is a human prayer for the power that Jesus Christ revealed by resisting the temptation to turn stones into bread. Thus the thought expressed in its meaning is approximately: Give us, in the present age, earthly bread permeated by your influence, even as the heavenly Word, for which we hunger and long, is imbued with your being.

While the fourth petition refers to the will processes of the metabolic system in the physical body, the fifth petition refers to the corresponding inner realm of activity in the ether body, which also has a kind of "metabolic" will organization. Its metabolism is expressed as its memory life; the experiences of the past continue to live in the ether body and fill it just as matter fills the physical body. Its will activity is expressed in the moral processes of "retaining" and" forgetting"—in the obliteration or strengthening of various experiences. The ether body thus carries the experiences that cause contraction through the flow of their cold currents as well as those that lead to expansion through irradiation by warmth. The *moral* side of retaining and forgetting in the ether body, in fact, is involved with whether the health-producing, positive contents have more radiant force than the disease-producing negative content. Human beings cannot do anything to alter it within a single lifetime; the past is immutable and irrevocable, its sins planted like pillars. And because human beings cannot change anything directly, they address the fifth petition of the Lord's Prayer to God the Father—but not in their own name and only personal guilt, but in the name of humanity and the guilt of all humankind. The essence of the petition is the hope of blotting out the negative past, which made humanity ill. The obliteration of the past as conscious, moral "forgetting" is the meaning of *forgiveness.* There can be no forgiveness on the part of the Father, however, unless a counterweight has been laid on the lower, human side of the balance. Thus, the condition for forgiving our trespasses is that we forgive those who have trespassed against us. When we learn in a moral sense (in our astral nature, where it is in our power to alter the content) to "forget" the negative in others, what is negative in us will be blotted out in the ether body, where we are powerless to change anything. When we obliterate *astrally* the guilt of others in our own astral body (as antipathy), then the essence of our own guilt will be correspondingly obliterated *etherically* in their ether body (as the deep-seated cause of disease).

As we have said, however, the fifth petition does not deal just with individual matters but with the concerns of humanity, which include all that is individual. Thus, it is not one or another particular trespass that is intended when one prays for forgiveness, but the human guilt from which individual guilt arises. This is the human guilt that was encountered as a possibility by Jesus Christ in the temptation in the wilderness—the temptation to take possession of the kingdom of the Earth at the cost of worshipping the lord of this world. Jesus Christ rejected that temptation; humankind, however, had succumbed to it long ago during the temptation in Paradise. So-called original sin is the consequence of the primeval guilt of humankind, who became the ruler of the Earth, on the one hand, while falling into a relationship of dependence on the lord of this world, on the other. Thus, forgiving the individual trespasses of others may annul the consequences of the universal guilt. Each time this is done, the petition unites with the voice of the Son to bring before the Father the intercessory plea: "Forgive them, for they know not what they do." The fifth petition of the Lord's Prayer is a petition, spoken by Jesus Christ on behalf of humanity, for healing from the consequence of original sin: "And forgive us our trespasses, as we forgive those that trespass against us."

While the fifth petition deals with the forgiveness of universal guilt and finds justification through the forgiveness by individuals of others' trespasses against them, the sixth petition deals with a number of trespasses of individuals. It deals with the *source* of individual trespasses of humankind. And it is the subject of the petition that makes such a condition of guilt possible, since *temptation* is the cause and the beginning of that state of guilt. The wording of the sixth petition gives the impression that the Father God might tempt human beings. While this is quite obviously unthinkable, the petition nevertheless says, "Lead us not into temptation." This contradiction is resolved when we comprehend more deeply the relationship between evil and the Father God as presented, for example, in the Book of Job in the Old Testament or in Goethe's *Faust* ("Prologue in Heaven"). There evil is allotted a fixed term, during which human beings may be tempted by evil and be tested. Such terms do in fact exist, both for individual lives and for the course of human history. For example, "Kali Yuga" refers to just such a term in the history of humanity.

Being led into temptation, therefore, indicates that the tempting forces are given the opportunity to enter, while, through the intervention of Lucifer, there is a natural tendency in the astral body to succumb to temptation. The human "I," however, is certainly able to resist this tendency. The human "I" holds its ground against spiritual temptation, which can be seen in the fact that it does not doubt the power of goodness and truth, not functioning as an external power, but through its own nature. Every recourse to seizing outer means of power (even with benevolent intentions) conceals doubt of the direct influence and force of truth and goodness—that is, unbelief in God. Such disbelief in the essential power of truth and goodness is clearly expressed in the demand that such power reveal itself *externally.* Karma had to be guarded as a secret from the consciousness of European humanity during the Kali Yuga period so that the people of that place and time might pass the test—that is, learn and prove through experience a belief in truth and goodness *themselves,* and not as a result of their karmic consequences. And during the period when the effects of karmic retribution were hidden, the temptation to evil assailed humankind in a *visible* way. Thus a situation arose that brought about great testing: goodness and truth seemed to have faded into mere human "ideals," whereas evil spoke with the thunderous voice of a natural force. Those who remained faithful to the "ideal" in that situation—those who, needing no outer "proof" of the power of goodness, nevertheless believed in the invincibility of truth and goodness because of their intrinsic value—thereby acquired the *right* to use of the sixth petition as a prayer for reciprocity of confidence between human beings and God. The unspoken part that justifies this petition may be thought of in this way: And, just as we do not tempt you, lead us not into the temptation of expecting an outer revelation of your power.

Again, we find a key to deeper understanding of this petition by looking at Jesus Christ's temptation in the wilderness. When the tempter approached Jesus Christ with the temptation that he should prove the reality of divine power by means of an outer miracle (by casting himself from a pinnacle of the temple), Jesus Christ rejected the temptation: "It is written again, Thou shalt not tempt the Lord thy God" (Matthew 4:7). And the petition to be spared temptation is justified by renouncing the human tendency to tempt God—to see him not as truth, but as an outer power that demonstrates and proves truth. While the fourth, fifth, and sixth petitions of the Lord's Prayer refer to the three temptations in the wilderness, the seventh refers to the great trial of Jesus Christ during his night in Gethsemane. There it was a matter of resisting the objective activity of the world's primal evil (*boese*), which can be called "evil" (*poneron*). This purely moral evil does not yet reveal itself in its own nature in human consciousness, but is active only as a remote force through the ahrimanic being, and its activity is expressed as a dark, sinister force in the body's subconscious.[6] In this sense, such activity is in complete contrast to that of the human "I," which brings out the brightest point in the human bodily organism, while this more outer evil induces the point of deepest darkness. Nevertheless, those who knowingly try to fight outer evil in the world can be delivered from it. The justification, or effectiveness, of the petition—"But deliver us from evil"—depends on whether those who use it do so in opposition to evil in the *world*. Therefore, this petition may be inwardly completed in this way: But deliver us from evil, as we do battle against the world's evil.

It is the moral and spiritual structure of the Lord's Prayer that gives the seven petitions the karmic weight of the three sacrifices and four types of resistance to temptation. The triangle of the Spirit and the rectangle of the earthly person form the basis of the Lord's Prayer and also express the capacity for sacrifice and resistance in the sevenfold human being. In harmony with these faculties is the weighing of the karmic balance of the new covenant, with its lower scale on Earth and its upper scale in the hands of the Father.

# Chapter 7

# The Signs and Miracles in John's Gospel

## The Moral Importance of Miracles in the Gospels

Our discussion of the three temptations of Jesus Christ pointed to the connection between overcoming each individual temptation and the three spheres of activity that thus arose. Proclamation of the Word, the performance of miracles, and the passion are the three levels of Christ's revelation, each made possible by overcoming a corresponding temptation in the wilderness. The most essential points in the proclamation of the Word were discussed in chapters devoted to the Sermon on the Mount (the nine Beatitudes and the Lord's Prayer), and now it is time to study the miraculous acts of Jesus Christ before studying the passion. Those who, judging with honest minds in the modern spirit, allow the miracles of Jesus Christ to pass before their souls as they are described in a specific intentional order in John's Gospel, for instance, might feel compelled to ask this sincere question: Why do the Gospels narrate the miracles? If the purpose is to show evidence of the divinity of the one who performed them, it contradicts the spirit of Christianity; such an assertion would use the very means that the tempter offered Jesus Christ in the wilderness and that he rejected—that is, using a miracle to convince the world of the power of truth. Moreover, the miracle argument is incompatible with the fact that Jesus Christ himself cautioned against speaking of his miraculous acts (Luke 8:56). If, on the other hand, the miracles are recorded for the purpose of showing special crises in the destinies of individual human beings or human groups, such experiences must, nonetheless, have a universal significance, for the sake of which they were included in a record designed for all humankind.

Do these miracles deal only with individual experiences in destiny or with individual destiny experiences that have significance for all? This leads us to another question—one designed to morally smooth the path toward solving the central problem of the miracles. This is the matter of the relationship between the universal and the individual—not from an abstract philosophical perspective, but from a moral and spiritual view. Indeed, from a moral and spiritual view, the life and history of humanity is repeatedly faced with this problem. No matter how simple and convincing the logical principle may seem (that is, the part is less than the whole), its application to the human moral sphere leads to fierce conflicts and moral cul-de-sacs. The stakes of the Inquisition, the guillotines of the French Revolution, and the horrors of "restoring social justice" today are all based on the principle that the part is less than the whole, as applied to the sphere of human morality. In fact, this principle is at the foundation of the deepest guilt of humanity, the crucifixion of divine humanity, an act determined by Caiaphas's argument: "It is expedient for us, that one man should die for the people, and that the whole nation perish not" (John 11:50). The greatest injustice in the history of the world relied on this argument; and Caiaphas' argument is merely a reformulation of the principle that the part is less than the whole.

Nevertheless, the Caiaphas principle governs a broad range of areas in human life. It is impossible to substitute any other principle, since contending that a part may be *greater* than the whole, or even equal to it, would be absurd. The Caiaphas principle cannot be argued; it must be investigated just as it is. In this world, it is not a matter of one principle against another, but of creative humanity against a mechanized humanity reduced to chaos. In this struggle, a very different meaning may be given to this principle applied to human relationships, depending on whether it falls into good or evil hands. Nonetheless, just as old age and death remain iron necessities of earthly life, so does this principle. Therefore, all human activity must exist under the tragic sign of needing to prefer the individual over the whole, thus proportionately diminishing the universal, or needing to devote itself to the universal, thereby overlooking the individual. When people wish to build a railroad, for example, they cannot make a detour round the cottage of some elderly couple; the line must go straight through. But can't we always compensate people for a destroyed home? Even so, actions can serve the universal will over individuals and their fate, while the forces limited to the individual are correspondingly withheld from the collective.

This is the cross borne by all human activity, and it is always accompanied by destruction or diminishing individuals. Our actions force us to take up either the cross of the robber or the cross of a common thief; they make us into the criminal crucified on the right, or the one on the left. No third kind of activity is directly possible to us; such a new activity will require a long path of Christianizing human thoughts and then feelings. It is the meaning and the intention of the central cross on Golgotha that, step by step, human beings will learn that third kind of activity. And this cannot be attained until a radical transformation takes place in human nature in terms of thinking, feeling, and willing, under the Christ impulse; only then will we be capable of acts that serve both individuals and the universal.

The need that this is "not only (individual) but also (universal)," however, was felt even at the time of the Mystery of Golgotha. An attempt was made then to oppose the Caiaphas principle with another that embodied protection of the universal as well as avoiding sacrifice of the individual. Pontius Pilate refused to hear the demand by the Council of the Elders and instead sent the Christ to King Herod, since he was a Galilean.

Whereas Herod found no fault in him that would require the death penalty, he nonetheless mocked him right along with his soldiers, dressed him in a beautiful robe, and returned him to Pilate. Beginning that day, Herod and Pilate became friends, for neither could find any fault in him. It was Pilate's suggestion that some form of physical punishment would be enough (Luke 23:8–17). The two became friends because they met on the common ground of an idea of justice both had conceived. This thought, however, was not the *true third*, which became possible only after the Mystery of Golgotha; rather, it was a compromise of "both." To avoid the death of an innocent, they wished to kill him morally by exposing him to mockery in order to shame him. But was he truly shamed? If so, why was he murdered?

Apart from the drawn sword of Peter, the argument of Herod and Pilate was the only one that humanity (human nature) had available to oppose the Caiaphas argument. Only the injustice of "the part and the whole" could oppose the compromise principle of "both." This shows with great clarity the character and disposition of human nature that has not absorbed the Christ impulse. This disposition of human nature is revealed in the words of Jesus Christ: "All that ever came before me are thieves and robbers" (John 10:8). The nature of the new type of activity can be comprehended, however, by studying the acts of Jesus Christ (passed down to us as miracles) in the light of questions about the relationship between the individual and the universal. The miracles recorded in the Gospels are, by their nature, exactly the "third activity" that rises as an entirely new possibility above the activity of the thief on the right and the thief on the left. The Evangelists have included details of Christ's miracles in the Gospels so that, through them, we might learn the possibility of this new activity. Hence the purpose was not to prove the divinity of Jesus Christ, but to show acts through which we might come to recognize a new possibility of future activity in the sense of Jesus Christ's words: "The works that I do shall he do also; and greater works than these shall he do" (John 14:12). The miracles of Jesus Christ reveal the secret of the influence exercised by individuals for the universal, and by the universal for the individual. This secret may be studied from many different perspectives.[1] In what follows we will study this subject from yet another point of view.

## The Miracles as Signs and Acts of Healing

The consequences of the fall of humanity are not apparent only in the fact that human consciousness has lost any real experience of the spiritual world; this fact is obvious, especially when people today pursue a spiritual path. Knowledge of these consequences in the spiritual history of humankind may be painful, but direct *experience* of them on the path to spirit is one of the most severe trials of the soul's endurance and courage. Arising in the realm of the soul's experience is the hard fact of the soul and physical organism with the many consequences of having become organic and alienated from the spirit.

The soul thus experiences not only the moral condition of human activity (as discussed), but also the coarseness of the human receptive faculty in relation to the spiritual world. The soul approaches the spiritual world not in a mood of confidence in the evolution of consciousness and an open road to infinite developmental potential, but as one who is sick and needs healing and reaches out to the health-giving springs of the spiritual world. Whether such individuals are sound in a medical sense, they experience the essence of human disease, inwardly and apart from any physical presence. As soon as a yearning for the spirit is awakened within, such individuals place demands on their inner forces and experience the essence of paralysis, blindness, disturbed balance, and so on. It is this yearning for spirit that reveals one sickness after another to human awareness.

And on the same path, people encounter the reality of the Christ impulse when spiritual miracles of healing take place. Initiation is not merely a process of knowing and of transforming human consciousness, but also a process of healing that leads to far-reaching changes in the human organism, affected as it has been by the consequences of the fall. These effects of inwardly experienced initiation are basically the same as those brought about by Jesus Christ in an outwardly visible way and handed down to us in the evangelists' records. The seven miracles recorded in John's Gospel represent the healing of the seven principal infirmities of human nature in both individuals and groups.[2] The Mystery of Golgotha, however, transferred the fruits of the healings to humanity as a whole. What does the Mystery of Golgotha mean to humanity? The traditional theological answer is "redemption from inherited sin." This is true, especially if it is understood not as a universal rule, but as an actual process of healing that goes through seven stages; these stages are the miracles recorded in John's Gospel. Thus, the true answer to the question of concrete consequences of the Mystery of Golgotha would state the possibility of healing the whole of humanity with the same hypotheses and conditions that were present in the seven miracles of John's Gospel.

This applies to the corresponding records of the other evangelists as well. We speak of John's Gospel only because it records Christ's miracles as more than initiation as a process of healing; the Gospel writer was very successful in making this view especially clear through the Gospel's form, style, and composition. In particular, we must consider John's Gospel in this chapter, because it plainly shows that the selected point of view is not arbitrary (of course, others might have been chosen); rather, it lies in the nature of the subject itself. If we allow John's Gospel to speak to our souls in silence, it tells us through its whole composition that the seven miracles of Christ are acts of healing that were performed for a few so that, after the Mystery of Golgotha, they might be manifested to the many. Thus those miracles are not *just* miracles; they are also signs of the future spiritual and bodily healing processes within the human organism, which is sick as a consequence of the fall of humanity. And Jesus Christ performed "this beginning of miracles [signs]" (*epoiesen archen ton semeion,* John 2:11) by changing water into wine at the marriage in Cana in Galilee. A superficial study of this first sign may easily lead one to ask: What does turning water into wine have to do with the works of healing we have been discussing? In John's record there is certainly no word of any of the guests being cured. Apart from new wine, the only result of this miracle mentioned in the Gospel is that Jesus Christ "manifested forth his glory" (*ephanerosen ten doxan autou*) and that "his disciples believed in him" (*kai episteusan eis auton hoi mathetai autou,* John 2:11).

Regardless of how commonplace and simple the particulars may appear in the Gospel, they represent important indications for those who understand the reality behind this "sign." That reality is not a *spatial* but a *temporal* matter. The influence of Christ's act was not limited to the wedding guests in that place and time, but at that hour and in that place it was a *sign* of the miraculous healing that would manifest during the years of destiny initiated by that wedding feast. The healing would manifest in the future, but when the sign was performed that predicted that future healing, it was most important to understand it and, in and through it, to perceive the great revelation of healing power (*ten doxan autou*), or "glory." So, the result of that hour was the disciples' belief; from the direct impression of the sign, they confidently foresaw the future healing. The healing itself would take place in the future, but for the moment, it caused only foreseen knowledge, or faith. The fact that this *was* the effect is stated clearly by the evangelist in his words about the future nature of healing.

But what is the healing activity that was both inaugurated and displayed by the sign of changing water into wine at that wedding? To understand this, we must first recognize that this was a real ceremony of wedlock in Cana when Jesus Christ was present as a guest. It was a matter of uniting the destinies of two persons who had been brought together by human love and human longing. And Jesus Christ took part in the feast of these two persons and their friends. Neither duty nor formality was the reason for his presence at this human festivity, but a desire to enrich it with his gift. Jesus Christ's presence as a guest at the wedding feast shows that a place where the union of human destinies is solemnized was certainly not alien to him; and it shows that he could work there in a miraculous way for healing and enriching that solemn occasion. Dreary preachers and teachers who voice the contempt of later centuries may say what they will; the friendly picture of that marriage in Cana is inscribed in bright colors in the world chronicle, and it can never be erased.

The gift presented by Jesus Christ to the bridal pair at Cana was the miracle of changing water into wine when the wine provision had been exhausted. To read this sign—to understand the future work of healing that it revealed—we need to study closely the dramatic flow of events: drinking and exhaustion of the natural wine; filling the vessels with water; changing that water into wine; and the wonder that the better wine was offered *after* the poorer quality wine. This series of images expresses a life secret without recourse to the (always doubtful) process of interpretation. Immersion in a series of pictures ordered intentionally provides their meaning in the same direct way that an orderly succession of letters produces a word. As is the case with reading, it is not a matter of interpretation, but one of simply *reading.* A similar process is involved when one's whole consciousness is immersed in studying a series of pictures; the series becomes a word produced by the pictures, just as a written word is produced by the letters of the alphabet.

Thus, the series of pictures of the wedding feast in Cana tells us that the important point is the *healing* of marriage itself, or the sacrament of wedlock. Indeed, it speaks of the transformation of that human relationship and its spiritual destiny. It was transformed so that a third level was added to that destiny; after the natural impulse through which Yahweh functions in the blood was exhausted, "water," the clear and cool element, appears at the next level, to replace the wine that stirs the spirit. The natural course of destiny would have reached its conclusion with the second stage, except that a third was added with the miracle of Christ's intervening impulse. With the third stage, the "water" was imbued with a force of love that was just as warm and stirring as natural love; in other words, he again turned the "water" into "wine." And the wonder of this transformation is heightened by the fact that, *as wine,* the second wine is better than the first, natural one. Here we are dealing with a secret of human blood, which can become a bearer of the Christ impulse, and the stages of that transformation are revealed in the processes of the sign at Cana.

Just as the miracle at Cana is concerned with the transformation of blood, the second miracle (also in Galilee, a land of mixed blood) dealt with healing heredity based on the blood connection between generations. The first miracle dealt with the relationship between bridegroom and bride, and the second with the relationship between father and son (John 4:46–54). By healing the son of noble heritage (*basilikos*), Jesus Christ healed the past, just as at the marriage in Cana he healed the future. The stream of heredity flows from past to future, and its function is to carry the past into the present and future. Indeed, the past is carried in such a way that the "I" and physical body of the father and the astral and the ether bodies of the mother represent the material of heredity passed on to the children. This occurs in reverse, however; the father's "I" influences the child's physical organism, and the father's physical body influences the child's "I." Similarly, the mother's astral body provides the heredity model for the child's ether body, while her ether body is the model for the child's astral organism. Thus, when the Bible tells us that the "sins of the fathers" will be visited upon the children (never mentioning the "sins of the mothers"), we should understand this to mean that one's "I" being "sins" and, further, that it is the father's "I" (not that of the mother) that decides heredity. Consequently, the Bible also speaks of Adam, not Eve, as the cause of original sin; in the case of inherited sin, the important point is not who made the sin possible, but who actually committed it—that is, the one whose "I" participated in it. Thus the Biblical account of original sin as an inheritance from the "old Adam" is far more accurate, justified, and true than are the nebulous theological ideas of today.

By recognizing that the "I" being of Adam participated in the original sin and thus became the physical destiny of the coming generations, one can understand the basis for the sickness and healing of the son of noble heritage. The very title *basilikos* (king's man) tells us much, because external things and circumstances that have no moral or spiritual significance for the event narrated are simply ignored in the Gospels; when a detail is mentioned, this is because it is connected to the spiritual moral meaning of the event described and helps express its meaning.[3] And this is why the story tells us that the father of the boy lying at the point of death was of noble heritage (*basilikos*). This fact shows an important circumstance for both the son's sickness and the act of healing; it indicates the character of the father's "I" being. To be a member of the nobility at that time—not merely as an outer position, but as a true servant of the king—meant being able to direct one's own being according to the "I" being of another. Individuals of nobility had to be satellites, with the King as their sun; the "I" had to be held in the background. Indeed, such a person had to possess an exceptional faculty for following an alien "I" being by suppressing one's own. The term *basilikos* indicates one who was unaccustomed to making decisions or acting independently and one who followed the initiative of the king (*basileus*). Such a custom, however, means weakening one's selfhood; in terms of heredity, it means weakening the physical body of one's child. This is exactly the weakness that appears in the case of the son of noble heritage in John's Gospel; his blood was not able to carry the "I"; his blood was too weak to be the organ of the "I." An illness thus developed and expressed itself as an inflammation of the blood, or a fever (*ho pyretos:* literally "burning fire").

Now the nobleman appealed to Jesus Christ. But Jesus Christ called on him to show a certain strength, the lack of which in the past had caused his son's illness. He said to him: "Except ye see signs and wonders, ye will not believe" (John 4:48). These words told the father that, out of the moral force of his "I" being, he must recognize the Christ being as the source of healing activity; he must believe without having seen signs and wonders. Faith, unsupported by external signs and wonders, is essential to an "I" initiative that leads to moral intuition. Complying with this demand, "The nobleman saith unto him, Sir [*kyrie*], come down ere my child die" (John 4:48). He believed the words of Jesus Christ: "Go thy way; thy son liveth" (John 4:50), and he went his way. At home the father discovered that his son had recovered at the moment when Jesus Christ said, "Thy son liveth."

It is also significant that after his conversation with Jesus Christ, the nobleman is given a new name by the evangelist; instead of *basilikos* (king's man), after he believed he is called *anthropos* (human being), and he was called *pater* (father) after he had confirmed, at home, the moment of that healing, and after both he and his whole household believed. Through the self-initiative of moral intuition he was no longer a "king's man," but had become a human being—one who had found his foundation in his own inner nature. And because his inner conversion was displayed so effectively that "his whole house" was convinced of the new truth, he became the *father* of the household in a true and profound sense. This meaning of the "father of the house" involves not just responsibility in the physical world, but also spiritual authority. Just as the mother is the soul of the home, the father must be its spirit. This is exactly what happened in the case of the nobleman who, once he had become a "human being," could become, in this sense, "father of his household" as well.

Thus, the healing of the son of nobility by Jesus Christ involved making the stream of heredity flow backward. Its direction had been from the past into the present, but Jesus Christ directed his work of healing from the present into the past—when the nobleman became a human being, and the human being a father—and from that healed past returned to the present by the healing of the son. The process can be visualized in this diagram:

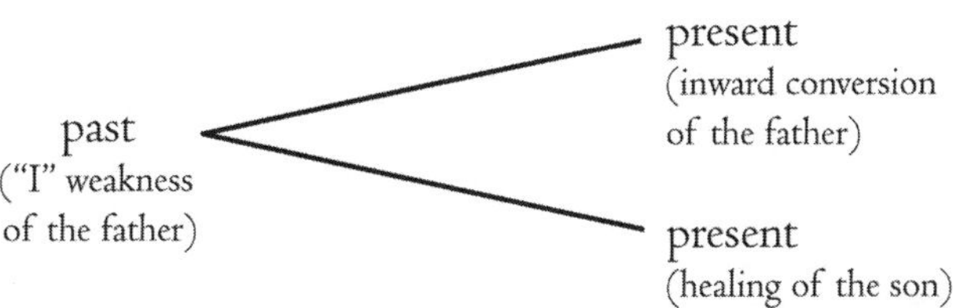


Like the first, the second Galilean miracle deals with healing the blood, insofar as it is related to marriage and heredity. The first healing referred to the future, while the second refers to the past and, in fact, to the past of moral causes and effects in successive generations.

The third miracle (John 5) also deals with the past, but with a more distant past of different construction. It deals with the past of the individuality affected by paralysis—his preceding earthly life. We see this in the words of Jesus Christ in connection with this act. Immediately after the healing of the man's paralysis, Jesus Christ speaks of the judgment that the Father has committed to the Son and about the dead who will hear the voice of the Son, even now. He also speaks of the Father—and now the Son—reviving the dead. In relation to the healing of the one who had lain motionless for thirty-eight years, it should be noted that the theme of death, judgment, and continued life indicates that the whole problem of karma—and thus repeated earthly lives—is opened up. If we focus on the series of images that the evangelist exhibited for this purpose, we are most likely to see that, in this case, we are actually dealing with karmic healing—that is, healing a disease whose cause lies neither in this life nor in heredity.

A healing spring is at the center of a five-rayed star, formed by the five approaches of the "house of mercy," into which an angel descends from time to time. Those who seize that moment and immediately step into the pool are healed. But those who have been lying for thirty-eight years and cannot do it for themselves are so alone in the world that they have no one to help; at the moment of healing, therefore, someone always steps into the pool ahead of them. Then comes Jesus Christ and asks if one wishes to become whole. Having been answered in the affirmative, Jesus Christ heals that one. This happens on the Sabbath day, when human activity must rest. The series of pictures provides unequivocal clarity about the nature of that individual's karma. With this "human being" (the term always used in the Greek original, never "man," specifically, or another title) it is a matter of karmic consequence whose causes were the opposite of those that led to the son's sickness. With the nobleman, it was a question of weak personality; here, however, the sickness was the result of an excess of this in a previous life. This was a person whose every movement welled forth from him alone, and whose motives were based entirely on self-consideration. As a karmic consequence of this, he became paralyzed and depended completely on awaiting the "mercy" of a spring that operated *outside.* One who was accustomed to prompt, self-centered action now had to lie and wait, hoping that someone would show up and help just when prompt action was necessary. But he lay there alone, because his earlier egoism had condemned him to loneliness. Since he had never cultivated any interest in others, others now passed him by without interest. In his former life, he had always refused to plan or act in conformity with his angel; now he had lain for thirty-eight years, yearning for contact with the angel who occasionally descended into the pool of mercy at the center of a building in the shape of a pentagram, the symbol of personality. He had despised them both in a former life, but now he needed both an angel and another person.

Jesus Christ approached the sick man and asked, "Wilt thou be made whole?" These words contain much more than one initially expects of such a simple sentence. The sick man understands the question very well and answers that he has no one to help him submit to the angelic power. This is what his answer means; the important point was not his desire be made whole (it stands to reason that if a sick man has come to a healing spring, he wishes to be cured); he was actually being asked whether he wished to be cured by the power of the angel—whether, despite thirty-eight years of waiting, he was discouraged or still had enough strength and humility to wait. And the answer was a real answer to the real question of Jesus Christ as it arises from the depth of those words: "Wilt thou be made whole?" In this question, the sick man heard much more than the words. They asked, "You have been lying here for thirty-eight years; do you still wish for healing from the pool of mercy? Do you, nonetheless, still believe that the mercy can come to you? Do you perhaps wish to appeal to some other possibility of healing—to some spring other than this pool of mercy, where the angelic power is manifested? Do you still hold the belief that *someone* will show up and bring you into contact with the healing angel? Haven't you lost faith in human beings by preserving your faith in the mercy of an angel?"

The answer of the paralyzed individual showed that he would not forsake his faith, whether in the spirit or in human beings, despite the many years of waiting. Then he was healed by one who represents both the world of angels and the world of human beings. At the moment of healing, Jesus Christ acted both as the long-awaited man and as the healing angel through whom healing might come. The words "Rise, take up thy bed, and walk" hold a collaboration of the *two* spheres of consciousness. "Rise" expresses the uplifting influence of the world of the hierarchies; "take up thy bed" expresses the horizontal orientation of the negative human past; but the command to "walk" combines the two cosmic directions, the vertical and the horizontal, in the *cross* of the human being walking—the one who stands erect while bearing the burden of the past. Thus the picture of the healed paralytic carrying his bed is a deep expression of human destiny: a walking cross, formed by the vertical of spiritual liberation and the horizontal of earthly bondage.

After the healing, Jesus Christ said in the Temple (*en to hiero*) to the one who had been healed, "Sin no more, lest a worse thing come unto thee" (John 5:14). With these words, Jesus Christ made it clear that the malady had arisen from moral causes in the past and, moreover, that the one who is healed is free to choose whether to bring about the same causes again. This reference to the connection between sickness and moral freedom shows clearly that, in the one who was healed, there was no question of either a weak character or an unhealthy soul life; that is, it was not a fault in the ether or astral bodies, but a misuse of moral freedom, which was exercised out of the "I," not the human organism.

The "I" is the member of the human being that continues on from incarnation to incarnation. The result of each incarnation continues to live in the "I," forming what is often called a "string of beads" in Indian symbolism, of which the individual "beads" are the "I" being of the various incarnations, while the "string" represents the continuity of consciousness from incarnation to incarnation. Thus the "I" being of former lives lives on and represents the "inner" past that is inseparable from an individual. This miracle of healing indicates a power that affected not only the present but also past "I" being—the "I" that passed through death with the responsibility for the previous life course. "I" consciousness of the past, which preserves its activity from the previous incarnation and in which many human beings live and act, is called consciousness of the "dead" in the Gospels, and those who live under the "I" impulse of the past are simply called "the dead." Thus, healing the paralyzed man involved more than merely the present "I"; the "dead," in particular, heard the "voice of the Son" and experienced a conversion in his past consciousness. "For as the Father raiseth up the dead, and quickeneth them; even so the Son quickeneth whom he will" (John 5:21). These words of Jesus Christ have a direct connection with the healing and refer to it. And words that follow express it even more clearly: "Verily, verily, I say unto you, The hour is coming, and now is, when the dead shall hear the voice of the Son of God: and they that hear shall live" (John 5:25). True, only a few of the dead had heard this voice—a fact expressed, for example, in these words: "Let the dead bury their dead" (Luke 9:60). This is the fundamental challenge to which we must respond if we wish to gain spiritual hearing. It is a summons to conquer ourselves again and again and, shutting out all personal impulses, repeatedly listen in silence to the voice of conscience. The sounds that the spiritual world uses to speak are moral and spiritual voices, not fixed "vibrations" for the purpose of being caught by a sensory organ. Those voices can be heard only after the soul has adapted to the voice of conscience; those who are prepared to follow the dictates of conscience without hesitation are thus prepared to hear the voices of cosmic conscience.

Jesus Christ characterizes his own suprahuman conscience in sublime words: "I can of mine own self do nothing: as I hear, I judge: and my judgment is just; because I seek not mine own will, but the will of the Father which hath sent me" (John 5:30). Just as Jesus Christ's moral judgment depends on hearing, or *inspiration* from the Father, his actions depend on seeing, or *imagination* of the Father's works. "Verily, verily, I say unto you, The Son can do nothing of himself, but what he seeth the Father do" (*an me ti blepe ton Patera poiounta,* John 5:19). The judgments of Jesus Christ were thus *inspirations* of the Father being, while the signs and wonders he performed were *imaginations* of the Father's activity. Through the feeding of the five thousand, the fourth miracle, our souls see a powerful example of an *imagination* of the Father's activity. This miracle, which is closely connected with the next—walking on the water—can illuminate the influence of the Christ impulse on the whole human race by both day and night. The feeding of the five thousand deals with a common daytime activity of the Christ, while walking on the water deals with a nighttime activity of the Christ. Together, these two signs (John 5) show the complete orbit of the Christic sun, through the day consciousness of the majority and (in the first example) the night consciousness of the few.

It is not important to interpret these miracles, but to concentrate directly on the spiritual moral element from which the pictures are not only woven, but in which, having condensed from it, so to speak, they float. So, first, let us place before our souls the pictures associated with the circumstances, and filled with meaning, as the Gospel shows them. On the far shore of the Sea of Galilee, Jesus Christ is on the mountainside and surrounded by his disciples. A great multitude has followed him, and the Passover feast is drawing closer, when unleavened bread would be eaten. When Jesus Christ saw how many people there were, he spoke of the need to feed them, and he gave the disciples five loaves and two fish that a boy had brought with him. And the disciples in turn gave these to the people. After everyone had been fed, enough leftovers were gathered to fill twelve baskets.

These are the main pictures shown in the first, *day* sign. Considered as a whole, these images express an important truth—of how the human senses are to be imbued with the Christ during the time of the consciousness soul. The conversion of the senses brought about by the Christ impulse is shown in the sign of feeding of the five thousand. It shows how *hungry* senses can become *productive* senses. After being blessed, the five loaves and two fish produced twelve baskets full of fragments; likewise, the five day senses and the two twilight senses having received the Christ impulse and taken it into the heart, lead to twelve creative currents that will flow from the heart and affect the whole sensory system. This sign deals mainly with the mystery of the human heart, which can receive the Christ impulse from without and, as a result, begin to radiate through all twelve senses.[4]

The Gospel also shows that the feeding of the five thousand deals with a deep-seated transformation in the human sensory system. At the beginning of the account, we are told that "a great multitude followed him, because they saw his miracles that he did on them that were diseased" (John 6:2). This passage makes two statements: first, neither philosophers nor occultists followed Jesus Christ, but "a great multitude" of ordinary people led by their senses; second, that multitude followed him not because of philosophic or occult motives, but because they saw the miracles he performed on those who were diseased. In other words, he had made an impression on them through their senses. The reaction of the multitude to that miracle was natural for those led by the senses: they wanted to make Jesus Christ a king (John 6:15). The attitude of Jesus Christ also corresponds exactly to the motive and the need of the multitude; as soon as he lifted his eyes and saw that a great many people had come to him, he raised the matter with his disciples of how they would feed this multitude. The very look of the multitude told him that *hunger* had brought them, and thus he asked his disciples how they might satisfy their hunger.

It is, of course, the nature of human senses to become hungry. Primarily, the senses are present to receive impressions, and they yearn for them. Sensory longing, however, need not be limited to physical impressions, since it is possible for the senses to perceive the moral and spiritual. Rudolf Steiner frequently spoke of *spiritualizing* sensory impressions, and "moral impressions" was the term he gave to sensory impressions of moral and spiritual phenomena. All healings performed by Jesus Christ were, by their very nature, this kind of moral impressions. The multitude that saw them did not see them merely as wonders, but more as *morally* wonderful phenomena. The impression made by those phenomena was a *moral* one. And the hunger that drove them to Jesus Christ was their hunger for moral impressions. Jesus Christ realized this as soon as he "lifted up his eyes, and saw a great company come unto him." The disciples did not understand this, however, until the miracle occurred. Only afterward did they understand it, which is expressed in Peter's answer to the question "Will ye also go away?" Peter answered for all twelve: "Lord, to whom shall we go? Thou hast the words of eternal life. And we believe and are sure that thou art that Christ, the Son of the living God" (John 6:67–69). This dialogue describes the final result of the whole sixth chapter containing the miracles of feeding of the five thousand and walking on the water—that is, the moral and spiritual result of the two signs and their effect as moral impressions on the disciples.

As a result of those acts, the disciples heard "words of eternal life." The multitude, on the other hand, wished to make Jesus Christ a king, because their hunger had been appeased. Thus began the great schism between the two types of Christianity that, later on, had infinitely tragic consequences for human history. Even fifteen hundred years after that event, the urge to bring Jesus Christ into power as king had not diminished. And just as then, later on the Christianity of freedom still had to be nurtured in small groups, in a ratio of perhaps twelve to five thousand. However this proportion may actually stand in history, the feeding of the five thousand showed severance in the destiny of those two streams of Christianity. For esoteric Christianity, it is not enough to receive moral impressions, because it is important that a corresponding free human response be given consciously from within. The twelve gave that response consciously in Peter's words, while the five thousand gave it unconsciously in the form of "twelve baskets of fragments." These twelve baskets were a result of the heart's productive activity as moral impulses radiating from the twelve gates of the complete sensory system. Peter's words, on the other hand, expressed the faith and recognition of the twelve that the essential being of Jesus is the Christ, the Son of God, operating not just in consciousness but in everything that lives. The title "Son of the living God" contains complete and concrete recognition; it states that this degree of divine revelation affects not only the "I" and astral body, but also the ether body. And the "words of eternal life" that Peter speaks carry their essence, drawn from the realm of eternity into the realm of life, or ether body, thus incorporating eternity within the ether body. The multitude experienced what the disciples not only experienced but also saw as revelation. Because they recognized it as such, they gained deep insight into the nature of the Christ; because the multitude experienced only the influence without seeing the true nature of Christ within it, they wanted to crown him king.

Recognition of the Christ's nature—perception that he truly is king in connection with feeding the five thousand—came to his disciples during the night that followed the day of the miracles. They experienced themselves as a small handful of men, driven here and there in a feeble boat, alone on the waves of life. It was dark that night; waves threatened to engulf them from the depths; unknown winds swept through the air. In life, they experienced an image of the true position of human beings within the cosmos; elemental forces and waves from subconscious depths affect them, and their consciousness is swept by the blasts of conflicting cosmic forces. At this moment, human beings have nothing to oppose that image of stupendous powers and raging cosmic waves in the subconscious, except the incomparably weaker force of their own personality; in this hour, heaven remains silent and veiled in darkness. Then everything depends on overcoming the fear evoked by that vision through the spring of one's inner forces. There is a force in this spring that will rush out at this moment, not manifesting as "personal" but as cosmic activity. Thus human beings must find within themselves a force of calm courage that can overcome the cosmic waves that assail the subconscious and the cosmic winds that sweep through one's consciousness. This force is contained in the words "I AM" once they have become a real experience of life. These words are the esoteric name of the Christ, who is the spring from which flows the strength of human "I" consciousness that can stand against the fear of cosmic forces.

The sign of walking on the water culminates with the Christ walking on the waves during the night experience of the disciples and saying, "It is I; be not afraid" (John 6:20). Thus the disciples find the strength and means to reach the shore. The words "It is I; be not afraid" contain a revelation of the true kingly nature of Christ. It does not call the Christ to govern (as the five thousand wished), but bestows on human beings the spiritual force of self-determination. The kingly nature of the Christ is his capacity not only to give humankind freedom, but also to give the needed strength to assert that freedom. In the spiritual moral sense, it would be proper to say that the royal nature of Christ involves giving kingly dignity to human beings.

Because the disciples had that night experience of the I AM as the true kingly nature of the Christ, they could say the following day those words spoken by Peter, which were just the opposite of what the five thousand had wished. The words of Peter express an intention that is different from that of the multitude. Jesus Christ confirmed it with these words: "Have not I chosen you twelve?" (John 6:70). Then he added, "and one of you is a devil" (*diabolos*). The added words point to the fact that within the circle of the twelve, there is one who will not follow the will expressed by Peter, but the will of the five thousand, which, at the critical moment, would make the Messiah an earthly king. Thus, the sign of feeding the five thousand contains both streams of Christian destiny as well as the seed of Judas' tragic destiny. That destiny of Judas arose (in that particular incarnation) because he was situated between two streams of will—that of the five thousand who wanted a king, and that of the disciples, who had experienced the "Son of the living God" as the I AM. Judas shared that night experience of the cosmic waves, but it had the opposite effect, leading him to become convinced that the "multitude" would never be able to withstand that trial. He could no longer believe that the many would ever be able to hear the voice of the I AM within, and the destiny of the multitude aroused his pity. So he took the side of the many, who (it seemed to him) would be sacrificed for an elect few. And because he had taken the side of the many, he believed, for example, that it would have been better to give the beggars the money that Mary, the sister of Lazarus, had spent on costly ointment with which to anoint the feet of Jesus Christ.

For Judas, it was not a matter of an individual human relationship to the needs of others; rather, his criterion was formed by an abstract idea of humanity in keeping with the principle that the whole is greater than the part. And this is why the evangelist tells us that Judas did not oppose Mary's action because he had the cause of the beggars at heart, but because he thought only in terms of the *quantitative* aspect: "This he said, not that he cared for the poor; but because he was a thief, and had the bag, and bare what was put therein" (John 12:6). Judas was a "thief" in the sense that, in reality, he deprived the community of what he aspired to receive for the community. This is exactly the tragedy of Judas: he did not wish to be a thief; he did not want to deprive the community (the many), yet it was this wish that made him a thief. Thus, in the beginning Judas was a thief in the cosmic sense of *diabolos* (a term used for "Lucifer" in the Gospels), then he became a murdering thief when *Satan* entered him—that is, when Ahriman appeared as the karma of Lucifer. The destiny of Judas among the twelve was to fully bear the two crosses of human activity: the cross to the left and the cross to the right on Golgotha. His apostolic mission to humanity (what he proclaimed to humanity) was the bitter truth about the nature of human activity *without* Christ. The mission of the twelve apostles was to bring the message of Christ to humanity from twelve perspectives. Judas, however, had the terrible mission of imparting knowledge of what human activity becomes when it is without the Christ. Judas represented one aspect of the Christ mystery—the negative side in the sign of the Scorpion. This is why he belonged to the circle of the twelve, although right after the feeding of the five thousand, Jesus Christ stated that, although he had chosen all twelve, nonetheless, one among them in their circle had the mission that *diabolos* (Lucifer) has in the circle of the zodiac.

But the miracles of feeding the multitude and walking on water dealt not just with the mystery of Judas. It also addressed the mystery of the twelve—not in the sense that they had consciously exalted themselves over or in opposition to the five thousand (although the vocation of the twelve apostles had been confirmed and their circle consciously formed), but in the sense that they revealed the nature of the Christ Sun acting through the twelve human senses by day and by night. The "five loaves" that fed the multitude represented the five effects of moral impressions that had to satisfy the hunger of the day senses. The "two fishes" were the effects of moral impressions on the two twilight senses; these no longer belong, as bread does, to the earth element of the physical world, but to the water element of the etheric world. The night experience of the twelve involved the reception of suprasensory moral impressions through the five night senses. The disciples' experience at the miracle of walking on water had five parts: the disciples experienced themselves as a group in the universe, united in one boat, driven over the waves by winds, and meeting with the Christ, who spoke to them. The whole night experience, culminating with the words "It is I," is thus made up of these elements:

awaking the disciples (self-awareness in sleep)
perceiving themselves as a group united in destiny (the boat)
threatened equilibrium (the waves)
forces pushing in a specific direction (the winds)
Christ speaking

These five experiences become an *inner* experience of the I AM and the sound from it.

After accomplishing the sign of feeding the five thousand, and after the disciples had experienced the night side of that sign, the multitude returned to Jesus Christ. He was asked, "What shall we do, that we might work the works of God?" (John 6:28). This question is actually the same as the one behind this meditation, which concerns the *third* kind of activity, by which one is neither a thief nor a murdering thief. The essence of the question asked of Christ was that they wanted to learn how to act in such a way that their actions would not follow the will of either Lucifer or Ahriman, but that of God. What can human beings do, out of themselves, so that their activity will be purely constructive, with no appropriation or destruction? This is the meaning of the question from the multitude. Jesus Christ's answer is staggering; he says there is *no* act in the realm of the physical body, no act in the realm of the ether body, and no act in the realm of the astral body that people can accomplish by themselves and entirely in harmony with the will of God. Only the human "I" can accomplish such an act; it can be done only in the realm of freedom in the human "I." "This is the work of God, that ye believe on him, whom he [God] hath sent" (John 6:29). This is the answer according to the wording of John's record. It gives a completely clear basis for human self-knowledge and for working toward its foundation in human action. It stresses the fact that the nature of the human organism is constructed so that it cannot, *on its own,* produce an act according to the will of God, and that, furthermore, the first, decisive action in this direction must proceed from the "I" by embracing faith in Jesus Christ. Embracing faith is the first of all the necessary changes in the human organism and destiny that lead to accomplishing the "works of God" in the physical world.

"Embracing the faith" does not (according to its real meaning) signify an acceptance of doctrines that we have no way of knowing are true; rather, it is an act of the human "I," performed in the realm of its origin, not in the sphere of its activity. When the "I" sends a current toward its source, it forms a union with the cosmic I AM, out of which the individual "I" proceeds like rays from the Sun. And the formation of this union with the spiritual, moral, cosmic Sun is precisely the process of "embracing the faith." From the light and warmth of that Sun, the "I" draws the substance and forces for its accomplishments in its sphere of activity—acts that can, in this way, gradually become "works of God."

The sixth and seventh miracles of John's Gospel lead further and deeper into the sphere of these questions, and they require a section devoted only to them. Accordingly, the next meditation will focus on the miracles of the man born blind and the raising of Lazarus.

# Chapter 8

# Healing the Blind Man and Raising Lazarus

## The Judgment that Gives Sight to the Sightless and Blindness to the Seeing

The previous meditation was devoted to the five miracles, from the marriage in Cana to walking on water. We now continue and conclude our consideration of miracles as signs and healings. The miracle that follows walking on water is healing the man born blind (John 9–10). First, we will read this sign in order to understand the healing. To do this, we must cover much ground, because the sign of healing the man born blind involves the whole problem of seeing in relation to hearing (John 9) and in relation to moral and spiritual aspects (John 10). The significance of blindness and seeing and of deafness and hearing in relation to the Christ impulse is revealed in the sign of healing the man born blind and in the words and incidents related to it.

To express all that is contained in the sign of healing the man born blind, however, we must cover much ground, as we said. To do this, we may first study the tragedy of Cain and Abel from a certain point of view. The primal differences in human cognition are shown in the tragedy of Cain and Abel. As the smoke of Abel's sacrifice rose vertically, and the smoke of Cain's rolled horizontally over the ground; likewise, the directions of human thought are twofold; it may rise to the heights or spread out horizontally. The flow that spreads out has the character of *seeing;* we speak of "broadening our view" in terms of thinking. The current directed upward is first experienced inwardly as a kind of *hearing;* there is, as it were, a question-and-answer dialogue, and it is the shadowlike sediment of this process of hearing or listening to the Word from above, or *Logos,* that people today call "logic." From a moral perspective, the vertical current expresses a devotional, respectfully silent attitude of the soul toward the world where all truth originates. The horizontal thought stream is that of one's own thinking—active apprehension of the world from within the "I." These two soul currents live in human beings like the two brothers of the old story; they are closely united yet oppose each other. The ascending flow of thought perception is killed perpetually by subjective thinking, whereas subjective thinking is ruled by the curse of Cain: "A fugitive and a vagabond shalt thou be in the earth" (Genesis 4:12).

The archetype of this opposition—whose roots go much deeper than just human thinking—is in celestial history before the Earth. It may be seen in the two paths adopted respectively by the Christ being and the Lucifer being at the very beginning of our cosmos. Christ renounced the *light* and, instead, listened devotionally to the Word of primal revelation of the wisdom of all preceding worlds. Lucifer, however, *became* the central point from which a world of light would be produced. While the Christ being devotionally absorbed the twelve final Words of the Father, Lucifer surrounded himself with the realm of color and form, which he projected from within himself. Lucifer's light concealed the Christ from the beings of the lower world and, as a result, became "a fugitive and a vagabond" in cosmic space. This is the origin of outer light in the universe, on the one hand, and on the other, the origin of the continuous orbits of visible planets—the "proscribed" products of Lucifer, as distinct from the quiescent planetary spheres around which the luciferic planets roam.

This cosmic drama was repeated in the destiny of Cain and Abel. But it had a further effect, with consequences even today. Those consequences appear in the two currents of thought force as described. Earlier, at the time of the Mystery of Golgotha, for example, they appeared in relation to the mysteries as two types of human beings with differing spiritual organizations. One type were those who were "blind," but had developed a sensitive capacity for hearing the spiritual Word; Homer, the "blind" poet of an even earlier age, is an example of this group. On the other hand, there were those who had sight but were "deaf" to the spiritual Word. In connection with the mysteries, these two groups relied on each other. By the time of the Mystery of Golgotha, an excellent collaboration had developed that bridged the gulf between Cain and Abel through the power of the Christ impulse. The "eye witnesses" and the "ministers of the word" (whom Luke speaks of at the beginning of his Gospel) actually collaborated to comprehend the Christ event and to make it intelligible to humankind; because of their collaboration, they showed the way to reconciliation for brothers in Christ, who is not only the Logos, but also the *true* Light Bringer.[1]

Although reconciliation of these two soul currents is accomplished by the Christ impulse, those who are called "ministers of the Word" make *knowledge* of the Christ possible to the others, the "eye witnesses." Only *hearing the voice* of Christ in a purely moral way could give direction to the vision of those who "saw." To believe without having seen was the true starting point of living dependence on Christ; all that followed was a consequence of this primary impetus.[2] The faculty of "believing, without having seen" is the capacity to hear and recognize, through the ascending thought current, the spiritual moral *voice* established in the front of the human head. And the *seeing* faculty is located in the same spot, but it is directed forward in a horizontal direction. The forehead, however, is the part of the human body that, because of its deep connection with a constellation of the zodiac, was named the Ram from the earliest times. Indeed, the brow's activity—which adapted to the subjective thinking of the human being and led to a kind of "horn" formation—was called "ram activity" in the proper sense of the word. On the other hand, the brow activity that silently acquiesced to hearing and obeyed the higher world was called "sheep," because its thinking was not subjective and thus produced no "horn" formation. It was those who had a preponderance of the principle of obedience, or hearing, whom Jesus Christ meant by "sheep" who hear the voice of the shepherd whom "he calleth his own sheep by name, and leadeth them out" (John 10:3). Such words point to those who were specially organized to receive the Christ impulse; indeed, some were able not only to hear the voice of the guiding being, but were also able to distinguish it from other voices. For such individuals, neither visions nor external signs and wonders were decisively significant; they heard and distinguished with certainty only the voice of the "Good Shepherd" from the voice of the "thief" and the "robber" (John 10:1). The sensitivity of their moral spiritual hearing also made it possible for them to hear the voices of Lucifer and Ahriman as alien voices, and thus *not* follow them, just as they heard distinctly and followed the Christ impulse as a familiar voice from the earliest times.

It is significant, however, that initially the vertical current produces only *hearing*, but later on it may become a kind of vertically directed *seeing*. This may happen if the current directed upward becomes, as it were, a channel through which an answering stream flows down from the spiritual world. It happens, for instance, when the answering current descends as far as the heart and even beyond, farther down. Perceptive hearing then becomes a kind of higher seeing. Those who had "ears to hear" will now have their "eyes opened." This process is enacted mainly in the astral and ether bodies. But it may also happen, for example, that the vertical current is so active in the ether body that the etheric forces needed for seeing are drawn into it. When this happens, etheric force is concentrated in a center above the root of the nose to such a degree that the two currents flowing right and left (the currents that supply the eyes) run dry, as it were. Then the process is reflected down into the physical organization, where it may appear as a physical disease, or *blindness*. This is what happened to the man born blind, whom we read about in the ninth chapter of John's Gospel. It was not the result of error on his part in a former life or negative heredity, but preparation for the future so "that the works of God *should* be made manifest in him" (*hina phanerothe ta erga tou Theou en auto*, John 9:3). In other words, he was meant to attain to the sight of God's works *within himself*. After Jesus Christ had said this to the disciples, he spoke the words that, in meaning and effect, contained the light current descending from above downward. In this case, the works of him who sent him was to be revealed in the I AM as the light of the world.[3]

In order to understand the healing of the man born blind, which followed these words—in other words, to understand the process of restoring the power of sight to the eyes of the blind—three conditions for that process must be understood. After the light of the I AM had produced a downward current by means of the "I" organization, three things remained that needed to happen that would lead to corresponding processes in the astral, ether, and physical organizations. Indeed, a Christian impulse to see had to be activated in the astral body, so that the faculty of sight in the eyes, healed by the power of the word of love, could make contact with outer, earthly reality.

Now, when we examine the impulse of sight as it exists in its natural state in human beings, we have to admit that it really has little to do with the *moral* life of humankind. We see, or should see, not exactly because we want to find our way on Earth to accomplish a moral and spiritual mission, but simply because the organ for sight is already there, so we may as well use it to accomplish our various intentions, good and bad, without distinction. Just as the Sun shines on both the bad and the good, likewise the eye looks out at the world for both good and evil intentions. This *neutral* service of our sense of sight, however, will not last forever. In the future, human beings will depend increasingly on morality, even in terms of the sense organs. With the progressing conversion of the astral body by the spirit, human beings will gain the faculty to see when they wish to see, for example, and *not* see when they do not wish to see. By contrast, however, human beings will lose the capacity to perceive any given area unless the moral will is present to do so. There will then no longer be an automatically given faculty of perception, once and for all, but one whose activity will be the expression of moral forces. People will not simply see, for instance, just because they have eyes; rather, they will have eyes because they have the moral impulse to see. That moral impulse to see will arise from the recognition, and the soul's immersion in the recognition, that the mission of humankind on Earth is to bring love to the world of nature. If people are imbued with an awareness of their purpose on Earth, immersing themselves, as it were, with their whole being into the awareness of this mission, they will gain a new motive for sight. The motive will be that love desires an eye to see what others need. In this sense, we can understand that, even though his sensory apparatus had been healed, the man who was born blind could not receive his sight until he had bathed in the Pool of Siloam (meaning "sent"). Once he had received a new impulse to sight into his astral body in the pool of human "sending," or missions, he could also receive his sight.

Before this could occur, however, his physical and etheric organisms were already healed by Jesus Christ. This healing was caused by a combination of earth (or clay) and saliva applied to the eyes of the blind man. In his lecture course on John's Gospel, Rudolf Steiner spoke on the concrete occult nature of healing in this miracle.[4] Here, the point is to add another morally lucid basis to this process of occult healing. Jesus Christ used *earth* and *saliva* for healing not just because they were effective remedies themselves, but especially because he could make them effective in a spiritual and moral way. And he was able to make them morally effective, because saliva and earth represent the final stages in the manifest realization of word and action.

The fact that saliva and earth can have this significance needs to be explained. We can comprehend their significance by beginning with two facts: the influence of hate and love on saliva, and the effect of the human *corpse* on the earth. One phenomenon may be important in helping us understand the influence of hate and love on the saliva. This is the fact that there is a malady that turns the saliva into a terrible poison. In the case of hydrophobia, or rabies, as it appears in dogs for instance, saliva is actually converted into a poison that is equally dangerous to human beings and animals. This change in the saliva is caused by an objective wave of hatred that wells up from the levels of the subterranean sphere and seizes the being. It is not the suffering creature that hates; rather, hatred functions in that organism with elemental force. It is the "evil word" that functions in this way; it cannot become a consciously spoken word and thus expresses itself as rabies. But the concrete, substantial expression of that evil is the *poison* in the saliva.

Today, this applies especially to animals; nonetheless, in the future we will be confronted by the fact (of which we will be conscious) that human saliva will have both positive healing properties and negative poisonous ones. And we will realize that those who are evil will possess an extremely dangerous substance in the form of their own saliva, whereas the saliva of those who have developed kindness and love in themselves will have healing properties. The secretion from the salivary glands will be seen as the essential expression of the blood's etheric activity. And because love and hate work down into the etheric level and then into the blood, saliva will be recognized as the silent word of love or hate. Whatever issues as a word of love or hate from the "I" organization or astral body will manifest externally and become, in the physical and ether bodies, either a wholesome, or a poisonous quality of the saliva. Thus saliva will become the visible carrier of condensed morality. And healing the man born blind relied on this action of condensed morality in the form of saliva. Jesus Christ first spoke the words of love, and *then* he allowed the result of these words—working down into the organic as saliva—to affect the sick man.

This act, however, was united with the activity of the earth, or clay. As we already mentioned, to understand this, we need to study the moral and spiritual connection of the human corpse with the earth. If the essential secretion brought about by the word of love becomes apparent in saliva, we may well inquire into what corresponding secretion might be caused by the moral element of a person's actions. The life of a human being on Earth, as a whole, is the sum of that individual's actions; indeed, as a whole, one's life is really a single act—the combination of many parts. And the secretion that results from this composite act is the human corpse, secreted at the time of one's death. The life act is accomplished, and the corpse remains as the substantial remainder of that act. It is not, however, just a material, amoral remainder of the life act; it also has a moral result that affects the earth. Just as saliva carries within it the condensed morality of the human being, the corpse carries the seed of a material and actively moral effect on the earth. Rudolf Steiner spoke many times of the fact that the Earth would have dried up and been petrified by now if the action of human corpses had not loosened it and preserved its life-bearing properties. This "loosening," which preserves the life-giving quality, is not mechanical, however, but a *moral* process. Every corpse (whether buried in the earth or cremated) makes an impression on the earthly substances that—however slight—reawakens and keeps awake the longing of all earthly substances to become like the substances in the human body. The impression that every corpse makes on the Earth's substances makes them long for the same relationship to one another as they have within the human organism. It is the desire to be the bearer of consciousness and to furnish means for human acts that keeps the Earth "loose" and gives earthly substances the strength to resist the rigidifying influences of Ahriman. That longing is constantly intensified by human corpses; and this forms the inner content of the "loosening" action of the human corpse mentioned so often by Rudolf Steiner.

In relation to the miracle we are considering, blindness had been a condition from birth. The man had never used his eye organism, which had therefore become hardened and rigid. The function of the clay, which Jesus Christ applied to the man's eyes along with the healing saliva, was to overcome that rigidity. In other words, the clay was to bring about a process similar to that of "loosening" the Earth's mineral matter by human corpses. The clay had to "loosen" the eye's rigidity, while the healing power of love in the saliva had to restore life to it. Jesus Christ thus healed the organic illness of the man who was born blind. Nevertheless, sight itself would not be available until he had bathed in the Pool of Siloam (the "*sent*")—that is, until the astral body had instilled a new impulse to sight into the healed etheric and physical organisms.

This is how the blind man received his sight. Before he could physically see, however, he received *spiritual* sight. First, his spiritual hearing, whose development had caused his spiritual and physical blindness, was raised to a higher level of spiritual sight, and only then was he given physical sight as well. This is clearly expressed in the Gospel; when the healed man encountered Jesus Christ again, Christ asked him whether he believed in the Son of God. "Jesus said unto him, Thou hast both seen him, and it is he that talketh with thee" (John 9:37). The Son of God cannot be seen with physical eyes, but only with spiritual sight; nonetheless, he could certainly *speak* through the human personality of Jesus. The *Word* alone could become flesh, not the Son of God. This is the meaning of the passage just quoted—the man born blind had first seen the Son of God, but then had to recognize his voice in the personality of Jesus. In other words, the "belief" about which he was asked included the task of uniting three areas of experience: What was first heard by the soul and what was then seen by the spirit had to be combined with what was now physically heard as a voice and seen as form. The man born blind had the insight to recognize that unity—that the Word (*Logos*) is the Son and that the Son has incarnated in Jesus. Thus he fell on his knees before Jesus Christ (John 9:38).

But the destiny of the man born blind has more than just individual significance; it is also universal. As Jesus Christ said, it is a manifestation of Jesus Christ's "judgment," applied to all humankind, by which "they which see not, might see; and they which see might be made blind" (John 9:39). Christ came into the world not to judge, but to open the way to everlasting life. The "judgment" mentioned in connection with healing the man born blind is thus not merely a condemnation, but extends the blessing of healing the man born blind to all humanity. It has to do with the effect of the Christ impulse on spiritual sight and hearing, and this effect is expressed karmically by the fact that those who possessed spiritual sight in anticipation of Christianity must lose it. They had to lose it in order to develop moral and spiritual hearing—the faculty of hearing the "voice of the shepherd." Hearing the voice of the shepherd is essential for a conscious acceptance of the Christ impulse, which is the voice of the shepherd sounding throughout history in the world. To consciously receive the Christ impulse, those who "saw" had to undergo reorganization that would make them dependent, for a while, on the vertical current of *hearing*. Afterward, however, they would be healed spiritually just as, nineteen centuries ago, the man born blind was healed physically.

Those who were already "blind" when they encountered the Christ impulse (those who received the Christ impulse through hearing the voice) received their sight. Those who clung to sight, however, became blind through the benevolent dispensation of judgment, or positive karma, so that they also might attain a morally free, conscious acceptance of the Christ impulse. This is what it means to say, "For judgment I am come into this world, that they which see not, might see; and that they which see might be made blind" (John 9:39). These words epitomize the universal significance of healing the man born blind.

## Raising Lazarus: A Sign of the New Life Impulse from the Life Spirit

The moral core of the miracle involving the man born blind was the new impulse to *perceive.* At the moral center of raising Lazarus, the seventh miracle, is the new impulse to *life* on the Earth as a whole. Lazarus' sickness involved a gradual drying up of the life spring within him, until he finally lost all will to live—to such a degree that even his breathing stopped. His death was conditioned by such an absence of life impulse, therefore, that even his breathing lacked any inducement to continue. Etherically, he was "bleeding to death." The ether body wasted away gradually, and his life forces abandoned the physical body. This was not a disease in the sense that the physical body suffered trauma or poisoning; he was in perfect health. The whole process was brought on by the ether body itself. A complete transformation occurred in Lazarus' ether body. Instead of working inward and bringing life forces to the physical body, it turned and poured them outward, thus losing the capacity to draw life forces from the natural environment—sunlight, plants, and food. Instead of a body that received, his body only gave. Indeed, it was devotion to the cosmic whole that caused his ether body to radiate out and reduced its capacity to replace what was given by taking from outside. This outpouring of life force was not corrected, and Lazarus languished.

This transformation of Lazarus' ether body was caused by his soul's devotion to the spiritual world, developed so strongly that it affected his ether body. This process points to the danger that exists when an inner life spring has not developed inwardly that can replace what is given out. A spring, into which a direct stream of life force flows from the spiritual world, was called the "glory of God" (*he doxa tou Theou*). The phrase "Glory of God" (as used in both the Old and New Testaments) refers to a direct radiation of the Godhead that shines down into the etheric. According to the New Testament, "Glory" (*doxa*), which not only illuminates but also gives life, is the special function of the Son—God the Son breathes life into what is created by God the Father and revealed by God the Spirit.

In this sense, the sickness of Lazarus was "not unto death, but for the glory [radiant activity] of God, that the Son of God might be glorified [revealed as actively radiant] thereby" (John 11:4). This emptiness of life force that afflicted Lazarus had the purpose of being filled with life radiating from the Son. Furthermore, this happened just as Jesus Christ called Lazarus out of the tomb. The cry of Jesus Christ was also a call to Earth, a call to life on Earth. Indeed, something happened even before this cry that points to the path on which the loosened link with Earth could be restored. This is the path indicated in the first part of Goethe's *Faust,* when the Easter bells sound and Faust speaks these significant words: "Tears flow—Earth holds me once again." Flowing tears express the new relationship of faithfulness to the Earth as established by the Easter impulse—established so that the soul remembers, morally, the Earth's need. In other words, it receives a new life impulse not because of the Earth's good things, but out of being conscious of its needs.

All things that are truly good for the soul are in the spiritual world; the Earth contains none of them. The very fact that the Earth is bare of the highest good, however, can become the soul's impulse to honor the Earth. This homage is the Easter impulse, which can become a new life impulse in a soul that has experienced, in some way, the reality of the words "I am the resurrection and the life" (John 11:25). Jesus Christ spoke these words to the sister of Lazarus as she stood at the tomb. As the representative of humanity, he wept, as did all those who were present. Then, as representative both of humanity and God, he called to life. The whole new purpose for life is contained in his cry, *"Lazare, deuro exo"* ("Lazarus, come forth," John 11:43). One may hear in it the warning of the great Guardian of the Threshold of humanity speaking to the soul: You have entered the spiritual world and experienced its riches; now look on the Earth and the human beings of Earth who are without such treasures. Remember the Earth, for the Earth does not possess what is now yours. Live on Earth, because the Earth and Earth's humanity do not possess the wealth that has been yours in the spiritual world. *Lazare, deuro exo!*

The cry was heard, and Lazarus, breathing once more, arose and returned to humanity and to human life. This new Christian purpose of life, its activity shown through Lazarus in this way, is the Word of the Son, affecting human beings, even into the ether body. The resurrection that Jesus Christ experienced happened in the realm of the *physical body.* This was possible because the *Father* was active in the death of Jesus Christ. In human beings, the Father's activity reaches into the physical body, whereas the sphere of the Son's activity is in the ether body. Hence, raising Lazarus was fundamentally different from the resurrection of Jesus Christ. In the resurrection of Lazarus, the reality of the human life spirit (budhi) was revealed, whereas that of Jesus Christ was the perfect consummation of the spirit body (atma), which, as the "phantom," has formed the seed of the human physical body since the ancient Saturn period. Similarly, the seed of the life spirit has formed the basis of the human ether body since the period of the ancient Sun. It is the source of the new life impulse that may take the place of the old life impulse originated at the time of the fall of humanity. When this happens, the old impulse dries up (the sickness of Lazarus), and a new one springs up to take its place (the resurrection of Lazarus).

On the path of Christian esotericism, this is a gradual process; the old eventually dies away and is replaced by the new. With Lazarus, however, the old died away quickly and, after a state of lifelessness, was suddenly replaced by the new. In this sense, that process was an exception, but one that elucidates and illustrates the essence of the normal process of the budhi revelation. The exceptional aspect of raising Lazarus was that it constituted a repetition, in a new form, of the ancient Egyptian mystery process.[5] What was typical is the fact that in the future ever-increasing numbers will experience this process, but in such a way that the gradual death and the new life go hand in hand. The symbolic sign for this concurrent process of gradual death and new life is the black cross with the seven shining, red roses. The spiritual movement that consciously nurtures this process is known (and misunderstood) as Rosicrucianism. True Rosicrucianism, through all its centuries of existence, has simply been the world stream that worked toward a renewal of the impulse to life. And it does so in this sense: that human beings should live not only by means of the instinctual life forces of the ether body, but even more so by means of the spiritual moral forces of the life spirit. Thus, the real core of Rosicrucianism is not a doctrine, tradition, or human community, but a certain etheric organization, imbued entirely by life spirit. That ether body is always active and protected against dissolution after death. This is why it is *forever* active, and thus the Rosicrucian "tradition" can be kept alive on Earth without interruption. It grows increasingly powerful, and the circles of its activity spread more widely with each new century.

The seventh miracle of John's Gospel was a sign and healing related to the human life spirit (the budhi principle). Healing the man born blind was a sign connected with the spirit self (manas). The Pool of Siloam (he who was sent), into which the man born blind had to immerse himself, is the moral spiritual essence of the union of consciousness and spirit self. The signs of feeding the five thousand and walking on water were related to the "I" from two points of view: the day and night experiences of the "I." They expressed the orbit of the "I" sun through the day senses and the night senses, showing the nourishing and strengthening of the Christ impulse in both spheres. The healing of the paralyzed man was concerned with a process that healed the astral body—the spiritual faculty of movement—on its way through the "I." Healing the son of nobility (also accomplished on the way through the "I") was, by contrast, a healing of the ether body, as the principle of the effect of heredity on the physical body. Finally, the sign of changing water into wine at Cana was concerned with the effect of the Christ impulse on the blood as the physical bearer of the "I."

The seven miracles and signs of John's Gospel represent the stages of Jesus Christ's healing activity. All the discourses and incidents recorded in the first twelve chapters of this Gospel are related to these seven events. But the healing activity of Jesus Christ is not exhausted by the seven miracles. Following the seventh miracle, the eighth took place: the resurrection of Jesus Christ after being crucified on Golgotha. That miracle and the associated steps of the passion will be the subject of our remaining meditations as the third stage of the Christ revelation, following those of the Word and the signs. At the same time, that eighth miracle (the Mystery of Golgotha itself) is the sun, so to speak, from which the seven rays of the preceding signs and healings radiate. Although the Mystery of Golgotha came after the seven miracles in the chronological sense, it is nonetheless their origin and cause. It is the basis of all the healings that preceded it temporally, and only it can give them meaning and human significance. The seven healings had no human significance until the Mystery of Golgotha, without which they would have remained isolated phenomena with no effect on humanity as a whole. Through the Mystery of Golgotha, however, they became signs. Those signs indicated the consequences of the Mystery of Golgotha for humanity, presaging the healing of the various human infirmities—a healing in which the *same* infirmities are morally and spiritually healed *in the same way,* as symptomatically foreshadowed in the seven miracles.

Humanity is sick and much in need of healing—just as much as those who were healed by Jesus Christ nineteen centuries ago. In the future, therefore, it will happen that more and more people will receive a new impulse to life, and many who are "born blind" will see. A great number in the fifth cultural epoch will receive moral impressions of Christ's activity, and for the twelve groups of humankind, contact with Christ's essential being will be a living experience of the I AM, and many who wait for moral healing from the angelic spring will receive that healing. And, in many cases, the sickness of family and marriage will be healed. What is needed to make this happen? What is expected of humankind so that the conditions behind these healings can be fulfilled?

The spiritual and moral condition required for each healing is indicated in the evangelic record itself; nonetheless, in every healing there is one essential thing that humankind can do. On the one hand, human beings must see the failure of their own forces and means; on the other, they must do their very best to overcome the condition of evil while maintaining an attitude confidently expecting helpful intervention from the spiritual world. Endeavor, freed of illusion and united with devoted expectation, is the spiritual moral element that most of all allows direct intervention from the spiritual world. Just as air is needed for breathing, the union of active penitence and confident expectation is the "air" that makes miracles possible. Self-righteousness and complacent satisfaction with our achievements are, by contrast, as detrimental to miracles as water is to fire.

To begin with, therefore, the most important thing in human destiny is to recognize our failure in all essential spiritual and moral spheres. The crimson dawn of coming spiritual events will not manifest through increased happiness and contentment but through the crimson blush of shame—elemental shame—that heralds their advent. Human beings will be ashamed of their achievements and failures, and those who are most ashamed will be the best. This is the necessary preparation for the state of mind in which humanity can receive help from the spiritual world. Everything great and elevating that is intended for humanity can be experienced only if we first experience self-knowledge in harmony with destiny. This self-knowledge is essential for healings like those described in John's Gospel.

# Chapter 9

# The Way of the Passion

## Foot Washing

Having studied the work of Jesus Christ in the Word and the miracles, we turn to the sacred, solemn way of the passion. What was true of the two other stages of Christ's work also applies here, but in an even higher way. No human being can deal exhaustively with any of these subjects; no one can comprehend and describe them in their full height, depth and width. This was the conviction behind the work of the writer of John's Gospel, for example. In the first sentence of his Gospel, when he defines the Word as the creative power of the universe and then points to Jesus Christ as the cosmic Word made flesh, he is saying even at the beginning of the Gospel what he clearly expresses at the end: "And there are also many other things which Jesus did, which, if they should be written every one, I suppose that even the world itself could not contain the books that should be written. Amen" (John 21:25). Here, the evangelist acknowledges that his work cannot be exhaustive, and that his subject offers breadth to all researchers and seers of the world. This is just as true today as it was then.

The conclusion that naturally follows from this is that every known truth concerning the Christ being and the work of Christ can be only an incentive to work toward knowing more of the truth. Hence, no one who has the right relationship to the Christ impulse will speak from knowledge with the intention of instructing. One's feeling will be the sort expressed by the question: Where and to what extent can speaking from knowledge be as fruitful as stimulating the efforts of others toward knowledge? Can what I know really serve anyone else? In other words, the only feeling with which we can speak about the influence of Christ's work—without a bad taste or striking a false note—is the feeling that arises when studying the "foot washing" scene. Our subject brings with it the very spirit in which it must be discussed. For example, we cannot speak of the Sistine Madonna in a spirit of politics, but only from a religious and artistic point of view; likewise, we must speak of the work of Jesus Christ in a spirit in which the soul wishes to be comprehended by the subject, not the other way round. This, however, presupposes a condition in which the soul essentially bows before the lofty nature of this subject.

When this happens, the soul gains the capacity of absorbing the subject in such a way that the soul becomes its mouthpiece. There is no other way of knowing the mysteries of Christianity as they are known in spiritual science. In the silence of the reverent soul, they shine out at the hour ordained by karma.

And it is not just one's attitude toward the passion mysteries that depends on karma, but also knowledge of their *meaning*. The images of the passion's stages reveal the path of Jesus Christ, without guilt, through the karmic consequences of the fall of humanity. The stages of the passion are also stages of the karma from the fall, which Christ took upon himself as the representative of humanity—or, as St. Paul expresses it, as "the new Adam." The effect of that sacrifice is that the consequences of the universal fall of humanity are annulled for every human being, insofar as each erases and makes good the consequences of one's own "individual fall into sin," or personal karma. Grace always begins once hard work has determined individual karma. "Who, ever striving, spares no pains, him can we well redeem." This passage from Goethe's *Faust* expresses precisely the fact that the intervention of grace that redeems the consequences of the fall—the karma from the Mystery of Golgotha—depends on ordering one's individual karma. This fact, artistically expressed in *Faust,* is also expressed through concrete spiritual science in Steiner's *How to Know Higher Worlds.* He describes spiritual evolution as a condition in which, along with the conscious evolution of half of the currents of the astral body's suprasensory organs, the other half belonging to these organs come into action on their own. This independent activity of the second half of these currents of the suprasensory organs, upon which all human faculties and knowledge depend, is the effective work of grace—the concrete result of the Mystery of Golgotha—as the act through which the universal karma of the fall of humanity was cancelled. But this cancellation cannot take effect until human beings have settled their own personal karma, the consequence of individual free initiative. Settling the consequences of the individual fall into sin is essentially the same sequence of experiences (though each circumstance will be at a different level and disposition) as those—enhanced to sublime heights—of Jesus Christ's passion. The steps of the path taken by the one without guilt must also be taken by human beings in their guilt. The stages of Christ's undeserved suffering are the well-deserved stages of suffering for those striving for truth and the life of the spiritual world in human existence. Nonetheless, when human beings consciously strive toward that goal, the stages of karmic balance become stages of knowledge, because karma is the great occult school of the world, not just a cosmic instrument of punishment.

There are those who knew that the karmic path of humanity includes an experience of the stages of Jesus Christ's passion. Using that knowledge, they created spiritual exercises that condense and simplify the essentials of this path. And, in this form, it was given to individuals in order to acquire the capacity to awaken within themselves the forces needed for the trials of the karmic path. Those exercises have changed in form (and only in form) according to the needs of human consciousness at the time; the moral essence of the exercise remains forever unchanged because, in fact, throughout the whole of Earth's evolution, everything depends on the Christ impulse. The spiritual and moral essence remains the same, whether we concentrate on Gospel images such as the crucifixion, burial, and resurrection or, for example, on the image of the Rose Cross; the Rose Cross is just as much an expression of death and resurrection as are the pictures of the Gospels we have discussed.

The images that expressed the moral and spiritual content had to be altered during the late Middle Ages, when they had to be drawn from observation of nature. Until that time, however, people had devoted themselves to pictures from the Gospels. This change had to happen, because the consciousness of later humanity had progressed and could no longer use the Gospels as a starting point. The Gospels became an *object* of knowledge instead of its source, as they had been thus far. The purpose of the images used for the newer exercises was nonetheless unchanged—they were still intended to waken the soul forces needed for foot washing, scourging, crowning with thorns, cross bearing, death, burial, and resurrection. In terms of changing the form in the exercises, the difference introduced on the path of evolution was this: people had previously used the Gospel pictures as their starting point and lived so intensively in them that they rose as *imaginations* before (or *inspirations* in) the soul. Later, however, people began with images that did *not* require an unconditional belief in the Gospel tradition; nevertheless, as a result of intensive work on them, they did lead to the rise of *imaginations* and *inspirations* that in turn revealed themselves as the pictures presented in the Gospels with their accompanying words. The mystical Christian path, which had required a belief in the evangelic tradition, led directly from traditional pictures that were handed down to seeing spiritual facts; the Rosicrucian path of knowledge, however, led from created pictures and images to seeing those same spiritual facts.

Seeing the spiritual facts of the path of Christian initiation, however, is not just a vision of them or mere comprehension; it has the added significance of a karmic stage, where the images seen represent commands and impulses for an inner soul attitude in certain life situations. For example, encountering the foot washing of spiritual science means experiencing both a principle and a fundamental force in the spiritual world. In this case, it means experiencing the relationship desired by the spiritual world between above and below—a relationship that also determines the whole method of the Christian occultism in the West. There are three pictures—three profoundly symbolic images—that show both the moral attitude and the ruling principles of the methods of the three occult streams; "fleeing upward," "mounting the throne," and "foot washing."

First, let us consider Indian yoga as practiced today. What is its main concern? Its intention is to alter, in certain ways, the system of currents of the human organism: the "kundalini fire," which dominates the abdomen, is awakened and guided up into the head, where its impact must be sufficient to press through the cranium and free one's whole consciousness from the spell that limits it within the skull. The point is to experience the body as a prison and, with the help of yoga practice, to flee that prison. The goal of yoga is to regulate the relationship between above and below in such a way that consciousness abandons what is below. Consciousness, driven out by the snake fire (or kundalini), is intended to escape upward on wings of thought. The image that forms the basis for the yogic method is the winged serpent, with the human head in flight from the land of enchantment.

Consider another method whose basis is a different image—a widespread attempt, through occultism, to gain power over human nature. Here, too, the idea is to regulate the system of currents in the human organism in a way that conforms to the goal. Here, however, it is not a matter of freeing consciousness but of handling and regulating the condensed and strengthened currents of the lower human being. Consciousness creates a firm foundation for itself in the human organism in order to develop power. It prepares for itself a support in the lower human being on which to rely. Consciousness does not depend on this support in the sense of morality, but in the sense of acquiring a supply of force to develop power. The practitioner makes, as it were, a throne and ascends to it without being crowned by anointing or empowering hands from above. *Ascent to the throne without crowning* is the picture behind this method, which, like Indian yoga, is widespread.

The picture of foot washing is very different from the two just described. To bow is just the opposite of a winged snake fleeing upward, and washing the feet is the polar opposite of ascending a throne. Just as images can contradict one another, methods of spiritual development—the principles expressed in those pictures—can be distinct both in terms of actual content and with respect to moral essence. Christian practice depends neither on flight from the body as a prison nor on exploiting the body to develop power. Its intention is to cause the forces of the higher human being to descend into the lower (even as far as the feet), thus shining through and transforming the lower forces. The goal of meditation practice for the Christian Rosicrucian school is that the light of consciousness shining from the head should be made so intense and forceful that it reaches from the head to the larynx, from the larynx to the heart, and finally from the heart to the feet, while having a purifying and transformative effect. Here, too, the aim is to purposefully regulate the system of currents in the human organism; this regulation, however, takes place in such a way that consciousness guides its currents downward to cause a gradual inner transformation of the lower human being in the direction of goodness, truth, and beauty. The relationship between above and below is regulated so that the higher bows before the lower, thus serving the lower as is depicted in the scene of foot washing.

In meditation, the principle of foot washing is the standard for spiritual events within the human organism; it is a real washing of the feet by the higher human being bending to the lower. In reality, the higher human being generally *desires* this and makes an effort to do it. Nevertheless, the stream of spiritual force flowing from the higher to the lower is sent as *grace* as an influence from the spiritual world. It is usually the guardian angel or another exalted spiritual being who bends to the one in meditation and "washes the feet." In other words, he sends down the strength of the spirit even to the feet of the one meditating. Foot washing is the essential attitude for beings of the spiritual world, where the higher serve the lower—archai serve archangels, archangels serve angels, and angels serve human beings.

The true process of meditation does not, therefore, involve just an *attitude* of the higher human being toward the lower in accordance with foot washing, but the actual act of foot washing on the part of spiritual beings toward the one meditating. It is of the utmost importance that the whole human being produces the conditions for becoming an object of foot washing by the spiritual world. Such inner processes, however, are only a preparation for another; human beings must also learn to give proof of the foot washing not just inwardly, but also through actions externally. It is one's task not only to be the *object* of foot washing, but gradually to become its *subject*—that is, to freely do for others what was done for oneself. Once people have recognized this duty, they will try to do more for humankind than is merely required by outer life, something that one resolves to do freely, just as one resolved, for example, to work at meditation. One then becomes devoted to an undertaking appropriate to the penetration of goodness, truth, and beauty—of entering an area of human existence in which goodness, truth, and beauty are not present naturally. Then, when those who have resolved to help human beings find one another, they may form communities that exist not for their own sake, but for the benefit of all humanity. Both small and large communities have thus come into being, manifesting the stream of Christian occultism in the world. They work in the world in a way that is almost as unknown and unrecognized as is the work among humankind by beings of the angelic hierarchy. Insofar as it is important, such work is based on the foot washing principle—the principle not just of the Christian Rosicrucian training, but the very basis of its whole work in the world. Other occult currents, by contrast, work on other principles that correspond to their particular methods; the nature of the work is the fruit of the training. Just as figs are the fruit of the fig tree, the influence of a spiritual school is the image of its methods of training.

Foot washing is certainly a fundamental principle of Christian spiritual activity; but, insofar as it is purely human, the actual effect of "foot washing" in the present time must be seen as only an ideal for the future. The activities of human beings themselves today reach no further than the "feet" of the higher human being, or "head" human. The "feet" of the head human are located in the human organism for hearing, where they touch the eardrums. And, as a rule, the effect of human "foot washing" reaches only this far—that is, to cleansing the "feet" located in the ears. In rare cases it may reach to the "feet" of the "thorax" human in the center of the body, but cleansing the hands of this second being is, in fact, still only an ideal to be worked for today. The feet of the *lower* human being, however (the real feet), will not feel the effect until the sixth cultural epoch, after the Maitreya incarnation has established the white magic of the individual human being. In the present age, the task of objective foot washing is limited by the injunction "He that hath ears to hear, let him hear" (Mark 4:9). It can be fulfilled only for the "feet" hidden in the ears. This, therefore, gives a special importance to the spoken word, or proclamation, in our present age. The "herald" must "bow" to the *ear* of the listener—to the other's power of comprehension. The possibilities of foot washing in the future will grow ever greater, until finally the sublime example of foot washing given by Jesus Christ himself is attained. At that point, it will be possible to transmit not only the purifying thought, but also the moral life of will from person to person. The *power* of goodness (not merely an understanding of it) will then be carried over from one person to another. This is the meaning of the foot washing as described in John's Gospel.

## Scourging

The inner encounter with spiritual "foot washing" represents the recognition of a basic law of the spiritual world and a principle of spiritual training according to the method of Christian Rosicrucianism. A similar encounter with spiritual "scourging" is the recognition of another law of the spiritual world and of Christian Rosicrucian training. Just as the foot washing deals with the relationship between above and below, scourging is a matter of the relationship between right and left. True regulation of the relationship between right and left in human beings and affairs—in keeping with divine will—is a task of great spiritual and moral scope, comprising a lengthy path of training and discipline. Essentially, it involves the same sort of adjustment in this relationship as is indicated in this precept: "Let not thy left hand know what thy right hand doeth" (Matthew 6:3). To understand what this precept requires (as well as the meaning of scourging), we must comprehend a condition frequently described by Rudolf Steiner—that the symmetry of the human form expresses the way luciferic and ahrimanic forces encroach from each side and hold a balance within the human being.[1] The "left human being" (the left eye, left ear, left hand, left leg, and so on) is the luciferic human, while the "right human being" is ahrimanic. Between these is a central septum that forms the arena for the "I" and for the spiritual and divine element that functions through the "I." In this sense, the right hand signifies the ahrimanic in the human being, and the left hand corresponds to the luciferic forces. Thus the principle that the left hand should not know what the right hand is doing comes to mean that knowledge should be present in the *third* principle, the divine human, but not in the left or right side. Neither should knowledge be in both sides at once, which would indicate an alliance between the luciferic and the ahrimanic in the human being, thus combining a consciously calculated goal together with passionate impulsiveness. Such a combination would require the worst description, representing the opposite of the precept quoted; the left hand would indeed know what the right hand is doing. It would mean that uprightness and honesty would be impossible; the soul's whole life would succumb to the taint of calculation.

The point is this: Both the right and the left hands should participate in one's actions, but they should not provide the *motivation* for those acts. Knowledge of what is being done belongs to the *third* aspect, whose consciousness is developed on the level of contact between the left side and the right side of the human being. Against this central human aspect, however, onslaughts are launched from left and right to establish a vacillation, swinging right or left. In the human organism, a continual struggle takes place, consisting mainly of a reciprocal conflict between the luciferic and ahrimanic elements, which is (after the spirit of foot washing has established the connection between above and below) nonetheless expressed as an attack from *both* sides on the center of one's being. The essence of an inner experience of *scourging* is this onslaught from both sides against the upright "Son of Man" who unites heaven and Earth within the human being. The point is that the true human being learns to stand in such a way that one swerves neither left nor right from the position of spiritual conscience. This "standing" is also the second spiritual moral principle of the Western Christian spiritual training. Such training is based on the moral attitude, between "rights" and "duty," in which *moral imagination,* as an expression of the creative spiritual conscience, has the final word. The Christ impulse is not a right or a duty but a free creative stream flowing from the cosmic spring of love. This act of creation is exactly what Rudolf Steiner termed *moral imagination* in his book *Intuitive Thinking as a Spiritual Path.*[2] The moral attitude indicated here also determines the actual method of spiritual discipline that uses this moral attitude as a requirement. Along this path, one's meditation exercise must be constructed so that it becomes neither an ardent absorption in prayer nor a sober reflection; rather, it should become a calm experience of consciousness, light, and life, with clear perception and strong thinking. It is important, therefore, that the living light radiating in one's central being not only shine outward; it should also stand firm in quiet determination against the onslaughts from left and right. The true value of a meditation exercise depends especially upon thoughtful, quiet steadfastness during the time spent in the light of a true and lofty thought.

Other spiritual movements use exercises that are very different from those described here. For example, there are exercises whose task is to develop shrewdness, one's gift of observation, and skills for dealing with the phenomena of physical existence. Such exercises are intended to give students an advantage over others in the physical world. Other exercises include practices of mystical absorption, or ecstasy. Their purpose is to enable clairvoyant, suprasensory experiences by suppressing or eliminating self-awareness. The first group of exercises is intended to train one's consciousness toward a higher esteem of the physical world, to become more connected with it than is normal; the second group, by contrast, attempts to suppress reason and intellect in order to attain, through ecstatic absorption, dreamlike experiences of suprasensory worlds.

The Christian Rosicrucian path, however, includes neither the strengthening of physical consciousness and physical reasoning nor an extension of one's dream consciousness into daytime; rather, it unites one's daytime consciousness with the spiritual world, and it maintains this union without deviating toward dreamlike or sensory consciousness. Maintaining this union with the spiritual world through the light ray of the spiritual conscience may increasingly become a necessity of life, even in the destinies of those who practice maintaining such union through meditation practice. It also happens, then, that the inner difficulties overcome in one's nature through meditation practice reemerge, as it were, and appear in one's "destiny organism." Onslaughts from right and left, which up until now had been strictly inner processes, now appear externally in one's destiny, which then assumes the nature of a constant dilemma. This dilemma is not one of *choosing,* however, but of proving one's capacity *not* to choose. As with Scylla and Charybdis, one is confronted by having to make a decision among *real* dilemmas that require a choice.[3]

What appears is a false dilemma against which one must stand firm, because it is not the *true* dilemma of good and evil.[4]

Destiny may then exhibit a further transformation. Perhaps false dilemmas urging one to this decision become real attacks and pressure from two sides. Slander and need, hostility and worry may become one's environment, and blow after blow may follow. The task is not to give in to resentment, anger, fear, or discouragement, but to stand firmly loyal to the spirit. No abstract belief will be of any use then, but only the awareness that, being guilty, we must fulfill the karma borne in incomparably greater measure by the one without guilt. And the strength of humility flows from this awareness, the only power needed in this situation, since the power of pride has been broken.

This experience of "scourging"—inwardly as meditation as well as in one's destiny—must be experienced by the portion of humanity that has decided for the Christ impulse in human history. And that portion of humanity *must* experience this historical "scourging," because the peoples and races of the world have no room for Christianity. Other ideals and other paths will be accepted by the world, and the nations will fight for those ideals and paths; in the end, however, they will all be of one mind: Christianity is, at best, superfluous. Within the human organism, the true human being has only a thin membrane available to defend against the onslaughts from left and right. And, similarly, all the "space" within organized humanity will be appropriated by other forces; truly spiritual Christianity will be allotted only a "thin membrane" *between* the right and left. "Ye shall be hated of *all nations* for my name's sake." This passage in Matthew (24:9) must be fulfilled for the very reason that humankind must bring about the same situation as that established within the individual through spiritual training. All the human organs of the right and left sides are owned by Lucifer and Ahriman, and all assaults on the spirit body without organs arise from them; likewise, all the peoples that make up humankind will be hostile toward anything that does not fit into that organization of humanity and toward any form of Christianity that does not originate with themselves. True Christianity is the conscience of humanity; it has no more to do with the various races and organizations than one's individual conscience has to do with different organs.

Because Christianity has been given only the vertical surface between right and left, it will have no room at all and be crowded out of anything that has the nature of an organization; the world will belong to everything organizational in nature, and Christianity will develop only in the consciousness of individuals and individual relationships. As its history progresses, Christianity will become literally a "kingdom ... not of this world" (John 18:36). For the first time it will display its power fully, because it will be true and absolutely free of compromise. The weakness of historic Christianity is the fact that it has been dirtied by the spirit of compromise. This tendency to compromise is seen mainly in the fact that human beings pin their hopes to something other than the spirit. People believe they will find allies in ideas, forces, and expedients drawn from *other sources.* So long as such illusions persist, Christianity can never be developed fully as an active force in human souls. The full development of one's soul depends completely on its complete devotion, which cannot be attained until the soul has been subjected to the test of scourging. This is the only situation in which the illusions of the spirit of compromise disappear; such compromise wants to rely on anything other than what flows in through the gates of conscience as a living revelation of spirit.

This test is also an *experience,* in which the reality of the Christ impulse is sensed in a clearer and more striking way than in any other situation. The consequence of this experience (for both the inner life of the individual and the spiritual history of humankind) is that the Christ impulse, which has been denied "room," obtains room for itself. It gains space in the human organism—not in any individual organ, but in the *blood* that flows through all the organs. Working from the blood, the Christ impulse gradually changes the whole organism, both the left and the right. Then this situation manifests: "Let not thy left hand know what thy right hand doeth." Knowledge will belong neither to the left side nor to the right side, but to the human conscience.

The consequences will be similar in history for Christianity that has experienced "scourging." When Christianity is experienced as "not of this world," it becomes a spiritually etheric current that flows, like the blood's circulation, through the organism of humanity as a whole. This current will flow through "all nations," as the stream of activity of the spiritual conscience inwardly transforms and emancipates the world from the bonds of group spirit and the trap of organizations. And to the extent that the people and groups of all nations respond to it, a new human cultural community will gradually arise—the community that the Revelation of John calls "Philadelphia." Spiritual science calls it the sixth post-Atlantean cultural epoch. In this period, culture will be that of the Christ impulse flowing through all humankind—no longer just a doctrine, but most of all a social force. This culture will have settlements in "all nations," a bond of friendly unity among humankind that binds nations and lands together all round the Earth. It will be the fruit of adjusting the relationship between right and left in the spirit of the experience that results from the trial by scourging.

## Crowning with Thorns

An inner experience of being crowned spiritually with thorns follows the foot washing and the scourging. It reveals essential spiritual facts and laws that are no less important than those disclosed by the foot washing and the scourging. It reveals the adjustment desired and intended by the spiritual world for the relationship between *front* and *back.* And this relationship will be no less consciously regulated under the Christ impulse than the relationships between above and below and between left and right are regulated by spiritual work, destiny, and world history.

To understand the basis for the relationship between front and back, we must first consider the human being from a certain perspective. We must, in fact, begin by considering, in terms of its spiritual stance, the "simple" fact that, in perception, speech, action, and walk, the spiritual being of a person is organized in a *forward* direction. The frontal human being is one who perceives, speaks, and uses the hands and feet, whereas the dorsal human being is blind, dumb, and unable to act. The human physical organization expresses the inner fact that an active person is provided for in front, and the passive person from the back. All the courage needed for life on Earth is not just expressed, but is the organs of the frontal human being; all devotion to the regulation of the higher and the unknown in existence is located in the dorsal human being. Nevertheless, human beings, as they have come to be since the fall, do not represent only courage and devotion. They are, on the contrary, organized so that the roles of *fear* and *shame* are just as important as courage in life and devotion to destiny. The two fundamental elemental forces that entered humankind through the fall are precisely fear and shame. The Bible indicates this fact by telling us that Adam hid himself from the Lord God, and that the first human pair saw "that they were naked." Indeed, their eyes were "opened," but they also became aware of their "nakedness." Lucifer certainly kept his promise that the senses of the frontal human being would be opened to the outer world; but shame, too, entered. It was the power of fear that forced the dorsal human being to flee Paradise. Ever since that time, the frontal human being has been filled with shame, while the dorsal human being is filled with fear. These two forces prevent human beings from experiencing "Paradise," on whose threshold stands the Guardian. Shame causes one to turn away from Paradise, and fear keeps one away from it. The activity of these forces, however, is for the most hidden part of the human subconscious, where they form the curtain that veils the spiritual world. Only a small part of those forces penetrates the experience of consciousness in the physical body. When consciousness rises into the ether body, however, it gains awareness of those forces. It meets them in the ether body in a way that corresponds to the nature of the ether body as the *time* body. It experiences shame as the elemental force that hides the past and fear as the force that hides the future. The human organization in the ether body is just the opposite of the physical organization. This applies not only to sex, but also to the relationship between "front" and "back" human beings; physically, human beings are constituted to look forward; etherically, they look backward. The seeing ("frontal") human being looks toward the past in the ether body; the "dorsal" human being faces forward, toward the future.

But this organization is more fully developed in a higher sphere during one's life after death; there we experience the kama loka state in a reversed direction, as well as the devachan condition on into the future. This arrangement, however, is not usually elaborated during the life between birth and death, because shame and fear conceal the spiritual world. These two forces are the "inner" karma of the luciferic and ahrimanic influences in human beings. They hold individuals back from consciously entering the spiritual world. But the same forces become wings to the soul when shame is converted into *conscience* and fear is converted into *reverence*. Shame and fear are rays that flash from the double-edged sword of the Guardian, who stands at the threshold of the spiritual world and prevents the unauthorized from crossing. Awakened conscience and reverence, on the other hand, are the wings upon which the Guardian lifts human souls into the spiritual world. Encountering the Guardian of the Threshold is thus the third principle of Christian Rosicrucianism. It determines the means of preparation and certifies knowledge gained of the spiritual world. Because the untransformed luciferic and ahrimanic influences are left on this side of the threshold, the experience on the other side is certain to be free of any intervention by forces that produce illusions.

Nonetheless, there are other paths that do in fact lead to spiritual experiences *without* encountering the Guardian of the Threshold. There are, for example, those who glorify the notion of blissfully resting in the light. They work to achieve this, however, by longing to experience the spiritual world as bliss. They elevate themselves by enhancing reverence to the level of light-filled blessedness in which everything is forgotten, including all human problems and suffering. In doing this they nevertheless disregard the Guardian's injunction to keep one's *conscience* awake. They certainly practice reverence, but chasing after blessedness (*ananda*) numbs the conscience. And because the conscience is dulled, one's awareness of meeting with the Guardian of the Threshold is also dimmed. Insofar as consciousness is concerned, that encounter never takes place; consequently, entry to the true spiritual world does not happen. The so-called enlightened blessedness experienced on this path is not the spiritual world that human beings enter after being purified in Kama Loka and on the path of initiation and after meeting with the Guardian of the Threshold. On the contrary, it is a distinct sphere of existence that may be called the "luciferic devachan." This region is a kind of "luciferic double" of Earth—filled with light but without truth.

Still others strive after occult knowledge by overcoming fear. What they develop in this way, however, is not courage as expressed by the conscience, but the courage of realism without reverence, gaining in this way the "unvarnished" truth of humankind and the cosmos. They do indeed learn the secrets of the subconscious in both human beings and the Earth organism; all forms of human egoism are, in this way, revealed to them, as well as many forces of the subterranean spheres. Courage really is needed to perceive such matters, but by its very nature it is a spiritually cynical courage lacking all reverence. And the human being identified with this path is not the true human being but a being of the lower subconscious. The world thus recognized is not the true spiritual world, but, rather, a reflection that has been distorted into its opposite as the spheres of the Earth's interior. It is impossible to penetrate the spiritual world by this path; the Guardian of the Threshold requires that all who enter there possess courage of true conscience and devotional reverence. If anyone avoids meeting the Guardian of the Threshold, such a one-sided endeavor leads not into the spiritual world but into the world of either Lucifer or Ahriman.

This is why meeting the Guardian of the Threshold is no less essential to the Christian Rosicrucian method than are the principles of foot washing and scourging. But meeting the Guardian of the Threshold has very definite consequences for those who experience it. Certain secrets of existence are revealed to them, and they themselves become "guardians" of these mysteries. Henceforward, the Guardian of the Threshold entrusts part of his mission to them. They are trusted with a share of the responsibility and task belonging to the Guardian of the Threshold. What the spiritual world confided to them they must now "guard" in the spirit of the task of the Guardian of the Threshold. What this means is that they are free to decide the way in which they will place their knowledge at the service of humankind. Such "guardianship" does not mean withholding or hiding such knowledge, but making it available in the right way to all who consciously strive for it and truly need it.

A new dignity is conferred upon human beings who pass the test of meeting the Guardian of the Threshold. They are assigned a "crown" that would draw the scorn and contempt of the world if it knew of it. For those who receive such a crown, it means renewed pain and greater trials. Just as they had to overcome shame and fear in response to the demands of the Guardian of the Threshold, now they no longer just represent the mysteries, but must also awaken shame and fear in others. They are now more than just liberal benefactors to others; they must also become a trial and a test for many. They must accept the fact that representing the truth before others often shames and frightens other people. It may even involve the need to remain silent under the eyes of many others—eyes that either greedily search for something in them that is unworthy of the truth they represent or look for something in their actions to prove that such truth is in fact false. Anxious not to be exposed, shame sharpens eyes for any deficiencies in those who represent spiritual truth; and fear, trying to stay out of sight, quickly offers to find contradictions in the represented spiritual truth. Once people have taken up the task of "guarding," or representing, spiritual truth, they are exposed to such scrutiny as this. And those who wear the "crown of thorns" must overcome shame and fear under the gaze of such eyes, just as they had to overcome shame and fear at the voice of the spiritual conscience representing the Guardian of the Threshold. They must not allow themselves to be drawn into polemical self-defense, nor must they shrink before the "keen and brazen gaze" of those who wish to expose them and cut to shreds all that they hold most sacred. They must not allow themselves to take a single aggressive step forward nor yield a step backward. The thorny crown of their task requires them to stand firm in the truth. This is the experience of new dignity—that of truth represented by human beings. And this is true human dignity, the dignity of the Son of Man.

In a general way, what we have attempted to describe here can be made clear and astonishingly alive by studying, from this perspective, many examples in the life of Rudolf Steiner. His life is certainly the best source for a profound understanding of foot washing, scourging, crowning with thorns, cross bearing, and the crucifixion. These stages in present-day spiritual history run through his life story, while showing the characteristics of the future spiritual history of humankind. Just as the scourging is a karmic necessity in the history of humankind's future, so is the crowning with thorns. Thorn crowning will be part of humankind's future spiritual history during the epoch when "white" humanity is pitted against ahrimanic humanity, following a complete severance of the two currents. "White" (or purified) humanity will then represent spiritual truth and, at the same time, reproach and warn the rest of humanity. But it will be standing before a humanity grown clairvoyant for all deficiencies and weaknesses—a humanity that will have the faculty not only of finding every imperfection but also of working through the doors of those imperfections. These words will then become historical truth: "Whosoever hath, to him shall be given, but whosoever hath not, from him shall be taken away even that he hath" (Matthew 13:12). All goodness to which the element of compromise still clings will be destroyed by the forces of the other portion of humanity; thus, "even that he hath" will be taken away from those who "hath not" an attitude freed of compromise.

Here we close our meditation on the first three stages of the passion and their significance for occult methods, karma, and the spiritual history of humanity. Nevertheless, it would not be out of place to give a short spiritual moral summary of the essentials on which these three stages are based, and this may be given in short sentences. In foot washing, we are dealing with the conquest of pride through service; in scourging, we are dealing with the uncompromising attitude that swerves neither left nor right; and in the crowning with thorns, we are dealing with a firm stand in the name of truth—neither going forward nor shrinking back.

Thus the first three stages of the Christian path may be summed up with these words:

> The First must be the servant of all.
> One's left hand must not know what the right hand does.
> One must recognize that the servant is not greater than the lord.

Further stages of the way of the passion will be considered in the next chapter.

# Chapter 10

# Higher Stages of the Passion

## Cross Bearing

In the preceding chapter we studied foot washing, scourging and crowning with thorns as principles of the Christian Rosicrucian method, as karmic necessities, and as future events of spiritual history. Although it could be addressed from numerous points of view, we approached our subject from the perspective of adjusting the relationship between above and below, right and left, front and back. Now, to apply this method of study to further stages of the passion, we need to understand the inner connection between the first three and the fourth.

The cross bearing results from a simultaneous experience of foot washing, scourging, and crowning with thorns. And just as the *cross* comprises all the spatial relationships we spoke of in connection with the first three stages of the passion, those three stages are comprehended in the stage of cross bearing. The "cross" to be carried is really one's own being. It is we who have formed within ourselves a cruciform system of currents—those of foot washing, scourging, and crowning with thorns. This gives us a new experience that is also a further test, because, up to this stage in our evolution, we always felt enlightened, strengthened, and *carried* by the spirit. Now, however, a fundamental change takes place. We now experience inwardly a higher, spiritual human being interpenetrating us in the form of the currents of the cross. This higher, spiritual human being, however, does not *carry* us as we previously felt carried by the spirit. On the contrary, we feel that it is we who must carry the higher human being within. The ordinary lower human being experiences the higher, spiritual "brother" inwardly, and throughout the whole course of our spiritual destiny we hear the command to be our brother's keeper (or guardian).

This command means, however, that individuals must experience themselves as a sheath and bearer for the other. The experience is such that individuals must surrender all the fruits of their toilsome work in acquiring knowledge on Earth and their earthly acts to others who do not in turn surrender the fruits of their spiritual experience and capacity to the lower human being, but place it at the service of humanity. Such individuals also sense that the inner higher human being continually exposes their inadequacies and imperfections. Indeed, they sense that this higher human being (in the form of a cross of light) causes the lower human being to appear in conscious reflections as the earthly cross of darkness. The physical organism now appears to be a wooden, dead organism, very poorly adapted to receive the spirit. Thus one's personal human consciousness stands between two crosses: the radiant cross of the higher human being and the dark cross of the bodily organization, both of which must be carried. In this situation, an inner resentment, or feeling of protest, always sets in. Such resentment may reach out in one of two directions: toward the higher human being or toward the human organism. Prompted by resentment, the personal consciousness may ask, "Am I my brother's keeper?" An urge may thus make itself felt in one's personal consciousness to cast off the cross of the inner higher human being—that is, to kill one's "brother."

On the other hand, one's personal consciousness may acquire a deep self-aversion, regarding itself as a philistine in body, temperament, and character. Self-hatred can arise and even lead to murder, just as surely as indignation arises against the higher human being. A temptation arises to cast off the cross of earthly personality, which then appears eminently worthless, commonplace, and cowardly.

Until we have experienced such trials, we can never understand the full significance of what went on in the depths of, for example, the souls of the two great suicides of the nineteenth century: Friedrich Nietzsche and Otto Weininger.[1] Nietzsche committed spiritual suicide by "killing" the higher Christian self within, casting off the shining cross. Weininger was unable to stand himself as an earthly being and laid the dark cross down by actually murdering himself. We mention those tragic figures not merely to show the seriousness of the cross-bearing trial, but also because an understanding of these catastrophes as a failed test is the main service we are bound to render to those who experience them. But the test that those men did not pass consisted essentially in developing the relationship to the bright cross and the dark cross, which is indicated in the words "love thy neighbor as thyself" (Matthew 22:39). These "simple" words in fact contain another fundamental principle of the Christian Rosicrucian method of initiation. It involves the unavoidable requirement to strive toward a practical solution of the problem "love of humanity—love of self." This must be worked toward so that one protects the higher human being—which lives for humanity—just as lovingly as one cares for the lower self. This means that we carry the bright cross not out of duty but out of love, and that we strive to lighten the dark cross through the kind of patient, voluntary training that is possible only through love.

People must not lack love toward their own souls and physical bodies; we must not, on the other hand, feel that our relationship with the higher human being, who is directed toward humanity, is merely a duty. The path toward a balance between these two poles is the personal consciousness between the two crosses—learning to share the love of the higher self for humanity so that our neighbor becomes as dear to us as is our own being, while affirming our own being (or earthly personality), because this is the only way we can actually manifest love toward our neighbor. The neighbor (the one who stands closest) is thus the school in which we learn to love humankind, while preserving self-love for new reasons. Love is not a quantity; at a certain point, learning to love makes it possible to vibrate in unison with the radiation of the inner higher human being toward the universal. On the other hand, those who have taken their neighbor unconditionally into the warmth of their hearts will never be cold toward their own being. Thus people must develop, awaken, and maintain three kinds of love simultaneously: spiritual universal love for humanity; love toward one's neighbor; and love toward one's own earthly personality. Once we make this a reality—once we fill spirit, soul, and body with love—no room remains inwardly for any hatred; however imperfect that love may be, one's being has no room for hate.

The crowning with thorns was a victory over shame and fear; likewise, carrying the cross is a definite victory over hatred, or resentment toward the higher and aversion to the commonplace. Hate must be overcome in the spirit of these words: Love thy neighbor as thyself; thus we achieve loving cooperation between body, soul, and spirit. Harmony of the three human aspects begins, and this harmony is both the fruit of passing the cross-bearing trial and the fulfillment of a fundamental requirement of Christian Rosicrucianism. The method of this occult path depends on the principle of harmony among spirit, soul, and body.

Other spiritual streams establish either the spirit of asceticism (denial of the body) or the principle of the earthly personality's supremacy (denial of spirit); yet the personality must follow the spirit if it wishes to go beyond what is transitory. The purity that Christian training strives for does not dominate human nature; rather, it ennobles human nature. As earnestness and courage flow more freely into human nature, it becomes clear that, indeed, *all* human faculties may serve the great work of goodness. Human freedom on this path involves learning to *love* one's spiritual duty.

These experiences of cross bearing, which may be encountered on paths of spiritual development and destiny, confront humankind during the epoch of the future during which "white" humanity will oppose ahrimanic humanity. By that time, however, such opposition will be characterized not only by faithfulness to truth, but also by a realization of responsibility toward the other portion of humanity. They will bear, as their cross, the portion of humankind that has succumbed to darkness. At the same time, each individual will be imbued inwardly by the cruciform rays of the spiritual human being borne by all. The "white" section of humanity will then assume the task of the angel, performing for ahrimanic humanity a service that is similar to that of the guardian angel toward human beings today. On the other hand, it will bear the higher human being inwardly, which will take the place of the guardian angel. The higher human being, however, will represent the guardian angel in such a way that one is not overshadowed; rather, it will manifest inwardly as an incorporated being. Because of this incorporation, the higher human being will, to some extent, be given over to one's personality. One will entrust the self to that being so that it will be one's "keeper." Humankind must always experience cross bearing in world history as a means of learning to overcome hatred and establish harmony of body, soul, and spirit.

## CRUCIFIXION

To understand the stage of crucifixion as a fundamental principle of Christian Rosicrucian initiation, we must begin with matters that seem to be unrelated. Phenomena of, for example, the law of metamorphoses must be considered insofar as they can be observed in human existence. Such phenomena may be seen in the inner sphere of human life as well as in the structure of bodily organs. In both areas, it is a valid rule that metamorphosis occurs through the alternation of limitation and freedom. Speech, for example, is a transformation of the capacity for movement through an enhancement of that faculty. This enhancement, however, could not take place until a limit had been placed on the outer movement; suppressed external movements became the concentrated movements of speech. Similarly, the faculty of thought is a development through metamorphosis of the movement faculty. Thinking is an enhancement of the speech faculty, which has been checked by suppression. We learn to think in silence, and we learn to speak through the limited urge to move.

This metamorphosis can, however, be taken further. Thinking can be enhanced to become a new, higher faculty. This may arise by consciously stopping thought movement—not through passive or deficient thinking, but by concentrating one's whole thinking force into a single point. Through such concentration, thinking is enhanced and transformed into the faculty of *spiritual seeing.* This transformation is brought about through meditation practice in which one moves from thinking to thought, and from thought to seeing. This progress depends, however, on efforts to curb through conscious self-limitation. Thinking must pass through the "needle's eye" of totally calm concentration before it can ascend to the "heavenly kingdom" of *seeing* as a force of perception. It must pass through a condition of complete restraint, or perfect immobility, before it can cross the threshold that separates the kingdom of visual experience from the kingdom of reflection. This principle of curbing the lower force so that it can be transformed into the higher is the principle of crucifixion (or initiation) in the Christian Rosicrucian school. It is the principle of ascent in meditation, but it is also the principle of the entire path of karmic evolution leading to a karmically determined initiation. Hence, on the karmic path of initiation, the soul must pass through an inner (and often an outer) situation where all its basic forces of feeling and willing are *bound.*[2] This is a situation in which the soul manifests a very strong desire and a very keen aspiration, but in which there is nevertheless not the slightest possibility of satisfying the desire or realizing the aspiration. Thus, longing and wishing are held motionless in the iron grip of necessity until they have been concentrated to a point and pass through the "needle's eye" of "mystic death." A "rich man" can never pass through that "needle's eye," but only one who is as poor as those who, on their deathbed, are at the point of passing through the gate of death.

The principle of curbing the lower with the intent of transforming it into the higher is called the "narrow way" in the Gospels, in contrast to the more commonly taken "broad way." These terms are not merely "poetic" in the Gospels; they are "technical occult terms," developed from a profound knowledge of occult facts. The "narrow way" is this kind of technical term; it describes the path on which "narrowing," or concentrating, one's soul forces takes place so that they may be changed (in accordance with the law of metamorphoses) into higher forces. This "narrowing" of one's soul forces culminates with the condition called "crucifixion." This appears when "cross bearing" has reached the point of uniting the two crosses, the bright spirit cross and the dark earth cross. When these two crosses interpenetrate so that (for individual human consciousness) absolutely no space exists between them, personal consciousness becomes a single point that collects its whole force, and from that it is poured into the cross. It dies by becoming a cross itself; it no longer *carries* the cross but unites with the human spirit and body. Thus its "spiritual duty," or higher human being, becomes flesh and blood; the human blood system becomes the organ of spiritual truth. Thus the higher becomes, so to speak, the lower, and the inner becomes the outer. The actual process of initiation is exactly this conversion; it no longer represents only the *harmony* of body, soul, and spirit as it does at the stage of cross bearing, but a complete *unity* of body, soul, and spirit. True, this process may be experienced in various degrees of intensity, and the different grades of initiation depend on those degrees. The process may be experienced in the Self (the "I" organization), or it may be experienced in the astral, the ether body, or even, to some extent, in the physical body. Jesus Christ alone experienced this *completely* in the physical body; those who have experienced it partially in the physical body are masters of the great initiates. Those who have experienced "crucifixion" in the ether body are called great initiates; and those who have experienced "crucifixion" in the astral body and the "I" come under the category of occult initiates and experts.

At the stage of crucifixion, one encounters the Greater Guardian of the Threshold, just as the stage of the thorn crowning is preceded by an encounter with the lesser Guardian of the Threshold. This "meeting" is really an experience of the spiritual crucifixion of the world; it was known to Plato, who spoke of the "crucified world soul." Here, however, it is not just ideational knowledge of the fact, but actual experience of the world conscience in the person of Jesus Christ. Then, indeed, one experiences the fulfillment of a promise: "Today shalt thou be with me in paradise" (Luke 23:43). Spiritually and morally, the experience is to become the malefactor crucified on the left and who is now in paradise; in the higher, spiritual world, it means experiencing "today" as the time in which the world conscience is *present* for one's being. One experiences, for the first time, true *presence:* "today in paradise." It is not just an earthly moment that links past and future, but a reality. We awake to an apprehension of the cosmic reality of the present when we pass through the experience on Earth of intense concentration on the moment of "mystic death," or "crucifixion." We experience this, however, just as the malefactor on the left did: the guilty looking on the innocent. This "looking on the innocent" is the essence of meeting the Greater Guardian of the Threshold as the crucified conscience of the world. This meeting is, at the same time, the experience of the *reality of the presence* (*die Gegenwart*), the reality of "today in paradise."

The "today" experienced in paradise is the present awaking of conscience to a sense of human responsibility for the whole past and future. The conscience, as a present knowing of the purpose past and the future, is the "great secret of initiation" that can never be betrayed. It cannot be betrayed because it cannot be expressed; it is absolutely incommunicable, whether in human language, that of suprasensory thought transference, or through signs and symbols. That "today" can rise only as a soul experience. It cannot in any way be given by a teacher. Consequently, the purpose of Christian Rosicrucian teachers is limited to helping students find a direction leading to this experience; the actual experience and the progression toward that goal must be left to the student. Rosicrucian students must live through this experience alone, just as they must pass through the gate of death alone.

Again, this is a fundamental principle of Christian Rosicrucian spiritual training; the relationship between teacher and student is based on the student's complete freedom. Both the guru who imposes on the inner life of the *chela* and the master who sets precepts in order to regulate the details of a student's life are far from the Christian Rosicrucian relationship between teacher and student. In this relationship, the teacher is neither a mentor nor a guardian, but an experienced friend who does not withhold advice when asked for it. The reason this relationship differs so much from these other methods is that they belong to the broad way. Such methods involve ways in which it is not a matter of transforming the consciously checked lower forces into higher but the development and use of existing forces as they are; thus, either the forces temporarily associated with the human being are freed, or existing faculties are strengthened and intensified. Either atavistic forces of the past are reanimated, or the existing forces of will and reason are strengthened and sharpened to a degree that makes it possible to use them in a way that is equivalent to "magical" practices. The broad way (expanding the development of what is already present) leads either to becoming a medium or to egoistic magic.

Nevertheless, there are many who walk the broad way leading to perdition and into the karmic community of the future ahrimanic humanity. This future ahrimanic section of humanity, however, will be faced likewise with a certain kind of crucifixion—that of the malefactor on the right. Through that crucifixion, ahrimanic humanity will lose the faculty of movement in the seventh epoch; they will be fixed to the Earth like plants. Those who have to carry the karma of becoming a medium this way (as victims of passivity) yearn to be freed, while those who have been placed in this unfortunate situation through the karma of black magic will cast reproaches and hatred against Heaven. Nevertheless, even in that situation there will remain the possibility of freeing many of those individuals from their bondage to Earth in a literal, physical sense. The yearning of those who have become victims of passivity will help to form a starting point. Thus, in the final hour of Earth's history, white magic (the force of love) will find a broad field of activity in which to loosen the bonds that bind human beings to Earth.

This effect of white magic will be possible because "white" humanity will have experienced a kind of crucifixion, as explained. In effect, it will then proclaim—with magic power—the message to the other portion of humanity: Do you not fear God, since you have been likewise condemned? It will be *fear*—fear of God's judgment—that will be the last guarantee of possible deliverance at the twelfth hour, even for those whose fate has been determined through the activity of black magic.

The karmic image of humanity's future in connection with the spiritual law of crucifixion, therefore, shows frightening abysses of misfortune, on the one hand, and on the other, the immense possibilities of help and deliverance that the providence of God has guaranteed to humanity.

## Entombment

The consequences of meeting the Greater Guardian of the Threshold are just as specific as those of encounterieng the first Guardian of the Threshold (or rather, the Guardian of the First Threshold). Human beings received a specific task from the First Guardian—to become keepers of the Threshold; likewise, human beings will be given a specific task by the Greater Guardian. This, too, involves conscious participation in the task of the Guardian; indeed, we claim for our own the aims of the Greater Guardian in world history and earthly evolution. These goals for Earth and earthly humanity may be summed up in the words of the Gospel: "Lo, I am with you alway, even unto the end of the world" (Matthew 28:20). One meaning of these words is that the Christ is leading humankind and the Earth through *inner* guidance. He does not guide as do, for example, the laws of nature, which enforce their consequences through external necessity. Christ works within human beings through the power of inner conviction. In place of the "old law," the "new law" acquires increasing force. The new law cannot acquire force, however, until the Christ impulse itself enters individual beings and, in this way, imbues human beings from within. The promise "I am with you" is thus a necessity that arises from the nature of the Christ impulse itself. It is in the nature of the Christ impulse not to forsake the Earth, but to draw it upward from within.

In this sense, the Christ impulse becomes a spiritual necessity of those who have experienced a meeting with the Greater Guardian of the Threshold. He resolves to stand by humankind and the Earth to the end—and in such a way that, within Earth's karmic relations, he will devote his force to advancing the *positive* tendencies of Earth's karma. The karma of Earth, however, is death, which is the only reality of everything that is purely of the Earth. And in the field of death, everything sown is reaped first by death. Those who truly understand this, therefore, cannot help feeling that the Earth is one vast grave. The poets may sing as much as they like about blossoms and springtime, but occultists know that Earth is really a grave. Such knowledge does not make them gloomy, however, because they do not hate that grave; rather, they consciously enter direct union with earthly life, just as naive human beings do so unconsciously. This conscious union with the Earth is precisely the stage of the spiritual path called *entombment.*

Hence, entombment is a repetition of cross bearing, but at a higher level; through it, one learns to no longer bear the cross of individual human karma, but that of Earth's karma. This represents an enormous difference not only in the scope of the trial, but also in its essence. The human cross is erected vertically, whereas the Earth's cross is horizontal. It forms a cruciform grave in which human beings must themselves lie. They do this in faith and in the hope that, by surrendering their whole being, gates will open, through which the power of cosmic grace will miraculously erect the Earth's cross again. They surrender to the grave in the hope of resurrection.

Entombment is not just a spiritual experience that occurs once; it is especially a condition in which human beings must, again and again, in a thousand cases, choose entombment. They must decide in the form of actions that *must* be unsuccessful in the given situations. They place them in the tomb of earthly events, hoping that in the future they will "rise again" as results. Thus, for example, Rudolf Steiner's activity toward a threefold social order was an entombment—one among many, but one in which we have become generally aware that it was so. And, gradually, it will dawn upon us that other things in the life and work of Rudolf Steiner were also entombments.

In this situation and at this stage, it is important to learn how to be a sower in the fields of death. We must also learn to act in ways that will not bear fruit until the distant future. This requires courage that no failure can daunt, because it means acting and working for *karma* and not merely for success. Such work for karma, or activity for the future, is a fundamental requirement for Christian occultists. Those who aim for success and want to change the world—not karmically, but directly—may accomplish much that is useful on their own, but they cannot be taken seriously as occultists. The serious nature of occultism is that of death. Its force is not an urge to act based on vital optimism but certainty in karmic knowledge, especially knowledge of the karma of the Mystery of Golgotha. This karma is the foundation for knowing that everything sown in the field of death will rise again one day.

Those with awakened spiritual conscience (as Christian occultists must have) dare not act today as if the Mystery of Golgotha had never taken place. They must strive (and cannot do otherwise) to unite their efforts with the karmic stream of the Mystery of Golgotha. Such efforts involve the necessity—in both experience and effective action—of not only foot washing, scourging, thorn crowning, cross bearing, and crucifixion, but also entombment. The "imitation of Christ" on the path of initiation *and* karma is not just the subject of a beautiful book of devotion by Thomas à Kempis, but also a basic principle of Christian Rosicrucian occultism, in the present as well as in the past and in all the future. There is only one "narrow way" that leads to the redemption of resurrection. The other paths belong to the broad way, which leads to death—becoming a component of Ahriman's being, the Lord of Death. Of course, he is not the lord *over* death, but is precisely named Lord of Death. In other words, there is no *annihilation;* death in the ahrimanic sense means to enter Ahriman's realm. Those who attain resurrection will be lords *over* death. The Lord of Death will reveal himself as the lord of hardening the individual, or rigidifying the personal. In the far future, therefore, entombment will occur as a karmic event in the form of rigidifying the section of humanity that has surrendered to Ahriman. Human beings will have become hardened parts of the hardened Earth, which will be, as it were, their common grave. The Earth will become one great tomb. But when this happens, the lord of death will perform one final, supreme act of mercy; the Earth as a planet will be destroyed and crumble to dust. It will succumb to the *other* death, which is not a hardening but decomposition and a crumbling of the rigid. It will be subjected to death that is the emancipation guaranteed by the lord of death. The Earth will die and arise as Jupiter. The ahrimanic portion of humankind will be given another chance to start fresh on the path to spirit. At the Venus stage, this chance will again be provided and, eventually, again on Vulcan.

## Resurrection

Resurrection is connected with entombment so closely that these two stages can hardly be studied separately; the courage needed for the trials of entombment is an expression of the hope of resurrection, which is based on knowledge of the Mystery of Golgotha—that it is not just the truth, but also the way and the life. Indeed, it is the way of the whole positive karmic future of humankind and the life that proves stronger than the rigidifying principle of death.

The experiences that we must consider in connection with this highest stage are the mysteries of *death* and of the Father. At this stage, we come to know the twofold form of death (its power to harden and dissolve) and the mystery of the Father in the realm of death. Indeed, it is experienced in such a way that it leads to recognition of the highest life in death, the highest light in darkness, and the highest companionship in complete loneliness. The soul plunges into the region that Rudolf Steiner calls the "cosmic midnight" in his mystery drama, from which it emerges enriched by a new experience. This emergence of the soul from the dark regions of cosmic midnight is the "resurrection" experienced on the path of initiation. In particular, it is the experience of resurrection in the human "I" and, in rare cases, even in the astral body and (most rarely in human spiritual history) in the ether body.

The process as a whole, however, was lived through only by Jesus Christ, in whom resurrection was experienced even by the physical body. Again, the depth of its significance to the initiated depends on the scope and the degree of consciousness of the resurrection experience, not only in terms of the stage of initiation, but especially in the possibilities of its spiritual efficacy. If the experience of crucifixion yields both the greatest certainty of knowledge concerning the mystery of human existence and an inner justification for arranging this knowledge as a teaching to guide others, the stages of entombment and resurrection produce effective spiritual forces that make possible the fulfillment of even higher tasks than guidance by proclamation. The possibility of encouraging all that is good in human beings through silent spiritual influence arises from the experience of plunging into cosmic midnight. In that midnight sphere (both dark for the outer and the inner eyes and silent for the outer and the inner ears), permeation of the soul occurs through the "dark lightning" and "silent thunder" of cosmic judgment. What is experienced there can be represented by human beings (who are bound to use a physical brain) only in the form of complete contradictions; they must translate it into concrete and logical thinking even for themselves. Such translation, therefore, is not usually attempted. It is not knowledge that enriches one's day consciousness that the soul brings when reemerging from cosmic midnight into the earthly sphere; rather, it is the force stirred in it when the Father forces of cosmic judgment flash and thunder through the soul.[3] The soul brings a portion of primeval force from the cosmic, creative depths of being, and this force enables the soul to develop an influence in the moral and spiritual activity of Earth that is equivalent to the spiritual karmic guidance of humanity.

Here we must end our meditation on the stages of the passion. First, however, we will summarize the stages of cross bearing, crucifixion, entombment, and resurrection, as we did at the end of the previous chapter on foot washing, scourging, and crowning with thorns. This time, however, our summary can be properly made only in the form of a picture. This picture is the Rose Cross, which epitomizes not only the higher stages of the passion but also, in fact, the whole path of Christian initiation. It is the symbol of the narrow way of sacrifice and the forces of resurrection that flower on this path. Death and resurrection are the two fundamental themes of the Christian spiritual path, and the two are united in the symbol of the Rose Cross.

Thus the black cross with the glowing red roses can summarize all we have said here about Christian initiation; it can stand, if only for a moment, before the inner eye of the reader's soul as a token of the solemn spirit world and, at the same time, as the author's Easter greeting to his readers.

The final two chapters on the New Testament will be devoted to the Mystery of Golgotha and to the Pentecost.

## Chapter 11

# The Mystery of Golgotha

### The Evolution of Love in the cosmos

In the previous two chapters, we considered the stages of the passion as fundamental principles and stages of the path of Christian initiation. Now it would be worthwhile to study the Mystery of Golgotha itself as a historical, spiritual, and cosmic event. In doing so, we will revisit the events of the passion, though from a different angle. We will no longer consider them as stages of initiation but in their spiritual and cosmic scope as the sacrifice of Jesus Christ. The significance of the Mystery of Golgotha is not limited to the transformations of human consciousness as they occur in initiation and in the course of karmic history; it is an event that concerns the whole Earth organism, the planetary system, as well as the spiritual hierarchies of good and evil. It concerns the universe; no being or group of beings in the universe is unaffected by the Mystery of Golgotha. And it concerns every being in the world, because it is the seed of a new cosmos. As it presently exists, and as it has evolved through the Saturn, Sun, Moon, and Earth periods up to the Mystery of Golgotha, it is a cosmos of wisdom that is to become a *cosmos of love.*

The statement that the present cosmos of wisdom is to become a cosmos of love contains a whole world of occult facts. And at the center of this host of facts is the Mystery of Golgotha; all other facts pertain either to the preparations for that mystery or to its aftereffects. The Mystery of Golgotha is itself the decisive factor; it is the purpose of this chapter to show both that it is a fact and the extent of this truth.

The present cosmos, as perceived by the senses, may be experienced as a kind of "frozen wisdom." The great moral impression made on humankind by the whole world structure is essentially a formation of wisdom congealed, as it were, into ice. Immense masses of wisdom have flowed into the world and have congealed into a Copernican *machina coelestis.* Wisdom is everywhere in the world; the world is saturated with wisdom. Every plant, every organism, all movements of the heavenly bodies bear witness to this; but the world is stark and chill and hollow to human souls. Nietzsche's words, "The world—a door to a thousand wildernesses dumb and cold," will echo in every human soul that inquires, not just about universal facts and laws, but also concerning the soul itself. Soul is not revealed in the universe; the laws of the universe bear witness to a wonderful wisdom—wisdom in whose presence human reason feels like a small and tiny creature—but the rigid lines of those laws are only the soul's coffin. It is not a dull, opaque coffin, but as transparent as a crystal; nonetheless, it is rigid and silent. At the same time, however, it bears witness to what it lacks. Just as cold bears witness to warmth and rigidity bears witness to movement, the cosmic coffin bears witness to the soul. In this sense, the crystal coffin "contains" the soul and demonstrates—through its coldness and rigidity—what the soul would have to be if it lived in the world; it reveals a dead soul.

Thus, the immensely meaningful fairy tale of *Snow White*—the crystal tomb with a dead maiden guarded by dwarfs—arises before the souls of those who see the universe as a "moral impression." This image expresses the fact that the present cosmos is one of wisdom, but one in which love is absent. This is the essential result of contemplating the universe from the *outside* as it appears to the consciousness between birth and death. Human beings can also come to understand the universe from the other perspective, the *inside;* they understand the inside of the universe either on the path of initiation or in the state of consciousness between death and a new birth. In either condition, human beings no longer experience the universe as merely rigidified wisdom, or as the *expression* of wisdom; rather, they have the sense of being submerged in a surging flood of wisdom. That flooding, flowing wisdom encircles and overwhelms the human soul so that, for the soul, it is not a matter of allowing wisdom to enter (as one does in the case of earthly consciousness); rather, is it important for the soul to assert itself as a soul, with the content of a soul, in this sea of purposeful wisdom.

The soul is plunged into this flooding turmoil, which threatens to make the soul feel insignificant and empty. The soul's environment is so full of light that the soul seems to be merely a shadow in the encircling radiance. The soul would, in fact, be condemned to a shadowy existence if not for the fact that it brings a force, or essence, from the Earth that makes it possible for the soul not to lose its being. This force was learned on Earth, and in the soul it becomes the capacity to love. After death, the soul receives the faculty of love as a force that is able to subsist side by side with cosmic wisdom. Earlier—in particular, in the time immediately before the Mystery of Golgotha—the soul had increasingly become a shadow after death. The "realm of shades" of the ancient Greeks was a reality, though not in the sense, of course, that that realm was dark, but because the souls of the dead were condemned to a shadowy existence. They could not bring anything with them from earthly existence into the spiritual world that was as significant as the light of that world's wisdom. Life on Earth could only reflect the wisdom of the spiritual world; consequently, the soul could bring into the spiritual world only a reflection, or shadow, of that world. Such a soul would feel like a mere shadow of a shadow, or semblance of a semblance.

The destiny of the human soul has changed, however, since the Mystery of Golgotha; now, when the human soul enters the spiritual world through the gate of death, it *can* bring something from the Earth that is not a reflection and a shadow but has essential value—something that carries inwardly the seed of a new world order. The old world order, that of wisdom, is expressed in the rule of measure, weight, and number, but since the Mystery of Golgotha a fourth element flows through the human soul and into the cosmic order—a new element that frees the other three from rigidity and at the same time restores to them their original purpose. Essentially, measure, weight, and number did not originally mean heaviness, limitation, and quantity. The celestial archetypes of measure, weight and number differ from their congealed expression in the lower world. What has become "weight" today was originally the primal force of *sacrifice* in the descent to the incarnation. But true weight was "betrayed" during the first post-Atlantean cultural (or ancient Indian) epoch; during that period a tendency originated that moved toward "weightlessness"—the attempt to betray Earth and be emancipated from it. As a karmic consequence of the fact that ancient India deserted its "first love"; weight lost its meaning as the "first love" (Revelation 2:4) and, under Ahriman's influence, became the "spirit of heaviness."[1]

Similarly, the original purpose of measure was not to limit or restrict as it does today, but to be the power that fulfills spiritual purpose on Earth: the *force of patience* in the created being. *Weight* originally meant the force of descent in the vertical direction of incarnation, whereas *measure* indicated the horizontal path of life toward the relationship between heaven and Earth that is the mission of earthly incarnation. Just as weight, in its original meaning, was betrayed by the ancient Indian civilization and given up to ahrimanic tendencies, likewise, during the ancient Persian cultural epoch, measure was betrayed when that civilization refused to complete the pure path indicated by the great Zoroaster, choosing instead to enter relations of compromise with the Turanian element. The consequence of that compromise was that, in the karma of humankind, measure became a restriction, or principle of confinement; indeed, it became the "prison" into which the tempter will cast "*some* of you" so that "ye shall have tribulation ten days" (Revelation 2:10).

The principle of "number," too, became purely quantitative because its original meaning was betrayed. This occurred during the Egypto-Chaldean cultural epoch, when the original meaning of *number* as the force of the essential structure of immortal beings was transformed into its opposite—an assembly of perishable bodily units. The celestial archetype (or truth of number) is nonetheless the fact that there are numerous individualities in the world. The very purpose for so many of them is that each has a qualitative meaning for the world that none other can have. If any individuality in the world did not exist, the world as a whole would be just as imperfect as a symphony that lacks an intended note. The unique nature of each individual has immense value because of that very uniqueness; this is the original meaning of number as intended in the heavens. The application of number, however, was diverted from the eternal individuality to the physical and thus materialism arose, one expression of which was mummification in ancient Egypt. The Apocalypse describes materialism in its original form as "the doctrine of the Nicolaitanes, which thing I hate" (Revelation 2:15). That doctrine was clearly the karma of the betrayal of number, just as the "prison" and "loss of the first love" were the karmic consequences of betraying measure and weight.

Now, however, every human soul that has received the Christ impulse (at least into the life of ideation) during earthly existence also brings something into the spiritual world that it changes there into the resurrection forces of original number, measure, and weight. Through the Christ impulse, the soul experiences the resurrection of number, measure, and weight—first in the spiritual world, then later, during the next incarnation, the power of the experience flows into the earthly existence and becomes the effective seed of a new world order. This is a new world order in which the wisdom tomb of the soul that was formed from the frozen number, measure, and weight will be melted, and the soul in number, measure, and weight will come to life. Then the human soul will experience, even during earthly existence (just as it can be experienced today in the spiritual world after death, or on the path of initiation), the fact that true weight, for example, is contained in foot washing; that true measure is contained in the words "not seven times, but seventy times seven times must forgiveness be granted" (Matthew 18:22). That true number is expressed, for instance, in the parable of the one lost sheep, the recovery of which brought more joy among the angels than did "the ninety and nine which went not astray" (Matthew 18:13). The Gospel, in the light of spiritual science, contains ensouled concepts of number, measure, and weight. Those concepts become *experiences* in the spiritual world, and these experiences become forces with which a new world can be built in keeping with the New Testament meanings of weight, measure, and number. When number, measure, and weight in the world gain soul, the new cosmos is present—the *cosmos of love,* which is to follow the dying cosmos of wisdom. The future cosmos will, however, manifest in stages; the Jupiter existence, which will immediately follow Earth existence, will be the stage of the conquered spirit of heaviness, the resurrection of *true weight.* The subsequent Venus phase will be the cosmic stage of ensouling of all measure in the universe. And the Vulcan existence will be the stage of the resurrection of number in its true meaning as a community of immortal individuals.

## The Redemption of Lucifer

The cosmos of love evolution began with the Mystery of Golgotha, the seed of the new cosmos. The whole future organism is contained in the seed, just as the whole future of the world is contained in the Mystery of Golgotha. This is why Rudolf Steiner frequently stated that the Mystery of Golgotha is the meaning of the Earth. The Earth is the arena where the decisive battle is fought between good and evil in the cosmos.

Initially, this conflict involves a very specific territory that includes everything in the universe upon which Lucifer works, has worked, or can work. The territory of Lucifer is the area of the world that may either succumb to Ahriman or be won back by the hierarchies of good. This territory includes, on the one hand, portions of the realm of the spiritual hierarchies and, on the other, the kingdoms of nature. Humanity is at the center of this arena, however, and has absorbed the luciferic. Thus, humanity is the central factor of the territory in dispute and, as such, connects the realms of nature and the hierarchies.

The struggle between good and evil initially takes place in luciferic territory, because the luciferic is not just inwardly opposed to the hierarchies of good and the ahrimanic, but it has also something *in common* with both sides; thus, for each side there is the hope that it may be completely won over. Lucifer has the *pride* of opposition in common with Ahriman, and he has *love* in common with the hierarchies of good. Lucifer is a Janus-like character: with one side of his nature he loves the Christ, while with the other he has affinity with Ahriman. Because of this, both sides have the possibility of winning the whole field of his activity; the spiritual hierarchies hope to acquire it for love, and Ahriman hopes to incorporate it into his dominion.

In the period directly preceding the Mystery of Golgotha, the situation was such that the whole luciferic field might be regarded as the assured prize of Ahriman. This was true for humanity as far back as A.D. 666, when a kind of "fantastic wisdom" (Rudolf Steiner's expression) emanated from Gondishapur, the spiritual center of the New Persian empire, and spread over the world. This type of wisdom was "fantastic" insofar as it was a combination of "iron logic" with a visionary perception of phantasms. It was not merely a matter of forms produced by human fantasy (which in themselves would have been relatively harmless), but rather of luciferic imaginations that Ahriman had given spectral existence; these were, therefore, really not fantasies, but actual specters. Thus the "logic" that was combined with mediumistic visions would not be the thought life that links the human head and heaven, but logic of the lower human being, or human metabolism; it would be a pragmatic logic of the will that, in conjunction with the visions, would produce a force against which humankind would be unable to stand. The essentially human element, the heart, would then not only be completely shut away (or "imprisoned"), but it would also be speechless and powerless; it would have no thought with which to make itself known, and it would have no influence over the will to act. The net formed by the visions and the logic of volition would have contracted around the heart, detaching it completely from the spiritual world, thus being forced to wither and abandon its realm of existence to Ahriman.

One characteristic of that "fantastic" wisdom would be that it produced no universal human truth at all; instead, importance would be attributed to "geographical" truths based on blood ties, whose origin is not in heaven but in earth and blood. For example, there would be one "logic" and worldview on American soil, and another on Eastern European soil. The visions of one group of human beings united by blood ties would be different from those that arise from the blood ties of another group. Different gods and demons, ascending from the blood fumes, would reveal themselves to different human groups and assume the direction of those groups with oracular authority. People would speak of the "awakening" of the gods and ancestors from the past, and the guidance of those gods and ancestors would be followed with implicit obedience. But such events did not occur—at least, they happened only partially and in a dulled and weakened way. The reason why this could not happen lay in the event when sacred blood flowed onto hallowed soil. With the Mystery of Golgotha, when the blood of Jesus Christ flowed onto the ground, a force was planted in human blood and in the Earth's soil; it counteracted the demonic element in the blood and the enslaving influence of the subterranean spheres that works through the soil. This counterinfluence causes human blood to carry not only the subjective illusions of demonic airs, but also the objective impulse of conscience. In addition, this influence not only robs the ground of its enslaving power, but it also speaks of nature's yearning and hope for redemption through humankind. Through it, human blood receives the capacity to reflect moral and spiritual truth, just as natural water reflects the sky; the ground, however, "receives blood," and thus the capacity of "groaning together with the whole creation." John's Gospel refers to this mystery of the Christ influence on blood and earth: "But one of the soldiers with a spear pierced his side, and forthwith came there out blood and water. And he that saw it bare record, and his record is true: and he knoweth that he saith true, that ye might believe" (John 19:34–35).

For humanity, however, this influence on blood and earth means the restoration of equilibrium in these regions and hence the establishment of *freedom*. Now it depends upon human beings themselves whether they will yield to the enslaving influence of earth and the phantasm-producing influence of blood, or whether they will view the whole earthly globe as the victim of the fall of humanity and make blood the bearer of conscience. The "fantastic wisdom" of Gondishapur no longer has power to simply overwhelm humankind with coercive force; it appears (and then incompletely) only when and to the degree that human beings cooperate with it.

The establishment of equilibrium (and with it, human freedom) is not the only result of the Mystery of Golgotha. It was also the beginning of a gradual retrieval of Lucifer's territory. The spirit who had severed this territory from the region of the hierarchies of good now experienced an inner conversion through the Mystery of Golgotha. True, that conversion initially concerned only Lucifer himself and not, say, the luciferic influence in human beings—which is still active in the old direction and can be changed only by human beings themselves. The prince of the luciferic hosts changed his course, however, because of the Mystery of Golgotha. The conversion took place within him when, looking at the crucifixion on Golgotha, it pierced him with the insight that it was in fact he who should have experienced those sufferings. And now the other was bearing them *in his place.* Pierced by that pain, a ceaseless longing for suffering and humiliation arose in Lucifer at that hour. To that proud spirit—the personification of the shining spirit of beauty—nothing since then has become more hateful than the incense of admiration for his character, which burns him like fire, and nothing has been more desirable than the recognition of his wrongful acts and the humiliation of his spirit, which is as balm to him and soothes his pain. He is filled with a passionate hope that at some time in the cosmos he may be allowed to experience martyrdom equal to that of the other. This hope of Lucifer was reflected in world history when, during the first centuries following the Mystery of Golgotha, there was a great wave of enthusiasm among people for suffering martyrdom. During those first Christian centuries, large groups of people were inspired by a current of willingness to be martyred and a yearning for martyrdom. Behind that aspiration was a longing to suffer as Jesus Christ had suffered; behind that longing was Lucifer, with his hope of a martyrdom to equal that of Christ. The spirit of self-aware beauty had recognized that the truest and highest beauty is sacrifice, and that when beauty continues to nurture itself after having seen the suffering of the righteous one of God, it is really ugliness.

This inner conversion of Lucifer began the retrieval of luciferic territory for the work of goodness, and with it sealed the fate of Ahriman, the "prince of this world."

## The Defeat of Ahriman

Before the Mystery of Golgotha, Ahriman's "hope" (or, more accurately, his expectation, since he has no soul) was to karmically "inherit" Lucifer's whole territory. All that is luciferic always leads (when carried through to a certain degree) to what is ahrimanic. The animosity of the luciferic for all that is ahrimanic is really animosity toward its own karmic future. Such hatred, however, constitutes one of the strongest of bonds, and this applies not only to spiritual beings, but also to human beings and nations of Earth. Even on Earth, those who represent the karmic future of others are the people and groups of people who are hated most. And this bond grows ever closer until the luciferic has slipped over into the realm of the ahrimanic to be swallowed by it. Devouring all that is, or has become, luciferic would mean not only that Ahriman's plan has been successful, but also that his natural urges have all been fulfilled. Ahriman would be merely a "spiritual machine" if he were unable to constantly devour other beings and forces as a kind of substitute for the soul life he lacks. The fact that Ahriman can have any living experience to fill his inner void is owed to his ability to devour. Because of Lucifer's inner conversion, however, not only has a limit been placed on this activity of Ahriman, but also the boundaries of the area in which he can devour have begun to contract. New luciferic beings continually attach themselves to Lucifer's view, thus diminishing the effective sphere of Ahriman's activity. Hence it is a fact that, *cosmically*, Ahriman has already been conquered in principle. Seen from the earthly perspective, however, this is not the situation. The decision of whether Ahriman will be overcome in the earthly (physical elemental) sphere does not belong to luciferic spirits but to human beings, on whose freedom it now depends.

Ahriman, however, cannot be overcome either by *attacking* the ahrimanic element or by trying to convert it externally. The ahrimanic influence can neither be coerced by force nor inwardly transformed. The point is to *recognize* the ahrimanic element, not fear it. A courageous glance of recognition is the sword that limits Ahriman in the outer world, and the courage of self-knowledge is the force that renders the ahrimanic double powerless in the human subconscious. As for Ahriman, the point is not to grant him power over the soul, and—with the weapon of recognition— to destroy all his attacks through uncompromising human courage. Stability and rocklike firmness are needed, not attacks or a desire to flee from ahrimanic onslaughts. The ahrimanic element is powerless if it cannot influence human beings with either fear or bribery. In such a condition of powerlessness, it receives no nourishment and disappears from the region, where it can no longer exercise power. Ahriman will be defeated, because he will not be nourished. His power in the universe looks enormous and overwhelming, but it is merely an illusion designed either to bribe or to frighten. Nonetheless, it is an *objective* illusion made up of *actual* external phenomena, but one that immediately shows itself as such when confronted by courageous recognition and incorruptibility—that is, a refusal to compromise, since all compromise is the result of bribery.

This has been shown as a fact of cosmic experience in the spiritual event of the Mystery of Golgotha traditionally called Christ's "descent into Hell." Just as the agony on the cross led to the inner conversion of Lucifer, likewise, the *kind* of death that Jesus Christ suffered led to a revelation of the secret of Ahriman. It was, as it were, an unmasking, laying bare the disguise of Ahriman's power both for the spiritual world and for those of Earth who stand in a right relationship to the spiritual world. This occurred because Jesus Christ died in a way different from any other human being. When human beings die, for about three days they are confronted by their life tableau. This is what they see during that period, and it conceals from them the *abyss*—the kingdom of Ahriman in the subterranean spheres. Through the goodness of the gods, before birth human beings are protected from seeing the luciferic sphere; similarly, at the moment of death they are protected by that same divine goodness from seeing the sphere of Ahriman. Before birth, the luciferic temptation to remain in the spiritual world is staved off by the sight of the karmic tableau of one's upcoming life; likewise, at death the soul is preserved from the confusion and perplexity of seeing the ahrimanic sphere when the tableau of the past life unfolds like a screen.

At his death, Jesus Christ *renounced* that vision of the tableau; he surrendered it to humanity, and it became the essence of what the disciples later "remembered" in the light of the Pentecostal flame. It was also what the evangelists contemplated from different viewpoints—the vision from which they wrote their records. The normal life tableau is given over to the gods—angels, archangels, and archai—by those who have seen it; the life tableau of Jesus Christ was not given over to the gods but to humanity—first to the apostles, the "eyewitnesses and ministers of the word" (Luke 1:2) and the initiates. Since then it has been the common karmic property of humankind; it is the unwritten "fifth Gospel," which can be read in the aura of the Earth.[2] A time will come, however, when (on the day of Earth's death) all of humankind will have the vision of this tableau; contemplation of it will begin the "final judgment." Thus Jesus Christ, as the representative of humanity, presented humanity with the tableau of his life, showing the human path to the spirit. In doing so, however, he renounced for himself the screen that conceals the subterranean spheres of "Hell." It is recorded that, at the hour of his death, "the veil of the temple was rent in twain" (Mark 15:38); this indicated that a new karmic balance had been established between good and evil when the curtain was lifted from Hell. Then, too, the curtain (or "veil") was lifted from the "Holy of Holies." Now, however, the consequence of this new karmic relationship is this: when the mystery of good and the secret of evil have both become available to human experiential knowledge, goodness *gains* by being known, while evil loses by being recognized as such. This is the essential difference between good and evil: good gains by being recognized; evil loses when it is recognized.

The most sublime act of cognitive courage occurred when Jesus Christ renounced the "veil of Hell" and (instead of witnessing the life tableau) descended with his whole being into the darkness of the subterranean spheres. That "descent into Hell" was an event that no human speech can describe. There is nothing more unsettling than the disappearance of Jesus Christ into the darkness of the lower spheres, out of sight of the beings watching from the spiritual world. A breathless expectation was maintained in the spiritual world; the world of the hierarchies became silent and breathless in expectation of either the most triumphant victory or the most disastrous catastrophe. During those days, only one thought and one question filled the whole world of the hierarchies: Will he return? Will he emerge from the abyss? Again, all human speech is powerless to give even the faintest reflection of the cosmic exultation that ensued when the risen Christ reappeared from the darkness of that abyss in the realm of twilight. Cosmic Easter was celebrated in the realms of heaven, a cosmic festival that continues for all time as the archetype of all human festivals on Earth.

That event proved cosmically and historically that Ahriman, even in his own kingdom, is powerless when faced with the wise courage of Christ—the courage that he pours into the souls of those spiritually united with him and his work. In the same way, the road has been laid and walked for knowledge of the secrets of the subterranean spheres; since that time, the ahrimanic secret of the interior of the Earth has been available to experiential knowledge. And beyond knowledge, the Earth's interior became accessible to the influence of the Christ impulse and its forces. The "gardener" who appeared to the woman made clairvoyant by grief was not a "gardener" from only *her* perspective. In a deeper sense, he was *truly* a gardener, because he had acquired the power to cause the Earth's soil to produce the fruits of goodness. From that time forward, the highest human initiates have likewise become "gardeners"; they work for the well-being of humanity—and not just the direct concerns of humanity, but also those that reach indirectly through nature and Earth's soil.

Jesus Christ's "descent into Hell" was the act that overcame Ahriman—not through superiority of power (that was not the issue), but by exposing the extent of Ahriman's true power over an alert and uncompromising consciousness. Since Jesus Christ walked that path, it has been proven that Ahriman's work in the world is hopeless, so long as people are willing to recognize and resist it. This attitude will continue into the future among those who do succumb to Ahriman, and in this way Ahriman will be "shackled." He will no longer have a point of attack and thus will become ineffective and passive. There will no longer be any motive for kindling activity, even in his consciousness, and (during the future Venus existence) Ahriman will sink into a kind of sleep. Of course, this will not be the end of his destiny, but, for the purpose of this particular meditation, when Ahriman "falls asleep," it may be viewed the final stage of human conflict with him. Ahriman will then enter the realm of karma that is fulfilled in him. Ahriman—who has always tried to lull human consciousness into a spiritual sleep and whose whole work was based on the hope that human beings would not be alert—will himself succumb to sleep, during which the things that happen to him will be the karmic counterpart of what he intended to do with the beings who became his prey.

In principle, therefore, the fate of the ahrimanic element is already sealed through the descent into Hell and the resurrection; the prince of this world is defeated.

## The Risen One

The risen one was the being who united in himself the experiences of the heavens, earthly life and suffering, and the subterranean spheres. These three kinds of experience in him represented our nervous, rhythmic, and metabolic systems. For us, however, they are *systems;* they involve an unconscious, autonomic aspect, whereas the body of the risen Christ consisted solely of moral, conscious currents. His risen body had nothing mechanical or autonomic in it, because its ahrimanic element had been overcome. Nonetheless, his body had not become merely a soul and thus alien to the realm of earthly activity, because its luciferic element had been transformed. It was, in any case, as capable of activity and influence as the physical body of any living person. Likewise, it was at least as full of moral soul life as the spirit body of anyone who had died and entered the devachan state. In the risen body, the gulf between life and death has been bridged; it is death become life. It bears inwardly the "tree of life" of the paradise legend; and those who "eat of its fruit" overcome the antithesis between life and death.

There is no other means of gaining an understanding of the resurrection body than by continuous, deep meditation. It is impossible to gain inwardly clear and factual knowledge of the resurrection body through concepts and conceptual relationships drawn from "ordinary" experience (that is, experience in the sphere that lies on *this* side of the threshold of resurrection). Thus a path of intimate spiritual concentration must be adopted—one that may have to be walked for many years before inner comprehension of the resurrection body shines out. We can begin with a passage that occurs in definite connection with this in John's Revelation: "These things saith the Amen, the faithful and true witness, the beginning of the creation of God" (Revelation 3:14). In repeated meditative concentration, this sentence may do more toward understanding the resurrection body than any abstract definition. This passage will be found especially fruitful if it is concentrated into the word *amen.* Thus a start may be made from the human Saturn body, which consists entirely of the warmth of will, "the beginning of the creation of God." Again, the object of concentration may be the fact that only this saturnine body has been, from the beginning, a witness to the whole cosmic evolution. Finally—after having studied it with respect to *space* and *time,* its nature may be considered in detail in relation to the word *amen,* which expresses its being. The special point here is moral concentration of the word's phonetic sound. The individual sounds of which it consists can lead to inner recognition of the individual currents of the resurrection body. Thus, the *a* sound leads to understanding the "risen head," or the current of relationship to the cosmic heights. The *m* sound reveals the "risen hands," or the current in cosmic space. The *e* sound leads to the inner life of the resurrection body, and the *n* sound reveals the force of its denial of evil—the strength of its resistance to evil—as shown in the descent into Hell.

The individual forces indicated by the individual sounds manifest with special power in particular situations of the life and work of Jesus Christ. The *n* force was especially revealed in the descent into Hell, and likewise the *e* force was revealed in the passion, especially the night in Gethsemane. The *m* force showed itself particularly in the healings and miracles, and the Jordan baptism is the particular point at which the *a* force is clearly perceptible. Thus the word *amen* is the epitome of the work of Christ, just as the resurrection body is the epitome of the cosmic evolution. This significance of *amen* was known to the evangelists; John summarizes his Gospel by concluding with this word, which holds the contents of all those books that must still be written in order to give a complete description of Christ's work—books that have never been written because "even the world itself could not contain them."

This word thus forms a link in the body of work with what these meditations on the New Testament offer as a contribution to Christology. The next, and final, chapter will be devoted to the Pentecost, an event that is not just the fruit of events recorded in the Gospels, but also an introduction to the future events of the Apocalypse.

# Chapter 12

# Pentecost

## The Organ of the Pentecostal Revelation

In our meditation on the Mystery of Golgotha, we tried to convey the spiritual fact that, as well as the written records of the evangelists, there is an "unwritten gospel," the life tableau of Jesus Christ, which has remained, in a sense, within the Earth's ether body. This indestructible and ineffaceable Gospel is the eternal source of knowledge of the Christ event nineteen hundred years ago, as it can be known on the path of *imaginative* vision, *inspired* knowledge, and *intuitive* experience. This "unwritten gospel," however, is not only important for the present and future; it also had tremendous significance for the past. Indeed, it became important immediately following the Mystery of Golgotha. During the forty days between the Mystery of Golgotha and the Ascension, the disciples experienced, in effect, scenes in the life tableau of Jesus Christ—the "teaching of the risen one." These were the instructions given to the disciples by Jesus Christ during the forty-day period after his resurrection; they included pictures that passed before their souls, each evoking another that represented a scene in the life and work of Jesus Christ *before* the Mystery of Golgotha, associating itself, in a sense, with the reconstructed pictures of the past. Consequently, pairs of pictures continued to arise before the souls of the disciples—one picture a revelation of the risen one and another from his life and work before the Mystery of Golgotha. It was always felt that the former involved the higher meaning and fulfillment, so to speak, of the latter. Thus the risen one led the souls of his disciples through the scenes of his life tableau, but in such a way that each scene was also experienced as an *imagination* of a higher spiritual truth. It was actually a course of instruction that taught them the essence of the unwritten gospel.

Thus it happened that the teaching they were receiving through *imagination* came to an end. The pictures vanished from the disciples' experience, along with the figure of the risen one. This happened on the day of ascension. That day was the beginning of a sorrowful time for the disciples; they felt forsaken and saddened. The world of imagery, having so much meaning, was blotted out, and their souls were plunged into silent darkness. Their grief during this time cannot really be compared to any pain we may experience in daily life. It was not the result of affliction or trouble but the absence of all that enlivened and motivated their souls. In such situations, *positive* suffering actually brings alleviation. Sharp pain is certainly an experience, but when life is merely an aching emptiness it is not really an experience but a soul condition that feels like a void. The disciples' experience of *soul death* preceded the event of Pentecost; it was a necessary preparation for it, since the *resurrection of the soul* during that event was an experience that could only follow the soul's death. That painful preparation for the Pentecost was alleviated, however, by one thing; the pain was shared by *all* of the disciples. Their feeling of loneliness was a spiritual experience; in a human sense, however, it united them as a group in the deepest way. Shared grief is the strongest means of binding people together, and the grief that the disciples shared would be the bond needed to unite them into the organ of Pentecostal revelation.

The group of disciples had to be unified in a special way to accomplish the revelation. That union had to be based not only on a common attitude, but also on a sense of community in the most profound depths of sentient life. The sentient bodies of the disciples had to be linked like the twelve currents of the suprasensory human heart in order to form the group into a single "organ," one that corresponded to the inner structure of the suprasensory heart. The resurrection of the soul must be experienced in the heart, but one that represents humanity. Such a heart had to be prepared; it was a heart of humanity, made up of a group of men whose sentient bodies were united through the suffering of a common grief, much the way the petals of a flower are joined. At the time of the Pentecost, therefore, the twelve apostles represented a twelve-petalled flower in which the individual "petals" were arranged around a central point. That point was represented by the one who occupied the central position as the thirteenth among that group. In ecclesiastical tradition, that figure is named and described as Mary, the Mother of Jesus; in the Gnostic esoteric tradition she is called the Virgin Sophia. "Mary Sophia" was the "heart of the heart"; she represented the central point in the circle of twelve, which became, at the hour of Pentecost, the "heart of humanity." During the early post-Christian centuries, and later on during the Middle Ages, knowledge was always present in regard to Mary Sophia's central importance in the circle of the twelve during the Pentecost. That knowledge was expressed even in the arts. The Pentecost is represented, for example, by a miniature in the Syrian Codex (A.D. 586), preserved in the Laurentian Library in Florence (see next page).

Mary is shown standing among the twelve, with the Holy Spirit in the form of a dove hovering above her head pouring a stream of revelation directly upon her, while the resulting tongues of fire shoot up over the heads of the twelve. Mary Sophia is represented in a bright purple robe (*maphorion*) over a blue tunic (*chiton*). The whole group is surrounded by a design of flowers in bloom, while above is the enclosing dome of an inverted chalice. This picture of the circle of twelve with Mary Sophia in the center leads us to a question that must be answered before the Pentecost can be understood: What is the nature of Mary Sophia and her role in bringing about the Pentecostal revelation?

## Sophia and the Pentecost

In our Old Testament meditations, we discussed the nature of the Sophia in relation to Solomon and to the Jordan baptism. There is no intention of repeating what was said there, but we must try to carry our understanding of the Sophia being a step further and deepen it. Actually, it is important not only to further our understanding of the cosmic nature of the Sophia, but also to evoke a feeling for the *tragedy* in the spiritual history of this being. Spiritual beings are not mere "principles," but living entities who have a kind of biography of their own; their biographies, however, extend through many thousands of years, whereas human biographies are limited to decades.

The first encounter with the reality of Sophia in our age occurs in human thinking when it strives to comprehend the divine Trinity as the cosmic revelation of a unity of three different principles. The recognition of the *unity* of the Trinity revealed in the cosmos is an event in human thinking that extends beyond the mere life of thought. It points to a meeting on the far side of it—one that favorably determines that thought life but is not really a product of it. This meeting in the depths of thinking may be the first experience of the Sophia's reality. In particular, the Sophia manifests for human consciousness by bringing about the harmony of all spiritual hierarchies, through which, in effect, the Father, Son, and Holy Spirit reveal themselves. What is called "synthesis" in the practice of abstract thinking becomes an experience of cognitive knowledge when the ascending thought life comes into contact with the Sophia being. Sophia causes cognitive perception of harmony in the spiritual, divine world; she does this in a literal sense since she is a being of *inspiration,* with whom the ascending human thought can meet. Before such an encounter can occur, however, consciousness must ascend (if only for a moment) two stages above ordinary objective consciousness. That ascent is needed because Sophia is actually without speech, both for objective consciousness and for *imagination* consciousness. She has no speech in these spheres because she does not possess the force of *imagination,* the faculty for creating *imaginations.* She does not possess this faculty because Lucifer robbed her of it. This happened during the period of Earth's spiritual history when the fall of humanity took place. Lucifer took for himself Sophia's *imaginations* by using them himself instead of serving her. And he used her *imaginations* as the materials needed to create a world.

This world, however, was to be constructed from Sophia's *imaginations* so that it would not reveal the harmony of the divine world but the grandeur of Lucifer himself. Thus Lucifer transformed the *imaginations* of Sophia into their opposite, and a world of *lies* arose. This world of lies became the so-called luciferic sphere that surrounds the Earth; clouds are the most external physically sensible expression of that sphere. The luciferic sphere is a *false* paradise, or false spiritual world, the source of those visions of egoistic bliss that manifest so frequently in popular religious life. The danger of that sphere is not so much that it encourages the egoism so deeply rooted in human nature, but, because it is actually made up of Sophia's *imaginations,* or pictures of comprehensive cosmic truth, it can have a tremendously corrupting effect on the faculties of knowledge that are not fully awake. A cosmic lie is not just a wild fantasy, but abused truth. And the truth of the *imaginative* revelation of Sophia was abused so that it was first broken into pieces and then reconstructed in a different pattern. The shining wisdom of God was changed into a glittering garment for Lucifer.

In this way, Isis Sophia, the "Wisdom of God," was killed for the lower worlds, since Sophia became a being without speech in regard to the two lower realms of existence. The creative force of *imagination* was taken from her, and, as a result, she became a colorless, ineffective being, barred from any activity in relation to earthly events. The figure of the *mater dolorosa,* or mourning mother, is the best expression of the tragic state of Sophia. She is generous in nature and inwardly filled with the gifts of wisdom, but she cannot give those gifts to human consciousness unless it rises to her sphere. Sophia cannot reach the lower worlds because she lost the *imagination* force, which was stolen by Lucifer.

The gifts that the Sophia bears within her are quite different from those of other hierarchical beings. She carries concentrated inner wisdom that is not only light of the Godhead shining through her being and not just the vista of the cosmic chronicle, or akashic record. The wisdom to which this being owes her name is neither a direct revelation of a higher divinity nor the epitome of the cosmic memory from the akashic record as presented to the gaze of hierarchic beings; rather, it is the memory of soul ascending from within; it is the wisdom of the soul's pure creativity and, at the same time, such that the whole experience of the past cosmos arises from the inner being as the primal intention, or "plan," for the present cosmos. Hence, Sophia is, for humanity, the spiritual archetype of the soul—not just in the sense of the tragic destiny of the soul growing more and more mute in the world, but also in the sense of that concentrated wisdom that is only possible in and through the soul. The tragic path of Sophia, however, has a counterpart in the human soul, since the human soul, too, has been deprived of the power of forming truth; the power of *imagination* has become subjective fantasy with an inner tendency to invent. Thus, the soul's capacity to inwardly imagine has lost the value of truth. The soul has grown silent, swathed in a sheath of egoistic interests that have overtaken the original force of *imagination.*

Thus there is a similarity of destiny between the true human soul being on Earth and Sophia's soul being in the spiritual world, In earlier times, human beings were aware of this similarity; consequently, an astral (or sentient) body was so purified from the sheath of egoistic interests that the true soul being could come to expression as the "Virgin Sophia." In this sense, Mary, the Mother of Jesus, was also the "Virgin Sophia." Because of extremely complicated influences and experiences coming from the spiritual world, Mary had an astral body that was so purified it could receive the revelations of Sophia and pour them out again as *inspirations* of the soul. This faculty was the very reason why, at the time of Pentecostal revelation, the Virgin Mary occupied the central position in the circle of the twelve. Without her, the revelation would have been *only* spiritual; there would have been twelve prophets, united in the Holy Spirit as was ancient prophecy. Through the cooperation of Mary, however, something more could happen; the disciples' *hearts* beat in harmony with hers while they experienced the Pentecostal revelation as personal human conviction. Through *this* experience, they became not prophets but specifically apostles. There is a great spiritual difference between prophecy and the mission of the apostles; a prophet proclaims spiritual revelation impersonally, whereas an apostle reveals the Holy Spirit within the soul. This was possible only because the spiritual revelation of the Pentecost could become soul through the Virgin Mary and be transmitted by her *as soul* to the disciples.

What took form in the earthly human sphere became a means to express what took place in the spiritual world. A great event occurred in the spiritual world at the hour of Pentecost; the Sophia's silence ended, and she regained her ability to reveal herself through speech. Moreover, she could reveal herself in such a way that not only could certain initiates rise to her sphere and receive her inspirations, but she herself could also descend and pour her influence into the ordinary day consciousness of earthly human beings. It was not that the Sophia had been reached by a certain group of human beings (which had happened before); the point now was that for the first time, on her side, she could reach down to a group of earthly human beings. This was important, because at the Pentecost Lucifer's opposition was overcome for the first time since the fall of humanity. At Pentecost, the barrier Lucifer had erected between Sophia and the realm of human day consciousness was cleared from the path. Union with the sphere of earthly destiny, which had been in bondage to Lucifer, could be restored. And this was possible because, on the one hand, there were again a number of imaginations present that had not been touched by Lucifer's influence, and, on the other hand, Lucifer conducted the revelation of the Sophia, undistorted, through his sphere of lies by means of the dedication of his whole being.

The following diagram may promote a clearer understanding of these matters. Although not complete (since the whole process is even more complicated), this sketch gives a picture of the cooperation among various forces at the time of Pentecost. It shows the interrelationship of the four regions of consciousness. In the area of waking

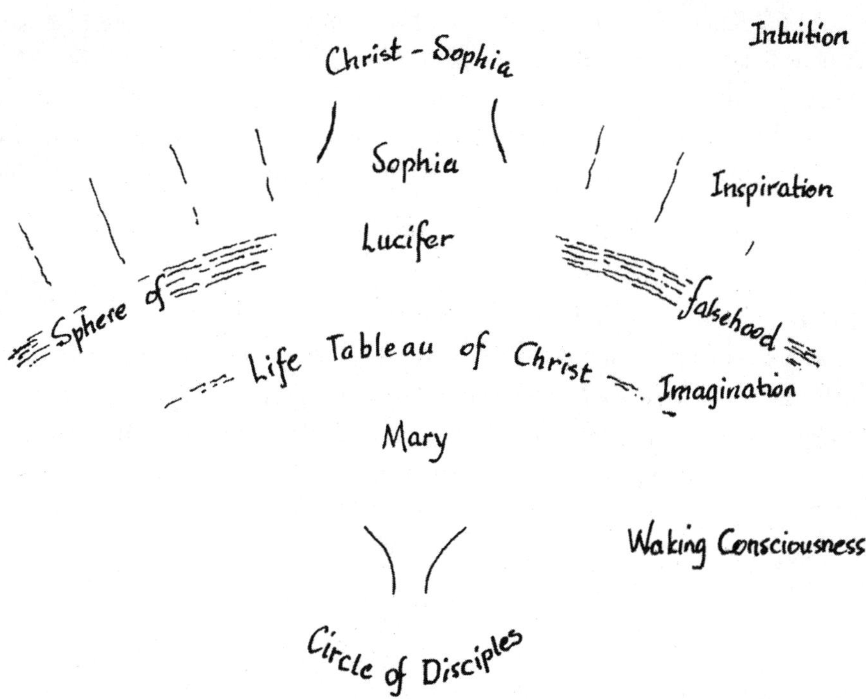


consciousness (below) is the circle of the twelve, with the open chalice in their midst that represents the Virgin Mary. Immediately above the group, in the area of *imagination* (at the boundary of waking consciousness), we see the life tableau that Christ left behind. That tableau replaces the stolen *imaginations* of Sophia, now appearing above in the area of Lucifer. It consists of *imaginations* that, because they were actual physical events as well, are not susceptible to luciferic influence. At the same time, they are the "missing link" between the areas of waking consciousness and Sophia's *inspiration.*

Then, between the area of the Sophia's *inspiration* and the *imaginations* of the life tableau of Christ, we find the luciferic sphere itself. At the time of the Pentecost event, however, that sphere became pervious to the Sophia revelation descending from above. This happened because of Lucifer's inner conversion at the Mystery of Golgotha. A penitent Lucifer became the humble bridge over the realm of lies he had created in the past. Thus the path of Sophia revelation led through the realm of Lucifer and, in fact, through the being of Lucifer himself. At the hour of Pentecost, Lucifer surrendered entirely to the Sophia impulse; he united with it and led it through his own being down to the life tableau of Christ, where it reached human souls. In reality, the influence of Sophia united with that of Lucifer. It is the unified influence of these two beings that John's Gospel calls the *Paraclete,* or the Comforter. The Paraclete is not just the Holy Spirit as the third hypostasis of the divine Trinity, but a *revelation* of the third hypostasis such as was effected by the combined influences of Sophia and Lucifer when Lucifer humbly submitted to serve the Sophia impulse.

Lucifer's attitude of service toward the Sophia impulse not only helped Sophianic revelation reach human souls undisturbed, but also led to the fact that Lucifer radiated an inspiring flame of enthusiasm and joy. The Paraclete was able to manifest as an effective reality only because the spirit who had brought about the isolation of souls now brought the enthusiasm for the reunion of souls. There is a hint of this in the Acts of the Apostles, when we are told that several bystanders received the impression that the apostles were "full of new wine." The Dionysian-like enthusiasm that was present led bystanders to associate their exaltation with the sort produced in the Bacchus cult with the help of wine. It was a misunderstanding, of course, but such a perception points to the significant fact that enthusiasm among the apostles was evoked with the cooperation of Lucifer.

Above the realm of Lucifer (returning the diagram), in the area of *inspiration,* the Sophia being is represented as an inverted chalice. In the area of *intuition,* she is united with the Christ and, through this union, brings about in the spiritual world what she must also bring about in the realm of earthly humanity—the realization of Christ's words, "Ye in me, and I in you."[1] The first purpose of the Mystery of Golgotha is that the Christ, who first stood *outside* as the disciples' master, now passed *into* their innermost souls. The path that Christ had to walk would lead from an outer position to living within. This happened at the Pentecost when the Christ entered the disciples' souls. And he did this in such a way that he was, as it were, born a second time; through the "heavenly Mother" Sophia, he was born in the souls of the disciples. Thus the "I" being of the disciples was filled with the Christ, who became the *Kyrios,* the group "I," as it were, of the disciples. That "I" was sheathed in the communal astral body of the Sophia; in the ether body, however, they bore the combined experiences of the life tableau of Christ; and, *physically,* the disciples represented a circle formed to become the means of the Pentecost revelation, with Mary as its center, whose esoteric name was the "Virgin Sophia."

## The Pentecost as the Realization of the New Testament

The theme of the Old Testament is the preparation and realization of the advent of Christ in the human body; that of the New Testament is the advent of Christ in the human "I." The "new law" is, in fact, no law, but the formation of the essence of a free human "I." This cannot happen unless the human "I" absorbs the being that is the "new law." This absorption must involve something that does not arise externally, but that comes from the depths of the world in which the human "I" is rooted. A plant receives its sap from the soil in which it is rooted, and likewise the being of the Christ impulse should enter the human "I" from the "soil" in which the "I" is rooted. The *means* to effect this in the disciples is the essence of Christ's farewell speeches as recorded in chapters 8 to 17 of John's Gospel. The gist of what was said is this: I was *with* you as your master; now I go to the Father, so that I may be *in* you, as the Father is in me. Consequently, the point was that the "I" being of Jesus Christ would pass into the "I" being of others; the

"I" that lived in the one human form must find a way to the inner "I" of others without encroaching, in the slightest, on the freedom of those others' "I" being.

Passing into the being of another "I" is possible only through the sphere that is the primal cause and the original dwelling of all human "I" being—the realm of the Father. From the Father, all human "I" being originated; and only from the Father realm can any influence be exercised within human "I" that is in keeping with the principle of freedom. This is why Christ had to take the path that leads, by way of the Father, into the human "I." Outwardly, this path was that of death; inwardly, however, it meant complete union with the Father. The path of death led to the resurrection; the Father path, however, led to the Pentecost. Death and the Father are two aspects of a single mystery; similarly, the resurrection and the Pentecost were two aspects of the Mystery of Golgotha. Indeed, the resurrection was the victory over Ahriman in the body, and the Pentecost was the victory over Lucifer in the soul. The resurrection meant a resurrection of the body, and the Pentecost meant resurrection of the soul.

Pentecost was resurrection of the soul in the sense that it brought to life wisdom that had united with the soul. Soul life did not arise out of mere feelings, but from powerful perceptions of the Christ mystery—perceptions that arise from the deepest ground of the heart. The real meaning of *heart* can be understood by studying the Pentecost; the common understanding of *heart* has the same relationship to the heart's experience of Pentecost as the Moon does to the Sun. The twilight of the heart's hopes and fears was replaced by the shining daylight of *knowing love.* The imperturbable inner certainty that the apostles possessed concerning the Christ mystery was not based on the authority of either the outer or the inner senses, but on their experience of the reality of love. Because the apostles experienced this reality in their souls, they also knew ways and means by which it had and would continue to influence the world. They knew, too, that what they now felt in their souls was the same experience that lived in Jesus Christ when he preached the Sermon on the Mount and performed the healings. They knew, likewise, that this force should live, through the Mystery of Golgotha, in human beings and overcome loneliness and death.

Out of this experience, the apostles spoke to those bystanders; and they all heard the disciples speak in their own language. This was possible because, in the apostles' speech, the divisions brought about by Lucifer had been overcome. Because Lucifer was vanquished during Pentecost, it was possible to speak in a way that was a kind of resurrection of original human speech. It was the risen *soul* that spoke; it used the language not of divided nations, but the language of the human soul. To understand the nature of the Pentecostal language, it is not enough to have a general idea of the victory over the divisions brought about by Lucifer. The true nature of the process by which that new language became possible in the human organism must be comprehended in a concrete way.

To get a more distinct view of this process, we must begin with the fact that human beings share their outer existence with the mineral world, their organic life with the plant realm, and their movement with the animal world. Nonetheless, human beings are distinguished from those three kingdoms by having speech, the fourth externally manifested attribute. Through this attribute, another member (aside from the physical, ether, and astral bodies) is revealed in human beings: the "I." This makes it possible for human beings not only to participate in physical existence by living and moving about, but also to *speak*. Although the human "I" is the actual source of the speech faculty, the existence of language nonetheless depends on the body's threefold makeup. The astral body is needed to combine the predicative with the attributive, the verb with the adjective; the ether body is needed to connect the verb with the substantive, or noun; and finally, the organs of the physical body are needed to make spoken language sound in the air. The speech impulse of the "I" passes through these three members of the body to reveal itself as spoken language; in the process, it not only influences those bodies but is also influenced by them. By making it as far as the physical body, the impulse is greatly transformed. In this metamorphosis, the predicative element in the astral body is weakened by the influence of the area of egoistic likes and dislikes, and by the unconscious likes and dislikes in this sphere that exercise a restrictive influence on speech. This restrictive influence then results in the speech impulse in the ether body that takes on a cultural or national tendency, eventually expressed in the sounds of a certain language through the organs of the physical body.

Thus, through the various languages, the original purely human speech impulse becomes a one-sided and relative phenomenon; this is because of Lucifer's influence in the human organism. If this influence is overcome, however (as it was, for example, at Pentecost), the speech impulse is freed from the restrictive influence of the organism to the degree that it is no longer forced to flow into the current of a single language; rather, it can move freely through the whole circle of human languages. This means that the speech impulse of the human "I" can contact the realm of influence governed by the whole circle of spirits of language (the luciferic archangels) to the extent that it has first acquired the faculty of uniting with the sphere of influence governed by folk spirits (the normal archangels). It was just this union with the whole circle of archangels (or folk spirits) that the twelve apostles established at Pentecost. This was possible because it is the host of archangels that spreads the revelation of the Christ mystery among all nations. What formed the essence of the Pentecostal revelation for human consciousness is poured into the life of the nations by the archangels, distributed according to the several parts or "words." Since the Pentecost, it has been the task of archangels, as folk spirits, to direct the flow of the Christ influence into the life of nations. The sum of their activity is the full Pentecostal revelation of the Christ mystery as experienced by archangelic consciousness, whereas the sum of the twelve apostles' knowledge at Pentecost is the full Pentecostal revelation of the Christ mystery as experienced by human consciousness. Hence, it was possible for the circle of apostles to unite with the circle of archangels. The Pentecostal revelation was an event not just in human consciousness, but also in the consciousness of folk spirits. Thus a circle was formed that received the "apostolate" of Christ. Then, just as the earthly human circle formed around one human being (Mary), the circle of archangels enclosed one archangelic being (Sophia).

The circle of human beings below and the circle of fire spirits (archangels) above together form the archetype of what is made real to human beings and nations by the New Testament. It is the true archetype of the *ecclesia,* the church, whose task is to bind humankind, as well as the beings of the spiritual hierarchies, as a unity in Christ. This unity is not meant to come about by means of organizations and edicts, but through the living flame of Pentecostal revelation. The essence of Pentecostal revelation is not just a comprehensive, intensified knowledge of the Christ mystery, but also the genesis of an archetype of every true community through experience of that knowledge.

Historically, the reality of the Pentecost was behind the *idea* of the church; that reality (though the impression of it gradually faded) became later the idea for a community of Christians that embraces all nations. The Pentecost was the real experience of freedom in world history—freedom united with the fraternity of humble equality in face of the sublime, all-embracing Christ mystery. Later in world history, however, that experience was no longer an idea, but the distorted caricature disguised as that monstrous human catastrophe, the French Revolution. That revolution was just the opposite of the Pentecost: a community of human beings, aware of their rights (*Ie droit humain*) gathered around the figure of *Glory*. What Mary Sophia was for the Pentecost event became the imaginary figure of Glory for the French Revolution; and the complete silence that pervaded the souls of those disciples who had passed through emptiness and loneliness now became a clamorous demand for rights.

The fact that the Pentecost became the object of both abstraction and distortion is simply an expression of its importance for the whole history of post-Christian times. The Pentecost reveals the true mission of the post-Christian period; everything revolves around the understanding, preparation, and realization of that event, as well as on the fading of its impression and the disguise and distortion of its outline. Because it is the mission of the fifth post-Atlantean epoch (the sixth epoch, the philadelphic, will be based on the Pentecost), it will be the object of every assault from the forces that try to accomplish other purposes. To understand the events of the last great section of world history, it is necessary to know that the Pentecost spirit will continue to wrestle throughout the centuries, constantly engaged in combat with powers that wish to obscure and distort it. This is the fulfillment of the New Testament in the same sense that the advent of Christ in a human body was the fulfillment of the Old Testament. This is because the mission of the New Testament event (the Christ event) is actually to cause the "new law" to shine from within human beings. Christianity is really not a doctrine but an *event* that will receive its full meaning once it has found a place not only on the arena of world history, but also within human hearts.

## THE PENTECOSTAL REVELATION AND THE APOCALYPSE

To understand the struggle of Pentecostal Christianity in the history of the present world and its consequences for the future, we must study closely the underlying essence of the Pentecostal revelation. The main lines of this revelation are indicated by Jesus Christ himself. In his farewell discourse he says: "If I go not away, the Comforter will not come unto you; but if I depart, I will send him unto you. And when he is come, he will reprove the world of sin (*peri hamartias*), and of righteousness (*peri dikaiosynes*), and of judgment (*peri kriseos*): of sin, because they believe not on me; of righteousness, because I go to my Father, and ye see me no more; of judgment, because the prince of this world is judged" (John 16:7–11). These words indicate the three most important things taught by the Holy Spirit of the Pentecostal revelation, the Paraclete. The first article of that teaching concerns the sin of not believing in Christ. This passage of John's Gospel has caused serious misunderstandings, but this is unnecessary if it is apprehended not superficially but in the depth from which Jesus Christ always spoke. What is called "belief" in this passage is a *moral action* of the human "I," not acceptance based on authority. "Belief" or "unbelief" in Christ are virtually synonymous with the presence or absence of the ideal of true humanity. This ideal is not dogma and can never be one, since it is the expression of the moral initiative of the human "I" being. When the human "I," out of its inner moral strength, fails to creatively seek out an ideal of humanity, it ceases to be awake in the moral and spiritual sense. But when the "I" encounters knowledge and truths of the revealed and realized ideal of true humanity and yet fails to accept it, it not only ignores something essential but also commits a morally destructive act. Hence, the point is not that we should "believe in" one thing or another, but that we should make a deeply rooted effort to feel the moral grandeur of the nature and work of Christ. The absorption of the Christ impulse is a free moral act of the "I"; likewise, rebuffing that impulse is an act that must be similarly assessed morally. In this sense, disbelief in Christ is a sin (*hamartia*).

Karma is intended to counterbalance sin through cosmic justice (*dikaiosyne*). But the law of cosmic justice had gone through a profound inner transformation as the result of the Christ event. Formerly, it had been governed by the Father principle, which is revealed in all external events. Thus it also functioned as an outer event in which punishments and compensations were revealed visibly. "An eye for an eye, a tooth for a tooth" was the Old Testament formula of justice—not just in the sense that such justice was *accurate* in number, measure, and weight, but also in the sense that its manifestations played a role in outer events just as clearly as did the misdeeds that brought it about. Thus the far-reaching changes in the administration of karma itself (which was to express the fact that Christ had gone to the Father) was bound to occur. It expressed the fact that he had entered the realm of cosmic judgment and now partook in the administration of cosmic justice—but in such a way that its effects did not make him visible. In New Testament times, karma functioned in such a way that it did not convince people through outer events of cosmic justice and controlling goodness; such conviction had to be gained independently. "Righteousness (or *justice*) because I go to my Father, and ye *see* me no more," is the profound formula of karma's function in the New Testament.[2] Christ is active in karma because he ascended to the Father, but the activity is such that he can be found only by those who seek him freely; he does not reveal himself visibly in outer events. Belief in punishment and reprisal and the fear of reprisal and hope of reward are not forces that lead to finding Christ; only the free love of goodness as such—regardless of any reprisal or reward—leads to knowing and recognizing the Christ who is *invisibly* active in karmic events. But the Christ who rules invisibly in karma will, nevertheless, one day clearly reveal himself as a cosmic judge, once the time has come when the "prince of this world" and all those who have allied their destiny with his must suffer the fate predetermined for them by their actions and aspirations.

The meaning of the third article of Pentecostal revelation, "The prince of this world is judged," contains a world of future events in the spiritual history of humankind. To unravel the processes by which the authority of Christ, in union with the Father, becomes visible in cosmic karma in the far future, we would have to reproduce the whole of John's Apocalypse. John's Revelation is the book of future *judgment,* which will follow the period when the full use or misuse of freedom will be possible, and the apocalyptic future will be the inevitable consequence of that use or misuse. Already determined are the consequences of the "sin of unbelief" and the misunderstanding of justice because the Christ works *invisibly* in it; the judgment has already taken place. This is why the Apocalypse could be written as a book that describes not only the individuals' trials of initiation, but also the future destiny of humankind and the Earth; the Apocalypse could be written because the "judgment" of "the prince of this world" has already taken place.

With these thoughts, the twelve meditations on the New Testament come to a close. They are to be followed by twelve meditations on the Revelation of John, the substance of which will develop the three sentences dealt with here as the essence of the Pentecostal revelation.[3]

## Addendum

The chapter devoted to the Pentecost, which closes our work on the New Testament, is the result of labor in which a group of people participated. It came into being in the spirit of the Whitsuntide (or Pentecost) as the festival of human community. The author owes the substance of this meditation to the cooperation of a group of friends who met in Tallinn, Estonia, to celebrate Whitsuntide together in the year 1938. At this meeting, the meaning and significance of the Pentecost was discussed by various people from different points of view. Part of what was said on that occasion has been included by the author in these meditations. This, of course, does not exempt the author from personal responsibility for what is expressed; it is merely his joyous task to mention the fact that a circle of friends collaborated in the production of this meditation.

# PART THREE

# ANTHROPOSOPHIC MEDITATIONS ON THE APOCALYPSE

# Chapter 1

# Weight, Measure, and Number in the Spiritual History of Humanity

## The Source of John's Revelation

For a long time, those involved in outer, material research have often looked for the sources of John's Revelation. Those sources have been sought in oral traditions, in the apocryphal writings of ancient Christendom, in the documents and traditions of the Judeo-Christian Gnosis, and even in abnormal and fantastic experiences based on atmospheric phenomena.[1] The essence of the Apocalypse itself, however, stands in rigid opposition to all such efforts; in its text the writer explains more than once that he "saw and heard" what it contains "in the spirit." The writer of the Apocalypse never wearies of pointing out unequivocally that the Apocalypse has nothing to do with the spatial and temporal horizontal nature of tradition, hearsay, or plagiarism; rather, he indicates that it manifested simply and solely on the vertical path of revelation from the spiritual world. Thus, the text of the Apocalypse begins with a specific statement about its source and author and the way it originated: "The Revelation of Jesus Christ, which God gave unto him, to shew unto his servants ... and he sent and signified it by his angel unto his servant John" (Revelation 1:1). In a distinct and solemn way, these words describe the *path* by which the Apocalypse came into being. It is one of descent from God to Jesus Christ, from Jesus Christ to the angel of Revelation, from the angel to John, and from John to the readers, hearers, and keepers (*hoi terontes*) of "the words of this prophecy."

It is impossible to get a serious concept of the origin of a document on human spiritual life without taking a serious look at the essence of the document itself. And it really would not be taking the *essence* of the Apocalypse seriously unless one made the very greatest effort to understand what the writer says about the origin of the work. It is certainly a fact that the content of the Apocalypse forces research to find ways and means that will render it possible to understand it; but such ways and means must not contradict the spirit and letter of the Apocalypse. To approach the question of origin from this vantage point, we must first overcome an obstacle that is certain to arise, whether consciously or unconsciously, at the very beginning. The essence of this argument may be expressed this way: The Apocalypse describes the *future* of humanity. Human beings are *free,* however, so how is it possible to give specific information about the future of humankind, since the structure of that future obviously depends on human freedom? This argument vanishes, however, when we recall that the Apocalypse describes *two* future paths; it shows the stages of paths that ascend and descend. Those *paths* are determined karmically. The freedom of each individual, however, determines *who* chooses which path. Indeed, those paths are already determined inasmuch as humankind has already lived through a long destiny. Today is not, of course, the first day of creation; a vast stretch of the karmic path lies behind humanity in the past.

The new, infinitely important factor that makes up part of human destiny is the fact that Christ has become the judge of that destiny. He has become the lord of karma.[2] Having become lord of karma, he not only determines the future of humanity, but is also the source of revelation concerning it. By contrast, the future is determined by the past, and judgment on the karmic past (insofar as it still has consequences for the future) likewise lies in the hands of Christ. For this reason, the "seven letters" to the seven "churches" refer not only to the future, but also to the past. In those letters, judgment was given not only on what was then the present and on the three future cultural epochs (or "churches"), but also on the three cultural epochs of the past: the ancient Indian, ancient Persian, and Egypto-Chaldean.

Before we begin to study the content of the letters to the seven churches, however, we must acquire a more specific idea of the source of John's Revelation. This, too, is in accordance with the writer's purpose, since the opening sentences of the Apocalypse not only indicate this source, but also in the first chapter the writer shows the spiritual figure of him who has invoked the Revelation (1:12–16). That figure was "one like unto the Son of man" (1:13) bearing the signs of the cosmic planetary forces just as they would be realized in the humanity of the future (the "Son of man") during the Jupiter period. The archetype of the Jupiter human being (the "Son of man" of the future) must be pictured thus: Arbitrariness will cease to be possible in the life of thought; streams of thought will flow down into the head, just as hair grows on its own. These thought currents flowing from the cosmos will not be *one-sided,* and they will have no distinct color, but will be "synthetic" in a deep and true sense. White light is a combination of the seven colors, and, similarly, the cosmic thinking of the future will be "white"—"white like wool, as white as snow" (1:14).

The force of "I" initiative will not manifest in the realm of thinking, which will be pure cosmic revelation. Rather, it will express itself in the illuminating and permeating of cosmic phenomena. "I" initiative will become the spiritual power of *vision,* filling things seen with its fire. *Seeing* will not be passive acceptance of outer impressions, but illumination and permeation that radiates from within external phenomena: "His eyes were as a flame of fire" (1:14).

The earthly life of volition will also be different, insofar as it will forfeit the flow of its driving force. It will instead bind the glowing ardor of fire with metallic rigidity. Human beings will no longer be compelled by waves of cosmic formative forces in the will, but stand on a stable foundation of conscious volition with the force of fire and the rigidity of metal. Human "feet" will be "like unto fine brass, as if they burned in a furnace" (I:15), and the waves of cosmic impulse and creative formative forces will pass over from the earthly human will into the human *voice*. The creative power of nature, functioning today as a compelling force in the human subconscious, will be lifted into the power of speech for future humankind. The human voice will be "as the sound of many waters" (*Hos phone hydaton pollon*).

The future human life of feeling will be such that, on the one hand, it will express the harmony of the heavenly *stars* and, on the other, be "sharpened" to the finest pitch of concentration on the creative *Word*. Human beings of the future will hold in their "right hand seven stars: and out of his mouth ... a sharp two-edged sword" (I:16). On the one hand, charity will flow as approval and understanding from the harmony of the seven stars, which are the spiritual beings of the seven "churches" of humanity, while, on the other, truth will find a rigid and sharp instrument as the "sword of the Word." But, precisely as an instrument of truth, this sword of the word will be double-edged; it will function in such a way that it strikes those who speak as well as those who hear. The Word will proceed from an awareness of the *unity* of humanity (from the "seven stars"), and thus its judgment will apply as well to the speaker as to the rest of humankind. The *Mars force* of the Word will indeed wage a war of annihilation against error and lies, but that annihilating conflict will produce an inner, as well as an outer, effect. Hence it will be free of any spirit of hostility. Thus the Word will be able to express the truth with inflexible decision and without the possibility of being used as a one-sided offensive weapon.

A complete picture of the human being of the future, however, is not limited to the changes we have mentioned in thinking, willing, and feeling. Those changes include not only the *inner* conditions of the soul forces mentioned, but also their relationships with one another. The interrelations of the soul forces in future human beings will have to change because the expanded Sun force of the heart will be raised into the head: "His countenance was as the sun shineth in his strength," while the formative and restricted force of the head will descend into the Sun region of the heart: Man will be "girt about the paps [breast] with a golden girdle" (I:16). And the will life will enclose the whole human being. In the realm of the *earthly* (or rather, of the *natural*, for in the Jupiter period the "earthly" will be different), it will become glowing metal. At the same time, however, it will flow down from the *higher* human to the *periphery* of one's being. This centrifugal direction of the will, by which it becomes a kind of sheath, is symbolized in the Apocalypse as "a garment down to the foot" (I:13).

Thus at the beginning of the Apocalypse we are shown the figure of the future human being who sends the "letters" to the seven churches. But he who reveals himself in this person is the "I AM," the "first and the last" of earthly evolution, the one who lives in that realm of cosmic evolution in which death rules (I:17–18). Christ himself, whose esoteric name is I AM for humanity, speaks through that person. He is the source of John's Revelation.

## Letters to the Churches of the Past

Because Christ is the source of John's Revelation, he is also the source of the positive soul currents that flow in humankind from past to future. The influence of Christ was already active during the ancient Indian cultural epoch; the positive fundamental impulse of that ancient culture of post-Atlantean humanity came from him. That impulse lived on below the surface in human souls, and those in whom its influence is especially strong and a determining factor form a community that the Apocalypse calls "church of Ephesus" (2:1). The purpose of the letter to the church of Ephesus is not merely to pass judgment on a long-past civilization; its purpose is really an appeal to the ancient Indian impulse that remains alive in souls today. Only this fact gives practical moral meaning in the admonition, "Remember therefore from whence thou art fallen, and repent, and do the first works" (2:5). Such an exhortation would really be meaningless if it were directed only to a long-past civilization, a human endeavor long ago sunk into silence. It is, however, also addressed to the present and to a future time—in fact, to eternity, since the letter begins with these words: "Unto the *angel* of the church of Ephesus write." These words express the fact that we are not dealing with a specific group of people living in the past or from the time it was written, but with the transcendent and comprehensive nature of a *message* of the ancient Indian culture. The messenger (the angel of that culture) is still active; such a culture does not manifest only to fall into oblivion; it existed so that a seed of revelation, the message of Heaven behind it, would sprout and grow through the ages in human souls, passing through many transformations brought about by cooperation with newly added influences, until it expands into a blossom and ripe fruit. This is why the mission of the essential message of the ancient Indian culture never ended. All that was begun then lives on, and the *messenger* of that culture, the angel of the church of Ephesus, continues to be associated with the flowing current of the effects and the consequences of the original message. The ancient Indian culture persists as a karmic stream, and the spirit of that culture is connected with that karmic current, living on as qualities, longings, and memories in human souls. It also lives in potential human limitations and in the human tendency to repeat earlier mistakes. And with it, the spirit of that culture is linked in the consciousness of shared responsibility.

What aspect of the ancient Indian spiritual life, then, is still present in human souls today? What is it that still functions as karma from that age? To answer this question, we must recall fundamental characteristics of the ancient "rishi" culture, especially the fact that it was an all-embracing *revelation culture,* from which sprang the basic impulse for the seven cultural epochs of the whole post-Atlantean evolution.[3] The revelation of the seven rishis was not just the revival of wisdom of the seven Atlantean oracles; it also planted the seven-colored wisdom from the seven epochs of the post-Atlantean age. It was the seven "vowels" of the cosmic Word (or Logos) that, by means of the rishis, flowed into human souls just as the twelve "consonants" of the cosmic Word were revealed at Pentecost.[4] And, just as there can be no speech without vowels, human souls would have been incapable of comprehending the Logos if there had been no revelation from the rishis of the ancient Indian epoch. The influence of the rishi revelation is felt even today as a certain inner longing and in the human ether body as "memories" of the ways and means to satisfy that longing.

The longing that lives in the depths of human souls as an echo of the rishi culture involves, above all, the efforts toward a comprehensive "synthetic" wisdom that is valid for everyone, wisdom that would harmonize one-sided tendencies, just as the revealed wisdom of the rishis during the ancient Indian epoch represented the harmonizing of the seven Atlantean oracles. The longing that lives in human souls corresponds to the light of the "seven stars" in Heaven, which became the light of the "seven candlesticks" on Earth. This longing lives in them simply because the light that shines in the seven stars, the constellation of the Great Bear, once shone also in seven men, the rishis, and for seven human groups associated in one community just as the seven candlesticks were joined in one light of wisdom. And the first letter is addressed to *this* longing, since it speaks of him "that holdeth the seven stars in His right hand, who walketh in the midst of the seven golden candlesticks" (2:1). The letter to the church of Ephesus proceeds from the one who can ease the longing, from the one who is the essence of the memory behind that longing, because the rishi revelation showed the comprehensive nature of Christ as the cosmic Word.

The future that is to result from this realization, however, is not merely to light the seven candles with the flame of the seven stars, but something that arises from this. What once existed as revealed wisdom will be the concrete *life* of future human beings. "To him that overcometh will I give to eat of the tree of life, which is in the midst of the paradise of God" (2:7). This expresses the positive future of the endeavor that moves courageously forward into the future from a reminiscent longing for the comprehensive wisdom of the past. "Overcoming" here means to overcome the desire for the past. True, it means living by a longing that arises from the past, but it must seek satisfaction not in the past but in the future. The drift of the soul's desire toward the past must be overcome permanently, but the *essence* of that longing must not only be nurtured but even be strengthened to an energetic striving toward the future. It will then be possible for wisdom to *become* life and for the wisdom originally revealed from Heaven to live in human beings. This transformation indicates the future evolution of the "moral ether" in human nature, and this "moral ether" will be just as full of light as was the original revelation of the wisdom of the rishis. Moreover, it will not only give light, but also function as does the life force. "Eating of the tree of life" means that the human system will absorb the power to give life.

The endeavor to master this life-giving force always existed, and it is developed in two special directions. One is toward asceticism, whose final expression is a kind of Indian yoga. The purpose of this type of asceticism is to send the life force in the human procreative faculty *upward* into the head, thus providing human spiritual life with the same creative life force as that of the procreative faculty. The second direction is called by the writer of the Apocalypse "the deeds of the Nicolaitans" (2:6).[5] Here the aim was to descend into the physical with such awareness that the instinctive forces of the physical body would be made to serve certain magical ends in an unnatural way. As with the first direction, the message of the Holy Spirit was distorted, because the spiritual force was not motivated by its inherent moral essence but by the influx of a force drawn from another realm of existence. So with the second direction, the purpose of the *human body* was distorted, because it was given a primary position by sensualizing the spirit.

Those who present themselves as sent by the spirit, and who nonetheless do not represent *pure* spirit, but a spirit mingled with forces from the body, are not truly sent by the spirit (as are apostles), but only believe themselves to be. And those who allow the spirit to become the prey of sensuality (as did the Nicolaitans) represent the other error in the search for "the tree of life." The fruit of the tree of life does not mean developing an activity of spirit at the expense of bodily forces, nor does it mean sensualizing the spirit; rather, it means developing pure spiritual force, increasing in strength so that it works with the strength of a nature force. Moral ether does not exist as a "latent force" of the body; it is a new force that will gradually be born in human beings out of the Christ impulse.

The hindrances that oppose the future birth of the *true* fruits of the tree of life are the efforts of liars, who claim to be apostles (sent by the spirit) but are not, and Nicolaitans. The angel of the church of Ephesus resists these two errors. Nevertheless, he had not remained entirely true to his mission, for he had "left his first love," the original pure impulse of post-Atlantean human evolution. That original impulse was love for the mission of humanity on Earth. It was a deeply rooted willingness of souls to incarnate truly and completely in order to completely fulfill the purpose of earthly existence. That will—the desire for complete earthly incarnation to fulfill the Earth's mission completely—is the real essence of "weight." Everything that involves a conscious, sacrificial descent is an expression of spiritual "weight." Thus, for example, any words that we may speak have more weight when they penetrate not only to the astral body, but down into the ether body as well. A human act has more weight when its moral essence penetrates right down into physical reality than it does when it touches only the upper levels of earthly existence. Seen from the physical side, there are two different manifestations of weight. One is the sacrificial "descent" already mentioned; the other is the phenomenon of the fall of humanity, or the expulsion from the spiritual heights. The second occurs as the karmic result of an unjustified attitude toward the spirit. True weight, then, becomes heaviness, and the descent, a downfall.

It was just this transforming of weight into heaviness that took place in the destiny of the ancient Indian cultural community. She forsook her "first love," and in consequence of this, the descent became a fall. "Remember therefore from whence thou art fallen (*ekpeptokas*), and repent, and do the first works" (2:5). With these words, the lord of karma expresses the karmic dispensation that became necessary because of the loss of the first love for the current of the ancient Indian culture. This is the effect of karma on all who are unwilling to incarnate fully, all who resist complete incorporation; they unwillingly *fall* into incarnation instead of *descending* by free moral force into the realm of karmic activity. For human beings, the scene of actions that determine karma is in the physical world; the working world is the area in which human acts acquire their greatest significance. The result is this warning to the angel of the church of Ephesus: "Remember therefore from whence thou art fallen, and repent, and do the first works (*ta prota erga poieson*)." This warning is addressed to all those who tend to energetically refuse to work in the area of action—all who are inclined to shirk the full measure of their share of responsibility for earthly events. Such people will not allow true *weight* to function in their souls—the weight of the spirit of sacrifice, which also gives weight to human effort and action in controlling the karma of the future.

To truly take the path into the future, beyond the spirit of sacrifice needed to produce weight in the soul, strength is also needed to carry that sacrifice to an end, persevering with it through trials. It is not enough to be prepared to descend into nether *space;* it is also necessary to take a path in that "space" leading to the goal. And it is necessary to remain faithful to the task through a given period of *time.* Following the ideal of the "first love" (the ability to love the earthly purpose of humanity) is the ideal of faithfulness to that mission throughout the trials of the earthly path in time. To realize this ideal is the purpose of the angel of the church of Smyrna, the mission of the ancient Persian spiritual impulse. This is why the letter to the angel of the church in Smyrna admonishes, "Be thou faithful unto death, and I will give thee a crown of life" (2:10). And this is also why this letter no longer comes from him "that holdeth the seven stars in his right hand, and walketh in the midst of the seven golden candlesticks," but from him who is "the first and the last, which was dead, and is alive." What flowed from Christ into human souls through the ancient Persian spiritual culture is the impulse of fidelity, the longing and the hope that all obstacles, even death itself, might be overcome. "The first and the last, which was dead, and is alive," is, therefore, a very concise formula that expresses the nature of the highest longing and hope that was the spiritual and moral life nerve of the ancient Persian culture; it persists today in the ancient Persian level of the human soul.

In its innermost essence, this ideal of fidelity is the spiritual essence of *measure,* just as the "first love" is the core essence of *weight.* The path that leads from "the first" to "the last," from "death" to "life," is the true *measure* of human fidelity and the magnitude of the earthly human mission. This measure can be perceived, recognized, and realized through the soul's free moral force; it then shines in the soul as the great, liberating goal of human earthly existence. If, however, it is not accepted freely and consciously, karma appears as a cramping and compelling influence rather than as a measure of spiritual heroism. The loss of the "first love" leads to the fall of humankind when true weight becomes heaviness; likewise, lack of fidelity leads to contraction. When true measure becomes a *constriction* of the soul "the devil shall cast *some* of you into prison" (2:10) to awaken an effort toward the free heroism of *true measure* through enforced confinement. Such imprisonment (brought about by Lucifer, or *Diabolos*) is actually the loneliness of the soul confined within itself because it refuses to unite with the great purpose of human evolution. Because the soul will not accept the *spiritual* measure, it must become, just as it is, the measure of its own consciousness; its nature will draw the line that confines its consciousness, its activity, and its world. The walls of the "prison" into which the soul has been cast by the luciferic impulse are the boundaries drawn by the soul itself; the soul's own egoism confines it to prison. Thus the soul is confronted by a choice of two possible measures: freely acknowledge the measure of the spirit, or accept the soul's own standard as the measure. Lucifer would guide the soul to the second choice, and this is why the Apocalypse tells us that Lucifer (*Diabolos*) "shall cast *some* of you into prison."

Those who have chosen the true path of fidelity to humanity's mission on Earth, however—that is, those who have chosen the spiritual measure—are called the "Jews" (*hoi Judaioi*) in this letter. This name simply refers to those human souls who are determined to minister throughout the ages to prepare for and realize the Christ impulse. This is the meaning of "eternal Israel,"[6] made up of twelve tribes; it is the karmic community of human souls united through many incarnations with the Christ impulse, first to prepare for it and then to realize it. Hence "Jews," in the sense of the Apocalypse, are not members of any nation but those souls who have decided to serve the Christ impulse. There is, however, a very difficult trial related to this—the "the blasphemy of them which say they are Jews, and are not, but *are* the synagogue of Satan" (2:9). The synagogue of Satan is the karmic antipode of the "eternal Israel," and the blasphemy of that community is in their imitation of all the power and activity of the Christ impulse in human life, while turning it into just the opposite. The activity of Ahriman (*Satanas*, in the Apocalypse) in human destiny is primarily the creation of a kind of caricature of the human community and order that the Christ impulse strives for. While Lucifer isolates human beings, "casts them into prison," Ahriman gathers them into a community (or synagogue), just as the Christ impulse unites them in a community (*ecclesia*). Instead of the egoistic isolation brought about by Lucifer, two communities based on "we" consciousness will appear in world history. One is the community of Christ, in which free "I" beings will unite in a free alliance; the other is its opposite, Ahriman's mass organization that swallows up the individual "I." The *blasphemy* involves the fact that the *true* "we" consciousness of spiritual fraternity is turned into its opposite by falsely mimicking "we" consciousness in the mass organization. Thus, on the one hand there are true "Jews"—free "I" beings striving toward community among themselves based on freedom—and, on the other, there are "we-oriented" people destined to be swallowed up by a mass organization. They believe, however, that "they are Jews [true individuals], and are not."

This polarity first appeared in world history in the relationship between Iranians and Turanians during the ancient Persian cultural epoch; it has persisted down the ages, however, and today, just as then, the two types of "we" consciousness confront each other as a trial of human faithfulness to their spiritual purpose on Earth. On the other hand, "imprisonment by the devil" also persists. It must last for "ten days," and that period is not yet ended, since the luciferic current will continue its karmic stream until the Christ Sun has shone ten times following the ancient Persian cultural epoch. This Sun shines at the beginning and at the end of each cultural epoch. It shines at the beginning as the fundamental impulse of the epoch, and at the end as a response to and a benediction on its positive result, however scanty it may be. Then it is "day," just as at the beginning there was the "day" of the cultural epoch. Ten such "days" will occur, until the sixth cultural epoch and those who are imprisoned either join the philadelphic community of loving friendship or are swallowed up by the "we" of ahrimanic humanity. The "prison," or isolation of self-reliance, will come to an end. They will then either become truly free or have to join the ahrimanic throng.

Thus the "church in Smyrna" must take a path on which it is tested by the "prison" of *Diabolos* and by the "synagogue" of Satan. Those who are "faithful unto death," however, receive the crown of life. That crown is not a mere poetic expression, but an exact description of the meaningful esoteric fact that, in the future, certain changes will take place in the system of spiritual currents in the human head. As a result, the "crown of death" will become the "crown of life." At present, human life forces concentrate increasingly in the head with age, and from there radiate upward as a kind of "crown." Then, if this concentration becomes complete, the heart ceases to function (even when there is no malady), and death supervenes. Now, however, another process may occur in the etheric organization of the human head—namely, a concentration in the head of downwardly radiating spiritual life forces that spread out with vivifying power into the rest of the human organism. The development of this "crown of life" is also a sign that the Christ impulse is active in the human body of life forces. Through this influence, the human life body is preserved from the "second death," or dissolution after physical death. The "crown of life" is the element of the life body that is not subject to "the second death." This is how we can understand the promise of the second letter: "He that overcometh shall not be hurt of the second death" (2:11).

The promise addressed to the karmic current called "the church in Pergamos" refers neither to the "tree of life" nor to the "crown of life," but to eating "hidden manna" and to a "white stone" engraved with a "new name ... which no man knoweth saving he that receiveth it" (2:17). The spiritual impulse behind the third (Egypto-Chaldean) cultural epoch, which has persisted in human souls since that time, is to strive for the experience of immortal individuality and for harmony among immortal individual beings. The "stone with a new name which no man knoweth saving he that receiveth it " is the immortal human "I" being. The name *"I"* is the one that can be spoken only in relation to one's self. "Hidden manna" is the community-forming force at work beyond the threshold of ordinary consciousness; it binds separate individuals into a human community. Thus Moses, for example, whose mission lay within the Egypto-Chaldean epoch, received the revelation of the "I AM THAT I AM" in the burning bush as the revelation of the source of "I" experience, whereas the Israelite community under his guidance ate of the "heavenly manna" that descended during the night and was "gathered" in the early morning. Moses led the community entrusted to him to the ideal of the "I" evolution; but he led it *as a community*, since it was united and held together as such by eating the "manna." The reality of the manas (or the "manna") influence manifests when human lives are based on the inner "I" and produce harmony. The *true* "we" cannot be realized without the influence of the manas (or spirit self) when "I" consciousness has gained rock-like firmness and solidity.

There is also an anti-manas current used to form communities. The force of community formation in this current is not drawn from the supraconscious regions, but from the subconscious. Together with the karmic union of individual beings brought into harmony by the "manna," there is yet another force that draws one to another and binds them; this is the urge that comes, not through the blood from the "I AM" impulse of Yahweh in the past, nor from the "I" as experienced today, but from the blood that is neither under Yahweh's influence nor determined by the "I." This force is the sexual urge. It was misused, for instance, by Balaam (Numbers 22–23) when he advised the Midianite prince Balak to substitute other principles for those of the Israelite community, so that, through the medium of the Midianite women dedicated to Baal, the Israelites might be drawn under the influence of the Baal cult. That influence was accomplished by arousing this urge through eating "meats offered to idols" (the flesh of victims prepared through ceremonial magic and invested with certain powers), thereby inducing alliances outside the network of positive karma. The "doctrine of Balaam" mentioned in the letter is the view from which "hidden manna" is sought not in the seclusion of the supraconscious but in the subconscious life of impulse.

The true harmony of manas activity can be falsified and superseded by the "doctrine of Balaam." Likewise, human striving for the experience of one's own "I" can be falsified and superseded by the "doctrine of the Nicolaitans." In the first instance there is a false kind of karmic union among people, and in the second there is a false "I" experience. Because the "Nicolaitan" stream we mentioned placed human consciousness right inside the body, it belived itself to be, for all practical purposes, independent and free within the body. Thus a substitute for the true "I" came into being, created by the confining influence of the body. A false "I" consciousness arose whose source was not the "I" but the body. And directed against these two errors is the double-edged sword from the mouth of the one who addresses the letter to the angel of the church of Pergamos; the sword of the word of truth strikes both immorality in the life of impulse and illusions in materialistic ideas and concepts.

The opposite of the two-edged sword of the future word of truth is the principle of black magic power working in silence, a principle that promotes, and is based on, the union of subconscious impulses with illusionary concepts. This is why the occult language of the Apocalypse speaks of this union as the "throne of Satan" (*thronos tu Satana*). The name signifies the evolution of Ahriman's power over humanity and that this principle ("throne") must be sought in the human metabolic system. On the other hand, there have been historical situations in which this "throne" was present outwardly and objectively, functioning as a center of power. The throne of Herod and Herodias, for example, was a point of departure for such activity. And the activity was manifested in the fact that those who came within the influence of that "throne" (or activity functioning through illusion and immoral impulse) were "beheaded." They were "beheaded" in the sense that they lost the "I" conscious center in the head and were thus exposed to the influence of the subconscious depths of the metabolic organization.

The only way to oppose this "throne" is to unmask the immoral "slavish" impulse springing from it and to overcome materialistic concepts by faithfulness to the spirit, even unto death. Every historical "throne of Satan" must always be opposed by "faithful witnesses" (*martys ho pistos*) of the spirit. This was also true of the throne of Jezebel and Ahab, whom Naboth withstood as the "faithful witness"; it was also true of the throne of Herodias and Herod, against whom John the Baptist was the "faithful witness"; each time the "faithful witness" had to overcome immorality through the word, and illusion through death. The immortality of human individuality is attested not only by teaching but by the fact that individual beings face death as "faithful witnesses" and that human individuality can be raised above death and is thus immortal. In this sense, not only John the Baptist, but also Socrates in Athens was a "faithful witness." This special mission of being a "faithful witness" against the "throne of Satan" has a name. In this sense, everyone who has such a mission to fulfill is an Antipas (2:13), one whose task is to suffer with the victims of the "throne" (or black magic). Thus, John the Baptist also suffered the fate of the victims of Herod's throne and was even "beheaded" physically, as other victims of that throne were "beheaded" inwardly in their souls. In this sense, John the Baptist is Antipas, the fellow sufferer, who withstood the "throne of Satan" as a "faithful witness"—and indeed, not only at that time, but also in the past during earlier lives.

Such "beheading" actually happens even today in a moral sense; it happens, for instance, wherever people are regarded and treated not as individuals but as a quantity, or number. When people are regarded merely as numbers, they are "beheaded"—the dignity of their "I" individuality is taken from them. When such units are added up and their sum stated, this is morally the opposite of forming a community through the power of the "hidden manna." What was originally black magical abuse of human impulses and materialized concepts has become statistical analysis of human units. Just as the sin of the church of Ephesus brought about the conversion of true weight into a fall consequent on heaviness; as the sin of the church of Smyrna brought about the conversion of true measure into "imprisonment" within the limits of egoism; likewise, the sin of the church of Pergamos caused the change of true number into the beheading and mechanical enumeration of human individuals. True spiritual number is a community of individual beings arranged according to "the glory of the stars," of which each is not merely a unit but a "new name" written into the white stone, "which no man knoweth saving he that receiveth it" (2:17). In the sense of true number, people should not, and cannot, be counted and added up; people should be called by their names and united into a community by the "hidden manna." The consequence of the sin of the Balaamites and the Nicolaitans is the substitution of a *sum* for manna and a *numerical unit* for the name.

Thus the statistics, which seem so innocent today, have antecedents; an example was established by tragic facts in spiritual history, and the state of mind that produces them owes its existence to past preparation through black magic. Considering the matter in this light, we can also understand why the spiritual world considered it so sinful for King

David to number people and why it brought such a severe punishment; what has now become common practice was then a terrible breach of faith in the idea of human community as desired by the spiritual world. Human faces and names should not be converted into numbers, which constitutes the sin of the third cultural epoch: "treason against spiritual number." Moreover, in this light we can understand how tragic is the beginning of the second chapter of Luke's Gospel, where we are told, "It came to pass in those days, that there went out a decree from Caesar Augustus, that all the world should be taxed [or counted]." We can understand the tragedy of Jesus being born during a national census and considered by the Roman state to be a mere "plus one" if we become truly aware of the real meaning of number as the harmony of the ineffable name of individual beings in contrast to the consequence of the "fall" of number into mechanistic ideation—that is, the abuse of impulses and illusions. Nonetheless, it was necessary for Jesus to be born in a time when weight, measure, and number had already been divorced from their true meaning; the birthplace of Jesus was a stable of animals.

The spiritual impulse and its history during that cultural epoch in which Christ Jesus appeared will be the subject of the next section.

# Chapter 2

# Letters to the Churches of Today

## The Letter to the Angel of the Church in Thyatira

The previous section dealt with both the true nature of "weight," "measure," and "number" and their "fall" in connection with the temporal missions and the eternal messages of the ancient Indian, Persian, and Egypto-Chaldean post-Atlantean cultures. From the standpoint of human nature, these three great principles contain the meaning of the human need to come to terms in the life body, sentient body, and sentient soul through the three axioms of human destiny: toil, suffering, and death. The three "curses of the Father" have hung over human destiny ever since the fall into sin and demand a spiritual and moral struggle in the life body, sentient body, and sentient soul. Indeed, human consciousness is obliged to evoke a sacrificial force in the life body in order to descend into the active world of physical existence. As the willingness to incarnate in a physical body, "weight" cannot be found in the physical world itself, but in the etheric realm, from which the physical is taken and shaped. The experience of the physical "toil" of earthly activity may occur in the etheric as love for the Earth's mission—as true "weight." Similarly, in the sentient body, human beings can consciously meet the "suffering" that they experience in the life body. Here we can be aware of its true essence and gain a conscious relationship with it. And here we can experience it as the temporal mission—as true "measure"—whereas the life body is time itself. It is only in the sentient soul, however, that we first encounter the tragic problem of "death." This is because it is only in the soul, and for the soul, that the external event and pain of death becomes an inner karmic question—one that involves the value and nature of the "number" of individual beings. It is a question of whether this number is an eradicable product of nature or rooted in the eternal Godhead (hence ineradicable).

Thus the main problem of the Egypto-Chaldean age was *immortality*, as clearly shown, for example, in the myth of Gilgamesh. And the main problem of the ancient Persian culture was the objective relationship between good and evil in the world and in the Zend Avesta.[1] Preserved until this day are echoes that show us that the important matter for the ancient Persian age was to feel the "cosmic year" as the measure of this relationship in the stream of time. Further, the main problem of the ancient Indian culture was the value of human activity in the physical world. For example, the Bhagavad Gita, though of later origin, is devoted entirely to this problem.

Added to these three problems—the value of the world of actions, the relationship between good and evil, and immortality—during the fourth, Greco-Roman, cultural epoch, a fourth was added: the problem of freedom. Human beings meet the first three in the life body, the sentient body, and the sentient soul, and they encounter the fourth, the problem of freedom, by awakening the intellectual soul. It is the intellectual soul that makes us aware of our position between what we know and will and yet cannot do, and between what we do not will and nonetheless do. It is difficult to find a better formula for this than that given by St. Paul: "For what I do, I allow not: for what I would, that do I not: but what I hate, that do I" (Romans 7:15). We find ourselves between impotent understanding and the hidden will when we experience ourselves within the intellectual soul. Our understanding presents us with the demands of the spirit, but gives us no power to fulfill them. Our subconscious nature, however, functions through impulses that are dark to one's consciousness. What we have seen to be true and good we recognize as necessity, or law; but what functions with natural force within us we see only as a result of acts already accomplished, which may also be regarded as a law (Romans 7:16–21). If we follow the claims of the spirit, the law, we must constrain our nature; if, by contrast, we follow our natural impulses, we are guilty of betraying our own convictions and of turning away from reason, which is, nevertheless, our guiding star. It is this real inner contradiction that raises the problem of freedom in the human soul. The question is: How can the light of insight shine in such a way that it can catch our natural impulses and shine through them? In other words, how can nature follow the spirit *freely*, and how can the spirit rise above the soul—not as a ruler, but as a benevolent sun?

In order to realize freedom, the light of the intellect must be more than mere light. It must receive the power not only to illuminate, but also to *kindle* action. The light must become fire; otherwise it will be impossible to make freedom a reality. By contrast, volition must become, as it were, a rigid light; it must become "metal." Just as the material of metals is light that has become rigid and heavy, the substance of the human will must become something that adds weight and solidity to the content of higher human knowledge. Consequently, the fourth letter, addressed to the angel of the church in Thyatira, establishes the ideal, or archetype, of freedom at the very beginning: "These things saith the Son of God, who hath his eyes like unto a flame of fire, and his feet are like fine brass" (2:18). Christ is the force that realizes the ideal of freedom, which is the conversion of light into fire and will into metal.

The path to realizing the ideal of freedom, however, lies in the love (*agape*) made possible by the Christ impulse. As love, the reality of the Christ impulse can overcome the opposition of intellect and impulses that hinder freedom. This is why the "angel of Thyatira" possesses not only the three needed qualities through which human beings come to terms with toil, suffering, and "death," but also the fourth, through which the realization of freedom becomes possible. If the necessity of toil requires conscious service (*diakonia*), the necessity of suffering requires patience (*hypomone*), and the necessity of death calls for faith (*pistis*). The angel of the fourth church possesses, besides these qualities, a fourth: love. "I know thy works, and charity, and service, and faith, and thy patience, and thy works; and the last to be more than the first" (2:19), says the letter to the fourth angel, indicating the fact of the "cross," for which those of the Greco-Roman epoch must be prepared. It is the cross of toil, suffering, and death that must be borne, and the dilemma appears in the manner of bearing that cross in the spirit of service, patience, faith, and freedom in love. This cross was erected gradually in the spiritual history of humankind. First, during the ancient Indian epoch, service was learned by dealing with the need for toil, by understanding the value of the world of action. Then patience was acquired during the ancient Persian epoch, when the important point was to recognize the objective relationship between good and evil in an age when humanity had to suffer the conflict between good and evil. During the Egypto-Chaldean cultural epoch, it was death in particular that people had to resolve and, by understanding immortality, attain faith. Finally, during the Greco-Roman period, the dilemma was experienced that Paul speaks of, and from this experience arose the problem of freedom and a longing to realize it through the force of love.

In the sense of the preceding meditations, the cross can also be represented as shown in the following diagram. Here the tests of weight, measure, and number lie in the karmic necessities of "toil," "suffering" and "death," and the forces acquired by passing those tests constitute the soul forces of service, patience, and faith. Freedom, however, is the reality of the true human "I," and this reality is revealed by the rays of the Sun force of love in human beings. Love is the essential revelation of true "I" being.

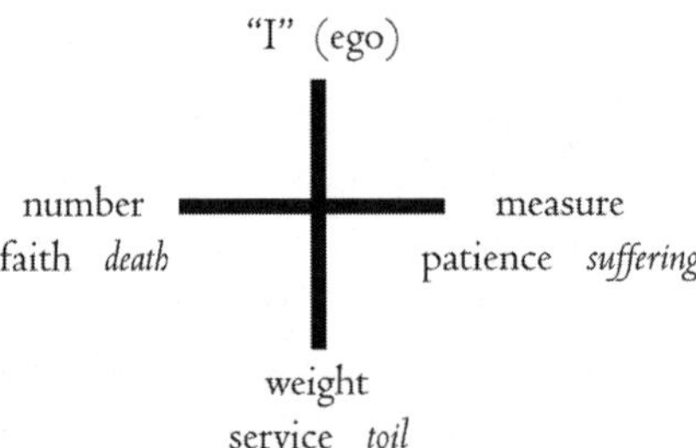


"I will put upon you none other burden. But that which ye have already hold fast till I come" (2:24–25). Bearing this cross is the task of the church in Thyatira, and it was the true mission of the fourth post-Atlantean cultural epoch. But opposed to that cross was the antithesis of the dilemma: overcoming suffering without toil, and fleeing from the tragedy of death and into the great unity. That spiritual tendency was based on the decadent sibylline school, the spiritual tendency of "that woman Jezebel, which calleth herself a prophetess" (2:20). The point connected with the Israelite queen Jezebel, who supported this tendency as an opponent of the prophets, was that the dilemma between reason and impulse could be bridged by submitting to guidance from the dark sibylline impulse. People are thus seduced into accepting the sibylline inspiration as a solution to the problem of freedom, and thus arrive at a condition in which the dilemma no longer exists because reason is excluded, and only nature is allowed a voice. This condition later developed into what is known today as channeling. At that time, it was not yet the modern trance condition, but nonetheless well on the way in that direction. On the other hand, the effect of the spiritual passivity thus fostered was that people became apathetic even toward suffering, because they had chosen a path that involved no toil. Such apathy toward suffering was achieved not through the genuine strength of patience, but by electrifying themselves so that they became fanatics through a process the Apocalypse calls "eating things sacrificed unto idols" (*phagein eidolo thyta*). Thus people became so inwardly "electrified" that they could endure a great deal without suffering. The "eating of things sacrificed unto idols" actually had a kind of narcotic effect; it numbed the soul's suffering by desensitizing it.

This spiritual tendency helped people overcome the karmic necessities of toil and suffering, and in the same way they helped themselves past the tragedy of death by trying to feel the "great unity" of all natural and spiritual life. Thus, they lost the sense of anything definite or individual, thus robbing death of its "sting." Such people lived with this attitude: All lives in all and leads through all to all; there is nothing to choose and nothing to lose, since all paths lead to the same goal—union with the active totality of nature. This peculiar sort of "monism" essentially denied the reality and significance of number. It avoided the conflict with "death" because individuality was not valued. The Apocalypse calls such deprecation of individuality and detachment from everything definite "committing fornication" (*porneusai*). It is a universal marriage of all with all, whereas the idea of individuality, the idea of true number, requires strict and definite organization. Here, only *one* way, leading to *one* ideal, is admissible. Thus the cross of Jezebel stands in opposition to the cross of the angel in Thyatira:

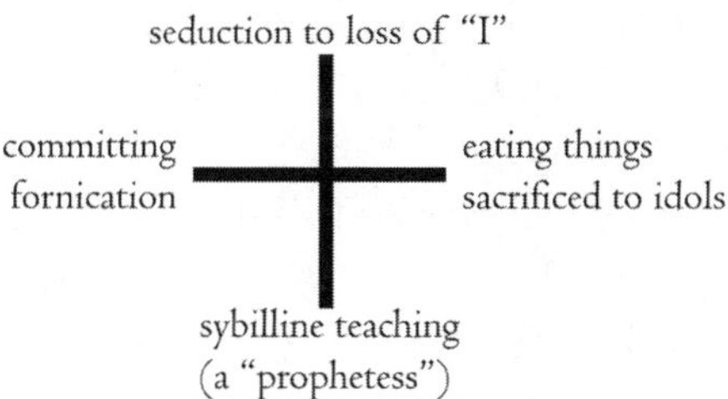


This cross is suggested in the Apocalypse: "Notwithstanding I have a few things against thee, because thou sufferest that woman Jezebel, which calleth herself a prophetess, to teach and to seduce my servants to commit fornication, and to eat things sacrificed unto idols" (2:20). And what is the karmic remedy for this sort of spiritual tendency? On the one hand, it is *time*—the chance to learn that the sibylline teaching that was once so high has become decadent. The sibylline teaching was once a true and pure source of spiritual revelation for humankind; that was the time when the gods stooped toward nature. Later, however, the gods withdrew to a higher realm, and the world of inspiration for the sibyls was taken over by demons. It became one of those realms that the Apocalypse refers to collectively as "the depths of Satan" (*ta bathea tou satana*). As a result, Jezebel was given "time to repent of her fornication; and she repented not" (2:21).

If knowledge of sibylline decadence is not enough to turn the spiritual "Jezebel" tendency in a different direction, however, destiny must intervene and end the possibility of sibylline revelation, on the one hand, and on the other, give greater power to "suffering" and "death" to heal the apathy toward those karmic human necessities. To render the sibylline revelation impossible, the vertical direction of that revelation (the line of teaching and seduction in our diagram), which runs from below upward, must become horizontal. Then the possibility of revelation from the subterranean realm ends; the sibyl becomes a person who can do nothing beyond ordinary human forces and has no knowledge beyond the memory of earlier sibylline experiences that might be reawakened. In any event, such a one is then completely under the control of "suffering" and "death." These matters are all clearly expressed in the Apocalypse. "Behold, I will cast her [Jezebel] into a bed, and them that commit adultery with her into great tribulation, except they repent of their deeds. And I will kill her children with death" (2:22–23). That destiny is the necessary remedy for the karmic tendency of Jezebel. The "diagnosis" on which that remedy is based, however, is obtained by searching the "reins and hearts" (2:23).[2] The two spiritual tendencies we are dealing with (that of "the angel in Thyatira" and that of "Jezebel") are distinguished precisely by the fact that, in the first, freedom through love is realized from the "heart," whereas the sibylline onslaught is made by the lower forces in the "reins." Hence the two currents involve different karmic paths. The current of the "reins" must take the path of losing the capacity for revelation while submitting to tribulation and death. The current of the "heart" must follow the path through which it will gain power in the realm of folk souls (*exusian epi ton ethnon*), while splitting them into fragments of separate units of consciousness, "as the vessels of a potter shall they be broken to shivers" (2:27). The "iron rod" of "I" consciousness will gain the power to loosen those bonds that unite the group soul, and to shatter the structures that originated *exclusively* within the group soul. In place of those group souls "broken to shivers," another principle of community formation will arise—Mercury, the Morningstar, which is the "star" of manas influence in the spiritual history of the Earth.[3] There are two main influences that direct the Earth's path: that of Mars and that of Mercury. The Mars influence is that of war, the division of humanity, the splitting up of community. The influence of Mercury, by contrast, is community formation and unification. The "rod of iron" mentioned in the letter is the rightful internalization of the Mars impulse, whose goal is the emancipation of personality from the group condition. If the personality gains independence and freedom by means of the iron rod (the influence of Mars on earthly matters), it will be reunited into community through the manas influence of the Mercury impulse (that of the Morningstar). Thus, at the end of the letter to the church in Thyatira, there is the promise of the Morningstar, under whose sign those freed from blood relationships will be reunited.

## The Letter to the Angel of the Church in Sardis

In the previous section, we saw a specific path that human beings must take to ascend from the trials of weight, measure, and number to freedom. The stages of that path lead from the life body to the sentient body, from the sentient body to the sentient soul, and from the sentient soul to the intellectual soul, at which point the problem of freedom arises. Even so, none of the stages in the human path is complete; ever since awareness of freedom awakened, post-Atlantean humanity has had to deal with death, suffering, and toil (the great tasks of number, measure, and weight) in the spirit of freedom. Indeed, in order to continue along that path, human beings must make the three primal necessities of human karma their own, so that these necessities are lifted into the realm of freedom and completely imbued with it. From this perspective, we can see the path for the post-Atlantean epoch of human evolution that might be illustrated in this way:

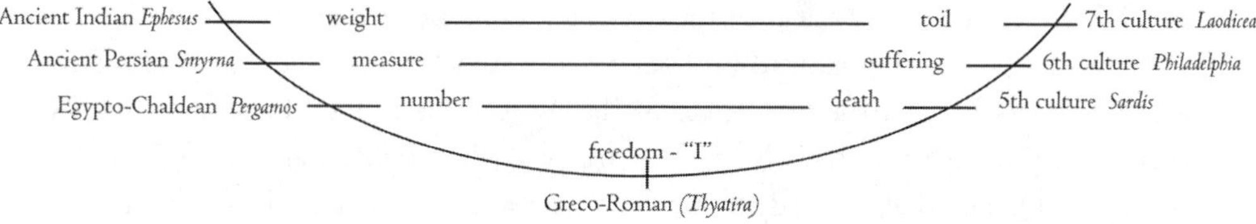


We make the three karmic necessities our own when we receive *within ourselves* what was previously approached from outside and then—creating in the spirit of freedom out of ourselves—transform it into higher forces and faculties. Thus again the mission of the fifth post-Atlantean epoch involves especially coming to terms with death, so that humankind can absorb its forces and learn to work creatively with and through them.

Although the present cultural epoch is still just beginning this task, we can already see the right and wrong paths related to the creative and controlling forces of death. Thus, for example, modern civilization owes its expansion to the cooperation of two forces: the force of dead abstract thinking and the mechanical forces of the material world. Almost all modern technological and scientific cultures have arisen through the influences of abstract human thinking combined with external mechanical forces. The faculty of abstraction is that of disconnecting actual life (light, color, rhythm, and warmth) from the realm of thinking. Essentially, modern, theoretical procedures involve killing the human thought life until it becomes a mere shadow, in order to handle that shadow freely and thus apply it to any desired area of life. Abstractions are believed to be without consequence and thus cannot influence the human soul. People can hold them in their hands and deal with them as they please. Similarly, modern human beings feel they can deal as they please with the mechanical forces of nature, especially those liberated through the disintegration of matter. The sub-organic forces of the outer world offer a field for developing power without restrictions like those imposed by the forces of living beings, in which there is always an uncontrollable element.

Working in this way with the forces of death, however, leads to two opposite results: on the one hand, it can free the inner forces of the soul and awaken them to a higher activity; on the other, it can mechanize human beings so that the inner forces of the soul go to sleep. The first takes place when souls in modern life demand and work toward another spiritually active area of existence. The very *emptiness* of the soul and spirit of modern civilization becomes a powerful motivation for developing an inner, creative activity to fill that emptiness. Then the arena of death forces supply abstraction and mechanism with a field for awaking the soul's deeper consciousness. It is natural for the mysteries of death to awaken higher awareness and bring clarity of consciousness. Certainly, this law is applicable: "He that hath, to him shall be given: and he that hath not, from him shall be taken even that which he hath" (Mark 4:25). Just as the wind makes a strong flame burn more brightly, it extinguishes a feeble flame. In this sense, we can understand how it affects the consciousness of a civilization when the abstract and mechanical take the lead. The deadly breath of abstract and mechanical tendencies can either stir the soul's creative consciousness to a powerful blaze or extinguish it altogether. This either/or effect of the death forces of modern civilization is the test of the present age and the main task of the fifth post-Atlantean cultural epoch. This is why the admonition of the fifth letter of the Apocalypse states, "I know thy works, that thou hast a name that thou livest, and art dead. Be watchful, and strengthen the things which remain, that are ready to die: for I have not found thy works perfect before God" (3:1–2). Those works (the sum of created cultural values) as seen inwardly (before God) are certainly not perfect (*ou pepleromena*). They are *empty* of divine life. In this situation, therefore, the first commandment is to be awake, on the one hand, and on the other to strengthen the things that remain and are ready to die. Dying and remaining awake are meant to balance each other; the more the one process is in evidence, the more the other must be also.

But awaking consciousness in facing death must take place in two directions: awaking to the true nature of the human being and awaking to the nature of the world. The latter must, indeed, be brought about by means of awaking and intensifying the memory, whereas knowledge of human nature must result from investigating the world. From the depths of consciousness, memory force must draw up knowledge of the "seven stars"; this is knowledge of the course taken by the grand "biography" of the cosmos through the periods of Saturn, Sun, Moon, Earth, Jupiter, Venus, and Vulcan.[4] The result of an awakened study of the universe is knowledge of the divine origin of the seven members of the human being—knowledge that the original entities of the physical, ether, and astral bodies, the "I," the spirit self, the life spirit, and the spirit body are really "the seven Spirits of God." These two consequences of awaking higher forces of consciousness are the purpose of the fifth cultural epoch. That is why, at the beginning of the letter to the church in Sardis, we find the ideal of the cosmic Christ, as of him "that hath the seven Spirits of God, and the seven stars" (3:1). The particular mission of the cultural epoch represented by the church in Sardis is to understand the Christ with the help of the seven stages of world evolution and the sevenfold nature of the human being. During this cultural epoch, Christianity based on knowledge of the cosmos is to arise, and then, having claimed the goals and purposes of cosmic evolution as its own, build the temple of the sevenfold human being as a home for the "seven Spirits of God."

Fulfillment of this task of the fifth post-Atlantean epoch necessitates following the path of awaking memory. And, of course, this awakening must not be only that of inward memory, but also the recognition of natural phenomena as the objective cosmic memory of past conditions in the evolution of the universe. Nature must remind us of the distant past; but we have to awaken our true nature inwardly through a "change of heart" (*metanoesis*), or repentance. There are two kinds of memory: horizontal, temporal memory, which can be awakened by nature, and vertical, spatial memory, through which we become aware of our own true character.

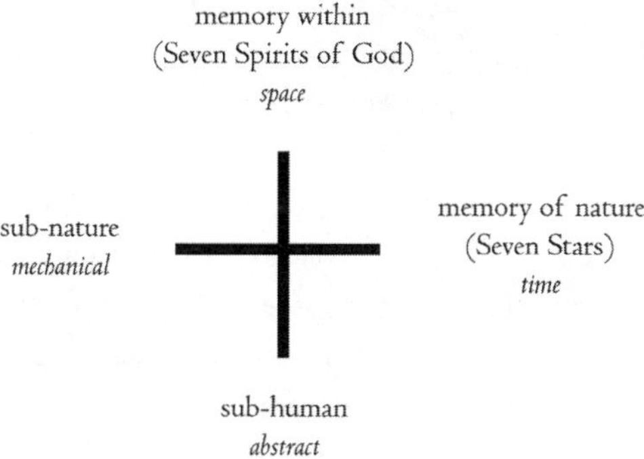


As we see from this diagram of the "cross" of the fifth post-Atlantean culture, two kinds of memory arise from the force of spiritual opposition to the sub-natural mechanical sphere, in the one case, and in the other, to subhuman abstraction. It awakens higher inner activity in opposition to the forces of death, both within and outside the human being. This awakening is complete once it has passed through three stages: images of spiritualized memory force; inner perception, or "hearing" of the soul; and purely spiritual reception into one's inner being. What is "received" in *intuition,* therefore, will be "heard" in the soul's *inspiration* and reappear in consciousness as memory. But once memory has descended from the sources of intuition along the path of *inspiration* to the *imagination* image, one is to translate it into an ordinary conceptual presentation so that it can remain a permanent possession of waking day consciousness. "Remembering" and "hearing" what has been "received" is followed by the injunction to "hold it fast"; in other words, make it a lasting possession of ordinary consciousness.

Thus the admonition of the letter to the angel of the church in Sardis contains the core essence of the spiritual method of the consciousness soul era: "Remember therefore (*mnemomeue*) how thou hast received and heard, and hold fast, and repent (*metanoeson*)" (3:3). Repentance, or a "change of heart," however, is behind this method; the moral force of "opposition" to the subhuman and sub-nature are to be awakened from the soul faculties that add the force of spiritual memory to thinking as a higher faculty of knowledge. In our age, it is the purpose of this higher faculty of knowledge (having been awakened to a consciousness based on the realm of death) to become aware of the great event of the second (etheric) advent of the Christ: "If therefore thou shalt not watch, I will come on thee as a thief, and thou shalt not know what hour I will come upon thee" (3:3).

The etheric second advent of the Christ is both the great hope and the great test of our time. It is the great hope, because it will exercise an influence that enables the soul to overcome the influence of abstraction and mechanization. Its influence will appear, for example, when a number of people overcome abstraction insofar as they can be stirred to the depths of the heart by pure thinking. This will not be an emotional relationship between the soul and thinking (as, for example, during the Middle Ages), but living activity of thought itself. Its influence will extend even into the human life body, and the life body, reanimated by the Christ, will give such life to thought that it will free it from abstraction. Such freedom cannot be attained, however, unless the conquest of abstract questioning precedes the conquest of abstract knowledge. Abstract inquiry, without the participation of the whole human being, merely tries to gain the comfort of a "flawless and incontrovertible system," but it will be replaced first by a new kind of questioning in which each question leads to another step toward awakened conscience. Then, the only questions will be those that arise from the soul's moral need. Then, too, questions will deal with the soul's happiness and unhappiness, though merely for the sake of increasing comfort. Nonetheless, this change in questioning must come before any real change in the area of knowledge can take place. Before the inner miracle can come to pass, there must be a period of tragedy in the questioning, inquiries in which the soul's complete happiness and unhappiness are at stake; and even when this has come to pass, it will not at first be *apparent.* The incapacity and failure of existing human moral and cognitive forces must be experienced fully before an actual event answers the one great question that sums up all separate questions: What are the *source* and the *means* of spiritual life force? More and more people and groups of people must begin to recognize that they have failed to do what they wished to accomplish. We have a task to fulfill, but we are not equal to it. We *cannot* do it, so how can we accomplish what we must?

We should not think that only those who are positively situated in modern materialistic civilization and science experience the tragedy of having "reached a dead end," and that those who devote themselves to, say, spiritual science are karmically immune from this problem. Everyone in turn will have to stand the test of experiencing failure, whether esotericists or not. The particular situations may be encountered on different levels of existence and in different states of consciousness, but no one is spared, just as no one person can overcome the general unhappiness of humankind in our age. It is the task of the initiates to experience the great crisis of human occultism, the task of the disciples to experience the crisis of community, and the task of modern culture's representatives to experience the crisis of the true moral value of modern views.

Rudolf Steiner spoke more than once of actual individual experiences of future meetings with him who will reappear with the etheric second advent. He spoke, for example, of the experience of a lonely individual sitting in a room in deep grief and helplessness, "not knowing which way to turn." Then one enters and speaks, and in place of despair comes light, strength, and life. Or, for example, there is a group of people at their wits' end. Again, the one appears among them and speaks words of comfort and hope.[5]

All the specific examples of future meetings with the etheric Christ that Rudolf Steiner gives have one thing in common: the people (whether alone or in groups) who experience such meetings are, in every case, at their wits' end, not knowing which way to turn; the encounter takes place at the very moment when one's consciousness requires it. That need is felt once the soul has been prepared through great pain of inquiry in order to be *awake* for that encounter. "Awake" in the soul means that it has experienced the questions of a conscience awakened to the transpersonal; it is the condition needed to know "the hour of his coming." *Not* knowing that hour—that is, remaining unaware of the event that is the concern of all humanity—is, nonetheless, not a punishment; if one's consciousness has no need of the Christ, neither will it have a conscious experience of meeting him. And one's consciousness does not need him if it is unaware of any question to which the Christ might be the truthful answer. Today, therefore, the most important issue at hand is to awaken human awareness to the questions at the very root of the soul's conscience. The most essential and the most urgent responsibility today is bringing consciousness, through spiritual science, of the "spirit's awakening call to the human soul."[6] That call is very different from those usually expected in the challenges of ordinary physical experience, because for ordinary experience the *strength* of the call determines its awakening effect. In the case of a spiritual call, just the opposite is true; the quieter and gentler the challenge, the more it is able to awaken the soul. The image of unhappiness joined by deep outer silence is the strongest spiritual call for awakening the soul's conscience. This call happens by means of a "voice awaiting free initiative on the part of the human soul"—in fact, so frequently that, whenever this strange, pregnant silence falls upon the spiritual world or any spiritual being, there is every reason for a person to ask, "What is expected of me? Let me try to see it in the light of my conscience."

Calls of the spirit are always images of unhappiness accompanied by pregnant silences. In this sense, there are three such awakening calls to all souls in the world that take the form of comprehensive demands of conscience. They are the unhappiness of nature, the unhappiness of humankind, and the unhappiness of the spiritual world. When St. Paul spoke of the "groaning of all creation," he meant the spirit's call to the human soul through nature. Nature depends on humanity; nature's well-being and suffering depends on the human race. Humanity can redeem nature by reuniting it with the spirit—or human beings can allow nature to fall ever more deeply into darkness and to become part of Ahriman's kingdom. The "awakening" that the Buddha experienced under the bodhi tree when he was roused to full Buddha consciousness was the result of becoming aware of the unhappiness of humanity. Birth, old age, disease, and death are the lot of all human beings and stages on the path of sorrow that constitutes human life. The Christ event had to happen nineteen centuries ago because the Buddha was correct in his assessment of human life.

For nineteen centuries, the crucifix has been a sign not only of what happened in history, but also of the condition of the spiritual world in general in relation to earthly events. If the cross of Golgotha stands for the healing of the human soul and body, it also implies a call, or challenge, to the free human "I." People took the *body* of the crucified Jesus from the cross, but what happened to his soul and spirit? Must not the liberator, himself, be liberated one day? The spiritual crucifixion continues; it is increasingly the destiny of the spiritual world. In fact, almost every guardian angel experiences crucifixion in the human being under his care. It is the task of the consciousness soul to become aware of those calls of the spirit; the questions connected with them must become a concern of the soul's conscience. This is the task of the soul: "wake up" to an awareness of the hour when the Christ will be present. That hour may be lived either as the "night" of consciousness or in such a way that consciousness goes with it. "But thou hast a few names in Sardis, which have not defiled their garments, and they shall walk (*peripatesousin*) with me in white, for they are worthy" (3:4). The possibility of "going together" or "walking with," however, depends on the condition described in the Apocalypse as names that "have not defiled their garments."

To understand this condition, we must study the two karmic areas of life and activities in the soul that constitute personal happiness and unhappiness, and we must consider the soul's meaning in the world. In every human being, we must distinguish between one's objective influence in the world and one's personal destiny—the destiny that is experienced within the narrow limits of a person's individual life. From very early days, the first area has been called the "name": the second is the karmic "body." Thus Goethe, for example, has both a "name" and a "body." His works, his influence on the world, and his knowledge both expressed and unexpressed all represent Goethe's "name"; his personal life, by contrast—his friendships and tastes, his character and temperament, his illnesses and health—constitute the "body." That "body" is and will remain hidden from the world by the garment of the "name," just as the physical body must be clothed before the eyes of the world. Thus, people may write biographies and draw attention to their "clothing name" (which is generally all that the world is interested in anyway), and they might also draw attention to the "body," which is covered by the "garment of the name." For example, Rudolf Steiner spoke of Goethe in a uniquely profound way; he shed light on his importance, his mission, and his influence on the present and future. Nonetheless, many have also written about the most personal matters in Goethe's life; they have thus "unclothed" him before the eyes of the world and revealed him in a way that is really no one's business. There is true wisdom and love in proclaiming a person's "name" to the world, but there is a certain indecency in showing a person's "body" to the world. Humanity owes to Rudolf Steiner (among others) knowledge of Goethe's true "name" as the source of the spiritual influence known as Goetheanism; but the trial of being deflected from what is essential to what is unessential is owed to several biographers.

It is not just biographers, however, who must learn to distinguish between a soul's objective influence and its intimate life; students of spiritual science must also do so, because the practice of "distinguishing the essential from the unessential" is the basic and fundamental requirement of spiritual development. The progress of such practice requires insight into the difference between the "name" and the "body," in the sense that the "name" is the concrete meaning of the revelation of manas (spirit self) by means of the human soul, whereas the "body" is the life of the soul itself, aside from its connection with the spirit self, which guides one from incarnation to incarnation. Whether one fulfills the mission (or objective task) of the soul in relation to the world is always revealed through the soul of the spirit self (and it is irrelevant whether the soul itself is aware of this); the purely personal, by contrast, is simply the expression of the personality itself. It is possible and permissible to interest oneself in the personality once the "name" has been recognized up to a certain point; one's vision is then pure, and one will not proceed without piety.

Nonetheless, we can treat our own "name" irreverently. This happens whenever we let personal motives and goals filter into the objective mission we have toward the world. These days, this sort of attitude toward one's purpose can be called "compromise." In the language of the Apocalypse, however, it is called "defiling" the name's garment. Compromise is the principle of false peace between the two opposites in human life; it also leads to darkening the system of spiritual current that "sheathes" the personal like a garment.

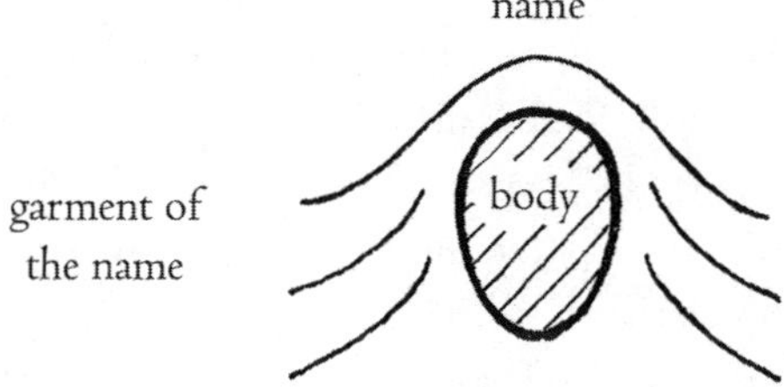


The introduction of the personal into the realm of objective purpose obstructs the spiritual light that streams down to help fulfill that purpose. The "light sheath" ceases to radiate its beams and becomes darkened.[7] This is the darkening that the Apocalypse calls defiling the garment of the name. Being "clothed in white raiment," by contrast, is the condition of being illumined by the light of the Spirit; thus, these whose activity is directed objectively outward stand with their impersonal, spiritual side toward the world. Strictly speaking, they do not merely "stand," but pursue a path laid down by Christ in the sense of the promise: "But thou hast a few names in Sardis that have not defiled their garments, and they shall walk with me in white, for they are worthy" (3:4). This describes the fulfillment of the particular task of the age of the consciousness soul; the important task for this epoch is that the consciousness soul should establish a proper relationship with the manas principle (or spirit self). The consciousness soul (like the other members of the soul) is developed by having not itself as the ideal and model, but a higher member of the human being. Development involves progress toward the future, and that future is manas, or the "name." The ideal hovering over the consciousness soul is to gain such an objectivity toward the world that all worldly matters become equal—not in the sense of dull indifference and excluding the life of the heart (as frequently found in a "scientific" outlook), but rather in the sense of a capacity to make, when necessary, everything in the world a personal, heartfelt concern. In such objectivity, the heart's life broadens enough to absorb every detail of world events, because the great purpose of those events has become a matter of the heart. This is the ideal that, for a healthy, progressive consciousness soul, gleams as a goal worth striving for. Efforts in this direction lead ever closer to the spirit self, and thus progress is achieved for the evolving consciousness soul.

The attainment of a conscious relationship with manas is described in the Apocalypse as being "clothed in white raiment" and "walking with Christ." It is a promise given in the letter to the angel of the church in Sardis, which is addressed both to the being whose mission involves the consciousness soul and to those who are especially connected with it. Similarly, the preceding letter is addressed to the being who represents the intellectual soul and to the associated "church." Once that provisional manas stage is reached, however (for the perfected manas stage will not be realized until the Jupiter period), this is what takes place. The name (the part of the astral body illumined by the spirit self) is projected into the life body, just as a seal is stamped into wax. The "name" is written in the "book of life." This transference of the illuminated part of the astral body into the ether body is an effect of the Christ impulse. The Christ impulse changes the "light" of the astral into the "life" of the etheric. The result of this change, however, is that the part of the ether body thus impregnated becomes immortal and does not succumb to dissolution after physical death. That individual's "name" is never "blotted out of the book of life" (3:5). But the words have another meaning as well; they refer also to the uninterrupted *memory* of the "name" retained by the individual being from incarnation to incarnation. Those whose ether body bears inwardly the "name" of the earlier incarnation also possess the memory of the spiritual core essence of that incarnation. One's "name" remains permanently in the "book of life," which one then also learns to read spiritually. Reading in the book of life is the faculty of memory made possible by the Christ; it is the capacity to draw vast stores of wisdom from past experiences out of one's ether body and to utilize them as ripe fruit for the benefit of humanity and the world.

Thus, through human freedom the problem of death (which, during the Egypto-Chaldean age, contained a tragic "sting") will be liberated during the fifth post-Atlantean epoch by a few "names" that have not defiled their "garments." By this means, too, this portion of humanity will be able to experience a new level of freedom. Freedom consciousness will be strengthened so that, with the "name written in the book of life" through Christ, one will become able to sustain consciousness of the Father's reality without injury to individual independence and freedom. Unless their "name" is written in the book of life by Christ and confessed before the Father and his angels, *consciousness of the Father's reality*—not just recognizing of the Father principle, but perceiving and feeling his actual spiritual cosmic activity and significance—cannot be borne by human beings; they would fall, crushed, to the ground. Along with the process of placing the "seal" in the ether body, *another* process also takes place; while the "name" (or the part of the astral body that has become manas) is projected *downward* into the ether body, the wisdom of that "name" is projected *upward*—also by means of the Christ—into the realm of the Father. The name that shall not be blotted out of the book of life is written at the same time that the name is confessed before the Father and his angels. Thus, human freedom is lifted into a new, higher realm, and the combined process that happens in two directions is initiation; it is the realization of a higher level of freedom and responsibility. "He that overcometh, the same shall be clothed in white raiment, and I will not blot out his name out of the book of life, but I will confess his name before my Father, and before his angels" (3:5). This promise proclaims a sublime prospect for the fifth post-Atlantean cultural epoch; it affirms that the ascent to true initiation will be made possible by the destiny, trials, and history of this epoch. What previously could be replaced only by means of an exclusive, esoteric mystery community is now (during the fifth post-Atlantean cultural epoch) accessible in any life situation through the karmic way of the "angel in Sardis"—by means of the open path of the spirit of the age. In this age, life itself will become an esoteric school for all who have not "defiled the garment" of their "name" by compromise.

The *reality* expressed by this promise in the Apocalypse is also at the foundation of the whole life work of Rudolf Steiner. The publication of his works (for example, *How to Know Higher Worlds*) would never have been justified, nor could they have been placed freely at the disposal of humanity, unless they had been based on the historical fact that, during the epoch of the consciousness soul, part of the path to a certain stage of initiation will be open to humankind. It is this consciousness that gives the concluding sentence of the letter to the church in Sardis even deeper meaning than that of the preceding letters—in particular, the exhortation, "He that hath an ear, let him hear what the Spirit saith unto the churches" (3:13).

We will devote the next chapter to the final two letters.

# Chapter 3

# Letters to Future Churches

## Letter to the Angel of the Church in Philadelphia

It is important for the fifth post-Atlantean cultural community to resume the struggle with death, which was taken up during the third (Egypto-Chaldean) cultural epoch. We have seen that this is essential for overcoming abstraction and mechanization through freedom from the bonds of materialism and selfishness. Similarly, it will be important for the sixth post-Atlantean cultural community to place the reality of *suffering* at the center of consciousness, just as during the second (ancient Persian) post-Atlantean cultural epoch it was the center of *destiny*. The fifth cultural epoch is a repetition of the third, and the sixth will be a repetition of the second. These "repetitions," however, do not mean that the outer aspects of the ancient Persian destiny, for example, will be repeated, but that the struggle with the "problem" of the ancient Persian cultural epoch will occur *inwardly* once again. This will happen in such a way that the repetition will be related to the spirit of ancient Persia, just as the spirit self (manas) is related to the sentient (astral) body. In other words, all the influences from the outer world at that time will emerge from human beings into the outer world as creative activity. For example, the God of Light (Ahura Mazda)—as the glorious revelation of the Sun—powerfully influenced souls from Heaven and will also influence the sixth cultural epoch. That influence, however, will no longer be poured from Heaven; the Sun influence will radiate from humankind and work through human activities.

The Ahura Mazda of Zoroaster will be just as surely the center of all spiritual life as he was in the time of ancient Persia; nonetheless, he will no longer shine from the Sun but from human hearts, because ever since that time he has followed the path that leads into human hearts. He became human and suffered human death. His path led him through death to resurrection, but not just to the resurrection that overcomes death in the human body, but also to the resurrection that overcomes death in the *soul*. The manifestation of Christ's resurrection in the human soul was the Pentecost. That event is the primal phenomenon of the sixth cultural epoch, which the Apocalypse calls the "church in Philadelphia." The community of Pentecost was no longer a circle surrounding Jesus Christ, but now a circle from which Christ revealed himself to the outer world. The language he used to reveal himself was such that people of all nationalities were able to understand.

The two main characteristics of the philadelphian spiritual culture are the immanence of the Christ in human consciousness and the cosmopolitan community that arises from that consciousness. In this sense, the sixth cultural epoch can be called the epoch of Pentecost. This name acquires even more meaning because the consciousness that leads to the culture of that time must stand the test of "keeping the word" and "not denying the name of Christ" (3:8); that is, it must be concerned with the word of Christ and with a relationship to his being as these become realities in the Pentecost. What was given then as a "dispensation of grace," however, must now be earned or submitted to before the cultural epoch of the spirit self can be realized. We must study the path that leads from the consciousness soul to the spirit self (manas) in order to understand the meaning of "keeping my word" and "not denying my name."

In relation to the seven stages of the passion of Jesus Christ (chapters 9 and 10 of our meditations on the New Testament), we saw that the Christ impulse finds no place either in the human organism or in the world as a whole. The human organism is filled with all sorts of substances, biological forces, and egoistic tendencies; in the areas of commerce, politics, and abstract intellectuality, human civilization is absorbed in profit, power, and pleasure. In fact, during this age of the consciousness soul, human life tends increasingly to eliminate all elements of real Christianity from its presence. Natural science, for instance, has already gotten rid of all Christianity from its area of influence, and business and politics are heavily involved in expelling Christianity from their realms as well. The banishment of Christianity from all areas of life goes on and on, and the "realities" of the physical world arrange themselves in stronger and stronger opposition to Christianity and in opposition to the love-filled light of wisdom that is just as essential to the human soul as are sunlight and warmth to a plant.

From this view of Christianity, the human world is empty and cold; in itself, however, it is overstuffed and stifling. Indeed, the "realities" of the physical world of humanity are gradually developing in a way that Christianity has been reduced to the same value and position that words have in that world. What Christian truth can manifest in present day life—that is, without having to protect itself everywhere through compromise? Only in the *word* can the Christ impulse become a reality among the people of today. True Christianity today has the same opportunity as does the word to live in the world without becoming adulterated and falsified by compromise; it is a time of great testing. The vast and powerful realities of today's Chastel Merveille are opposed only by the word and nothing else at all.[1] The millions of Christians cannot and must not be arrayed to do battle with the organized antichristian millions. Antichristian forces cannot and must not be fought through the use of their own weapons. Power, number, and organization—all are opposed only by the word borne by the human voice. The test is this: Despite everything, we must never say, "These are mere words; they are not the realities." Rather, because they can be only words, the *whole* reality of the Christ impulse must be experienced *in* them.

Because the great mass of antichristian and unchristian forces fills our entire life sphere, we must allow the power of thought, the life of the heart, and the feeling for truth to live in the word and to oppose the hostile world with the other world that can be experienced in the word. This *can* be done if we are truly aware of the fact that in the beginning the Word was with God; that *all* things were made by the Word, and that the Word that was once divine with God is now human and with humanity. Then, when human beings are wholeheartedly united with him who became man and spoke words as man—to him who instills divine forces into the human word—then humankind will know that the spirit-filled word of experienced and recognized spiritual truth can stand against the whole massive stronghold of "realities" of human physical existence.

This is the position between a world that seems to be able to live only in the word and exercise influence through the word, and a world whose rapacious power is eager to show that it can stifle and swallow up all free spiritual life. This position between two worlds (in fidelity to the world that initially seems to have no power or influence other than the word spoken by the human voice) is referred to in the Apocalypse as "keeping the word of my patience."[2] This is exactly the path that the soul must follow in order to make the transition from the consciousness soul to the spirit self. It involves an immense strengthening of awareness in the consciousness soul and, at the same time, a specific orientation toward the spirit self. This strengthening of awareness is attained by resisting the world of "facts," on the one hand, and, on the other, by not being led astray by the notion that nothing as "weak" and "insignificant" as "mere word" could be chosen to outweigh this world of facts. Awareness is not strengthened by contrasting physical facts against physical facts, but through the *awareness* of truth finding, according to *content,* the inner strength to see through the lies and illusions of the world of facts, and to face them without wavering or being deceived. By arraying the remaining "small strength" against a power that is still colossal, awareness joins forces with the "little strength" in the world, because it represents *truth* and rejects the "colossal power" of the world, seeing it is a lie having nothing but its sheer magnitude with which to convince.

If we understand the test that is applied to the awareness of the consciousness soul once it has declared for the spirit self, the words of the letter to the church in Philadelphia acquire amazing significance: "I know thy works: behold, I have set before thee an open door, and no man can shut it: for thou hast a little strength, and hast kept my word, and hast not denied my name" (3:8). Once it has been recognized as truth by human awareness, what was originally "only word" now becomes an "open door" to a world; it becomes the capacity for *constant* awareness and reciprocal interchange with the spiritual world, an ocean in which the physical world floats like an ice floe. Before this can happen, however, consciousness must not only side with the "little strength" against the "great" and "keep the word," but it must also refrain from denying the "name" of Christ.

This means that it is not enough to be faithful as a mere idealist to a universal world of ideas or the like, but to be faithful to a world of which the center is a Sun dispensing radiance and warmth like the physical Sun—a world at whose center shines not an idea, but the Christ sun, radiating warmth and light. For it is only so that converse with the spiritual world can become converse with *actual entities* (human and hierarchic). Then it is no longer merely a knowledge of truths and interdependences. When such conversation takes place in a light that makes the "appearances" of spiritual beings visible and their individual "voices" audible, then it becomes a real conversation with actual individuals. And the light that causes the individual in the spiritual world to stand out clearly from the universal ocean of impersonal morality and truth is to be obtained not by "keeping the word" alone, but also by "not denying the name of Christ." This signifies that the "keeping of the word" described above not only means that ideals are to be held aright in the face of external realities; it also has the special meaning that the ideals arising from knowledge are to be filled and permeated by the moral life of the Christ impulse.

The etheric Blood of Christ must convert ideas into ideals; only those ideas that spring from the soil of Christ's work in the universe have the faculty of pouring life forces into the soul. In *How to Know Higher Worlds,* Rudolf Steiner stated this principle: "Every idea that does not become an ideal for you kills a force in your soul, but every idea that becomes an ideal for you creates forces of life within you" (p. 25). We can understand this to mean that every idea comprehended in the spirit of the Christ impulse creates life forces; every idea not comprehended in that spirit kills the life forces. When it comes to understanding ideas, the point is not to spin them into a system of logic, but to root them firmly in the spiritual moral organism of Christ's cosmic work. In the Apocalypse, such work is called the "name of Christ," and "not denying" his "name" is the soul attitude that accepts as true only ideas indebted not just to logic, but also *always* to the moral forces. Not to deny the "name" is moral logic, just as amoral, formal knowledge is itself a denial of the name of Christ, since it excludes the voice of goodness from the realm of knowing.

The faculty of the *word* and that of *moral logic* (keeping the word and not denying the name) will be most highly developed at the beginning of the sixth epoch, the philadelphian, when the Maitreya Buddha, the "Bringer of Goodness," will appear. The special task of Maitreya Buddha is to develop what has "little strength"—the *word* and the *thought*—into a power that will regain a position in the world that allows a cultural community to evolve. This moral force of the word will live and work so powerfully in Maitreya Buddha that human beings will be stopped and experience a spiritual conversion, not only through their own efforts and meditation, but also through the magical, moral influence of the word. Thoughts will no longer merely explain the nature of goodness, but actually transmit it. The Maitreya Buddha will not merely *show* goodness; he will awaken it in the soul. Therefore, the effect of his word, as a great movement among humankind, will become the foundation of a new culture. This was the effect on those whom Gautama Buddha referred to when he spoke the prophecy concerning the Bodhisattva Maitreya, who would become the next Buddha: "He will be the leader of a band of disciples, numbering hundreds of thousands, as I am now the leader of bands of disciples, numbering hundreds."[3] From those hundreds of thousands will emerge the power to determine the life forms of the sixth post-Atlantean epoch—life forms that express the new Pentecost experience and the Pentecostal influence of the word. A single form of wisdom will inform and fashion all. There will no longer be opinions and worldviews; people will yield to progressive stages of receptivity for revealed *one* wisdom.

Thus, within that cultural community, the main source of culture will not be the *synthesis* of views, not mutual *opposition.* The unity of religion, art, and science—which were embraced during the very ancient past within the primal wisdom of the mysteries—will arise again and determine the whole cultural life of humanity. The meaning of that primal wisdom in the past can be understood from the testimony of the six centuries surrounding the beginning of our chronology. Plutarch, for example, wrote of the Egyptian Isis and Osiris and was convinced that they referred to Dionysus. Apollonius of Tyana (according to his biographer Philostratus[4]) visited Babylon, India, and Egypt and was able to offer advice everywhere in temples and schools. Both of these facts point to *universally* revealed wisdom that was still in existence, or at least as believed to be at the time. A similar universally recognized wisdom will be inherent during the sixth cultural epoch; the difference will be that, whereas the old mysteries looked back to the past as the stream of revelation already dwindling to its end, the sixth cultural epoch will deal with a current of ever-increasing apocalyptic wisdom of the future. People will not look back to the past to see a plan and pattern of perfection; they will look forward for knowledge and wisdom to shape the future, which will replace the authority of the past.

The position described here is not abstract and remote; what should be accomplished in the culture of one age must be experienced and realized in the occultism of the preceding age. The occultism of the present represents what must be realized in the universal culture of the future; this is exactly where we find its occult character. Hence the essence of today's occultism anticipates the essence of the whole sixth cultural epoch, the "church in Philadelphia." Therefore, the true occultism of the present is based not on being faithful to the past but on fidelity to the future. The purpose of occultism is to introduce to the future the growing current of revelation of "occult knowledge of the Grail."[5] This implies, however, that the higher must be awaited and sought tomorrow, not yesterday. Now, one's attitude depends largely on the content of one's spiritual knowledge. Rudolf Steiner said more than once that the occult stream of the Rose Cross is distinguished from others that flow from the past by its "apocalyptic" nature—its specific orientation toward the future. This does not imply a lack of interest in the past; it means, on the contrary, an awakening of *true* interest in the past. People do not have a true interest in the past unless they are looking at it for the causes that shape the reality of the future. They are then practically and morally impressed by the value that the past contains for the future; they look back to the past with an eye for the future tasks of the world karma that arise there. Further, from such a retrospective view, the most valuable gift that the past can give is bestowed upon the soul—that is, the kindling of the will to fulfill that task that knowledge of the past presents to the soul. Present-day occultism exists under the sign of increasing revelation, which human beings must respond to by bringing an increasing sincerity and selfless enthusiasm to their quest for truth. The development of today's expanding occultism depends on two factors: the influence of the spiritual world and the degree of sincere research and selfless intellectual force with which people meet that influence. In regard to what is needed for the higher side of this progress, cosmic karma has already determined that there should be a progressive enhancement of spiritual revelation. If that enhancement is not occurring at this time, it is because efforts have proven inadequate; in other words, research lacks earnestness, and intellectual pursuits lack altruism.

Nonetheless, regardless of how the streams of revelation may be dammed from *below* for now, the "'hidden' Grail knowledge will become evident; as an inner force, it will increasingly permeate the manifestations of human life" (Ibid., p. 389). This permeation of all of life's manifestations will extend again as far as it did during the age of the mystery culture. "For the duration of the fifth cultural period, knowledge of suprasensory worlds will continue to flow into human consciousness; when the sixth period begins, humanity will have been able to reacquire the non-sensory perception it possessed in a dusklike way in earlier times—but now on a higher level and in a form that is quite different from the old perception" (Ibid., 389). Also at this higher level, consciousness will develop an impetus toward a new culture, and space will be found on Earth for something that has had no place for a long time. The ancient mystery wisdom had temples all over the world; in them, the divine could still find a place, and once again will there be a place where the divine can live. Thus the Apocalypse calls the place recovered in the future for the divine a "temple," where the one who "overcometh" will become a "pillar" and "shall go no more out" (3:12).

This "temple" is also a state of consciousness and a cultural community foreshadowing the Jupiter existence ("the new Jerusalem, the city of my God") in the human realm of Earth. As a state of consciousness, it is a new relationship between the part and the whole, between humankind and the cosmos, between the individual and the community. This relationship may be described in this way: In the past, the mental and moral attitude of human beings toward the spiritual world was such that they felt lifted by it; their feet were on the ground, but the spiritual world made them "lighter" and prevented them from sinking into it. Now, by contrast, the relationship between human beings and the spiritual world is such that they feel that, standing on the ground, they support the spiritual world, just as a supporting pillar must be firmly positioned on the ground. It is not the solid earth, however, that supports human beings, but their "I" being. People experience their "I" as a point of support that bears the weight of the spiritual world, just as a temple's pillars support the vaulted dome above. Thus, those who have manas consciousness will have a much stronger "I" consciousness than they now have, because they will feel the "I" to be the only firm ground on which a world can be supported. Nonetheless, they will also not feel alone but a part of a wonderful "temple building," where each individual must take up a post as "pillar of the temple."

The consciousness of being a "pillar in the temple of God" (manas consciousness) is both individual to a large degree and more universal than is experienced at the level of the consciousness soul. Essentially, manas (or "name") consciousness has three stages. The Apocalypse describes them as the writing of three names on the pillar of the temple of God—the name of God, the new name of Christ, and the name of the new Jerusalem, "the city of my God ... which cometh down out of heaven from my God"(Revelation 3:12[6]). Each of these three "names" indicate a level of manas consciousness that corresponds to the three higher stages of the ancient Persian initiation. The three (of seven) higher stages of the Persian initiation, whose names were preserved in the later Mithras mysteries, were called Persian, Sun hero, and Father—the stages of the expanding consciousness of the sphere of one's responsibility. To be a Persian was to become aware of the spheres of responsibility for a nation; one recognized the mission of a folk spirit (an archangel) toward humankind and consciously devoted oneself to the fulfillment of that mission. To be a Sun hero was to recognize humanity's mission toward nature—that is, to absorb the Sun being of Christ into the human "I" to the degree that it would radiate healing forces into nature, bringing spiritual light and moral warmth as the Sun gives ordinary light and warmth. To be an initiate at the level of Father was to become aware of humanity's mission in relation to the world's evil—the transformation of evil into the highest form of good. These ancient Persian stages of initiation (like the spiritual culture of the ancient Persian age in general) will be resurrected. The stages (the name of the city, the new name of Christ, and of the name of God) essentially repeat those stages at a higher level.

The attainment of true social consciousness for humanity is linked to the aspect of apocalyptic wisdom related to the future Jupiter period of existence. This foreshadowing of Jupiter existence in human social life shows the mission that people will become aware of at the first level—the task that arises from knowing that the basis of social community is the spirit functioning in all of humanity. Only on this basis can the formation of justice and commerce take place in a way that corresponds to the spiritual revelation. In this sense, the first stage of manas consciousness will also be that of the Holy Spirit. The second stage takes place when human beings become aware of not just the social mission toward humanity, but especially the human mission toward nature. Humanity will cease to regard nature as an object of exploitation and will become aware that nature is awaiting redemption through human beings. During that cultural epoch, there will be a great deal of activity in the service to nature. The ancient attitude of service to nature will reemerge, yet people will not worship nor expect omens and oracles from nature, but serve for the purpose of healing nature. The capacity will be provided for bringing healing forces to nature, just as during previous times nature was able to bring forces of healing to humanity. People at this level of consciousness will represent the new name of Christ, because once the fifth sacrifice has been accomplished in the present age, the new name of Christ will be completed through the healing of the elemental, or natural, world. When the etheric Christ comes to Earth, he will not come only for humankind; his sacrifice will be for nature as well. Christ will receive a new name, because his healing activity will be new. Those who realize this and take it into their souls will arise as the new "Sun heroes" of ancient Persia—that is, as legions of the Son and the "brethren of Christ." The third stage of manas consciousness will be represented by those who have widened their sphere of responsibility to the degree that they become aware of the activities of the Father God of the world and devote themselves to him. But this will involve working in the realm of the greatest evil in order to transform it into goodness. Those who are at this level, which represents the Father's mission, will become the resurrected "Fathers" of the ancient mysteries of Persia.

The basis of manas consciousness and manas culture is only the first stage—the level of being aware of social community arising from the universal spiritual revelation common to all. Such individuals, who make up the group of the Holy Spirit, will be the true representatives of the sixth cultural epoch. The main characteristic of their consciousness will be (as indicated) a new relationship with the spiritual world and, at the same time, a new relationship with humanity as a whole. They will be profoundly self-dependent pillars in the temple of God, on the one hand, but, on the other, they will have the true social "we" consciousness. This true "we" consciousness (in contrast to unsocial individualism) will be based on a sincere feeling of responsibility toward the assigned station of each human being, which no one else can fulfill. Only this kind of self-dependence—in which individuals stand erect and on their own two feet—can such consciousness of community arise; this is the sense of fraternity that may be called "Philadelphia." Only those who know they hold a position in a community of harmonious work can also know that they hold a position in relation to others who also stand at their posts. Such awareness is the source of true fraternity, the Philadelphia that will form the basis of the culture during the next epoch.

Our meaning of the "next epoch," however, refers to the cultural community that responds to the call to "keep the word" and "not deny the name of Christ." Numerically, that community will nonetheless begin as a small minority in contrast to the great masses of humanity. To begin with, the majority will not be able to keep pace with the spiritual progress of the smaller portion of humanity; it will lag behind. The fact that the majority of human beings will lag behind does not imply merely a slow pace of evolution on their part; rather, it is the result of a karmic entanglement in the network that is spread purposefully by evil intelligences. Such a network is based on the principle of an inverted copy, or reversed reflection. Evil accomplishes the intentions of good in a false way; this is its only means of deceiving human consciousness. Evil appeals to the soul's prenatal memory impressions of the true tasks of the age; it also provides a *direction* that, though easier, lies entirely within the realm of evil. In opposition to the philadelphian cultural community, therefore, another community will form that, likewise, gives reality to "we" consciousness and sociality. The old antagonism of the ancient Persian epoch (the antagonism between the Iranian and Turanian cultures) will reappear.

In the letter to the church in Philadelphia, the Apocalypse uses the name applied to that hostile community in the letter to the church in Smyrna (referring to the ancient Persian culture): the "synagogue of Satan," Ahriman's congregation. In each case, it names the ahrimanic cultural community that, during the sixth cultural epoch, will again be separated off as a second, hostile culture. The essence of that culture will be the inverted reflection of the philadelphian culture. It will likewise include "we" consciousness, but not as a conscious expression of being "pillars in the temple of God" but of being the "nuts and bolts of a machine." Individuals will be welded into an impersonal power structure and will employ their forces to further its effectiveness. They will likewise stand at their appointed posts and share the weight of the whole, but they will not be supported by "I" consciousness but by the forces of subterranean strata. They will find the ground giving way beneath their feet, but they will not receive support in their "I" being; they will "sink" into the ground, because their support is really *beneath* the ground. This "sinking" of those who believe they are the community chosen to manifest the truth—"which say they are Jews and are not, but do lie" (3:9)—will lead to a relationship between the two groups in which the highest individual in one will occupy the position of the lowest in the other. A relationship will develop in such a way that those of the ahrimanic community will be able to understand and absorb only that aspect of the philadelphian community that can flow into their limbs and into their very feet.

In a sense, the head of ahrimanic individuals will have access only to the part of the philadelphian individual that has been able to work its way down into the feet. Only those forces of good that have strength to fill the entire human being from head to foot will be able to make an impression on ahrimanic individuals; everything else will seem unintelligible and illogical. Thus we can also say that the head of Ahrimanic individuals will be in the position of the feet of philadelphian individuals. Only a stream of true love of Christ (which *alone* can fill one from head to foot) will be able to offer conviction to Ahrimanic individuals. This is expressed with pregnant precision in the Apocalypse: "Behold, I will make them of the synagogue of Satan, which say they are Jews, and are not, but do lie; behold, I will make them to come and worship before thy feet, and to know that I have loved thee" (3:9). This acknowledgment of love's reality at the "feet" does not, however, imply only humiliation; it also describes the way knowledge of goodness may yet come to ahrimanic individuals. They will be able to attain such knowledge only in exact proportion to the degree that philadelphians are able to fill themselves with enough of the Christ impulse that it reaches the feet. *That* impulse will then enter an area accessible to the intelligence of ahrimanic human beings, who are sinking (only morally at first) into subterranean spheres. Nevertheless, this current of spiritual force working downward will not be present just occasionally; it will be a life condition of the manas person. Standing as "a pillar in the temple of God" does not mean only that one must maintain a vertical relationship with the spiritual world; it also means that one who stands in this way should become a channel for the descending flow of revelation from the spiritual world. The flow of such revelation, like one's continuous physical breathing, will be uninterrupted, because an "open door" will be provided (3:8).[7] "Open door" is the term applied to the level of consciousness that has already created the conditions, and assumes one's capacity, for conversation with the spiritual world. That faculty insures unhindered communication with the spiritual world and experiences consciousness as an "open door." To the spiritual eye (directed to the outer form of one thus endowed) this faculty appears to be a special formation of the individual's etheric head. It appears as a "radiant crown" upon the head—an expression of the ascending and descending spiritual currents that reveal the capacity of the "open door." That "crown," however, is associated with certain risks; it runs the risk of a one-way development of the currents that form it—development of only the ascending currents. As practiced in our age, yoga cultivates this; thus, consciousness may be detached from the body by this means, and higher consciousness may simply float away. Those who accomplish this have entered the luciferic path. Their "crown" will then be taken from them by another (3:11).

The crown must be "held fast," fixed firmly within the physical and etheric bodily organization. It then forms a doorway for the descending Christ impulse, which is always near the "crown" and always ready to provide an answer "quickly" upon any "questioning" current. Now we can understand this verse in the Apocalypse: "Behold, I come quickly: hold that fast which thou hast, that no man take thy crown" (3:11). Here, we can comprehend certain concrete facts of occultism instead of the usual poetic and moral definitions given to it. Similarly, we can understand, as a concrete spiritual reality, the aspect of the Christ being that is the ideal of the philadelphian culture, as shown in the introductory sentences of the letter. Each letter is introduced by an aspect of the comprehensive Christ being; this is the aspect revealed for the cultural epoch being considered. In this sense, the Christ concept of the sixth cultural epoch is revealed with these words: "And to the angel of the church in Philadelphia write; These things saith he that is holy, he that is true, he that hath the key of David, he that openeth, and no man shutteth; and shutteth, and no man openeth" (3:7). The Christ being will be experienced most of all as the force that leads to truth and morality (the holy and the true), to be felt and to function as a unity. The Maitreya Buddha of the sixth epoch will reveal exactly the new relationship between the "holy" and the "true," or between logic and morality, which are identical in the Christ being. "Moral logic" arises from an experience of the Christ impulse as it appears in the beginning of the letter to the angel of the church in Philadelphia—the impulse causing knowledge and morality to operate as a unity. It is this unity that "opens the door," bestowing the karmic faculty that makes possible communication with the spiritual world. This karmic capacity based on fidelity to the future is called the "key of David," since David's character answered the manas consciousness described earlier. The Christ of the sixth cultural epoch appears as the *initiator* who opens the door—that is, as the Greater Guardian of the Threshold, whom the sixth cultural epoch has the purpose of meeting. The Christianity of that period will be characterized especially by the fact that Christ is recognized and experienced under the aspect of the Guardian of the Threshold.

## The Letter to the Angel of the Church of the Laodiceans

Whereas the sixth cultural epoch had to recognize the Christ as the Greater Guardian of the Threshold, the seventh post-Atlantean epoch must become aware of another aspect of the Christ being. To understand this side of knowing the Christ, we must consider the past epoch that the seventh cultural epoch will "resurrect." Just as the sixth cultural epoch will "resurrect" the ancient Persian period, the seventh will likewise "resurrect" the ancient Indian epoch. Again, this will occur in the sense that the revelation and inspiration that flowed into human intellect during the old Indian epoch will now have to be learned and acquired through the effort of the intellect. The seventh cultural epoch will be related to the first post-Atlantean epoch just as the life spirit (budhi) is related to the ether body. The essence of the ancient Indian revelation will reappear in such a way that "seven candlesticks" on the Earth will no longer receive their light from the "seven stars." There will no longer be seven human beings inspired by the divine revelation; the content will appear as that *conscience* reveals itself in human beings. Everything involved in the ancient Indian period was a revelation from Heaven, and it will "rise again" during the seventh cultural epoch as the inner conscience of human beings. The word *conscience* is not used here as generally understood today—as moral judgment of one's actions—but in the sense of a kind of certainty. It is the certainty that can arise in the soul from comprehensive, formless, and silent knowing; it arises not from outer sensory impressions, speculative thoughts, or clairvoyant perception, but from the deepest level of ones being. "Conscience," in this sense, is the result of internalizing the experiences of numerous past incarnations. It is the great moral and spiritual synthesis of all experiences and revelations that the soul has received. During the age when Christianity began, such comprehensive vision from within outward was indicated by the word *amen,* which is defined today as "it is certainly true." This interpretation is justifiable insofar as it indicates an untranslatable word, as in the case of *Adm* in Sanskrit or the *Tao* of Taoism. If something is known as a certainty to be true, yet it is based only on the spoken word itself, having no meaning that can be found in ordinary experience, then the meaning hidden in his own nature has been revealed and the *certainty* arises from this revelation.[8]

In connection with the karmic history of the great Zoroaster, Rudolf Steiner offered an example of how this all-embracing inner wisdom, or the Amen, comes about.[9] He stated that, during the ancient Indian period, Zoroaster followed a path that prepared for his mission, from the ancient Persian period on, as the great teacher of the post-Atlantean mysteries. During that time, he passed through seven incarnations, in each receiving the revelation of one of the rishis. By this means, he absorbed the whole revelation of the seven Rishis. After that, he appeared in an eighth incarnation, blind and deaf. It was thus impossible for him to receive any sensory impression from the outer world. In that eighth incarnation, the great Zoroaster had to rely entirely on his own inner resources. As a result, the whole "memory" of the revelations from the seven rishis arose within him. He did not merely recall the Rishis' revelations; rather the revelation was resurrected from his "I" being as a unified whole. That unified whole then became an organ with the capacity to receive, during the next incarnation, a new revelation from without; this was the revelation of Christ as the Sun being, Ahura Mazda. Zoroaster's path was, in fact, the archetype of the path followed by all of post-Atlantean humanity, when many souls had typically absorbed the ancient Indian revelation and were taking the one path that led toward the spiritual world through blindness and deafness. The result of following this path, however, will be the resurrection from within of the original revelation and of all the experience it produced. Indeed, this resurrection will not merely repeat the arising of combined and enhanced past wisdom, but resurrect it as an "organ" for accepting the Christ being as the living essence of that wisdom. Christ is the core of the essence of that wisdom. He is the Amen, hidden in "the beginning of the creation of God" (3:14). The Christ being will be recognized as the Amen during the seventh cultural epoch—recognized as the one who is related to the resurrecting comprehensive wisdom just as the Sun is related to its light. Human beings become aware of the Sun by means of its light, unless of course they see nothing beyond the light and imagine themselves to be its source; likewise, in this revivified wisdom, they will possess an organ with which to receive the very essence of that wisdom. Hence, in the letter to the angel of the church of the Laodiceans, the Apocalypse speaks of Christ coming in to sup, or share a meal, with human beings. "Behold, I stand at the door, and knock: if any man hear my voice, and open the door, I will come in to him, and will sup with him, and he with me" (3:20). "Sup with him" expresses the fact that his entry leads to the closest conversation with the Christ being. Supping comes after hearing of the voice; *intuition* knowledge of Christ follows *inspiration* knowledge. The shared supper indicates converse of intuitive knowledge. Human beings take Christ into their innermost being, just as, in the physical world, we take in food; similarly, the Christ takes the human being into himself. The point is this: the meal is *shared*. In *intuition* knowledge, in addition to knowing, one is known. The "bread" eaten in this communion is offered mutually.

Before this can happen, however, one must pass the test that involves resurrecting inner wisdom from the past. The deeply imprinted memory that arises from within may affect the soul in such a way that it feels "rich," possibly becoming so satisfied that it asks for nothing further. Consequently, a disastrous error may follow; instead of using the rising memory as an organ (or doorway) for admitting the living being—whose very shadow contains all wisdom—and rather than turning a questioning gaze from the light toward the Sun that sheds it, one may be completely satisfied with the wisdom that has already been absorbed, possibly saying, "I am rich, and increased with goods, and have need of nothing" (3:17). In this way, those who experience wisdom and believe themselves "rich" do not recognize that they are "wretched, and miserable, and poor, and blind, and naked" (3:17) in terms of the real purpose of all wisdom. Although he became a radiant star of "wisdom from within himself," the great Zoroaster did not stop short at his comprehensive understanding and consciousness of bearing all wisdom within him; rather, he found the strength of true humility to use that wisdom as an "eye" that, forgetting itself, looks outward (as does a physical eye) toward a higher being. Similarly, those of the seventh cultural epoch will not consider the wealth of wisdom arising within them as an end in itself but as a doorway (and initiates at the corresponding level of occultism must do the same today). This organ is as selfless as the eye or ear; from the hidden heights, it receives the living essence of the Amen. The physical eye—a structure filled with tremendous wisdom—does not observe itself, but selflessly forgets its own being and submits to the outer world; this is the way people of the seventh cultural epoch must repeat the act of the great Zoroaster many thousands of years earlier. They must sacrifice their wise wealth of intensified memory in order to fashion something higher, just as Zoroaster did when he shaped it into a faculty through which to absorb the Sun spirit, Ahura Mazda.

The test of the seventh post-Atlantean cultural epoch will involve overcoming one's temptation to be content with riches derived from the past. If such a sense of contentment is not overcome, it will stall evolution with the result that the soul will become "neither cold nor hot" (3:15). This state of mind feels neither the coldness of loneliness and darkness nor the warmth of hope and endeavor for the future; it is a condition in which the soul actually rests, completely satisfied with itself. For the divine love of the providence that watches over the progress of humanity, this state of mind is a condition that offers just one alternative: the use of catastrophic blows of fate to restore the soul to a sense of cold and hot. Only such heavy blows can reawaken the spiritual humility that feels none of its knowledge and circumstances to be ends in themselves, or "riches," but regards each—however excellent and advantageous—to be a gift entrusted to the soul solely for the purpose of the work to be accomplished in the world under the unfailing guidance of the Christ being. Far from lingering in tranquil enjoyment of his spiritual treasures, the great Zoroaster became a prophet of the approaching Christ, feeling all the yearning of expectation and all the pain of a world that continued to await him.

Nonetheless, regardless of how edifying it might be to pass such a test, it is important to study those individuals in the spiritual history of humanity who had to experience the error of this great temptation. Thus, during the first century of our chronology, a much-maligned man lived and worked who nevertheless enjoyed immense authority and fame among his contemporaries. His fame spread throughout almost the whole known world of those days, from India to Spain. He was an initiate who, through his extensive travels (to Babylon, Egypt, India, and Spain), evoked within himself, layer by layer, an enhanced resurrection of the wisdom of the past. Step by step, comprehensive wisdom sprang up in him as he wandered. First there was the whole combined wisdom of the Greek mysteries; then there was an equally complete synthesis of the Chaldean and Egyptian wisdom. Later, after a glimmer of the ancient Persian wisdom (strangely weak compared to the others), the old Indian wisdom arose and outshone them all. Later, he traveled to the West, to Spain, to experience a rekindling of Western guidance, the path of Atlantean wisdom. This cooperation between external destiny and his inner life of knowledge led to a kind of consciousness that included a magnificent, intensified synthesis of the pre-Christian mystery wisdom. Thus, during the first century of our calendar, Apollonius of Tyana became, as it were, a living synthesis of all past mysteries, endowed with faculties that the entire world admired. This sage cared nothing for power or wealth and had practiced countless acts of compassion; he knew all the mystery schools and had learned all the traditions and had even visited most of the temples. The strange thing is, however, that this sage would pass blindly by the greatest events—and not just those of his age, but the most significant events of all world history.

Apollonius of Tyana ignored the Mystery of Golgotha. He never occupied himself at all with Christianity or with the Jewish mysteries. If we ask ourselves the reason of this strange circumstance, we have to conclude that it was the very wealth of his wisdom that "blinded" him to the Mystery of Golgotha. Apollonius was put to the test of viewing his accumulated wisdom not as the goal but as the means of attaining a higher level at which the fulfillment of all mystery wisdom can be found. The outcome of that initiation test was tragic. Owing to his remarkable wisdom and destiny, and obvious to all the world, Apollonius could have bestowed on humanity—with whom he had so much sympathy—the most profound knowledge of the Mystery of Golgotha. Instead, he left the impression that the world of his day had no use for the Mystery of Golgotha. If the mission of Apollonius of Tyana had not taken such a tragic turn, the almost indescribable tragedy of Julian the Apostate would never have had to happen. The gulf that opened at the time between exoteric Christianity and a mystery principle devoid of hope—a gulf created by the partisan spirit forced upon the Church by Julian—would never have existed at all if Apollonius had discovered and revealed the link between mystery wisdom and the event through which it was fulfilled. Christianity would not have become exoteric, and the mystery principle would have become an "eye" through which humankind could gaze with knowledge upon the Mystery of Golgotha.

Nonetheless, Julian was beloved by that spirit, the Sun Spirit, whom he also loved and who was present at that time on Earth. This fact made it impossible throughout the tragic course of his destiny for him to rely contentedly on his wealth of wisdom. In his destiny, the words of the Apocalypse became real: "As many as I love, I rebuke and chasten" (3:19). It may be seen in the destiny of Julian how suffering made it impossible for him to be either hot or cold, yet he lived in the most intense cold of loneliness as well as in the fire of his hopeless longing to reawaken the spirit of the mysteries. Thus, through the example of two different individuals (Apollonius and Julian) we can see the danger of resurrecting the memory of past wisdom and how protection may be available with the help of the lord of karma.

Nevertheless, those who withstand this test and overcome the temptation to relax in the light of wisdom achieve rest of a different kind in the very being from which that wisdom radiated. Love itself is the being on which wisdom depends, and those who overcome the temptation involved in wisdom enter the hidden realm, the Amen of wisdom; they become rooted in the very being of Christ. Being rooted in Christ is true rest, since it does not mean resting satisfied with past results, but rather a condition of security that taps into the inexhaustible springs of patience and courage to fulfill the Christ mission throughout the ages. This is the state of sharing Christ's sources of strength, where the soul rests in such a way that it becomes ever stronger for ever greater efforts of sacrifice. This condition is described in the Apocalypse as sitting in the throne with Christ. This letter ends with a promise: "To him that overcometh will I grant to sit with me in my throne, even as I also overcame, and am set down with my Father in his throne" (3:21).

This inner intuitive relationship to the Christ being will be the positive outcome of the seventh cultural epoch, whereas the negative outcome will be the antithesis of the supping together. Christ will "spue" from his mouth those elements of the seventh cultural epoch that have rigidified into a state of self-satisfaction. This spitting out, however, is a process that means not only being separated from the Christ, but also—and above all—being *aware* of that condition. It will be experienced in such a way that they will experience a "plunge" into cold and darkness. That plunge will include a shock that may be salutary in the sense of awakening them to "cold" and "warmth" in the soul—in the sense of being liberated from resting in self-satisfaction. That shock was also experienced in the past on the path of karma in earthly life. It was experienced, too, in life after death. In the future, however (especially during the seventh cultural epoch, which will end with the "war of all against all"), for the great majority of humankind such a shock will be the only cure for the condition of false rest. Further, the war that will bring about the destruction and end of the whole post-Atlantean culture will be karmically necessary to shock humanity into realizing that they are not "rich, and increased with goods, and have need of nothing," but are instead "wretched, and miserable, and poor, and blind, and naked" (3:17).

# Appendix

# The Four Sacrifices of Christ

## and the Reappearance of Christ in the Etheric

*Based on seven lectures by Valentin Tomberg*
*December 1938 to January 1939, Rotterdam*

## CONTENTS

1.

# The Cosmic, Primeval Acts of Christ

Anthroposophia, as a living being of spirit in the world, is like any other being living in time; it has a past and a future. In other words, what arises from the nineteenth century affects anthroposophic work; on the other hand, future prospects for the end of the twentieth century are still before us. It is up to us to choose a direction and guide the work from the past into the future. Rudolf Steiner has often pointed out the important aspects of future anthroposophic work. The transition from all that is most prosaic of the nineteenth century to all that the future holds is offered by the spiritual manifestation of Goetheanism, which indeed constitutes a bridge for the transition from nineteenth-century quantitative thinking to a more qualitative and descriptive thinking. This transition leads to spiritual science. Here it is not just a matter of being able to think qualitatively, but also of bringing the moral element of thinking to the foreground. By comparison, one could say that Goetheanism is related to Anthroposophy, or spiritual science, just as the organic world is related to the soul world. The organic calls for qualitative thinking; the soul world calls for the formation of moral concepts.

Spiritual science has a future and must form a bridge. It has a central, or core, question, and spiritual science exists for the sake of resolving this. Rudolf Steiner stated several times that all of spiritual science has been called into being to bring about an understanding of the Mystery of Golgotha. Everything we learn from spiritual science is to help us progress ever further in deepening our knowledge of the Mystery of Golgotha. One could say that, in all spiritual scientific work, Christology occupies a position that has the same relationship to individual questions as the relationship of the Sun has to the planets; it is central. In *An Outline of Esoteric Science,* Rudolf Steiner tells us that the future of the spiritual scientific movement (in the fifth cultural epoch and on into the sixth) will be based on a growing Grail wisdom, which will stream increasingly into the spiritual life and culture of humankind. Indeed, much is stated here; when we look to the past, the beginning of our era, we find echoes of a primeval wisdom. At that time, people looked to the past for a model of what would come in the future; wisdom was waning.

Today is the time when a spiritual stream exists that is increasing; it is a time when the important factor is the continually growing Grail knowledge flowing down into human consciousness. There is a fundamental difference between the old mystery wisdom and what Rudolf Steiner calls the apocalyptic wisdom of the Rosicrucians. mystery wisdom was based on the past; it held what had existed earlier as the ideal. Apocalyptic wisdom, however, is based on the future; in this case, the more perfected is yet to come. Just as the authority of mystery wisdom was carried by what had proved itself with time, similarly in the stream of apocalyptic wisdom, increasing authority will be based on what proves fruitful for shaping and understanding the future. When Rudolf Steiner chose the term "Grail knowledge," he meant the main characteristic of this apocalyptic, ever-growing stream of wisdom—knowledge of the Christ mystery. It is the Grail mystery: the mystery of Christ continually working and progressing. This is the situation for the history of the spiritual movement.

Furthermore, if we direct our attention even higher, we can comprehend the fact that the three foregoing periods of ancient Saturn, Sun, and Moon evolution were stages of preparation for the event of Golgotha. We must look higher than human history and lift our gaze to cosmic history; we begin with the understanding that the Mystery of Golgotha is the very purpose of Earth's evolution. These meditations are intended to consider the acts of Christ, in their various stages, from this perspective. First, however, we must ask ourselves the most important question concerning the being of Christ: Who is the Christ in the cosmos? This question is justified to the extent that there are very different and seemingly contradictory indications regarding the Christ being. You can read in the work of Rudolf Steiner, for example, that Christ is the "fullness of the elohim" and, furthermore, that Christ was a being active during the ancient Sun period as leader of the hierarchy of archangels; again, we read that Christ is the *Logos* who created the cosmos. All such concepts must be interwoven as a comprehensible whole that can be investigated.

To understand the being of Christ, an example, or analogy, may provide real help—an analogy of the human breathing process. The breathing process involves four aspects: we breathe in, we pause when the lungs have filled with air, we breathe out, and we pause when our lungs are emptied of air. These are the four stages of the breathing process. With this analogy, we can approach the Christ mystery from four points of view. First, imagine that Christ is born from the Father's essence; the Christ being is the Father's "breath"; the Christ essence arises from the Father. Here you have the concept of the Son who is in the Father, who is one with the Father, as breath in the primal breathing being. Next, imagine the essence as being present itself, just as the air-filled lung is present itself. You see, once a word is spoken it is outside and external. The spoken word lives on. This is the second aspect, the Logos. The Son is always being born of the Father, but once the word is born, it stands for itself; that is the Logos. Now, if this Logos emanates for the salvation of beings—if this Logos "breathes out" and enlivens beings—then we have the Christ as a being that gives life and heals. We have Christ, the Savior; the Christ who acts as a redeemer for the beings of the world.

Now, a fourth element arose, a being that can be designated as Jesus Christ since the Mystery of Golgotha. This is not only the Logos, or the Christ, but a new being who arose because the Christ passed through a human body. A fourth good, a primal good, has thus arisen in the world. On ancient Saturn, the decisive act was done by the Father;

on ancient Sun, the Son was at the center of all activity; and on ancient Moon, the Holy Spirit led the world. Now you can see the fourth principle of primal good arise in Earth evolution; something new has entered the world. The Rosicrucians knew about this. In the Rosicrucian writings of Hinricus Madathanus Theosophus, you find not only the Trinity (the secret figures there contain not only the "three"), but also a fourfold being, or quaternary.[1] Indeed, this quaternary involves the Father, the Son, the Holy Spirit, and the "Person" of Jesus Christ. What arose through Jesus Christ is the divine being of the Personality. It is something new that came into being through him. Thus we can compare this fourth entity with the fourth stage of the breathing process, the stage at which the lungs, now emptied of air, rest, and complete independence has been realized. So when we speak of the Christ, we must always distinguish what we mean—a countenance of the Trinity, the Son; the Logos; the Redeemer, Christ; or the one who arose *after* the Mystery of Golgotha, Jesus Christ.

Now, after this introductory consideration of the Christ being, let us try to consider the cosmic prehistory of the Christ being until the Mystery of Golgotha, so that we may gain, in broad outline, a plan for our further meditations. When we follow the course of cosmic evolution described in Rudolf Steiner's *Outline of Esoteric Science*, many important questions arise. For example, during each cosmic stage of development (the periods of Saturn, Sun, Moon, and Earth), one hierarchy passed through an experience resembling that of humankind. The human stage of humanity itself is connected with a sacrifice we call the Mystery of Golgotha. Could it be true that the foregoing stages of human experience in the world—when archai, archangels, and angels experienced their human stage of development—happened without a corresponding sacrifice? The answer is this: A gradual intensification of sacrifice through each cosmic stage did, in fact, take place. The Mystery of Golgotha was a unique event, since it involved a passage through death, but it did contain various stages that recapitulated those that took place as sacrificial acts at the other levels of cosmic evolution.

Thus, we might ask: What was foremost for the beings who went through the human stage during Saturn evolution? They went through their human stage by being placed between coldness and warmth. During the Sun stage of evolution, the beings who went through their human stage were placed between light and darkness. This is the difference. The descending Saturn evolution, until halfway through it, involved the fact that, through cold, the principle of hardening continually increased. After the midpoint of Saturn evolution, an ascent began that led ultimately to the action of the thrones, the spirits of will, which planted the seed of the spirit body (atma) into the essence of the physical body. The transformation that took place at mid-descent (the change in direction of development) was not a mere rotation of the wheel; nothing in the world turns itself. Every event in the world involves actions—acts of beings and groups of beings. If, then, Saturn evolution experienced an ascent, this indicates an action. What took place there was the act of a secret being in the middle of Saturn evolution (in the iciest cold), causing the transformation of that cold into the warmth of will. One has to imagine that the trial of Saturn evolution consisted in the fact that will was "banned," or immobilized, and that a being of Saturn evolution caused a turning point by offering the sacrifice of entering that immobility of icy coldness and "standing" there. Steadfastly "standing" within the persistent, motionless will led to the turn in Saturn evolution. When Jesus Christ was nailed to the cross, it was a distant echo of this Saturn event when he said, *"Eli, Eli, lama sabachthani"* ("My God, my God, why hast thou forsaken me?" Matthew 27:46). Calling upon "Eli" recalls, or repeats, the event on Saturn that was the primordial crucifixion of the world. And when the Father later sent the Son down to Earth so that he would die by crucifixion, this was known by the Father being; it was something that had already been realized on old Saturn.

If we continue on and consider Sun evolution, we can ask: What event caused the turning point toward ascent during Sun evolution, so that descent did not continue eternally? What act allowed an ascent to take place? (For nothing happens on its own; there are always actions at the roots of every event.) The answer is this: During the Sun period of evolution, there was tension between light and darkness. When this condition is translated into the soul's terms, it signifies the essence of joy and misery. At that time, when the archangels were going through their human stage, everything that can be experienced in the soul as a state of joy and misery composed itself into the tension between light and darkness. The essence of happiness involves the fact that there is a "relationship." The essence of misery in the soul involves the possibility of complete loneliness in the world; the darkness of loneliness is the essence of misery. It was in these polarities of "loneliness" and "togetherness" that archangels experienced their human stage of evolution.

As we know from the literature of spiritual science, Christ became the leader of the Sun evolution. This does not mean, however, that he was the most powerful among all the beings during that stage of evolution, but that he nonetheless offered the greatest sacrifice during the Sun evolution. The sacrifice that was offered when the archangels went through their human stage of development was this: One archangel had inwardly united with the being of Christ, and this union created a still point—the still point of complete aloneness within the overall experience of loneliness. The center of the radiant Sun was morally and spiritually fashioned when the Christ being plunged into the darkness of loneliness. In this way, the Sun radiated its own light from this center, while the center point itself was in total darkness and loneliness. What happened then, during ancient Sun, was repeated during the Mystery of Golgotha. Just as the physical crucifixion was a repetition of the sacrifice that took place during Saturn evolution, the night in Gethsemane was a repetition of the sacrifice on ancient Sun. That night repeated what caused the turning point for ancient Sun evolution.

Most important for the ancient Moon period of evolution is the fact that the Moon had two sides; ancient Moon existence was also situated in a tension between two polarities. One side was turned toward the Sun, while the other was dark. In *An Outline of Esoteric Science*, Rudolf Steiner describes the changes in consciousness of the Moon inhabitants.[2] He describes how they had a consciousness directed toward the Sun on the light side and, on the dark side, had a pictorial consciousness. This led to the pendulum-like oscillation between a resounding Sun and silent perception of the lunar environment. The danger that threatened Moon humanity then involved the fact that it could be torn apart into two separate kinds of humankind; one kind would have outer perception, and the other would have Sun awareness. Consequently, a mystical humanity and a materialistic humanity would have eventually arisen on Earth. This would have begun on old Moon if a sacrifice had not again taken place. The sacrifice performed by Christ on old Moon was essentially his union with the same archangelic being whom he had united with on old Sun. Thus he went to the dark side of the Moon to awaken the memory of the Sun and eliminate the danger of forgetting. On old Moon, the sacrifice was that of descent into oblivion so that memory could arise from oblivion. That sacrifice, too, was reflected in the events of Golgotha. And at the Last Supper, when Jesus Christ was with the circle of his disciples, he broke the bread and gave it, saying, "Do this in memory of me" (do this to reawaken the memory of me). The Last Supper thus recapitulated the sacrifice on old Moon, the mystery of the resurrection of memory out of oblivion.

Now, when we come to Earth evolution, the fourth cosmic stage, we find that sacrificial acts of the Christ being have taken place here, too. The first took place during the Lemurian epoch. Christ again united with the archangelic being with whom he had united on ancient Sun, causing a change in the human organization that manifested as the upright stature of the human being. (Here we will consider this only as needed for an introductory overview of the whole cycle of events.) Human beings at that time became upright. One could say that, in their physical volitional organization, a stream of will was activated, which raised humankind from a horizontal position to the vertical. The sacrifice consisted in the Christ uniting with the Archangel Jesus to the degree that he stood immobile, as it were, like a pillar. Christ brought about an absolutely vertical stature at that time. He was stretched out from the Father to the Earth in an immobile column of will. The effect of this sacrifice, which was a repetition of the one on Saturn, was that human beings now stood upright; a stream of volition arose in the physical body. The primordial Saturn volition was awakened. Human beings stood upright and thus became truly human.

At the beginning of the Atlantean period, the danger arose that human soul life might be completely absorbed into the organic life processes, thus the soul was lifted out of the life processes of the ether body. Again, behind this action was a sacrificial act by the Christ. Whereas the first sacrifice by Christ during the Lemurian epoch was completely static and vertical, or obelisk-like, the Christ's sacrifice at the beginning of the Atlantean epoch was an activity of outstretched arms, expanding the soul horizontally. The soul was lifted out of the life processes when a stream of expansion entered it. Consequently, the independent sounds of human speech arose. Speech came into being when isolation, or loneliness, was overcome. Every word that a person speaks is overcoming loneliness. Speech, or lifting the voice to make a sound, overcomes the condition of being alone. This took place at the beginning of the Atlantean evolution; human beings had left the "paradise" state and experienced a sense of loneliness, and speech was born out of this. The pain of loneliness invoked the first human vocal sound. Again, this event reflected, or repeated, the event on old Sun, when the cosmic "night in Gethsemane" took place at the midpoint.

Toward the end of Atlantean evolution, the third earthly sacrifice by Christ took place. This sacrifice caused the human "I" being to be lifted out of the human astral realm of thinking, feeling, and volition; this was the result of the Christ's sacrifice. The actual act of sacrifice, again, involved uniting with that same archangel so that a stream arose in the human organization that primarily loosened the human thinking capacity from the astral body; thus, the "I" was able to establish itself there as its prime area of activity. This sacrifice also affected memory, since the power of *imagination* was covered over; the faculty for inner perception of the ether body was concealed through this sacrifice. As the memory capacity of Atlantean human beings became increasingly weakened, a new faculty arose—the ability to use consonants in speech, or human speech as we know it. In fact, human beings cannot speak unless they have lost the capacity for complete, unforgetting memory. Just consider what it would be like if we had all of our past experiences displayed continuously before us. We would be unable to say anything. We cannot speak, however, unless the whole of the treasury of memory has been extinguished; speech draws upon the dark content of the forgotten and manifests from the darkness of forgetting as creative memory. One cannot speak unless inner memory has been silenced and darkened; one must allow the memory to be resurrected through the creative activity of the human "I," which can not only to give expression to the human soul, but can also report objective, outer events. This sacrifice took place at the end of the Atlantean epoch and recapitulated the Moon sacrifice on Earth. On ancient Moon, it had been necessary, through forgetting, to bring about the resurrection of Sun memories; now it was necessary for memory to be resurrected as human speech. These three sacrifices of Christ on Earth therefore represent acts of cosmic prehistory that took place in the past.

The fourth sacrifice, the Mystery of Golgotha, was not prefigured in the past; it was completely new beginning the moment Christ died and descended into the interior layers of the Earth. The Last Supper had a cosmic precedent; the night in Gethsemane had a cosmic precedent; the crucifixion on Golgotha had a cosmic precedent; but the descent into the realm of death was new and had no precedent. Thus, we have the Mystery of Golgotha as a process that did not involve a recapitulation. The Mystery of Golgotha has karmic consequences, one of which is the need for Christ's return in the etheric, the *fifth* sacrifice of Christ. Just as the three previous sacrifices of Christ were to some extent a recapitulation in the earthly realm of past sacrificial acts, the fifth sacrifice of Christ will also prefigure the future. The Mystery of Golgotha, in terms of Christ's descent into the Earth, is unique and has no precedent; nor does it prefigure the future. The fifth sacrifice of Christ, on the other hand, anticipates the future Jupiter evolution.

The reappearance in the etheric has significance not just for humanity, but also for nature. The purpose is to bring something new into being. After death, the human ether body "dissolves"; nevertheless, at the same time an extract survives death and goes with the individuality from one incarnation to the next. Likewise, nature will also acquire a realm related to ordinary nature, just as the extract of the human ether body relates to the ether body itself. The extract of the human ether body is, in fact, budhi, or life spirit. Similarly, a realm of life spirit will also arise in nature as a result of the etheric second coming of Christ.

In these meditations, we will go into the details of the Christ's sacrifices. Here we could give only a general outline to prepare for all that will follow. In this study, we have presented introductory considerations, and in the following six meditations we will try to assemble the cosmic building stones we need to understand the return of Christ in the etheric; the etheric return of Christ manifests as a need of the karma of worlds past and from the Mystery of Golgotha. This is the task we have assumed.

2.

# The First Sacrifice of Christ during the Lemurian Epoch

We spoke previously about the cosmic prelude of the Mystery of Golgotha, in the sense that the three sacrifices of Christ took place on Earth before the Mystery of Golgotha and have a cosmic prehistory. Certainly, an act of sacrifice was performed on old Saturn that gave that period of evolution an upward direction. On old Sun, an act of sacrifice by the Christ took place that is reflected in the second sacrifice of Christ on Earth, just as the first earthly sacrifice was a reflection of the Saturn sacrifice. And the third sacrifice of Christ on Earth was a reflection of the Moon sacrifice of the Christ being. These three cosmic sacrifices took place in the past and reappear together in the Mystery of Golgotha. Thus, the Last Supper, the night in Gethsemane, and the crucifixion on Golgotha all have a cosmic prehistory. The point is this: The stillness of the crucifixion was the essential element of the Saturn sacrifice; the solitude of the Night in Gethsemane repeated the essence of the Sun sacrifice; and the Last Supper, as an act for the resurrection of memory, repeated the sacrifice on the old Moon. Moreover, we discussed the fact that the cosmically new element that took place with the Mystery of Golgotha was Christ's death and descent into the Earth, or "descent into Hell."

Now we will consider the first earthly sacrifice of Christ during the Lemurian period. What we have already mentioned (and Rudolf Steiner confirms) is that the first, the Lemurian sacrifice, and also the sacrifices that followed, led to the being of Christ becoming united with the Jesus being. If we are to understand the sacrifice, we must consider the way this union took place. We must begin by asking: Who is this Jesus being? By raising this question, we must consider two elements. First, there is the Archangel Jesus; he is one of those archangels who experience a descending development, who make the sacrifice of descending from a higher stage to a lower stage. Second, we have to consider the so-called sister or brother soul of Adam. Not all of humankind fell into sin when the fall of humanity took place; a portion remained outside that fall and is designated the brother or sister soul of Adam. As Rudolf Steiner indicated, this is an etheric being, which is to say that it is the life spirit of humankind. It is the being who bears the budhi life body of Adam. The Archangel Jesus united with this sister soul of Adam and became a single entity, and later he surrendered it to the Christ as the vessel for the Christ being. Because of the unification of these three beings, the Christ was able to act not only in the third hierarchy, but also in the fourth hierarchy, or that of humanity. If the sister soul of Adam had not been an element of the Jesus being at the time of the sacrifice, the sacrifice of Jesus Christ would have affected only the third hierarchy. It was necessary, however, for it to affect humanity and thus a human element was incorporated into this being of Jesus when he allowed himself to be permeated by Christ. Consequently, the being of Christ affected humanity through the sister soul of Adam, which represented the portion that had not fallen, while maintaining a karmic and spiritual connection with the fallen.

Now, however, we are faced with more questions: How is it cosmically and karmically possible for there to be such a being of humanity that had not fallen? And how should we understand the fact that, after the fall of humanity, a portion of this being of Adam was able to remain behind in the spiritual world, on the other side of the threshold? There is, however, a great cosmic secret, or cosmic event, behind this fact. You will recall that, at the very beginning of world evolution and during the time of ancient Saturn evolution, there was a sacrificial surrender of the thrones to the cherubim; the thrones, or spirits of will, sacrificed their will to the cherubim. This volition, flowing out of the thrones to the "feet" of the cherubim, was accepted, on the one hand, and, on the other, was rejected. The whole world manifested because the sacrifice was not accepted; the will was rejected. What we call the "substance" of the world originated because the Thrones' volition was rejected by the cherubim. Nevertheless, another part was certainly accepted by the cherubim. Here we have a cosmic treasure that allows the possibility of redemption through this activity of grace—the element in the substance of the world that had not fallen, the will of the thrones that the cherubim accepted. We can say, therefore, that part of the world substance streamed down into the material world; this is the part that was rejected. There was another part that was, in fact, accepted by the cherubim; this is the primal portion that did not fall into the world of sin.

What does this mean? It means that, at every stage and for every hierarchy, there is still a possibility of remaining guiltless at a certain spiritual level in order to descend and function, later on, in a redemptive way at cosmically critical points in time. From the very primal beginning of world evolution, therefore, we have the karmic realization of the possibility of help in the future: redemptive action in the world. Something that remained beyond the karmically conditioned realm would be able to intervene later on in a way that redeems.

For the same reason, this provision is also valid for the human hierarchy. When the fall into sin occurred during Earth's evolution, part of the human being was held back in the spiritual world for the work of redemption. Since then, through the countless thousands of years of further human development on Earth, the sister soul of Adam has had the function and the task of allowing the power of Christ to flow down into the realm of human existence. This was also true of the first sacrifice of Christ. The Christ was able to work into the human hierarchy only by uniting with the guiltless sister soul of Adam, thus changing the human physical organization. We must imagine the being that carried out the sacrifice during the Lemurian epoch as a vessel formed from the being of the archangel, that this vessel was replenished from the higher worlds by the being of Christ, and that this vessel then established a connection with humanity through the sister soul of Adam. The effect of the first sacrifice during the Lemurian epoch was (as Rudolf Steiner indicated) the harmonization of the human sensory system, on the one hand, and, on the other, the attainment of a physical upright posture for human beings.

Now we will try to gain a deeper understanding of what this means. When we consider the human senses today, we find the peculiar characteristic that they are "selfless." The eye, this wonderful structure, does not contemplate itself, but selflessly devotes itself to the outer world. We perceive the outer world because the eye does not perceive itself. The other senses, as well, surrender themselves selflessly; they are forgetful of their self. At the same time, however, today's senses are dead. They represent the element in the human being that comes closest to being mechanical and machine-like. They function as marvelous mechanisms, but there was a time during the Lemurian epoch (before the fall of humanity) when the senses were much more alive than they are today. They were constituted in such as way that, when a color was perceived, for example, it was not just a simple, objective perception that said, "This object is green." Instead, the whole human being was moved by the perception. When those individuals perceived blue, they expanded; when they perceived red, they contracted. Human beings "breathed" colors through the senses. The senses had a much more intimate relationship to the objects that were perceived. Every sense had an intuitive relationship with the outer world. In an extreme sense, we could say that, through all their senses, human beings were able to "eat" the world as though it were food. This was the original process.

Later, however, an enormous danger arose after the fall of humanity—after the luciferic element had entered. This danger was that human beings would not only fall to Earth, but fall even further, into the interior of the Earth. After the entry of the luciferic element, humankind could succumb completely to Ahriman. If the human senses had maintained their original intuitive quality, Ahriman would have gained control immediately over all of humanity. Ahriman entered Lucifer's shadow and thus into the whole nature of the Earth. If human senses had maintained the same relationship to the Earth, at the moment human beings touched the Earth's surface with their senses and Ahriman approached, they might have been swallowed up by Ahriman. Consequently, that intuition of the senses had to be covered over. You are familiar with the expression that there was once an atavistic clairvoyance and that such clairvoyance gradually diminished. That decrease, however, was gradual; it happened through specific stages. First, human beings had atavistic *intuitions* that arose through the physical body, just as there were atavistic *inspirations* that came through the etheric body. Now there was the danger that these clairvoyant capacities would manifest at a time when human beings were unable to offer resistance, since harmonization of the senses had not yet taken place. Therefore, atavistic *intuition* had to be extinguished first.

The other thing that happened to humankind is connected with our upright posture. Human beings stood upright, crowned with the head. What does this mean? When the first sacrifice of Christ occurred, a moral, magical act took place. The essence of that moral, magical act was that Jesus surrendered himself to the Christ. The archangelic being, Jesus, in union with the sister soul of Adam, surrendered himself to Christ, and this capacity for self-surrender poured itself out among humankind. This is how the human senses became selfless; they were able to give themselves to the world, just as the soul of Jesus had surrendered to Christ. The fact that this became an organic attribute of human beings was made possible though the surrender of one being to another. That surrender was reflected in the human organization, and thus today we have eyes that can see. By contrast, the Christ being gave himself to the Father. In the first sacrifice, the thought, or formula, involved doing the will of the Father spirit. We could say that this is the idea of the first sacrifice in the Lemurian epoch—doing the will of the Father spirit. The Christ being united with the Father spirit; thus, one element was the surrender of Jesus to the Christ, which mirrored the selflessness of the senses, whereas the other element was Christ's surrender to the Father reflected in the fact that human beings rose to a vertical position, much as an obelisk, so that the head formed above. Obedience was implanted in the will that shaped the physical body; this is the basis for the brain's formation. At the time when human beings began to bear a head, something was implanted that denotes obedience to cosmic destiny. We would never be able to think if we failed to listen to the objective life of thoughts; we had to become silent in face of the spiritual world. This was brought about when human beings stood upright and opened themselves to the world of the fixed stars in order to perceive them inwardly.

We can represent the Christ sacrifice during the Lemurian epoch by saying that humanity then lived in the "horizontal" position of the Moon-Earth current. The vertical direction supervened through Christ, and the round shape of the head above was formed as a reflection of the primal Saturn state, or the fixed-star sphere of that time. As you know, in the Egyptian mysteries, the *crux ansata,* or *ankh,* was the most sacred sign that the Egyptians carried in their consciousness—the sign of the Christ sacrifice during the Lemurian epoch.[3] That was the time when human beings began to stand upright, and the human head was formed.

In addition to the formation of the human head at that time, the question of the senses' "defenselessness" arose. It had become necessary for the senses to be inaccessible to the ahrimanic attack upon them. This can be imagined as follows. Human being became inwardly "hot" and thus became filled with luciferic cravings and desires. From above, a cool layer of Saturn cold was poured over this heat; that coldness, however, was imbued with selflessness. Because of their desires, a cool selflessness came to enclose and surround human beings; thus, the human skin came into being. What we experience as our skin is the physical result of the event through which the human senses were harmonized. The senses were initially a unity that was "poured out upon" the human skin. This "stream" that surrounded human beings was the flowing altruism that radiated from the selfless devotion of the Jesus being toward the Christ.

So it can be said that in the book of Genesis, when Moses says that, after the fall of humanity, people made themselves garments of skin and hide, he is actually describing how human beings first received skin when the life of the senses began. "His eyes were opened," and at the same time the life of desires was covered over by selflessness flowing from the first sacrifice of Christ. This selflessness materialized and became the skin's sense of touch; the other outwardly directed senses were formed from the skin's sense of touch. As already mentioned, there would have been the danger of humankind being swallowed up by Ahriman if these two effects of the sacrifice of Christ had not happened—specifically, the upright human posture and the selflessness of the human senses. Something similar would have happened to the whole of humankind as happened to Judas. What might have happened to all human beings would have been the same that occurred when Judas received the "morsel" from Christ; he took the morsel and then went out into the night. Even today Ahriman works from without; he stupefies human beings but does not compel them inwardly. If human senses had remained as they were during the Lemurian epoch, the outpouring effects of Ahriman would flow directly through the senses into human beings, and in this way they would succumb completely to Ahriman's power. Thus the meaning of the first sacrifice is that humankind was rescued from the danger of being completely engulfed by Ahriman.

Something else happened in connection with this sacrifice of Christ, through which human beings became selfless, upright beings—an event in the human ether body. Let us try to get a better understanding of the means by which human beings became selfless beings in their senses and upright in bodily posture. The life ether and sound ether were lifted beyond the limits of arbitrary human will and outside the realm of Lucifer's rule during the Lemurian epoch and with the fall of humanity (as you may read in Steiner's lectures on Luke's Gospel[4]). Thus, the life ether and sound ether were protected. To the same degree that the life ether was raised out of the inner human being and arbitrary caprice, selflessness simultaneously flowed down and into the periphery of the human being. This selflessness was etherically imbued with something we could call a "death ether." Death entered the human organism. We read in Genesis about the three "curses" of the Father: that human beings will die, suffer, and have to labor throughout life; these are the results of the fall of humanity into sin. Nonetheless, the entry of death was gradual. The senses that were initially akin to life processes such as nourishment and breathing began to be inflicted, or injected, with the process of death; death first entered the human senses. As humankind became increasingly upright beings, the skeleton had to physically carry the upright posture that served then as a concentration of the death process. Thus, at first, death entered the skin and later spread out and took possession of the human skeleton. At the beginning of the Atlantean period, human beings did not have bones. Gradually, human beings became increasingly "mortal," but only after long periods of time; thus, the skeletal system developed. From the periphery, or skin, death increasingly entered the interior of the human body.

This process was mitigated by a beneficial act of grace from the Christ. This grace involved the fact that, whereas death certainly entered the human being, selflessness also entered at the same time. Indeed, fate was inflicted upon humankind, but at the same time obedience toward fate was also implanted. Human beings became mortal through the will of the Father, but they were helped insofar as selflessness and obedience were implanted in the will streams of the physical body itself. The agony of the physical body at death would be completely unbearable if these streams were not present in the body, if obedience and selflessness were not imprinted in the physical body. Thus "the will of the Father Spirit be done" (John 5:30) was the basis for the human head and human skin formation during the Lemurian epoch. That is the moral and spiritual essence of the first sacrifice of Christ.

When the second sacrifice of Christ took place at the beginning of the Atlantean period, something occurred that separated the soul life from the life processes of breathing, warmth, nourishment, and so on; the soul life was lifted out. What does this mean? Suffering and illness entered humankind as the results of the fall of humanity. By raising the soul life out of the life processes, human beings gained the possibility of rising above mere illness as such, since they were able to develop a soul life that was not consumed by the conditions of illness and of health. Thus, at the beginning of the Atlantean period, human beings came to bear the cross of illness when illness and pain came into being. The soul was raised out of the life processes and thus had to experience the flow of life processes as involuntary functions, in which the soul had no say. The soul became the bearer of the cross. But something else also manifested—something that could exist beyond the process of illness. Help was given that helped one endure the effects of karma. Suffering, the second "curse" of the Father, was mitigated in this way.

Once the third sacrifice of Christ had taken place, and the Atlantean power of memory was extinguished, the human power of consonantal speech arose; the word was created through thought. This was spiritualized labor that, at the same time, contained the joy of creativity. At the end of the Atlantean period, labor as such began on the Earth. With the loss of memory, human beings had lost the power of control over nature. They had to work the earth as we still do today. Laborious toil, the third "curse" of the Father, then came into effect; this was mitigated through the third sacrifice of Christ, which resulted in the harmonization of the human soul forces. Thus the possibility arose of resurrecting, through creative forms of speech, what had been extinguished in the past. This became "labor" that could be a free, creative act.

Thus, we can see that the three sacrifices of Christ are connected with the three primordial karmic decrees of the Father; we see that the Christ's acts of sacrifice each signify an act of mitigation. Next, we will discuss, in much greater detail, the second sacrifice of Christ, which occurred at the beginning of the Atlantean period.

3·

# The Second Sacrifice of Christ during the Atlantean Epoch

Our discussion of the first sacrifice of Christ showed both how humankind came to an upright position and how the senses were harmonized so that, from that time forward, selflessness and obedience were instilled in the human organization. Because of these spiritual and moral events, the human head and skin have become as they are today. The first sacrifice was needed to protect humankind from the danger of succumbing completely to Ahriman. Previously, it was possible for human beings, because of their physical body, to experience a primal *intuition,* but this had to be covered over and prevented, since this made it possible for Ahriman to penetrate the human body into the human will. Nonetheless, another danger still existed involving the mixture of life processes in the ether body with the soul's life. This made possible an inspiration of evil to the degree that human beings could again succumb to evil. This inspiration, however, would no longer come only from Ahriman, but from both Ahriman and Lucifer working together; this possibility arose when the life processes of the human ether body were permeated completely by the soul life.

There are seven life processes (as Rudolf Steiner describes them[5]). First, there is the breathing process; we breathe air into ourselves from the outside. The second life process is warming; we need inner and outer warmth. The third life process is nourishment, or nutrition. The fourth is the separation of "secretions" in the food we consume to build the body. The fifth process occurs when those separated secretions are used to maintain the body; this is the process of sustenance, but not merely a matter of maintaining the organism, but also helping it to grow. Growth is the sixth process. The seventh involves reproduction, the human capacity to create another human organism. All of these processes were originally united with the human soul life. At that time, life processes did not occur outside the soul life as they do now; rather, they took part in determining the soul life. Breathing and warmth were penetrated especially by thinking, whereas nourishment, secretion, and maintenance were imbued more with feeling; growth and reproduction, by contrast, were more volitional. Because the life processes intermingled with the soul life, it was possible for "bad" *inspiration* to be exerted by the combined activities of Lucifer and Ahriman; the human soul life was completely susceptible to their influence. Whereas evil descended from the astral into the etheric (the luciferic influence), an influence also began to be exerted from the outer world

(Ahriman's activity). These two streams could merge as a common *inspiration* through the seven life processes.

What does it mean to say that the soul life was completely connected with the seven life processes? Those familiar with Rudolf Steiner's readings of the akashic chronicle know that, for a long time, the ancient Atlanteans retained power over the growth processes. The nature of those Atlanteans (especially during the first epoch) enabled them to alter their shape according to the strength and content of their volition. By expressing a strong will, they could become physically strong and large; in terms of its growth forces, the body responded to the will. Volition and growth were thus mixed as a unity. The giants of Greek mythology and various Eastern and Western occult traditions are examples of such persons in whom the element of will influenced growth.

Through another example, we clearly see what comes into play in another life process. We must say that these life processes were not separated from the soul life all at once; this came about gradually so that, through the whole Atlantean time, there were those who retained the old connection. Even during the post-Atlantean periods, atavistic conditions still existed. Imagine the acts of sacrifice as coming into effect gradually rather than suddenly. We can recognize and understand, with the help of an example, the preservation of this atavistic consciousness, in which a mixture of breathing with human thinking still functions. The Indian practice of hatha yoga has survived to the present day; it is based on the ideas that breathing and thinking are a single process and that one actually tries to experience *inspiration* when breathing in physically. During Atlantean times, however, the unity of breathing and thought perception was a natural gift.

We can cite another example. There are those who have remained at the Atlantean stage of development; the Chinese are such a people. For them, a tradition has survived that is derived from the Atlantean period—the occult tradition of a Chinese school of initiation. Chinese occultism is based on the fundamental principle that nourishment, secretion, and maintenance of the body can be used for knowledge and magic. Chinese occultism is involved with the inner processes of nourishment. We can say that these cultivated processes of the "central" human being (the "mean" between the upper, or head, and the lower growth and reproductive processes) forms the fundamental principle of Chinese occultism. It is the false heart—completely united with the nourishment processes—in which the Chinese individual lives. Together with these life processes, spiritual knowledge is gained and forces released for the purposes of effect. Exoteric Chinese tradition uses the symbol of the dragon. The Chinese dragon is neither wholly luciferic nor wholly ahrimanic, but both luciferic and ahrimanic in nature. This is a false "mean" between two opposites. It points to the historic cultural reality that Chinese tradition has preserved knowledge and practice based on the fact that nourishment, body maintenance, and secretion were once connected with the human life of feeling, or the life of soul between the human spirit and body. Thus, the *inspiration* in Atlantis that endangered all of humankind has been realized to a certain, but weakened, degree. It has been preserved, though in a weakened form.

In order to protect humanity from this danger, the second sacrifice of Christ took place at the beginning of the Atlantean epoch. That sacrifice again involved the fact that the Christ being united with the Jesus being, the archangelic being who had united with the sister soul of Adam for the duration of these acts of sacrifice. This union was different from the first. Every sacrifice of Christ entails a special "union," each representing a different kind of sacrifice on the part of Jesus. The Jesus being surrendered his "I" during the first sacrifice of Christ in the Lemurian epoch; it was a surrender of the "I" principle. And so when we spoke of this formula: "The will of the Father spirit be done." It was the formula through which this "I" being placed itself wholly within the Father stream through devoted surrender to the Father principle during the Lemurian epoch. With the second sacrifice of Christ at the beginning of the Atlantean epoch, it was then a matter of surrendering the astral body; the astral body was given up by the Jesus being to Christ. Let us try to understand the meaning of this.

If we are to understand this, we must consider something that seems to be unrelated. Nonetheless, it can help shed much light on what really happened during this second sacrifice of Christ. The physical human being, when passing through the portal of death, pursues a long path, since dying involves more than separating from the physical body at a certain moment. The stages of dying continue on in the spiritual world as the "liberation" of the individual members of the human being proceeds. Thus, it is not just a matter of death in the physical world, but also additional stages of dissolution of, or lifting away, the "parts" of a human being. After three days of contemplating the life tableau, one grows to gigantic size and the etheric body dissolves into the cosmic ether. After Kama Loka, where the astral body finally dissolves into a general sympathy for the world, the second member of the spiritual human being separates.[6] After this the "I" rises to the realm of cosmic midnight, the sphere of Saturn. "I" consciousness is lost in the excess of spiritual content, into which it must immerse itself before rising again and beginning the path of descent to a new incarnation. Thus we have the death of the physical body, the dissolution of the ether and astral bodies, and the loss of "I" consciousness in the sphere of cosmic midnight.

The first sacrifice of Christ occurred when the Jesus being completed through sacrifice what present-day human beings experience in the sphere of cosmic midnight after death. Human beings surrender their "I" consciousness to the worlds of the Father beyond the sphere of Saturn; this sacrifice must proceed until consciousness is lost. The sacrifice of Jesus to the Father spirit of the world happened in a similar way. Thus the way of Jesus Christ goes through the stages of dying (though in the opposite sequence). During the Lemurian epoch, the sacrifice consisted in the fact that his surrender went so far that the "I" lost consciousness in the sphere of cosmic midnight.

In the second sacrifice of Christ, the astral body of the Jesus being—imbued by the Christ being—expanded so much that it went through the same type of death that the human astral body experiences. That death was in the Sun sphere, where human beings also shed the astral body. This process of the continually expanding astral body was the basis of the saying (or, more correctly, the thought) that may be expressed in this way: The feeling of the cosmic soul will live alone. This idea was realized in the second sacrifice of Christ. The astral body expanded to enormous size, and this event reflected itself in the human soul; thus, the powers of the soul were lifted out of the life processes. Through the power of its expansion, the soul body was freed from the seven life processes. As a result, the miracle happened that human beings gave inner birth to a "language" of vowel sounds, the language that expresses triumph over solitude. The fact that a voice sounds and a soul expresses itself in this way means that the soul is seeking a relationship with other beings who will understand it. This overcoming of solitude was made possible by the second sacrifice. This second sacrifice of Christ was essentially a passage through the sacrificial experience of the second stage of human dying, as seen from above.

Then came the third sacrifice of Christ at the end of the Atlantean epoch (which we will speak about in greater detail in the next study). The third sacrifice had the significance that the Jesus being experienced what a human being experiences during the first days after death while viewing the life memory tableau. That tableau then passes away into distant cosmic spaces. With the third sacrifice, Jesus Christ gave up his ether body; the tableau of memories was extinguished and delivered up. Thus in humankind, as a mirror of that sacrifice, the imaginative ability—the capacity for memory possessed by the ancient Atlanteans—was extinguished. And at the same time, "consonantal" language—a truly human language that still exists—was born.

Finally came the Mystery of Golgotha itself, the fourth sacrifice of Christ, which reflected a kind of summary of the three previous sacrifices. The Jesus being, now ascending again, had given up his astral body to the Christ and, with this part of his being, had experienced death of the physical body.

We see that the path through the various stages of dying was the path of the Christ's sacrifices. The Saturn sacrifice was repeated in the first sacrifice of Christ during the Lemurian epoch. Cosmic midnight—the darkness in which the human "I" must immerse itself after death—was experienced first by the Jesus being. The second stage was surrender of the astral body, and this repeated the astral body's spreading out in sympathy with the whole world. That was the Sun sacrifice, the second sacrifice of Christ. The third stage of the way of Jesus in connection with the Christ sacrifice consisted in Jesus giving up his ether body, or memory. Again, this was the experience of that portion of human destiny through which everyone must pass immediately after physical death. This was a repetition of the Moon sacrifice, which corresponded also to the human being's experience of death in the Moon sphere. As the fourth stage, we have the passage in the astral body, which had united with the Jesus Christ being in such a way that, having passed through the gate of physical human death, it physically incarnated.

After each of the four sacrifices of Christ there was an aftereffect that embraced a long period of time before being fully realized. Each aftereffect included a division of humankind, because these effects were not accepted by all the beings of primitive humanity to the same degree and at the same time. So it was that the first sacrifice of Christ during the Lemurian epoch (which formed humankind into upright beings) lifted only a portion of humanity out of the domain of the animal kingdom. New forms thus arose in the animal kingdom through the decadent human forms that could not be reshaped in an upright position. Part of humanity separated from the rest and sank into animal existence. (Please note, however, that we are speaking here of the bodily organization, and not the souls themselves.) With the second sacrifice of Christ, the division into Atlanteans and Lemurians took place. Because the second sacrifice was taken up intensively by one portion of humanity (and very little or not at all by another portion), the "advanced" Atlanteans and the "retarded" Lumurians emerged. Once the third sacrifice of Christ had taken place, the representatives of humankind again separated into two streams. Those who completely accepted the sacrifice of Christ were the hosts of Atlanteans who emigrated with Manu.[7] The others were those who increasingly rejected the effects of the third sacrifice of Christ.

Now, having these spiritual historical facts as a foundation, we can consider the future and understand that the other acts of Christ—especially the Mystery of Golgotha—must also have aftereffects whereby humankind will be divided further. When Rudolf Steiner speaks of two opposing cultures coming into existence in the sixth post-Atlantean cultural period, about two races emerging later, and about the time when Earth is to be divided into two planets, he is talking about the continuation of a process that began in the time of the first sacrifice of Christ during the Lemurian epoch.

Next we will consider the third sacrifice of Christ. It is hoped that through the present study, the stages of the way of Jesus (passing through all the stages of death) will provide a living basis for further considerations. These are matters that can help us understand the etheric return of Christ, which is the subject of our final study.

# 4.

# The Third Sacrifice of Christ during the Atlantean Epoch

We already discussed the second sacrifice of Christ in connection with the path of the Jesus being—the path by which, with each sacrifice, the Jesus being went through one stage of dying. That being first experienced the loss of "I" consciousness in the Saturn sphere; then came the dissolution, the expansion of the astral body into the cosmos in the Sun sphere, and after that the surrender of memory in the Moon sphere. These three cosmic acts of sacrifice that took place on Saturn, Sun, and Moon reflected themselves in three sacrifices of Christ. First, the purpose of the "I" was the sacrifice through an offering of "I" consciousness. Second was the liberation, or dissolution, of the astral body. Third was the separation of the etheric body.

Now we will consider the third sacrifice, which involves separation from the etheric body. When we go through the gate of death, first we are confronted inwardly by the tableau of our life; the sum of our remembered life experiences simultaneously face us in a spatial perspective. Typically, after three days this tableau begins to disconnect from the observing soul. It grows ever larger and, assuming gigantic dimensions, loses clarity and eventually disappears owing to its huge dimensions. The inner experience of this event corresponds to the separation of the human soul from the ether body. And what is the result of this event? The experiences of one's human life are taken up by the "thinking" of the world; the experience of the single human life is assimilated into the world's thinking for consideration. As a consequence, it happens that the human soul forces (which had been engaged completely in the tableau) become the object of experience and perception. That is the kama loka state, which involves the human "I" gaining the ability to perceive what its soul forces bear inwardly. The human "I" frees itself from the soul forces and experiences a judgment of them. One then learns what was good in life and what was bad.

A similar event happened in the third sacrifice of Christ at the end of the Atlantean epoch, when the human "I" was liberated from the soul forces. At the beginning of the Atlantean epoch, the soul forces were mingled with the life processes; likewise, the "I" was mingled with the soul forces before the third sacrifice of Christ. Through this sacrifice, however, the "I" was released from the soul forces and gained the ability to independently direct its gaze on the world. Thereby a state of being could arise in humankind (which, again, took a long time to develop completely) whereby human beings could express their "I" being through sound; the language of the human "I" arose inwardly as the capacity for thinking and outwardly as consonantal language. The most striking difference between human beings and animals is the human ability to not only experience but also to give an account of that experience. This capacity, which so clearly distinguishes the human from the animal kingdom, arose because human beings not only have physical, ether, and astral bodies, but also "I" being, independent and separate from the astral body. Before this came about, human beings were unable to perceive events in the astral body. Consequently, human beings were also unable to speak in a consonantal language, nor could they think, which is inner human speech.

After death, human beings give up their memory pictures to the cosmos. These are taken up by the world thinking soul as material to be worked on; thus the Jesus Christ being surrendered his memory. That memory was resurrected in humankind as the capacity for judgment and for thought inwardly, and outwardly as the capacity to speak a consonantal language.

Just as before, a certain formula and geometrical figure corresponds to this act. The basis for the first sacrifice of Christ is outwardly simple but inwardly profound: a vertical line. The figure for the second sacrifice of Christ is also outwardly simple though inwardly profound: an expanding horizontal line. Likewise, the third sacrifice of Christ has a distinct geometrical figure as its basis. This figure can be compared to a spiral, which expands outwardly in concentric circles. Here we have a complete representation of the three sacrifices: the figure of the cross with the ever-expanding circle. This is a form in movement that may indicate memory spreading out into the world and uniting with the world thinking soul. Thus, we can say that the third sacrifice of Christ took place according to a specific formula: The thinking of the world thinks. This "world thinking" assumed the faculty for memory, and among human beings this process is mirrored in the gradual disappearance of the atavistic faculty of memory. Externally, this was expressed when the etheric body (formerly towering above the human head) gradually contracted into the physical human head. Inwardly this was expressed by the fact that humankind lost the power of memory that enabled one to look back into the past through the generations. This power transformed itself into the capacity for thought and consonantal language.

The danger that then threatened human beings, who were protected through the third sacrifice of Christ, was that humanity no longer faced temptation but, instead, the inescapable danger of being completely taken up into the realm of Lucifer. If that atavistic capacity for *imagination* had remained and had not been eliminated at the end of the Atlantean epoch through the third sacrifice of Christ, matters would have reached a point where, from the beginning through the end of the Atlantean epoch, the inclination would have increased in human beings to cultivate this capacity for memory and look back into images of the past. It would have no longer been a matter of simply looking back to the actual past on Earth, but rather a situation in which luciferic caprice would have falsified the pictures so that memory would have formed a bridge to the sphere of Lucifer, which then formed an astral ring around the Earth.

The sphere of Lucifer has a very peculiar power, since it is, in fact, essentially wisdom; at the same time, however, it is imbued with a moral content that is contrary to the intentions of the gods. Let us try to understand this; remember the saying that we constantly repeat—that, as a microcosm, the human being is an image of the macrocosm. The human being is a small world, a microcosm, and a symbol of the great world, or macrocosm. Thus we can gain self-knowledge by knowing the world. This is the way of such knowledge today. If the third sacrifice of the Christ had not taken place, because of luciferic temptation, human beings would never have troubled at all to understand the external world in order to gain self-knowledge. Rather, human beings would have realized that the human individual is a world and that all wisdom is already within; they would have allowed themselves to spread throughout the world; everywhere they would perceive self-reflections; they would have stifled, dazzled, and deafened the world with their own being. That would have led to a state of self-enjoyment for all eternity—self-contemplation and self-reflection that would have ended any further progress.

The legend of Narcissus expresses this condition. The young man assumed the form of a plant and descended to a lower realm of existence, because he was fascinated by his own reflection and delighted in his own beauty. The Narcissus danger threatened humankind at the end of the Atlantean epoch. This temptation to self-reflection continues, but through the sacrifice of Christ the power of this danger, which human beings would have been unable to withstand, was weakened to the point where we can face it freely as a mere temptation. If the third sacrifice had not taken place, this would not have been merely a temptation but a compelling necessity. Because the ancient Indian culture still continues today, through certain aspects of it we can imagine the situation during the Atlantean epoch when that danger threatened. At the basis of the Indian manner of thinking lies a particular psychological tendency—an effort toward bliss while at ease inwardly. Their ideal of bliss (to be free of the changing forms of existence and to rest in oneself) derives from the luciferic sphere. It is not a human task to rest anywhere. It is our task to ascend continually to higher powers of sacrifice and to find peace within activity. If this danger had not been prevented through the third sacrifice of Christ, a point would have been reached where human beings would ascend over the bridge of memory tableau into the luciferic sphere, thus experiencing themselves as a microcosm and ignoring the macrocosm. Human beings would have found enjoyment in themselves. Such a condition of humankind would have prevented any post-Atlantean development from taking place. The Aryan epoch of development would not have taken place. Human evolution on Earth would have reached an end. That is the danger of the atavistic faculty of *imagination*, which was overcome by the third sacrifice of Christ. Thus a view into the outer world was opened up for humankind; by stepping out into the spiral, human beings could seek thoughts that come from without. The great world gained meaning for human beings, and, through this, the danger that human beings might find enjoyment only in themselves was overcome.

Those who had developed the strongest capacity for thinking were also the ones who had followed the great Manu out of Atlantis and into desert areas, where everything was new and unrelated to past memories, where one was reminded of nothing, and where the outer world in no way reminded them of Atlantis. These people were *Manushyas,* or thinkers. They formed a new race that has continued its development until today. The danger that threatened humankind at the end of the Atlantean epoch is essentially the same one that later appeared as the first temptation of Jesus Christ in the wilderness. When the tempter led Jesus Christ up onto the high mountain and showed him all the grandeur of the world (which he would be given in exchange for worshipping the tempter), it means that he was tempted by possessions. In reality, we possess only what reflects us outwardly. This was the danger—that the microcosm would spread out over the macrocosm. This could be expressed as, "O human being, how glorious you are!" There would have been only a reflection of one's being in all of the surrounding world.

The danger of atavistic *inspiration* was overcome through the second sacrifice of Christ, so that it never went beyond temptation to become a danger with real power. The danger of *inspiration* through the life processes means what actually transpires through the second temptation as described in the Gospels; when Jesus Christ was led onto the pinnacle of the temple to throw himself down, a miracle might have occurred through the intervention of angels who were supposed to support him. This image of falling from the pinnacle means, literally, to cast oneself out of the head and into the subconscious, in the hope that forces will be found there to carry and support one. To abandon oneself entirely to *inspiration* that works through the life processes is the essence of the second temptation. It means to rely blindly on the life processes, where angels are active and make danger impossible.

We can say that, if this danger had not been overcome by the second sacrifice of Christ, something else would have happened to humankind. Atavistic *inspiration* would have increasingly become a domain where Lucifer and Ahriman work together. And if humankind were forced to succumb to that *inspiration,* it would have caused a condition for human beings in which they could not be redeemed as a whole. Part of the human essence would have had to share the fate of Ahriman for all eternity, and another part the eternal fate of Lucifer. This would mean that if Lucifer were to be redeemed in the future, only a portion of the human being could be redeemed; and if Ahriman were to be redeemed, then again only a part of the human being could be redeemed; the whole human being would never be redeemed. This is the danger of the seven life processes. The upper three (breathing, warmth, and nourishment) would have passed to the fate of Lucifer; the four lower (secretion, maintenance, growth, and reproduction) would have fallen prey to Ahriman. This problem of being torn apart into two realms of existence was averted through the second sacrifice of Christ.

By overcoming the danger of atavistic *inspiration,* human beings were safeguarded from the second temptation; likewise, by overcoming the danger of atavistic *intuition* through the first sacrifice of Christ in the Lemurian epoch, human beings were safeguarded from the third temptation in the wilderness—to turn stones into bread. What does it mean to turn stones into bread? It means that something dead is to be experienced consciously as though it were alive. If the human senses had retained the capacity for *intuition*, which humankind had during the Lemurian epoch, human beings would have become united with the outer world to the degree that they would have sunk through the senses into the outer world and finally been devoured by Ahriman, who was entering the world. Humankind would have sunk beneath the Earth's surface and become a citizen of the subterranean sphere. The Earth, being a "stone," would have thus become "bread" through the devoured humankind. Again humanity was freed from this danger through the first sacrifice of Christ. Thus we see how everything reappears, tremendously concentrated, in the accounts of the Mystery of Golgotha, in the activity of Jesus Christ on Earth nineteen centuries ago. Jesus Christ had to withstand these three temptations. It was also, however, a summary of the whole evolution of humankind on Earth.

The fourth danger that threatened humankind after the Atlantean epoch (around the seventh century after the Mystery of Golgotha) was the possibility that all three temptations would simultaneously approach each individual. That was the grave danger that faced post-Atlantean humanity. What does it mean to say that all three temptations would simultaneously approach human beings? To understand this, we must go off on a tangent and return to the beginning of these meditations. We discussed the fact that the divine is no longer to be understood as a Trinity, but rather as a quaternary, in that the divine personality arose at the fourth stage of Earth's development. Because Jesus Christ lived and died, a new element arose in the world: the eternal personality. And along with this, it must be said that evil, too, has a plan, but this plan of the "evil one" can never, in essence, be creative. This is the deep inner difference between evil and good in the world. Evil cannot create but only imitate. For this reason, the plan of the "evil one" (I do not mean the details of its execution) consists in an imitated inversion of the plan that the gods have for the evolution of the world.

It is a deep secret of spiritual life that the Antichrist is not simply Ahriman and not simply Lucifer, nor Ahriman and Lucifer together, but something that came into being as "evil personality." The Antichrist is the opposite of Jesus Christ. The Antichrist has to inwardly unite all three temptations into a fourth, allowing the temptations in the wilderness to rule in the world as an outer means of working. This danger means that human beings have to meet the totality of the three temptations along with a hidden fourth that is veiled in darkness—the "evil personality" in the guise of absolute freedom. This is the one who lives and works in its own name and only for itself.

What did the three temptations in the wilderness mean in relation to Jesus Christ? Here, we must have the cognitive courage to acknowledge that it was a matter of turning the Christ into the Antichrist. The three temptations approached Jesus Christ because the "evil one" had hoped that Christ would reach an understanding with him. If that had happened, the Christ would have become the evil personality. But the three temptations were rejected and overcome by Christ. Through the death on Golgotha, Christ became a personality who had overcome death.

Thus the fourth danger is averted; it is the fourth sacrifice of Christ in the history of humankind.

Around the time of the Mystery of Golgotha (and a little earlier), the human "I" was constituted in such a way that one might say that the higher "I" and the lower ego were mingled, just as earlier on, at the end of the Atlantean epoch, the "I" was mixed with the astral body; or, earlier still, the life processes were mingled with the soul forces; or, in the Lemurian epoch, the physical senses were mixed with the outer forces. It was necessary for the human "I" to be harmonized; only a harmonized "I" being can stand up to an encounter with the Antichrist. The meeting with the Antichrist will take place; it must come about. But it will be only a temptation for human beings, not a takeover; humankind remains free. Jesus Christ has not rid the world of temptation, because we must choose for ourselves. He did, however, provide for freedom insofar as, at every stage, there is the possibility of withstanding temptation according to the degree of possible freedom. The "evil one" was permitted to retain only the moral weapon, but not the weapon of *compulsion.* If we will it to be, we can discriminate. The possibility that we will be able to distinguish the Antichrist when we meet him will not happen unless the lower ego and higher "I" are separated as independent members, just as the "I" was separated from the astral body with the third sacrifice of Christ.

Next we will speak about the Mystery of Golgotha, the fourth sacrifice, which establishes the element of human freedom and enables human beings to meet and stand against the Antichrist, who is a historical necessity.

5.

# The Mystery of Golgotha

We have been able to see that, essentially, the whole spiritual history of humankind has revolved around the fact that dangers have threatened human beings and that these were averted through the sacrifices of Christ. Those dangers had to do with atavistic clairvoyant capacities with which human beings were endowed originally. The first sacrifice of Christ overcame the first danger—that, through atavistic *intuition*, humankind would have succumbed to the power of the third temptation of Christ in the wilderness. The second sacrifice of Christ prevented the second danger that threatened humanity, which involved the fact that, through atavistic *inspiration*, humanity could have fallen under the power of Lucifer and Ahriman, the power of the second temptation of Christ in the wilderness. And the power of the first temptation of Christ in the wilderness was overcome at the end of the Atlantean epoch by the third sacrifice of Christ; thus atavistic *imagination* came to an end. As a result, the power of temptation was broken, and human beings have become what they are. All that remained was the possibility of moral temptation; no longer was there the force of compulsion that had previously threatened humanity.

In our previous study, we discussed the fourth sacrifice of Christ (the Mystery of Golgotha), whose significance has been that humankind was saved from the power of a fourth danger—specifically, the power of all three temptations together, collectively attributed to the antichrist principle. This fourth sacrifice, the Mystery of Golgotha, was an act of Jesus Christ through which the human "I" was harmonized, just as the preceding acts of sacrifice harmonized the human astral, etheric, and physical bodies. Just as the physical body was threatened by the power of the third temptation, then the ether body was threatened by the power of the second temptation, and finally the astral body was threatened by the power of the first temptation of Christ in the wilderness, likewise, the human "I" was threatened by the power of what we can call the fourth temptation. This temptation may be understood as the confrontation with the Antichrist. It is immediately directed toward the human "I" and not through the medium of the physical, etheric, or astral body, but directly to the human "I" being. This temptation would cause the human "I" to develop self-determination, which would make it an expression of the antichrist principle. In other words, an ideal of freedom would arise in the human "I" in terms of absolute self-determination—an ideal of freedom from God, which is not in harmony with the intentions of the deity. This temptation will, nonetheless, confront humankind.

When Rudolf Steiner said that the fifth post-Atlantean epoch will end with the war of all against all, this is based on the fact that a large portion of human beings—human "I" beings—will reach such a degree of self-determination that they will, in fact, cause a war of all against all. This danger of self-determination in the human "I" involves, especially, the fact that the "I" was mingled with the spirit to the same extent that, earlier, the soul was mixed with the life body. At one time, the life processes were unified with the soul forces, and later the "I" was still unified with the soul; likewise, at the time of the Mystery of Golgotha the human "I" being was inwardly mingled with the spirit. The self-determination that could have entered the human "I" at that time would have been a kind of "spiritual poisoning." Just imagine what this really means; we can picture being poisoned physically—even poisoning the soul—but try to imagine a spiritual poisoning, whereby the spirit would be completely poisoned, thus becoming a "machine." This would have happened if something had not happened to separate the spirit from the "I," just as the previous sacrifices separated the "higher" from the "lower."

Now try to understand this process further. At the time of the Mystery of Golgotha, the mysteries were in a difficult situation. In particular, this difficulty involved the fact that the human "I" was incapable of knowing the spiritual world. Philosophies were certainly possible, but spiritual experience through the human "I" was not. "I" being stood between the human soul and the spirit world as a concealing factor. The "I" had to be extinguished before an experience of the spiritual world could arise. The "I" was essentially a closed door when one wanted to experience the reality of the spiritual world. Consequently, the mood that reigned in mystery centers was one of almost unutterable despair. On the one hand, it was obvious that the "I" was becoming increasingly powerful, whereas there was also a growing conviction that any future for the mysteries was impossible. The "I" was egocentric, but in the spiritual world one must develop the capacity for self-sacrifice. Thus people would have been caught in a cul-de-sac with no way out. This situation would have continued if a miracle had not occurred. That miracle was the Mystery of Golgotha, the fourth sacrifice of Christ in world history. The Mystery of Golgotha altered human nature to such a degree that the human "I," which previously concealed and closed the way to the spiritual world, now became an open gate into the spiritual world. This is what Rudolf Steiner calls the harmonization of the "I." Human "I" being was altered so that it became possible, without extinguishing the "I," to see into and experience the spiritual world through the "I" itself.

So how did this come about in the human being? The higher "I" was separated from the lower ego. One was lifted, and the other had to descend gradually, so that the lower ego could no longer influence, or govern, the higher "I." Thus a relationship that we are all familiar with arose among human beings—that is, the relationship between one's consciousness and one's conscience. The voice of conscience stands and calls out in judgment over us, and we can come into conflict with our higher "I," or conscience. Conscience arose as a result of the separation between the two essential elements of the

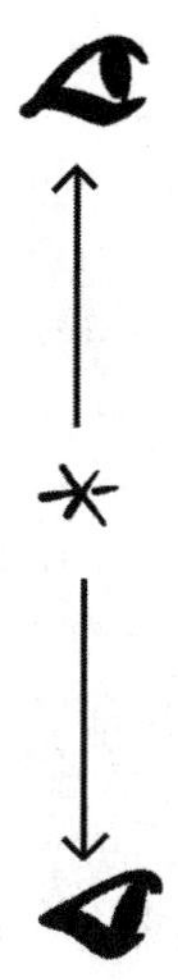

human "I." Perhaps we can best picture these two essential parts as "eyes"—an upper and a lower one arranged vertically, in a straight line. If I draw an upper eye and a lower eye and connect them with a vertical line, we have a representation of the higher "I" and the lower ego. From the point where they were previously mixed together, the higher "I" ascended, and the lower descended; this is a reflection of the act of Christ.

Here we are touching upon a deep mystery of the Christ's death. Jesus Christ himself says in his parting words that he is going to the Father, yet he is going to death—in fact, he is going to Hell, the subearthly realm. He went in two directions simultaneously: he went into death, yet, for his consciousness, this meant the other direction. This is the truth of the words, "I and my Father are one" (John 10:30). It was both an ascent and a descent, a fusion with the Father and a descent into the Earth's interior. These "two" resulted in the resurrection. A reflection of the way Christ ascended into the realm of the Father and descended into the realm of death occurred in the human "I" and continues to occur increasingly there. Part of the human "I" (the conscience, independent of human caprice) has been lifted; the other part has now descended much more deeply into the physical body than it was at the time of the Mystery of Golgotha.

Nonetheless, it is not the purpose of the human "I" to manifest a duality; this is only a stage through which humanity is passing. It is not the ideal but a path whose goal is to realize unity. This division into an upper "I" and a lower ego, which was brought about by Christ, is described in the Gospel as the "sword." "I came not to send peace, but a sword" (Matthew 10:34). When you read these mysterious words, it means that the human "I" will be divided into upper and lower parts. The significance of this division into two "eyes" is that one eye looks to the realm of goodness while the other looks into the domain of the outer world—increasingly the expression of evil. Thus we can say that the "upper eye" means knowing the intentions of goodness, and the "lower eye" means knowing the power of evil; seeing with both "eyes" at the same time means complete wisdom. Our task is to see into both domains at the same time; this is the inner requirement for true freedom.

This simultaneous sight through the upper and lower "eyes" is possible only when a relationship exists between them, and the bond between knowing goodness and knowing evil is the Christ impulse in the human "I." Christ, therefore, divides the upper from the lower and reunites them. He joins them so that, at the center where the spiritual and the egoistic were formerly mingled and then divided, "seeing together" is made possible through the love principle. This is why the formula for the fourth sacrifice of Christ is the "I AM." Rudolf Steiner stated that the esoteric name of Christ, the I AM, is really the harmonization of the human "I," which is first split into two polarities and then reunited. Lower and higher knowledge join in unity to develop love. This is also the reason why we should not believe that the purpose of human beings is to assume the shape of chalices in order to be filled with grace. Neither should we extinguish the lower ego just in the higher. Instead, the real task is this "seeing together" with the higher "I" and the lower ego. "Seeing together" is true gnosis, the essence of the new mysteries. At the time of the Mystery of Golgotha, the human "I" was a hindrance to knowing the spiritual world; now it has become the means—the way through the divide between the higher "I" and lower ego toward uniting the two in the Christ impulse and the power of the I AM. The I AM is the axis of vision for these two "eyes," the upper and the lower. It is the principle of the new mystery, which is profoundly different from the old mystery.

How did it happen that the new path into the spiritual world was opened just as the old, atavistic clairvoyance (*imagination, inspiration,* and *intuition*) was extinguished, and had even become dangerous? Indeed, atavistic clairvoyance is a great danger even today. Can we visualize how knowledge of the spiritual world is possible—not only through cognition of the "I" (which can know only through *intuition*), but also through the human members that can know through *imagination* and *inspiration?* To answer this question, we must consider the inner aspect of the events connected with Christ's sacrifice in the Mystery of Golgotha.

We discussed the fact that the Mystery of Golgotha contained a repetition of the cosmic sacrifices as well as the preceding earthly sacrificial acts. The Last Supper, therefore, was a repetition of the third sacrifice of Christ; the night in Gethsemane repeated the second sacrifice; and the crucifixion was a repetition of the first sacrifice. Death and descent into the interior of the Earth, however, was a new element. We also spoke of the third sacrifice of Christ as a renunciation of memory and liberation from the ether body; it was a sacrifice of the ether body to "cosmic thinking," which, in fact, happens to everyone during the first three days after death. Christ told his disciples, during the Last Supper, what they must do in memory of him (in order to resurrect memory, since they forgot everything with his death). This means that he had given up his memory, which was now intended to arise again. During the night in Gethsemane, he gave up the astral body. With the crucifixion, he gave up his "I" being, as happens after death in the sphere of the cosmic midnight, and as it happened on ancient Saturn as the first cosmic sacrifice.

Then a descent into the interior of the Earth occurs, a process that takes death farther than normally experienced by human beings; Christ died in a more profound sense. He descended into the sub-material, into the sphere of Earth's interior. What actually happened each time through these stages of death in the ether body, astral body, and "I" being (from the Last Supper to the descent into Hell) is that Christ renounced the beneficial element connected with death. We all experience liberation of our memory, but at the same time we experience the "tableau of memories" in the soul; this is a power we take with us. Christ renounced the sight of his life tableau at death; he left it for his disciples. Seen inwardly, Christ's ether body became a part of the Earth's ether body; it became the eternal and indestructible "fifth gospel." Consequently, in the future, when the capacity for *imagination* has reopened for human beings, we will not see the sphere of Lucifer, but experience the life tableau of Jesus Christ, and we will remember that the

Christ was there. Human beings will experience the essence of the Gospels as their own memory. Books will be unnecessary, because humankind will read the book inscribed into the etheric aura of space—the life tableau of Christ—which he leaves to everyone, since he renounced viewing it himself.

The kama loka state of the soul is the second experience after viewing the tableau during an ordinary passage through the process of death. This has both a painful and a beneficial aspect. During this time, we are able to distinguish good and evil and become tremendously wise in this respect. Christ renounced what was rewarding and positive in this state. When He experienced the night in Gethsemane, he went through all the pain of Kama Loka for all of humankind. What did He renounce? He renounced the cognition that arises with that experience. Thus, the experience was planted in the astral aura of the Earth, as tones that ring out there as words. When human beings ascend to *inspiration* in the future, they will not encounter the joint temptation of Lucifer and Ahriman, but instead see the essence of Christ's experience of the kama loka condition. They will be able to see the eternal apocalypse, the story of the future of humankind, of which John's Apocalypse is only a part. It describes the good and the evil fate of humankind, which will occur as a karmic result of the fall into sin. Those who ascend to *inspiration* will be able to read that eternal apocalypse and find the judgments and sentences of the Lord of karma over human destiny. There, one gets to know the mysteries of good and evil as the powers that form destiny for the future. The fifth gospel towers above the works of the four Gospel writers, and likewise the eternal apocalypse towers high above the one John was able to write. New parts will always be added to this, just as new parts will always be added to the Gospels.

Because Christ renounced the beneficial fruits of the devachan state, the third condition that we encounter in our passage through death, the temple of humanity was built in the spirit of the Earth. Because the Christ descended into Hell and renounced the experience of devachan instead of ascending into the heavenly world, the temple of humanity was built. He spoke of that temple himself: "I will destroy this temple that is made with hands, and within three days I will build another made without hands" (Mark 14:58). This means that he would pass through death in such a way that a new temple would be built in place of the old. His descent into the Earth's interior and his ascent, in fact, built the temple of humanity, the true state of future humankind. Everyone who ascends to the level of *intuition* will encounter that temple.

Through the Christ, experiences were realized that human beings will encounter, in essence, through the experiences of *imagination, inspiration,* and *intuition.* Christ's acts of sacrifice caused realities to be brought into the world, and those realities will protect future capacities of *imagination, inspiration,* and *intuition.* If human beings guide themselves with true heartfelt reverence for the life of Jesus Christ and follow the Christ impulse when inquiring into matters of spirit, they will not encounter the temptations of Lucifer, but instead perceive the life tableau of Christ. When human beings rise to the level of *inspiration,* they will not meet Ahriman and Lucifer; rather, by listening, they will encounter the apocalyptic revelation. This will grow constantly; it is the wisdom of the future that will always grow. This apocalyptic wisdom is indeed the essential effect of Christian Rosenkreutz's activity. And when human beings ascend to the level of *intuition,* they will not take in Ahriman but, through *intuition,* meet the temple; they will realize the highest ideal of humankind.

The Mystery of Golgotha was a deliverance from the danger of the egoistic, self-directed "I," on the one hand, and, on the other, it reopened the doors to the spiritual world. This passage is through the "I" itself, which was harmonized by separating the higher "I" from the lower ego (like two eyes) and their consequent reunion in the I AM. What these "two eyes" perceive are the higher and the lower mysteries. Through Christ's acts of sacrifice, these were prevented from becoming a source of temptation. Instead, human beings would perceive all that guides them toward the good. They would perceive the fifth gospel and the eternal apocalypse and then, at the stage of *intuition,* enter the temple. These are the results of the Mystery of Golgotha—consequences viewed here from only one side. You know from the works of Rudolf Steiner and from the work that we have attempted here that there are numerous sides. In connection with the work of these meditations, however, it has been a question of just this one side.

Following the Mystery of Golgotha was a time of working out of the karmic consequences of that mystery. It works on the human organization most fully when we find a conscious relationship to the Mystery of Golgotha. What I have described does not happen automatically, but only as the result of a consciously formed relationship to the Mystery of Golgotha and to the being of Christ. Thus, we may ask: How can everyone truly realize the fact of Christ and of his sacrifice? Must we preach it everywhere? Is this the only way? The question remains: Is it *possible* for everyone to experience the reality of Christ as a cosmic being? The Mystery of Golgotha, as we have discussed it, took place especially for humankind. But what was accomplished for nature? This is the other question. Again we are faced with an open question. The significance of the next sacrifice of Christ, his etheric return, will be the answer to these two main questions. This will allow everyone to know Christ and create a conscious relationship to him. And something will also happen in and for nature that is necessary for its redemption.

In the following meditations, we will discuss the karmic consequences of the Mystery of Golgotha and the appearance of Christ in the etheric. We will try to understand Christ's return as a necessary and inevitable event that needs to be understood not simply as a prophecy, but as the result of the past destiny of humanity and of cosmic karma.

6.

# The Karmic Consequences of the Mystery of Golgotha

In this series of meditations, we have considered the four sacrifices of Christ in the light of their inner connections, whose purpose is to harmonize the human physical, etheric, and astral bodies and "I" being. Each of these sacrifices was necessary because of a particular danger; these are the dangers described in the Gospels as the three temptations in the wilderness. We described the fourth danger, which is the appearance of the total power of all three temptations simultaneously; these were noted as the antichrist principle. So the first three sacrifices of Christ took place for the purpose of saving humankind from the danger of succumbing completely to Ahriman, to both Ahriman and Lucifer, and finally to Lucifer. The Mystery of Golgotha was intended to save humanity from the eminent doom of the encounter with the Antichrist. Humanity would not have stood up to such an encounter if not for the Mystery of Golgotha.

The Mystery of Golgotha brought about the division of the human "I" into "upper" and "lower" aspects, so that what we called "two eyes" were formed. The upper eye, the so-called higher "I," was to perceive the mysteries of goodness, and the lower eye, or lower ego, was intended to recognize the mysteries of evil. The capacity to perceive both mysteries simultaneously was the "line" joining the two views; this "line" was created through the words of Christ: "I AM." This simultaneous perception is the basis of the new post-Golgotha mysteries; it is the only way to acquire knowledge of the spiritual world without extinguishing the "I," as was the case in pre-Christian mysteries. Human beings were thus again able to experience, in waking consciousness, knowledge of the higher world, because now the higher "I" is able to relate to lower ego in such a way that there is a mutual reflection of experiences. The new stages of *imagination, inspiration,* and *intuition* are possible because the old, atavistic *imagination, inspiration,* and *intuition* were extinguished through the first three sacrifices of Christ; these stages will be attained in the future when the higher "I" and lower ego are able to relate with each other in a particular way. Each of these three stages implies a unique interrelationship between the higher "I" and the lower ego.

Another consequence of the Mystery of Golgotha is the fact that, if the stage of *imagination* knowledge, for example, is achieved, then the danger of falling prey to the realm of Lucifer is no longer a threat. Those who have worked toward *imagination* knowledge, from the basis of the Christ impulse, do not perceive the sphere of Lucifer, but the "fifth gospel." In other words, one perceives the life tableau of Jesus, the view that Jesus Christ renounced during his death for the benefit of humankind. In the future, if the stage of *inspiration* is achieved, one will not be exposed to the joint power of Lucifer and Ahriman; instead, one's "hearing" will take in the judgments of humanity's karma. One will read the eternal apocalypse, written in the astral sphere of the Earth and inscribed there by Christ at his death for the benefit of humankind.

Now consider more closely the way that these three potential future experiences of *imagination, inspiration,* and *intuition* have been brought about by the sacrifices of Christ. When Jesus Christ broke the bread and handed it to his disciples, he accompanied that act by saying, "Do this in remembrance of me." He performed a deed with a truly deep and symbolic significance. It has the meaning that, when we take up the Christ impulse, that impulse can actually awaken memory—specifically, the memory of Christ's life during the three years he was incarnated in a human form. By taking up the Christ impulse, it can lead us to the level of *imagination* that perceives the "fifth gospel," or the life tableau of Christ spread out in the etheric sphere of the Earth.

Furthermore, Christ descended into the sphere of oblivion when his closest disciples forgot him. When Peter was told, "Surely thou also art one of them," and he began "to curse and to swear, saying, I know not the man" (Matthew 26:73–74), at that moment Christ descended into the sphere of oblivion. The consequence of this, however, is that the memory of what happened to Jesus and of what he experienced is preserved for all of humanity. Thus, the memory pictures of Jesus Christ remain permanently in the etheric realm, and future Christians will no longer simply repeat what they have learned from previous generations, but will be authentic witnesses to the reality of Jesus Christ.

It is more difficult to understand how the Apocalypse came to be inscribed in the Earth's astral body. Kama Loka actually involves the fact that whatever we experience during the day is experienced again during the night; it is experienced in the light of conscience but remains in darkness. The judgments of our daytime experiences by the spiritual world during the night thus remain dark. This is the moral essence of sleep. All of this lights up in human consciousness during Kama Loka. In Kama Loka, human beings consciously experience what they experienced in the night as echoes of daytime experiences. This is, in fact, the judgment of the spiritual world upon what was done during the day.

With all due respect, we may now ask: What about the sleep of Jesus Christ during the three years he worked on Earth? The Gospels tell us only about his waking state. We are also told of his waking state in Rudolf Steiner's lectures that are referred to as the "fifth gospel" (and are, in fact, based on the fifth gospel).[8] Nonetheless, we must also ask this question: What was nighttime like for the Christ? How did he sleep? Sleep for Jesus Christ was different from what it is for others. People fall asleep in order to be judged by the spiritual world. Christ, by contrast, lifted himself out of his body to judge other beings and humanity; he was not the one to be judged, but pronounced judgment on others. This was because he was himself the spiritual Sun of the world, present on Earth. Thus, when you read of his meaningful conversation with Nicodemus during the night—a conversation that Rudolf Steiner said took place in suprasensory consciousness—you will find that in Nicodemus it illuminated his memory of a conversation with a being whose voice could be heard, but whose countenance could not be seen. That conversation was a "ray" from the nighttime activity of Christ reaching human consciousness. When Christ faced Nicodemus and spoke to him of the need to be born of water and of the Spirit, he asked, "Art thou a master of Israel, and knowest not these things?" (John 3:10). This question was both a reproof and instruction; it expresses the activity of the Christ being that, during the night, was addressed to many.

Jesus Christ spent only one night as a human being. It was nevertheless a night without sleep; this was the night in Gethsemane. During that night, Christ renounced the "beneficial" element of the nocturnal knowledge of good and evil. He renounced the positive aspect of Kama Loka, going into death in order to descend into the Earth and into Hell. Christ renounced the essence of everything he had experienced during the nights of his three years of earthly life. Just as his life tableau remains, this essence also remains; it is inscribed into the "night sphere" of the Earth. The words of Christ remain in the astral sphere of the Earth, and thus the Apocalypse of John could be written as part of the eternal apocalypse. The eternal apocalypse will remain for as long as the Earth survives; this is one aspect of the secret expressed in these words: "Heaven and Earth shall pass away: but my words shall not pass away" (Luke 21:33). This means that these words are written in the eternal; they are not just daytime words, but are also words spoken by night. The essence of the Apocalypse is the judgment of human destiny. Every human being of the future who reaches the stage of *inspiration* will be able to experience the sphere of this Apocalypse. Such individuals will experience the fruits of the Kama Loka of Jesus Christ, the fruits that Christ himself renounced.

When Christ renounced the ascent into the devachan state at his death and, instead, descended into the subterranean interior of the Earth, the fruits of that experience became available for the good of humankind. In the spiritual realm of the earthly body stood the temple that Christ said he would destroy and rebuild in three days. This is not merely relative or a figure of speech, but a fact. The ideal of future humanity was built because of Christ's descent into the interior of the Earth, the realm of evil, and his ascent as the resurrected one. All knowledge of good and evil was realized through that act. The temple was built by Christ as a result of his renunciation of the devachan state. All those who set forth out of the Christ impulse and reach the stage of *intuition* will be able to read in that temple. There, they will be able to perceive and investigate the secrets of good and evil. Along with much else, these are the karmic consequences of the Mystery of Golgotha for humankind.

Now we may ask: What could the karmic consequences of the Mystery of Golgotha have been for the being of Christ himself? Christ became a man, lived in a human body, went through a human death, and thus entered the field of human karma. He set in motion a human karmic stream that will work itself out in the future. During the time that Jesus Christ was a man on earth, he established a certain relationship with humanity. He had a circle of students—indeed, three circles of students. He had a secret circle, with whom he could converse "spiritually"; the circle of twelve, who traveled with him "physically"; and the circle of seventy mentioned of in the gospels.[9] This was one relationship that humanity had with the Christ being. The other relationship was the one expressed in his trial and condemnation. Humanity judged the Christ being; humanity condemned him and found him worthy of punishment by death. Their behavior toward him was such that, through his death, they eliminated him from their world.

Now, if we consider the stages of his judgment—when He was scourged, crowned with thorns, laden with the cross, and crucified to die on the cross—we must not believe that this process took place only once, nineteen centuries ago, and then ended. In fact, it happened again and continues today. "Inasmuch as ye have done it unto one of the least of these my brethren, ye have done it unto me" (Matthew 25:40). If these words of Christ are true, it means that everything that happens to those who are in any way connected with the Christ impulse—as representatives of the Christ impulse—is also experienced by the Christ being. Do not believe that Christ has become insensitive to what happens to his own in the world. Every blow received by one who stands faithfully as a representative of the Christ impulse in the world also strikes Christ as it happened in those days. The path of Christ's sacrifice has not come to an end. Because it is the Christ who experienced the scourging physically, he experiences it with everyone who lives according to his impulse. When you read a work, say *Ecce Homo* by Nietzsche, that hurls blows and thrusts with inner cruelty and scornful criticism at the one who seemingly cannot be reached (and whole streams of thought exist just to carry this on), let no one imagine that the one who wrote with the hand of that unhappy victim, Friedrich Nietzsche, did not know who felt those blows. Do not think that Ahriman believes, even for a moment, that his blows strike only empty air. He knows well that such scourging reaches an actual being, that of Christ, who suffers along with all those who are in any way connected with him.

This is why we should simply note that everything is present; all of the past belongs to today. In other words, the matters we are discussing do not belong only in the area of historical research; they are wholly topical. If we discuss the historical event of Christ's passion, it is because we want to understand the karmic consequences of the life that belonged to the specific person who was Jesus Christ; it is not a matter of ignoring what is happening now. Nineteen centuries ago, when he was a man, the Christ was scourged, crowned with thorns, laden with the cross, and nailed to the cross to die. In terms of karma, that has certain specific consequences. There is no thing or event in the world that does not have consequences. Now let us try to understand those consequences.

Nineteen centuries ago, the Christ came in a certain way; he descended from the heavenly spheres and into the interior of the Earth. We know that the earthly life of the Christ began with the baptism in Jordan, following which he descended further into his bodily organization. And he went even deeper—into the sub-bodily, or sub-physical, and on into the Earth's interior spheres. In a spiritual and moral sense, he went from above downward in order to ascend with the resurrection. His path was thus vertical.

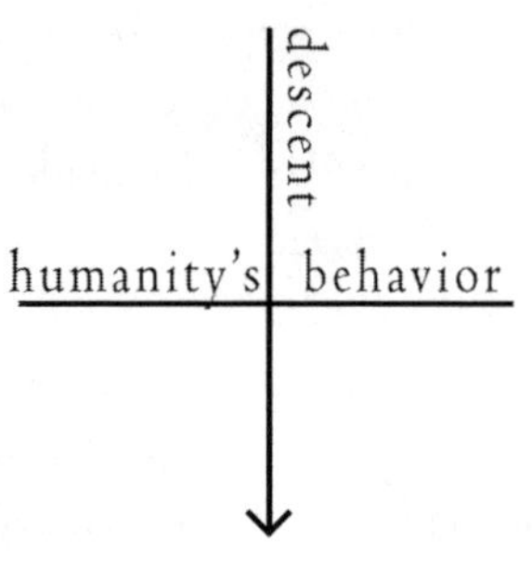


Christ's sacrifice, however, is related to a cross. The horizontal line, which is missing from the line of descent and ascent, was not his path; he did not create it himself and did not go in that direction, but took only the path of descent and ascent. The horizontal line, in contrast to the line of descent, was created by Christ's relationship to humankind. When humanity pronounced judgment upon him and then abused him with scorn and death on the cross, the horizontal line was created; it is linked to the path of descent, thus forming a cross. This was the relationship between humanity and the Christ; the cross was thus formed (see figure). That relationship was expressed in the behavior of humanity toward the Christ as the stages of judgment, scourging, crowning with thorns, cross bearing, and crucifixion; human striving cut across his path. As a consequence, this fact can bear karmic compensation; a correction can occur in the world toward the man Jesus Christ.

The deed done to him by humanity took place nineteen centuries ago. At that time, Jesus Christ had moved in a small circle on the small portion of Earth where he lived. Unlike the "wise" ones of his time, he did not go on distant journeys. He was active only in one area, the tiny Palestine. This was because, spatially, he did not have the horizontal dimension at his disposal for his work; his only direction was descent. Those who joined him on this path were few. Christ was unable to visit the greater portion of humankind spread out over the Earth's surface during his time because the world was filled by the presence of Lucifer and Ahriman. The important and shattering consequence of meeting only a sample of humanity in that small corner of the Earth is that the Christ suffered as the result of an unjust condemnation by human beings. The karmic consequence is that the horizontal breadth that was aggressively denied him by humanity nineteen centuries ago is now at his disposal. The same number of steps through which humanity persecuted him is now at his disposal to move spatially in the world. This is why an etheric return of Christ can take place. It is the reason why Rudolf Steiner could say with certainty that there will be an etheric return of Christ in the world; nothing can prevent this. It is karmically determined through his path of suffering. This karma is eternal, because the power of the Father is behind it, which up to now has known no opposing power. So you can see that it is not a matter of mere prophecy but knowledge arising from initiation science, which gives certainty about what will be.

We have now acquired a concept of the fundamental nature of the etheric return of Christ and why it must come about. Nineteen centuries ago, Jesus Christ was able to meet only a small number of people, and only they were able to join him on the path of descent and ascent. He had only a limited corner of the Earth for his activity then, but now he has the possibility of visiting all of humanity in the horizontal dimension. The coming of Christ then was limited in space; now the necessity follows and, karmically, the possibility arises for Christ's movement in space. The etheric return of Christ differs from his physical incarnation in that it will happen in the horizontal dimension. This time, however, humanity will have to create a vertical relationship to it. There will be a great difference between the way Jesus Christ manifested nineteen centuries ago and the way he will work today.

Let us briefly consider the steps that the Christ will take in the space available to him because of the karma of the Mystery of Golgotha for humanity—the karmic result of humanity's past behavior toward him. Humanity judged Christ; now he has the possibility of judging humanity. Judgment by Christ does not mean retribution, however, since the Christ must end the principle of retribution in the world. Christ's judgment means that he will awaken the conscience; he will be able to work spatially and take steps that awaken the conscience of human beings. The first inkling of the Christ's return in the etheric will be a wave of elemental feelings of conscience. Feelings of shame will seize people with elemental power. A consuming power of shame will arise, and people will not know its source. Thus we can say that Christ's appearance in the etheric will be heralded by a red glow of human shame. People will experience an overwhelming force of disappointment in the values they have treasured as "truth" and "beauty." In a sense, people will have to reassess all the values in their souls. In the state of Kama Loka, one has to experience a reversal of life's values, owing to rays of the cosmic conscience; now people will have to experience a reversal of all their values, because they will experience those values through the effect of Christ, who will function in horizontal space.

Because Christ was scourged and crowned with thorns in the past, another step in space is now at his disposal karmically. Christ will not only awaken the human conscience, but also move people. Just as he received the blows of scourging, he will likewise be able to reach, touch, and move people. He will touch those who are in despair and instill comfort and courage in them. This moving touch is a consequence of the scourging, and it will cause courage to flow for a new effort of creativity. Some will say: We'll begin afresh, because everything we have created thus far will not stand up to his light. To a certain extent, the first day of creation must begin within the human kingdom. People will not gain courage out of themselves; rather, they will gain it from the emotional disturbance that comes from the Christ as karmic consequence of the scourging he experienced. And because Christ was crowned with thorns in the past, he will give tasks to individuals and groups of people and show them how to serve his work. He will crown people with duties of love. We know that there are certain concepts of "duty" that do exist in the world. Nevertheless, "duty" will eventually lead humankind to catastrophe, because everything evil that enters the world will, in fact, be pursued by people out of a sense of duty. When he returns in the etheric, however, Christ will assign tasks of love to people and groups, whereas the notion of "duty"—a giant with feet of clay—will fall and be shattered into a thousand fragments. Instead of duty, there will be a love for one's task.

In the past, Christ had to carry the cross on which he would be crucified; now Christ will heal people's infirmities when he reappears in the etheric; there will be a healing of destinies. Those who carry their crosses will have the strength to carry them through the healing of soul and body.

At the Mystery of Golgotha, when Christ was crucified, he said, "Father, forgive them; for they know not what they do" (Luke 23:34). These words contain what he wishes to accomplish in the space, and what was granted to him as karmic consequence of the crucifixion—that people might become conscious of what they do. The karmic result of the crucifixion will not be to bind human beings as though they were crucified, but to open their eyes. A new clairvoyance will be stirred through Christ, so that all human beings will be able to see and know what they do. This is karmic clairvoyance—seeing karma. When people act today, they do not know the karmic consequences of that act. In the future, however, people will know what they are doing. Karmic clairvoyance is Christ's answer to the crucifixion, because people did not know what they were doing. These are the karmic steps of Christ in space; their cause goes back to when he was a man and had to walk the path of suffering to which human beings had condemned him. Thus Christ changes the negative into the positive. The return of Christ in the etheric is his response to the way he was treated when he lived among humankind as a man.

Nineteen centuries ago, when Christ was limited to the vertical path of descent, he was imperceptible to the world of nature. He was unable to work in the realm of nature, because nature perceives only in the horizontal plane. His appearance then was intended only for humanity. Now, however, he will move in space horizontally, thus his appearance will also affect nature, the realm that has nearly lost all hope of redemption. Hope for nature's redemption will be renewed through the return of Christ in the etheric. And much will take place in human consciousness as a result of his reappearance in the etheric. In our next study, we will speak of how Christ's reappearance in the etheric will affect human consciousness and world of nature.

# 7.

# Christ's Return in the Etheric

Previously, we discussed the effects of the Mystery of Golgotha, especially in relation to its karmic results. We began by asking: What were the consequences, both for humanity and for Jesus Christ? Christ, too, was human and thus created human karma. What were the consequences of the fact that he was judged, scourged, crowned with thorns, forced to bear the cross, and then crucified? We also tried to understand the matter of how, nineteen centuries ago, Jesus Christ worked on Earth in such a way that his path involved a continued descent from the heights into the Earth's interior, and how, across this vertical Christ line, a horizontal line was formed by the way human beings acted toward him. Christ took the vertical path of descent. It is crossed by the horizontal line of humanity, which expresses the fact that humanity judged and condemned Christ to death on the cross. The karmic consequence of that human relationship to Jesus Christ means that, in the future, Christ will be able to reappear not only in the vertical line of descent, but especially in the horizontal dimension; in other words, space is karmically at his disposal, having become available to him through his suffering and the unjust judgment by human beings. He will be able to take as many steps horizontally toward humanity as human beings took against him through their aggression. We have indicated that, because he was judged, he will appear as a judge—not to dole out retribution, but to awaken the human conscience.

Through his visitation to all human beings on the Earth, the first step of his return will manifest as feelings of shame, followed by a reassessment of all the values held by human souls. And because Christ was scourged, jostled, and struck, he will be able to reach out and touch and move the people of our time. This will be expressed as increased courage in human hearts—courage to begin everything anew once people have reevaluated their values. The karmic consequence of having crowned the Christ with thorns will be expressed in Christ's next step; he will assign tasks, or labors of love, so that there will many guardians of the Christ mystery. Those guardians of the Christ mystery will bear witness to meeting him; in addition to seeing him, that meeting will involve receiving tasks from Christ. The fact that, nineteen centuries ago, he had to carry the cross will lead karmically to healings, so that dry, "wooden" human ether bodies will be enlivened and reanimated. A rich inner life will arise for those who, because of their dried and shriveled ether bodies, previously had no basis for such an inner life. And, finally, another karmic consequence will be that Jesus Christ will awaken a new capacity in human souls;

this will be a faculty for a new, etheric clairvoyance. This new, etheric clairvoyance will have an inner connection with the words Christ spoke during the crucifixion: "Father, forgive them; for they know not what they do." This clairvoyance, which can also be called "karmic clairvoyance," will arise so that people will be able to be conscious of what they do. People will be given the possibility of acting in such a way that they will realize how their acts relate to the past and their consequences for the future.

Now we will try to understand these things further and consider Christ's steps, spatially, from yet another perspective. If we view this series of steps as the way Christ uses the karmic consequences at his disposal from the Mystery of Golgotha, and if we look at the five possibilities that will approach human beings, then we can read something from our soul pictures. It is really a matter of another repetition of the preceding sacrifices (we have mentioned these manifestations several times). We have seen that the Saturn, Sun, and Moon sacrifices were "repeated" prior to the Mystery of Golgotha, and that the fourth and new sacrifice was the Mystery of Golgotha. We have also seen that, on this occasion, all of Christ's sacrifices were also repeated in the Last Supper, the night in Gethsemane, and on Golgotha during the crucifixion. It is the same for the etheric return of Christ; the preceding acts of sacrifice will again be repeated.

Now we can understand that the awakening of conscience in the human soul corresponds to what happened earlier in the physical nature of humankind. This was during the Lemurian epoch, when human beings first stood erect. The first sacrifice of Christ repeats again—not physically this time, but in the human soul organization. Human beings become upright psychologically, or in the soul, when the conscience is awakened; they will feel the eye of the spiritual world upon them. That experience will awaken the human conscience—first as elemental feelings of shame, and then as a reassessment of all values.

In the second step of Christ's return will awaken courage for new creativity. This means that the conscious higher part of human beings will be lifted out of the experience of remorse and despair; people will gain the courage to begin afresh, despite everything they have experienced in the sense of despair. People will have experienced great failure in every area. Today we can be satisfied with one thing or another, but in the light of Christ, we will be unable to rest content. Despair will arise, but the creative aspect of human souls will be released from that despair. This will correspond to the second sacrifice of Christ, when the soul body was released from the life processes.

The third step of Christ is experienced by human beings when tasks are assigned, as though people are given crowns of thorns by the Christ; this will lead to a new way of representing the spiritual world and the being of Christ in the world. We all know about the Guardian of the Threshold, who has the responsibility of guarding the threshold to the spiritual world. Some of his tasks will be transferred to human beings—those who are willing to accept them.

Consequently, just as the third sacrifice of Christ involved consonantal speech, now the capacity for a new spiritual language will arise. This will no longer be merely a language of vowels and consonants, but one containing a new element of intonation. This element will have the ability to imbue ordinary concepts and words with an essence that vibrates inwardly and reveals more than the mere word one uses. People will learn to speak thoughts with words; those thoughts will be embodied in one's words that now carry something greater. We can say that moral tone, or moral substance, will flow into speech and give the power of conviction to language. Then not only will words based on experience be convincing, but also those simple words and sentences based on the delicate breath of moral values. This will flow in through the new way of representing the spiritual world—a way of speaking in the name of the spirit world.

With the fifth step of Christ, a certain element is repeated—the element connected with the crucifixion, death, and resurrection. This will open human eyes for karmic clairvoyance. For the first time, the Mystery of Golgotha will be repeated, but now with an added new element. It will consist of what corresponds to the fourth step, insofar as human ether bodies become endowed with the vitality needed for the development of a rich inner life. In addition, a new "karmic clairvoyance" will be evoked through the activity of the Christ being. This etheric clairvoyance will be entirely new and not a repetition; it will be the result of the fifth sacrifice of Christ.

Try to understand this new, fifth sacrifice (the preceding ones were repetitions). The earlier sacrifices involved harmonizing the physical, ether, and astral bodies and the "I." The fifth sacrifice, however, harmonizes the human manas organization, or spirit self. Harmonization of the form always comes before the harmonization of the essence, which can take effect later and develop on the foundation thus created. This is precisely a matter of harmonizing the manas, the relationship between the "I" that ascends and the ego that descends. It is the harmonizing of the two "eyes"; the upper eye sees the mysteries of goodness, the future, and the world of spirit, while the lower eye perceives the mysteries of evil. The manas organization is harmonized by uniting these "eyes" in the I AM of the Christ impulse. This is their axis of vision, which includes potential

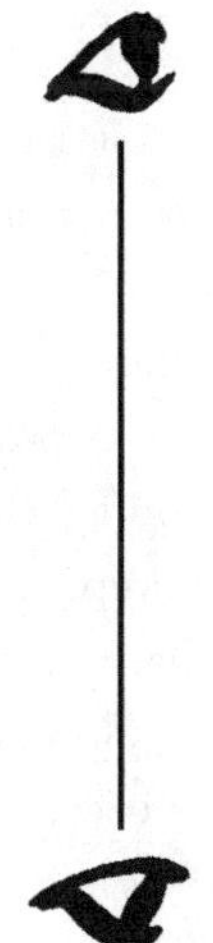

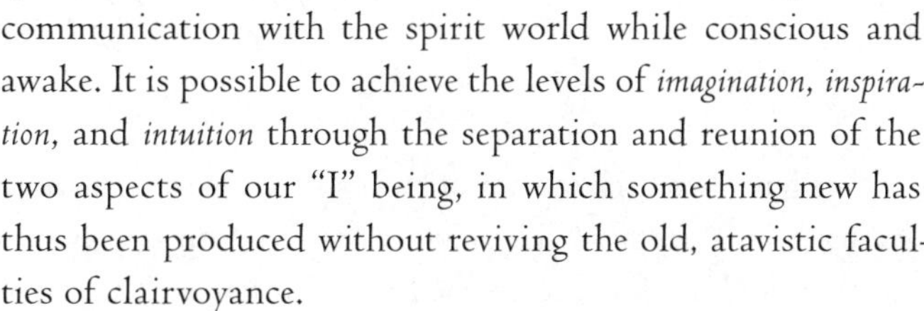

communication with the spirit world while conscious and awake. It is possible to achieve the levels of *imagination, inspiration,* and *intuition* through the separation and reunion of the two aspects of our "I" being, in which something new has thus been produced without reviving the old, atavistic faculties of clairvoyance.

We can draw this image of two "eyes" with the visual axis uniting them (see figure). This union will become permanent in harmony with the human spiritual organization, and not something that existed only at certain times during special states of meditation. The harmonization of the manas organization gave rise to a permanent connection between the upper "I" and the lower ego. This axis of vision of both "eyes," or axis of vision in the manas organization (with the upper seeing into the upper world and the lower seeing into the lower world), unites both as a continuing, ever-present faculty.

With Christ's etheric return, therefore, we are dealing not only with a memory of the past, but also a new "memory" of the future. In other words, the awake human daytime consciousness would perceive both what the upper "eye" is able to perceive in the future of the spiritual world (the spiritual world is always in the future), and what the lower "eye" would remember from the past by "reading" the etheric body, thus gathering knowledge from earlier incarnations. This attainment of knowledge from the past and knowledge of the future through the activity of the two "eyes" is linked by a unifying memory stream. Rudolf Steiner once wrote a mantra that begins, "In the beginning was the power of memory." For the human organization, the significance of the etheric return is expressed in these words; it will permanently link the upper and lower worlds within human consciousness, a link that makes possible the intended power of memory. By awaking memory, the possibility of recognizing karma arises.

What is karmic clairvoyance? Rudolf Steiner stated that, at the beginning of the 1930s, a small number of people would have this clairvoyance, and that, eventually, the number of such people would increase. This question can be answered to some extent by the previous diagram of the manas organization coming into being. The following drawing will help further.

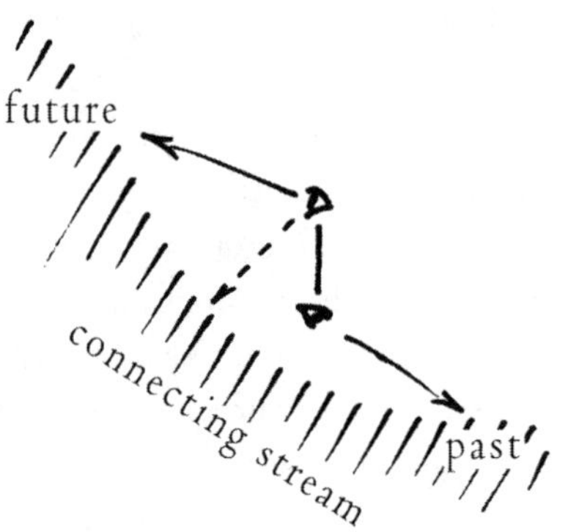


Imagine, here, the stream of the spiritual world descending, and the lower ego looking back into the past. The connection between two points can be seen through this image of looking forward to the future in the spirit world and looking back to a point in the past and to what has happened then on Earth. For example, say a man experiences something in the past through the lower "eye." With both "eyes," he seeks a corresponding "distant" point in the future. Then he discovers what is to happen on Earth as the karmic result of these two factors. We can say that it is a matter of building a certain figure whereby the future is seen and the temporal and spatial place is discovered where the karmic result of the past can be realized. This faculty will arise not as a kind of trick or acquired dexterity; rather, it will have varied degrees of clarity exactly because it will be a faculty instead of a mere skill. Through this concept of karmic clairvoyance, we can understand that people will increasingly begin to know what they are doing in the stream of karmic events. They will experience and recognize karma in such a way that an event of the past will always be experienced in connection with a future event. This will not be a general theory of karma but real knowledge of concrete, specific karmic configurations. This ability will indicate the etheric return of Jesus Christ for humankind.

We mentioned that the etheric return of Christ will also have significance for the world of nature. When Christ appeared nineteen centuries ago, he came for the benefit of humanity. His descent took place vertically in the sphere of human existence. The consciousness of nature, however, is on a horizontal plane. Consequently, the effects of the Mystery of Golgotha are accessible to nature only through human beings. The world of nature does not experience the being of Christ directly, and, because of this, a certain sense of hopelessness is becoming stronger for nature. We can say that humankind is the destiny of nature; we must bring salvation to the world of nature, because we have the moral connection with the spiritual world. But nature has a dynamic connection with the spiritual world; it must obey the world of spirit. Nature can experience the warmth that comes from the Sun, but not moral warmth, which can come only from human beings. Unfortunately, this does not happen. Because of this, misfortune occurs again and again in the elemental world.

The Bible mentions the primordial chaos (*tohu wa bohu*). The Genesis of Moses portrays the earth's becoming, particularly from the view of the elemental world. At that time, the beings of nature, the animals, were brought before human beings, who gave them names. Through this act, a certain influence proceeded from humankind toward the beings of nature, and this determined their karma; human beings determined nature's karma. This occurred during the Lemurian epoch, and the post-Atlantean epoch is a reversed reflection of that Lemurian epoch. Chaos is again arising in the elemental world. It is the duty of humankind to return order into that chaos by using moral powers. All of this chaos makes possible certain influences upon humanity. For example, when Rudolf Steiner spoke of Bolshevism, he said that there are cruel elemental beings behind men—elemental beings who goad human beings to commit acts of cruelty. It is our human task to cure the world of those illnesses. Still, human beings do almost nothing in this way for nature, and thus much of nature has less and less hope for redemption. The etheric return of Christ will signal a restoration of hope for nature; it will be a sign of resurrection for nature. Christ will be active throughout the horizontal spatial realm. He will visit all the regions of the Earth, and this will lead to a meeting with the beings of nature and an active moral force in the world of nature. In the past, this happened through the vertical plane for humankind; today it happens on the horizontal plane for nature.

How can we picture the effect that the Christ will have on nature through his movement through the spaces of that realm? Much is taking place, and anyone who is truly paying attention can see this. In nature, much happens every year that increasingly contradicts the whole traditional process of nature in the past. Springtime is different from what it used to be. Summer, autumn, and winter are changing as well. In March, we experience the sultry days of summer. People talk of mysterious manifestations; the whole divine revelation of spring, summer, autumn, and winter is mixed up. Chaos is setting in, and this comes not from Heaven, but from the interior of the Earth. People think that these are merely climate changes, but this is not the case. When orderly changes take place again in nature, these will be the outer signs of Christ's etheric return. Each spring will then breathe warmth and healing, not evil and sultry days. The summers will include two harvests. Nature will breathe out goodness and offer her fruits as though presenting gifts. Now, however, nature does not exude goodness; there is something in nature that is withering. Every year, that withering process increases. Nature has not yet become poisonous for humanity, but the times of spring have become increasingly evil.

Three years will come during which nature will radiate goodness. For example, when people are in despair they will find remarkable consolation in trees. Goodness will flow from plants into human souls. People will have the experience that trees bend before them in goodness and generosity. Goodness will be felt in nature to such a degree that people will not forget it; it will be remembered as a natural marvel. Phenomena such as thunder and lightning will not occur. A breath of goodness will flow from the world of nature, and human nature will feel it as regeneration and healing. The movement of Christ will progress spatially in concentric circles, and science will designate certain phenomena "ozone streams." Tubercular patients will feel better and, in whole regions, be cured simultaneously. People will speak of lines of ozone in the atmosphere, but it will really be the breath of Christ moving in a certain direction over the surface of the Earth. For a short period of three years, there will be reconciliation between humankind and the world of nature. This is the second event that will take place for nature in relation to the coming of the etheric Christ.

Now we are confronted by a third question: What will happen before these three years and how can we prepare an understanding for these events? Before these events (which, according to Rudolf Steiner, have begun already in the 1930s), they are being prepared for within human souls. An angel loses consciousness in the world of spirit; in selflessness, he sacrifices himself to humankind in such a way that his consciousness can be rekindled only when it lights up in the inner human being, in the conscience. It lights up in human beings when the angel's astral body, streaming down to earth, is received. This angel's ether body will remain an empty cup and able to receive the Christ, who will move through space in the form of that angel—the same angel with whom he was already connected four times before during his previous sacrifices. Thus, first, the consciousness of the angel is lost, somewhat like fainting spiritually. And on Earth, humankind's moral life must be quickened as a means of preparation. There must be awareness of this moral stream that flows down. It will resurrect in human consciousness only when the deep-seated moral questions of human beings come to meet it.

The order of events now is the reverse of their occurrence nineteen centuries ago. The series begins now with the Pentecost; the actual meeting with Christ, as an experience, comes later. At the time of the Mystery of Golgotha, Christ first descended into the realm of death, and then the Pentecost followed as the last in the series of events. Pentecost was a resurrection in the human soul; this time it happens in reverse. First, the Christ must be understood in his return in the etheric. Then the meeting in space with Christ, moving in the etheric, can happen consciously. The significance of his etheric return must now come first to human beings inwardly; only then will people be able to perceive Christ in the etheric realm. Consequently, it is extremely important that these questions remain at the center of our inner efforts and search; in this way, the return of Christ will not go unnoticed. To realize this, a general knowledge of spiritual science (knowledge of the ether body, karma, and so on) is not enough; people must concern themselves with the matters and connections we have been discussing, and intensive work is needed in relation to this event. Christology today is not an area of knowledge that may or may not be cultivated according to one's preference; it is a need of human destiny, so that we can avoid the misfortune allowing these events to go unnoticed by human consciousness.

The Pentecost of our time is the beginning; it is the arising warmth of awakened moral conscience; it is the dawn of understanding the meaning of the etheric return of Christ. The etheric return of Christ as a fact will be perceptible to the extent that this knowledge lives. First the knowledge comes, then the fact. This knowledge is the resurrection of that angel in the inner life of human beings; this is the angel who sacrifices his consciousness to humanity. This is the Pentecost that must precede the meeting with Christ. First come the resurrection and Pentecost, then the coming of Christ himself to live in the sheath of the ether body, which is held ready by that angel.

This return will occur in stages as Christ descends through various spheres. Even during the nineteenth century, it was possible to meet him on the level of *intuition*. This is why Rudolf Steiner could declare with certainty that this would happen, as well as when it would happen, because he experienced that meeting with the descending Christ on the level of *intuition*. Now it can be experienced on the level of *inspiration*. Later on, Christ will arrive in the sphere of *imagination*. Then people will perceive him in visions that they will surely have, as Rudolf Steiner has described.[10] It is not a matter of a prophecy; we can know from cosmic karma the way one sacrifice of Christ always has the next one as its consequence—how the Mystery of Golgotha was the inevitable consequence of the four preceding sacrifices, and how the fifth sacrifice is determined by the Mystery of Golgotha. The fifth sacrifice of Christ is karmically determined by the essence of the Mystery of Golgotha. Thus, one can know for certain that it will happen. This is not a prophecy based on trust, but a matter of certain knowledge from all that makes up Anthroposophy.

# Notes

## Part One

### *Chapter 1*

1 The angels who visited Abraham in Mamre were spoken of as "men" who ate Abraham's food and went to Sodom, where they spent the night in Lot's house.

2 The name is derived from *Turan,* an ancient Persian name for Turkistan, the area of the Turkic languages in Central Asia.

3 *Ashtaroth* is the Hebrew plural form of *Ashtoreth,* the name of the Canaanite fertility goddess and consort of Baal. Her name is spoken in Greek as "Astarte." She was worshiped at various local shrines, and there are a number of references to her in the Bible.

### *Chapter 2*

1 See *An Outline of Esoteric Science* (Anthroposophic Press, Hudson, NY, 1997), pp. 125–239.

2 The "Eighth Sphere," or Planet of Death, is seen esoterically as both a globe and a condition of being wherein utterly and irredeemably corrupt human souls are attracted, to be dissipated as earthly entities. These "lost souls" have, through lifetimes, lost their link with their inner god and so can no longer serve as a channel for those spiritual forces (see *Encyclopedic Theosophical Glossary,* www.theosociety.org/pasadena/etgloss/ea-el.htm). For a somewhat different discussion of the Eighth Sphere, see also C. G. Harrison, *The Transcendental Universe* (Lindisfarne Press, Hudson, NY, 1993), lecture 5.

3 We cannot speak here of Lucifer's relationship to the Eighth Sphere; its complexity demands an explanation that would lead us beyond the scope of these studies. — V. Tomberg

4 This applies only to the present. In the future, from the sixth cultural epoch on, human beings will be able to develop forces of "white magic" through their own power. — V. Tomberg

5 Yet even in the present epoch it is possible to work together with Yahweh after death, but only the highest initiates can make use of this possibility. — V. Tomberg

6 *Kama loka,* desire world; a semi-material plane, subjective and invisible to us, the astral region penetrating and surrounding the earth. It is the original Christian purgatory, where the soul undergoes purification from its evil deeds and the material side of its nature.

### *Chapter 3*

1 See, for example, Exodus 3:6 and 15, and Exodus 4:5.

2 *Christ and the Spiritual World: The Search for the Holy Grail* (Rudolf Steiner Press, London, 1963), lecture 3, Leipzig, Dec. 30, 1913.

3 See Rudolf Steiner, *According to Matthew: The Gospel of Christ's Humanity* (Anthroposophic Press, 2003), lecture 4, Berne, Sept. 10, 1910, pp. 69ff.

4 These three terms refer to levels of initiate consciousness as used by Rudolf Steiner. When used in this way, the words will be italicized. For more about these terms, see Rudolf Steiner, *A Psychology of Body, Soul, and Spirit: Anthroposophy, Psychosophy, and Pneumatosophy* (Anthroposophic Press,

Hudson, NY, 1999), especially part 3, lecture 3, Dec. 15, 1911, in which he discusses these levels of initiation specifically.

## *Chapter 4*

1 See, for example, Rudolf Steiner's lecture, October 7, 1923, on the Easter Concept.

2 Prentice Mulford (1834–1891), an influential figure in the New Thought movement, frequently wrote on building and maintaining one's life forces, as in the following quote: "Goodwill to others is constructive thought. It helps build you up. It is good for your body. It makes your blood purer, your muscles stronger, and your whole form more symmetrical in shape. It is the real elixir of life. The more such thought you attract to you, the more life you will have."

3 The reference here is always to the sphere of the Holy Spirit before the Mystery of Golgotha. After the Mystery of Golgotha, a second sphere of the Holy Spirit manifested, on this side of the luciferic sphere, which began the process of transforming the Earth into a new Sun.

4 See, for instance, Rudolf Steiner *Karmic Relationships: Esoteric Studies,* vol. 3 (Rudolf Steiner Press, London, 1977; CW 127); and Steiner's lectures in Neuchatel, September, 1911, in *Esoteric Christianity and the Mission of Christian Rosenkreutz* (Rudolf Steiner Press, 2005; CW 130).

5 Regarding these terms, see Rudolf Steiner, *Theosophy: An Introduction to the Spiritual Processes in Human Life and in the cosmos* (Anthroposophic Press, Hudson, NY, 1994; CW 9), pp. 50–61.

## *Chapter 5*

1 Rudolf Steiner, *Esoteric Christianity and the Mission of Christian Rosenkreutz* (Rudolf Steiner Press, 2005), the lectures in Neuchatel, September, 1911 (CW 130).

2 Rudolf Steiner, *The Deed of Christ and the Opposing Spiritual Powers: Lucifer, Ahriman, Asuras, Mephistopheles, and Earthquakes* (Steiner Book Centre, North Vancouver, BC, 1954), 2 lectures, Berlin, January 1 and March 22, 1909 (CW 107).

3 To better understand these ancient evolutionary periods, the stages of consciousness, and the spiritual beings involved, see Rudolf Steiner, *The Spiritual Hierarchies and the Physical World: Zodiac, Planets & Cosmos* (SteinerBooks, 2006), 10 lectures, Düsseldorf, April 12–18, 1909 (CW 110).

## *Chapter 6*

1 Carl Unger, *The Language of the Consciousness Soul: As a Basis for the study of Rudolf Steiner's "Leading Thoughts"* (St. George Publications, Spring Valley, NY, 1983), chapter 5.

2 *How to Know Higher Worlds: A Modern Path of Initiation* (Anthroposophic Press, 1994), p. 62.

3 *The Christ Impulse and the Development of Ego Consciousness* (Anthroposophic Press, 1976), 7 lectures, Berlin, Oct. 25, 1909–May 8, 1910 (CW 116).

4\. *Devachan* (Sanskrit): The "dwelling of the gods." An intermediate state between two earthly lives, into which the "I" (atma, budhi, and manas) enters after the disintegration of the lower principles on Earth.

5 See, for example, *The Christ Impulse and the Development of Ego Consciousness,* lecture 1.

## *Chapter 7*

1 Rudolf Steiner, *Founding a Science of the Spirit* (Rudolf Steiner Press, 1999), 14 lectures, Stuttgart, Aug. 22–Sept. 4, 1906 (CW 95); previous edition, *At the Gates of Spiritual Science.*

2 Rudolf Steiner, *From Jesus to Christ* (Rudolf Steiner Press, 2005), 11 lectures, Karlsruhe, Oct. 4–14, 1911 (CW 131).

3 See Rudolf Steiner, *Anthroposophical Leading Thoughts: Anthroposophy as a Path of Knowledge* (Rudolf Steiner Press, 1998), "The Apparent Extinction of Spirit-Knowledge in Modern Times," March 25, 1925, pp. 206–209 (CW 26).

4 Rudolf Steiner cites examples in his lectures presented in 1924, *Karmic Relationships: Esoteric Studies* (Rudolf Steiner Press), 8 vols. (CWs 236–240).

5 See Rudolf Steiner, *Christ and the Spiritual World: The Search for the Holy Grail* (Rudolf Steiner Press, 1963), 6 lectures, Leipzig, Dec. 28, 1913–Jan. 2, 1914 (CW 149), especially lecture 4.

6 See Rudolf Steiner, *According to Luke: The Gospel of Compassion and Love Revealed* (Anthroposophic Press, 2001), 10 lectures, Dornach, Sept. 1909 (CW 114). Here, Steiner speaks of the relationship between Phinehas and Elijah in these lectures.

7 Rudolf Steiner, *Truning Points in Spiritual History,* (Garber, Blauvelt, NY, 1987), 6 lectures in Berlin. 1911 (CW 60).

## Chapter 8

1 Rudolf Steiner, *According to Matthew: The Gospel of Christ's Humanity* (Anthroposophic Press, 2003) 12 lectures, Berne, Sept. 1–12, 1910
(CW 123)

2 Rudolf Steiner, *Genesis: Secrets of Creation* (Rudolf Steiner Press, 2002) 11 lectures, Munich, August 16–26, 1910 (CW 122).

3 See, for example, lectures 3 and 4 of Rudolf Steiner, *The Riddle of Humanity: The Spiritual Background of Human History* (Rudolf Steiner Press, 1990) 15 lectures, Dornach, July 29–Sept 3, 1916 (CW 170).

## Chapter 9

1 See Rudolf Steiner, *According to Matthew,* lecture 2.

2 "Thou hast proved mine heart; thou hast visited me in the night; thou hast tried me, and shalt find nothing; I am purposed that my mouth shall not transgress" (Psalms 17:3).

3 Sulamith's name does not appear as such in the Bible. Rather, she is a character in the opera *The Queen of Sheba,* by Karl Goldmark (1830–1915). Sulamith is portrayed as a daughter of the high priest and a member of Solomon's court who is engaged to marry Assad, Solomon's emissary to the Queen of Sheba. — Ed.

## Chapter 10

1 *According to Matthew: The Gospel of Christ's Humanity,*

2 See Rudolf Steiner's lecture cycle, *The Truth of Evolution: Inner Realities* (SteinerBooks, 2006); also *Evolution in the Aspect of Realities* (Garber, 1989) 6 lectures, Berlin, November 1911, (CW 132).

3 14 lectures, Stuttgart, August 22–September 4, 1906 (CW 95), Rudolf Steiner Press, 1999 (also *At the Gates of Spiritual Science,* Anthroposophic Press, 1986).

4 The Yahweh method and its contrast to the Baal method were discussed in meditation 8.

5 See Rudolf Steiner, *According to Matthew,* lecture 1.

6 One aspect of this event has been fully considered in study 8, "Moses." Here it will be dealt with from a different perspective.

7 A relevant idea of this inversion is given, from an etheric standpoint, in Dr. Günther Wachsmuth's *Etheric Formative Forces in cosmos, Earth and Man: A Path of Investigation into the World of the Living,* Anthroposophic Press, 1932.

8 It might be argued by those versed in the ancient human history, especially that of Atlantean humanity, that it was the egoistic self-deification of the

ancient Turanians that provided the karmic seed for the Turanianism of the post-Atlantean epoch, and that therefore the "we-consciousness" mentioned here cannot be thought of as characteristic of ancient Turanianism. This objection, however, falls apart when we reflect that egoism makes people much more alike than does altruism, which instead nurtures individuality. The "masses" are the result of the inbred egoism of the past. Thus, Turanian "we-consciousness" can be traced to the ancient Turanian self-assertion of the Atlantean epoch. — V. TOMBERG

9 See Rudolf Steiner, *The Gospel of John* (Anthroposophic Press, 1984), 12 lectures, Hamburg, May 18-31, 1908 (CW 103).

10 See lecture 2 in Rudolf Steiner, *According to Matthew: The Gospel of Christ's Humanity.*

## Chapter 11

1 See Rudolf Steiner, *How to Know Higher Worlds,* chapter 10.

2 See, for example, Ezekiel 2:1–3; 3:1–3 and 10; and 4:1.

3 "The Sons of Twilight" and "Sons of Life" are terms Rudolf Steiner uses for the hierarchy of angels in *An Outline of Esoteric Science,* p. 146.

4 Joseph Ernest Renan (1823–1892), French philosopher and theologian; David Friedrich Strauss (1808–1874), Bible scholar, theologian, lecturer, cleric, teacher, and writer in Germany and Continental Europe; Vladimir Solovyov (1853–1900), Russian philosopher, poet, pamphleteer, and literary critic who played a significant role in the development of Russian philosophy and poetry at the end of the nineteenth century.

5 Vladimir Solovyov, *Lectures on Divine Humanity,* edited by Boris Jakim, Lindisfarne Press, 1995.

6 Ibid., *War, Progress, and the End of History: Three Conversations, Including a Short Tale of the Antichrist,* Lindisfarne Press, 1990.

7 See Rudolf Steiner, *Secret Brotherhoods: And the Mystery of the Human Double* (Rudolf Steiner Press, 2004), 7 lectures, in St. Gallen, Zurich, and Dornach, November 6–25, 1917 (CW 178).

8 *Sophia Achamoth:* the daughter of Sophia and the personified astral light, or the lower etheric plane.

## Chapter 12

1 *From Jesus to Christ,* (Rudolf Steiner Press, 2005), 11 lectures, Karlsruhe, Oct. 4–14, 1911 (CW 131).

2 "And so it is written, The first man Adam was made a living soul; the last Adam was made a quickening spirit" (1 Corinthians 15:45).

3 See, for example, chapter 9, "The Idea of Freedom" (esp. pp. 148ff) *Intuitive Thinking as a Spiritual Path: A Philosophy of Freedom* (Anthroposophic Press, 1995), written 1894 (CW 4).

4 "I indeed baptize you with water unto repentance: but he that cometh after me is mightier than I, whose shoes I am not worthy to bear: he shall baptize you with the Holy Ghost, and with fire" (Matthew 3:11).

5 *Enstasy* was a term used by the Russian orientalist Professor Rosenberg of Petrograd University. He coined the term to distinguish between Buddhist "submersion" and Zarathustrian "emergence from the self." Frequently attributed to Mircea Eliade, who used the word in his 1954 book on yoga to describe yogic samadhi. *Enstasis* means "standing within"; it can be contrasted with *dis-stasis* (non-standing); it can also be contrasted with *ecstasy* or *ec-stasis* (standing outside of).

6 "Which was the son of Enos, which was the son of Seth, which was the son of

Adam, which was the son of God" (Luke 3:38).

7 "Every valley shall be filled, and every mountain and hill shall be brought low; and the crooked shall be made straight, and the rough ways shall be made smooth; And all flesh shall see the salvation of God" (Luke 3:5–6).

8 "Remembering without ceasing your work of faith, and labour of love, and patience of hope in our Lord Jesus Christ, in the sight of God and our Father; Knowing, brethren beloved, your election of God" (I Thessalonians 1:3–4).

### *Addendum*

1 See lecture 5, January 19, 1915, *The Destinies of Individuals and of Nations* (Anthroposophic Press, 1986), 14 lectures, Berlin, Sept. 1, 1914–July 6, 1919 (CW 157).

2 Friedrich Rittelmeyer, *Rudolf Steiner Enters My Life,* The Christian Community Bookshop, London, 1940.

3 Rudolf Steiner and Edouard Shuré, *The East in the Light of the West / The Children of Lucifer and the Brothers of Christ* (Garber, 1986), 9 lectures, Munich, August 1909 (CW 113), lecture 9.

4 Rudolf Steiner, *Life Between Death and Rebirth* (Anthroposophic Press, 1968), 16 lectures, various cities, Oct. 26, 1912–March 2, 1913 (CW 114), lecture 3.

5 Rudolf Steiner, *The Apocalypse of John: Lectures on the Book of Revelation* (Anthroposophic Press, 1993), 12 lectures, Nuremburg, June 18–30, 1908 (CW 104), p. 142.

6 Rudolf Steiner, *The Mission of the Folk-Souls: In relation to Teutonic Mythology* (Rudolf Steiner Press, 2005), 11 lectures, Oslo, June 7–17, 1910 (CW 121).

7 The author begs the reader to remember that it is not a question here of showing how he has arrived at his concept of the three teachers and the three branches of occultism, but of showing through one example that his views are based on Rudolf Steiner's teachings. — V. Tomberg

8 Rudolf Steiner, *The Challenge of the Times* (Anthroposophic Press, 1979), 6 lectures, Dornach, Nov. 29–Dec. 8, 1918 (CW 186), lecture 3.

9 C. G. Harrison, *The Transcendental Universe: Six Lectures on Occult Science, Theosophy, and the Catholic Faith,* p. 81.

10 Rudolf Steiner, *The Christ Impulse and the Development of the Ego-Consciousness,* lecture 7.

11 Rudolf Steiner, *Earthly and Cosmic Man,* (Garber, 1986), 9 lectures, Berlin, Oct. 23, 1911–June 20, 1912 (CW 133).

12 Rudolf Steiner, *An Outline of Esoteric Science,* pp. 388–389.

## Part Two

### *Chapter 1*

1 James H. Leuba (1868–1946), a psychologist on the faculty of Bryn Mawr and the founder of its psychology department, was an outspoken atheist and the author of *The Psychology of Religious Mysticism* (1929). William James (1842–1910) taught psychology and philosophy at Harvard and identified himself as a "pragmatist." His books include *The Principles of Psychology* (1890), *Pragmatism: A New Name for Some Old Ways of Thinking* (1907), and *Some Problems of Philosophy* (1910).

2 B. P. Vysheslavtzeff, professor of moral theology at St. Sergius (d. 1954), former professor at Moscow University. His articles may be found in *Kirche, Staat und Mensch, Russisch-orthodoxe Studien, Studien und Dokumente* (Geneva, 1937), along with those of Berdyaev, Bulgakov, Fedotov, and others. See also, S. Bulgakov, *The Holy Grail and the Eucharist* (Lindisfarne, 1997), and N. Berdyaev, *The Russian Idea* (Lindisfarne, 1992).

3 What Lucifer sows falls to Ahriman as the harvest; human beings wish to surrender to Lucifer but, instead, become the victims of Ahriman. — V. Tomberg

4 "If thou therefore wilt worship me, all shall be thine" (Luke 4:7).

5 "Wherefore I say unto you, All manner of sin and blasphemy shall be forgiven unto men: but the blasphemy against the Holy Ghost shall not be forgiven unto men" (Matthew 12:31).

## *Chapter 2*

1 In chapter 10 of our Old Testament meditations, we discussed in detail the so-called three curses of the Father from the perspective of the history of mystery wisdom. In this study we shall speak more of this from a different point of view. — V. Tomberg

2 See *According to Luke,* lecture 7.

3 See Rudolf Steiner, *The Effects of Esoteric Development* (SteinerBooks, 2006), 10 lectures, The Hague; March 20–29, 1913 (CW 145).

4 Rudolf Steiner, *Mystics after Modernism: Discovering the Seeds of a New Science in the Renaissance* (Anthroposophic Press, 2000), written 1901 (CW 7).

5 *Intuitive Thinking as a Spiritual Path.*

6 Rudolf Steiner, *Christianity as Mystical Fact* (Anthroposophic Press, 2006), written 1902 (CW 8).

## *Chapter 3*

1 See sections on The Lord's Prayer (October 20, 1904; Jan. 28, February 4 and 18, and March 6, 1907) in *The Christian Mystery* (Anthroposophic Press, 1998), a collection of Rudolf Steiner's early lectures and writings on Christianity.

2 This is the image of the "rosy cross" meditation, as described by Rudolf Steiner in *An Outline of Esoteric Science* (chapter 5, "Knowledge of Higher Worlds—Initiation").

3 These words are within quotes, because they do not refer to more than characterizations and include the activities of the Word, as indicated in the first section of this chapter. — V. Tomberg

4 Here, the figure of "need" includes the figure of want, which with guilt, need and care, appears in the scene of Faust's blindness. — V. Tomberg

## *Chapter 4*

1 Rudolf Steiner, *According to Matthew,* lecture 8, p. 140.

2 The term used in the original Greek text is *penthountes,* which means one who "mourns" or "bemoans," not one who "suffers" or "weeps" in a general sense. *Penthountes* is the participle of *pentheo* (Lat. *lugeo*), which specifically means "I bear sorrow," or "I bemoan," indicating the suffering of a bereavement.

3 See Rudolf Steiner, *The Christ Impulse and the Development of Ego-Consciousness,* lecture 5, "Correspondences between the Microcosm and the Macrocosm."

4 See Rudolf Steiner, *Karmic Relationships: Esoteric Studies,* vol. 3 (Rudolf Steiner Press, 2002), 11 lectures, Dornach, July 1–8, 1924 (CW 237), especially lectures 7–11.

5 See Rudolf Steiner, *An Outline of Esoteric Science,* pp. 318–319. Also, this and many other of Steiner's spiritual exercises are contained in Rudolf Steiner, *Start Now! A Book of Soul and Spiritual Exercises,* SteinerBooks, 2004.

## *Chapter 5*

1 On the topic of spirit self, life spirit, and spirit body, see chapter 1, "The Essential Nature of the Human Being," in Rudolf Steiner, *Theosophy: An Introduction to the Spiritual Processes in Human Life and in the*

*Cosmos* (Anthroposophic Press, 1994), written 1904 (CW 9).

2 *Eirenopoios* from *eirene,* peace, and *poios,* a creator, means a peacemaker or peace founder; thus, definitely one who *establishes* peace, not merely one *agreeing* to peace, as it appears in the Lutheran translation.

3 Those who compare Rudolf Steiner's "Foundation Stone Meditation" with what has been said will be able to see how the last three Beatitudes have risen again today in a different way through Steiner's teaching. The three passages (dealing with the Father, Son, and Holy Spirit) are concerned with a resurrection of the last three Beatitudes. — V. Tomberg

4 The term *nature* is not used here in Goethe's sense. When he spoke of nature, he meant especially the activity of the elohim, dynamis, and kyriotetes, through the third hierarchy. *Nature,* here, refers to the existence and destiny of the three natural kingdoms and the hosts of elemental beings behind them—ahrimanic, luciferic, neutral, and those devoted to the gods.

5 "Rejoice, and be exceeding glad: for great is your reward in heaven: for so persecuted they the prophets which were before you" (Matthew 5:12).

## Chapter 6

1 See lecture 2, Rudolf Steiner, *Karmic Relationships: Esoteric Studies,* vol. 3.

2 Here the Christian concept is opposed to the corresponding theosophical view of the "causal body." See, for example, Charles Leadbeater, *Man Visible and Invisible,* Quest Books, 1969.

3 In the Gospel of Matthew, the Lord's Prayer is placed specifically under the sign of Libra. Luke's Gospel, by contrast, places it under a different sign, but recognition of this cannot be fruitful for the understanding of the Lord's Prayer unless it has already been understood under the sign of Libra. — V. Tomberg

4 The discussions that follow assume the reader's acquaintance with Rudolf Steiner's *Lord's Prayer, An Esoteric Study* (Anthroposophic Press, Spring Valley, 1970) will be assumed. The author knows of no other work dealing with this subject on the same lines. — V. Tomberg (This and similar works are contained in Rudolf Steiner, *The Christian Mystery* [Anthroposophic Press, 1998], a collection of early lectures.)

5 "If thou therefore wilt worship me, all shall be thine. And Jesus answered and said unto him, Get thee behind me, Satan: for it is written, Thou shalt worship the Lord thy God, and him only shalt thou serve" (Luke 4:7–8).

6 This is addressed in greater detail in the fifth of our Old Testament studies.

## Chapter 7

1 See, for example, Rudolf Steiner, *The Bhagavad Gita and the Epistles of Paul* (Anthroposophic Press, 1971), 5 lectures, Dec. 28, 1912 to Jan. 1, 1913 (CW 142), lecture 6; and *The Gospel of John: And Its Relation to the Other Gospels* (Anthroposophic Press, 1982), 14 lectures, Kassel, June 24 to July 7, 1909 (CW 114), lecture 9.

2 The sevenfold number of the miracles of healing refers to the human organization belonging to the *day* (that is, serving daytime consciousness). Nevertheless, Jesus Christ's works of healing are not confined to this; his healing power is also effective in the world beyond waking awareness—for example, in Christ's descent into Hell.

3 The greater part of the four Gospels has arisen from seeing, hearing, and participating in the akashic record. But there are spiritual moral threads that associate the human consciousness with certain scenes of the akashic record. Such consciousness perceives no more

than is needed to establish a moral and spiritual connection. Hence all the details of events described in the Gospels have moral and spiritual significance. This is why the descriptions given by each individual evangelist differ. — V. Tomberg

4 Regarding the human senses, see Rudolf Steiner, *A Psychology of Body, Soul, and Spirit: Anthroposophy, Psychosophy, and Pneumatosophy* (Anthroposophic Press, 1999), 12 lectures, Berlin, 1909–1911 (CW 115), especially the first four lectures, "Anthroposophy," Oct. 23–27, 1909.

## *Chapter 8*

1 This Gnostic formula is relevant here: "*Christus verus Luciferus.*" Rudolf Steiner tells us of ancient times:

> The Yahweh principle worked in the blood relationship; hence, the feeling of belonging to one another. By means of this blood relationship, Yahweh brought about order and harmony; and the forces working against him were the luciferic beings who directed their strongest attacks against the principle of the blood relationship. They always wanted to center human beings within their own personality—tearing them away from their blood relationships—before Christ came and perfected the development of the human personality, giving humankind its most inner power and making wisdom and grace the deepest impulses of the human being. The luciferic beings had prepared humankind for this throughout very long ages. Not until Christ appeared on Earth had humanity become mature enough to match the requirements of those luciferic beings. Those who understood this knew very well what they were saying when they spoke the words *"Christus verus Luciferus,"* Christ the true Lucifer. This is an esoteric saying (*Universe, Earth, and Man,* 11 lectures, Stuttgart, August 4–16, 1908, Rudolf Steiner Press, 1987, lecture 6).

2 "Jesus saith unto him, Thomas, because thou hast seen me, thou hast believed: blessed are they that have not seen, and yet have believed" (John 20:29).

3 "I must work the works of him that sent me, while it is day: the night cometh, when no man can work. As long as I am in the world, I am the light of the world" (John 9:4–5).

4 See lecture 9, Rudolf Steiner, *The Gospel of John: And Its Relation to the Other Gospels.*

5 Rudolf Steiner described the resurrection of Lazarus from this perspective in lecture 8 of *The Gospel of John: And Its Relation to the Other Gospels.*

## *Chapter 9*

1 See, for example, *The Balance in the World and Man, Lucifer and Ahriman: The World as Product of the Working of Balance* (Steiner Book Centre, 1977), 3 lectures, Dornach, Nov. 20–22, 1914 (CW 158).

2 *Intuitive Thinking as a Spiritual Path.*

3 Ulysses had been warned by Circe about two monsters, Scylla and Charybdis. Scylla lived in a cave high on the cliff, from which she thrust her long necks (she had six heads), each with a mouth able to seize one crew member of every vessel passing within reach. The other terror, Charybdis, was a gulf at nearly water level. Three times each day, water rushed into a chasm and was disgorged. Any vessel coming near the whirlpool when the tide was rushing in would be engulfed. When approaching the haunt of these dread monsters, Ulysses watched carefully for them. The roar of the waters as Charybdis engulfed them gave warning at a distance, but Scylla could not be discerned. While Ulysses and his men anxiously watched the dreadful whirlpool, they were not sufficiently on guard against an attack by

Scylla, and the monster, darting forth snaky heads, caught six of his men and carried them away shrieking to her den.

4 Again, it must be pointed out, however, that true dilemmas may appear, along with false dilemmas, and that one must not only go through a test that requires one to stand firm and make *no* choice; one must also go through the test of deciding when a choice *should* be made.

### *Chapter 10*

1 Friedrich Wilhelm Nietzsche (1844–1900), a German philosopher, is probably best known for his work *Thus Spoke Zarathustra* (1885); see Rudolf Steiner, *Friedrich Nietzsche: Fighter for Freedom* (Garber, 1985) and *Autobiography: Chapters in the Course of My Life, 1861–1907* (SteinerBooks, 2006). Otto Weininger (1880–1903), an Austrian philosopher, published *Sex and Character* in 1903, which became popular after his theatrical suicide at the age of twenty-three.

2 There is no more to be said at this point about *thinking*, because thinking must have already passed through corresponding stages. At this stage it is really *willing* that is especially important. —V. Tombereg

3 The experience of passing through the cosmic midnight, described here as an inner meeting with the Father principle, may seem to contradict the facts found in lectures 5 and 6 of Rudolf Steiner, *The Inner Nature of Man and the Life between Death and a New Birth*, Vienna 1914 (CW 153), English translation unavailable. There, consciousness of the cosmic midnight is associated with the *spirit* principle. In fact, however, there is no contradiction here; in that sphere, God the Spirit is the source for the alertness of consciousness, whereas what the consciousness experiences is under the activity of the Father. —V. Tomberg

### *Chapter 11*

1 "Nevertheless I have somewhat against thee, because thou hast left thy first love" (Revelation 2:4).

2 See Rudolf Steiner, *The Fifth Gospel: From the Akashic Record* (Rudolf Steiner Press, 1995), 13 lectures, Oslo, Oct. 1, 1913–Feb. 10, 1914 (CW 148).

### *Chapter 12*

1 "At that day ye shall know that I am in my Father, and ye in me, and I in you" (John 14–20).

2 More on the New Testament type of karmic functioning may be found in chapter 6 on the Lord's Prayer.

3 Only three studies were actually completed.

## Part Three

### *Chapter 1*

1 N. Morosow, "Revelations in Storm and Tempest" (in Russian).

2 We tried to show the inner meaning of this fact in our section of the New Testament, especially the part devoted to the Lord's Prayer.

3 For more on the "holy rishis," see, for example, Rudolf Steiner, *Egyptian Myths and Mysteries,* 12 lectures, Leipzig, Sept. 1908 (GA 106), Anthroposophic Press, 1971.

4 See New Testament meditation 12.

5 *Nicolaitans:* literally, *nicao* = to conquer or dominate; *laos* = the people, or laity.

6 See the first part of our "Studies of the Old Testament."

## Chapter 2

1 The holy book of Zoroastrian tradition; see, for example, *The Zend-Avesta* (translated by Abraham Anquetil-Duperron and introduced by Robert D. Richardson, Jr.), Garland, New York, 1984.

2 *Reins,* literally the kidneys or the loins, the area of the kidneys; traditionally the seat of feelings, or passions. — ED.

3 "Mercury" in esoteric terms, whereas astronomy names that planet "Venus," the Morningstar. See Georg Unger, "Concerning the So-called Interchange of Mercury and Venus," in Rudolf Steiner, *The Spiritual Hierarchies and the Physical World: Reality and Illusion* (Anthroposophic Press, 1996), 10 lectures, Düsseldorf, April 12–18, 1909 (CW 110), and 5 lectures, Berlin, October 31–December 5, 1911 (CW 132).

4 Here, as in all examinations of the Apocalypse, some acquaintance with Rudolf Steiner's works is assumed, especially *The Apocalypse of St. John* and *An Outline of Esoteric Science.*

5 See Rudolf Steiner, *The Reappearance of Christ in the Etheric: A Collection of Lectures on the Second Coming of Christ,* SteinerBooks, 2003.

6 Compare these passages from Rudolf Steiner's *Anthroposophical Leading Thoughts.*

> The lives of human beings unfold in the middle, between two regions of the world. In the development of the physical body, human beings are members of the "lower world"; in soul nature, they are the "middle world"; and in spirit faculties, they continually strive upward toward the "upper world." Human beings owe their bodily development to all that nature has provided; they bear soul being inwardly as their own portion; and, inwardly, they discover spirit forces as the gifts that lead outward and to participation in a divine world.
>
> The spirit is creative in these three regions of the world. Nature is not void of spirit. We lose even nature from our knowledge if we do not become aware of the spirit in nature. Nonetheless, in nature's existence, we find the spirit "asleep." Yet, just as sleep has its purpose in human life—just as the "I" must be asleep at one time in order to be more awake at another—the world spirit must be asleep in nature in order to be more awake elsewhere.
>
> In relation to the world, the human soul is like a dreamer when it ignores the spirit at work inwardly. The spirit awakens the dreams of the soul from their endless weaving in the inner life, to active participation in the world in which the true being of humankind has its origin. Just as human beings become involved inwardly and close themselves off from the surrounding physical world when dreaming, the soul would lose its connection with the spirit of the world and its source if it turned a deaf ear to the awakening calls of the spirit within. (leading thoughts 17–19, translation revised)

7 Rudolf Steiner describes this light sheath as the third kind of aura—the spiritual aura, side by side with the physical and the astral:

> Inside the spiritual skin, the spirit body is alive; it is built up by a spiritual life force in the same sense that the physical body is built up by a physical life force. Therefore, just as we speak of an ether body, we must also speak of an ether spirit for the spirit body. We will call this ether spirit the life spirit. The spiritual constitution of the human being is thus subdivided into three

members, the spirit body, the life spirit, and the spirit self.

For someone who can "see" in spiritual regions, this spiritual constitution is a perceptible reality—the higher, truly spiritual portion of the aura. A seer can "see" the spirit body as life spirit inside the spiritual skin, can see how the life spirit constantly grows larger by taking in nourishment from the outer spiritual world, and can also see how, as a result, the spiritual skin continues to expand and the spirit body becomes larger and larger. Of course the spatial concept of "getting larger" is only an image of the actual reality. Nevertheless, in picturing this, we are directed toward the corresponding spiritual reality. The difference between the human being as a spiritual being and as a physical being is that physical growth is restricted to a fixed size while spiritual growth can continue indefinitely. What is taken in as spiritual nourishment is of eternal value.

It follows that the human aura is made up of two interpenetrating parts, one of which is given form and color by our physical existence, the other by our spiritual existence. The "I" provides the separation between the two: The physical relinquishes its distinctive character to build up a body that allows a soul to come to life, while on the other side the "I" does the same, allowing the spirit to have a life within it. The spirit in turn permeates the soul and gives it a goal in the spiritual world. Through the physical body, the soul is confined to physical existence; through the spirit body, it grows wings that give it mobility in the spiritual world. (*Theosophy*, pp. 55–56)

## *Chapter 3*

1 Rudolf Steiner had this to say on this subject:

> We have on the one hand the kingdom of the Grail, and on the other the evil kingdom, Chastel Merveille, with all that came from the pact between Klingsor and Iblis playing into it. And here we can see, expressed in a wonderfully dramatic form, all that the most independent and innermost of the soul organs, the intellectual, or mind, soul, has had to endure in face of attacks from without. In the fourth post-Atlantean period, this soul principle had not yet become as inward as it had to become in the fifth epoch. It retreated more from the life of the outer world that prevailed in Greco-Roman period and back into the inner part of human beings, becoming freer and more independent. Because of this, it was much more open to attack by all the powers than it had been in the Greco-Roman epoch. The whole change that had taken place in the intellectual soul is portrayed haltingly and through legend, yet it stands dramatically before us as the antithesis between "Montsalvat" and "Chastel Merveille." We sense an echo of all the sufferings and conquests of the intellectual soul in the stories related to the Holy Grail. Everything that had to be changed in the human soul during more recent times is revealed to those who have come to know the nature of the mysteries. (lecture 4, February 7, 1913, *The Mysteries of the East and of Christianity*, 4 lectures, Berlin, Feb. 3–7, 1913 [CW 144], Garber Publications, 1989)

2 "Because thou hast kept the word of my patience, I also will keep thee from the hour of temptation, which shall come

upon all the world, to try them that dwell upon the earth" (Revelation 3:10).

3 *Cakkavattisuttanta,* quoted in Hermann Oldenberg, *Buddha: His Life, His Doctrine, His Order* (1882), Taylor & Francis, 1971.

4 Flavius Philostratus, *The Life of Apollonius of Tyana,* 5 vols., Harvard University Press, 1912.

5 In *An Outline of Esoteric Science* Rudolf Steiner states:

> "Hidden" knowledge was now flowing, although imperceptibly to begin with, into people's ways of thinking. It is self-evident that intellectual forces have continued to reject this knowledge right into the present. But what must happen will happen in spite of any temporary rejection. Symbolically, this hidden knowledge, which is taking hold of humanity from the other side and will do so increasingly in the future, can be called "the knowledge of the Grail." If we learn to understand the deeper meaning of this symbol as it is presented in stories and legends, we will discover a significant image of what has been described above as the new initiation knowledge with the Christ mystery at its center. Therefore, modern initiates can also be known as "Grail initiates." (p. 388)

6 "Him that overcometh will I make a pillar in the temple of my God, and he shall go no more out: and I will write upon him the name of my God, and the name of the city of my God, which is new Jerusalem, which cometh down out of heaven from my God: and I will write upon him my new name" (Revelation 3:12).

7 "I know thy works: behold, I have set before thee an open door, and no man can shut it: for thou hast a little strength, and hast kept my word, and hast not denied my name" (Revelation 3:8).

8 *Amen* (also *amon*) in the language of ancient Egypt means "hidden"; similarly *amenti* ("kingdom of the dead") refers to something that hides. — Ed.

9 See lecture 6, Rudolf Steiner, *The Gospel of St. John.*

## Appendix

### *The Four Sacrifices of Christ*

1 Hinricus Madathanus Theosophus published *The Secret Symbols of the Rosicrucians* (1785). See, for example, Rudolf Steiner, *The Secret Stream: Christian Rosenkreutz and Rosicrucianism* (Anthroposophic Press, 2000) a collection of lectures, p. 129; also Rudolf Steiner, *Esoteric Christianity and the Mission of Christian Rosenkreutz* (Rudolf Steiner Press, 2005), 23 lectures, 1911-1912 (CW 130), lecture 1.

2 See "Cosmic Evolution and the Human Being" ("Moon," beginning p. 165), *An Outline of Esoteric Science.*

3 The Tau (or T-shaped cross) was applied to the Egyptian *ankh,* a Tau with an inverted drop shape added to the top. It was the symbol of life for ancient Egypt, and it is often thought that the early Christians of Egypt designed their own cross after earlier "pagan" models of that region. The *ankh* symbol is known as the *crux ansata,* or *ansated* cross. The word *ansated* is derived from the Latin for "having handles" or something in the form of handles.

4 See *According to Luke,* especially lecture 7, "Christ, the Great Mystery of Earth Evolution."

5 See Rudolf Steiner, *The Riddle of Humanity: The Spiritual Background of Human History* (Rudolf Steiner Press, 1990), 15 lectures, Dornach, July 29 to Sept. 3, 1916 (CW 170), lecture 9.

6 In Theosophical terms, *Kama Loka* (Sanskrit) means "desire world," a

partially material realm that is usually invisible to human beings. It surrounds and encloses our physical Earth and is the dwelling place of the astral forms of dead human and other beings. It is in Kama Loka that the second death takes place, after which the liberated part of the human being enters Devachan.

Rudolf Steiner discussed Kama Loka in a number of lectures, especially during the years when he was closely associated with the Theosophical Society in Germany. In one lecture, he described it this way:

> When someone has gone through the gate of death, what place does that individual experience? One can answer this question by asking, "Where is an individual during the kama loka period?" This can be expressed spatially in words that express our physical world. Imagine the space between the Earth and the Moon, the spherical space described when the orbit of the moon is taken as the outermost path away from the Earth. Then you have the realm in which the human being, loosened from the Earth, dwells during Kama Loka. (*Life between Death and Rebirth,* [Anthroposophic Press, 1968], 16 lectures in various locations, Oct. 26, 1912 to May 13, 1913 [CW 140], p. 63)

7 In *Egyptian Myths and Mysteries,* Rudolf Steiner described the mission of Manu:

> That little handful of whom we have already spoken, who were led by the greatest initiate (generally known as Manu) and his pupils deep into Asia and thence fructified the other cultures, just this handful, being composed of the most advanced human beings of that time, first lost the ancient gift of clairvoyance for the ordinary relationships of life. For them the true day consciousness, in which we see physical objects sharply contoured, became ever clearer. Their great leader led this group farthest into Asia, so that they could live in isolation; otherwise they would have come too closely in touch with other peoples who still preserved the old clairvoyance. Only because they remained separated from other peoples for a time could they grow into a new type of human being. A colony was established in inner Asia, whence the great cultural streams could flow into the most varied peoples.
>
> Northern India was the first country to receive its new cultural current from this center. It has already been pointed out that these little groups of cultural pioneers nowhere found unpopulated territory. Earlier still, before their great migration from west to east, there had been other wanderings, and whenever new stretches of land rose from the sea, they were peopled by the wanderers. The persons sent out from this colony in Asia had to mix with other peoples, all of whom were more backward than they who had been led by Manu. Among these other peoples were many persons who had retained the old clairvoyance. (lecture 3, "The Old Initiation Centers: The Human Form as the Subject of Meditation")

8 Rudolf Steiner, *The Fifth Gospel.*

9 "After these things the Lord appointed other seventy also, and sent them two and two before his face into every city and place, whither he himself would come" (Luke 10:1).

10 See Rudolf Steiner, *The Reappearance of Christ in the Etheric.*

# Bibliography & Relevant Literature


## By Valentin Tomberg

*Early Articles,* Spring Valley, NY: Candeur Manuscripts, 1984.

*Group Work,* Spring Valley, NY: Candeur Manuscripts, 1985.

*Inner Development,* 7 lectures, Rotterdam, August 15–22, 1938, Hudson, NY: Anthroposophic Press, 1992.

*Lazarus, Come Forth! Meditations of a Christian Esotericist on the Mysteries of the Raising of Lazarus, the Ten Commandments, the Three Kingdoms & the Breath of Life,* Great Barrington, MA: SteinerBooks, 2006 (former edition, *Covenant of the Heart,* 1992).

*Meditations on the Tarot: A Journey into Christian Hermeticism* (published anonymously), New York: Tarcher Putnum, 2002.

*Studies in the Foundation Stone,* parts 1 & 2, n.d., no publisher; part 3, Spring Valley, NY: Candeur Manuscripts, 1982.

## On Valentin Tomberg

Heckman, Liesel, *Valentin Tomberg: Leben-Werk-Wirkung. Eine Biographie,* Band 1.1 1900–1944. Schaffhausen: Novalis Verlag, 2001.

———, *Valentin Tomberg: Leben-Werk-Wirkung. Eine Biographie,* Band 1.2 1944–1973. Schaffhausen: Novalis Verlag, 2005.

———, (Herausgeben von Ramsteiner Kreis) *Valentin Tomberg: Leben-Werk-Wirkung.* Band 2 *Quellen und Beitrage zum Werk.* Schaffhausen: Novalis Verlag, 2000.

Prokofieff, Sergei O., *The Case of Valentin Tomberg: Anthroposophy or Jesuitism?* London: Temple Lodge, 1997.

———, *Valentin Tomberg and Anthroposophy: A Problematic Relationship,* London: Temple Lodge, 2005.

## By Rudolf Steiner

*According to Luke: The Gospel of Compassion and Love Revealed,* 10 lectures in Dornach, September 1909, Great Barrington, MA: SteinerBooks, 2001 (CW 114).

*According to Matthew: The Gospel of Christ's Humanity,* 12 lectures, Berne, September 1–12, 1910, Great Barrington, MA: SteinerBooks, 2003 (CW 123).

*Ancient Myths and the New Isis Mystery,* 8 lectures, Dornach, 1918, 1920, Hudson, NY: Anthroposophic Press, 1994 (CWs 180 & 202).

*Anthroposophical Leading Thoughts: Anthroposophy as a Path of Knowledge: The Michael Mystery, written 1923–1925,* London: Rudolf Steiner Press, 1998 (CW 26).

*The Apocalypse of St. John: Lectures on the Book of Revelation,* 12 lectures, Nuremberg, June 17–30, 1908, Hudson, NY: Anthroposophic Press, 1993 (CW 104).

*Approaching the Mystery of Golgotha,* 10 lectures, various cities, 1913–1914, Great Barrington, MA: SteinerBooks, 2006 (CW 152).

*Autobiography: Chapters in the Course of My Life, 1861–1907,* written 1924–1925, Great Barrington, MA: SteinerBooks, 2006 (CW 28).

*Background to the Gospel of St. Mark,* 13 lectures, Berlin, Munich, Hanover & Coblenz, 1910–1911, London: Rudolf Steiner Press, 1968 (CW 124).

*The Balance in the World and Man, Lucifer and Ahriman: The World as Product of the*

*Working of Balance,* 3 lectures, Dornach, Nov. 20–22, 1914, N. Vancouver: Steiner Book Centre, 1977 (CW 158).

*The Bhagavad Gita and the Epistles of Paul,* 5 lectures, Dec. 28, 1912 to Jan. 1, 1913, Hudson, NY: Anthroposophic Press, 1971 (CW 142).

*The Book of Revelation: And the Work of the Priest,* 18 lectures plus conversations, Dornach, September 1924, London: Rudolf Steiner Press (CW 346).

*The Challenge of the Times,* 6 lectures, Dornach, Nov. 29–Dec. 8, 1918, Hudson, NY: Anthroposophic Press, 1979 (CW 186).

*Christ and the Spiritual World: The Search for the Holy Grail,* 6 lectures, Leipzig, Dec. 28, 1913–Jan. 2, 1914, London: Rudolf Steiner Press, 1963 (CW 149).

*The Christ Impulse and the Development of the Ego-Consciousness,* 7 lectures, Berlin, Oct. 25, 1909–May 8, 1910, London: Philosophical-Anthroposophical Publishing, 1926 (CW 116).

*The Christian Mystery: Early Lectures, 1905–1908,* Hudson, NY: Anthroposophic Press, 1998 (CW 97 & others).

*Christianity as Mystical Fact,* written 1902, Great Barrington, MA: SteinerBooks, 2006 (CW 8).

*Deeper Secrets in Human History: In the Light of the Gospel of St. Matthew,* 3 lectures, Berlin, Nov. 1909, Hudson, NY: Anthroposophic Press, 1985 (CW 117).

*The Destinies of Individuals and of Nations* 14 Lectures, Berlin, Sept. 1, 1914–July 6, 1919, Hudson, NY: Anthroposophic Press, 1986 (CW 157).

*Earthly and Cosmic Man,* 9 lectures, Berlin, Oct. 23, 1911–June 20, 1912, Blauvelt, NY: Garber, 1986 (CW 133)

(and Edouard Shuré), *The East in the Light of the West / The Children of Lucifer and the Brothers of Christ,* 9 lectures, Munich, August 1909, Blauvelt, NY: Garber, 1986 (CW 113).

*The Effects of Esoteric Development,* 10 lectures, The Hague; March 20–29, 1913 (CW 145); 1 lecture, Berlin, Feb. 3, 1913, Great Barrington, MA: SteinerBooks, 2006.

*Esoteric Development: Lectures and Writings,* collected lectures, 1904–1923, Great Barrington, MA: SteinerBooks, 2003.

*The Fifth Gospel: From the Akashic Record,* 13 lectures, Oslo, Berlin, Cologne, Oct. 1913– Feb. 1914, London: Rudolf Steiner Press, 1998 (CW 148).

*The Foundation Stone Meditation,* London: Rudolf Steiner Press, 2005 (CW 260).

*Founding a Science of the Spirit,* 14 lectures, Stuttgart, Aug. 22–Sept. 4, 1906, London: Rudolf Steiner Press, 1999 (CW 95); previous edition, *At the Gates of Spiritual Science.*

*From Jesus to Christ,* 11 lectures, Karlsruhe, Oct. 4–14, 1911, London: Rudolf Steiner Press, 2005 (CW 131).

*The Four Sacrifices of Christ,* 1 lecture, Basel, June 1, 1914, Hudson, NY: Anthroposophic Press, 1981 (CW 152).

*Friedrich Nietzsche: Fighter for Freedom,* written 1895, Blauvelt, NY: Garber, 1985 (CW 5).

*Genesis: Secrets of Creation,* 11 lectures, Munich, August 16–26, 1910, London: Rudolf Steiner Press, 2002 (CW 122).

*The Goddess: From Natura to the Divine Sophia* (collection), London: Sophia Books, 2002.

*The Gospel of St. John,* 12 lectures, Hamburg, May 18–31, 1908, Anthroposophic Press, 1984 (CW 103).

*The Gospel of St. John: And Its Relation to the Other Gospels,* 14 lectures, Kassel, June 24–July 7, 1909, Hudson, NY: Anthroposophic Press, 1982 (CW 114).

*The Gospel of St. Mark,* 10 lectures, Basel, September 15–24, 1912, Hudson, NY: Anthroposophic Press, 1986 (CW 139).

*How Can Mankind Find the Christ Again? The Threefold Shadow-Existence of Our Time and the New Light of Christ,* 8 lectures, Dornach, Dec. 1918–Jan. 1919. Hudson, NY: Anthroposophic Press, 1984 (CW 187).

*How to Know Higher Worlds: A Modern Path of Initiation* written 1904–1905, Hudson, NY: Anthroposophic Press, 1994 (CW 10).

*The Influences of Lucifer and Ahriman: Human Responsibility for the Earth,* 5 lectures, 1919, Hudson, NY: Anthroposophic Press, 1993 (GAs 191 & 193).

*The Inner Nature of Man and Life between Death and Rebirth,* 6 lectures, Vienna, April, 9–14, 1914, Spring Valley, NY: Anthroposophic Press, 1959 (CW 153).

*Intuitive Thinking as a Spiritual Path: A Philosophy of Freedom,* written 1894, Hudson, NY: Anthroposophic Press, 1995 (CW 4).

*Isis Mary Sophia: Her Mission and Ours,* a collection, Great Barrington, MA: SteinerBooks, 2003.

*Karmic Relationships: Esoteric Studies,* vol. 3, 11 lectures, Dornach, Jul. 1–Aug. 8, 1924, London: Rudolf Steiner Press, 2002 (CW 237).

*Karmic Relationships: Esoteric Studies,* vol. 8, 6 lectures, Torquay & London, Aug. 12–27, 1924, London: Rudolf Steiner Press, 1975 (GA 240).

*Life between Death and Rebirth,* 16 lectures, various cities, Oct. 26, 1912–March 2, 1913, Hudson, NY: Anthroposophic Press, 1968 (CW 114).

*The Mission of the Folk-Souls: In relation to Teutonic Mythology,* 11 lectures, Oslo, June 7–17, 1910, London: Rudolf Steiner Press, 2005 (CW 121).

*Mystics after Modernism: Discovering the Seeds of a New Science in the Renaissance,* written 1901, Great Barrington, MA: Anthroposophic Press, 2000 (CW 7).

*The New Spirituality: And the Christ Experience of the Twentieth Century,* 7 lectures, Dornach, Oct. 17–31, 1921, Hudson, NY: Anthroposophic Press, 1988 (CW 200).

*An Outline of Esoteric Science,* written 1910, Hudson, NY: Anthroposophic Press, 1997 (CW 13).

*Polarities in the Evolution of Mankind: West and East, Materialism and Mysticism, Knowledge and Belief,* 11 lectures, Stuttgart, 1920, Hudson, NY: Anthroposophic Press, 1987 (CW 197).

*A Psychology of Body, Soul, and Spirit: Anthroposophy, Psychosophy, Pneumatosophy,* 12 lectures, Berlin, 1909–1911, Hudson, NY: Anthroposophic Press, 1999 (CW 115).

*The Reappearance of Christ in the Etheric,* 13 lectures & writings, 1910–1917, Great Barrington, MA: SteinerBooks, 2003 (CW 118).

*The Riddle of Humanity: The Spiritual Background of Human History,* 15 lectures, Dornach, July 29–Sept 3, 1916, Rudolf Steiner Press, 1990 (CW 170).

*Secret Brotherhoods: And the Mystery of the Human Double,* 7 lectures, St. Gallen, Zurich, & Dornach, Nov. 1917, London: Rudolf Steiner Press, 2004 (CW 178).

*The Spiritual Hierarchies and the Physical World: Zodiac, Planets & Cosmos,* 10 lectures, 1909, Great Barrington, MA, 2006 (CW 110).

*The Sun Mystery & the Mystery of Death and Resurrection: Exoteric and Esoteric Christianity,* 12 lectures, various cities, March 21–June 11, 1922, Great Barrington, MA: SteinerBooks, 2006 (CW 211).

*Theosophy: An Introduction to the Spiritual Processes in Human Life and in the Cosmos,* written 1904, Hudson, NY: Anthroposophic Press, 1994 (GA 9).

*Truth of Evolution: Inner Experience,* 5 lectures, Berlin, Oct. 31–Dec. 7, 1911, Great

Barrington, MA: SteinerBooks, 2006 (CW 132).

*Turning Points in Spiritual History*, 6 lectures, Berlin, 1911, Blauvelt, NY: Garber, 1987 (CW 60).

*Universe, Earth and Man*, 11 lectures, Stuttgart, Aug. 4–16, 1908, London: Rudolf Steiner Press, 1987 (GA 105).

## On Russia

Bulgakov, Sergei (Sergius) Nikolaevich, *The Bride of the Lamb*, Grand Rapids, MI: Eerdmans, 2002.

———, *The Holy Grail and the Eucharist*, Hudson, NY: Lindisfarne Books, 1997.

———, *Sophia: The Wisdom of God: An Outline of Sophiology*, Hudson, NY: Lindisfarne Press, 1993.

Carlson, Maria, *"No Religion Higher than the Truth": A History of the Theosophical Movement in Russia 1875–1922*. Princeton: Princeton University Press, 1993.

Florensky, Pavel, *Iconostasis*, Crestwood, NY: St. Vladimir's Seminary Press, 1996.

———, *The Pillar and Ground of the Truth*, Princeton, NJ: Princeton University Press, 1997.

———, *Salt of the Earth: An Encounter with a Holy Russian Elder*, Platina, CA: St Herman of Alaska, 1987.

Leighton, Lauren G. *The Esoteric Tradition in Russian Romantic Literature: Decembrism and Freemasonry*, University Park: Pennsylvania University Press, 1994.

Rosenthal, Bernice Glatzer, *The Occult in Russian and Soviet Culture*, Cornell: Cornell University Press, 1997

## On Sophia

Baring, Anne and Jules Cashford, *The Myth of the Goddess*, New York: Penguin, 1991

Bock, Emil, *Threefold Mary*, 3 lectures, Great Barrington, MA: SteinerBooks, 2003.

Matthews, Caitlin, *Sophia: Goddess of Wisdom*, London: Harper Collins, 1991.

Powell, Robert, *The Most Holy Trinosophia: The New Revelation of the Divine Feminine*, Great Barrington, MA: Anthroposophic Press, 2000.

———, *The Sophia Teachings: The Emergence of the Divine Feminine in Our Time*, New York: Lantern Books, 2001.

Prokofieff, Sergei O., *The Heavenly Sophia and the Being Anthroposophia*, London: Temple Lodge, 2006.

Schafer, Peter, *Mirror of His Beauty: Feminine Images of God from the Bible to the Early Kabbalah*, Princeton, NJ: Princeton University Press, 2002.

Schipflinger, Thomas, *Sophia-Maria*, York Beach, ME: Weiser, 1998.

## Works by Other Authors

Bamford, Christopher, *An Endless Trace: The Passionate Pursuit of Wisdom in the West*, New Paltz, NY: Codhill Press, 2003.

Harrison, C. G., *The Transcendental Universe: Six Lectures on Occult Science, Theosophy, and the Catholic Faith*, Hudson, NY: Lindisfarne Press, 1993.

Leviton, Richard, *The Imagination of Pentecost: Rudolf Steiner & Contemporary Spirituality*, Hudson, NY: Anthroposophic Press, 1994.

MacDermot, Violet, *The Fall of Sophia: A Gnostic Text on the Redemption of Universal Consciousness*, Great Barrington, MA: Lindisfarne Books, 2001.

Rittelmeyer, Friedrich, *Rudolf Steiner Enters My Life*, London: Christian Community Bookshop, 1940.

Solovyov, Vladimir, *Lectures on Divine Humanity*, edited by Boris Jakim, Lindisfarne Press, 1995.

———, *War, Progress, and the End of History: Three Conversations, Including a Short Tale of the Antichrist*, Lindisfarne Press, 1990.

# Index

## a



## b

## d



## e

## i

## q



## r



## s